Sectionalism and
American Political Development
1880–1980

Sectionalism and American Political Development 1880–1980

Richard Franklin Bensel

THE UNIVERSITY OF WISCONSIN PRESS

Published by

The University of Wisconsin Press
114 North Murray Street
Madison, Wisconsin 53715

The University of Wisconsin Press, Ltd.
1 Gower Street
London WCIE 6HA, England

Printings 1984, 1987

Printed in the United States of America

Library of Congress Cataloging in Publication Data
Bensel, Richard Franklin, 1949–
  Sectionalism and American political development,
  1880–1980.
  Includes bibliographical references and index.
  1. United States Congress. House—Voting—History.
2. Political parties—United States—History.   3. Section-
alism (United States)—History.   4. United States—
Politics and government—1865–1900.   5. United States—
Politics and government—20th century.   I. Title.
JK1316.B43   1984   320.973   84–40145
ISBN 0–299–09830–3
ISBN 0–299–09834–6 (pkb.)

To Elizabeth, Millie, and Seth

Contents

Maps	ix
Figures	xi
Tables	xiii
Author's Note	xviii
Preface	xix
1 Introduction	3
2 Overview	22
3 Tariffs, Elections, and Imperialism: 1880–1910	60
4 War, Agricultural Depression, and the New Deal: 1910–1940	104
5 War Mobilization, Farm Legislation, and Civil Rights: 1940–1970	175
6 The Decline of the Core Economy: 1970–1980	256
7 The Bipolar Democratic Coalition and the Rise and Decline of the Congressional Committee System	317

8 The Changing Sectional Base of the Congressional
Party System and American Ideology   368

9 Conclusion   403

Appendix: Methodology   415

Notes   451

Index   475

Maps

2.1   Opposing Sections in the 49th Congress (1885–1887)   39
2.2   Opposing Sections in the 54th Congress (1895–1897)   40
2.3   Opposing Sections in the 59th Congress (1905–1907)   41
2.4   Opposing Sections in the 64th Congress (1915–1917)   42
2.5   Opposing Sections in the 69th Congress (1925–1927)   43
2.6   Opposing Sections in the 74th Congress (1935–1936)   44
2.7   Opposing Sections in the 79th Congress (1945–1946)   45
2.8   Opposing Sections in the 84th Congress (1955–1956)   46
2.9   Opposing Sections in the 89th Congress (1965–1966)   47
2.10 Opposing Sections in the 94th Congress (1975–1976)   48
2.11 The Bipolar Structure of American Politics, 1880–1980   54
3.1   Persons Receiving Military Pensions as Percentage of County Population, 1887   68
3.2   House Vote on Passage of the Lodge Bill, July 2, 1890   80
4.1   Naval Appropriation Bill—Amendment to Increase Expenditures, June 2, 1916   126
4.2   Major Economic Territories of the United States, 1925   138
4.3   Passage of the First McNary-Haugen Bill, June 3, 1924   144
4.4   Passage of the Third McNary-Haugen Bill, February 17, 1927   145
5.1   Proposed Freeze on Agricultural Price Supports and Allotments, March 20, 1958   202
5.2   Passage of the Voting Rights Act of 1965   227
5.3   Passage of the School Busing Amendment, July 24, 1979   252
6.1   Labor Surplus Areas in the Fourth Quarter, 1978   282
6.2   Congressional Support for the Blouin Amendment to the CETA Formula, February 10, 1976   286
6.3   Congressional Support for the Roybal Amendment to Change the Formula Allocating Fuel Subsidies for the Poor, August 27, 1980   296
6.4   AFDC Recipients as a Percentage of the Total Population by County, 1978   306

8. 1   Sectional Base of the Party System: 67th Congress (1921 – 1923)   376
8. 2   Sectional Base of the Party System: 89th Congress (1965 – 1966)   377
8. 3   1968 Presidential Vote for George Wallace   389
8. 4   1980 Presidential Vote for John Anderson   390
A. 1   1885 Trade Area Boundaries   423
A. 2   1895 Trade Area Boundaries   424
A. 3   1921 Federal Reserve Branch Bank Territories   432
A. 4   1925 Trade Area Boundaries   435
A. 5   1935 Trade Area Boundaries   436
A. 6   1945 Trade Area Boundaries   438
A. 7   1955 Trade Area Boundaries   439
A. 8   1965 – 1975 Trade Area Boundaries   440

Figures

3.1 Tariff Revenue as a Percentage of Total Government Receipts,
    1880–1930   69
3.2 Mississippi Voter Participation and Presidential Voting Pattern,
    1872–1980   82
3.3 Copy of a Ballot Used in a Virginia Congressional Election, 1894   86
4.1 Percentage of U.S. Cotton Production Exported to Foreign
    Markets, 1880–1980   120
5.1 Gross National Product, 1939–1946   177
5.2 Wartime Expansion in the United States, 1939–1944   178
5.3 Relative Percentages of the Two Major Party Memberships
    Favoring Civil Rights Legislation, 1922–1981   231
5.4 Percentage of Rules Committee and House Democrats Favoring
    Major Civil Rights Legislation, 1922–1981   239
5.5 Sectional Stress and Civil Rights Legislation, 1922–1981   245
6.1 Union Shop Status, Energy Advantage, and Population Change as
    a Percentage of Annual National Growth, 1946–1982   265
6.2 Changes in AFDC Dependency in Five Selected Cities and the
    Nation, 1971–1980   307
7.1 Percentage of First-Term Members in the House of
    Representatives, 1881–1981   337
7.2 Prior Service of Members of the House of Representatives,
    1881–1981   338
7.3 Average Number of Committee Assignments per Member,
    1885–1981   347
7.4 Political Roots of the Seniority System, 1880–1965   349
7.5 How Seniority Was Maintained   350
7.6 Retention or Promotion of Most Senior Member to Highest Rank
    on Committee Party List, 1885–1977   350
7.7 Deterioration in Seniority Norms, 1965–1982   354
7.8 Roll Calls per Legislative Day, 1885–1975   363
7.9 Floor Amendments to Appropriations Bills, 1963–1977   365

8.1 Sectional Stress in the Membership Base of Congressional Parties, 1881–1984   378

8.2 Percentage of Southern House Seats Held by Democrats, 1877–1984   382

8.3 Southern Democrats as a Percentage of All Democratic House Seats, 1877–1984   383

8.4 The Democratic Party as a Vehicle for Southern Influence in National Politics, 1877–1984   384

Tables

2.1 Vote-Trading Arrangements 27

2.2 Presidential Administrations and Corresponding Congresses, 1881–1982 32

2.3 Method Used to Isolate and Identify Regional Poles 33

2.4 Major Trade Area Alignments, 1885–1976 34

2.5 The Bipolar Structure of American Politics: Trade Area Alignment with the Industrial-Commercial Core, 1885–1976 36

2.6 Average Sectional Stress and Distribution of Scores on Competitive Roll Calls, 1880–1980 53

2.7 National Public Policy and Sectional Competition, 1880–1980 57

3.1 Composition of the Expenditures of the United States, 1880–1934 67

3.2 Trade Area Delegation Support for a Protectionist Tariff Policy, 1880–1930 71

3.3 Regional Shares of Federal Expenditures for the Salary and Expenses of Special Deputy Marshals at Congressional Elections, 1877–1893 83

3.4 Contested Elections in the House of Representatives, 1881–1931 85

3.5 Trade Area Voting on Imperialist Policy Decisions, 1894–1907 94

4.1 America's International Balance Sheets, 1914, 1919, 1929 108

4.2 Contracts for War Materiel and the Stock Market, 1914–1915 114

4.3 Congressional Action on Military Preparedness and Neutrality, 1916 123

4.4 Trade Area Delegation Support for the Development of Muscle Shoals, 1916–1933 132

4.5 Trade Area Delegation Support for McNary-Haugenism, 1924–1929 147

4.6 The New Deal, the Committee System, and High Sectional Stress, 1933–1939 154

4.7   The New Deal, the Committee System, and Low Sectional
      Stress, 1933–1939   156
4.8   Voting on the National Industrial Recovery Act: Change in the
      Road Money Formula, May 26, 1933   157
4.9   Voting on the Wage and Hour Bill: Motion to Recommit,
      December 17, 1937   163
4.10 Voting on the Works Progress Administration: Striking
      Amendment to Narrow Regional Wage Differences, February 2,
      1939   166
5.1   Comparison of Pre–World War II Industrial Production and
      Wartime Facilities Expansion   182
5.2   Trade Area Delegation Voting on Selected High-Stress, Closely
      Contested Roll Calls, 1945–1946   185
5.3   Trade Area Delegation Voting on Major Farm Policy Decisions,
      1954–1958   201
5.4   Trade Area Delegation Voting on Selected Commodity
      Programs, 1951–1959   205
5.5   Classification of Trade Areas by Economic Type   207
5.6   Voting on Basic Commodity Supports, 1956–1959   210
5.7   Percentage of Urban Core Party Members Supporting Basic
      Commodity Support Programs   217
5.8   Trade Area Delegation Voting on Major Civil Rights Bills,
      1922–1968   226
5.9   Legislative Consideration of Civil Rights Bills, 1922–1981   236
5.10 Percentage of Members Supporting Passage of Discharged Civil
      Rights Legislation, 1937–1945   237
5.11 Signers of Discharge Petitions on Civil Rights Legislation, 1937
      and 1960   240
5.12 Congressional Voting on Anti-Busing Riders to Appropriations
      Bills (1968–1977) and the Proposed Constitutional
      Amendment to Ban Busing (1979)   248
6.1   High-Stress Legislative Decisions Concerning the Redistribution
      of National Wealth and Nationalization of Social Welfare
      Programs, 1971–1980   270
6.2   Trade Area Delegation Voting on Passage of the New York City
      Aid Bill, December 2, 1975   277
6.3   Voting on Maybank Amendment Repeal, 1961–1980   281
6.4   Alternative Formulas under Title VI, Part B of the
      Comprehensive Employment and Training Act   285
6.5   Unemployment Rates in Major Metropolitan Areas and Voting
      on the Blouin Amendment   285
6.6   Analysis of Voting on the Blouin Amendment   287
6.7   Voting on the Community Development Block Grant Formula   289

6.8 Effect of Floor Amendments on Education Formulas Contained in Bills Reported by the Education and Labor Committee, 1973–1978 291

6.9 1978 Aid Formula Proposed by the Education and Labor Committee 291

6.10 Voting on Floor Amendments to Federal Education Formulas, 1973–1978 292

6.11 Trade Area Delegation Response to the Regional Redistribution of Wealth Produced by Rising Energy Prices, 1976–1980 295

6.12 Voting on the Maguire Amendment to the Revenue Sharing Formula 300

6.13 Percentage of Labor Force Belonging to Unions in Selected States 301

6.14 Congressional Support for Organized Labor: Selected Decisions, 1965–1976 302

6.15 National AFDC Caseloads, 1971–1980 305

6.16 Welfare Dependency in Democratic and Republican Constituencies, 1978 309

6.17 Analysis of Voting on the 1979 Welfare Reform Bill 310

7.1 Manufacturing Belt Members as a Percentage of 1981 Standing Committee Assignments 320

7.2 Subcommittees Containing Constituencies with the Highest Median and Mean AFDC Populations, 1979 322

7.3 Subcommittees Containing Constituencies with the Lowest Median and Mean AFDC Populations, 1979 323

7.4 1976 Campaign Contributions by Organized Labor to Subcommittee Members in the House of Representatives 326

7.5 1976 Campaign Contributions by Individual Labor Unions to Selected Subcommittees in the House of Representatives 328

7.6 Trade Area Delegation Voting on Six Major Precedents in the House of Representatives, 1890–1965 330

7.7 Growth of Committee Assignments, 1949–1979 342

7.8 Cross-Assignments Allowed During Each Post-Reorganization Period 343

7.9 Cross-Assignment Patterns by Group, 1949–1979 344

7.10 Number of Exclusive and Cross-Assignments among Democratic Congressmen, 1949–1979 345

7.11 The Four Basic Rules of Seniority 347

7.12 Major Restrictions on Committee Autonomy, 1965–1981 355

7.13 Major Changes in Democratic Party Rules Governing Committee Assignments, 1965–1979 356

7.14 Floor Reciprocity in the 93rd Congress (1973–1974) 358

7.15 A Comparison of the Voting Records of Members Deposed from

and Promoted to Chairmanships by the Democratic Caucus in
1975 359

7.16 Intra-Committee Success and Party Affiliation, 93rd Congress
(1973–1974) 360

7.17 Majority Leader Support and the Success of Democratic
Committee Members, 93rd Congress (1973–1974) 361

7.18 Number of Rules Committee Defeats on Special Orders,
1929–1980 365

7.19 Membership Characteristics and Institutional Supports for a
Strong Committee System in Five Legislative Periods 366

8.1 Sectional Stress in the Membership Base of Congressional
Parties, 1881–1984 374

8.2 Sectional Base of the Party System, Metropolitan Districts, 67th
and 89th Congresses 375

8.3 Sectional Stress in the Congressional Party System and Critical
Presidential Elections, 1880–1966 380

8.4 Sectional Stress in the Congressional Party System and the Size
of the Republican Party in the House, 1881–1984 380

8.5 Sectional Stress in the Congressional Party System, Critical
Elections, and the Size of the Republican Party in the House,
1880–1966 381

8.6 Sectional Stress in the Congressional Party System and the Role
of the Democratic Party as the Vehicle of Southern Political
Influence, 1881–1984 384

8.7 Congressional Districts with Split Election Results: Districts
Carried by a Presidential Nominee of One Party and by a House
Nominee of Another Party, 1900–1980 386

8.8 Comparison of Sectional Stress in the Membership Base of
Congressional Parties and Presidential Elections, 1920–1980 387

8.9 1970 Membership of the Americans for Democratic Action, by
State and Region 394

8.10 Average ADA Scores for Democrats in Leading Periphery
Delegations and for Republicans in Leading Core Delegations,
1945–1976 396

8.11 Correlation between Liberalism and Support for the Industrial
Core, 1945–1976 399

A.1 Population (1880, 1890) and Reserve Status (1883, 1900) of
Leading Trade Area Urban Centers 425

A.2 Amount of Capital and Surplus in Cities Considered for Federal
Reserve Center Status and Tabulated Vote on Designation 429

A.3 Size and Wealth of Federal Reserve Districts as of March 4,
1914 430

A.4a Identity of Major Trade Centers and Size of Congressional Trade
Area Delegations, 1885–1975: The Northeast 444

A.4b Identity of Major Trade Centers and Size of Congressional Trade
Area Delegations, 1885 – 1975: The Midwest   445
A.4c Identity of Major Trade Centers and Size of Congressional Trade
Area Delegations, 1885 – 1975: The South   446
A.4d Identity of Major Trade Centers and Size of Congressional Trade
Area Delegations, 1885 – 1975: The West   448

Author's Note

This introductory note to the paperback edition provides an opportunity for a restatement of the major themes and purposes of the book. The most important contention is that sectionalism is and has been the most significant and fundamental influence in American political development. This theme is, I think, clearly presented and maintained throughout the book.

Upon reflection, two other themes are not as clearly elaborated. First, political competition between the nation's great sections is not the only explanation of political development in the United States. I contend, instead, that sectional stress has been the *fundamental* developmental influence upon which the richly-textured interaction between party competition, institutional structure and political ideology has rested. These other factors have independently and jointly determined the way in which sectional stress has found expression in the policies of the central state. Though these arguments are made at various points in the text, they might bear repetition again at the outset of the book.

This is also an attempt to present the "best case" for the primary importance of sectionalism. In that sense, the book is both a theoretically focused account of American development and an invitation to other scholars to craft competing explanations of similar scope. I can easily imagine alternative interpretations of development that would rest on political parties, ideology, or the institutional structures and policies of the central state. (I must confess that I cannot easily imagine a cultural explanation of similar explanatory power.) Each of these alternatives, I believe, would ultimately be revealed to be less fundamental than sectional competition. Put very simply, an explanatory framework resting on the regional division of labor can encompass these other factors but not vice versa. Nor can they, either singly or jointly, be invoked as co-equal explanations. To maintain co-equality would be to assert the existence of a simultaneous and exact interdependence which is implausible even as speculation. Thus this book is a challenge, albeit an imperfect one, to those who maintain the fundamentality of an explanatory factor other than sectionalism.

At the request of my son, who is now old enough to regret the impetuous generosity of his youth, I now reclaim responsibility for any errors that may still appear in the text.

June 1987

Preface

In most accounts of American political development, sectionalism in the political arena is described as a fading anachronism, a primitive impulse that owes much of its influence to a dimly remembered civil war. In its place, class conflict and ideological beliefs are said to determine the alignment of interests and direct the energies of the modern national state. The central argument of this book is that sectional competition—grounded in a geographical division of labor between the economically advanced northern core and the underdeveloped southern and western periphery—has been and remains the dominant influence on the American political system. Despite the frequent masking of regional claims in class or ideological rhetoric, the development of government institutions and the party system cannot be properly understood without a clear recognition of the persistent impact of this sectional competition.

The broadest area of concern affecting the organization of this book was the intensity and consistency of regional conflict in national political institutions, primarily the House of Representatives. The evidence demonstrates that the geographical alignment of sectional competition has undergone very little change in the last one hundred years. These pages also describe political conflict surrounding ten major public policy disputes that have significantly influenced American political development. The analysis of each of these disputes stands alone and can be read as an individual "vignette" in political history, as well as an episode in the continuous political rivalry between the northern core and the southern and western periphery. Later chapters investigate the impact of sectional competition on the American party system, ideology, and the institutional development of the modern state. An appendix describes both the construction of the sectional stress index and the trade area delineations used in the analysis of each historical period. The text relies on a relatively uncomplicated methodology in the belief that such a presentation will permit cross-national and historical comparison and make the text accessible to readers from a range of academic disciplines.

During the years in which this manuscript was written, I was extremely fortunate to have the encouragement and constructive criticism of a number of colleagues—particularly, Bob Bernstein, Steve Chan, Edward Harpham, and Theodore Lowi. I owe the greatest debt to my wife, Elizabeth Sanders, of Rice University. I would not have undertaken this project without her support and every page of this book bears the imprint of her absolute dedication to rigor and clarity. Her task—the most difficult of all—was to combine intellectually honest criticism with the unconditional encouragement of a loving spouse. I hope I can do as well.

The Institute for Humane Studies provided crucial support during preliminary research, and its assistance allowed me to spend two summers in Menlo Park with access to the Stanford University Libraries. I owe a special debt, also, to the Wisconsin State Historical Society Library which I very profitably exploited for several summers during completion of the manuscript. The University of Texas at Dallas provided research support during the academic year 1982–83, and, at UTD, Cynthia Kaheley and the staff of the School of Social Sciences patiently typed several drafts and revisions of the entire work. My research assistants, Dieter Lehnortt and Bill Stolberg, helped with data collection and carefully proofread the text. John Milton Cooper reviewed the manuscript for the University of Wisconsin Press and saved me from several errors of interpretation and emphasis. Brian Keeling, my editor, was understanding, thorough, and professional.

I have dedicated this study to Elizabeth in recognition of her help and support in its preparation. I have also dedicated the book to my mother-in-law, Millie Sanders, for her care of our son during the drafting of the first four chapters and for the courage and support she gave even while she herself was not in good health. Seth was born just as I began work on the manuscript and is included in the dedication because he likes books and because he has cheerfully accepted sole responsibility for any remaining errors in this one.

Sectionalism and
American Political Development
1880–1980

1

Introduction

Of all internal threats to national integration, sectional stress is the most serious. By dividing a nation into two or more cohesive regions with incompatible political goals, sectional stress carries with it the possibility of secession. The disruption of national ties is the clearest solution for a region which consistently loses its battles within a sectionally polarized nation. The history of the modern nation-state is littered with examples of partitioned political systems in which intense sectional conflict preceded national disintegration; outside the United States, one must look no further than Canada or the United Kingdom for examples of sectional stress in the modern world.*

In many modern political systems, sectional stress remains associated with ethnic identity and religious rivalry. In these nations, the promotion of ascriptive cultural and ethical values is expressed through regional competition because adherents are regionally concentrated and the political system is

---

*V. O. Key recognized this possibility: "Sectionalism, or conflict along territorial lines, may threaten national unity as sectional cohesion tightens and the lines of cleavage between sections deepen. The way of life of a region may lead its citizens to look upon the 'outsider' as an 'alien'—a feeling not unlike that of the people of one nation toward those of another. Territorial differentiation and conflict in extreme form may pose for the politician the problem of manufacturing a formula for the maintenance of national unity. Only once did the American politicians fail in this endeavor . . ." *Politics, Parties, and Pressure Groups* (New York: Thomas Y. Crowell, 1964), p. 233. On Canada, Mildred A. Schwartz has written: "It appears that political cleavages are potentially most troublesome for the development of a viable nation-state when they are set apart by territorial boundaries . . . regional strife has a weapon not available to other groups— secession." *Politics and Territory* (Montreal: McGill-Queen's University Press, 1974), p. 107. See also Richard Simeon, *Federal-Provincial Diplomacy* (Toronto: University of Toronto Press, 1972); R. W. Jackman, "Political Parties, Voting, and National Integration: The Canadian Case," *Comparative Politics* 4 : 4 (July 1972): 511–36; and Kenneth D. McRae, "Empire, Language and Nation: The Canadian Case," in S. N. Eisenstadt and Stein Rokkan, eds., *Building States and Nations*, vol. 2, *Analyses by Region* (Beverly Hills: Sage, 1973), pp. 144–76. For a comparative account of national disintegration, see Stein Rokkan, "Geography, Religion, and Social Class: Crosscutting Cleavages in Norwegian Politics," in Seymour M. Lipset and Stein Rokkan, eds., *Party Systems and Voter Alignments* (New York: Free Press, 1967), pp. 367–444. On the United Kingdom, Michael Hechter's work is the most suggestive: *Internal Colonialism* (Berkeley: University of California Press, 1975).

based on spatial representation. While the regions are often economically differentiated, the economic implications of political decisions are not the primary cause of sectional conflict.* Because most Americans share a common language, a common political culture, and a common religion, however, even the most serious ethnic or religious disputes have never seriously threatened to dismember the nation. The comparative lack of religious or ethnic rivalry between the American regions has meant that sectional stress in the United States has usually been grounded in economic competition. For these reasons, interregional competition should be interpreted as a struggle for control over the national political economy.† At stake for each region is its immediate economic welfare and, in the long run, the preservation of the social and political institutions which sustain the regional economy.

Formally defined, sectional stress is political conflict over significant public decisions in which a nation is divided into two or more regions, each of which is internally cohesive and externally opposed to the other(s).‡ The cause

---

*These political systems are most commonly studied within a center-periphery perspective. Sidney Tarrow describes one formulation of this approach: "Many . . . see the periphery primarily in terms of cultural diffusion, of the growth of empathy, and of the extension of urban values from center to periphery. Both Western philosophical thought and modern social science have contributed to this 'diffusionist' perspective, which inevitably characterizes the periphery as isolated, distant from the center, and traditional in its perspectives." However, Tarrow himself sees the problem another way: to "the older peripheralism of territorial and cultural isolation has been added a second peripheralism of economic and social marginality. . . . Especially in nation-states that failed to liquidate the ethnic, linguistic, or religious cleavages between regions during their formation, this notion of the marginal periphery has gained great relevance as an internal counterpart of the theory of international economic dependency that has come out of the Third World in recent years." *Between Center and Periphery: Grassroots Politicians in Italy and France* (New Haven: Yale Press, 1977), pp. 15–16. From this perspective, "regionalism can be most fruitfully studied as an element in the hegemony of the modern capitalist state, one that cushions the constraints of the market with a consensus built around regional ideology and modifies it through give-and-take of center-periphery political negotiation. Whether it is the market or the state that is ultimately dominant, one cannot say. But regionalism mediates between government policy and peripheral response in many ways, one of which is to provide an ideological umbrella for policies of increased central domination." Sidney Tarrow, "Regional Policy, Ideology, and Peripheral Defense: The Case of Fos-sur-Mer," in Sidney Tarrow et al., eds., *Territorial Politics in Industrial Nations* (New York: Praeger, 1978), p. 99.

†This conception of political economy is similar to that proposed by John R. Commons: "the state also proportions the factors over which it has control. It opens up certain areas, localities or resources, instead of others. It does this, not directly as individuals do, but indirectly through working rules which guide the transactions of individuals. It encourages or protects certain businesses or classes of businesses, certain occupations or jobs, rather than others. It restrains certain activities deemed detrimental to the whole. Its proportioning of factors is the proportioning of inducements to individuals and associations of individuals to act in one direction rather than other directions. This proportioning of inducements, by means of working rules, to individuals and associations is *Political Economy.*" *The Legal Foundations of Capitalism* (New York: MacMillan, 1924), p. 387. For numerous examples of the relationship between sectionalism and the national political economy, see Stanley D. Brunn, *Geography and Politics in America* (New York: Harper and Row, 1974).

‡In V. O. Key's words: "In an extreme form sectionalism might be taken to refer to a

of regional conflict may lie in ethnic, religious, or economic rivalry, or, more likely, some combination of the three. Where sectional conflict is a serious threat to national integration, regions channel competition into political parties and enlist ideological belief-systems in support of their respective positions. The development of separate political parties, distinct supporting ideologies, and high intraregional cohesion characterizes political systems on the verge of disintegration. For these reasons, a historical study of sectional stress yields an account of state-building and national decay.* The existence of sectionally based political conflict constitutes the most massive and complex fact in American politics and history.† Sectional stress is impossible to deny as a

---

condition of absolute sectional solidarity in which the people of the South, say, were united in opposition to the North. To be sure, such a high degree of sectional cohesion and inter-sectional antagonism rarely occurs within a working polity. Nevertheless, a sectional politics commonly involves a sharing of interest and attitudes by people of all sorts in a major geographical region against a similar clustering of interests and attitudes of the people of another region." *Politics, Parties and Pressure Groups* (New York: Thomas Y. Crowell, 1964), p. 232. The terms "section" and "region" are used interchangeably.

*Most of the following analysis is applicable only to democratic political systems. Frederick Jackson Turner saw political parties as generally conducive to national unity: "The one tragic exception in America to the unifying influence of parties and a common legislative body lies in the Civil War, when parties did become sectional." "Sections and Nation," *Yale Review* 12 (October 1922): 1–21. In addition to the United States both before and after the Civil War, contemporary Canada has also possessed a party system aligned along sectional lines. For example, after the 1972 general election, the Liberals controlled 76 percent of the seats from Quebec, 41 percent from Ontario, 31 percent from the Atlantic provinces, and only 10 percent from provinces in the West. After the same election, the Progressive-Conservatives held 61 percent of the seats from the West, 69 percent from the Atlantic provinces, 45 percent from Ontario, and only 3 percent from Quebec. The Social Credit party won seats only from Quebec (20 percent). The Co-operative Commonwealth Federation/New Democratic parties won seats only from Ontario (12 percent of the total) and from the West (29 percent). Data from Colin Campbell, *Canadian Political Facts* (Toronto: Methuen, 1977), pp. 91–92. On sectionalism and state-building, see Seymour M. Lipset and Stein Rokkan, "Cleavage Structures, Party Systems, and Voter Alignments: An Introduction," in *Party Systems and Voter Alignments* (New York: Free Press, 1967), pp. 1–64; Stein Rokkan, "Cities, States, and Nations: A Dimensional Model for the Study of Contrasts in Development," in Eisenstadt and Rokkan, eds., *Building States and Nations*, vol. 1, *Models and Data Resources*; and Stein Rokkan, "Dimensions of State Formation and Nation Building," in Charles Tilly, ed., *The Formation of Nation-States in Western Europe* (Princeton: Princeton University Press, 1975), pp. 562–600.

† The concept of a "complex fact," as opposed to a falsifiable scientific theory, is discussed in a letter to the editor in *Science* 212:4496 (May 15, 1981): 738. In that letter, biological evolution is described as a possible example of such a "fact": "In any case, evolution can be considered a complex fact rather than a theory. What is in dispute is not the existence of the fact but the mechanism through which it works." In a letter to the *New York Times* (March 17, 1981, p. A16), Ashley Montagu had previously suggested the concept as a possible rebuttal to the "creationist" claim that evolution was still a hypothetical theory:

"There are theories concerning the exact mechanisms of evolution, but concerning evolution there can no longer be any doubt as to its reality.

"The method of science is falsification, the attempt to disprove by every possible means the theory which appears to explain the fact. If that attempt fails, the scientist knows that he has something. . . . because we have innumerable evidences of the reality of evolution, both of a

coherent fact not only because of its magnitude but because of the constancy of its shape: the ebb and flow of political conflict across the American nation has almost always produced the same basic geographical pattern. That pattern, representing the alignments of competing sections, indicates—without explaining—the structural imperatives of the American political system. These imperatives are rooted in the economic geography of the nation and dictate the spatial form of political conflict.

In the United States, sectional stress has been grounded in an interregional division of labor established by geographical proximity to the advanced industrial economies of Europe and the location of deep harbors, inland transportation routes, and industrial raw materials. The sectional alignment of political conflict has been extraordinarily stable, as stable as the economic divisions upon which it is based. Although expressed in cultural or religious terms at times, the historical alignment of sectional competition in America is primarily a product of the relationship of the separate regional economies to the national political economy and the world system.*

The first purpose of this study is to provide an empirical framework for the analysis of sectional stress in the United States. That framework should be sufficiently general to allow cross-national and historical comparison between and within individual nations. The second purpose is to establish the fundamental underlying structure of sectional political competition and its historical consistency in American politics. Sectional stress must be seen, in the first instance, as a "massive fact" of both extreme complexity and basic spatial or geographical simplicity. The consistent spatial form of sectional stress in history belies the complexity of its influence on the evolution of American political institutions, the growth of the state, the development of party competition, and the emergence of national ideological belief-systems.

The third and final purpose of this study is to propose a general theory of sectional stress. In a sense, this theory is an attempt to explain the "massive fact" by reformulating its fundamental structure in general terms and redescribing large blocks of American political history from this new perspec-

---

premeditated and unpremeditated (natural) experimental kind, evolution is no longer a theory but one of the best-authenticated facts within the whole realm of science. The fact of evolution is beyond dispute."

*For directly competing interpretations, see Daniel J. Elazar, *Cities of the Prairie: The Metropolitan Frontier and American Politics* (New York: Basic Books, 1970); and Paul Kleppner, *The Cross of Culture: A Social Analysis of Midwestern Politics, 1850–1900* (New York: Free Press, 1970). For the relationship between the settlement of individual ethnic groups and regional economic differentiation, see Martin M. Katzman, "Ethnic Geography and Regional Economies, 1880–1960," *Economic Geography* 45:1 (January 1969): 45–52; and David Ward, *Cities and Immigrants: A Geography of Change in Nineteenth Century America* (New York: Oxford University Press, 1971). For a somewhat analogous examination of political development in France, see Edward Whiting Fox, *History in Geographical Perspective: The Other France* (New York: Norton, 1971), particularly his distinction between "trade" and "commerce" and the politico-institutional characteristics associated with each.

tive. Contemporary political conflict will be reinterpreted as a product both of historical sectional tensions and of regional competition arising within the present political economy.

The present study focuses on the House of Representatives in the United States over the last century (from 1880 to 1980). While the House of Representatives is a political system in its own right—a dimension which will be discussed in some detail—for most purposes it will be viewed as a composite mirror of the American polity. As members of a national legislative institution, representatives regularly take positions on most of the important public issues that arise within each political period. These positions reflect congressmen's interpretations of the interest of their districts on each public policy, but they must also be seen in the context of the partisan and institutional constraints under which members operate.

Along with the Senate, the House of Representatives controls the statutory base of the national government. Throughout history, the roughly 400 members of the House (fewer in the latter nineteenth century, 435 after 1912) have been compelled to publicly reveal their preferences on specific, narrowly framed questions of public policy. Their preferences have been frequently expressed and directly connected to proposed changes in the statutory base of the government. For these reasons, legislative voting in the House of Representatives has accurately recorded the historical sectional struggle for control over the national political economy.*

Frederick Jackson Turner and Sectionalism in American History—The Traditional Approach

In a series of articles written near the end of his life, Frederick Jackson Turner proposed a sweeping reinterpretation of American history based on the political importance of sections.[1] His statement of the problem and the general approach, though ultimately less fruitful than his work on the American frontier, attracted a number of scholars and for several decades before mid-century was considered a major theoretical perspective on American history.

Turner's sectional interpretation did not abandon or contradict his frontier thesis. Instead, he viewed the two approaches as complementary.

> The frontier and the section are two of the most fundamental factors in American history. The frontier is a moving section, or rather a form of society, determined by the reactions between the wilderness and the edge

*The only plausible substitute for roll call analysis as a measure of sectional stress would be the study of election returns, but such data have two comparative deficiencies. Not only are primary and general elections infrequently held, but the implications drawn from the returns are usually based on the large, inarticulate lumps of policy positions contained in the respective party platforms. Thus, compared to roll call voting on specific statutory alternatives, party platforms and election returns are a much weaker source of information concerning regional policy preferences.

of expanding settlement; the section is the outcome of the deeper-seated geographical conditions interacting with the stock that settled the region.[2]

As the country became settled, the influence of the frontier disappeared from American politics, but sectionalism persisted—largely because of these "deeper" geographical and economic conditions which underscored regional differences.*

Turner's sectionalism possessed several characteristics. First, sectional political conflict was inevitable. The United States was as vast and diverse as the European subcontinent, and only the colonial origins of the American state prevented a similar degree of political fragmentation.† "We have become a nation comparable to all Europe in area, with settled geographic provinces which equal great European nations. We are in this sense an empire, a federation of sections, a union of potential nations."[3] Second, in his view, geographical features and their corresponding economic implications were the most important influences on sectional political competition. Turner cited class and ethnic factors which could mute the political expression of economic interests or even "reverse" political positions, but his interpretation remained implicitly grounded in an undeveloped geographical determinism. Finally, his sections were collections of place-names—an ever-changing amalgam of proper-

---

*Turner was not entirely consistent on whether sectionalism would remain a primary force in American politics. In 1908, he wrote: "in the long run, as American society loses the mobility stimulated by the artificial and transient opportunities of free land and the demand for labor in sparsely occupied areas, the sectionalism due to physiographic conditions, economic interests, and constituent stocks of settled societies, will persist, if sectionalism persists at all" (*Sections in American History*, p. 290). But by the 1920s he had come to believe: "That sectionalism is not dying away in the United States will be clear enough to anyone who examines the newspapers and reads the debates in Congress, not to speak of analyzing the votes in that body" (*America's Great Frontiers and Sections*, p. 63).

† Turner carried this comparison to great lengths: "The United States is imperial in area. If we lay a map of Europe upon a map of the United States constructed to the same scale, the western coast of Spain would coincide with the coast of southern California; Constantinople would rest near Charleston, South Carolina; Sicily, near New Orleans; and the southern coast of the Baltic would fall in line with the southern coast of Lake Superior. Thus, in size, the United States is comparable, not with a single nation of Europe, but with all of Europe, exclusive of Russia. It is also comparable with Europe in the fact that it is made up of separate geographic provinces, each capable, in size, resources, and peculiarities of physical conditions, to be the abode of a European nation, or of several nations. American history is in large measure still colonial history—the history of the exploration, conquest, colonization, and development of these physiographic provinces, and the beginnings of a process of adaptation of society to the section which it has occupied." *Sections in American History*, p. 289. As a consequence, sectionalism was likely never to vanish completely: "There will be a decline in the movement of inter-state migration, men will be more accustomed to living provincially in their own section; the improvement of transportation will assist in breaking down the importance of the state, the radio will diminish localism, but the very fact that we are continental in our breadth will probably continue to emphasize the section as the state declines." *America's Great Frontiers and Sections*, p. 62.

named states, river valleys, mountain ranges, drainage basins, and ethnic provinces. He could recognize persistent political cleavages between many of these sections, but his quest for a single dominant geographical characteristic upon which to base a unified historical theory was unrewarded. Since Turner viewed sectional differences as slowly-evolving or even static, this failure to identify effective sectional units was extremely frustrating.[4]

While sectional feeling always carried with it the potential for national disintregation, Turner saw two factors in the American political system which worked to hold the nation together. The first of these was the party system, and, as he viewed it, the necessity to maintain majority or potential majority coalitions.

> National party, then, has been in America a flexible bond, yielding in extreme cases to sectional insurgency, yielding often, in the construction of bills, to sectional demands and to sectional threats, but always tending to draw sections together toward national adjustments by compromise and bargain. A common language, law, and institutions, absence of sectional concentration of religions and races, absence of historical hatreds, have helped to prevent America from splitting apart and falling into European conditions; but regional geography, quasi-continental parties, and a national, that is, intersectional (our equivalent of international), congressional organization by which sectionalism could express itself in voting instead of by war—these are important factors in the contrast between European and American ways of settling difficulties, and are important explanations of our continued unity.[5]

In a country as diverse as the United States, no section could entirely dominate a majority party. Furthermore (and this constituted the second unifying factor), no section was entirely homogeneous, and this heterogeneity decreased the political intensity and cohesiveness of each section. "The existence, within each of the large sections, of smaller sections or regions which did not agree with the views of their section as a whole, constituted a check both upon party despotism and upon sectional arrogance and exploitation of other sections."[6]

Sectional conflict was revealed most regularly and consistently in the halls of Congress. There, Turner felt, sectionalism pervaded the less public and more informal political processes of the committee chambers, cloakrooms, and the Committee of the Whole.*

---

*The House of Representatives never recorded the roll call positions of its members in the Committee of the Whole during Turner's lifetime. For that reason, Turner used roll call data drawn from votes on recommittal or final passage as the main support for this thesis. Even though these votes were all that were available to him, he still felt that they revealed extremely striking and persistent regional cleavages. From his perspective, however, the lack of comparable data from other parts of the legislative process (where sectional feeling was even more intense) hampered a full treatment of the topic.

Party policy and congressional legislation emerge from a process of sectional contests and sectional bargainings. Legislation is almost never the result of purely national or purely sectional considerations. It is the result of sectional adjustments to meet national needs. For the most part, such adjustments take place in the formative stages of bills, in the committee rooms, and in the process of framing the measures by amendments. It is in these stages that the bill is most easily affected by sectional interests. The vote on the third reading of the bill affords opportunity for dissent; but after the completion of the measure, party discipline and party loyalty assert themselves and, in spite of discontent, usually furnish the necessary votes to pass the measure.[7]

However, even though parties could usually call in the votes of dissident members on final passage, in some situations a congressional party could more or less permanently split into blocks or factions.

Within the same party a section may possess the instruments of legislative power such as the speakership, the chairmanships of important committees, etc. If this ruling section has sought to use its power primarily for its own advantage, party voting will often give way to sectional voting, to the formation of alliances or working agreements between the aggrieved sectional wings, or blocs may be formed as for example by the union of insurgent Republicans in the West-North Central states with the Democratic South. . . .[8]

While one section could come to dominate a majority party and thus provoke a factional split, minority parties could also come to coincide with a section.

This [political alignment] will result from resistance to the domination of another section or sections when they completely control the machinery of the victorious party. Obviously, this type of sectionalism cannot be successful short of the use of force because it is by its very nature a minority section unwilling to make sacrifices and combinations. As a rule it is a step in [the] reorganization of parties.[9]

During the early part of the twentieth century when Turner was working, the Democratic party was the primary political vehicle for the South in national politics—particularly when the party was in the minority. The Republican party served to represent the Northeast and most of the industrialized Midwest. In the political system which revolved around these two sectional poles, the insurgent farm bloc of progressive Republicans never found a place until the New Deal brought them into the Democratic party.

Though Turner used roll call positions to illustrate sectional competition on important political issues and though he believed this competition was even more intense in the hidden recesses of the legislature, he never developed a general account of congressional behavior and organization from a sectional perspective. While Turner viewed sectional stress as a ubiquitous political phenomenon, obvious to anyone willing to see it, his general thesis has remained underdeveloped and, for want of objective theoretical underpinnings, unexplored.

V. O. Key, Julius Turner, and Political Analysis—
The State of the Art

In one of his most important works, *Politics, Parties and Pressure Groups*, V. O. Key set out a theoretical basis for American sectionalism that recognized and sought to resolve the "determinist" implications of an economic-geographical interpretation of political history.

> At times the notion of geographical influence has been pushed to the form of an extreme geographical determinism; more recently students have pointed out that man may affect geography as well as geography, man. The geography of the South did not predestine it to cotton culture and slavery; a complex of cultural factors—a demand for cotton, the availability of slaves, the existence of attitudes condoning slavery— brought about the utilization of southern soil by a slavocracy.[10]

In his interpretation, sectional differentiation in the distribution of natural resources gives rise to economic specialization and divergent interests among the various regions.* These divergent economic interests, in turn, produce political competition between the sections. Geographical features and climate alone do not determine the actual course that sectional economic development and political competition follow, but important economic and political differences of some kind are bound to develop between regions with sharply distinct geography and climate.†

---

*"The conditions of temperature and rainfall in Louisiana and Florida give us the politics of sugar cane, though it might be more accurate to say that politics gives us sugar cane in Louisiana and Florida, since the crop could not be produced without political protection. The seat of political activity of the extractive industries—mining and petroleum production—is determined by the geographical location of those resources. The juxtaposition of the raw materials for steel influences the location of the metal industries and, hence, the sectional locus of manufacturing." Key, *Politics, Parties, and Pressure Groups*, p. 238.

† Any political analysis which adopts an analytical framework grounded in geographial concepts skirts, if it does not openly imply, a philosophical position approximating physical determinism. In its extreme form, geographical determinism asserts that the course of human events is fully caused by climate, land forms, and the location of natural resources. This approach to historical interpretation not only overstates what can be explained through the use of geographical concepts but calls up an intellectual tradition which has been substantially discredited. Edward Fox solves this problem by viewing geographical features as limitations on human possibility and not deterministic channels that the course of history must follow: "The fact that the potentialities as well as the limitations of human action, in any geographic situa-

Like most historians and political scientists, Key saw sectionalism in the United States primarily in terms of a North-South division. This sectional dualism was preceded by the frontier period in American history, in which the settled and capital-exporting eastern seaboard areas were in political competition with a rapidly expanding and debtor West.[11] Slavery, economic specialization in cash crop cultivation, and the social maturation of western settlements developed the North-South cleavage which led to secession and the Civil War. The historical events surrounding the Civil War and Reconstruction, the preservation of segregation and its associated political implications, and a continued dependence on a largely agricultural, cash crop economy produced a South whose distinctiveness within the American nation was matched by its political cohesion in opposition to northern interests.

Following the Civil War, the two great political parties came to rest on this sectional dualism.

In the North the hegemony of the Republican party rested on the skillful maintenance of a combination of manufacturers, industrial workers, and farmers. The protective tariff, opposed by the South, provided a common bond for manufacturers and workers in protected industries. The same policy created difficulties in holding the grain growers of the Midwest in the Republican ranks.[12]

In the South, the Democratic party was almost the only political force, and political competition was shunted into the Democratic contests for nomination to political office with little or no Republican opposition in subsequent general elections.* Between the two regions, each defined by the complex of economic interests concentrated within them, lay a large and rather variegated "border" region. Tilting toward the Republican party, the midwestern farm belt portion of the border has historically split away from party policy on agricultural subsidies and internationalism. Tilting toward the Democratic party, the mountain West and those "slave" states which remained in the Union (Kentucky, West Virginia, Maryland, and Delaware) have nevertheless often opposed the free trade and anti-labor positions of the South.

Furthermore, both the North and the South had even more extreme sectional centers. Within the South, Key noted that the complex of historical events and socioeconomic factors which gave the region its distinctiveness found their purest political expression in the Black Belt. This rural plantation area characterized by high farm tenancy, cotton cultivation, a rich, black loam,

---

tion, reside in man himself eliminates the false threat of determinism. Men act on, or within, their environment, while geography—in terms of human experience—is inert. Any given men, at any given time, in any given geographical setting, will, in a very practical sense, be limited by the environment . . ." *History in Geographical Perspective*, p. 23.

*The unique sectional expression of the South in national politics, however, was at least partly produced by the restrictive suffrage requirements then in force in many southern states. See V. O. Key, *Southern Politics in State and Nation* (New York: Knopf, 1949).

and a highly concentrated black population consistently delivered the largest
Democratic majorities in the nation in both congressional and presidential
races. In the Republican North, the medium-sized industrial centers and rural
hamlets of New England formed a slightly less cohesive foundation for the
Grand Old Party. These central regions and particularly the core sub-regions
within them

> gain a disproportionate influence in the party and thus assure that these
> interests will be amply represented in party councils. Democratic Sena-
> tors and Representatives from the Solid South, re-elected term after
> term, gain positions of power in congressional committees under the
> seniority rules. Similarly, in national conventions and in the formal party
> councils these persons, through long service in party affairs, gain posi-
> tions of vantage from which to defend and promote the interests of their
> region. Likewise, Republican leaders from the Northeast climb,
> through seniority, to positions of power in their party.[13]

Thus, for Key as for Frederick Jackson Turner, sectionalism operating through
the two major parties came to dominate the institutional structure of
Congress.

V. O. Key viewed sectionalism, by 1964, as a political influence of declining importance. In its strongest form, sectional political demands arose
out of resource-based, extraction-dependent economies. As the United States
industrialized and urbanization proceeded apace, interregional competition—
he believed—would evolve into a class-based party system.

> As the southern trends suggest, the changes associated with urbanization
> undermine the structure of historic agrarian sectionalism. A great area
> producing a major crop may be expected to carry along with it in na-
> tional politics its small cities and villages that forage on the countryside.
> But a great industrial city has a political character of its own: it contains a
> variety of economic, racial, and social interests, often with little unity of
> purpose.[14]

Only with the development of an indigenous competitive Republican party
would the South—the most agricultural and least industrialized section—
finally move into the "mainstream of American politics" as a result of these
trends. To Key, the two-party system of the North represented the political
future of the South.*

---

*Key apparently saw this transformation as inevitable: "Economically based section-
alism in its more extreme form tends to be agrarian and rural. When a single interest
dominates a huge area both economically and politically, the probabilities are that social pressures for political conformity result in a structure of partisan attitude with special powers of self-
preservation. Even when sectional interests begin to change, the heritage of political faith may
lag in its adjustment to the new state of affairs." Key, *Politics, Parties, and Pressure Groups*,
p. 243.

In 1951, Julius Turner published the major work of his career, *Party and Constituency: Pressures on Congress*. In 1970, this study was extensively revised and updated by Edward Schneier.[15] The revised edition contains the best available longitudinal analysis of sectional influence on voting behavior in the House of Representatives.

With some reservations, Turner and Schneier saw political parties, urbanization (or metropolitanization), ethnicity, racial composition, and sectionalism as distinct and separable "pressures" each of which, to a measurable extent, influences the policy positions assumed by congressmen. They viewed sectionalism, therefore, as only one of a number of exclusive and competing factors operating on congressmen, and one of the goals of their analysis was to determine the relative significance of each factor. Aside from the analytical assumption of causal independence between party and region, their account of sectionalism closely resembled Key's description.[16]

Turner and Schneier began their analysis by segregating the membership of the House into the two major parties. They then located the major sectional cleavage within each party by investigating the roll call behavior of the members by region. In the Democratic party, Turner and Schneier discovered the traditional North-South split in American politics.

> There is one alignment in American politics, however, in which the factor of tradition is strong, and which apparently cuts across a number of issues. That is, of course, the division between North and South. The North-South conflict has a long history, cuts deep into party ranks on some issues, and has been a major divisive force in Democratic politics at both the congressional and national levels.[17]

Included in the South were the eleven states of the old Confederacy plus Oklahoma. All other states were classified as northern. The influence of sectionalism on congressmen, according to Turner and Schneier, was substantially weaker than party but stronger than urbanism, ethnicity, or racial composition.*

The most original part of their analysis, however, was reserved for the Republican party. Turner and Schneier found that the Republican party has

---

*Like Key, Turner and Schneier find that southern sectionalism is strongest in rural Black Belt areas: "The general bloc structure of the southern delegation has traditionally pitted the heartland of Dixie against the rim, urban against rural, and Black Belt against border." Turner, *Party and Constituency: Pressures on Congress*, rev. ed., p. 179. Also, like Key, they expect sectionalism to decline in the future: "With these shifts [industrialization, black migration to the North, and urbanization], with the rise of the Republican party in the South, and with the electoral emancipation of the Negro, we are beginning to see the emergence of a southern political system in which party labels mean roughly the same thing as they do nationally. The more the South moves in this direction, the less we will see of the bipartisan conservative coalition, and the less regionalism will be a factor in Democratic politics in the House of Representatives." Ibid., p. 186.

passed through two sectional cleavages over the 1920–64 period. In the first, the West Central section (North and South Dakota, Nebraska, Kansas, Minnesota, Iowa, Missouri, plus Wisconsin) was opposed to the remainder of the nation. In this cleavage, progressive farm and isolationist policies divided the two sections. Later on, the first cleavage gave way to a second which separated the coastal states (the New England, Middle Atlantic, and Pacific census regions) from the interior (the remainder of the nation). A wider range of policies—more or less closely associated with a liberal-conservative alignment—divided the party in the later period, and members from the coastal region were generally more "liberal" than their conservative colleagues in the interior. Both cleavages were generally weaker than the North-South division in the Democratic party.

Turner and Schneier summarized their findings by pointing out the similarity between the sectional voting blocs which appeared in both the early and late periods of their longitudinal analysis:

> . . . the basic sectional alignment in modern times strikingly resembles that of earlier periods. As in the nineteenth century, an inter-party alliance of southern Democrats and interior Republicans has appeared on a significant proportion of recent roll-call votes. The nineteenth-century insurgency of west central Republicans, of course, did not always place them in the camp of the regular southern Democrats. Nor is the insurgent South of the mid-twentieth century consistently allied with the Republican interior . . . the lines of sectional cleavage in the two parties have flowed through overlapping, but by no means identical, lines of stress. For the Democrats, the Negro, immigration, states' rights, foreign aid, and labor issues have produced the most frequent disagreements. For the Republicans, foreign affairs and farm policies have been central to sectional rivalries.[18]

Because the shortcomings of the Turner and Schneier investigation are generally shared by other works in the field, the following critique also applies to most contemporary congressional analysis. The decision to conduct separate investigations into sectionalism within each party has several untoward implications. For periods when only a handful of Republicans were elected from the South (e.g., most of 1920–64), the major sectional cleavage in American politics, the North-South division, is left largely unanalyzed because it occurs *between* the parties where no examination is undertaken. The Turner-Schneier assumption of causal independence between section and party,* be-

---

*Causal independence may not completely describe their philosophical position, which seems to be one of complete causal simultaneity among the several political, demographic, and geographic variables that they use. From a sectionalist perspective, geographic variation and the economic differences implied by that variation are the first (though not always the most salient) "cause" of both party structure and political competition.

cause it led them to neglect interparty sectional divisions, obfuscated most of the historical impact of sectional stress by "holding constant" its most important political vehicle, the major American party.

Furthermore, because of this assumption, Turner and Schneier misinterpreted some important political events. For example, they interpreted the waning of West North Central insurgency in the Republican party in a way that suggested the disappearance of rural progressivism. However, midwestern rural progressives did not vanish during the New Deal, they moved into the Democratic party. In their new party, these progressives and the sectional interests they represented could not be isolated by Turner and Schneier. When the rural progressives moved into the Democratic party, the eastern Republican conservatives who constituted their most salient opponents were left behind in the GOP. Within the Democratic party, the distinctive character of midwestern progressivism was completely overshadowed by the dominant North-South cleavage. Even if the North-South division had not been comparatively dominant, Turner and Schneier could not have isolated the regional identity of midwestern Democratic progressives because their approach lumped these members together with those from the East and West.

A similar criticism concerns Turner and Schneier's treatment of the North-South split in the Democratic party. As the Republicans elected more members from the South (particularly after 1960), the North-South cleavage within the Democratic party has declined as the more irreconcilable districts most opposed to the national party position switched parties. From their perspective, Turner and Schneier saw declining sectionalism within the Democratic party as a decline in sectionalism generally; in reality, the Strom Thurmonds of 1948 have simply changed parties.

Finally, the Turner and Schneier study relied on state boundaries and standardized census categories such as North, South, West North Central, etc. If sectional stress evolves to take on a new geographical configuration substantially different from the old one captured by the great census divisions, conventional political analysis may not be able to identify the new sectional "poles" and may, instead, record a general decline in sectional competition. Furthermore, these great sectional divisions contain sub-regions which possess extremely divergent economic interests and political inclinations. Even when the regional organization of economic and political interaction is accepted, these static definitions inadequately record the social evolution of regional life because they preclude the examination of cycles of intrasectional cohesion and dissension.

The standard reference works in the field, the *Congressional Quarterly Weekly Report* and *Congressional Quarterly Almanac*, suffer from analytical difficulties similar to those of the Turner-Schneier approach. The *Quarterly* classifies roll calls by dividing the Democratic party into two sections, North and South (the eleven states of the Confederacy plus Kentucky and Oklahoma), while leaving the Republican party intact. The editors then analyze the incidence of North-South divisions within the Democratic party as their only indicator of sectionalism.

When a majority of Republicans vote with a majority of the southern Democrats in opposition to the northern Democratic wing, the *Congressional Quarterly* assumes that a "conservative" coalition has occurred between the Republicans and southern Democrats. One of the implications of this analytical assumption is that no southern representative can align with the "liberal" northern Democrats when the House of Representatives is perfectly divided along an "ideological" cleavage. The combination of partisan distinctions and the ideological interpretation assigned to the conservative coalition completely transforms what is basically a sectional competition (in V. O. Key's terms) into an amalgamation of partisan allegiance and ideological predispositions. Even more so than Turner and Schneier's conceptualization, the approach taken by the *Congressional Quarterly* is inflexible and inextricably confuses party, region, and ideology.

The delineation of regional boundaries based on the concept of "trade areas" avoids most of the difficulties associated with conventional treatments of sectionalism. Whereas broad census divisions like North-South are atheoretical, rigid, static, and rooted in a particular, unique national experience, trade areas are flexible, evolutionary, suitable for cross-national analysis, and firmly grounded in socioeconomic theories of industrial location and central place organization.[19] The theoretical case for the use of trade areas in the analysis of sectional stress and a description of their historical development are presented in the Appendix. The theories upon which their definition is based are extended to include the "core-periphery" interpretation of American political development that will be formally proposed in chapter 2.

As the "massive fact" of American political development, sectional stress appears to be primordial. The existence and form of sectional conflict in the United States can be seen as inevitable and, in a complex sense, almost "predetermined" by the geographic shape and content of the country. American sectionalism, viewed from this perspective, is the progenitor of noneconomic cultural, social, and political differences between the regions. Thus, party competition and ideological belief-systems are the epiphenomena of inevitable sectional competition and are subordinate factors in the evolution of American politics. Firmly grounded in the economic geography of the nation, the sociocultural and political differences between the sections encourage a continuous struggle for control of the national political economy. The implementation of public policies produces new economic conflicts and differences between the sections which overlay the preexisting, fundamental pattern.

Immanuel Wallerstein and the World-System

Immanuel Wallerstein divided history into three distinct "structures": social geography, civilizations, and the social economy. The most persistent and deepest of these, he believed, was social geography, which described the "eco-logical underpinnings of our social relations." Though ultimately finite in their temporal influence, the structures of social geography were nonetheless millennial in nature. Overlaying geography were the structures of civiliza-tions, "the cultural forms in which we clothe our social action." The "cultural barriers" erected by civilizations were multisecular but not millennial and further narrowed the course of human development. The more transient struc-tures of the "social economy" were "the modes of production which determine the constraints within which social action occurs." However, even the social economy was multisecular and, for most periods in history, constituted an unchallenged and unquestioned feature of human experience.[20]

In his own work, Wallerstein focused on the structures of the social economy in their most significant form: the world-system.

> A world-system is a social system, one that has boundaries, structures, member groups, rules of legitimation, and coherence. Its life is made up of the conflicting forces which hold it together by tension, and tear it apart as each group seeks eternally to remold it to its advantage. It has the characteristics of an organism, in that it has a life-span over which its characteristics change in some respects and remain stable in others. . . . What characterizes a social system in my view is the fact that life within it is largely self-contained, and that the dynamics of its development are largely internal. . . . If the system, for any reason, were to be cut off from all external forces (which virtually never happens), the definition implies that the system would continue to function substantially in the same manner.[21]

As long as each world-system was relatively isolated from others and consti-tuted a "closed system" in terms of its own evolutionary dynamics, more than one could coexist at the same time.

In the past, world-systems have taken two different forms. World-empires, such as Rome, Byzantium, and China, imposed a single political rule—an imperium—on the entire geographical extent of an interregional economy. World empires gathered economic "surplus" from conquered or sub-jugated regions in the form of tribute and, thus, redistributed wealth to the political center. The rise and fall of world empires exhibited a cyclical pattern in which the political system expanded in size "to the point where the bu-reaucratic costs of appropriating the surplus outweighed the surplus that could, in socio-political terms, be effectively appropriated, at which point decline and retraction set in."[22] World-systems also took the form of a world-economy.

> [A] world-economy is defined as a single division of labor within which are located multiple cultures—hence it is a *world*-system like the world-empire—but which has no over-arching political structure. Without a

political structure to redistribute the appropriated surplus, the surplus can only be redistributed via the "market," however frequently states located within the world-economy intervene to distort the market. Hence the mode of production is capitalist.[23]

Before the emergence of the modern world-economy, these systems were extremely fragile institutions which usually developed and decayed within less than a hundred years. Prior to the late fifteenth century world-economies often disintegrated because subordinate or relatively disadvantaged regions withdrew from the system. In the pre-modern world such withdrawal was possible both because economically advanced nations within the system were not sufficiently strong to impose participation and because transport technology did not permit the development of a critical level of interdependence between widely separated regions. If centrifugal forces were not sufficiently powerful to destroy a pre–sixteenth century world-economy, then it inevitably succumbed to an expanding imperium which extended its boundaries to the limits of the interregional division of labor. In this way a transient world-economy was transformed into the cyclical dynamic of a world-empire, and capitalist appropriation by relatively advanced regions was transformed into tribute redistributed to the political center.[24]

The modern world-economy, now five hundred years old, dates from the late fifteenth century and originated in the (at that time) new "discontinuity between economic and political institutions . . . made possible by the creation of capitalist forms of production, not only in commerce and industry, but most important of all, in agriculture."[25] Like world-systems before it, the modern world-economy possesses three characteristics: a world division of labor between nations and regions within one unified economy, a hierarchical interregional order based on a core-periphery functional dualism, and a constantly expanding penetration of remaining unintegrated territory.

The geographical extent of the world-economy is determined "largely by the state of technology," which also determines which goods are exchanged and the direction of trade between regions. Technology determines the relative cost of transport to the value of product and, thus, the extent to which an interregional division of labor can emerge. The state of technology also determines which types of goods will be created by relatively "high-wage, high-profit, high-capital intensive" methods of production. The "unequal exchange" between the higher-order core and lower-order periphery economies redistributes wealth—an economic surplus—from the latter to the former.[26] In the sixteenth century, for example, the world-economy exhibited a particular form of functional dualism.

The core areas were the location of a complex variety of economic activities—mass-market industries such as there were (mainly textiles and shipbuilding), international and local commerce in the hands of an indigenous bourgeoisie, relatively advanced and complex forms of agriculture (both pastoralism and high-productivity forms of tillage with a high component of medium-sized, yeoman-owned land). The peripheral areas, by contrast, were monocultural, with the cash crops being produced on large estates by coerced labor.[27]

Wallerstein's model implicitly assumes that all nations and regions will attempt to retain core-state status (if they are already at the higher levels of the interregional order) or strive to improve their position (if they are relatively disadvantaged). The world-economy is clearly dynamic in that nations and regions can both change their place in the world order and, subject to significant constraints imposed by the world-system itself, can meaningfully influence their relationship with the remainder of the world-economy (e.g., through tariff policy). Wallerstein maintains that the original core-periphery allocation of functions between northwest Europe and the remainder of the (largely European) world-economy of the sixteenth century was a largely "accidental" conjunction of technological development and political change. However, the emergence of an interregional functional dualism was predestined because any difference, however small, between higher and lower regional economies would inevitably redistribute capital and, thus, rapidly increase the relative advantage of the emerging core through investment. A core-periphery allocation of functions had to emerge in the new world-economy; northwest Europe, through no action or strategy of its own design, became the center of higher-order functions.[28]

Wallerstein, though he does not directly discuss the relationship between them in his major works, seems to view the geographical "firmament" as a relatively unimportant element in the development of the world economy. The spatial dimension is clearly fundamental to the core-periphery model, but the content of that dimension (harbors, mineral resources, etc.) is rarely mentioned. For example, an economic-geographical determinist would probably maintain that northwest Europe was almost predestined to become the emerging core of the world-system given the state of technology and distribution of raw materials.

Wallerstein insists that the development of an individual nation must be viewed in the context of a continually evolving world-economy. This position, which in a less rigorous formulation is undoubtedly correct, seems to prohibit study of individual nations outside of the broadest historical and international context. Indeed, such studies are not included among his proposed five areas of future research: the internal functioning of the capitalist world-economy as a system, the origins of the capitalist world-economy, the historical coexistence of capitalist and noncapitalist world-systems, the alternative modes of production in various types of social system, and the development of the new world-socialism.

The theoretical approach of the present investigation into sectional stress in the United States is indebted in many ways to Wallerstein's model but differs in two important respects. First, it will be maintained that sectional stress follows the development of a core-periphery allocation of functions within the nation. While Wallerstein does maintain that core-states "because of their complex internal division of labor" can reflect the pattern of the world-system as a whole, this internal functional dualism does not play a prominent role in his analysis. Second, sectional stress along an ecologically predetermined core-periphery axis will be viewed as the major political dynamic determining the relationship of the nation to the remainder of the world-economy. In order to demonstrate this connection, the major focus must remain on the United States, and the world-economy can be only briefly treated.

The methodology and units of analysis utilized in the next eight chapters, including the historical evolution of "trade areas" in the United States and their relationship to the core-periphery model, are described in the Appendix. The reader will need to refer to this material at some point in the course of reading the book. The following chapter is an overview of American political development between 1880 and 1980 and presents evidence on the bipolar form of sectional competition and the varying intensity of regional competition throughout the last century.

2

Overview

Sectionalism is a fundamental and persistent factor in American politics. In the shaping of congressional legislation and even in the formation of the platforms of our national parties, the influence of conflicting sectional interests is of prime importance. The precise nature of such sectional conflicts and the alignment of the various sections upon the leading policies of the time are clearly revealed by an analysis of the votes and debates in Congress on outstanding issues of national importance. Such votes, mapped by congressional districts, show that again and again party lines are broken by the force of sectional interest and that both Republicans and Democrats divide into sectional wings.

Hannah Grace Roach, 1925.

Several claims about the nature of American politics will be examined in these pages. Perhaps the most important of these claims is that the seetional alignment of political forces upon which the American system rests has remained unchanged for at least a century. Since 1880, one pole of the sectional axis around which American politics has revolved has been the industrial and commercial-seaport cities of the Northeast and Midwest. At the opposite pole have been the interior distribution centers of the plantation South. The geographical consistency of this regional competition establishes its fundamental theoretical role in explaining American political development. Most accounts of American development have interpreted political change as the result of party system dynamics or one aspect of an evolving nexus between ideology, culture, and government. However, the unchanging aspect of American sectionalism strongly suggests that it is one of the primal "causes" of political development. In Braudel's words, the underlying axis of sectional competition is one of the deep "structures" of history upon which more transient social institutions rest (such as the party system or ideology).*

*Fernand Braudel interprets history as largely the product of three "waves" or *durees*: the *longue*, the *moyenne*, and the *courte*. The *courte duree* "is the subject and substance of the newspaper and in ages past of the chronicler." These short waves are the political froth or turbulence on the

22

A corollary argument is that the observed, historical consistency of sectional conflict arises out of a basic incompatibility between the economies of the industrial core and the agrarian periphery, an incompatibility that has its origins in the radically different orientations of the two regions toward the world-economy. This difference, for example, determined the political alignment over the protective tariff and imperialism in the closing decades of the nineteenth century and the early years of the twentieth. Later, differences between the social structures that characterized the industrial core and the agrarian periphery produced substantial variation between their internal political development. In the industrial areas of America, class conflict had developed by the New Deal period and led ultimately to the sharing of power by the lower classes and the industrial-financial elite. In the agrarian periphery, destabilization of the plantation Bourbons came almost forty years later and was accomplished from without by the intervention of the central state. But, as with all other changes in the relative political and economic positions of the two regions, the emergence of class conflict in the twentieth century did not alter the underlying axis of sectional competition. Though the policy content and context of political conflict was transformed by the New Deal and, later, by the civil rights movement, sectional conflict over the new agenda still pitted the industrial Northeast against the southern periphery.

A second corollary arises out of the relationship between sectional conflict and secondary social structures such as the party system, ideological belief-systems, and the central state. Sectional conflict, driven by the conflicting economic imperatives of the industrial core and agrarian periphery, has

---

surface of the historical ocean. They are made up of diplomatic intrigues and negotiations, coronations and elections, colonial annexations and territorial cessions, and economic pacts and military alliances. Such events capture the attention of most men in any society and most people remain unaware of the longer trends or waves in human history. The *moyenne durée* is located at the edge or limit of human consciousness during any historical period. Furthermore, comprehension of this wave seems to follow its occurrence and, thus, most people cannot anticipate its direction or result. As "causes" of particular political events (the *courte durée*), the *moyenne durée* is not entirely free of interdependence or "feedback." The *longue durée*, however, is the great swell of history on which the intermediate (*moyenne*) and short-term (*courte*) are mounted. To most people in any particular period, the elements composing the *longue durée* are permanent and fixed features of the sociopolitical environment. As causes of short-term events or intermediate trends, the structures of the *longue durée* are entirely free of interdependence or feedback. These elements are the "givens" of man's political and social life within any period and are completely static within the range of human consciousness. While Braudel allows for the potential inclusion of technology, social structure, and administrative capability among these long-term structures, in his most important work he discusses only the geographical featurs of the *longue durée*. The physical environment becomes, for Braudel, the arena crucially defining and limiting possibilities for the unfolding of human history. See *The Mediterranean and the Mediterranean World in the Age of Philip II* (New York: Harper and Row, 1973). See also J. H. Hexter, "Fernand Braudel and the *Monde Braude Uien*," *Journal of Modern History* 44:4 (December 1972); and Samuel Kinser, "*Annaliste* Paradigm? The Geohistorical Structuralism of Fernand Braudel," *American Historical Review* 86:1 (February 1981).

clearly influenced and, at some points in history, completely remolded these secondary structures in American development. While sectional conflict has been clearly dominant, these secondary structures have in their turn affected the form and strength of sectional influence in the political system. The political expression of sectional economic conflict was muted, for example, by the New Deal coalition between the southern plantation elite and the industrial working class. Somewhat earlier, the payment of military pensions to Union veterans helped to solidify political support for the protective tariff and the Republican party in the agrarian plains of the Midwest. While important in their own right, these events did not disturb the underlying axis of sectional competition.

The fundamental role of sectionalism in American political development determines the place of other potentially competitive explanatory factors. Three of these factors are political institutions, party competition, and ideological beliefs. Of the possible explanatory factors, sectional conflict has exhibited the greatest persistence and consistency in American development.

Explanatory Factor	Historical Duration	Example
Sectional conflict	Long-term (century or more)	Core-periphery competition
Political institutions	Intermediate (half-century)	Strong congressional committee system
Party competition	Intermediate (half-century)	New Deal Coalition
Ideological beliefs	Short-term (quarter-century or less)	Nativism, pacifism, religious movements

Less durable than sectional conflict, the major political institutions that control the course and strength of the central state have been crucially influenced by regional competition. The clearest case is the pervasive decentralizing tendency in almost all areas of federal policy. Other examples would include the congressional committee system, civil service recruitment and classification of the central state bureaucracy, and a large, permanent military establishment. Each of these institutions, in turn, affects the political expression of sectional conflict. However, this feedback effect is much more transient and less significant than the original influence of the underlying regional alignment.

In this scheme, the dynamics of party competition occupies a position somewhat similar to political institutions. Included here are a wide variety of legal and organizational mechanisms which structure the electoral process. The most important effect of these legal and organizational arrangements is to make certain coalitions of interests likely while making the effective expression of other interests difficult or impossible. The white primary, poll tax, and literacy tests which were common in the South between 1890 and 1965 effectively strengthened the political dominance of the plantation elite in the region. The two-thirds rule governing Democratic presidential nominations, repealed in 1936, gave the southern periphery veto power over potential candidates placed before the national convention. To take a third case, the decline of the urban machine in the North has made accommodation between the two sectional wings of the New Deal coalition more difficult. In the past a secure electoral base allowed northern Democrats to resolve even the most intractable disputes within the national party by compromise and logrolling. Freewheeling primaries have now replaced machine-controlled nominations, and the core electorate can deny renomination to incumbents who become too accommodating to periphery interests.

Ideological belief-systems are probably the most malleable aspects of the American political system. Ideology becomes a significant explanatory factor when important political divisions in society do not coincide with the coalition structure of the major parties. When the party system parallels the fundamental sectional alignment, ideology (e.g., progressivism) tends to span regional cleavages. When the party system is not regionally polarized, however, ideology tends to reflect the imperatives of the underlying sectional conflict. Such is the function of modern strains of liberalism and conservatism. Ideological belief-systems thus articulate political demands which are not adequately expressed within the party system, and they are effectively destroyed by conjunction with one or the other of the two parties (as happened with populism in 1896 and progressivism from 1912 to 1916). One of the most important functions of American ideologies is to provide labels for political actors and governmental actions that reflect the most pervasive cross-party cleavages (as, for instance, "liberal Democrat" and "progressive Republican"). The role of political institutions, party, and ideology as explanatory factors will be extensively considered in each of the substantive chapters and, separately, in chapters 7 and 8.

Roll Call Voting and Sectional Stress

Though many different types of data are presented, the basis of this study is the roll call behavior of congressmen in the House of Representatives. Perhaps the most significant assumption that has been made concerning this behavior is that most voting decisions in the House reflect the economic interests of the members' constituencies. In many cases, such as the grant-in-aid formula fights that captured national attention in the 1970s, the connection between constituency interest and voting decisions can be unambiguously demonstrated. But when policy alternatives are less clearly defined, so are the direct interest of constituencies and the indicated position of their congressmen. Furthermore, in many instances a district's interests may be intimately linked to the corresponding interests of surrounding districts. For example, the Wichita consumer's direct interest in cheap bread may be outweighed by an indirect interest in maintaining rural prosperity in the Kansas hinterland (through high government price supports for wheat). A sizeable portion of the Wichita economy services the collection and distribution needs of the surrounding agricultural community and is thus dependent on that community's economic health. Finally, congressmen regularly trade votes and in so doing greatly complicate the connection between economic interest and voting patterns. In summary, there are at least three ways in which the connection between economic interest and congressional voting can be loosened without necessarily violating the assumption: interdependency with surrounding districts, unclear policy alternatives, and vote trading.

Most of the interdependency between congressional districts has been captured by the trade area definitions discussed in the Appendix. Interdependency between urban centers and their tributary hinterlands lies at the very heart of sectionalism as an analytical theory and constitutes the theoretical basis of the trade area concept used in the sectional stress index and in tables throughout this book.

The clarity of policy choices is closely connected to the latitude or breadth of executive and bureaucratic discretion. In Chapters 4 and 8 it will be argued that the rise of executive and bureaucratic discretion after 1930 made the New Deal coalition possible by intentionally avoiding public positions on specific legislative alternatives. Generally speaking, executive discretion strengthens party-centered logrolling arrangements (which are brokered by the presidential administration when the party controls the White House). The rise of bureaucratic and executive discretion since the New Deal is probably responsible for some portion of the secular decline in sectional stress over the last fifty years.

Vote-trading takes place at many different levels of specification and over widely varying time horizons. Only one thing is certain about logrolling behavior and that is that we can explicitly recognize only a small proportion of the individual cases in which it takes place. A number of different types of vote-trading can be described. The six categories of vote-trading arrangements included in table 2.1 are not in any sense mutually exclusive. In fact, economic interests, as defined by the position of individual constituencies within the national political economy, comprise the driving force underlying each of them. Furthermore, any specific legislative decision will include aspects of all six types of vote-trading. For example, the vote by which federal aid was extended to New York City was of direct interest to the city and state, involved future trades between individual members of the Banking Committee, was partially brokered by the leadership of the Democratic party, was chosen by the Americans for Democratic Action as a "liberal" test vote in their annual ratings, was supported by the Banking Committee majority, and provoked a sharp regionally polarized cleavage within the House membership (see chapter 6).

In most situations, identifying a single motivating factor which explains

Table 2.1. Vote-Trading Arrangements

Type of Vote-Trading Arrangement	Trading Partners	Degree of Specification	Time Horizon
(Direct Constituency Interest)	(None)	(No Trade)	(No Trade)
Individuals	Individuals	Usually High	Usually Short
Party Organizations	Party Members	Moderate	Medium-Term
Ideology	Perceived Colleagues	Usually Low	Long-Term
Institutional Norms	Reciprocity between Committee Majorities	Very Low	Very Long-Term
Sectional Alignment	Members in Core or Periphery	Extremely Low	Extremely Long-Term

a congressman's decision to desert his constituency's direct interest is an impossible task. The congressional voting calculus is structured at different levels of specification and with different time horizons. At the lowest level the congressman supports his district's immediate interest. This may or may not be compatible with his chosen party, ideological allegiance, or other characteristics which define his position within the House of Representatives. The only defining feature of this category is that the member's position on the roll call does not necessarily imply a trading or pooling of political influence at any level. For example, when a member from Manhattan cast his vote in support of the New York City aid bill, he might have ascribed his decision to party loyalty, ideologically based beliefs, or institutional reciprocity norms. The outside observer only knows that these influences need not be invoked in order to explain the congressman's decision.

On many roll calls, however, either a majority of the members deviate from the direct economic interests of their constituencies or the policy alternatives presented to the members are more or less indistinct. Deviations from direct interest probably indicate a trading of votes with those members who are also directly interested but vote consistently with their own constituency interest. For example, the least complex description of a rural Arkansas district's interest in New York City aid is that it involves a slightly higher potential or actual tax burden. If the Arkansas member votes in favor of federal aid, it can be assumed that this choice was dictated by a sensitivity to one or more of the other categories. At the individual level, the Arkansas member may have traded his vote with one or more members of the New York delegation. Because they lack organizational, institutional, or ideological frameworks, such trades are usually explicit and, therefore, short-term. In this case, the New York side of the bargain might have been support for a rice subsidy measure on the following day. At the party-centered level, formally designated party leaders broker the interests of the various factions. These leaders usually promise organization support for measures without explicitly committing individual

votes. For the Arkansas member, such support might include favorable sched-
uling of the rice subsidy legislation and the designation of the bill as a "priority" goal of the party. Without promising that specific individuals will reciprocate for the Arkansas member's support on the New York aid bill, the
party leadership promises a favorable outcome on the rice bill or a very similar
measure in the near future.

Ideological coalitions draw their importance in the political system from
several features of their organization and their constantly evolving belief-
systems. First, ideology independently influences coalition-building and the
pooling of political influence because it offers an alternative bargaining framework to party organizations. When the interests aligned on a policy issue
are distributed in such a way that major parties do not offer particularly helpful or effective templates for constructing a majority coalition, the liberal-
conservative spectrum is often the most useful alternative. An ideological
belief-system is an effective alternative because it represents a constantly evolving search for the lowest common denominator between constituencies located
at one end of the ideological spectrum. For example, aid to New York City
became an ADA-endorsed measure because of the historic role of the city as the
national center of liberalism. If Dallas had been placed in exactly the same
situation, the ADA probably would have ignored its plight. By backing New
York, the aid package was included in the other positions the ADA supports,
which, taken together, compose the political economy of liberalism (just as
there is a political economy of conservatism). Contemporary "liberal" positions include support for the nationalization and expansion of the American
welfare state, opposition to agricultural subsidies and increased defense spending, support for federal aid for mass transit programs, selected regulatory
reforms, resistance to restrictions on the availability of abortions, and opposition to prayer in the public schools.

Considered as a whole, the economic interests and social attitudes that
the ADA endorses are concentrated in a group of congressional districts that
might be designated the heart of American liberalism. In recent years, this
class of congressional districts has coincided almost exactly with the industrial
core and has therefore comprised a sectionally based, alternative coalition to
the depolarized party system (see chapter 8). Traditionally members of Congress have played a central role in the construction of the ADA liberalism
index from roll call data. It is therefore possible that these members could play
a brokering role roughly similar to that played by the party leadership (by
designating bills such as the New York aid measure as "tests" of liberalism).
Generally speaking, however, ideological coalitions represent a pooling of political influence with a significantly lower level of specification and longer time
horizon than party-centered arrangements. In part, these differences can be
traced to the homogeneous nature of economic interests represented within an
ideological coalition, compared to the party-centered alternative.

Institutional norms compose yet another way in which members can
pool their political influence. Respect for institutional norms represents a tacit

acceptance of institutional officers—as opposed to party leaders or ideological groups—in the role of political brokers. The incentives underlying this acceptance are quite complex but are relatively enduring. These incentives are further explored in chapter 7. The most prominent institutional norm is reciprocal respect by the various committees for each panel's proposals. In the example given above, the Arkansas member supports the majority position of the Banking Committee (passage of New York City aid) *and* many other measures supported by the relevant committees; in return, the Arkansas member expects floor support for his rice subsidy measure *if* he wins majority approval from his own Committee on Agriculture. Committee reciprocity norms thus operate on behavior in nearly all roll call decisions, and the time horizon of this pooling of influence—the period in which a member expects something back—spans nearly the entire length of a congressman's career.

At the foundation of the political system lies the fundamental coreperiphery sectional alignment which continually reshapes the comparatively ephemeral forms of other proto-coalitions. In certain historical periods (e.g., 1880–1930), the party system closely coincides with the core-periphery alignment, and party-centered vote-trading arrangements are then the most effective and visible type of influence pooling. In these periods, ideological coalitions (such as populism or progressivism) represent policy issues which obliquely cut across the fundamental sectional alignment. In other periods, the geographical distribution of ideological belief-systems most closely coincides with the core-periphery cleavage (1965 to the present). In these years, the party system is sectionally depolarized and ideological pools of influence appear to be dominant.

In almost all legislative situations, an increase in the amount of executive or bureaucratic discretion involved in the policy alternatives presented to congressmen will increase the strength of pooling arrangements which cut across the fundamental sectional alignment. During the progressive era, for example, statutory specification tended to strengthen party-centered brokering arrangements, to the chagrin and disappointment of the bipartisan alliance of Republican insurgents and Democratic progressives.[1] Highly specified and detailed policy alternatives tend to increase the proportion of "direct economic interest" votes compared to more discretionary and broadly worded alternatives. Where these direct interests comprise major parts of the political system, the distribution of those interests tends to coincide with the underlying core-periphery alignment. From this observation, it is not surprising that the secular rise of the bureaucratic state and the "imperial" presidency has lessened the intensity of contemporary sectional conflict.

After 1933 and up to at least 1965, executive and bureaucratic discretion strengthened the hand of the party leadership and the influence of institutional norms. During the same period—particularly the latter half—ideologically based pooling arrangements and the influence of the underlying sectional alignment were correspondingly weakened by the delegation of legislative authority to the executive branch. Throughout this period, it should be noted, the party controlling the presidency was consistently more favorable to the granting of executive discretion than was the party out of power.[2] As with the other relationships that have been described in this section, the effect of the bureaucratic state on sectional conflict should not be considered in isolation. Instead, the American bureaucratic state is the end product of the New Deal Democratic coalition's attempts to retain political power in the face of the incompatible policy demands put forward by the southern plantation elite and the industrial working classes (see chapters 4 and 8).

From an analytical perspective it is usually not very productive to compare the influence of the different pooling arrangements on a specific vote or group of roll calls. They operate on totally different levels. Direct constituency interest, for example, influences the voting pattern solely on the immediate roll call. On the other hand, explicit trades between individuals influence at least two roll calls on different policy issues in which the bargain is consummated. Both party organizations and ideological groups influence more or less open-ended sets of roll calls. On the New York City bill, for example, the influence of party-centered pooling arrangements might carry over onto many seemingly unrelated decisions (such as the rice subsidy measure) which might span several years. Institutional norms implicate almost all roll calls and an even longer time horizon. At the most fundamental level, the underlying sectional alignment of economic interests and political forces shapes the structure and influence of these pooling arrangements, whether or not there is explicit recognition by the political actors involved.

Furthermore, these pooling arrangements overlap both in terms of membership and policy implications. For instance, the institutional norms which have supported a strong committee system were also indispensable to the maintenance of the New Deal Democratic coalition. Most of the members benefiting from a strong committee system were Democrats after 1932, and the decentralization of legislative decision-making in effect allocated political power among the party's competing factions. The fates of the institution and of the party were thus intertwined. Finally, a member can obviously participate in more than one pooling arrangement at the same time (as the hypothetical Arkansas member might have done).

While direct comparison of the influence of different pooling arrangements is difficult, we can more easily measure the importance of one pooling structure on various roll calls. For example, the relative influence of ideological beliefs can be gauged by noting the correspondence between roll call cleavages and conventionally measured ideological predispositions (e.g., the ratings published by the Americans for Democratic Action). For party organizations, unity scores and differences in party voting provide evidence for such comparisons. Regional competition is measured by the sectional stress index described in the Appendix. While sectional polarization over particular political issues or within isolated periods of American history has often been noted, most accounts of regional conflict have over-emphasized the importance of transient political events as the immediate cause of regional competition and, as a result, underestimated the continuity and influence of the underlying structure of sectional stress.

The Fundamental Alignment of Sectional Stress

Throughout American history there have been distinct periods in which certain critical issues have dominated political debate. While no study could hope to cover all of these periods or the policy conflicts that have colored their political life, one way to trace the rise and fall of major political currents is to sample the political activity within each decade and analyze the controversial roll calls that divided the House of Representatives.

The evidence to be presented was drawn from a survey of political behavior within ten separate Congresses, each of which met during the middle years of its respective decade (see table 2.2). In each survey, an analysis of legislative roll calls was used to describe the form and intensity of sectional stress and to identify the types of policies which provoked high levels of sectional political conflict. For each period, a central "theme" emerges which characterizes the connection between the contemporary policy decisions that generated sectional stress and the long-term evolution of the national political economy. In chapters 3 through 6 the distinctive theme of each Congress is subsequently extended by relating the economic and political impact of these policies to similar ones in other historical periods.*

Even though this procedure is not exhaustive, it balances several competing analytical goals. It allows legislative behavior to be interpreted within the unique institutional context that characterized each Congress while also treating government policies as a part of the historical development of the political system and the growth of the nation-state. In addition, the sampling procedure allows the isolation and identification of the underlying structure of sectional stress that was the common foundation for political conflict in all of these periods.†

*The sampling procedure unavoidably biases the analysis in chapters 3 through 6 toward policies which provoked high levels of sectional stress in their respective periods. The decision to proceed in this manner was made for several reasons. First, in most periods contested policy decisions which provoked low sectional stress scores concerned relatively trivial matters such as adjournment from one day to the next, committee funding requests, non-binding resolutions, or omnibus measures with conflicting implications. (A number of low-stress decisions are, however, considered in the analysis of regional competition during the New Deal.) Second, the high-stress decisions in each period identified policy areas of unquestionable saliency to American political development (see table 2.5). Though the reader can almost certainly identify important themes that have not been covered, this sampling is both broad enough to draw a general outline of sectionalism in American history and narrow enough to allow a full examination of the basis of sectional competition in specific areas of the national political economy. What this research design highlights is the linkage between the primacy of sectional stress in roll call voting, the relatively unchanging axis of regional competition over the last century, and the policy analysis of political conflict in each of the ten periods.

† As a first step in the analysis of policy issues in each of the ten Congresses, the level of sectional stress was measured on all roll calls for which the winning margin was less than or equal

Table 2.2. Presidential Administrations and Corresponding Congresses,
1881–1982

Congress		Presidential Administration
47th	1881–83	Garfield (R) and Arthur (R)
48th		Arthur (R)
49th	1885–87 (1st Period)[a]	Cleveland (D)
50th		Cleveland (D)
51st		Harrison (R)
52nd		Harrison (R)
53rd		Cleveland (D)
54th	1895–97 (2nd Period)	Cleveland (D)
55th		McKinley (R)
56th		McKinley (R)
57th		McKinley (R) and Roosevelt (R)
58th		Roosevelt (R)
59th	1905–7 (3rd Period)	Roosevelt (R)
60th		Roosevelt (R)
61st		Taft (R)
62nd		Taft (R)
63rd		Wilson (D)
64th	1915–17 (4th Period)	Wilson (D)
65th		Wilson (D)
66th		Wilson (D)
67th		Harding (R)
68th		Coolidge (R)
69th	1925–27 (5th Period)	Coolidge (R)
70th		Coolidge (R)
71st		Hoover (R)
72nd		Hoover (R)
73rd		Roosevelt (D)
74th	1935–36 (6th Period)	Roosevelt (D)
75th		Roosevelt (D)
76th		Roosevelt (D)
77th		Roosevelt (D)
78th		Roosevelt (D)
79th	1945–46 (7th Period)	Truman (D)
80th		Truman (D)
81st		Truman (D)
82nd		Truman (D)
83rd		Eisenhower (R)
84th	1955–56 (8th Period)	Eisenhower (R)
85th		Eisenhower (R)
86th		Eisenhower (R)
87th		Kennedy (D)
88th		Kennedy (D) and Johnson (D)
89th	1965–66 (9th Period)	Johnson (D)
90th		Johnson (D)
91st		Nixon (R)
92nd		Nixon (R)

Table 2.2. (continued)

Congress	Presidential Administration
93rd	Nixon (R) and Ford (R)
94th 1975–76 (10th Period)	Ford (R)
95th	Carter (D)
96th	Carter (D)
97th 1981–82	Reagan (R)

[a] The ten Congresses analyzed in this study are indicated by period.

Table 2.3. Method Used to Isolate and Identify Regional Poles

1. Sectional stress scores are calculated for all competitive roll calls taken during a given Congress. Competitive roll calls are those in which the majority of those voting is less than or equal to 55 percent.
2. The ten roll calls with the highest sectional stress scores are identified and the positions of each trade area delegation with more than four members are noted.
3. Regional poles are identified by isolating sets of regional delegations which are opposed on every one of the ten highest roll calls.
4. Where more than one set of regional poles emerges from the analysis, the "major alignment" is that set involving the largest number of members.

---

to 55 percent. The winning margin criterion was adopted for a number of reasons. First, some standardization in roll call margins was necessary in order to develop the polar designations described in this chapter. In addition, a closely competitive roll call is usually associated with calculated and carefully considered political behavior because individual congressmen are likely to influence the outcome. Furthermore, a close vote is often a critical watershed for the policy under consideration and indicates in a general way the probable composition of a "minimal winning coalition" in that policy area. Finally, but not least in importance, a closely competitive roll call divides the nation into two roughly equal parts. Given issues upon which the level of sectional stress is approximately equal, the more evenly balanced the size of the two regional coalitions, the more serious are the implications of that level of sectional stress for national integration and unity.

Given this data base of closely competitive roll calls, the "poles" of sectional stress within each period were identified by a procedure involving three steps. First, scores on the sectional stress index were calculated for each roll call and the ten votes with the highest stress scores were identified. Second, the position of every trade area delegation on each of the ten roll calls was noted and compared. Finally, the "poles" of sectional stress were determined by isolating sets of trade area delegations whose majorities took opposing positions on all ten roll calls (see table 2.3). Where more than one set of sectional poles emerged from the analysis, the "major alignment" was that set of delegations involving the largest number of congressmen. It should be noted that this procedure could theoretically produce a pattern which contained as many different poles as there were trade area delegations or a pattern which contained no poles at all.

Table 2.4. Major Trade Area Alignments, 1885–1976

				Congress					
49th 1885–87	54th 1895–97	59th 1905–7	64th 1915–17	69th 1925–27	74th 1935–36	79th 1945–46	84th 1955–56	89th 1965–66	94th 1975–76
				Core					
Albany Boston Buffalo Grand Rapids Minneapolis Omaha Philadelphia Pittsburgh Portland, Me. San Francisco Syracuse	Columbus	Chicago Cleveland Minneapolis Omaha Pittsburgh	Boston Buffalo Chicago New York Philadelphia Pittsburgh San Francisco	Boston New York Philadelphia Pittsburgh Toledo	Boston Philadelphia	Columbus Indianapolis	Boston New York Philadelphia	New York	Boston New York Philadelphia
				Periphery					
Atlanta Memphis Nashville New Orleans Richmond St. Louis	Atlanta Charleston, S.C. Memphis Nashville Richmond	Atlanta Birmingham Dallas Houston Jacksonville Little Rock Louisville Memphis New Orleans Richmond	Atlanta Birmingham Dallas Houston Jacksonville Kansas City Little Rock Louisville Memphis New Orleans Oklahoma City Richmond St. Louis	Atlanta Birmingham Fort Worth Little Rock Memphis Nashville Oklahoma City	Seattle	Birmingham Charlotte Dallas Little Rock Memphis Nashville New Orleans Richmond San Antonio	Birmingham Dallas Memphis	Charlotte Dallas Knoxville	Atlanta Birmingham Charlotte Dallas Memphis New Orleans

Trade area poles (i.e., consistent regional opponents) appeared in each of the ten periods between 1885 and 1976 (for the major alignments, see table 2.4). In five Congresses (the 54th, 59th, 64th, 79th, and 94th), the major trade area alignment was the only one that developed. In the other five, the minor or secondary alignments that also appeared usually involved only two or three delegations and voting patterns very similar to the major alignments of those Congresses. For example, a minor alignment developed in the 1885–87 period which differed from the major voting pattern on only one roll call. This secondary alignment placed the Milwaukee and Kansas City delegations in opposition to Charleston (South Carolina); the former trade areas generally— aside from the deviant roll call—supported the core while the latter aligned with the periphery. These alignment patterns are more extensively treated in the sections devoted to each of the periods.

The bipolar structure of sectional stress in American politics is a reflection of the internal core-periphery continuum around which the economic life of the country is organized. At one end of the continuum, the oldest and largest industrial centers and seaports in the nation are concentrated. In American economic history, these regions have dominated the national political economy through control of the state apparatus and the domestic financial community. As the nation developed, the policy imperatives of the industrial-commercial core—policies viewed by the political representatives of the section as necessary for the maintenance or advancement of its interests in the national political economy—have often changed. However, whenever the implementation of those policy imperatives has provoked a high level of sectional stress, the industrial-commercial core has been opposed by the interior-hinterland periphery.

The specific positions of the trade area delegations on the core-periphery continuum can be assessed on the basis of their long-term voting records (see table 2.5).* When twenty-four major delegations are ranked according to their support for the industrial-commercial core, Philadelphia, which supported the core in 96 of 100 high-stress votes, comes out on top, and the

---

*The twenty-four trade areas included in the table met two conditions: each was identifiable as a trade area in at least eight of the ten periods between 1881 and 1981, and in each of those periods the delegation contained at least four congressmen. The trade area approach, by design and theory, produces constantly changing units of analysis. While these twenty-four trade areas were relatively constant over the last century, their boundaries and the number of congressmen in their delegations changed with each decade as the urban network grew or contracted. Altered population patterns (based on census returns), congressional reapportionment (either adding or subtracting members, or merely altering district lines), and—most important—new trade area boundaries could singly or together radically restructure a trade area delegation designated by the same urban center name. The table gives the voting record of trade area delegation majorities for each of the ten Congresses and a summary score in the far right column. Within each Congress, a score of one hundred means that the majority of the trade area delegation supported the industrial-commercial core position on each of the ten "high stress" roll calls; a scope of zero indicates that the respective delegation majorities never supported the core and always aligned with the interior-hinterland periphery.

Table 2.5. The Bipolar Structure of American Politics: Trade Area Alignment with the Industrial-Commercial Core, 1885–1976

	Agreement with Industrial-Commercial Core on High-Stress Roll Calls (%)[a]										
Trade Area	1885–87	1895–97	1905–7	1915–17	1925–27	1935–36	1945–46	1955–56	1965–66	1975–76	100 Roll Calls, 1885–1976
Philadelphia	100	80	90	100	100	100	95	100	95	100	96.0
Boston	100	65	80	100	100	100	70	100	95	100	91.0
Buffalo	100	70	85	100	95	—	90	90	85	65	86.7[b]
Chicago	90	80	100	100	80	60	45	85	90	80	81.0
New York	25	50	90	100	100	70	60	100	100	100	79.5
Detroit	20	65	90	80	90	90	80	70	90	90	76.5
Pittsburgh	100	80	100	100	100	10	75	60	85	55	76.5
San Francisco	100	50	60	100	85	35	40	90	65	95	72.0
Cleveland	75	90	100	55	50	75	40	90	50	70	69.5
Omaha	100	75	100	65	25	—	90	50	45	—	68.7[b]
Cincinnati	75	80	80	60	85	95	85	60	40	20	68.0
Minneapolis	100	75	100	90	80	45	85	20	35	40	67.0
Indianapolis	35	90	—	—	25	50	100	60	40	75	59.4[b]
Kansas City	90	50	90	0	45	60	75	25	30	20	48.5
Denver	—	15	—	25	80	10	85	30	60	20	40.6[b]
St. Louis	0	80	30	0	15	40	85	40	60	25	37.5
Baltimore	10	60	15	25	25	30	20	85	—	—	33.7[b]
Louisville	15	25	0	0	90	60	—	—	25	10	28.1[b]
Richmond	0	0	0	0	20	40	0	30	20	10	12.0
New Orleans	0	5	0	0	20	10	0	10	30	0	7.5
Birmingham	—	—	0	0	0	20	0	0	25	0	5.6[b]
Atlanta	0	0	0	0	0	15	5	10	10	0	4.0
Memphis	0	0	0	0	0	10	0	0	20	0	3.0
Dallas	—	—	0	0	5	15	0	0	0	0	2.5[b]
Correlation[c]	.729	.760	.892	.898	.762	.668	.725	.810	.821	.865	

[a] Where a trade area split evenly on a high-stress roll call, the delegation was viewed as half "in-agreement" with and half "opposed" to the polar position. Otherwise, the trade area majority determined the position of the delegation.

[b] Table 2.5 does not report the sectional alignment of trade areas that did not appear consistently in trade area systems between 1880 and 1981, nor does the table record the position of delegations containing fewer than four members. In eight of the twenty-four delegations, the trade area either did not exist as a separate entity or had fewer than four members in one or more of the ten Congresses. In these eight cases, the performance of the trade area delegation in the remaining Congresses was pro-rated to one hundred.

[c] Relationship between roll call behavior in the indicated Congress and behavior in the nine other periods (the summary scores were recalculated to exclude the indicated Congress).

The column on the far right summarizes the voting records of each trade area delegation over the last century in terms of their support for the commercial-seaport core. Since ten high-stress votes were analyzed for each of the ten periods, the summary score was based on one hundred roll calls. Using these scores, the twenty-four delegations were ranked on a core-periphery continuum.

Memphis delegation, which opposed the core on 97 of the same role calls, ranks next to the bottom (behind Dallas with a pro-rated core support score of 2 ½). From their summary scores, we can conclude that the Philadelphia and Memphis delegations opposed each other on *at least* ninety-three of the one hundred high-stress roll calls from 1885 to 1976.

Because the summary scores span a century and generalize the results of roll calls taken on a wide variety of issues, the resultant ranking of trade area delegations can be interpreted as accurately reflecting the fundamental geographical structure underlying the American political system. Viewed in traditional terms, the main axis of sectional stress has run between the Northeast and the Deep South and the poles or ends of the sectional continuum have exhibited great stability over the entire period. Viewed in terms of the core-periphery dichotomy, one pole has been anchored in the large commercial seaports of the nation, a category which includes centers like Chicago and San Francisco, located at some distance from the eastern seaboard. Seven of the eight trade areas which have summary scores greater than seventy contain urban centers characterized by commercial, industrial, and export-import trade prominence (Pittsburgh, the only exception, is primarily industrial). At the other end of the sectional stress axis, six of seven trade areas with core support scores under thirty are located in the interior, away from the nation's coastline (the only exception here is New Orleans).

The political dynamics of economic competition between the two poles have revolved around a constantly changing set of policy issues. Largely created and given political prominence by core or periphery representatives, these issues have always had the same relationship to the political economy imperatives of the industrial-commercial and interior-hinterland poles; what the core supported, the periphery opposed. The two most fundamental causes of their political incompatibility are the regional division of labor and the relation of each section to the larger world-economy. While the composition of the two poles has exhibited little change over the last century, the middle ranges of the axis have been unstable. The trade areas located in the middle of the continuum share some characteristics typical of the core and other typical of the periphery. Because they straddle both poles, these delegations have been extremely sensitive to the specific issue or policy content of high-stress roll calls in any given Congress. When the content of these roll calls touches upon features of their economic structure that they share with the core, these trade area delegations align with the industrial-commercial pole; when the roll call implicates political economy imperatives shared with the periphery, the region tilts toward the interior-hinterland pole.

The extent to which different political settings or periods correspond to the underlying structure of sectional stress can be calculated by correlating the scores for each of the ten Congresses with composite scores made up of trade area positions assumed over the remainder of the last century. For example, trade area support for core positions during the 74th Congress (1935–36) can be correlated with core support over the ninety high-stress roll calls recorded in the other nine Congresses. Because each individual Congress is thus isolated, the resulting correlations are statistically independent. All ten correlations are extremely high. Of the ten Congresses, the 59th (1905–7), the 64th (1915–17), and the 94th (1975–76) replicated the underlying sectional structure most accurately. In 1905–7, the issue content of high-stress roll calls concerned statehood and American imperialism and resulted in a correlation of .892 with roll call behavior in the other nine periods. The policy theme for the 64th Congress was mobilization carried out in preparation for American entry into World War I. The correlation here was .898. For the latest period (1975–76), policy proposals that were intended to stem or reverse the economic decline of the core regions dominated the political arena and yielded a correlation of .865.

Political alignments strayed farthest from the underlying structure in the 49th (1885–87), the 74th (1935–36), and the 79th (1945–46) Congresses. In the 49th Congress, the House of Representatives was preoccupied with private bills intended to grant military pensions to specific claimants. The voting pattern nevertheless correlated at the .729 level with the summary stress scores. The New Deal was at flood tide during the 74th Congress (which produced a correlation of .668), and policy decisions growing out of war demobilization dominated high-stress roll calls in the 1945–46 period (a correlation of .725).

These correlations follow what will become a familiar cyclical pattern. The passing of Reconstruction, the consolidation of local power by the southern plantation elite, and tariff-protected industrialization all combined to intensify and mold political conflict along a single sectional axis. As the core and periphery elites increased their dominance over the industrial-commercial and interior-hinterland poles, the correlation between the policy conflicts associated with each political period and the underlying structure of sectional stress steadily increased from 1885 to 1917. Later the farm crisis of the twenties and the New Deal introduced "cross-cutting" cleavages in regional conflict, and the correlations fell between 1917 and 1936. From the point of greatest deviance in the 1930s, the correlation at each subsequent period has increased. The explanation for this cyclical pattern of resurgence and abatement as well as for peculiarities in the sectional alignments of each Congress, will be treated in following chapters.

Sectional Alignments in Each of the Ten Periods

Maps 2. 1 through 2. 10 show the sectional alignment of all trade area delegations, including those containing fewer than four members, during ten Congresses. Since the high-stress roll calls upon which these maps are based are closely competitive, the procedure tends to divide the nation in half (without, of course, specifying in which half any trade area delegation will fall).

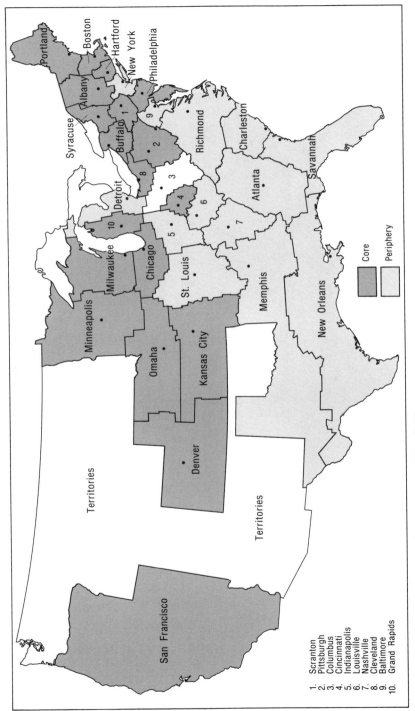

Map 2.1. Opposing Sections in the 49th Congress (1885–1887)

Core   Periphery

Portland
Boston
Hartford
New York
Philadelphia
Albany
Syracuse
1   Buffalo
9
2
8   3
Detroit   4   6
10   5   7
Milwaukee
Chicago
Minneapolis   St. Louis
Richmond
Charleston
Savannah
Atlanta
Memphis
New Orleans

Omaha   Kansas City

Denver

Territories

Territories

San Francisco

1.   Scranton
2.   Pittsburgh
3.   Columbus
4.   Cincinnati
5.   Indianapolis
6.   Louisville
7.   Nashville
8.   Cleveland
9.   Baltimore
10. Grand Rapids

39

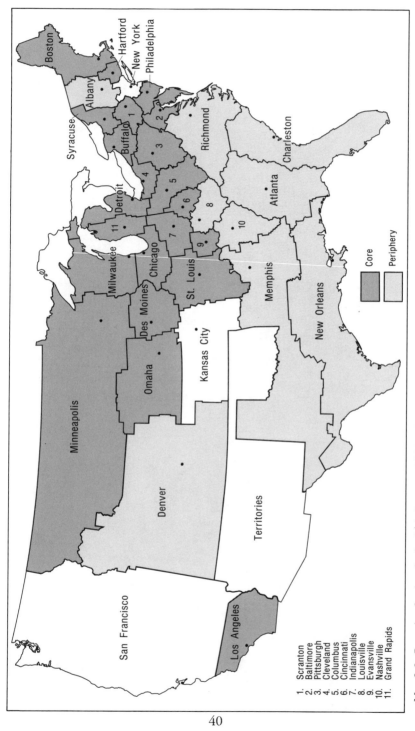

Map 2.2. Opposing Sections in the 54th Congress (1895–1897)

1. Scranton
2. Baltimore
3. Pittsburgh
4. Cleveland
5. Columbus
6. Cincinnati
7. Indianapolis
8. Louisville
9. Evansville
10. Nashville
11. Grand Rapids

Core

Periphery

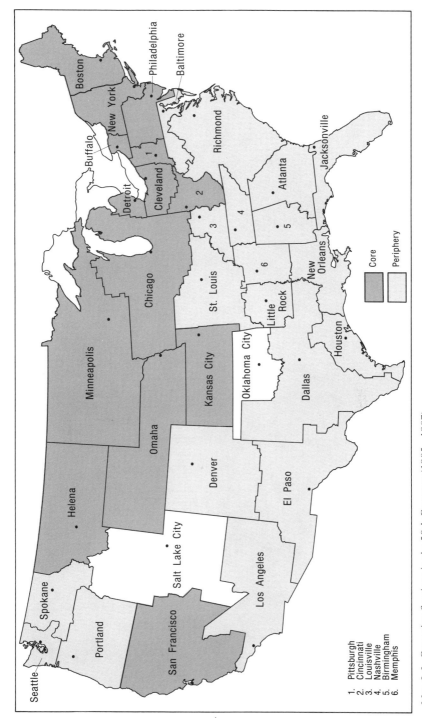

Map 2.3. Opposing Sections in the 59th Congress (1905–1907)

1. Pittsburgh
2. Cincinnati
3. Louisville
4. Nashville
5. Birmingham
6. Memphis

Core
Periphery

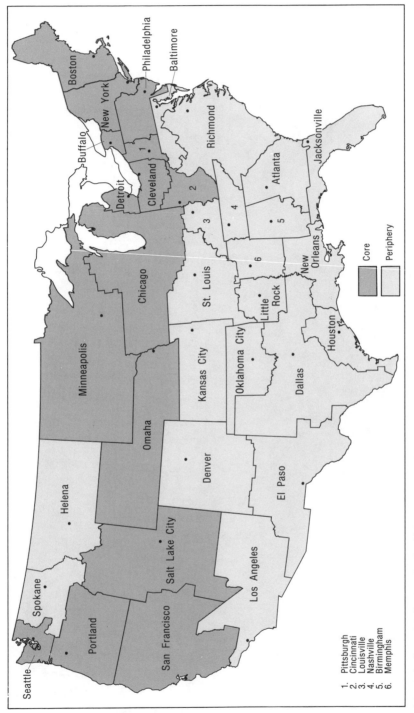

Map 2.4. Opposing Sections in the 64th Congress (1915–1917)

Core

Periphery

1. Pittsburgh
2. Cincinnati
3. Louisville
4. Nashville
5. Birmingham
6. Memphis

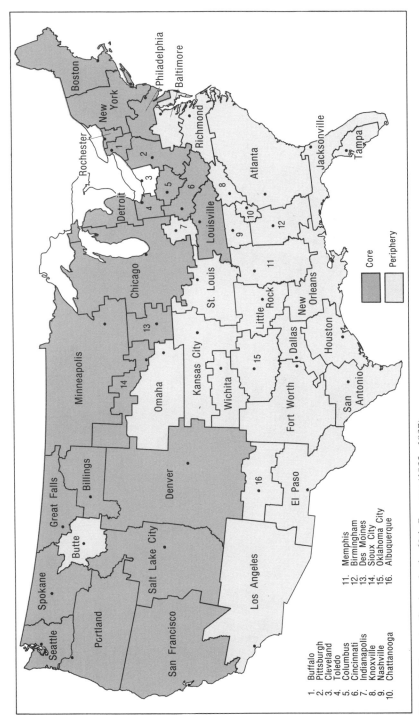

Map 2.5. Opposing Sections in the 69th Congress (1925–1927)

1. Buffalo	11. Memphis
2. Pittsburgh	12. Birmingham
3. Cleveland	13. Des Moines
4. Toledo	14. Sioux City
5. Columbus	15. Oklahoma City
6. Cincinnati	16. Albuquerque
7. Indianapolis	
8. Knoxville	
9. Nashville	
10. Chattanooga	

Core   Periphery

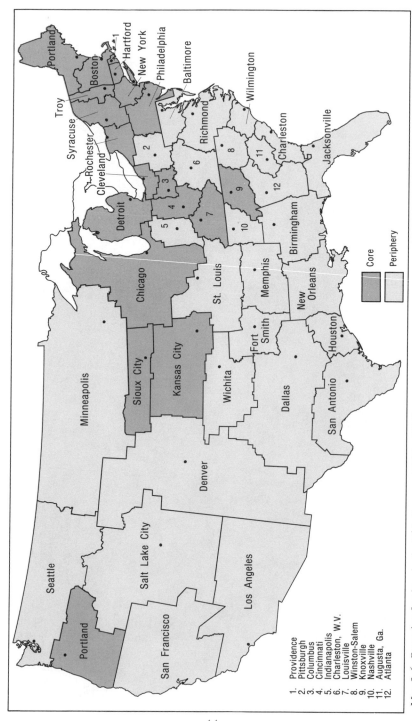

Map 2.6. Opposing Sections in the 74th Congress (1935–1936)

Core

Periphery

1. Providence
2. Pittsburgh
3. Columbus
4. Cincinnati
5. Indianapolis
6. Charleston, W.V.
7. Louisville
8. Winston-Salem
9. Knoxville
10. Nashville
11. Augusta, Ga.
12. Atlanta

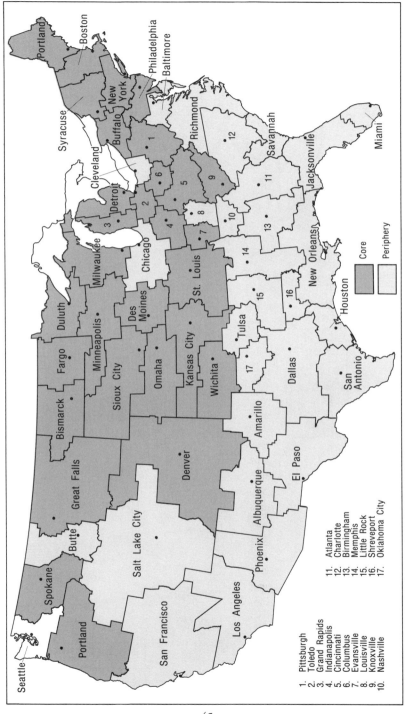

Map 2.7. Opposing Sections in the 79th Congress (1945–1946)

Core

Periphery

Portland
Boston
Philadelphia
Baltimore
New York
Syracuse
Richmond
Savannah
Buffalo
Jacksonville
Cleveland
Miami
Detroit
Milwaukee
Chicago
New Orleans
St. Louis
Houston
Duluth
Des Moines
Minneapolis
Fargo
Sioux City
Omaha
Kansas City
Tulsa
Bismarck
Wichita
Dallas
San Antonio
Great Falls
Denver
Amarillo
El Paso
Butte
Salt Lake City
Albuquerque
Phoenix
Spokane
Portland
San Francisco
Los Angeles
Seattle

1. Pittsburgh
2. Toledo
3. Grand Rapids
4. Indianapolis
5. Cincinnati
6. Columbus
7. Evansville
8. Louisville
9. Knoxville
10. Nashville
11. Atlanta
12. Charlotte
13. Birmingham
14. Memphis
15. Little Rock
16. Shreveport
17. Oklahoma City

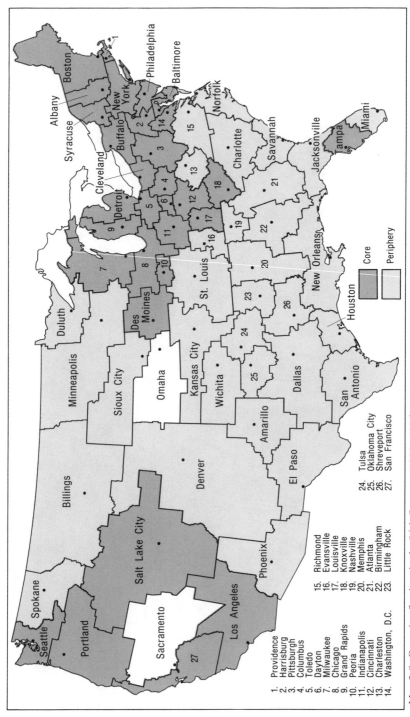

Map 2.8. Opposing Sections in the 84th Congress (1955–1956)

1. Providence
2. Harrisburg
3. Pittsburgh
4. Columbus
5. Toledo
6. Dayton
7. Milwaukee
8. Chicago
9. Grand Rapids
10. Peoria
11. Indianapolis
12. Cincinnati
13. Charleston
14. Washington, D.C.
15. Richmond
16. Evansville
17. Louisville
18. Knoxville
19. Nashville
20. Memphis
21. Atlanta
22. Birmingham
23. Little Rock
24. Tulsa
25. Oklahoma City
26. Shreveport
27. San Francisco

Core

Periphery

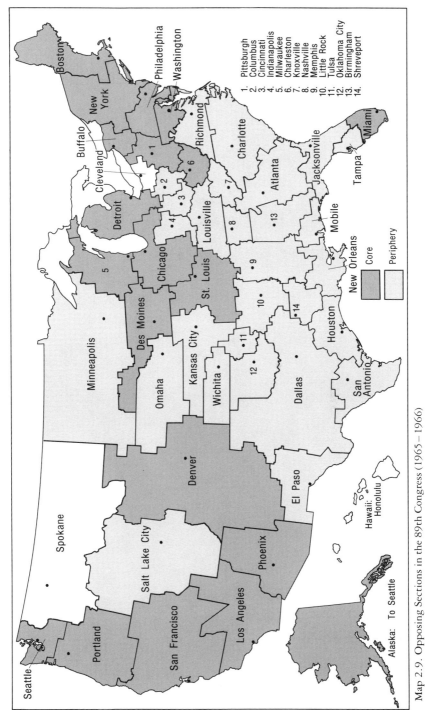

Map 2.9. Opposing Sections in the 89th Congress (1965–1966)

Core

Periphery

1. Pittsburgh
2. Columbus
3. Cincinnati
4. Indianapolis
5. Milwaukee
6. Charleston
7. Knoxville
8. Nashville
9. Memphis
10. Little Rock
11. Tulsa
12. Oklahoma City
13. Birmingham
14. Shreveport

Seattle
Spokane
Portland
San Francisco
Los Angeles
Salt Lake City
Phoenix
El Paso
Denver
Minneapolis
Des Moines
Omaha
Kansas City
Wichita
Dallas
San Antonio
Houston
Chicago
St. Louis
Louisville
Detroit
Cleveland
Buffalo
New Orleans
Mobile
Atlanta
Jacksonville
Tampa
Miami
Charlotte
Richmond
Washington
Philadelphia
New York
Boston

Hawaii: Honolulu
Alaska: To Seattle

47

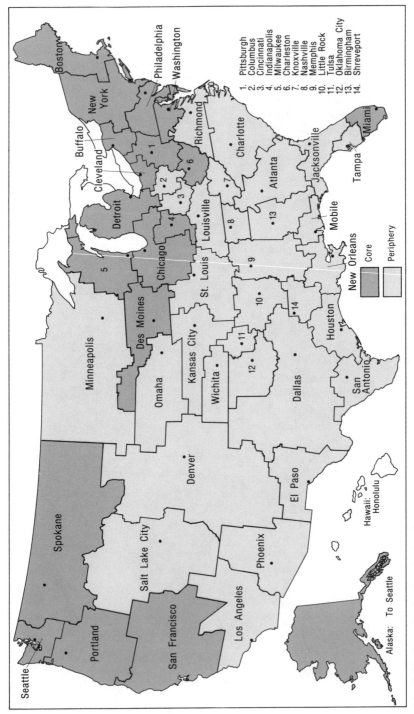

Map 2.10. Opposing Sections in the 94th Congress (1975–1976)

Core

Periphery

1. Pittsburgh
2. Columbus
3. Cincinnati
4. Indianapolis
5. Milwaukee
6. Charleston
7. Knoxville
8. Nashville
9. Memphis
10. Little Rock
11. Tulsa
12. Oklahoma City
13. Birmingham
14. Shreveport

Over the last century, there has been but one exception to the close cohesion of northeastern trade area delegations to the industrial-commercial pole: the Democratic Tammany machine that dominated New York City politics at the end of the nineteenth century led the New York trade area (and Albany in the 54th Congress) into a temporary alliance with the southern periphery. Tammany was able to take New York out of its otherwise "natural" alignment with other core regions for several reasons. First, the city dominated the nation's export-import trade to such an extent that New York adopted a "free" trade position on the protective tariff. Both the role of the city as the port of entry for most foreign imports and its position on the tariff (compared to other major urban seaports) were unique. Second, the high percentage of foreign-born ethnic groups in the city's population meant that Civil War veterans, and consequently pensioners, composed a relatively small part of the population compared to other northern regions. This fact allowed Tammany representatives to assume a position either of ambivalence or of outright opposition to the pension program that dominated domestic economic policy in the late nineteenth century.

Because the United States developed into a continental nation, the economy was potentially autarchic, a condition that allowed the nation to industrialize by establishing a high tariff to protect emerging sectors from foreign competition. This temporary withdrawal from the world-economy, Wallerstein argues, is a necessary stage in the emergence of any core state from a semi-peripheral or peripheral position in the world system. The withdrawal, in the American case, clearly benefited the industrializing regions, including most of the northeastern core. However, these regions could not—by themselves—impose protection upon the country without additional political support. That support was "purchased" by redistributing the income derived from a high tariff to Union veterans of the Civil War. Since these veterans resided almost exclusively in northern trade areas, this massive tariff-pension engine of economic development fused the interests of industrializing urban centers with rural native populations which had a high percentage of Union veterans. The sections that clearly "paid" for these development policies were the cash-crop exporting South and, unique among major industrial areas of the North, New York City.

For these reasons, New York developed a strong political machine that was able to assume a pivotal role in bipolar sectional competition during the late nineteenth century. This calculated political brokerage was made possible by the unique economic imperatives of the region, the limited political horizons and expectations of the electorate, and the closely balanced competition between the respective sectional alignments. At the national level, the margin of victory for the Democratic party was often provided by Tammany representatives—a balance of power role which colored the New York City delegation's interpretation of electoral reform (e.g., the proposed Force Bill of 1890).

Southern trade areas were, without major exception, closely allied with other regions of the interior-hinterland periphery throughout the century. In many periods, southern delegations dominated the periphery pole of the major alignment. Only Knoxville and south Florida (beginning in 1955) have intermittently defected toward core policy positions.

Industrialized port regions outside the Northeast have generally aligned with the core. Both the Great Lakes industrial basin and the major ports of the Pacific coast have participated in the formation of core political coalitions. The only exceptions to the pattern have been Los Angeles, a center of support for periphery policies since its emergence in the mid-twentieth century, and interior regions in Indiana and southern Ohio.

The only trade areas that have shifted between the two poles have been those of the Great Plains and mountain states. From 1885 through 1917, the section stretching south from the Canadian border between Wisconsin-Illinois and the Rocky Mountains was consistently aligned with the core. In the 69th Congress (1925–27), the farm crisis and World War I demobilization measures divided the plains trade areas between the poles; beginning in 1935, the section has given periphery policies consistent support. Only the World War II demobilization policies of the 79th Congress (1945–46) temporarily returned these trade areas to their former allegiance to the core. Throughout the century, the Great Plains have been economically dependent on the production of grains and livestock. These commodities could be largely consumed in the domestic market or exported to colonies (e.g., the Philippines) within the high protective tariff wall. Thus, during the early decades of the period, the Great Plains supported core policies because they created a larger working-class and domestic market for foodstuffs, captured foreign markets through imperialist colonization, and redistributed revenue to the large numbers of Union veterans residing in the section. By 1925, however, grain production exceeded the consuming capacity of the domestic and colonial markets, and pension benefits were "nationalized" by attrition of Civil War recipients combined with the extension of the program to Spanish-American War and World War I veterans.

Perhaps no section has been more inconsistent in its affections than the Rocky Mountain states. While the southern tier of the region (e.g., Phoenix and Albuquerque) has generally supported periphery policy positions, the remaining trade areas have followed a highly variable pattern. The mountain regions have been dependent on an extractive economy which is alien to the remainder of the country. In addition, the federal government, through its massive ownership of public lands in the West, has dominated economic development and made influence over the Departments of Interior and Agriculture a major goal of the region's congressmen. Furthermore, the mineral and agricultural economy has been highly diversified internally even while the region as a whole has been distinct from the remainder of the country. Finally, the section has been apportioned relatively few congressmen for most of the period. All of these factors have imposed upon mountain trade area delegations a political role generally characterized by continuous and intense bargaining with members of the two great sectional alignments. In many respects the West has traded away influence over most of the national political economy in the pursuit of parochial control of federal land and resource policy.

Because the United States has been a continental nation, the American economy has re-created on a national scale the core-periphery division of labor that typifies the modern world-system. The core regions of the United States have been characterized by their entrepôt functions as gateways between the national and world economies, by their dominance over private investment decisions both within the nation and abroad, and by their role as urbanized areas in which comparatively higher forms of economic activity take place. The American periphery, on the other hand, has been a net importer of domestic private investment with little participation in foreign capital markets, has been integrated into the world-economy as a producer and exporter of extractive raw materials, and generally has performed lower-order economic functions within both the national and world systems. While this sectional division of labor was extremely well defined during the last decades of the nineteenth century, lower transportation costs and increasing ease of communication have led to the relocation of some higher economic functions in the periphery and increasing penetration of interior economies by the world-system. These changes, while they are reversible, have generally reduced the stark contrasts of the sectional division of labor, decreased the homogeneity of the economic base of the various trade areas, and made control over government policy a less efficient means of affecting regional prosperity.

Political competition between the core and periphery is and has been inevitable because the economic imperatives of the two polar regions are in almost total conflict. Sectional competition over control of the national political economy has had two major results. First, the national political system has performed a "tribute gathering" function. In the late nineteenth and early twentieth centuries, the national state, dominated by the industrial-commercial core, compelled the periphery to bear the costs of industrialization and imperialism, destabilized periphery elites through electoral reform, and imposed an internal free market—with extensive federal protections for interregional investment—throughout the nation. While the "tribute gathering" effect of these policies was clearly to redistribute wealth from the periphery to the core in the early decades, more recent federal policies have had a wide variety of redistributive consequences. For example, urban redevelopment programs generally benefit the core while public works projects redistribute wealth to the periphery. Unlike the early period, when the great sections either won or lost over almost the entire range of national policy simultaneously, in the modern era trade areas have prevailed on some and lost on other national issues during the same Congress.

The national state apparatus has developed by playing off sectional elites against one another. For example, the rapid growth of the federal bureaucracy since the onset of the New Deal has been the result, in part, of its crucial role as arbitrator between the competitive claims of the sectional wings of the Democratic party. While the bureaucratic heart of the national state has been ostensibly neutral and perhaps has served to increase national integration by pursuing and supporting the expansion of central government powers for their own sake, the national state apparatus has been, on the whole, more favorable to the interests of the core than it has been to the periphery. This favoritism is a product of three factors: the comparative wealth of the core regions, the resistance of the periphery to the expansion of national state authority, and the recruitment of a disproportionate number of higher-level civil servants from core regions. The comparative wealth of the commercial-seaport core enables it to penetrate periphery economies and influence the political positions of a critical minority of periphery representatives. Control of the national media and other forms of cultural influence have achieved the same purpose. Thus, the periphery has historically viewed the national state apparatus with some suspicion. When the inability of the periphery to control national policy has translated into periphery resistance to state expansion, the central state bureaucracy has considered the core its strongest sectional ally. There have been major exceptions to this pattern, such as the Wilson administration and the early years of the New Deal, which will be explored in later chapters. These exceptions were partially the product of temporary periphery penetration and control of the higher levels of the national state bureaucracy during periods of intense class conflict within the core.

In following the evolution of sectional stress over the last century and its influence on the growth of the national state and the party system, the amount of change in the economic imperatives of the two polar sections should not be exaggerated. The same bipolar alignment that prevailed just after Reconstruction still dominates the present-day political system, even though the policies over which the sections now battle could not have been comprehended by late nineteenth-century politicians. Specific policy positions have changed over time. For example, the core began the period as an enthusiastic supporter of a protective tariff; after the emergence of the United States as a mature core state in the world-economy, the core supported free trade and anti-colonial policies; and now, with the declining competitiveness of heavy industry, some parts of the core have once again sought protection. In all of these permutations, the core position has been opposed by the periphery.

American Political Development and the Intensity of Sectional Stress

The average level of sectional stress on competitive roll calls has generally declined over the last century (see table 2.6). For example, sectional stress in all five post-1930 Congresses analyzed here has been lower than that for any of the five Congresses before 1930.

Table 2.6. Average Sectional Stress and Distribution of Scores on Competitive Roll Calls, 1880–1980

Congress (Years)	Average Sectional Stress	Percentage of Competitive Roll Calls on Which Sectional Stress Index Was:						N
		Over 70.0	60–69.9	50–59.9	40–49.9	30–39.9	20–29.9	
49th (1885–87)	55.0	0	40.6	34.3	14.1	9.4	1.6	64
54th (1895–97)	48.5	0	12.5	33.3	41.7	12.5	0	24
59th (1905–7)	58.8	0	47.6	42.9	4.8	4.8	0	21
64th (1915–17)	54.9	3.6	21.4	53.6	21.4	0	0	28
69th (1925–27)	55.1	0	20.0	53.3	26.7	0	0	15
74th (1935–36)	44.5	0	0	27.8	33.3	33.3	5.6	18
79th (1945–46)	48.1	0	2.2	45.7	39.1	13.0	0	46
84th (1955–56)	47.5	2.9	2.9	28.6	40.0	25.7	0	35
89th (1965–66)	39.4	0	0	5.7	39.6	45.3	9.4	53
94th (1975–76)	39.9	0	.6	7.1	41.0	44.2	7.1	156

SOURCE: Calculations from roll call data.

The declining level of sectional stress on House roll calls has been partially caused by the same institutional developments that supported the New Deal coalition in the Democratic party. A strong committee system allowed the representatives of the core and periphery regions to carve up the national political economy into sectors which the sectional poles could then control. The periphery came to dominate committees holding jurisdiction over defense, agriculture, and public works; the core controlled education, labor, judiciary, and banking panels. This strong, sectionally based committee system had several effects on roll call voting and public policy. First, it decentralized policy decisions by removing them from the floor into committee chambers and, ultimately, into closed, covert working relationships between committee members and that part of the executive bureaucracy that fell within their jurisdiction. The decentralization of policy deliberation was enhanced by a general decline in statutory specification and a corresponding rise in executive discretion. Thus, congressmen were increasingly presented with ambiguous policy choices on the floor of the House of Representatives as the committee system developed. At the same time, the decentralization of policy decisions encouraged committee reciprocity in floor voting. These developments were clearly reinforcing. The ambiguity of post–New Deal statutes allowed members to vote for policies that, if specified in law, they would have been compelled to oppose on the basis of local economic interest; executive discretion strengthened the effectiveness of a committee system that depended on committee reciprocity in floor voting. Committee reciprocity, in turn, was dependent on the leeway allowed congressmen in voting on ambiguous, discretionary policies. In later chapters, after an examination of the types of policies that have provoked sectional stress over the last century, this interpretation of institutional change and certain developments in the national

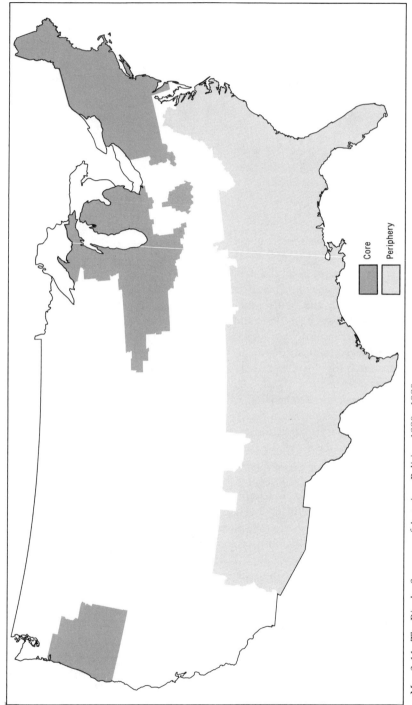

Map 2. 11. The Bipolar Structure of American Politics, 1880–1980

Core

Periphery

54

political economy which may have reinforced the secular decline in sectional stress will be explored.

Use of Terms

In this study, roll calls exhibiting sectional stress scores in excess of sixty on the index will be described as examples of "extremely" or "very" high levels of regional polarization. As a group, such roll calls composed on the average slightly more than 15 percent of the competitive roll calls within each of the ten analyzed Congresses. The highest level of sectional stress uncovered during the course of this investigation occurred on a 1959 proposal to extend the life of the Civil Rights Commission (for a description, see chapter 5). The vote on that proposal registered 88.9 on the sectional stress index. Maps depicting the geographical distributions associated with high and low levels of sectional stress are provided in the following chapters (for example, see maps 8.1 and 8.2).

Descriptive Term	Score on Index	Average Percentage of Competitive Roll Calls, 1880–1980
Extremely or Very High-Stress	Over 60	15.4
High-Stress	50–59.9	33.2
Moderate-Stress	40–49.9	30.2
Low-Stress	30–39.9	18.8
Very Low-Stress	20–29.9	2.4

In describing the bipolar structure of American politics, the terms "core" and "periphery" will be extensively relied upon to indicate the economic and geographical basis of sectional competition. Though the lines of political conflict are often altered, sometimes significantly, by changes in the public policy focus of regional competition, the geographical alignment underlying sectional stress has most often found an industrial, commercial-seaport core pitted against an agrarian periphery oriented toward the nation's interior. While the boundaries of the respective poles should not be taken too literally, and while geopolitical coalitions have historically varied with changes in the national political economy, the two polar regions depicted in map 2.11 give an idea of the geographical content of the core/periphery dichotomy.*

*Map 2.11 is based on voting patterns on sectionally divisive issues in the House of Representatives over the last century. However, the core-periphery dichotomy can be more directly linked to the economic structure of the nation. If the per capita value added in manufacturing in 1919 is calculated for each of the federal reserve branch bank territories (see map A.3), the resulting pattern closely resembles the geographical alignment pictured in map 2.11. Those areas in which the value added in manufacturing exceeded $300 per capita compose the industrial core: Boston, Buffalo, New York, Pittsburgh, Philadelphia, Cleveland, Detroit, and Seat-

National Public Policy and Sectional Competition (1880–1980)

Chapters 3 through 6 will explore the changing relationship between sectional stress and control of the national political economy. In analyzing this relationship, ten separate public policy themes are articulated—one for each of the Congresses that serve as the basis of this study (table 2.7). The policy category containing the largest number of the ten highest-stress roll calls is identified for each Congress, then connected to the contemporary structure and processes of the national economy. The broader theme that emerges for each category is then investigated in the years both preceding and following each particular Congress: for example, in chapter 3, the continuity of political coalitions supporting the protective tariff from 1880 to 1930.

A number of underlying threads run through the chapters. One is the connection between the relative positions of the sections within the world-economy and the policy implications of regionally polarized legislative decisions. For example, in at least six Congresses (all but the 54th, 74th, 79th, and 89th) the economic imperatives of the industrial core and agrarian periphery cannot be understood apart from their role in the world-economy. Another thread is the relationship between sectional stress and extra-constitutional political institutions. The most important of these institutions are political parties and the congressional committee system. Before the New Deal, the dynamics of a strong party system were closely tied to intense sectional conflict between the industrial core and the agrarian periphery. During and after the New Deal period, the emergence of a largely autonomous committee system gradually began to encourage the regional depolarization of the party system, and party organizations became less effective vehicles for the expression of sectional interests in the national political economy.

Yet another theme ties the separate political periods together: the consistent hostility of the agrarian periphery to the creation and expansion of a permanent central state bureaucracy. In the early, post–Reconstruction Congresses, most opposition can be explained as an attempt by the South to prevent the creation of a large military establishment within the federal government. A large standing army appeared to threaten the internal political autonomy of the South; in its absence, the plantation elite proceeded with the disfranchisement of blacks and the lower classes and, subsequently, erected the

---

tle. Those areas under $200 make up the periphery: Birmingham, Atlanta, Jacksonville, New Orleans, Nashville, Memphis, Richmond, Baltimore, Louisville, St. Louis, Minneapolis, Helena, Oklahoma City, Kansas City, Little Rock, Omaha, Denver, Houston, Dallas, El Paso, Los Angeles, Salt Lake City, and Spokane. Between these poles lie the territories drawn around Cincinnati, Chicago, San Francisco, and Portland, Oregon. All figures are calculated from data taken from the 1920 Census of the United States. Very similar results can be derived from data on the capital utilized in manufacturing in any census from 1880 to 1920.

Table 2.7. National Public Policy and Sectional Competition, 1880–1980

Congress	Largest Category of High-Stress Roll Calls	Relationship to National Political Economy	Primary Reasons for Sectional Tension
49th (1885–87)	Private pension bills.	Military pensions broadened political support for the protective tariff which, in turn, promoted industrialization.	Only Union veterans were eligible for military pensions (20–40% of federal expenditures from 1880 to 1900); the tariff provided over half of federal revenue while protecting northern industrial expansion.
54th (1895–97)	Contested congressional elections.	Contested election cases became the primary federal response to southern disfranchisement of blacks and poor whites.	Contested elections were used by the Republican representatives of northern industry to expose the "undemocratic" election practices of the South and to destabilize the political regime of the southern plantation elite.
59th (1905–7)	Naval expenditures and Oklahoma statehood.	The issues associated with imperialism and statehood determined the size and strength of the central government.	Representatives of the northern industrial core supported territorial expansion, imperialism, and larger naval expenditures; members from the southern agrarian periphery held that colonies considered ineligible for statehood should be abandoned and that the federal government should not impose extraordinary preconditions on the entry of western territories into the federal union.
64th (1915–17)	Military preparations for World War I.	Military expansion increased the size of the central government and reinforced trade and cultural ties between the northern industrial core and Western Europe.	The southern and western periphery opposed expansion of the standing army and navy as "militarism" and promoted government operation of war production facilities in order to reduce the involvement of private capital in the arms trade and domestic government purchases.
69th (1925–27)	Agricultural relief and denationalization of government-owned war production facilities.	Proposals for government intervention in support of the severely depressed agricultural sector were intended to reallocate national income from industry to agriculture.	The northern core opposed and the southern and western periphery supported McNary-Haugenism (use of the tariff and other mechanisms to artificially raise the price of major agricultural commodities) and government development of Muscle Shoals (subsidized fertilizer production for southern agriculture).

Table 2.7 (continued)

Congress	Largest Category of High-Stress Roll Calls	Relationship to National Political Economy	Primary Reasons for Sectional Tension
74th (1935–36)	Distributive decisions relating to public works expenditures and government regulation.	The creation of new government programs and agencies strengthened the emerging congressional committee system and reinforced the Democratic New Deal coalition	The Republican representatives of the industrial core elite opposed New Deal programs which put in place the necessary elements for the maintenance of a bipolar coalition in the Democratic party between the southern plantation elite and the urban lower classes of the industrial core.
79th (1945–46)	Governmental controls related to the war effort and reconversion to a peacetime economy.	Governmental controls redistributed national income among major sectors of the economy and regions of the nation.	Industry and labor in the northern core and agriculture in the southern and western periphery attempted to manipulate wartime controls and reconversion measures in order to benefit their relative position in the national political econoy.
84th (1955–56)	Farm legislation.	Agriculture price supports and production controls raised the income of southern and western producers.	High price support programs and weak restrictions on agricultural production promoted the development of strong political ties between representatives of the major regional commodities and northern urban members of the Democratic party.
89th (1965–66)	Civil rights.	Federal desegregation and voting rights measures undermined the regional hegemony of the southern plantation elite.	Federal control of southern electoral machinery and the dismantling of segregated school systems/public facilities produced a deep sectional split within the Democratic party and a much weaker role for the congressional committee system in the legislative process.
94th (1975–76)	Federal grants and regulations which benefit particular regional economies.	Federal revenue-sharing formulas, regulatory law, and direct subsidy programs were manipulated in order to retard the relative decline of the industrial core economy.	Open contests for advantage in the national political economy between the northern core and southern and western periphery underlined the progressive deterioration of the congressional committee system and emphasized the deepening economic crisis of the industrial core.

pervasive social and political codes that effected race segregation throughout the region. Later proposals to expand the national civilian bureaucracy were scrupulously reviewed with reference to their impact on segregation. Except for policies with extremely remote implications for the southern caste system (such as the Federal Reserve System), permanent expansions of central state authority were consistently resisted. Even with the dismantling of segregationist institutions in the 1960s and 1970s, periphery opposition to the expansion of bureaucratic power continues to play a central role in American political development.

Chapter 6 describes the sectional alignment of the 1970s. In this exploration of the political response to the gradual decline of the industrial core economy, the economic basis of the emerging post–industrial era is examined in light of the historical, interregional division of labor. From this perspective, the decline of the core economy is connected to the future evolution of the fundamental sectional alignment in the American nation.

3

Tariffs, Elections, and Imperialism: 1880–1910

In the years between 1880 and 1910 the United States created the industrial infrastructure and developed the military strength that allowed the nation to emerge as a mature and powerful member of the international community of nations. While the United States clearly possessed the size and natural resources that were necessary preconditions for industrialization, the rapid development of the country was also the product of a calculated manipulation of the domestic political economy. In this respect, three policies stand out: the military pension-tariff engine of national development, the national control of federal elections, and the imperialist expansion of the United States in the late nineteenth–early twentieth century.

Because all three policies were directly related to the emergence of the United States as a world industrial and military power, they should be interpreted as different aspects of the same phenomenon. Taken together, these policies reflected the dominance of the northeastern-midwestern core in a struggle with the southern periphery and the mountain West for control of the national state apparatus. The protective tariff was proposed and enacted by the industrial core as a means by which the United States could "withdraw" from the world-economy. This withdrawal was viewed as a necessary stage in the development of modern industry on a scale large enough to effectively compete with the advanced nations of Western Europe. One result of the high tariff wall which the industrializing core built around the country was that customs duties became the major source of national revenue. Because pension recipients allied themselves with the core industrial elite and thus formed a coalition large enough to successfully defend a high tariff as a part of the national political economy, the redistribution of this tariff revenue through the Civil War pension system became a major element in the political strategy of development.

Like military pensions, the national control and supervision of federal elections was in one sense inherited as an archaic artifact of disunion. However, in spite of the fact that Reconstruction had ended in 1877 with the withdrawal of federal troops from the South and the readmission of the states that had formed the Confederacy, a renewal of federal control of the southern political system loomed as a very real threat to the sectional hegemony of the plantation elite. While this potential federal control was never actually exercised, the northern core did overturn the official results of southern elections on a case-by-case basis. Throughout the period—though with decreasing frequency after the turn of the century—these contested election cases and potential federal control of the political system threatened to destabilize the dominant position of the plantation elite in the South and forced the section's representatives, on occasion, to acquiesce in developmental policies which they would have otherwise opposed. After 1896, when the South had completed the disfranchisement of blacks and upland whites, the possibility of federal intervention in local electoral arrangements became remote and the plantation elite could be much more aggressive in national politics.

The imperialist expansion of the United States was supported by the northern industrial core for several reasons. Core congressmen believed that territorial possessions were an important element in the extension of American commercial interests, industrial markets, military power, and opportunities for capitalist investment. The northern core also believed that these possessions should accept a subordinate or "inferior" position within the national political system either as colonies administered outside of the constitutional framework, territories which would be in practice ineligible for statehood, or states admitted into the Union only after particular preconditions and requirements determined by Congress had been satisfied. The southern periphery opposed imperialist expansion primarily because the policy required the development of a large military establishment and a strong central government. These potential developments reminded the South of Reconstruction and the possibility that the experience might be repeated. Imperialist administrative practices also set a precedent for unequal membership of periphery regions within the federal republic. Perhaps most important, the position of the plantation South and mineral-rich West in the world-economy made the extension of free trade arrangements within the world-economy a far more beneficial strategy than northern-dominated imperialist expansion.

In the remainder of this chapter each of these policies, the military pension-tariff developmental coalition, federal control of elections, and imperialist expansion, is discussed in turn. In each case, the level of sectional stress on closely related policy decisions was extraordinarily high and clear references to sectional content and implications were frequently made in and out of congressional debate. In every instance also, the regional alignment followed an identical pattern, with the northern core supporting tariff protection, supervision of elections, and imperialist expansion and the southern periphery opposing all three.

Civil War Pensions, the Tariff, and the 49th Congress

Between the end of Reconstruction and the First World War the United States became a major industrial power by using what Immanuel Wallerstein has called "the classic technique of mercantilist semiwithdrawal from the world-economy":[1] the protective tariff. High tariffs on manufactured goods protected infant, developing industries from the stultifying competition of the technologically advanced economies of Western Europe. Given the size of the American nation—as Walter Dean Burnham has said, "The United States was so vast that it had little need of economic colonies abroad; in fact it had two major colonial regions within its own borders, the postbellum South and the West"[2]—the protected domestic economy provided a market large enough to permit full exploitation of industrial economies of scale. In addition, because customs duties were regressive, the wealthy were freed from a potential tax burden and the tariff thus increased the rate of social savings and reinvestment.[3] At the end of the period of industrialization following World War I, the United States could compete in the world-economy on more-than-equal terms.*

The protective tariff was, therefore, a policy which furthered the interests of the commercial-industrial core regions of the United States. The tariff in effect imposed a twofold tax upon the nonindustrial periphery; wealth was redistributed from the periphery to the core in the form of higher prices for manufactured goods and from the periphery to the national treasury in the form of customs duties. In fact, customs receipts during the period not only repaid the federal debt resulting from the Civil War but also created a politically significant budgetary surplus.

Core industrial interests were not strong enough to impose the tariff upon the nation without additional political support. In its "classic" phase, the political coalition which erected and maintained the high tariff barrier to world trade was composed of five groups: the core industrial and financial elites, industrial labor, Civil War veterans, agrarian producers dependent on urban markets in the core, and a small group of commodity producers who could also take advantage of tariff protection. Of these five, the first three were the most significant and the intertwining of their interests within the "pro-economic development" coalition intimately tied together three seemingly unrelated policies: the protective tariff, the disposal of the treasury surplus, and military pensions. The machine that supported industrialization used the protective tariff to produce revenue which then was distributed, in a fashion

---

*After 1910, the American economy had reached the stage of relative maturity in world markets that Great Britain had attained in the middle of the nineteenth century. The unit costs of many manufactured products made in the United States were lower than comparable European production. See Frank W. Tuttle and Joseph M. Perty, *An Economic History of the United States* (Cincinnati: South-Western, 1970).

that encouraged fraudulent claims, to hundreds of thousands of Civil War veterans and their survivors.

All three groups, elites, labor, and pensioners, were located in the North and, thus, this section retrieved the "taxes" it paid through imposition of the tariff. The tax imposed by the higher costs of manufactured goods was recaptured by regionally repatriated profits and customs duties were recaptured by the payment of military pensions. The developmental engine left the southern periphery to shoulder almost the entire cost of industrialization; Confederate veterans were not eligible for federal pensions and no indigenous product (save sugar) was protected by the tariff. The periphery was drained while the core prospered.

Of the ten high–sectional stress roll calls taken during the 49th Congress (1885–87), eight concerned the plight of the Union veteran in some respect and seven of these were taken on the passage of private pension bills.[*] In 1862 the federal government instituted a disability pension program that contemplated compensation for almost any imaginable wartime service ailment, to be paid to the veteran, his widow, orphans, or other dependents. Under the 1862 program, enrollment peaked in 1873 and had subsequently begun a slow decline. The administration of Civil War pensions then remained relatively noncontroversial until the 1879 Arrears of Pensions Act.[4] That act provided that every successful applicant could recover the entire amount that he would have been paid if his pension had been granted at the time his disability occurred even if his first claim was filed many years after the war had ended. The promise of a huge lump sum award for a successful applicant led many "old soldiers whose wounds were long since healed . . . to discover that, after all, their injuries had been very serious." The promise of a commission on a large award led pension claim agents and attorneys to scour the country for both legitimate claimants and individuals willing to conspire to defraud the government. Before 1879, new claims had been filed at the rate of 1,600 a month; after the new act took effect, new claims rose to over 10,000 a month.[5]

The Pension Bureau after 1879 became a graft-ridden political machine identified with and controlled by the Republican party. During political campaigns and especially in areas where the election result was uncertain, the Republican appointees who directed the bureau allowed claims that were particularly suspect and even dispatched special agents into the field to encourage potential recipients to apply.[6] The Grand Army of the Republic (GAR), the major association of Union veterans, provided an additional link between potential pensioners and the Republican party.[7] By the time Grover Cleveland assumed the presidency in 1885, a quarter of the existing pension list of

---

[*]Passage of the Interstate Commerce Act of 1887 and adoption of a Senate amendment to grant the public printer and his employees fifteen days annual leave produced the remaining two high-stress roll calls.

345,000 veterans and survivors was generally thought to be based on fraudulent claims.[8]

Under Cleveland, Democratic appointees charged with the administration of the bureau removed "politics" from the pension system by emphasizing the objective criteria and proof that the law demanded as a condition for eligibility. In the view of the GAR and claims attorneys, this overly "technical and irritating construction of the pension law" led the bureau to deny many meritorious claims.[9] In order to properly compensate these veterans, the Republican members of Congress introduced an increasing number of private pension bills. Each of these bills added a specific individual to the pension roll when enacted into law. While private bills had always been used by unsuccessful claimants to appeal an unfavorable decision by the Pension Bureau, this category of legislation had been but a minor part of the congressional agenda prior to Cleveland's administration. Cleveland interpreted the bureau as analogous to a pensions court which should give all applicants a fair hearing and objective decision in light of the law. He argued that Congress should either rely upon the bureau or reorganize it to better meet legislative goals. Having adopted that position, Cleveland proceeded to do what no Republican president before him had ever done: he examined every private bill passed by Congress and vetoed those that he believed to be based on fraudulent evidence or doubtful constructions of the law.[10] He rejected 233 private pension bills during his first term.*

Cleveland's action set the stage for a terrific confrontation with the northern-dominated Congress. In the first six months of the Democratic administration over 4,000 pension bills had been introduced into the House of Representatives. In Friday night sessions set aside specifically for the purpose, the House would consider these bills en masse by voice vote and on occasion enacted them "with a jubilant whoop."[11] Some of the claims represented by these bills bordered on the absurd. For example, HR 5603 would have granted a pension to Mrs. Catharine McCarty because, in the words of the bill's sponsor, Representative James B. Weaver of Iowa, her husband "was asked by one of his comrades to taste of some medicine which he had in a bottle. The soldier did taste of it and it killed him."[12] Although the bill's supporters conceded that the death did not occur in the line of duty and certainly did not fall within the general pension law, the House of Representatives sent the bill on to the Senate by a narrow margin. Cleveland later vetoed the bill.

Cleveland vetoed a similar bill which would have increased the size of a

---

*Between 1862 and 1893, seven Republican presidents served a total of twenty-seven years in office. During that period, Republican chief executives vetoed only five private pension bills, *Congressional Record*, 54:1:4342, April 23, 1896. Although most of the private pension bills Cleveland vetoed had been unanimously passed by the House of Representatives at these Friday night sessions, the Democratic members almost always reversed position and opposed any attempt to override. Only one of Cleveland's 233 pension vetoes was overridden during his first term.

pension already allowed to John W. Farris. In his message, Cleveland noted that Farris had originally filed for a pension in 1881, sixteen years after his discharge from the service, claiming that he was afflicted with chronic diarrhea which had been contracted in the Army. This claim was allowed in 1885. In September of the same year, he filed a new claim for an increase in his existing pension alleging that his eyesight had been damaged as a result of his previous ailments. Cleveland concluded: "The ingenuity developed in the constant and persistent attacks upon the public Treasury by those claiming pensions and the increase of those already granted is exhibited in bold relief by this attempt to include sore eyes among the results of diarrhea." [13]

The roll calls that attended the passage of Mrs. McCarty's bill and the attempt to override Cleveland's veto of the Farris petition were among the ten high–sectional stress votes recorded during the 49th Congress. The core trade area delegations voted to grant relief to the applicant; the periphery voted to uphold the decision of the Pension Bureau. Neither bill, however, received as much notoriety as the case involved in a third high-stress roll call: a petition for the relief of Sallie Ann Bradley. According to Mrs. Bradley's petition,

> her husband and her four sons had been Union soldiers. Two of the sons were pictured as slain on the field of battle, a third had his arm torn off by a shell, and the fourth lost an eye in the gallant defense of his country. Her husband was described as a fighting member of a fighting regiment, the 24th Ohio, later transferred to the gallant 18th Ohio, only to fall, terribly wounded, in "Pap" Thomas' fight before Nashville. Maimed, but still heroic, he had dragged out his shattered life until 1880, drawing the pitiful pittance of four dollars a month; and then, worn out by wounds that would not heal, had passed to the other shore, leaving his wife, poor, broken by sorrow and sickness, and compelled to live on charity as an inmate of the County Infirmary, because her surviving sons were too crippled to earn enough to sustain her in her declining years.
>
> Upon the face of the facts as stated, Sallie Ann Bradley certainly merited a liberal pension, as the widow of a hero whose death had been due solely to wounds received in battle. All she asked was eight dollars a month, and Congress had approved her prayer; but the President, having taken the trouble to investigate the facts, vetoed the bill, and was promptly denounced. The Clinton County *Democrat* of Wilmington, Ohio, on July 29, 1886, having investigated the case, sustained the President, giving its readers the following summary of the actual facts, as gathered from the neighbors of the widow, and from an inspection of what remained of her shattered family:
>
> "The husband's name was T. J. Bradley. He was not in the battle of Nashville, and could not, therefore, have fallen terribly wounded in 'Pap' Thomas' fight. He choked to death on a piece of beef when gorging himself while on a drunken spree, and, therefore, did not go to camp on

the other shore when worn out with wounds and old age. So much for the old man.

"There were four sons who were in the service, viz.: Robert, John, Carey, and James. They all came home from the war, so that two of them could not have been shot dead on the battle field. Two of them, John and James, are living, so that they could not have been the ones who are said to have been shot dead. Of the others, Robert died of yellow fever in Memphis several years after the war, while Carey committed suicide when on a spree a few years ago at his home in Bentonville, Adams County, Ohio. They were not shot on the battle field.

"Now for the eye and arm story. John is the one about whom the anecdote is told that he had his eye shot out. . . . He is a shoemaker by trade, and the Democratic postmaster of Bentonville, and lost his eye while working at his trade from a piece of heal nail striking it when repairing a pair of boots. James was shot in the arm at Nashville, but it was not torn off by a shell. Mrs. Bradley never was in the County Infirmary, and her boys are not unable to support her by reason of disabilities produced from wounds received in the army. The Republican Senate twice rejected the bill to pension Mrs. Bradley, one of the bills having been introduced by that valiant lover of the soldiers, Alphonso Hart."[14]

As a result of his veto policy, Cleveland was berated by claims agents and the GAR as being a "mere tool of the South."[15] During his successful campaign to replace Cleveland, Benjamin Harrison argued that it "was no time to be weighing the claims of old soldiers with apothecary's scales." Once the Republicans were victorious, Harrison was reported to have gleefully declared, "God help the surplus," and the Pension Bureau under his administration reopened old cases, rerated existing pensions upward, and generally rewarded political allies and supporters.[16]

For most of the late nineteenth century, expenditures under the pension system accounted for more than a quarter of the federal budget; in fact, between 1890 and 1894, military pensions consumed 37 percent of total federal spending. This percentage declined dramatically just before World War I, and the pension system never returned to the political and fiscal preeminence it enjoyed during the last decades of the nineteenth century (see table 3.1). Civil War pensions "became a dependable source of income for the northern section of the Union" from which the South was clearly excluded.[17] While map 3.1 clearly illustrates the geographic concentration of pension recipients in the core regions of the North, even that representation of the pattern fails to do justice to the facts. Hundreds of counties in the southern periphery did not contain a single pensioner, while in hundreds more in the North recipients composed at least 4 percent of all eligible voters (adult males). Most pensions granted southern applicants were for service in the Mexican-American War or carpetbag supporters of the Republican party. The only areas of the North

Table 3.1. Composition of the Expenditures of the United States, 1880–1934

	Function					
Years	Civil (%)	Military (%)	Indians (%)	Pensions (%)	Postal Deficiencies (%)	Interest on the Public Debt (%)
1880–84	20.3	19.3	2.2	21.2	1.2	35.8
1885–89	29.8	21.1	2.4	27.0	2.0	17.8
1890–94	28.0	21.5	2.8	37.3	1.7	8.6
1895–99	20.9	30.0	2.9	34.8	2.5	8.8
1900–4	24.9	39.5	2.1	26.7	.9	5.9
1905–9	23.9	43.6	2.4	24.1	2.2	3.8
1910–14	24.3	46.2	2.8	23.2	.3	3.2
1915–19	38.9	46.0	1.4	10.8	.3	2.4
1920–24	37.1	28.8	1.1	6.3	1.2	25.5
1925–29	41.8	23.2	1.3	7.2	1.4	25.3
1930–34	57.7	18.5	.6	5.5	2.9	14.9

NOTE: Figures are averages for the five-year periods indicated. The Civil category includes civil expenditures in the War and Navy Departments through 1915 (when they are shifted to the "Military" heading). The military category includes both the War and Navy Departments in addition to expenditures on rivers and harbors and the Panama Canal. "Pensions" includes only payments to Army and Navy pensioners who saw service prior to World War I. "Postal Deficiencies" represents advances from the Treasury to meet deficiencies in postal revenue.

SOURCE: Percentages computed from *1936 Annual Report of the Secretary of the Treasury on the State of the Finances* (Washington: Government Printing Office, 1937), table 5, "Receipts and expenditures for the fiscal years 1789 to 1936," pp. 362–63.

where recipients were relatively scarce were in the heart of the largest urban centers where a large portion of the population was composed of postwar immigrants and a few regions on the frontier (northern Minnesota and the Far West) which had similarly attracted recent arrivals into the country. Even as late as 1910, some twenty-three years after the 49th Congress closed its doors, the northern New England states of Maine, Vermont, and New Hampshire were receiving a per capita share of pension expenditures twenty times as great as that received by South Carolina.[18]

In the four decades before World War I, the major source of revenue for the federal government was the protective tariff (see figure 3.1). The greatest dependence on this source occurred in the five-year period between 1886 and 1890, when 57.7 percent of all federal income was derived from customs duties. As it had sponsored the expansion of a liberal pension system, the Republican party came to support the protective tariff, and ultimately the two policies became intimately linked. The Republicans argued that "a high tariff was indispensable to the very existence of infant industries and to specialization in industry." Furthermore, the party claimed that:

It guaranteed high wages for labor and a home market for the farmer and the manufacturer; it provided that concentration of population in cities

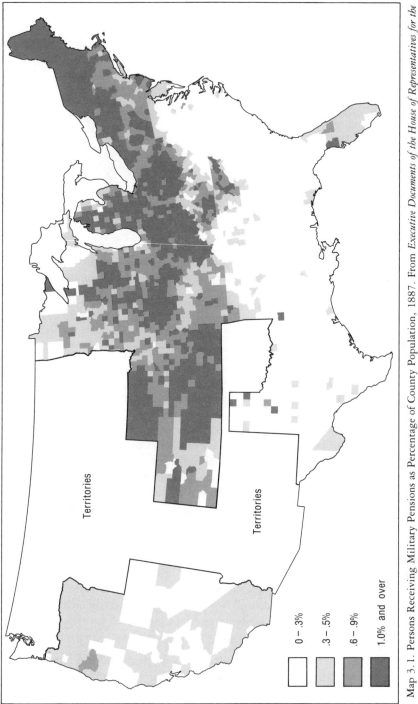

Map 3.1. Persons Receiving Military Pensions as Percentage of County Population, 1887. From *Executive Documents of the House of Representatives for the First Session of the Fiftieth Congress*, Serial No. 2542, Washington: Government Printing Office, 1889, and *Abstract of the Twelfth Census of the United States, 1900*, United States Bureau of the Census, Washington: Government Printing Office, 1904, and calculations by the author.

Territories

Territories

0 – .3%

.3 – .5%

.6 – .9%

1.0% and over

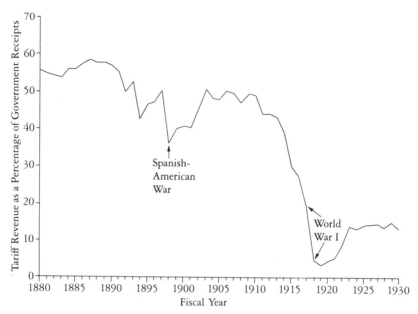

Figure 3.1. Tariff Revenue as a Percentage of Total Government Receipts, 1880–1930
SOURCE: Compiled from data contained in *Historical Statistics of the United States*, vol. 2 (Washington: Bureau of the Census, 1975), p. 1106.

and towns which was essential to cultural and social growth; it compensated the American producer for differences between the cost of production at home and abroad; and it stood between the American worker and the "pauper" labor of Europe and Asia. Protection, the argument ran, was necessary for the maintenance of a high standard of living, of a balanced economy, even for the preservation of our national independence.[19]

Some historians believe that the protective tariff was enthusiastically embraced by the Republicans because Grover Cleveland clumsily committed the Democrats to a free trade policy in his annual message to Congress in 1887.[20] Prior to that year, the primary difference between the parties had been over the amount, not the advisability, of the tariff. After 1887, the Democrats argued that the tariff was "the mother of trusts," that it was no longer needed to "protect" highly developed American industry, and, therefore, the major effect of contemporary tariff policy was higher domestic prices.[21]

For most of the last quarter of the nineteenth century, revenue from the tariff was sufficiently large to support the current operations of the government and to repay the national debt. As debt service expenditures became an increasingly smaller portion of the budget, the "surplus" of revenue over expenditures became a politically embarrassing side-effect of a high tariff. The Democrats campaigned against the surplus by advocating a tariff "for revenue only" manipulated to meet budgetary requirements. In short, the party would have eliminated the surplus by reducing income. The Republicans, committed to protectionist duties, moved to increase expenditures and, using the pension system as their conduit, had no difficulty in eliminating the surplus. Between 1889 and 1893, after the Republican party had regained the White House, military pensions rose from an annual rate of $88,000,000 to $159,000,000.[22]

The interests of high tariff men and pensioners were completely integrated during Cleveland's administration, and by 1888, Senator James Beck, a Kentucky Democrat, could declare that the proposed pension bill of that year was "a shrewd scheme by which the protected interests proposed to use up the surplus and prevent a revision of the tariff."[23] Of Republican solicitude for infirm and aged veterans, the senator remarked, "they want to save the soldiers from going to the poorhouse by absorbing all the surplus revenue, when in fact they are really seeking to save the tariff in order to enrich a few men that are making princely fortunes out of it at the expense of the great mass of the people."[24] "The real object is artfully concealed" because "the protected barons who are now perfecting the trusts . . . devised under tariff protection to plunder the country by all sorts of illegal schemes, could not invent a better way to do it [than] under the guise of a patriotic purpose."[25]

After Cleveland committed his party to tariff reform, a political coalition that included veterans, their relatives, claim agents and pension attorneys, and local shopkeepers (who anticipated that pension money would ultimately reach their tills) rose up to aid the core industrial elite in the struggle against tariff revision.[26] The leaders of veterans' organizations publicly campaigned for the protective tariff on the ground that any reduction in federal revenue might reduce opportunities for further expansion of the pension system.[27] For their part, the manufacturing interests of the nation "looked upon the pension system as a most satisfactory means of returning . . . embarrassing surpluses to general circulation among the people."[28]

Between 1880 and 1930, the House of Representatives voted on ten separate tariff bills (table 3.2). The voting pattern clearly indicates the great stability of the sectional alignment engendered by the tariff. For example, the Philadelphia trade area adopted a protectionist position on every tariff bill between 1880 and 1930, while Memphis, Atlanta, New Orleans, Richmond, and Louisville just as consistently favored a free trade policy. Comparatively few regions—the most significant being New York—exhibited inconsistent or erratic voting patterns on the tariff, and the historical record of all trade area delegations was very similar to their respective positions on Civil War pensions.

Sectional stress on these ten tariff roll calls averages 51.1, with a high

Table 3.2. Trade Area Delegation Support for a Protectionist Tariff Policy,
1880–1930

Trade Area	Tariff Revision Proposal									
	1883	1884	1886	1888	1890	1894	1897	1909	1913	1921
Philadelphia[a]	P[b]	P	P	P	P	P	P	P	P	P
Boston	P	P	P	P	P	P	P	P	FT	P
Buffalo	P	P	P	FT	P	P	P	P	S	P
Pittsburgh	FT	P	P	P	P	P	P	P	P	P
San Francisco	S	P	P	P	P	P	P	P	P	P
Omaha	P	P	P	P	P	P	P	P	FT	P
Minneapolis	P	FT	P	P	P	P	P	FT	P	P
Chicago	P	P	P	P	P	S	P	P	P	P
Kansas City	P	S	P	P	S	FT	FT	P	P	P
Cleveland	FT	P	P	P	P	FT	P	P	FT	P
Cincinnati	P	P	P	S	S	FT	P	P	FT	P
Indianapolis	P	FT	FT	P	FT	FT	P	—	—	P
New York	P	FT	P	FT	FT	FT	P	P	FT	P
Detroit	P	FT	FT	P	P	FT	P	P	S	P
Louisville	FT	FT	FT	FT	FT	FT	FT	FT	FT	FT
Baltimore	FT	P	FT	FT	P	FT	P	P	FT	P
St. Louis	FT	FT	FT	FT	S	FT	P	FT	FT	P
Richmond	FT	FT	FT	FT	FT	FT	FT	FT	FT	FT
New Orleans	FT	FT	FT	FT	FT	FT	FT	FT	FT	FT
Atlanta	FT	FT	FT	FT	FT	FT	FT	FT	FT	FT
Memphis	FT	FT	FT	FT	FT	FT	FT	FT	FT	FT
Sectional Stress	51.7	52.4	60.7	49.0	54.4	42.1	62.1	51.9	22.4	64.6
Party Stress	54.1	29.3	55.6	47.8	54.7	39.2	53.6	57.0	26.4	70.7

[a] Trade areas are in descending order of support for the core position on high-stress
roll calls during the 49th Congress (1885–87). These high-stress votes generally dealt
with private pension bills, and the core position in every instance was in favor of the
claimant; thus, trade area delegations are ranked in order of their support for a "liberal" interpretation of pension law and an expanded system.

[b] "FT" indicates that a majority of the trade area delegation supported a "free trade"
position; "P" indicates that a majority supported protectionist policy; and S indicates
that the delegation split evenly on the roll call.

SOURCE: Computations from roll call data.

score of 64.6 on passage of the Fordney-McCumber schedule in 1921 and a low
of 22.4 on the Underwood Tariff of 1913. The sectional stress scores generally
reflect the extent to which the proposed bill would have protected the American home market; the upward revisions of 1890, 1897, 1909, and 1921 averaged 58.2 on the stress index while attempts to lower trade barriers (in 1888,
1894, and 1913) produced a mean of 37.8. In part, this pattern seems to result
from the dynamics of the party system. Sectional stress in the congressional
party system averaged 48.8 during the ten years in which tariff revisions were
proposed. This moderately high average was only slightly lower than the cor-

responding mean for the tariff bills themselves, and individual stress scores for the geographical distribution of party members and patterns of support for the tariff generally paralleled one another. In years when major upward revisions were proposed, stress in the party system averaged 59.0, while party polarization during attempts to significantly lower barriers produced a 37.8 mean. The relationship between the party system and the tariff should not be surprising given that trade policy was probably the single most significant issue separating the parties during the period and that downward revisions of the tariff were only attempted when the Democrats controlled the House. In order to capture the House, the periphery party was forced to exploit class conflict in the core—a strategy which ultimately reduced sectional polarization in the party system (see chapter 8).[29]

In periods of Democratic dominance the periphery members of the party were able to construct a platform which could successfully exploit class cleavages in the core electorate. Based on agrarian radicals, ethnic groups, and industrial labor, exploitation of these class cleavages produced a Democratic majority which combined a cohesive and monolithic periphery bloc with a wide scattering of members from most regions of the northern core. Since the auxiliary issues which allowed the party to break out of the periphery always turned out to be ephemeral, northern core representatives who voted for a platform which combined class-based issues and a low tariff usually had short congressional careers. Thus, the cross-policy coalition which supported attempts to lower the tariff seems to have been inherently unstable while the cross-policy coalition which maintained the protective tariff exhibited more persistence over the 1880–1930 period, drew majority support during "normal" elections, and produced significantly higher levels of sectional stress in roll call voting.

By the beginning of the First World War, the United States had emerged from its isolation in the world-economy and assumed a position at or near the top of the international division of labor. From that point, the mighty engine of national development composed of Civil War pensions, a chronic budget surplus, and the protectionist tariff began to decay. By 1898 the United States was exporting more manufactured goods than it imported. While American manufacturers still pled their case, the domestic economy was so efficient and export-oriented that the tariff was for many products no longer a significant factor in their market price. The distribution of pension benefits was "nationalized" by the natural attrition of Civil War veterans and dependents and by the extension of eligibility to include Spanish-American War and World War I veterans. When combined with the passage of income tax legislation in 1913 which loosened the link between tariff revenue and pension expenditures, the nationalization of eligibility made southern politicians vulnerable to veterans' lobbies. World War I also eliminated the chronic surplus, and the stronger federal state that surfaced after the war pursued such a wide variety of new activities with unprecedented vigor that the place of both military pensions and the tariff became increasingly unimportant.

Contested Elections, the Force Bill, and Political Hegemony

Of the ten high-stress roll calls recorded in the 54th Congress (1895–97), one concerned a private military pension bill, two dealt with appropriations to private institutions—a home for Union veterans, Howard University, and miscellaneous charitable and educational organizations—one occurred on a bill to establish a national bankruptcy code, and a fifth was taken on legislation to provide for federal enforcement of laws governing imitation dairy products. The remaining five votes were taken on contested election cases and this, the largest category, provides the theme for the second period.

Following the Civil War, northern financiers invested heavily in the southern economy and came to control the industrial development and transportation system of the periphery South and West.[30] This dominant economic role had become so pronounced by 1890 that a Massachusetts Republican, Representative Elijah Morse, could respond to a silver bimetalist with the following words:

> During this debate I have heard from gentlemen on the other side derisive words spoken of the businessmen, manufacturers, bankers, and capitalists of New England and Massachusetts. They have been derided in these halls as "bloated bondholders," "gold-bugs," "shylocks," etc.
>
> Neither New England nor Massachusetts needs any eulogium or defense at my hands. . . . Eliminate from the West and South the capital and enterprise of these same men, and I tell you the unbroken prairie and the primeval forest of creation would stand in place of some of your cities and populous towns. Who builds the Western railroads that develop that great and growing section of the country? Who joined the Atlantic and Pacific Oceans with a railroad? Who builds the lofty buildings, whose summits pierce the sky, in your Western cities?
>
> I answer. . . . New England enterprise and New England capital. . . .
>
> When the yellow wings of the pestilence flap themselves in a Southern sky, when fire or famine or flood devastate any section of the country, where do they go for funds to relieve the distressed? What section gives more than any other section? What merchants pour out their money like water to relieve distress? Why, these same bloated bondholders, bankers, gold-bugs of Boston and Massachusetts.[31]

Until 1877, the economic penetration of the southern periphery by northern capital was furthered and protected by Reconstruction governments supported by the force of federal arms. In order to maintain the political power of the northern industrial elite and the Republican party against the resurgent "white supremacy" claims of the southern Bourbons, Congress enacted four laws intended to enforce recognition of black civil and political rights between 1870 and 1875. The first of these acts authorized federal courts, marshals, and district attorneys to prevent and penalize interference with registration or voting in congressional elections by states, groups, and individuals, and empowered the president to use military force to implement the act. This act of May 31, 1870, primarily renewed the Civil Rights Act of April 9, 1866.

A second federal election law was passed in 1871 and provided for election supervisors appointed by the federal courts. A third law, also passed in 1871, extended these earlier acts, provided additional federal penalties, and authorized the president to make summary arrests. Under this act martial law was declared in nine South Carolina counties six months after passage. A fourth act was intended to protect black civil rights in public accommodations. The law was passed in March 1875, but the Supreme Court in a series of rulings declared this law unconstitutional and significantly narrowed the scope of the other three. In 1877, federal troops were withdrawn from the section as the price of Hayes' election in the disputed 1876 contest, and the southern plantation elite embarked on a course which gave them undisputed political hegemony in their section by the turn of the century.[32]

Following the withdrawal of federal troops from the South and the reversion of the Supreme Court to Calhoun's doctrine that most questions involving race relations fell within the police power of the individual states, the region more or less openly revolted against the remnants of radical Republicanism and, often through violence, intimidation, and fraud, "redeemed" southern governments for the white race. The federal government turned its attention away from this process for a number of reasons. While the ideological justification for radical Reconstruction was a belief that the national government should control race relations, the underlying purpose was to keep Republicans in power. As it became clear that Reconstruction goals would require the permanent occupation of the South by northern armies, the financial and political costs were increasingly perceived by northern political and economic interests as excessively burdensome. When "the strange and daring experiment of compelling racial equality by the use of arms" became linked in the public mind with the "rogues, knaves, thieves, and incompetents" who were employed in Republican rule, political support for military occupation of the South dwindled away.[33] Fourteen years after Hayes' election, a Wisconsin Republican decried the methods used by southern Bourbons to regain political supremacy and the inability of the northern core to resist the process. Occupied with the contested election decisions then before the House of Representatives, Representative Nils P. Haugen was moved to write, "No fair man can sit in Committee as I have done and hear the testimony and arguments in seventeen contested cases without becoming thoroughly convinced of the absolute lawlessness in elections in a large portion of the South."[34]

In 1889 and for the first time in fifteen years, the Republicans controlled the presidency and held absolute majorities in both chambers of Congress. Even though their numbers were rapidly dwindling, the remaining radical Republicans in the national party seized this political opportunity to propose one last attempt to construct a two-party system in the agrarian South. With the periphery party in the minority in all parts of the federal government, these Republicans saw a chance—albeit a slim one—of reversing the consolidation of southern political power in the hands of the indigenous economic elite.[35]

With the support of President Benjamin Harrison, Representative Henry Cabot Lodge of Massachusetts introduced what became known as the "Force Bill" in March 1890. The law was to become operative on the petition of one hundred citizens in an entire congressional district or any city of 20,000 or more inhabitants or on the petition of fifty citizens in any part of a congressional district; three regional election supervisors representing both major parties were to be appointed by federal district judges in each qualifying congressional district. These regional supervisors were to assist a chief supervisor (appointed for every federal judicial circuit) and were empowered to inspect registration books, attend elections, and perform other functions. In the larger towns, they were required to inform registrants of the procedure, place, and time of voting by way of a house-to-house canvass of the city. After the election, a board of canvassers, appointed by the circuit court, was to examine and certify the election returns as presented to it by the federal supervisors. If the candidate certified by the federal board of canvassers differed from the winner as determined by the state election officials, the board's decision was *prima facie* evidence of election though it could be appealed to a federal circuit court (in which case the court's decision was intended to be conclusive).[36] Lodge publicly claimed that one of the major problems that would be resolved by the act was the increasing number of contested election disputes that preoccupied the Congress.[37]

The legislation was also intended to regulate jury selection, and the president was given the authority to use military force if implementation met with violent resistance. This last provision gave the bill its name, and southern whites, including many Republicans, left nothing to the imagination. "If you are determined to pass a federal election law, then you must prepare to enforce it with Federal bayonets and possibly Federal bullets," said Hamilton Coleman, the Republican congressman from Louisiana.[38] Representative Allen Candler of Georgia affirmed in debate that:

> we will never surrender our government into the hands of an inferior race. . . . We wrested our State government from negro supremacy

when the Federal drum-beat rolled closer to the ballot-box and Federal
bayonets hedged it deeper about than . . . will ever again be permitted in this free Government. . . . Though the cannon of this Republic thundered in every voting district of the South, we still should
find in the mercy of God the means and the courage to prevent its
establishment.[39]

The prospect of federal enforcement of suffrage rights provoked anger, frustration, and fear in southern whites and immediately produced a dramatic
upsurge in violence against southern blacks.[40]

Republican support for the Lodge bill was founded on a variety of principles or presuppositions. Relatively few Republicans, among them Harrison, sincerely "cared about the plight of the party in the South or the fate of
the Negro."[41] Instead, the primary purpose of the legislation was to secure
Republican control of the national government by recapturing marginal
areas in the South. The president viewed federal protection of the black vote
as the only way to promote a Republican revival in the region and believed
that such a revival "would create a permanent majority for the protective tariff in Dixie and prevent Southern tactics of intimidation at the polls from
spreading northward." Thomas Reed of Maine, the Republican Speaker of
the House, claimed that it was "just as fair for the Republicans to poll ignorant Negroes in the South as for Democrats to poll ignorant immigrants in
the North."[42] Northern Democrats believed that the ultimate Republican
goal was "to pack Congress with fraudulent majorities in order to pass economic legislation" which would favor the interests of the core elite.[43]

Even if the federal election bill had been only partially successful, the
legislation would have had two consequences favorable to the North. Federal
enforcement would have destabilized southern white elite control of the periphery political system and thereby forced the diversion of political energy
toward the maintenance of local dominance. On the national level, periphery
representatives and senators would have been compelled to bargain over implementation and enforcement even if they had continued to prevail in most
election contests. Furthermore, the lower classes of the periphery—most obviously the black but also the upland white—would have been absolutely
dependent on the support given them by the party of the core elite. Where
Republicans were elected from the periphery, their voting records—as was
true in the Reconstruction era—would not have differed noticeably from
their northern comrades even though the economic interests of their constituencies would have been radically different. Given passive support for the
policy from northern electorates, Republicans could have benefited even from
lenient and sporadic enforcement of the law. Finally, of course, the Force Bill
was a convenient political issue—a "bloody shirt" in which to dress up the
protective tariff and military pensions. As it turned out, however, the Democrats seem to have made more political capital out of the opportunism of the

Republicans than the GOP could squeeze out of the "disloyalty" of the Democracy.[44]

Within the Republican party itself, the most important source of opposition emerged from the timidity of northern commercial interests that had extensive trade connections or investments in the southern periphery. These interests feared that federal enforcement of voting rights and control of election machinery would lead southern whites to retaliate against the northern economy by boycotting goods produced in the North, by sabotaging northern investments in the South, and by diverting federal revenues to the support of military operations in the periphery. The costs of an occupation army would reduce funds available for military pensions, public works, and subsidies to private enterprise—all of which served the needs of an expanding core economy.[45] Of all the explanations for the relative apathy of the Republican party, this unwillingness to disturb the now pacified southern periphery and thus destroy the stable economic environment for northern investment and commerce was probably the most important. *

The Democrats interpreted the Force Bill as an open bid for power by the Republican party and, aware of the timidity of northern commercial interests, emphasized the intensity with which the southern white would resist enforcement. A recurring theme in southern rhetoric was that the Lodge bill was an imperialist policy comparable to English subjugation of Ireland or India.[46] Representative William Breckinridge of Kentucky stated one version of this view.

> It is a measure modeled after the force bills passed by an English Parliament for Irish constituencies and defended on precisely the same grounds.

---

*A few Republicans opposed the Force Bill on the ground that enforcement would unite southern whites in opposition to the "black" Republican party and suppress all latent class and producer differences within the region. Hirshson, *Farewell to the Bloody Shirt*, pp. 213, 223. Some of the congressmen who adopted this position painted an optimistic picture of racial and political progress in the post-Reconstruction South. For example, Republican Representative Hamilton Coleman of Louisiana claimed:

"The principal influence which holds the white people of the South together is the old Democratic war-whoop of 'negro supremacy' and 'Africanization.' Remove from the eyes of the people the scales of ignorance of and prejudice to the Republican party, and let them realize that the bugaboo 'yawps' and war-whoops of the Democratic politicians are without foundation, then the shotgun squad will disband, and the negro will be protected in his political and civil rights by Republican ex-Confederates, ex–White Leaguers, and ex-Democrats.

"In several if not all those States where bulldozing, intimidation, or ballot-box stuffing prevails we find feuds and divisions among the leaders of the Democratic party, and there are undoubted signs of disintegration, owing in many cases to the personal ambition of rivals for political position or patronage.

"We find movements operating under the name of wheels, Alliance, and Labor party, whose leaders and adherents have been voting with the Democrats. Pass a Federal election law, and many who are now willing to separate from the Democratic party will immediately get back into the so-called 'white man's party' rather than risk 'negro supremacy.'" *Congressional Record*, 51:1:6773, June 30, 1890.

Mendacious slanders of the people of the weaker sections; exaggerated and sensational reports of occasional acts of violence; passionate appeals to the people of other sections; petty persecutions and irritating annoyances by an unscrupulous constabulary; offensive and insulting charges thrown at the representatives; urgent party persuasion characterize in common those who pass force bills there and press force bills here.*

Even southern Republicans could sometimes view the imperialist policy of their own party as counterproductive. Representative Hamilton Coleman of New Orleans complained, "In distributing patronage, shake off the old Reconstruction barnacles, and do not treat Louisiana as a colony and a conquered province by appointing men to fill Federal positions who were outside of the State on Election day." [47]

The Force Bill was clearly aimed at northern Democratic machines as well as the plantation South, and in cities such as New York with its Tammany Hall, the legislation could have been used to reshape the electorate to Republican political advantage. To meet the threat on both fronts, the national Democratic party developed a bisectional strategy based primarily on a "states' rights" philosophy. They maintained that the federal government should not attempt to regulate race relations, and their position in favor of a decentralization of race policy allowed the party to pursue entirely contradictory political strategies in the core and the periphery. In the South, the party became the political vehicle for white supremacy and, after disfranchisement, the plantation elite. The northern wing of the party tolerated the southern strategy as a necessary price of political unity and out of a "conviction that whites should exercise political power in the region, albeit through persuasion rather than force." [48] Unlike the South, however, the core Democracy appealed to the lower classes of the North, which were alienated by industrial and commercial influence within the dominant Republican party. In the post–Civil War period, the northern wing of the Democratic party acquiesced in Reconstruction amendments to the Constitution, supported state legislation protecting civil rights, distributed patronage to influential blacks, and, under Cleveland, appointed scores of additional blacks to federal positions. [49] However, this "liberal" race policy was never extended to include voting rights in the South.

The national Democratic party denounced the Force Bill as an unnecessary and dangerous concentration of power, an indication of Republican distrust of local democratic rule, an attempt to stir up sectional and racial hostility, and a threat to American economic prosperity. [50] When the legislation

---

Congressional Record, 51:1:6856, July 1, 1890. In support of the periphery interpretation one Tammany Democrat, Representative Amos Cummings of New York City, compared the legislation to the English penal code for Ireland, adding: "This is imperialism outright. It is machinery to hold on to power instead of returning it to the people every two years. Juarez would have had just as good a chance in running against Maxmilian for Emperor of Mexico as a Democrat would have in running for Congress in a fairly close district under the provisions of this bill." Ibid., 51:1:6683, June 23, 1890.

finally died with Cleveland's reelection in 1892, the New York *Sun*, a news-paper allied with the Tammany machine, was exultant:

The message which went over the wires this morning is worth a thousand millions of dollars to that section [the South] of our great republic.
"No force bill! No Negro Domination!"
Every patriot in the land must rejoice that the black cloud which for several months has overhung the free and prosperous South is at last and forever dispelled.
"No Force Bill! No Negro Domination!"
A new bond unites the Democracy of the Southern States with their brethren of New York, Indiana, and New Jersey. Together, they have won the great and final battle for home rule and honest elections, free from Federal bayonets and hired Republican bulldozers.
"No Force Bill! No Negro Domination!"
. . . There will be no Force bill. There can be no return of the black days of Negro Domination.[51]

The House of Representatives recorded fifteen roll calls on the Lodge bill between June 25, 1890 (the day the legislation was made the subject of a special order), and July 2 (the day the bill passed and was sent on to the Senate). Though the roll calls concerned amendments and procedural matters in addition to passage, the patterns of support and opposition were almost identical for each vote. The sectional stress index scores ranged between 57.2 (the special order) and 60.9 (one of the amendments). On passage, the stress index was 60.8—a score greater than eight of the ten high-stress roll calls recorded in the 54th Congress. Republicans supported the bill by a margin of 154 to 2; Democrats opposed it unanimously (147 to 0). One Union Labor congressman from Arkansas also supported the bill, and the final vote thus stood at 155 to 149—almost a perfect party-line split. (For the geographical voting pattern produced by the Force Bill, see map 3.2.)

In the Senate, the Lodge bill met with increasing Democratic hostility and Republican apathy. Ultimately, the Democratic members traded votes with pro-silver factions and with Republicans interested in tariff revision and thus won postponement of floor consideration of the bill. Finally, the 51st Congress expired and with it disappeared the last significant attempt to per-manently "reconstruct" the South.*

*The bill's experience in the Senate clearly illustrated the kind of political "rent" that the Force Bill and similar election legislation could impose upon the southern periphery. Even the threat of federal intervention was sometimes sufficient to gain periphery support for core policies such as the tariff, and the South was clearly vulnerable to such threats from the end of Recon-struction until the end of the civil rights movement of the 1960s. If the Force Bill had been enacted, such "rent" could have been collected much more regularly but at a higher cost (e.g., military intervention). For a description of the bill's demise in the Senate, see DeSantis, *Republi-cans Face the Southern Question*, pp. 208–9, 213; Hirshson, *Farewell to the Bloody Shirt*, pp. 226, 228–30, 232–33; Oberholtzer, *A History of the United States Since the Civil War*, 5:117.

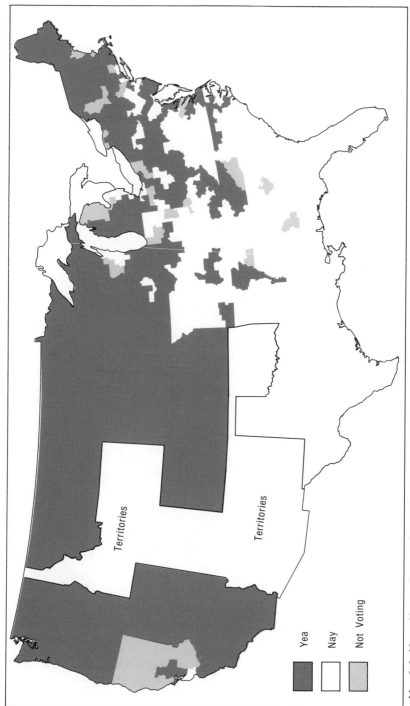

Map 3.2. House Vote on Passage of the Lodge Bill, July 2, 1890

Yea

Nay

Not Voting

Territories

Territories

Even as Congress debated the Force Bill, the South began to alter the conditions of the franchise and to replace a system which excluded the black man through fraud, intimidation, and violence with one that accomplished the same end "legally." In 1890, Mississippi drew up a new constitution which instituted a poll tax and made the exercise of suffrage rights conditional upon the ability to read or understand the Constitution. Of the 147,000 blacks of voting age, only 37,000 were estimated to be literate and only 8,600 were able or willing to register to vote under the new law. For the first time since the Civil War, white voters were legally in the majority.[52] Before the compromise of 1877, voter participation in Mississippi exceeded 70 percent. During the next decade, voter turnout dropped to less than half of the potential electorate as the white plantation elite moved to power (figure 3.2). With the constitutional reform of 1890, participation dropped another twenty-five points and hovered around 15 percent for the next six decades. The low point came in the 1920 presidential election, when more than nine of every ten voting-age Mississippians failed to exercise the franchise. As long as the national party tolerated the southern caste system and race code (that is, until 1965), the Democratic party dominated the state in almost inverse proportion to the size of the active electorate.

Other southern states soon enacted versions of the Mississippi plan: South Carolina, 1894–95; Louisiana, 1897–98; North Carolina, 1899–1900; Alabama, 1901; Virginia, 1902; Texas, 1902; Georgia, 1908.[53] The results were everywhere the same: almost all blacks and most poor whites were disfranchised and the plantation elite achieved hegemonic control over the region. Electoral reform simultaneously released the Bourbons from the twin threats of federal intervention and agrarian, class-based radicalism. In 1893, as a new Democratic majority in the House of Representatives was considering repeal of the last remaining Reconstruction statutes, a Republican minority report summarized the new status quo in the South:

> Whatever may have been the necessity for the enactment of Federal statutes supervising the elections in the large Northern cities, an added necessity has arisen in the South, because of State laws and their operation. Through Kuklux violence in nearly all the Southern communities the Democratic party gradually gained control of every branch of the State governments. The murders and assassinations committed have passed into history. Through these the State governments were seized; then came the enactment of the Southern force laws, by which usurped power is retained in all of the late Confederate States. Although there are still occasional instances of violence, this is no longer necessary because the laws are so framed that the Democrats can keep themselves in possession of the governments in every Southern State. The details of the laws of the various States differ, but the purpose of all is the same.*

Congressional Record, 53:1:2348, October 9, 1893. The southern response to these

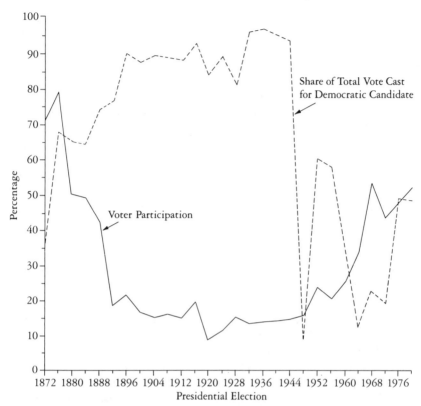

Figure 3.2. Mississippi Voter Participation and Presidential Voting Pattern, 1872–1980

SOURCE: U.S. Bureau of the Census, *Historical Statistics of the United States, Colonial Times to 1970*, part 2 (Washington: 1975), p. 1072; U.S. Bureau of the Census, *Statistical Abstract of the United States, 1980* (Washington: 1980), pp. 501, 517. "Voter Participation" is the percentage of the voting-age population (males only before 1920) that actually voted in the general election.

---

charges usually included a claim that blacks were not, if they ever would be, "ready" for suffrage. For example, during the debate on the Force Bill, Democratic Representative Allen Candler of Georgia argued: "The truth of the matter, Mr. Speaker, is that the average plantation negro has never appreciated his responsibility as a citizen. The ballot was thrust upon him when he was utterly and totally unprepared for it. He regards election day as a public holiday. He goes to the polls as he goes to the circus or to a public execution—for a frolic." *Congressional Record*, 51:1:6703, June 28, 1890.

Table 3.3. Regional Shares of Federal Expenditures for the Salary and Expenses of Special Deputy Marshals at Congressional Elections (%), 1877–1893

Section	Fiscal Year			Total, 1877–93	Amount in Dollars
	1877	1885	1893		
New York State	56.0	40.1	56.4	54.1	610,324
North and West[a]	14.1	45.0	34.0	32.2	363,169
Border[b]	22.4	8.9	5.8	8.4	94,472
Former Confederate	7.5	6.0	3.8	5.3	59,631
Total	100.0	100.0	100.0	100.0	1,127,596

[a] Does not include New York.
[b] Former slave states that did not secede from the Union.
SOURCE: Adapted from a table prepared by the First Comptroller's Office of the Treasury Department, reprinted in the *Congressional Record*, 53:1:2095, October 3, 1893.

The Republicans were not slow to connect the political issue to the economic. Representative William Hepburn of Iowa made the connection explicit:

> I can see, too, gentlemen, that you have a motive in repressing black suffrage [in] the South. You have an interest in so doing. It is not, in my judgment, because you fear their domination. The whites are the class of wealth, intelligence, and power. You do not fear the blacks. You have, as a rule, but a single industry there. It is an industry that does not require skilled labor, but one which you think requires cheap labor, and the certainty of labor at particular seasons of the year. The man who has the ballot values himself, values his manhood, and learns to value labor. That you do not want. This is not altogether a political question with you, it is an economic question, the question of how you can maintain the cheap labor that is necessary to enable you to produce cotton in competition with the cheap labor of other parts of the world.[54]

In the years following the compromise of 1877, the federal election machinery created by the Reconstruction legislation of the 1870s came to have as its major purpose the harassment of Tammany Hall and seldom applied to the South. From 1877 to 1893 over half of all federal appropriations for the provision of supervisors and deputy marshals to oversee voter registration and the conduct of elections was spent in New York State (see table 3.3). Throughout the debate on repeal in 1893, the Democrats complained about John I. Davenport, the federal supervisor for congressional elections in New York, while the Republicans concentrated their defense of election oversight on reported abuse in the South. The inconsistency between the rationale for and actual administration of federal election law led Democratic Representative Barnes Compton of Maryland to complain, "Now, if these laws were made for the protection of the poor helpless colored man of the South, in God's name why was not the money spent in that section?"* Representative Andrew Hunter, an Illinois Democrat, saw three additional reasons for federal election policy. He charged that the Republicans used the appointment of deputy marshals at five dollars a day as a cheap form of patronage to hold the loyalty of weak party members, that particularly "brutal and desperate" men were selected to intimidate "timid" voters, and that, if all else failed, appointments on the day of election constituted an outright bribe.[55]

Even as Republican Charles Boutelle observed that "any man who has sat in the gallery of the House during the past ten days has seen the sheeted ghosts of the Confederacy flitting in and out of these doors, striding up and down these aisles, and gibbering the discordant shibboleths of a defeated conspiracy," the Democratic majority was moving repeal toward final passage.[56] On October 10, 1893, the repeal of federal election laws cleared the House of Representatives by almost a two-to-one margin (201-102) after two hostile Republican amendments were voted down. All three roll calls were along party lines and their sectional stress scores, ranging from 39.8 to 42.2, reflected the underlying sectional structure of the party system after the 1892 election. When enacted into law, the repeal bill lifted the yoke of federal supervision from Tammany and quieted the lingering fear of renewed political "imperialism" still felt by the southern periphery.

In the 54th Congress (1895–97), five of the ten high-stress roll calls were taken on contested election cases then before the House. All of these cases arose out of alleged irregularities involving southern congressional elections and reflected the continuing attention the Republicans paid to the periphery political system even after 1894. In fact, of the twenty-five Congresses held beginning in 1881 (the 47th) and ending in 1931 (the 71st), the 54th Congress contained the largest number of election contests (thirty-one—twice as many as the second-ranked Congress), the greatest number of successful challenges (eleven), and the largest gain for the majority party (nine seats—tied with the 51st Congress, which reported the Force Bill).

Election contests in the House of Representatives were highly partisan (table 3.4). In sixteen of the twenty-five Congresses, the successful contests

---

Congressional Record, 53:1:2140, October 4, 1893. For comparable data on supervisors of congressional elections, see ibid., 53:1:2024, October 2, 1893. For the years 1891–93, 40 percent of federal expenditures for the salary and expenses of supervisors was spent in New York State. Most of these expenses were incurred in the southern district of the state, which included New York City. New York Republicans realized the consequences of repeal for their own political fortunes. Representative George Ray made the most articulate observation: "From the inner chambers of Tammany wigwam are issued the edicts that are to control the party. . . . It was Tammany Hall that set on foot the proposition to repeal these laws. . . . 'Give us New York City,' said Tammany, 'and give us absolute sway on election day in that city freed from fear of responsibility and accountability to the Government of the United States, and we will give you New York State every time.' This perfect political machine, like the car of Juggernaut, is dragged over the people of that great city crushing out their political liberty and life. . . . They only fear the laws of the United States and John I. Davenport." Ibid., 53:1:2231, October 6, 1893.

Table 3.4. Contested Elections in the House of Representatives, 1881–1931

Decade	Average Number per Congress			Percentage of Total Contests Involving Former Slave States
	Number of Contests	Successful Challenges	Net Gain for Majority Party	
1881–91				
Republican Control	12.5	8.0	6.5	88.0
Democratic Control	6.0	2.3	1.7	38.9
1891–1901				
Republican Control	16.3	5.7	4.7	83.7
Democratic Control	5.0	2.0	2.0	50.0
1901–11				
Republican Control	6.0	1.0	1.0	66.7
1911–21				
Republican Control	4.5	2.0	.5	33.3
Democratic Control	7.7	1.0	.7	34.8
1921–31				
Republican Control	4.8	.4	.4	42.9
Average, Both Parties, Entire Period	7.5	2.3	1.8	62.8

SOURCE: Computations from data in *Biographical Directory of the American Congress: 1774–1961* (Washington: Government Printing Office, 1961).

resulted in a net gain for the majority party. Even though nine Congresses left the majority unchanged, in no Congress did the minority party experience a net gain through successful election challenges (on three occasions the minority did win individual seats).

Before the plantation elite had legally disfranchised their lower classes, the vast majority of election cases came from the South. An example of these contests is the case involving Jacob Yost and H. St. George Tucker, which produced two high-stress roll calls in the 54th Congress. The disputed election took place in 1894 in central Virginia. The Republican contestant, Jacob Yost, claimed rightful possession of the seat on three general grounds. First, he asserted that ballots should be counted which were, under a strict interpretation of the law, improperly marked but which clearly, if improperly, indicated the intention of the voter.[57] The major decision rule in contested election cases was to somehow replicate an accurate ballot count from the information available. This process was complicated by the fact that Democratic election officials had destroyed impaired ballots immediately after the election. Even after a portion of the improperly marked ballots had been awarded to Yost, however, he was still short of a plurality. The second allegation was that special constables which, under Virginia law, were to assist illiterate voters often failed to do so when Republican voters requested help. The Committee on Elections awarded no ballots to the contestant on this ground.

The final allegation was also the most unusual and set the case apart from others of the same period. Yost maintained that "schools" for illiterate and semiliterate Republican voters were formed throughout the district and that in these schools the party's supporters were taught to recognize the name "J. Yost" in Roman letters. These voters "were instructed to study the formation of the letters; to count the letters in the name, and to see that it contained only five; to compare the length of the name with other names of candidates, it being the shortest, and to so familiarize themselves with its appearance that they would be able to recognize it." In addition, "tens of thousands" of slips bearing the candidate's name—again in Roman type—were scattered "broadcast" in order to assist Yost's supporters. Last, "it was understood at the opening of the polls that an intelligent Republican would vote first, and then come out and tell those who had not voted the location of the contestant's name on the ballot."[58] The Democrats in several counties got wind of the well-laid Republican strategy and printed the ballots in what Yost called a "German" text which might as well have been "Greek" to his supporters (figure 3.3). Not only was the ballot set in a rather bizarre style of type, but the Democratic electoral board then transposed the order of the candidates' names in seventy-five different permutations so that no "intelligent" Republican could guide the rest. As one Democrat testified, "My object was to enforce the law strictly, and to a man unable to read, the German type was as intelligible as any other."[59] While the committee acknowledged the accuracy of the allegations (even the

FOR MEMBER OF THE HOUSE OF REPRESENTATIVES OF THE UNITED STATES from the Tenth Congressional District of Virginia.

Edmund R. Cocke,

H. St. Geo. Tucker,

James Seldon Cowdon,

J. Yost,

C. H. Grove,

Figure 3.3 Copy of a Ballot Used in a Virginia Congressional Election, 1894

Democrats admitted the facts) and called the action "reprehensible," no votes were allowed the contestant. Thus, Yost was, in the committee's view, still short of a majority in the district and the full House subsequently retained the incumbent, Tucker, by a narrow majority (127 to 119).

Generally speaking, election contests were much more frequent between 1881 and 1901 than after the turn of the century and more frequent still during Republican as opposed to Democratic control of the House. Through the power of the House to rule on the qualifications of its members in these cases, the party of the northern core attempted to impose standards of election conduct that the party was unwilling or unable to enforce through a resort to arms. As a result of this attempt, election contests were inevitably partisan and the outcome of the case was often as loosely related to what might be termed the "objective circumstances" of the election as the certified vote total was to the actual distribution of voters in the district. All too often even conscientious members and, indeed, the contestants themselves were unable to replicate or recount the events that surrounded the disputed election.

Contested election cases, from the perspective of the Republican party, had three purposes. They used the discretionary power of the House of Representatives over the credentials of its members as a substitute for direct federal supervision of elections. To some extent, the threat of a successful challenge may have compelled southern election boards to be more circumspect in the manipulation of suffrage rights and election machinery. However, the effect could not have been very significant, if only because periphery elites had much more powerful and legitimate means of controlling election outcomes (e.g., constitutional provisions setting registration requirements). Successfully contested elections also provided a small increment to the majority party coalition. That marginal increase in the size of the majority perhaps—and again to a relatively slight extent—decreased the possibility of political stalemate in the lower chamber of Congress. The parties during this period were extremely cohesive, and if the membership was closely divided, one or two additional members would have made it much easier for the majority to prevail. The most important purpose of election challenges, however, was undoubtedly to publicize the nefarious election practices of the minority and thereby to gain political advantage. In this respect, contested elections were only a pale shadow of Reconstruction and the Force Bill.

After 1891, the Republican party turned away from the southern "question" and became concerned, when it thought at all about southern politics, only with the dispensation of patronage and the appointment of delegates to presidential nominating conventions.[60] As Senator Benjamin "Pitchfork" Tillman of South Carolina put it, "The brotherhood of man exists no longer, because you shoot Negroes in Illinois when they come in competition with your labor, and we shoot them in South Carolina when they come in competition with us in the matter of elections."[61] As Elihu Root, one of the architects of American imperialism, observed in 1903, "I fear we are compelled to face the conclusion that the experiment [of giving the negro citizenship and suffrage and equal rights] has failed . . ."[62] The northern core was to leave the periphery caste system more or less intact for three-quarters of a century.

Territorial Expansion: Statehood and Imperialism, 1905–1907

During the 59th Congress (1905–7), almost all of the high-stress roll calls dealt with some aspect of territorial expansion by the United States. Four of the ten high-stress votes occurred on various solutions to the question of statehood for Oklahoma, New Mexico, Arizona, and the Indian Territory. These votes raised two issues important to core-periphery relations: the terms under which the respective states would enter the Union, and the number of seats they would receive in the U.S. Senate. Four additional roll calls concerned the registration of foreign-built naval vessels in the United States, government manufacture of supplies purchased by the United States Navy, and a construction cost differential which would have allowed the Pacific coast to compete effectively with Atlantic seaboard shipyards for the construction of naval vessels. Each of the latter policy decisions related in some way to the maritime expansion and growing naval power of the United States that formed a major part of imperialist policy between 1894 and 1917.

One of the ten roll calls was over an amendment which excepted aliens working on the Panama Canal from a proposed eight-hour law for laborers and mechanics engaged in public works construction. The decision reflected a larger political division over the legal status of overseas possessions under the Constitution and American law. The last high-stress roll call occurred on legislation which authorized the board of education of the District of Columbia to maintain a series of free evening lectures. The political division reaffirmed a reluctance on the part of the southern periphery to see precedents set for national control of education. In most areas of social legislation, which of course included race relations, the exercise of federal police power in the District of Columbia served as a model for a time when similar policies might be expanded to the nation as a whole. From Reconstruction down to the 1970s, the southern periphery has generally opposed innovative policies and local control in the District for fear that such actions might support a centralization of social policy in the future.

For most of the 1894–1917 period, the issue of territorial expansion of the United States and the implications it held for the national economy and political development was one of the two or, at most, three preeminent issues before the country.* In the early part of this period, the political conflict over

---

*The earlier date was chosen as one limit to the period studied in this section because 1894 was the high tide of Populist insurgency, one of the deepest points in the economic depression of the 1890s, and includes the first serious attempt by Congress to confer statehood to

American foreign policy competed for public attention with the Populist response to the agrarian crisis of the 1890s and the silver issue—free, unlimited monetization of silver at a ratio of 16 to 1 with the value of gold.* In later years, the saliency of imperialist policy must be compared to "progressivism" (of which it formed one component) and to military preparations for American intervention in World War I.

In a general sense, imperialism is a national policy of territorial expansion which involves the taking and holding of colonies and an ideology which justifies the political suppression of colonial populations (which usually belong to a different racial-ethnic stock).† In the American case, imperialism was based on an almost universal concern with penetration and control of foreign markets following the prolonged and severe economic depression of the 1890s.[63] "Both in the farming districts and in industry, the general opinion was that the crisis had been the result of over-capacity and over-production and that the only hope for recovery lay in new markets for American products and capital—in expansion. This conviction was as rooted in the agrarian South and West as in the industrial Northeast . . ."[64] All sectors of the economy and sections of the nation believed in the necessity of commercial expansion, in the utility of foreign bases and coaling stations (for maritime trade and for the projection abroad of American naval power), and in the superiority of (Anglo-) American civilization and the Anglo-Saxon race.[65] While the ends of American foreign

---

the territory of New Mexico. The later date was chosen because World War I significantly altered both the structure of the national economy and the role of the United States in the world community.

*Stanley L. Jones, *The Presidential Election of 1896* (Madison: University of Wisconsin Press, 1964). Both nineteenth-century populism and the silver issue were themselves highly sectional movements. The Populists ultimately failed in their attempt to exploit latent class conflict in the agrarian regions of the core and the periphery (upland and mountain). The party was crushed between the two great, elite-dominated parties and decimated by disfranchisement in the South and emigration from the wheat belt of the North. Gabriel Kolko, *Main Currents in Modern American History* (New York: Harper and Row, 1976), pp. 28–29; John D. Hicks, *The Populist Revolt* (Minneapolis: University of Minnesota Press, 1931). When agrarian radicalism reemerged in the second decade of the twentieth century as one strain of "progressivism," the accommodation to northern core industrial interests was clear; progressive insurgency within the Republican party never possessed the destabilizing potential of the Populist political program and rhetoric. Gabriel Kolko, *The Triumph of Conservatism* (New York: Free Press of Glencoe, 1963).

†This conception of "imperialism" is drawn, in part, from *Webster's Third New International Dictionary* (Springfield, Massachusetts: G. and C. Merriam, 1961), and is adapted to complement Goran Rystad's description of "globalism" in chapter 1 of *Ambiguous Imperialism: American Foreign Policy and Domestic Policy at the Turn of the Century* (Stockholm: Scandinavian University Books, 1975). Hans Daalder's discussion of the term in the *International Encyclopedia of the Social Sciences*, ed. David L. Sills, vol. 7 (New York: Macmillan and the Free Press, 1968) indicates some of the many difficulties and complexities of modern usage, including its strong emotive connotations. Use of the term is unavoidable in any discussion of American expansionist policy at the turn of the century if only because the political participants of the period relied so heavily on the concept in public debate.

policy were consensual, the political debate over the means produced one of the most intense and prolonged sectional conflicts in American history.

The struggle over the course and extent of American territorial expansion can conveniently be described as a contest between "continentalism" and "imperialism."* As a political theory, continentalism was the ideological position assumed by the southern periphery and the political vehicle through which its interests were expressed: the Democratic party. The theory was composed of four basic principles. First, continentalists maintained that the Constitution and laws of the United States followed the national flag. The most basic practical consequence of this view was that all regions controlled by the United States were either territories or states. The concept of a "colony" that lay beyond the reach of general laws governing the tariff, immigration, bankruptcy, etc. was seen as unconstitutional (although conquered lands might be ruled temporarily under martial law).[66] If populated lands were acquired by the United States, the continentalists felt that they must, in addition to being administered as territories, be perceived as viable candidates for statehood at some time in the foreseeable future. If not (and the reason usually given was the "incompatibility" of the racial stock with Anglo-Saxon civilization and a consequent "inability" on the part of the subject race to adapt to the American political system), then the region should be abandoned immediately and left to fend for itself. In rare cases, the United States might, however, shield the region from the predatory designs of other imperial powers.†

Similarly, all territories admitted into the Union should be accorded equal political rights. No new state should be bound by conditions or requirements that did not apply equally to all states. Finally, the continentalists maintained that commercial expansion did not require the acquisition of new lands either as colonies or territories but only the successful promotion of "free trade" principles in the international economy.

"Imperialism," or "globalism," was the ideological competitor that confronted the continentalists. As a political theory, imperialism rationalized the interests of the northern industrial core, their agrarian allies in the Great Plains, and the Republican party (as a vehicle for attaining core political goals). The imperialists held that the Constitution did not necessarily follow the flag. Ultimately this position was to prevail within the Supreme Court in a series of decisions conventionally described as the Insular Cases. As Foster Rhea Dulles summarized the court's opinions:

*Rystad, *Ambiguous Imperialism*, ch. 1. This notion of "imperialism" corresponds to Rystad's "globalism." These concepts have been adapted and enlarged upon in order to encompass the combination of issues analyzed in this section.

† "The Democrats constantly stressed the difference between old-style continentalism and the new imperialism. On the one hand territories were incorporated into the Union, covered by the Constitution, and prepared for ultimate statehood; on the other, territories were acquired which were not incorporated but governed outside the Constitution, not considered a part of the United States, [and] excluded from ultimate statehood." Ibid., p. 156.

An almost mystical theory was evolved. The new possessions were said to be territory appurtenant and belonging to the United States but not a part of the United States. Their inhabitants, so long as such territories remain "unincorporated," were not entitled to all the rights and privileges of American citizens, but only to such fundamental rights as were derived from natural law. While such rights included those relating to the protection of life, liberty, and property, they did not necessarily embrace the constitutional provision that all duties, imposts, and excises should be uniform throughout the United States [and similar provisions governing interstate commerce and immigration].*

The governing agent in this extra-constitutional administration was the almost absolute power of Congress to acquire a possession and to "keep it like a disembodied shade, in an intermediate state of ambiguous existence."[67] From this successful defense of "colonialism" under the Constitution, it seemed to follow that territorial possessions acquired by the United States could be held indefinitely without any prospect of ultimate statehood and, for the duration, groomed for independence and self-government. This aggressive interpretation of congressional power was extended to include political requirements that could be imposed upon prospective states as a precondition for admission.

Finally, the imperialists adopted a neo-mercantilist attitude toward commercial expansion that interpreted military power, national prestige, and economic wealth as different aspects of the same phenomenon: a predestined, dominant role for America in world civilization. This perspective on national policy had two important components. Imperialists asserted, first, that sea power, both civil and military, was the only secure foundation for national economic growth. In order to assume its rightful place in the first rank among nations, the imperialists felt that the United States should pursue a calculated, long-term policy of naval construction and the strategic acquisition of foreign bases and coaling stations. The leading exponent of this view, Captain Alfred Thayer Mahan, was quite specific concerning the location of these bases and resupply depots. He wanted the Sandwich Islands (Hawaii), Samoa, Puerto Rico, Cuba, a canal linking the Atlantic and Pacific Oceans, and, later when the opportunity was presented, the Philippines. While the naval bases Mahan contemplated did not necessarily imply "colonialization" of the entire island or archipelago, imperialists were easily persuaded that colonial control would enhance the strategic security of such stations because these colonies would not only allow the United States to penetrate remote foreign markets but would

---

*Foster Rhea Dulles, *America's Rise to World Power* (New York: Harper, 1955), pp. 56–57. "A false step at this time . . . might be fatal to the development of what Chief Justice Marshall called the American Empire," stated a justice in one of the decisions. Dulles adds that the cases "clearly reflected the conversion of the Supreme Court to overseas extension." For a concise description of these cases and their consequences, see Hicks, *The American Nation*, pp. 342–44.

also provide opportunities for the reinvestment of "surplus" capital.[68] The imperialists believed that the depression of the 1890s revealed the inadequacy of domestic markets and the necessity of international expansion. The depression also pointed out the need for American competition in the race for overseas possessions. In short, they believed that "profits are, other things being equal, higher where the least capital has previously been invested—that is, in undeveloped areas—and the fruits of economic expansion naturally seemed more secure if only a government controlled by the capitalists themselves had to be dealt with."[69]

The southern periphery opposed such an imperialist policy for a number of reasons. Perhaps most important, the policy differences between the northern core and periphery can be traced to their respective positions in the world-economy. Unlike the industrial core or its close regional allies in the wheat and corn belts of the Midwest, the South and mountain West produced raw materials that on the whole sought industrial markets (e.g., cotton and metals) either in the United States or abroad. While undeveloped colonies could provide markets for the foodstuffs and manufactured goods produced in the northern core, these same colonies held little promise for the disposal of "surplus" cotton by the southern plantation elite. Concerning the development of overseas markets, the goal of the agrarian southern periphery and mountain West was increased competition among buyers of their products, not the paternalistic exploitation of "native" consumers or expanded opportunities for the export of surplus capital. In fact the periphery during this period was composed of debtor regions which imported huge amounts of capital from the northern core. Instead of neo-mercantile imperialism, the periphery required the development of free trade in the world-system, which could only occur with the destruction of tariff barriers and elimination of exclusive exploitation of colonial markets by the major imperial powers.*

Because they dominated the national state apparatus, the imperialists of the northern core were not apprehensive about the growing power of central government. The southern periphery, on the other hand, feared the two most

---

*Core and periphery goals in the world-economy are generally incompatible. Core economies usually develop exclusive relationships with a variety of peripheral states so that, while the core enjoys something approaching a competitive market both in purchasing raw materials and selling manufactured goods, the periphery is usually at the mercy of only one core state or an oligopoly of core states. See Johan Galtung, "A Structural Theory of Imperialism," *Journal of Peace Research* 8 (1971): 81–117; and Steve Chan, "Cores and Peripheries: Interaction Patterns in Asia," *Comparative Political Studies* 15:3 (October 1982): 314–40. The best treatments of agrarian interests in imperialist expansion are William Appleman Williams's *The Roots of the Modern American Empire* (New York: Vintage Books, Random House, 1969), and *The Contours of American History* (Cleveland: World Publishing, 1961). His emphasis on midwestern grain producers and the relative paucity of evidence presented for the southern periphery indirectly supports the distinction drawn between foodstuffs and industrial raw materials. On the subject of overseas exports and investment, see Dulles, *America's Rise to World Power*, p. 46; Foner, *The Spanish-Cuban-American War*, 1:287–88, 295; Rystad, *Ambiguous Imperialism*, pp. 12, 16–17, 29–34, 36.

likely consequences of imperial policy: militarism and the political suppression of peripheral territory. Imperialist expansion openly embraced militarism as an essential element of America's emergence as a world power. The continentalists, however, saw in large standing armies and naval flotillas the potential for coercion of underdeveloped areas within the nation itself. While the Northeast dreamed of the sun never setting on the American flag, the South remembered the interventionist provisions of the 1890 Force Bill and, of course, the Civil War.

Within the national economy, the northern core was overwhelmingly dominant at the turn of the century, and, as we have seen, that dominance was translated into influence over the political economy (military pensions, the tariff, etc.). The periphery resisted, but could not prevent, these developments. However, it sought to prevent a subordinate economic role and political disadvantage from being translated into a permanent feature of the republic. It is this goal that explains periphery hostility to extraordinary preconditions on admission into the Union for new states and extra-constitutional status for colonial possessions.* While the northern core argued in favor of paternalistic training of subject races in the intricacies of self-government and the assimilation of alien cultures into the American political system, the periphery viewed these policies as parallel to northern administration of the slave states during Reconstruction and the sentiments expressed from time to time concerning the proper development of citizenship qualities in the southern black.

The debate over expansionism was won by the northern core. As Foster Rhea Dulles has explained,

> The imperialists held almost every advantage. Theirs was the positive, active policy which reflected the new sense of power of the American people, and the compelling idea that to surrender wartime gains was somehow to impair the national prestige established by trial of arms.

---

*On a strictly political level, the continentalist and the globalist played unusual roles in the constitutional debate. When the continentalist argued that the Constitution followed the flag, he implied that foreign colonies would flood the American market with cheap, non-white labor (because of unrestricted immigration) and with cheap raw materials that would be in permanent competition with periphery producers in the national market (because of the elimination of tariff barriers). Because the consequences of this "legitimate" interpretation of the Constitution were disastrous, the periphery argued that the United States should not try to hold overseas possessions. When the core argued that Congress could administer possessions outside of the Constitution, they indicated that "inferior" races would not be incorporated into the Union through immigration or statehood and that tariff barriers would protect the home market of domestic producers (most prominently sugar). Thus, imperialist policy would be made compatible with major political allies of the industrial core: domestic labor and sugar beet and cane producers. See, on the Philippines, Hicks, *The American Nation*, pp. 345–48; and, in general, LaFeber, *The New Empire*, p. 207; Rystad, *Ambiguous Imperialism*, pp. 159, 168; Smith, *Economic History of the United States*, pp. 429, 441–42; and Christopher Lasch, "The Anti-Imperialists, the Philippines, and the Inequality of Man," *Journal of Southern History* 24:3 (August 1958).

Table 3.5. Trade Area Voting on Imperialist Policy Decisions, 1894–1907

Trade Area[a]	Education in English—New Mexico Statehood	Recognition of Cuban Republic	Annexation of Hawaii	Platt Amendment	Philippine Independence	Oklahoma, Arizona–New Mexico Statehood
Chicago	Imp[b]	Imp	Imp	Imp	Imp	Imp
Pittsburgh	Imp	Imp	Imp	Imp	Imp	Imp
Cleveland	Cont	Imp	Imp	Imp	Imp	Imp
Omaha	Imp	Imp	Imp	Imp	Imp	Imp
Minneapolis	Imp	Imp	Imp	Imp	Imp	Imp
Philadelphia	Imp	Imp	Imp	Imp	Imp	Imp
New York	Cont	Imp	Imp	Cont	Imp	Imp
Detroit	Imp	Imp	Imp	Imp	Imp	Imp
Kansas City	Imp	Cont	Imp	Cont	Imp	Imp
Buffalo	Imp	Imp	Imp	Imp	Imp	Imp
Boston	Imp	Imp	Imp	Imp	Imp	Imp
Cincinnati	Cont	Imp	Imp	Imp	Imp	Imp
San Francisco	Cont	Cont	Imp	Imp	Imp	Cont
St. Louis	Cont	Split	Cont	Split	Cont	Cont
Baltimore	Imp	Imp	Imp	Imp	Imp	Imp
Louisville	Cont	Cont	Split	Cont	Cont	Cont
Richmond	Cont	Cont	Cont	Cont	Cont	Cont
New Orleans	Cont	Cont	Cont	Cont	Cont	Cont
Birmingham	—	—	—	—	Cont	Cont
Atlanta	Cont	Cont	Cont	Cont	Cont	Cont
Memphis	Cont	Cont	Cont	Cont	Cont	Cont
Dallas	—	—	—	—	Cont	Cont
Sectional Stress	57.8	63.2	53.0	55.5	70.1	72.8
Party System Stress	39.2	53.6	53.6	58.7	62.4	61.9

[a]Trade area delegations are ranked in descending order of their support for the core position on the ten high-stress roll calls recorded during the 59th Congress (1905–7); see table 2.5.

[b]"Imp": Imperialist; "Cont": Continentalist; Split: the delegation divided evenly between the Imperialist and Continentalist positions.

SOURCE: Computations from roll call data.

The stand taken by the anti-imperialists was necessarily a more negative one. They appealed to the past, to tradition, to the Constitution—to the well-tried principles of a century of experience. It was not, however, the risks of foreign entanglement growing out of overseas expansion that most alarmed them. It was the violation of republican principles in seeking to establish rule over an alien people. They condemned any colonial policy as a repudiation of the basic tenets of American democracy. Emphasizing the national commitment to liberty which had been advanced as justifying intervention in Cuba, they lost no opportunity to stress the irony of having a war to overthrow Spanish colonialism lead to the creation of an American empire.[70]

One roll call related to the continentalist-globalist dispute was recorded on an amendment to legislation providing for the admission of New Mexico into the Union. (See table 3.5 for the voting pattern on this and five other major policy decisions related to the struggle between continentalism and globalism.) The amendment, proposed by the Republican party, would have required that New Mexico stipulate in its constitution that the English language be taught "as a branch of study in all public schools" as a precondition for admission. The Democratic party supported admission and opposed the amendment. The Republicans opposed admission and supported the amendment. One Republican, John Van Voorhis of Rochester, New York, argued, "it is utterly absurd to try to bring this nation of greasers in as a state."* The continentalists opposed the language requirement as a discriminatory precondition on statehood placed by the northern core on a periphery territory.

On April 13, 1898, the House of Representatives adopted a joint resolution which authorized President McKinley to use the land and naval forces of the United States in order to "stop the war in Cuba." Given the foreign situation at the time, the immediate effect of the resolution was equivalent to a declaration of war on Spain, and the measure marked the beginning of the Spanish-American War. While both parties supported the joint resolution on passage, the Democratic minority tried to amend the legislation by substituting language which would have recognized the independence of the "Republic of Cuba." As Representative Hugh Dinsmore of Arkansas, the ranking minority member of the Foreign Affairs Committee, put it, the Democratic substitute would have assured the Cuban revolutionaries that the United States was "not going to force upon you a government that may be a 'carpetbag' government, run by somebody else outside of your own dominion."[71] The intent of the substitute was to prevent any prolonged military occupation or

---

*In debate, typical comments regarding the equality of states in the federal union can be found in the *Congressional Record*, 53:2:6910–11, June 27, 1894. Van Voorhis's comment appears on p. 6918. All congressmen agreed with the assessment of Representative Charles Boatner, an Alabama Democrat: "I take it that the Anglo-Saxon element in the Territory of New Mexico will dominate. They have done it everywhere else and they will do it here." *Congressional Record*, 53:2:6915, June 27, 1894.

ultimate colonization of the island following the war with Spain. The continentalist position supported adoption of the amendment.*

Two months after the House passed the joint resolution concerning Cuba, the chamber deliberated the question of annexing the Hawaiian Islands.† As the continentalists pointed out, the proposed annexation and similar designs on the acquisition of the Philippines were rapidly converting a war of "liberation" into a "contest for empire," with potentially unfavorable consequences for the United States. During debate a comparison with English policy was made by Representative John F. Fitzgerald, a Massachusetts Democrat:

> It is true that the sun never sets upon British possessions, but it is also true that history does not record one instance of greater oppression enacted in the pursuit of territorial expansion than has been exercised by England upon the Irish, the Boers, the Maltese, the Hindoos, the Bermese, and the Chinese. She finds herself today beset by foreign foes in the East. Her wicked aggressions upon national rights and her continued assaults on weaker nations, resulting in the absorption of their territory, has left her without a friend or an ally among the nations of Europe.[72]

The Republican globalists responded, "The Anglo-Saxon race must grow. England, cooped up on the island known as Great Britain, would not be a fourth-class power. Centuries ago her statesmen opened the way for her children, until the English race is today found in every clime and her colonies present the

---

*Support for the Spanish-American War was almost universal in the United States but was motivated by a variety of factors. Evidence on the fundamental economic rationale for U.S. intervention was provided by an article in *World's Work* written by Frederick Emory, chief of the Bureau of Foreign Commerce of the Department of Commerce, in January 1902: "Underlying the popular sentiment, which might have evaporated in time, which forced the United States to take up arms against Spanish rule in Cuba, were our economic relations with the West Indies and the South American republics. So strong was this commercial instinct that had there been no emotional cause, such as the alleged enormities of Spanish rule or the destruction of the Maine, we would have doubtless taken steps in the end to abate with a strong hand what seemed to be an economic nuisance. . . . The Spanish-American War was but an incident of *a general movement of expansion which had its root in the changed environment of an industrial capacity far beyond our domestic powers of consumption. It was seen to be necessary for us not only to find foreign purchasers for our goods, but to provide the means of making access to foreign markets easy, economical and safe.*" Cited in Foner, *The Spanish-Cuban American War*, 1:286. Emphasis added.

Before final passage, five additional roll calls occurred on direct and indirect attempts to amend the joint resolution. On the sectional stress index, these votes ranged from 59.7 to 62.8 and duplicated the trade area pattern displayed in table 3.5.

† The McKinley administration first proposed a treaty with the Hawaiian "government" that would have annexed the islands to the United States. When the treaty failed to receive the necessary two-thirds majority in the Senate, annexation was reproposed to Congress in the form of a joint resolution requiring a simple majority in both the House and Senate. Subsequently, on April 30, 1900, Hawaii was given full territorial status. For a background and history of this stage in American imperialism, see Dulles, *America's Rise to World Power*, pp. 43–44; LaFeber, *The New Empire*, pp. 204–6, 208–10, 362–67, 369; and Pratt et al., *A History of United States Foreign Policy*, pp. 172, 186.

grandest system of governments, outside of our own, to be found on earth." [73] Throughout the debate, references to the future development of American civilization indicated the Democratic view that territories must ultimately become part of the Union (with, in the case of Hawaii, disastrous consequences) and the Republican belief that colonial expansion was an almost inevitable national destiny.*

A Kentucky Democrat, John S. Rhea, summed up the continentalist view of the Hawaiian people. "The Hawaiian religion is the embodiment of bestiality and malignity that frequently lapses into crimes of lust and revenge. The various legends of their gods abound in attributes of the most excessive animalism and cruelty. Lewdness, prostitution, and indecency are exalted into virtues." [74] While the globalists in the House argued that Rhea had exaggerated the benighted state of Hawaiian society, they did not feel annexation necessarily implied ultimate statehood. On several occasions, Republican speakers drew parallels between the sugar planters in Hawaii and their Asian laborers and the southern cotton planters and their black laborers. The comparison implied that a governmental arrangement might be developed in Hawaii similar to the "Mississippi plan" of disfranchisement. Representative John Sharp Williams of Mississippi, later minority leader of the Democratic party, responded, "the very same possibility of preserving civilization from negro domination and yet not violating the Constitution of the United States, which has been wrought out and does happily exist in Mississippi, could not be wrought out and could not exist amongst the race known as the kanakas in the Hawaiian Islands." [75] Disfranchisement could only follow statehood, which neither party favored.

Narrow economic motives supported the positions of the respective parties. The Democrats maintained that annexation would bring unrestricted immigration of "coolie races" that would harm native American labor and open the national market to Hawaiian sugar. The Republican globalists asserted that these consequences, if indeed they transpired at all, were greatly

---

*Fitzgerald asserted that "The climatic conditions of this country [the United States] are such as to produce the highest intellectual, moral, and physical development, and it is absurd to suppose that the inhabitants of Hawaii, situated as it is in the tropical zone, can begin to keep pace with the magnificent civilization of this nation; rather must they always stifle our growth and impede our progress." *Congressional Record*, 55:2:5968, June 15, 1898. A Louisiana Democrat, Adolph Meyer, who was accused of opposing annexation because he feared increased competition for sugar cane producers in his state, agreed: "I deny that you can have a colonial system, with inferior and mongrel races and mongrel governments, and standing armies to hold and defend them, without giving up your grand American system of free government with limited powers, State rights, local self-government and individual freedom. This proposition is self-evident. It requires no argument and no elucidation" (p. 5985). Representative Amos J. Cummings, a Tammany Democrat from New York, countered these arguments. "Territorial acquisition is the desire of every people. With the English-speaking race it is not only a passion, but the source of all their strength and greatness. . . . A higher power than that of the sugar kings has decreed that these islands shall become an integral part of the United States. It is the decree of the King of Kings, the Ruler of the Universe" (p. 6012).

exaggerated by the continentalists. The Democrats offered a substitute amendment which would have recognized the independence of the American-dominated planter government and guaranteed military protection for the islands against any act of foreign aggression.* The continentalists favored adoption of the amendment (see table 3.5).

In September 1900, President McKinley ordered the election of a Cuban constitutional convention as a first step toward independence, and by February 1901, the convention had framed a document very similar to the American Constitution. The Republican imperialists were unsatisfied with the Cuban constitution, however, because it failed to recognize the "special relationship" the new government should have to the United States. In order to indicate to the convention the type of provisions that should be included, the Senate (and subsequently the House) added the Platt Amendment to the 1901 Army Appropriation Bill. The Platt Amendment advocated:

1. That the government of Cuba should never by treaty with a foreign power impair its independence.
2. That it should keep its public debt within its capacity to pay from the ordinary revenues of the island.
3. That the United States should have the right to intervene for the preservation of Cuban independence and the maintenance of a government adequate for the protection of life, property, and individual liberty.
4. That the acts of the American military government during the period of occupation should be validated.
5. That the plans for the sanitation of Cuba already begun should be carried out by the new government.
6. That the Isle of Pines should be omitted from the proposed constitutional boundaries of Cuba, and its title settled by treaty with the United States.
7. That Cuba should sell or lease to the United States lands necessary for coaling or naval stations.
8. That all these special provisions should be embodied in a permanent treaty with the United States.[76]

The appropriations bill became law on March 2, 1901, and the Cuban convention included the Platt Amendment as an appendix to the next constitution and subsequently ratified the treaty suggested in section eight. Thus, the amendment appeared in American law, the Cuban constitution, and in a treaty between the United States and Cuba. The most important provision, section three, assured that Cuba was "not quite free; its status could be described more accurately as that of a protectorate of the United States."[77] After Cuba became autonomous in 1902, the Platt Amendment was invoked on several occasions. The most serious of these began in 1906 when President Taft

---

*Subsequently the House passed the annexation bill. The sectional stress index on passage was 52.5.

ordered an American occupation of the island that lasted for several years. Franklin Roosevelt abrogated the treaty during his administration, but by then, "American investments in Cuba had made of the island an economic, if not a political, dependency of the United States."[78]

When the Platt Amendment was debated in the House of Representatives, Representative Edward Hamilton of Michigan explained the globalist interpretation of section three: "Our obligations in regard to stable government do not necessarily cease upon our withdrawal from the island. The first establishment of government in the island of Cuba is necessarily experimental and may utterly fail. The ability of the people of Cuba to govern themselves will be on trial."[79] The continentalist argument articulated by Charles Littlefield of Maine was that an amendment which "clearly intends to perpetuate our control over the island and its inhabitants" was unconstitutional, and would probably be invoked in the name of "foreign capital" when its interests might be threatened in some way by the Cuban government.[80] In a roll call taken on adoption of the Platt Amendment in the House (table 3.5), the continentalists opposed the amendment.

In 1902, the same year American forces were withdrawn from Cuba, the House of Representatives considered legislation to create a permanent civil government for the Philippines.* The United States had acquired the islands as one of the results of the Spanish-American War and was engaged in an extremely bloody suppression of a native insurrection at the time the bill was considered.† The revolt was largely quelled, but smoldered on until 1905. Over 30,000 Philippine natives were killed by American occupation forces over the four-year period from 1898 to 1902.[81]

In supporting the Philippine bill, the Republicans, through Governor

---

*The United States gained possession of the Philippines following Commodore Dewey's victory over the Spanish fleet in Manila Bay. Dewey had been ordered by Theodore Roosevelt, then Assistant Secretary of the Navy, to proceed immediately to the Philippines following the outbreak of hostilities with Spain. As a result, the first battle in the war to "liberate" Cuba was fought to capture colonial territory in the Far East. See Dulles, *America's Rise to World Power*, p. 42; LaFeber, *The New Empire*, pp. 382–83; and Pratt et al., *A History of United States Foreign Policy*, p. 179.

†One of the best summaries of the economic interpretation of U.S. Philippine policy is provided by an opponent of the perspective, Richard E. Welch: "The evolution of industrial capitalism in the United States saw the growth of trusts and brought increasing political power to the representatives of Big Business. The quest for aggrandizement that stimulated industrial combination at home inspired a policy of expansion abroad, for by the 1890's the capitalist economy of the United States appeared threatened by its own productivity. Manufacturers sought new markets, as did American investors desirous of a higher rate of return, and the Philippine archipelago was judged a most valuable possession. Not only would the islands provide a new market for American goods and capital, but they would serve as an entrepot for the still more important market of China. Business consequently favored a policy of territorial colonialism and demanded the annexation of the Philippines. As the needs of capital expansion had inspired McKinley's Philippine policy, Business praised that policy and supported the military effort to subjugate the Filipinos." *Response to Imperialism: The United States and the Philippine-American War, 1899–1902* (Chapel Hill: University of North Carolina Press, 1979), p. 75.

General William Howard Taft, argued that "there is not the slightest probability that the Christian Filipinos will be ready for self-government in any
period short of two generations."[82] The Democrats believed that American
control of the islands threatened the survival of the republic and offered an
amendment which, in return for a cease-fire, offered the Philippines self-
government and independence within four years (for the vote, see table 3.5).
The continentalists favored adoption.*

The final roll call on that amendment is closely related to the four high-
stress roll calls on the admission of Oklahoma into the Union. In the years
immediately preceding Oklahoma's admission, the Republicans—particularly those "east of the west line of Kansas" as one member put it[83]—
attempted to combine the Arizona and New Mexico territories into one state
and tie Oklahoma's admission into the Union to that of a proposed state of
Arizona. The clear purpose of the Republican plan was to combine the "alien"
population of New Mexico with the "Anglo-Saxon" residents of Arizona in
order to guarantee that the new state would preserve and uphold American
institutions.† The combination of territories had the additional, and perhaps
more important, advantage of reducing potential Senate representation from
four to two seats.‡ Periphery congressmen argued that neither Arizona nor
New Mexico desired admission under those conditions and that the core
should not fear the creation of "Pacific Coast senators." In their attempt to
sway periphery Republicans, the Democrats charged, "the Republican party is
dominated and controlled, body and soul, by northern and eastern influences,
ever watchful and farsighted in their own interest, but without the slightest
regard for the interest of the country at large."[84] In the vote on the Republican
proposal (table 3.5),§ the continentalists opposed the legislation as a denial of
periphery claims to representation and local self-government. Though House

---

*The vote on passage of the Republican plan after the Democratic amendment had been
defeated was very similar. The sectional stress index on passage was 69.1.

† In reply to Republican insinuations of "alien" influence in his territory, New Mexico
delegate Bernard Rodey recounted, "Why, sir, two or three years ago, after a session of Congress,
I went down to Rockaway Beach, adjacent to New York City. I witnessed there the crowds
coming down from New York and bathing in the ocean day after day. It takes an ocean to clean
such a people. I went among those people and I talked to them, or tried to talk. They spoke every
language ever dreamed of at the Tower of Babel or anywhere else, except the English language.
Those people do not know any place on earth except the particular place in the old country where
they came from—Bohemia, Turkey, or somewhere else—and New York City. Yet those jack-
legged foreigners become citizens and voters in New York in five years, and some, it is said, do
on arrival." *Congressional Record*, 58:2:5146, April 19, 1904.

‡ The combination of "Anglo-Saxon" Oklahoma and "alien" Indian Territory served the
same purposes from the perspective of core Republicans.

§ Two subsequent votes on the Republican plan were taken on February 17, 1905, and
January 25, 1906, in which the sectional stress index was 68.4 and 66.8 respectively. The four
high-stress roll calls overlap these votes and displayed almost identical patterns of trade area
support.

Republicans prevailed on this particular vote, Arizona and New Mexico were, of course, admitted as separate states eight years later in 1912.

Trade area delegations exhibited great consistency on these six roll call votes. Nine of twenty-two delegations (table 3.5) supported the imperialist position on every decision. Six trade areas (including Birmingham and Dallas) consistently supported the continentalist alternative. Even the delegations which presented a partially "mixed" voting record showed little ambivalence on the imperialist-continentalist questions: Cleveland, New York, Kansas City, and Cincinnati seldom deviated from the imperialist position, and St. Louis and Louisville just as consistently sided with the continentalists. Only the San Francisco delegation, which voted against the northern core on statehood measures but supported overseas imperialism, straddled the deeply polarized House. In four of the six votes, imperialist policy provoked a higher level of section stress than existed in the underlying party system of the period. On the six imperialist policies, sectional stress scores averaged 62.1—substantially above the party system average of 54.9. A comparison of table 3.5 with table 3.2 and map 3.2 demonstrates the continuity of political support for imperialism with that for military pensions, the tariff, and federal supervision of southern elections.

Conclusion

All three policy systems discussed in this chapter—military pensions and the tariff, contested elections and Reconstruction, and imperialist expansion—were interrelated. Civil War pensions expanded political support for the protective tariff by creating a dependent constituency (pensioners) and by advantageously redistributing a potentially embarrassing budgetary surplus. During this period, national income was systematically redistributed from the southern periphery to the northern core. The South paid for northern industrial development either directly in the form of higher prices for domestic goods or indirectly in the form of duties on imported products. In the first case, southern income was redistributed directly to northern industry. In the second, southern income flowed through the federal treasury to Union veterans, almost all of whom resided outside the South. The export of southern cotton to the industrial economies of Europe thus provided much of the foreign exchange necessary for northern development.

The consequent economic subordination of the periphery was reinforced by federal restrictions on southern political autonomy. At first, these restrictions took the form of northern resistance to the resumption of regional political dominance by the southern plantation elite. Later, through the mechanism of contested election cases, representatives of the northern core commanded southern acquiescence in national economic policy as the price of southern political autonomy in election laws and race relations. The implicit threat underlying contested elections was a return to Reconstruction policy and the creation of a dependent, pro-development constituency within the South itself, composed of blacks and poor upland whites.

American imperialism at the turn of the century combined both of these themes: the expansion of domestic markets protected from foreign competition and the political subordination of the American periphery. Like imperialism—at least in its classic form—the military pension-tariff developmental and contested election policy systems became much less salient in national politics after the First World War. The attrition of Civil War soldiers and the addition of Spanish-American and World War I veterans "nationalized" the distribution of military pensions while the new federal income tax dramatically reduced the importance of the tariff to federal revenue. Simultaneously, the southern plantation elite legitimated their regional hegemony through constitutional reform, and contested elections lost their importance in national politics.

The plantation elite controlled the political system of the southern periphery until the passage of a second "Force Bill," the Voting Rights Act of 1965. The act formed part of a massive federal assault on the racial caste system of the South and provoked the same sectional polarization in Congress that the political conflict over election law, expiring Reconstruction measures, and contested elections had produced in the 1890s. Like these nineteenth-century precedents, voting rights legislation in the 1960s destabilized plantation elite control by expanding the authority of the central government. Unlike the 1890 Force Bill, however, the 1965 Voting Rights Act precipitated a division in the Democratic party. This split starkly illustrated the emergence of the northern wing of the party as the new vehicle of northern core interests, and demonstrated the impending dissolution of the New Deal coalition that combined the plantation elite of the southern periphery with the lower classes of the industrial core.

Following the disastrous consequences of the Philippine insurrection and the emergence of the United States as an advanced industrial economy in the world system, America ultimately pursued a "free trade" policy of economic penetration of overseas markets without colonial oppression. In this sense, Woodrow Wilson's denial of imperialist expansion as an American diplomatic goal during World War I signaled a significant shift in U.S. policy.[85] However, free trade did not become a central theme in foreign policy until the Roosevelt administration altered American tariff policy and negotiated the dismantling of the British Empire during World War II.[86]

One of the most important consequences of imperialist expansion was the close relationship that developed between the United States and Great Britain. As William Fox described this developing, informal alliance,

> The withdrawal of the British Caribbean squadron to waters nearer home, the dismantling of fortifications in the Caribbean and in Canada,

the renegotiation of the Isthmian Canal question to permit the United States to build and operate the Panama Canal alone, and finally the sacrifice of the Canadian claim in the Alaskan boundary dispute, all were evidence of British retreat. Henceforth, the way was open for Anglo-American collaboration, especially since the United States did not challenge British interests in Europe or other parts of the world.[87]

As Anglo-American cooperation increased, the United States found that not only could the nation move more easily and with more confidence upon the world stage, but the country was inevitably being drawn into the politics and squabbles of the core states of Europe.

4

War, Agricultural Depression, and the New Deal: 1910–1940

In several respects the sectional struggle over American intervention in the First World War was a continuation of the politics of imperialism. Anglo-American cooperation during the opening decade of the twentieth century predisposed United States foreign policy toward support of the Allies in their conflict with the Central Powers and many Americans viewed the British imperial navy as a barrier to a hostile German expansionism which might otherwise threaten national interests in the Far East, Latin America, and elsewhere. Both imperialism and intervention required the creation and maintenance of a strong military establishment and a central government powerful enough to pay for the equipment and salaries that military expansion would necessitate. To the southern periphery, increasing government expenditures seemed to imply a higher tariff schedule; a larger standing army also seemed to threaten a possible reoccupation of the South similar to the Reconstruction experience. Furthermore, the respective positions of core and periphery economies within the international system reinforced the political postures each assumed with relation to both imperialist expansion and intervention.

But there was one significant change. During, and partially as a result of, the First World War, the industrial core of the United States reached maturity in relation to the developed nations of Western Europe. While a protective tariff survived the war, American imperialism—at least in its expansionist, colonial form—did not, and over the ensuing decade political support for a "free trade" policy which promised an expansion of the international market for domestic manufactured goods increased. The last years of protectionism were marked by a collapse in the foreign market for American agricultural products and a severe agricultural depression which persisted throughout the 1920s. The farm crisis brought on an attempt by midwestern and southern agrarians to construct a "tariff for agriculture" and to secure government subsidies which would reestablish equality for agriculture within the domestic economy or, at least, limit industrial preeminence.

While the McNary-Haugen plan and agrarian proposals for the development of Muscle Shoals were never enacted, the growing cooperation between the plains, mountain, and southern periphery regions during the 1920s provided the foundation for passage of the Agricultural Adjustment Act and the creation of the Tennessee Valley Authority in the New Deal. During the twenties, this cooperation assumed the form of explicit logrolling agreements. After the onset of the Great Depression and the opening of the New Deal, political cooperation between agrarian regions began to assume the form of intracommittee bargaining with committee reciprocity on the floor. In this new institutional environment, members increasingly tended to support the position taken by a majority of the reporting legislative committee. The rapid increase in the volume of legislation and the ever-broadening scope of administrative discretion during the Roosevelt era not only strengthened the agrarian alliance, but also made possible the development of a New Deal coalition between the industrial working classes of the North and the southern periphery elite. While the New Deal coalition never eliminated the fundamental division between core and periphery policy goals, the decentralization of public policy deliberations into the committee system and the concurrent development of floor reciprocity made possible the coexistence of both factions within the Democratic party. The implications of this New Deal coalition for the form of public policy, the institutional structure of the House of Representatives, and the political system generally are examined in this chapter.

Militarism, Neutrality, and the First World War, 1915–1917

Of the ten closely contested roll calls which exhibited the highest levels of sectional stress in the 64th Congress, six occurred on legislative motions which were related in some way to American military preparations for entry into the First World War. Four of the six were taken between March 23 and May 8, 1916, on H.R. 12766, legislation which expanded the size of the regular army and reserves, increased the discretionary power of the president, and provided for a government-owned plant to produce nitrates for munitions. These high-stress roll calls were recorded on amendments specifying the relationship between reserve and regular army service and expanding the standing army from 140,000 to 220,000 men, on a motion to recommit the bill without instructions, and on an amendment which would have permitted the president to construct a nitrate plant with private capital. The remaining two high-stress votes were taken on an amendment to greatly increase naval appropriations and on a privileged resolution offered by a South Carolina representative. The resolution would have printed in original form a colloquy critical of the Secretary of War and his decisions relating to the posting of troops along the Mexican border. The issues of military preparedness, American neutrality, and intervention in the world war—represented by H.R. 12766 and the naval appropriations bill—provide the theme for the 1915–17 period.*

In order to understand the response of the American political system to the First World War, military preparedness and neutrality measures must be interpreted in terms of their effect on the expansion of central government power, their continuity with earlier imperialist policies, and the emergence of the United States as a mature and formidable industrial nation. In the years preceding American intervention, the southern periphery still viewed a large standing army with deep mistrust. The resistance of southern representatives to an aggressive expansion of American forces was a legacy of the 1890 Force Bill and, even farther back, the Civil War. By 1915, this southern suspicion of centralized military power had combined with an agrarian antipathy (shared by midwestern congressmen) to the growing industrial and financial dominance of the East. The result in the periphery was an almost pacifist resistance to Wilson's war policies. The sentiment was well expressed by Texas Democrat Oscar Callaway's remarks to the House in 1916. Callaway alluded in floor debate to the sectional interest of the East in promoting war "hysteria." He lamented the cultural dominance of the East in national politics and connected support for military preparedness to American colonial policy.

> One of the ridiculous phases of this preparedness agitation is the attitude of the New Yorkers, Bostonians, and Philadelphians. They are all for preparedness; and what they mean by preparedness is what the Army and Navy bluntly ask, "all they can get." The money is poured out along the Atlantic seaboard. It goes straight into the pockets of the Bostonians, New Yorkers, and Philadelphians, and other places along the Atlantic coast. Of course, they are for preparedness. It is money to their locality. They have had books written, moving-picture shows staged showing New York, Boston, and Philadelphia taken without the firing of a gun or the loss of a life; but when the question of turning loose the Philippine Islands—the most dangerous military liability the United States Government has—came up every mothers son of them voted against it. They are not only a liability from a military and naval standpoint—they cost this Government a hundred million dollars a year—but there is some trade to New York, Boston, and Philadelphia in them, and some citizens

---

*The other four high-stress roll calls occurred on a motion to recommit a bill to revitalize certain war claims against the federal government with an amendment to restrict eligible claims to those owners who could prove loyalty to the United States during the Civil War, on a motion to discharge the Interstate and Foreign Commerce Committee from further consideration of a bill to continue the investigative authority of the so-called "Newlands" committee, on approval of a conference report on an agriculture appropriations bill, and on the passage of legislation which would have provided for the removal of federal circuit and district court judges upon the age of seventy and after ten years of service upon the suggestion of the president and the approval of the Senate.

of those places have investments there. It has cost us since we have had them more than a billion dollars, yet these scared ones from Massachusetts, New York, New Jersey, and Pennsylvania fought desperately against turning this scarecrow loose. Are they scared? Their wail to me has the sound of self-interest and hypocrisy.[1]

The agrarian regions of the Midwest had previously been allied with the industrial-commercial centers of the Northeast and Great Lakes on American colonial expansion but now broke with the industrialized East over preparedness. For some congressmen this break implied a repudiation of United States expansionist ambitions. During the debate on the American declaration of war, for example, Senator Robert LaFollette of Wisconsin rhetorically asked his fellow senators, "Are we seizing upon this war to consolidate and extend an imperial policy?" A month earlier, Senator William Stone of Missouri had asked, "When did it come to pass that Uncle Sam must lay his head on the palpitating breast of Uncle Johnny Bull with a timid sense of dependence?"[2] The truth was that the United States had long since tied its own imperial ambitions to the corresponding aspirations of the British.

Midwestern agrarians interpreted the world war as the outgrowth of a rivalry among European powers for colonial possessions, a rivalry in which the "Allied powers were as bad as if not worse than Germany in terms of autocracy, secret diplomacy, militarism, and imperialistic ambitions."[3] Well-known eastern scholars and major newspapers like the *New York Times* published repeated warnings that Germany constituted a hostile threat to U.S. interests throughout the world, assured the public of an enduring Anglo-American "community of interests," and connected American security to the preservation of British naval supremacy.[4] While the demands of American imperial policy were not by any means the most important factors shaping political alignments over United States involvement in the European war, much of the rhetoric and ideology of the earlier struggle over imperialism found its way into the sectional debate over intervention.

In the decade before the war, the United States had an average international trade surplus of 450–500 million dollars. Until the war, the trade surplus was largely the result of agricultural exports, mostly to Europe. Since the United States still protected its own domestic market in manufactured goods behind a prohibitively high tariff wall, European powers paid for these agricultural exports with the dividend and interest income that they received from investments made in the American economy. Within the prewar world-economy, the United States was a debtor nation that paid its way by exporting raw materials and agricultural products.[5]

As a result of the war-inflated economic boom, the American trade surplus climbed to over three and a half billion dollars in 1917 and manufactured goods captured over 60 percent of all exports between 1916 and 1918.[6] Because the United States still maintained the protective tariff and because of the

Table 4.1. America's International Balance Sheets, 1914, 1919, 1929 (Foreign Assets and Liabilities in Millions of Dollars)

Items	July 1, 1914	December 31, 1919	July 1, 1929
Assets (Private Account):			
Securities	862	2,576	7,839
Direct Investments	2,652	3,880	7,553
Short-Term Credits	0	500	1,617
Total	3,514	6,956	17,009
Liabilities:			
Securities	5,440	1,623	4,304
Direct Investments	1,310	900	1,400
Sequestrated Properties	0	662	150
Short-Term Credits	450	800	3,077
Total	7,200	3,985	8,931
Net Assets Privately Held	−3,686	2,971	8,078
Intergovernment Debts:			
To the U.S. Government	0	9,982	11,685
From the U.S. Government	0	391	0
Net Assets on Government Account	0	9,591	11,685
Total Net Assets on Private and Government Account	−3,686	12,562	19,763

SOURCE: Adapted from Cleona Lewis, *America's Stake in International Investments* (Washington: Brookings Institution, 1938), pp. 447, 450.

demands placed on European manufacturing sectors by the war, the Allies were not able to pay for these American goods by expanding their own exports to the United States—hence the surplus in the American account. Some of America's exports to Europe were paid for in gold, but most were reimbursed from the proceeds accruing from the liquidation of European investments in the American economy. During World War I both the French and British disposed of about 70 percent of their respective holdings in American shares and bonds. All together, foreign investment in the United States was reduced from 7.2 billion dollars in the summer of 1914 to under 4 billion dollars at the end of 1919 (see table 4.1).[7]

World War I transformed the United States from a debtor nation with net liabilities of 3.7 billion dollars (in 1914) into a creditor nation with 3 billion dollars more in foreign assets than foreign interests owned in the United States. Intergovernment debts of nearly 10 billion dollars swelled this American advantage to a grand total of 12.5 billion dollars, but these government-to-government loans were never repaid. Although their existence and huge size underscores the emerging industrial and financial strength of the United States, these intergovernment debts were important primarily as a means of funding foreign purchases of war material and for the impact they had on international trade when foreign countries did attempt to repay their obligations to the United States.

As a result of the world war, the United States ceased to be a periphery nation which provided opportunities for foreign investment and raw materials for mature European core-economies. Instead, it began to seek out expanded markets for its own manufactured goods and "surplus" capital. Because the great imperial powers had already carved up the globe into exclusive possessions, much of American foreign economic policy in the remainder of the twentieth century became oriented around anti-colonial and free-trade principles. From this perspective, the protectionist tariff—maintained into the early thirties—became a counterproductive anachronism. Not only did American protectionist policies invite retaliation by foreign nations, but the persistence of high tariff barriers also prevented the repayment of war debts by the Allies. Combined with the liquidation of foreign assets in the United States, they destroyed the economic basis for export of the American agricultural surplus.[8] In the long run, U.S. intervention in the First World War was a net plus for the core regions of the domestic economy and a disaster for the export-oriented and extraction-dependent economies of the southern and western periphery.

The First World War began on August 1, 1914, with Germany's declaration of war against Russia. Other nations rapidly followed suit, and by the end of the month the lines of battle were drawn within Europe. On August 19, President Wilson appealed to Americans to be "impartial in thought as well as deed," and the administration embarked on a foreign policy which combined "neutrality" with domestic military "preparedness." Even though related, the issues involved in American neutrality and military expansion must be viewed separately. American neutrality was ultimately a policy dominated by the executive and a frustrated Congress played a clearly subordinate role. The historical debate over the meaning of "true" neutrality and President Wilson's motives and prejudices began even before the United States entered the war and continues today. Arthur S. Link, himself relatively sympathetic to Wilson's motives and measures, has described the historical school that has taken a dimmer view of the Wilson administration during the prewar period:

> He [Wilson] has been most condemned by that group of historians highly censorious of his policies, generally known as revisionists, on this score—for becoming the captive of pro-Allied influences within his administration, for condoning such sweeping British control of neutral commerce that the Germans were forced to resort to drastic countermeasures, for permitting American prosperity to become dependent on loans and exports to the Allies, in short, for permitting a situation to develop that made it inevitable that the United States would go to war if the success of Allied arms was ever seriously threatened.[9]

Most sympathetic interpretations of Wilson's policies cite the "legitimate" economic interests of the United States, the possible long-term threat that a German victory would have constituted for American security, the detrimental effects which alternative measures would have had on national prestige, and Wilson's intention to create a just and permanent international system.[10] From this perspective, the gradual involvement of the United States was primarily the result of the increasing probability of a German victory and German opposition to a negotiated peace. For as long as he was able, Wilson pursued a balance of power policy toward the European belligerents, and tilted toward the Allies only when uncontrollable events made a continuation of neutrality detrimental to American interests.

Contemporary congressional opponents of the war consistently advocated a far more rigidly neutral policy: an embargo on the sale of munitions and the extension of credit to belligerent powers, a prohibition on the entry of armed merchantmen into American waters, and a ban on the travel of American citizens on belligerent vessels.[11] From their persective, growing American involvement in the war could be traced to changing administration attitudes toward the extension of credit to Great Britain and France. On August 15, 1914, the United States had announced that "loans by American bankers to any foreign nation which is at war are inconsistent with the true spirit of neutrality." However, on November 4, 1914, the administration advised a New York bank that the government would not object to a pending grant of short-term credit to France. By September 1915, Wilson had acquiesced in the extension of general loans to the Allies. In that month alone, 500 million dollars was raised by Great Britain and France. On March 5, 1917, the American ambassador to Great Britain warned Washington of the impending economic collapse of the Allies. He suggested the possibility of a world financial crisis and surmised, "Perhaps our going to war is the only way in which our present preeminent trade position can be maintained and a panic averted."[12] Less than a month later, President Wilson delivered his war message to Congress. His address emphasized the necessity of making available to the Allies the "most liberal financial credits" and the "materials which they can obtain only from us or by our assistance."[13]

When the Allies began their purchasing program (funded largely by the extension of credits and the liquidation of American assets), the United States economy was in recession. In December of 1914, for example, more than half of America's steel furnaces stood idle. Business activity quickly recovered, however, and a year later the steel industry, fueled by war orders from the Allies, was operating at full capacity. In the following two years, economic prosperity became increasingly linked to the demand originating from the Allied war effort. J. P. Morgan & Co. became the exclusive purchasing agents for Great Britain and France and began "parceling out orders beyond the wildest dreams of great American manufacturing corporations."[14] Exports of war-related goods such as cartridges (from 3.5 million dollars in 1914 to 40.2 million in 1916) and gunpowder (from 200 thousand dollars in 1914 to 147.9

million in 1916) expanded tremendously before American intervention.* Though many agricultural products also benefited from war purchases by the Allies, much of the upsurge in activity was concentrated in the heavy industrial sectors of the economy. As Charles Beard later described the transformation: "Loan after loan was floated to pay Americans for American goods. As the days and weeks passed the fate of American bankers, manufacturers, farmers, merchants, workers, and white-collar servants became more deeply entangled in the fate of the Allies on the battlefield—in the war."† For critics such as Beard, international trade in war-related material combined with the extension of financial credits to the Allies to produce a political and economic environment in which war with Germany was inevitable.‡

Ultimately, Wilson's foreign policy required an expansion of American military power. Unlike his neutrality measures, which by and large did not need congressional approval (even though opposition on Capitol Hill was sometimes strong), military preparedness legislation necessitated congressional acquiescence. In submitting his proposals to Congress, Wilson ran up

---

*As did American exports of automobiles (33.2 million dollars in 1914 to 121.7 million in 1916) and brass goods (4.8 million in 1914 to 123.4 million in 1916). See Minnesota Representative Sydney Anderson's insertion in the *Appendix* to the *Congressional Record*, 64:1:1727–30, August 11, 1916.

†Cited in Cohen, *The American Revisionists*, p. 183. Foster Rhea Dulles was later to repeat this interpretation of America's drift toward war: "this expanding commerce had become such an integral factor in the national economy of the United States that its interruption would have had almost disastrous domestic consequences. Much was made in congressional debates in 1916, and again twenty years later, of the role played by the munitions makers and international bankers in blocking every move to place an embargo on munitions and thereby keeping the nation on the road to war. The fact was that the entire country was greatly concerned in a trade that embraced not only munitions but other manufactures and such basic farm products as wheat, cotton, and beef. Once it had been allowed to develop as it did, the people as a whole— farmers, industrial workers, businessmen—were unwilling to forego the commercial activity which largely accounted for their domestic prosperity." *America's Rise to World Power*, p. 96.

Charles Callan Tansill had earlier placed American intervention in a slightly different context: "In America the rise of 'big business' had produced a vast industrial organization that could fill war orders in an amazingly short time, and the very fact that this organization was severely suffering from a widespread business depression meant that these orders would receive special attention. It was not long before immense exports of American munitions were crowding British ports. In 1916 the value of American war supplies to the Allied Governments mounted to more than a billion dollars, and the intimate economic ties thus created served to supplement the sentimental bonds that had long attached America to the side of the Entente Powers." *America Goes to War* (Boston: Little, Brown, 1938), p. 32. See also pp. 53–55.

‡Other prominent revisionists believed that economic interests had little to do with the decision to intervene. For example, Warren Cohen summarizes Charles Tansill as having argued that "the real battle in the years 1914–17 was a battle between British shrewdness and realism on the one hand and American naivete and idealism on the other. The United States was handicapped throughout this battle by a pro-British administration in Washington and by the pressures of Anglophile advisers on Wilson who, though pro-British himself, sought desperately to remain objective in his judgment of the belligerents." *The American Revisionists*, p. 199.

against the intense and at times emotional antipathy of southern and mid-western members of his own party. Texas Democrat Rufus Hardy stated clearly what many of his colleagues from the periphery believed:

> Compulsory military training and conscription . . . would establish a centralized military system, five hundred thousand strong at first, per-haps a million or two million strong later. A system more vicious and dangerous in a Republic than in a monarchy, a system easily mobilized and used by powerful interests with a friendly administration to crush and oppress the people.[15]

Even though a rigid neutrality or even isolationist policy agreed with the deep-seated convictions of many congressional Democrats, party loyalty prevented these members from presenting a consistent alternative to the robust militar-ism and pro-Allied sentiments of the Republican party.[16] Although Wilson's program probably represented the majority opinion—such as it was—of the American people and could have been interpreted as a compromise necessary for the reelection of a president belonging to the (normally) minority party, Democratic anti-militarist feeling was so intense and widespread that Wilson had to proceed carefully in order not to side openly with the Republicans.[17] A majority of the opposition party in Congress represented the industrial and commercial core regions of the Northeast and Midwest; preparedness and even interventionist sentiment in these areas ran high.

Two bitter critics of Wilson's war policies were the Democratic Speaker of the House, Champ Clark of Missouri, and the House Democratic majority leader, Claude Kitchin of North Carolina.[18] As chairman of the Ways and Means Committee, Kitchin used his power over majority party committee assignments to fill vacancies on the Military and Naval Affairs Committees with members opposed to military preparedness legislation.[19] On the eve of defeat for the McLemore Resolution, Kitchin wrote, "Confidentially, I think the President is anxious for the war with Germany—his sympathies are so strong with the Allies."[20] Outflanked by the president and bellicose Republi-cans, Kitchin complained that his party was violating principle with no pros-pect of political gain: "If we [Democrats] try to make politics out of it [preparedness] to catch these war traffickers, jingoes, munition plants, and their 'patriotic societies,' the Republicans are just smart enough to outbid us every time."[21] While most Democrats sympathized with their party leader, a minority also responded to patronage and the pull of party loyalty. A few members strongly criticized party dissidents,* and Democratic anti-

---

*For example, Democratic Rep. William Schley Howard complained: "Some would have you believe that in the twinkling of an eye the President has become enamored of the goddess of war; that he has been transformed from a clear-headed, cool, and conservative, though firm, being into a rabid declarant of belligerent tendencies, and that he would plunge this Nation into the European cataclysm, and that he is wandering about grasping at a diplomatic straw to involve us in war. . . .

preparedness sentiment provided political ammunition for prominent Republican newspapers.*

Ultimately, Wilson was able to skillfully play off potential Democratic dissent against the prospect of even more extreme preparedness measures if he were forced to rely on Republican support. That the president belonged to the Democratic party was a fact that effectively neutralized what otherwise would have been a powerful and perhaps dominant political force in support of rigid neutrality. In the absence of an effective political opposition, the president consolidated and expanded his power over the mobilization of national resources necessitated by the American war effort.†

"Let me say to those who affiliate with the Democratic Party that if it is your purpose to capitalize your campaigns in the coming election by taking stock in a political propaganda other than that of President Wilson and his administration, you are taking stock in a bankrupt political machine. Your success depends upon your upholding your President and my President at this critical moment in the history of the United States." *Appendix* to the *Congressional Record*, 64:1:482, March 8, 1916.

*For example, on February 25, 1916, the *New York Times* editorialized: "Woodrow Wilson should have the help and support, not the hostility, of his countrymen, of all true Americans. He is in a position of extraordinary difficulty and responsibility. Criticism is free to all, but at a time when he is seeking to maintain the dignity and honor of the Nation and the rights of its citizens it should be helpful and sympathetic, not factional, partisan, and obstructive.

"The Republicans in Congress are better disposed toward him than the Democrats. They, at least, seem to put the feeling and the consciousness of nationality above the petty concerns of party. It is the Democrats who are divided; some of them are hostile to the President altogether. They expose themselves to the suspicion of seeking to compass his downfall, even though the accomplishment of their ends would involve peril and discredit for the Nation. President Wilson, with loyal support, will guide the country through the difficulties that beset him. He will carry his party through the campaign to triumph in the November election if his party will let him do it. In the Democratic Congress lies the peril to the Democratic Party." Inserted in the *Congressional Record* by Democratic Representative Thetus W. Sims of Tennessee, 64:1:3156, February 25, 1916.

†Herbert Agar has described Wilson as a "constitutional dictator" who "not only took the full 'war power' of the President as developed by Lincoln; but he added immense further authority which he persuaded Congress to delegate to him. Whereas Lincoln preferred to meet his emergencies by lonely Executive action, Wilson preferred to ask Congress for specific laws to stretch his authority. In this way he gained a control over the nation's economy which would have caused a second civil war if Lincoln had attempted it. Lindsay Rogers described Wilson as combination of King, Prime Minister in control of legislation, Commander-in-Chief, party leader, economic dictator, and Secretary of State for Foreign Affairs. The Lever Act of August, 1917, is an example of how Congress gave him his head.

"Under the terms of this statute the President . . . could regulate the importation, manufacture, storage, mining and distribution of any necessaries; could requisition foods, fuels, and other supplies . . . could purchase, store, and sell certain foods; could fix a reasonable and guaranteed price for wheat . . . could take over and operate factories, mines, packing houses, pipe lines . . . could fix the price of coal and coke and regulate their production, sale, shipment, distribution. . . ." *The Price of Union* (Boston: Houghton Mifflin, 1966), p. 671. For an analysis of congressional attitudes toward measures extending Wilson's discretionary power, see Richard F. Bensel, "The Origins of the Discretionary State: Statutory Articulation and Political Insurgency, 1895–1917" (paper presented at the Annual Meeting of the American Political Science Association, New York, 1981).

Table 4.2. Contracts for War Materiel and the Stock Market, 1914–1915

Corporation Name	Headquarters (city)	Center of Operations (state)	Total Outstanding Stock (Millions of Dollars)	War Orders, Contract Value (Millions of Dollars)	Estimated[a] Earnings on War Orders (Millions of Dollars)	Stock Quotations July, 1914	High, 1915
Aetna Explosives[b]	New York	Pa.	7.6	40.0	10.0	37	171
American Can	New York	Calif.—Ill.	82.5	80.0	20.0	27	68
American Locomotive	New York	N.J.—N.Y.	50.0	35.5	8.9	30	75
Baldwin Locomotive	Philadelphia	Pa.	40.0	100.0	25.0	45	154
Bethlehem Steel	Newark	Pa.	29.8	150.0	37.5	42	600
Bliss, E. W.	New York	N.Y.	1.3	75.0	18.8	85	450
Carbon Steel	Pittsburgh	Pa.	5.0	12.7	3.2	20	135
Colt Firearms	Hartford	Conn.	2.5	30.0	7.5	120	950
Crucible Steel	Pittsburgh	Pa.	49.6	17.0	4.3	16	110
DuPont Powder	Wilmington	N.J.	45.5	147.5	36.9	122	1,000
Electric Boat	New York	N.J.	7.7	30.0	7.5	15	560
General Electric	Schenectady	Mass.—N.Y.	101.5	105.0	21.3	147	185
Hercules Powder	Wilmington	N.J.	12.4	20.0	5.0	120	450
New York Airbrake	New York	N.Y.	10.0	20.2	5.1	62	165
Pressed Steel Car	New York	Pa.	25.0	23.0	5.8	43	78
Savage Arms	New York	Pa.	1.0	38.6	9.7	120	490
Studebaker	South Bend	Ind.	41.0	17.0	4.3	29	195
Westinghouse Airbrake	Wilmerding, Pa.	Pa.	19.6	20.0	5.0	130	143
Westinghouse Electric	E. Pittsburgh	Pa.	41.0	100.0	25.0	74	141

[a] Calculated at an arbitrary rate of 25 percent profit.
[b] Company incorporated in November 1914.

SOURCES: Adapted from the *Standard Financial Digest*, January 12, 1916, cited in the *Congressional Record*, 64:1:8971, May 31, 1916. Headquarters and center of operations data from *Moody's Manual of Railroads and Corporation Securities*, vol. 3 (New York: Moody Manual, 1917).

In sectional terms, the struggle over American foreign involvement divided the nation into three regions. In the industrial and commercial core of the Northeast and Great Lakes, Republican congressmen and a smaller majority of their Democratic counterparts supported an aggressive foreign policy and military expansion that substantially exceeded Wilson's proposals. In the Great Plains and mountain West, predominantly Republican delegations usually opposed preparedness legislation but were often divided by considerations of party loyalty and their party's commitment to military expansion. In the southern periphery, opposition to preparedness measures was more intense and consistent, with the significant exception of the McLemore Resolution.

The northeastern core delegations, which included members from the trade areas of Philadelphia, Boston, Buffalo, New York, and Pittsburgh, supported an aggressive assertion of American rights (unlimited and unrestricted trade with the Allies) and also military and naval expansion. Perhaps the most subtle reason for this stance was the region's physical proximity to Europe and the consequent extent of cultural penetration by the centers of European civilization—particularly Great Britain and France. For a region bound so closely to the Allies by cultural ties, the prospect of a spectator role in a battle to determine the future course of world history was repugnant. The major commercial and industrial centers had also supported American expansionist measures at the turn of the century, and the United States had tacitly—at times, explicitly—coordinated its imperial policies with the British. Core congressmen and commercial interests believed that major economic and trade advantages would result from continued cooperation with Britain in the future.

In the major commercial centers of the Northeast were located the large financial institutions which extended credit directly to the Allies, floated their bonds with the American public, and held substantial investments in the European nations of the Entente. Here, too, was the center of industrial production of war materiel which had been greatly expanded by Allied war demand. Eighteen of the nineteen corporations believed by the *Standard Financial Digest* to possess the largest war contracts had their headquarters in core regions of the Northeast (see table 4.2).[22] Extensive financial investments in these and similar firms were held by residents of the region, and fabulous profits were to be made off the common stock of war-related industrial corporations. The common stock of Bethlehem Steel alone soared from $41.62 a share in July 1914 to $600 at its high point in 1915.* Mass public opinion, at least as represented by a poll published in the *Literary Digest* in January 1915, seemed to confirm the region's support for an aggressive assertion of neutrality rights.[23]

---

*Nearly two decades later a sensational inquiry by the Senate Munitions Investigating Committee stressed the fantastic profits made by American financiers and armament producers during World War I and attempted to connect American intervention to covert efforts by representatives of their interests. Daniel M. Smith, *American Intervention, 1917* (Boston: Houghton Mifflin, 1966), p. 215.

Core interests were also served by the vast mobilization and coordination of industrial capacity, the suspension of anti-trust regulation, and government tolerance and even encouragement of corporate consolidation. Of the war effort, Murray Rothbard has written:

> It was a 'war collectivism,' a totally planned economy run largely by big-business interests through the instrumentality of the central govern-ment, which served as the model, the precedent, and the inspiration of state corporate capitalism for the remainder of the twentieth cen-tury. . . . With the return of the railroads to private operation in March 1920, war collectivism finally and at long last seemed to pass from the American scene. But pass it never really did; for the inspiration and the model that it furnished for a corporate state in America continued to guide Herbert Hoover and other leaders in the 1920s, and was to return full-blown in the New Deal, and in the World War II economy.[24]

Finally, while northern financiers and industrialists did not openly voice these sentiments, they probably anticipated both economic independence from the European interests that had influenced American development since coloniza-tion, and an increasingly dominant position within the domestic economy as possible results of United States participation in the Allied war effort.

Congressmen from the Great Plains and interior regions of the Midwest held to an isolationist position in foreign affairs which was influenced by the remnants of the populist and progressive movements. Ray Billington has described the historical continuity of prewar isolationism with agrarian radicalism:

> To them the defeat of inflation, which doomed them to a continuing struggle with poverty and debt, could be laid at the door of eastern and British capitalists. From this belief stemmed several prejudices which became entrenched in western thought. One was a dislike for England. Another was an intensified sectional antagonism which inclined farmers there to look with disfavor on anything sanctioned by easterners. Thus, if the East favored intervention in world affairs, they would automati-cally swing in the opposite direction. The third and most important prejudice was directed against eastern bankers and industrialists. This "money power" had been hated by the frontier since the days of Andrew Jackson, and now the three hatreds seemed confirmed. Its wealth not only had defeated inflation but had engineered imperialism, after the Spanish-American War, for its own selfish ends. These antagonisms were strengthened by the violent anti-trust agitation of the Progressive era, and by the unfolding Caribbean policy which seemed to increase the poor man's taxes for the benefit of a few wealthy corporations. Thousands of westerners came to believe that intervention was only another tool of the trusts in their battle against the people.[25]

By 1914, the Midwest was the most self-sufficient region of the nation. The domestic economy consumed most of the foodstuffs produced in the section and the manufacturing sector was largely oriented toward the needs of the immediate agricultural market.[26] This increasing self-sufficiency of the grain cash crop economy freed the midwestern farmer from the imperialist policy of the industrial East and reinforced the confluence of agrarian radical and isolationist beliefs.

These areas of the nation, in addition, were comparatively isolated from the economic and cultural contacts the East enjoyed with Western Europe. As a consequence, neither congressmen nor their constituencies felt as keenly the urgency of aiding the Allies. Furthermore, increased foreign demand did not benefit the cash crop economy to the same extent as it did the heavy industrial base of the eastern seaboard and Great Lakes, nor were domestic agricultural markets likely to expand with American intervention in the war. Overlaying the complex of ideological antipathies and economic considerations were ethnic loyalties; the midwestern regions contained the largest concentrations of first- and second-generation German populations, some of whom openly favored the Central powers.

Intertwined with the pacifist perspective of the Midwest were several related themes. Many congressmen believed that American exports of war materiel made intervention more likely without increasing the security of the United States.* Agrarian representatives from mountain and midwestern districts attributed the preparedness movement to an industrial elite that concealed their very tangible interests under the heavy cloak of patriotism.† Antipreparedness sentiment ran strong in those states west of the Mississippi where the Populists had once waged their most effective campaigns. A *Literary Digest* poll of newspaper editors discovered that over half of all responding editors from those states "saw militarism as a real danger" compared with 11 percent in the East and 28 percent in midwestern cities and towns east of the Mississippi.[27]

Many representatives, among them Wisconsin Republican William J. Cary, connected the preparedness movement to an older evil: the trust. As

---

*Along with Republican Representative Edwin D. Ricketts of Ohio, many members believed that American exports of war materiel made intervention more likely. "If there is one thing more than another that will eventually drag the people of this country into war or cause an invasion or an attempted invasion of the American soil by a foreign foe, it is this cruel and blood-cursed traffic on the part of the rich corporations and war trusts of this nation." Republican Representative Edwin D. Ricketts of Ohio, *Appendix* to the *Congressional Record*, 64:1:266—68, February 9, 1916.

†More than a few congressmen agreed with Progressive-Democrat Representative James H. Mays of Utah when he asserted: "Men profiting greatly from the manufacture of armor plate and implements of destruction have organized 'Navy Leagues,' 'National Security Leagues,' and other alleged patriotic societies designed to increase military establishments for their own profit." Ibid., 64:1:1218, June 2, 1916. Another Democrat, Iowa Representative Thomas J. Steel, put forward a similar interpretation on August 15, 1916. Ibid., pp. 1884—85.

populists and progressives had prophesied before him, Cary predicted that "the people . . . will rise in righteous wrath" if the wages of their toil were diverted in order

> to fatten the swollen fortunes of the Steel Trust, the Armor-Plate Trust, or the Powder Trust, while the Army and Navy are neglected, mismanaged, or, what is worse, still controlled and ruled by bureaucrats who are either hide-bound to old and obsolete methods or wedded to a very suspicious alliance with the moneyed corporations that control the supplies which the defensive forces of the country most need.[28]

The trusts were connected, in turn, to the conspiratorial machinations of the great barons of Wall Street—the Morgans, Rockefellers, and du Ponts.* Two months before American entry into the war, when intervention seemed all but inevitable, Democratic Representative Clyde H. Tavenner of Illinois explained the downward slide toward active participation in one paragraph:

> Wall Street first demanded preparation for war, and when it got appropriations for the Army and Navy increased by hundreds of millions of dollars it started in for the real thing, war. Wall Street has its billions tied up with the cause of the Allies, and it is a tradition that the heart and sympathy of Wall Street will invariably be found sojourning in the vicinity of its money bags.[29]

From a denunciation of Wall Street, the trusts, and the trade in munitions,† it was but a short step to attack the entire eastern section of the country.‡ One representative, Charles A. Lindbergh—a Minnesota Republican and father of the legendary pilot—believed that an "invisible government" had been constituted in secret committees and party caucuses that met behind "closed doors." This "invisible government," Lindbergh maintained, sought

---

*Cohen, *The American Revisionists*, p. 12. In opposing Wilson's proposal to declare war on Germany, Senator George W. Norris, a Nebraska Republican, stated, "We are going into war upon the command of gold."

†The most extreme assault came from William Cary of Wisconsin: "The New York City newspapers on the first day of this year gave graphic accounts of the New Year's Eve revelry, and the bacchanalian orgy in the high-life districts of the metropolis exceeded the extravagance, dissipation, and indecency of any previous scene of the same sort even in that lively city. The enormous amounts of money spent were naively accounted for by the big profits made in war-stock speculation, so that it is easily seen who profits by this blood money—the idle, vicious, and degraded class, who are to-day not only the laughing stock of the world, but the shame and disgrace of American manhood and womanhood. A fitting end and a fitting place for such wealth to go." *Appendix* to the *Congressional Record*, 64:1:933, May 9, 1916.

‡One such attack was delivered by Republican William Ramseyer of Iowa on February 5, 1916: "The Middle West is usually put down as against preparedness. That depends on what you mean by preparedness. The East has gone insane on munitions profits. They consider any legislation that would decrease the blood-money prosperity of the last eight months as unpatriotic." Ibid., pp. 247–49.

to spread its "sinister influence" by undermining American democratic institutions and replacing them with a "monarchical and plutocratic system." * Such attacks were so bitter and widespread that some scholars have argued they constituted an unprecedented assault on the capitalist system and the expression of a belief that the war itself was a "capitalist plot."[30]

Like the agrarian Midwest, the southern periphery also had little cultural interaction with the European Allies and, accordingly, little sympathy with their cause. Furthermore, the South had opposed the Anglo-American imperialist policies pursued by core Republicans and attributed at least part of the support for American colonial expansion to the covert influence of British interests. When the cotton market was destroyed by the eruption of World War I, southern congressmen displayed indifference or hostility to the Allied war effort and even urged aggressive American measures to end restrictions on trade with the Central powers. Furthermore, many southern congressmen believed that Wilson's preparedness program would evolve into a militarism that would ultimately endanger the republican foundations of the nation.

On the eve of American intervention, Representative George Huddleston, an Alabama Democrat, identified five classes which were imposing conscription upon the country: (1) a "military satrapy" bent on making a free citizenry into a "senseless human machine with which the superior may work his absolute will"; (2) "the great financiers . . . who hate democracy" and desire "a free hand" in imposing monopoly and exploitation upon the people; (3) "war traffickers" and "munitions makers . . . who coin their profits out of human blood"; (4) the "parasite press . . . insidiously seeking to discredit the common people"; and (5) "sycophants and snobs . . . who hang upon the coattails of the great." † While the opponents of military preparedness in the Midwest and South often made common cause and shared a similar philosophical interpretation of the "forces" supporting intervention, the

---

*Under the new political system Lindbergh believed that "it will be the privilege of a few to rule in splendor and the fate of the many to spend their lives in unrequited toil." *Congressional Record*, 64:1:1837, July 5, 1916. At least one southern congressman, Democrat James H. Davis of Texas, agreed with Lindbergh. Davis inserted a letter that he had written to one of his constituents in which he claimed to have uncovered a conspiracy between the breweries, Morgan, and President Wilson: "The invisible government that rules this country from the headquarters of the money devil in New York has made a deal, through a group of its agents and satraps, the Steel Trust and 'war traffickers' generally to sell Texas (and perhaps the whole country) to that chief of abominations, that superlative aggregation of scoundrelism, known as the liquor traffic." *Appendix* to the *Congressional Record*, 64:1:365–68, February 18, 1916.

†*Appendix* to the *Congressional Record*, 64:2:113, January 10, 1917. Representative Martin Dies, a Texas Democrat, traced the origin of militarism back to the Persian Empire and noted the comparative superiority of the "volunteer soldiers" of the Greek city-states. In support of his position, he cited de Tocqueville: "All men of military genius are fond of centralization, which increases their strength; and all men of centralizing genius are fond of war, which compels nations to combine all their powers in the hands of the government." *Congressional Record*, 64:1:1691–95, January 28, 1916.

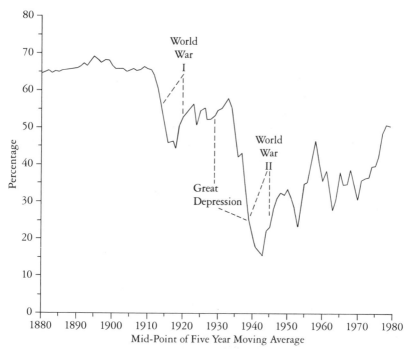

Figure 4.1. Percentage of U.S. Cotton Production Exported to Foreign Markets, 1880–1980
    SOURCE: Five-year moving average computed from data in U.S. Department of Agriculture,
Agricultural Statistics (Washington) vol's. 1936, 1948, 1959, and 1971. U.S. Bureau of the
Census, *Statistical Abstract of the United States: 1982–1983*, (Washington: 1982).

agrarian radicals of the plains and mountains emphasized the economic roots of
war (the "trusts," "Wall Street," etc.) and the pacifists of the southern periphery dwelled on militarism and the centralization of government power. Although congressmen from both sections borrowed rhetoric from each other
almost indiscriminately, these were distinct motives for opposing the war. The
economic orientation of the prairie originated in the Greenback and Populist
movements of the late nineteenth century, while the roots of southern ap-
prehension concerning the emergence of militarism were to be found in the
Civil War, Reconstruction, and the Force Bill.
    Another important factor in southern opposition to military prepared-
ness measures was the dependence of the South on European (particularly British) markets for the periphery's biggest export: cotton. In every one of the
thirty-five years prior to the outbreak of war, the percentage of the cotton crop
marketed abroad exceeded 60 percent of the total (see figure 4.1). In over half
of the harvests during that period, exports totaled two-thirds or more of do-

mestic production.* More than any other region of the country, the South depended on exports for economic prosperity. Almost all exported cotton was shipped to Europe and almost half of all cotton sold abroad was purchased by Britain alone.

Upon the outbreak of war, the immediate concern of most southerners was the disruption of export markets.[31] Within a week, most important cotton exchanges closed their doors. Among the most important factors underlying the "cotton panic" were reports that the American harvest would be the largest in history, an anticipated decline in normal British demand, and fear that an expected British blockade would prevent American cotton from reaching the Central powers.[32] During 1914, southern planters suffered a cash loss of 300 million dollars because of the disruption of normal markets and international trade.[33] The hardship that this loss imposed upon the cotton belt and the economic uncertainty that accompanied British policy on contraband aroused considerable anti-British sentiment.† During the summer of 1915, a senator friendly to the Allies, John Sharp Williams of Mississippi, warned in a letter to President Wilson that southern demands for retaliation against the British were so great that every politician in the South was compelled to adopt an anti-British attitude.[34] Even when the cotton market had recovered, many congressmen remembered the panic and attributed responsibility for it to Great Britain. As Democrat James H. Davis of Texas put it,

> For more than two years she forbade us to trade with her enemies, dragged our commerce from the seas, and with pusillanimous perfidy kept us from trading with Germany and Austria, and, through her minister of munitions and international financial agent in this country, Pierpont Morgan, she killed the cotton market of the South, robbed the Southland of nearly $400,000,000, [and] bought our cotton on a dead market at 5 and 6 cents a pound.[35]

*Of all major cash crops, only tobacco, with an average export percentage of a little over forty, rivaled cotton. In most years, less than 20 percent of the wheat crop and less than 5 percent of the corn harvest entered international markets. Edwin G. Nourse, *American Agriculture and the European Market* (New York: McGraw-Hill, 1924), pp. 246, 283.

†The British recognized the impact of their policies upon the course of domestic American politics and moved carefully. When they finally imposed a total blockade on cotton exports to the Central powers, the British artificially supported the price of cotton through purchases on the open market. "To the British, the gravest threat of all was the possibility that the powerful southern bloc in Congress would combine with pacifist and pro-German groups to create an irresistible demand for an embargo on the export of munitions to the Allies or for positive efforts to break the British blockade." Years later, as the United States entered the war, it remained clear that the "cotton crisis of 1914–15 left deep scars upon the South and a residue of intense anti-British sentiment. Combined with the prevailing rural pacifism, southern resentment at the British maritime system made the South one of the chief centers of resistance to military and naval expansion and to strong diplomacy vis-a-vis Germany between 1915 and 1917." Link, "The Cotton Crisis," pp. 132, 138. For a concise synopsis of British policy, the American response, and the prevailing tenets of international law, see John D. Hicks, *The American Nation* (Cambridge, Mass.: Houghton Mifflin, 1941), pp. 476–79.

In the prewar period no congressional delegation was more stridently and cohesively opposed to military preparedness and the munitions trade with the Allies than were Texas Democrats. But congressmen were drawn to the pacifist standard from throughout the southern and western periphery. Thirty members from largely rural districts stood at the center of pacifist opposition within the Democratic party.[36] These members followed Claude Kitchin of North Carolina, the majority leader.*

Of the most significant roll calls on the issues of neutrality and preparedness, only the first, the vote on the McLemore Resolution, was directly related to Wilson's diplomatic policy (see table 4.3). Of the other four roll calls, three dealt with amendments to the National Defense Act of 1916 and the last decided the size of the construction program in the naval appropriations bill. All five roll calls were recorded during the first session of the 64th Congress.

The McLemore Resolution was named after Representative Jeff McLemore, a Texas Democrat, who had drawn up the legislation early in 1916 in response to Wilson's diplomatic policy. The resolution requested, without the force of law, that the president warn American citizens who chose to travel on armed belligerent ships that they did so at their own risk. Though the resolution reflected a popular position within the House of Representatives and was later to present one of the most serious challenges to Wilson's leadership during his years in office,[37] it probably would have never reached the floor of the House had not the president indicated on February 21, 1916, that he would hold Germany to "strict account" if a submarine without prior warning sank an armed ship upon which American citizens were traveling.[38] To some congressmen "it seemed that the administration was almost asserting the right to travel unmolested on belligerent warships, a totally unreasonable claim, unparalleled in the history of warfare."[39] In response to the president's position, the Democratic members of the Foreign Affairs Committee in the House agreed unanimously to request consideration of the McLemore Resolution.† When the House Democratic leadership consulted with Wilson at the White House on February 25,[40] the president indicated that he would break diplomatic relations with Germany if a submarine were to sink an armed merchant-

---

*The *New York Times* alleged that Kitchin had assured southern colleagues that "since the Northeast had been responsible for the preparedness program, he would see to it that those above the Mason and Dixon line would pay for it in taxes." Reported in Richard L. Watson, "A Testing Time for Southern Congressional Leadership: The War Crisis of 1917–1918," *Journal of Southern History* 44:1 (February 1978): 7. For Kitchin's half-hearted denial, see *Congressional Record*, 64:2:2129–30 and 2316–17, January 27 and 30, 1917. Most of those who persisted in their opposition to the war after America entered the conflict, however, lost their seats in the 1918 election as cotton prices rose under the influence of British purchases and United States government price-setting. Tindall, *The Emergence of the New South*, p. 64. See also Seward W. Livermore, "The Sectional Issue in the 1918 Congressional Elections," *Mississippi Valley Historical Review* 35 (June 1948): 29–60.

†Though they themselves favored the resolution, Speaker Clark and Majority Leader Kitchin asked their colleagues to delay until they had met with the president. Link, *Woodrow Wilson and the Progressive Era*, pp. 211–12.

Table 4.3. Congressional Action on Military Preparedness and Neutrality, 1916

Trade Area[a]	McLemore Resolution (March 7, 1916)	Expansion of Standing Army (March 23, 1916)	Expansion of Standing Army (May 8, 1916)	Volunteer Army (May 8, 1916)	Naval Appropriations (June 2, 1916)
Philadelphia	Int[b]	Int	Int	Neut	Int
Boston	Int	Int	Int	Int	Int
Buffalo	Int	Int	Int	Int	Int
New York	Int	Int	Int	Int	Int
Pittsburgh	Int	Int	Int	Neut	Int
San Francisco	Neut	Int	Int	Int	Int
Chicago	Neut	Int	Neut	Neut	Int
Minneapolis	Neut	Int	Neut	Neut	Neut
Detroit	Int	Neut	Neut	Neut	*Split*
Omaha	Neut	Neut	Neut	Neut	Neut
Cincinnati	Int	Neut	Neut	Neut	Neut
Cleveland	Int	Neut	Neut	Neut	Neut
Baltimore	Int	Neut	Int	*Split*	Neut
Denver	Neut	Neut	Neut	Neut	Neut
Kansas City	Int	Neut	Neut	Neut	Neut
St. Louis	Int	Neut	Neut	Neut	Neut
Louisville	Int	Neut	Neut	Neut	Neut
Richmond	Int	Neut	Neut	Neut	Neut
New Orleans	Int	Neut	Neut	Neut	Neut
Birmingham	Int	Neut	Neut	Neut	Neut
Atlanta	Int	Neut	Neut	Neut	Neut
Memphis	Int	Neut	Neut	Neut	Neut
Dallas	Int	Neut	Neut	Neut	Neut
Sectional Stress	35.0	62.4	61.4	55.7	64.8

[a] Trade area delegations are ranked in descending order of their support for the core position on the ten high-stress roll calls recorded during the 64th Congress (1915–17); see table 2.5.

[b] "Int" (Intervene) indicates that a majority of the trade area delegation supported a position which was generally interpreted as increasing the immediate likelihood of American involvement in the First World War; "Neut" (Neutral) indicates that the delegation supported a position which reduced the immediate likelihood of involvement; *Split* indicates that the delegation divided evenly on the roll call.

SOURCE: Computations from roll call data.

man with Americans aboard and that such action would probably be followed by a German declaration of war against the United States.*

Even though many Democrats disagreed with the president's course of action, they also agreed with the interpretation of the vote put forward by Representative Cyrus Cline of Indiana: "the question presented in this context

*This "Sunrise Conference" convinced many congressmen that Wilson was embarked upon a course which led inevitably toward war, but the adamant position taken by the president made adoption of the McLemore Resolution a test of party loyalty. McLemore himself an-

is whether we shall stand by the President in this crisis or not. This is the issue for us to settle, and not whether we want war or whether we do not want war."[41] A motion to table, and thus kill, the McLemore Resolution was successful (table 4.3). Supporting the motion (and Wilson) were 182 Democrats, 93 Republicans, and 1 Progressive. On the other side were 33 Democrats, 102 Republicans, 5 Progressives, 1 independent, and 1 Socialist.[42] The voting pattern is interesting for two reasons. First, the level of sectional stress, in contrast to the roll calls on preparedness legislation, was relatively low. Second, the core delegations of the Northeast and the periphery congressmen of the South were aligned against the agrarian plains and West. Since Republicans dominated the northeastern and midwestern delegations, the split between the Philadelphia-Boston-Buffalo-New York and Chicago-San Francisco-Minneapolis-Omaha-Denver delegations can be interpreted largely as a reflection of differing sectional attitudes toward the war and neutrality.* The South, however, was almost exclusively represented by members of Wilson's own party and swung in line behind the president only out of loyalty to the Democracy and after application of the party whip and the related withholding of patronage. Even then a majority of the Texas delegation cast votes against the tabling motion.† In addition to the conflicting motives of members of the two parties and their respective distribution among the various sections, the fact that the resolution purported to be only a non-binding indication of House sentiment minimized sectional tensions on the tabling motion.

In contrast, sectional stress on the four preparedness roll calls was comparatively high. Three of these votes occurred during House deliberations on

---

nounced that he would not work for a vote on his resolution, but Wilson claimed that his ability to conduct the foreign affairs of the United States would be hampered if the legislation was not publicly rejected. Link, *Wilson: Confusion and Crises, 1915–1916*, pp. 176–78, 188–93.

*The voting, according to John Milton Cooper, "demonstrated the respective pressures put on Democrats by officeholding and on Republicans by opposition. Many Democrats who favored the principle behind the McLemore resolution voted to table it out of loyalty to the Administration. Party ties held Southerners in particularly tight rein, with even Kitchin and Page joining in the substantial Southern vote for tabling. The Democratic holdouts were almost all radical agrarians, including Bailey, Slayden, and 'Cyclone' Davis. The Republicans presented a mottled picture. Some ideological division was evident both in Republican support for tabling, which came primarily from northeastern conservatives, and in the opposition, which included most of the party's well-known progressives. Yet such redoubtable conservatives as Cannon, Longworth, and Mann also opposed tabling." The latter, it must be suspected, did so out of a desire to embarrass the president. *The Vanity of Power*, pp. 230–31.

†Texas Democrat John H. Stephens stated their position when he declared: "Neither presidential persuasion nor coercion can force me to cast a vote that my conscience and my judgment tells me may force this Nation into a cruel, bloody, and wasteful war, and I believe in the end will make our Republic a military autocracy or a Prussianized depotism." *Appendix* to the *Congressional Record*, 64:1:495, March 9, 1916. All three voting members of the Houston trade area delegation opposed the party on the resolution along with five of the eleven voting Texans in the Dallas delegation. The Houston voting record is not shown in table 4.3.

the National Defense Act of 1916 which, according to one scholar, "represented one of the most sweeping extensions of national power in American history."[43] When finally passed by Congress, the act created the Army of the United States, which was to be composed of the Regular Army (doubled in size), a new Volunteer Army, a new Reserve Force, and the National Guard. The legislation also established a national ROTC program, conferred sweeping emergency powers over the economy upon the secretary of war, and provided for government production of nitrates at Muscle Shoals in Alabama (discussed in the following section).

The first significant roll call on the act took place on an amendment offered by Republican Representative Julius Kahn of California. Kahn's amendment would have expanded the size of the standing (regular) army from the 140,000 ceiling provided in the committee version of the bill to a maximum of 220,000 men. The amendment was defeated by thirty-one votes (185 to 216); 149 Republicans (over half from the Northeast) joined 30 Democrats (three-quarters from the Northeast) and six Progressives in support of Kahn's motion. Thirty-four Republicans (over 80 percent of these from the Midwest) combined with 181 Democrats (two-thirds of whom represented southern districts) and one Socialist to defeat the expansion.[44]

The second roll call in this series was recorded on May 8, 1916, when the House refused to accept, by a substantial margin (142 to 221), a Senate amendment which would have expanded the standing army to 250,000 men. On the same day, the House also rejected a Senate amendment authorizing the War Department to raise and train a national volunteer force of up to 261,000 men (109 to 251). The House later compromised with the Senate on these issues and, in its final form, the National Defense Act gave Wilson practically everything he requested.[45]

Another vote occurred on an amendment offered to the naval appropriations bill on June 2, 1916 (table 4.3). The alternative offered by preparedness advocates provided for a much larger construction program than the Naval Affairs Committee had reported to the floor. Though members opposed to military expansion objected, they "never feared navalism as the same dire threat to American institutions as militarism."[46] Much of the debate on the bill focused on the differing capacities for the construction of capital ships in the shipyards of the nation.* New York, Norfolk, and Bremerton, Washing-

---

*Even so, many pacifist representatives, including Democrat Joseph B. Thompson of Oklahoma, carefully calculated the cost of preparedness in economic and human terms: "It requires a half million bales of cotton to construct one battleship. . . . The entire production of cotton in my district would build about one-fifth of one battleship. . . . It is time someone was turning from the gold and tinsel, the epaulets and braid, the music, and the fanfare of militarism and casting a glance at those back home who pay the bills. . . . Think of all the tragedies wrapped up in that cotton, of the little barefooted children toiling through the long summer days to cultivate it and shivering in the frost of the November morning to gather it!" *Appendix* to the *Congressional Record*, 64:2:801–6, March 3, 1917.

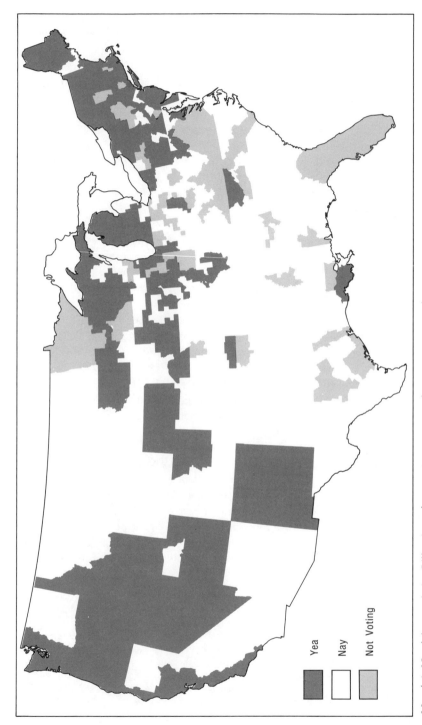

Map 4.1. Naval Appropriation Bill—Amendment to Increase Expenditures, June 2, 1916

Yea

Nay

Not Voting

ton, all were affected by both the quantity and quality of the expansion program, and their representatives squabbled on the floor of the House over the design and content of the naval budget. The expansion amendment was finally defeated by six votes (183 to 189) and the sectional alignment took a now familiar form (see table 4.3 and map 4.1). The members from metropolitan New York City voted overwhelmingly for the amendment (24 to 3), as did the members from Philadelphia (6 to 0), Pittsburgh (4 to 0), Boston (7 to 0), and Chicago (7 to 1). For all of these urban centers, the members from the tributary hinterlands followed the lead of the metropolitan contingent. Only in rural districts tied to Chicago did significant opposition develop. The southern periphery, with the exception of abstaining members from port districts in Virginia, North Carolina, Florida, Alabama, and Texas, gave almost unanimous support to the smaller naval program sponsored by the committee. A majority of the congressmen from the remaining interior regions also supported the smaller committee version.[47] The Senate later amended the House bill by greatly expanding naval spending and, under heavy pressure from Wilson, the House caved in to Senate conferees. Upon passage of the conference report, one of few Democrats resisting the president, Majority Leader Kitchin, protested, "Approval of this building program means that the United States today becomes the most militaristic naval nation on earth."[48]

With the exception of the McLemore Resolution, congressional opposition to American intervention and military preparedness reflected the cumulative influence of the sectional alignments of the three preceding periods. The warning resolution constituted an exception in the early twentieth-century political system—the demands of a president who drew upon the periphery for most of his political support but needed to penetrate regions allied with or composing the core in order to remain in office. In the struggle over military preparedness, the waning of the developmental coalition which had been based on military pensions and the tariff could be seen in references by midwestern and western representatives in congressional debate to "trusts" and eastern "predatory" wealth.[49] The prewar sectional alignment reflected the diametrically opposed positions of the core and periphery in the national and world economies (the export-oriented South and the tariff-protected, industrial East).

Periphery resistance to military preparedness measures was consistent with earlier opposition to Reconstruction and to the 1890 Force Bill. The South continued to see military power in the hands of the central government as a threat to "republican liberty," by which they meant regional political autonomy. The core regions were correspondingly indifferent to these larger implications of military expansion. Finally, the more recent sectional conflict over imperialism continued into the prewar years. The industrial core sought to coordinate American foreign policy with the British and to interpret American interest in a manner compatible with needs of the British Empire. American intervention was a method of gaining leverage or influence over the design of the postwar world order—an order in which the core regions of the United States would reach maturity in the world-system and maintain domestic hegemony. The agrarian periphery, which after the dissolution of the Republican developmental coalition included the midwestern plains, saw these events as potentially disastrous.

The Farm Crisis, 1925–1927

Two types of issues dominated the ten high-stress, closely contested roll calls of the 74th Congress. The first group that provoked high levels of sectional stress in the mid-twenties related to the gradual and continuing decontrol of the American economy from the government mobilization of the nation's resources in World War I. Four of ten recorded votes occurred on legislative motions concerning appropriations for the federal Shipping Board and the Emergency Fleet Corporation. These agencies had constructed and operated federal merchant ships as part of the war effort, and political conflict over their continued existence in the postwar era sparked sectional conflict between the "free-enterprise" Northeast and the agrarian periphery. A fifth roll call on passage of a bill which sought, at government expense, to construct a railway and tram road on the Seward Peninsula in Alaska raised a similar debate over the proper role of government in the American economy. All of these decisions were part of a larger effort to prevent mothballed remnants of the war effort from falling into the hands of the "interests." The movement behind government control and ownership of the Muscle Shoals hydroelectric installation between 1916 and 1933 was part of that effort and produced the most intense and prolonged dispute over the respective roles of free enterprise and public operation in American history.*

Three other high-stress roll calls were recorded on farm legislation. Two of these occurred on the McNary-Haugen farm bill (which is discussed below), and the third decided the fate of an amendment which would have added cotton seed to a bill regulating and restricting the importation of alfalfa and red clover seeds. All three votes reflected the agrarian response to the deepening agricultural depression of the decade following the First World War and

---

*While the Shipping Board and the Emergency Fleet Corporation both represent important legislation, "nothing," as Karl Schriftgiesser notes, "was more basic to the clash of interests of the 1920's than the fight over Muscle Shoals." *This Was Normalcy* (Boston: Little, Brown, 1948), p. 227. Arthur S. Link has said the McNary-Haugen movement "was a milestone in the development of a comprehensive political doctrine that it was government's duty to protect the economic security of all classes and particularly depressed ones," while the Muscle Shoals project "signified a deviation from the older traditions of mere regulation . . . and the triumph of new concepts of direct federal leadership in large-scale development of resources." "What Happened to the Progressive Movement in the 1920's?" *American Historical Review* 64:4 (July 1959): 833–51.

the emerging alliance between congressional representatives of the nation's wheat, corn, and cotton belts.*

The conflict over American neutrality and preparedness left behind a heritage of agrarian resentment against the industrial and commercial interests of the East—a resentment that was gradually reinforced by a growing disillusionment with the results of American involvement. The changing international economic order brought on by the war also contributed to an ever deepening domestic agricultural depression—the most severe in American history. McNary-Haugenism was "a last-ditch stand against industrial and commercial domination."†

With passage of the Fordney-McCumber tariff in 1922, the United States became one of the most highly protected markets among the major industrial powers of the world. This tariff, like previous protectionist legislation before it, not only constituted a barrier to imports but probably restricted exports as well. Until the First World War, foreign nations were able to purchase American exports by remitting earnings on investments in the United States economy. The Allied war effort, as described in the preceding section, resulted in the liquidation of foreign holdings and transformed the United States from a debtor to a creditor nation.[50] In addition to the postwar renewal of protection and the liquidation of foreign investment, the United States put pressure on the Allies to repay their war debts with the limited dollars their exports to America earned them.[51] All of these factors reduced the foreign marketability of the American agricultural surplus in the postwar period.

Several related developments combined to contract foreign demand for the largest American export: cotton. In absolute terms, American cotton exports to Great Britain peaked in 1911, and while Britain had imported up to 80 percent of its domestic consumption from the United States prior to World War I, the expansion of cotton cultivation in India, Egypt, and the Sudan—all parts of the British Empire—reduced British dependence on American cotton to about 50 percent of its consumption in the two postwar decades. In addi-

---

*One of the two remaining high-stress roll calls occurred on a proposed rules change that practically eliminated the discharge petition in House proceedings and thus consolidated procedural power in the hands of the core-oriented Republican leadership. The other vote was recorded on legislation that provided for an "automatic" reapportionment of the membership of the House of Representatives following the 1930 census (Congress had failed to authorize reapportionment after the 1920 census). Passage of the legislation promised to reallocate representation away from the agrarian states of the periphery and toward the industrial core regions of the Northeast, Great Lakes, and Pacific Coast, and the 1930 reapportionment ultimately had that effect.

†Gilbert C. Fite, *George N. Peek and the Fight for Farm Parity* (Norman: University of Oklahoma Press, 1954), p. 122. John D. Black, a contemporary scholar, described the movement as "agriculture's stand against the domination of its affairs and the affairs of the country by the commercial and industrial interests." "The McNary-Haugen Movement," *American Economic Review* 28:3 (September 1928): 405. See also Darwin N. Kelley, "The McNary-Haugen Bills, 1924–1928," *Agricultural History* 14:4 (October 1940): 170–80.

tion, cotton manufacturing shifted out of Europe into the cheaper labor markets of Japan, China, India, and Brazil, which were closer to foreign sources of raw cotton fiber. In competition with foreign labor and the opening up of virgin land, American production costs were higher than foreign sources and the United States steadily lost ground in the world market. Finally, the emergence of competing fibers such as rayon decreased world demand in absolute terms.[52] World agricultural markets also suffered from overproduction stimulated by the exceptional demands of wartime economies and the increased productivity brought on by mechanization.[53]

The deteriorating condition of the international marketplace was only one factor in the agricultural depression. The agricultural sector's main difficulty, according to Gilbert Fite, was its "growing position of inferiority in the over-all economy of the nation."[54] The economic stimulation that agriculture had received during the war had led to overinvestment in land and capital, increased agricultural indebtedness, and ultimately expanded commercial farming for a cash market.[55] All of these developments combined with the withdrawal of wartime price supports to produce a precipitous decline in farm income. The price of a bushel of wheat in Minneapolis, for example, fell from $2.94 in July to $1.72 in December, 1920.[56]

One political result of increasing agricultural distress was the formation of a farm bloc in Congress that cut across party lines.* During the remaining years of the decade, the farm bloc—first its midwestern wing and subsequently the South—became converted to McNary-Haugenism: "a doctrine of extreme economic nationalism" which was based "on the one method of governmental interference with the price mechanism that had the approval of tradition, the tariff."[57] The goal of the McNary-Haugen movement was to "make the tariff work" for agriculture, a goal which agricultural representatives believed would be easier to achieve than a reduction of import duties on those goods and services the farmers purchased in the domestic market.[58]

Before the McNary-Haugen proposal foundered on the reefs of presidential vetoes, its support became intertwined with that of the government complex at Muscle Shoals, Alabama. As part of the National Defense Act of 1916, Congress had authorized the construction of a plant to manufacture synthetic nitrates at Muscle Shoals, taking advantage of the potentially abundant supply of hydroelectric power available at the site. The nitrates produced at Muscle Shoals were to be used in making explosives in wartime and would relieve the United States of its dependence on foreign suppliers. During peacetime, the government plant was originally intended to produce fertilizer, but

---

*William Allen White believed that the "Progressive bloc in the Senate was rooted in the decay of Republican leadership. That decay began with the introduction of the direct primary and the direct election of United States Senators by the people." *A Puritan in Babylon: The Story of Calvin Coolidge* (New York: MacMillan, 1938), p. 263. See also Christiana McFadyen Campbell, *The Farm Bureau and the New Deal* (Urbana: University of Illinois Press, 1962), pp. 33–35.

when President Wilson attempted to convert the plant to that purpose after the war, an intense and sometimes violent controversy over government-versus-private operation of the complex broke out and continued almost without intermission until the New Deal created its successor: the Tennessee Valley Authority. The regional group most directly interested in the fate of the complex were the representatives of the Southeast who saw in Muscle Shoals a possible source of relatively cheap fertilizer. While they consistently advocated the development of the site for that purpose, these members did not particularly care whether the government or private enterprise carried out the project as long as it did not fall into the hands of the Alabama Power Company or the "fertilizer trust."[59]

Of seven roll calls that decided the fate of Muscle Shoals between 1916 and 1933, the first was recorded on an amendment which would have eliminated the funding authorization for Muscle Shoals from the National Defense Act of 1916 (table 4.4). The amendment passed the House on March 23, 1916, by a substantial margin (224 to 180), but the project, strongly supported by both the Senate and President Wilson, was later restored in conference and subsequently approved by the House. At this time the proposed complex was considered a possible precedent for the government manufacture of munitions which many agrarian pacifists felt would decrease the economic pull toward intervention, and aside from the fact that agrarian forces were weaker on this roll call than they were on other preparedness votes, the sectional alignment follows the prewar regional pattern. This vote was one of the ten high-stress, closely contested roll calls recorded in the 64th Congress (1915–17).

On March 4, 1918, Republican Nicholas Longworth of Ohio offered an amendment to restrict nitrate production to quantities "needed for munitions." The amendment was offered to legislation which authorized federal condemnation of land at Muscle Shoals, and although the government was to complete the construction of two nitrate plants at a total cost of eighty million dollars before the end of the war, most congressmen already foresaw that the major purpose of the complex, if it was to have any function at all, would be the production of fertilizer.[60] Regional representatives, such as Democrat J. Thomas Heflin of Alabama, pushed for expansion and completion of the project as part of the overall war effort. Heflin pleaded, "Let us vote for this measure and vote for it quickly and get behind the President and have unity of purpose and concerted action in the righteous work of winning this war."[61] Noting that the huge hydroelectric installation that was to become Wilson Dam was far from finished, most northern members were skeptical of the project's relevance to the war effort. Republican Clarence Miller of Minnesota spoke for many of these members when he responded to Heflin's plea:

> Under the guise of doing something to help our military efficiency we are, in effect, erecting a gigantic enterprise in a certain part of the South

Table 4.4. Trade Area Delegation Support for the Development of Muscle Shoals, 1916–1933

Trade Area[a]	Nitrate Plant Construction (May 8, 1916)	Fertilizer Production Ban (April 4, 1918)	Tie Funding to Vote on Ford Proposal (June 24, 1922)	Fertilizer Quota for Ford (March 10, 1924)	Government Operation of Site (May 25, 1928)	Government Operation of Site (May 28, 1930)	Creation of Tennessee Valley Authority (May 17, 1933)
Philadelphia	Priv[b]	Priv	Gov	Gov	Priv	Priv	Priv
Boston	Priv	Priv	Gov	Gov	Priv	Priv	Priv
New York	Priv	Priv	Gov	Gov	Priv	Priv	Gov
Pittsburgh	Priv	Priv	Gov	Gov	Priv	Priv	Gov
Buffalo	Priv	Priv	Priv	Gov	Priv	Priv	—
Detroit	Priv	Priv	Priv	Gov	Gov	Priv	Gov
Louisville	Gov	Gov	Priv	Priv	Gov	Priv	Gov
San Francisco	Priv	Gov	Priv	Priv	Gov	Priv	Gov
Cincinnati	Priv	Gov	Gov	Priv	Split	Priv	Gov
Chicago	Priv	Priv	Gov	Gov	Gov	Priv	Gov
Minneapolis	Priv	Priv	Gov	Gov	Gov	Gov	Gov
Denver	Gov	Gov	Gov	Gov	Gov	Split	Gov
Cleveland	Priv	Gov	Priv	Gov	Gov	Priv	Gov
Kansas City	Gov	Gov	Gov	Gov	Gov	Priv	Gov
Omaha	Priv	Priv	Gov	Split	Gov	Gov	—
Indianapolis	—	Split	Gov	Gov	Gov	Gov	Gov
Baltimore	Gov	Split	Priv	Priv	Priv	Split	Gov
Richmond	Gov	Gov	Priv	Priv	Priv	Split	Gov
New Orleans	Gov	Gov	Priv	Priv	Gov	Gov	Gov
St. Louis	Gov	Gov	Gov	Priv	Gov	Gov	Gov
Dallas	Gov	Gov	Priv	Priv	Gov	Gov	Gov
Birmingham	Gov	Gov	Priv	Priv	Gov	Gov	Gov
Atlanta	Gov	Gov	Priv	Priv	Gov	Gov	Gov
Memphis	Gov	Gov	Priv	Priv	Gov	Gov	Gov
Core Position	Priv	Priv	Gov	Gov	Priv	Priv	Priv
Periphery Position	Gov	Gov	Priv	Priv	Gov	Gov	Gov
Sectional Stress	64.7	55.8	65.3	54.6	46.5	44.1	27.2

a "Trade area delegations are ranked in descending order of their support for the core position on the ten high-stress roll calls recorded during the 69th Congress (1925–27); see table 2.5.

b "Priv" (Private) indicates that a majority of the trade area delegation supported the "private enterprise" alternative; "Gov" (Government) indicates support for the "government intervention" alternative; Split indicates that the delegation divided evenly on the roll call.

SOURCE: Computations from roll call data.

for the manufacture and production of fertilizer. . . . It will take years to build the plant; the war will have ended long before this plant can be used. The purpose is to have the Government provide cheap fertilizer for the South.[62]

The sectional alignment on the roll call, though exhibiting a moderately lower level of overall stress, followed the pattern of the 1916 vote. Slightly greater support in the Pittsburgh, Cleveland, and Cincinnati trade area delegations and in the Far West gave the southern periphery sufficient strength to defeat the amendment, and progress at the site continued. At war's end, however, Congress cut off all appropriations, and further work on the still uncompleted dam was halted.*

At the end of construction at Muscle Shoals, the government had spent 150 million dollars on the two nitrate plants, the unfinished dam, and site improvements. As part of Harding's return to "normalcy," his secretary of war entertained proposals by private enterprise to lease the complex if they guaranteed a fair return to the government on its investment. The most serious bid was made by Henry Ford, the automobile industrialist; it promised, in return for a one-hundred-year lease, to pay one and a half million dollars in yearly rental fees, annually produce forty thousand tons of nitrates for the manufacture of cheap fertilizer, and build a city that would stretch for seventy-five miles along the banks of the Tennessee River.[63] Southern congressmen, whose major interest in the project was its potential for reducing the cost of fertilizer, became Ford's strongest supporters.†

Legislation that would have enabled the government to accept Ford's offer was reported out of the Military Affairs Committee of the House of Representatives, but consideration of the proposal by the full chamber was blocked by the Republican leadership.[64] During the ensuing delay, Ford charged that "selfish Wall Street interests" were conspiring to defeat his proposition, and the battle lines between core and periphery delegations rapidly jelled.[65] Mem-

---

*Among core congressmen there was frustration with the "discriminatory" executive administration of war mobilization programs and with the persistence of government "interference" in the private economy after the war ended. This frustration was reflected in the words of Nicholas Longworth of Cincinnati: "Yet today, though our Army is disbanded and our Navy reduced to a peace footing, all the war powers of the Executive continue in full force and vigor. Trade and commerce are out of joint. War boards and war commissions flourish, and thousands upon thousands of useless employees and chair warmers abound in the land." *Congressional Record*, 66:2:5467, April 9, 1920. Longworth was speaking on a resolution which would have unilaterally terminated the state of war that still existed between the United States and the Central powers and thus abolished the emergency powers that had been conferred upon the president as part of the mobilization program. Upon its passage by Congress, Wilson vetoed the resolution, and it was not until July 2, 1921, that the United States officially ended the war.

† However, "Ford was chiefly interested in the power available at Muscle Shoals, which he was proposing to obtain at a ridiculously low figure." C. Herman Pritchett, *The Tennessee Valley Authority: A Study in Public Administration* (Chapel Hill: University of North Carolina Press, 1943), pp. 9, 13.

bers from the northeastern commercial and industrial core supported the Republican leadership and urged outright rejection of the Ford proposal as a "fraud." Though their positions are depicted as the "government" alternative in table 4.4, many of these members actually supported competing private bids from corporations such as the Alabama Power Company. At this point, northern Republicans reversed themselves and urged completion of the Wilson Dam by offering an amendment authorizing the resumption of work to an appropriations measure then before the House. Southern members interpreted the Republican move as an attempt to further the interests of the "fertilizer" and "power trusts" by sabotaging the provisions of the Ford proposal (one of which was an offer to complete construction of the dam).

On June 24, 1922, Representative George Huddleston, an Alabama Democrat, offered an amendment to the Republican measure which would have delayed further work at the site until Congress had an opportunity to vote on Ford's bid. A clear attempt to force the Republican leadership to bring the Ford offer to the floor, the Huddleston amendment was narrowly turned back (118 to 132). The sectional alignment was highly consistent with earlier votes (table 4.4) even though the "government" and "private" designations were reversed. The level of sectional stress was extremely high (65.3 on the index).

On March 4, 1924, the Ford offer reached the floor of the House for the first time. During debate, southern congressmen again railed against the "powers of Wall Street," but many progressive Republicans refused to support the agrarian position for two reasons. First, progressives opposed the Ford proposal because acceptance would prevent public development and control of the hydroelectric potential of the site and, some visionaries maintained, the entire Tennessee Valley. These members made common cause with industrial core representatives who were even more hostile to public power than they were to Henry Ford's plan. Second, Ford's campaign against the "minions of high finance" had boiled over into overt anti-Semitism which caused revulsion among many progressives.* Other members, including many midwestern agrarian representatives, could recognize the interest of the South in the development of Muscle Shoals but just couldn't see what was in it for their own districts. Republican James G. Strong of Kansas spoke for these members when he noted:

> Now Kansas does not use any fertilizer at the present time. I realize this is a bill to secure nitrates for the cotton farmers of the South, and I hope it accomplishes that. I have always gone along to help the farmers of the

*Representative Fiorello LaGuardia of New York reflected the growing revulsion of progressive members everywhere when he replied to charges of Wall Street complicity: "The only man who has hatred in his heart is Henry Ford, based on his ignorance of history, literature, and religion. And Henry Ford has done more, I will say, owing to his bigoted hatred, to create strife and hatred in this country among the races than any man in the United States . . . the wealth and ignorance of Henry Ford . . . has made . . . possible . . . a nefarious warfare against the Jews." Hubbard, *Origins of the TVA*, pp. 119–20. See also pp. 116–22.

South. I have voted for everything you have had before the Congress to help the farmers of the South, and I want to help you to pass this bill if it can be amended so that it will be fair, but I can not go along with a bill that has been drawn by Henry Ford's attorneys and in which we are not allowed to change a single thing in the interest of the people of my section.[66]

Of all the major agricultural regions of the United States, the greatest expenditures for fertilizer occurred in the Atlantic and Gulf coastal plains and in the piedmont cotton and tobacco regions. Almost nothing was spent on fertilizer in the western stretches of the wheat and corn belts.[67]

The closest test of strength between the two sides came on an amendment which would have voided the sale and lease of facilities at Muscle Shoals if Ford failed to produce 40,000 tons of fertilizer on an annual basis in two consecutive years. If adopted, the provision would have clouded Ford's title to the property and possibly induced him to withdraw his proposal. If rejected, the provision was intended to politically embarrass agrarian supporters of the bid who had defended Ford against charges that his commitment to produce cheap fertilizer was insincere. Somewhat ironically, therefore, southern members opposed the condition imposed by the amendment in the interest of increasing the prospects for fertilizer production at the site. The amendment was defeated on a recorded vote (176 to 197). The level of sectional stress remained quite high on this fourth contest (table 4.4), and the regional pattern was consistent with earlier votes. The House later passed the Ford proposal, as did the Senate, but the two chambers were unable to reach a compromise and the legislation expired at the end of the 68th Congress (1923–25).

Meanwhile, the government continued to sell the electricity generated at Muscle Shoals to the Alabama Power Company, completed the construction of Wilson Dam, and maintained the two idle nitrate plants. In the following years, the McNary-Haugen movement, which started in the Great Plains, expanded to include representatives of the cotton and tobacco belts. This developing alliance between the plains and southern periphery first appeared in the American Farm Bureau Federation but soon influenced the internal politics of the congressional farm bloc.[*] In return for midwestern support for the public development of Muscle Shoals, southern members promised votes for the McNary-Haugen plan.

On May 25, 1928, the House of Representatives approved the conference report on legislation which would have created a federal corporation to operate the existing site, to construct a second dam at Cove Creek, Tennessee,

---

[*] "The strength of the South lay in its agricultural population, which gave it political power. The strength of Midwestern agriculture lay in its wealth, which gave it economic as well as political power. Each in its own way was therefore the leading agricultural section, and the alliance of the two through the Farm Bureau and through the harmonious relations of their leaders gave the A.F.B.F. power which no other farm organization in the United States could hope to match . . ." Campbell, *The Farm Bureau and the New Deal*, p. 60. See also pp. 38–40.

to produce and distribute fertilizer, and to market surplus power. This was popularly known as the Norris bill, after the progressive Republican senator from Nebraska. In spite of substantial majorities in the House (211 to 147) and Senate, President Coolidge killed the bill with a pocket veto. The roll call on which the conference report was adopted clearly reveals the emergence of coalition ties between the midwestern and southern periphery. Not all members, however, honored the tacit terms of the alliance, and the level of sectional stress declined from previous scores.[68]

In the following Congress the public power proposal was again considered by Congress. In the House, the decisive vote on the issue occurred on May 28, 1930, when the chamber substituted an administration plan to establish a commission which would evaluate the facilities and award a fifty-year lease to a private party subject to the approval of the president.[69] The administration substitute passed in spite of the pleas of southern congressmen for "reciprocity." Democrat Niles Allgood of Alabama made the clearest appeal for agrarian solidarity:

> I am pleading that you adopt this amendment . . . so that you will guarantee to the farmers of the South that in the operation of this plant we will have a maximum production of fertilizer. Personally I can not see why men who are familiar with the conditions and needs of the South were not placed on the subcommitee to write this bill. I am a member of the Committee on Irrigation and Reclamation and I voted for the Boulder Canyon Dam, and I followed the lead of the men from the West, who knew the problems of the West. I think it but fair to the South that you give leadership to men who know the problems of the South.[70]

Although the skeletal outline of the farm bloc alliance still persisted on the roll call (see table 4.4), numerous agrarian defections allowed the administration position to prevail. The Senate again passed the Norris plan for public development of the site and the subsequent conference between the chambers labored over a compromise for nearly a year. Finally, the House conferees capitulated to the Senate position and a public power bill was once more submitted to a Republican president, this time Herbert Hoover. On March 3, 1931, the legislation was again vetoed.

Thus the Muscle Shoals complex, still largely mothballed and undeveloped, endured the hostility and indifference of three postwar Republican administrations. Upon the return of the periphery party to power under the leadership of Franklin Roosevelt, the Norris plan for a public corporation was transformed into the vast regional authority now known as the Tennessee Valley Authority. The political system of the New Deal, spawned by the economic emergency of the Great Depression, brought together the representatives of agrarian regions with a cohesion that prior, explicit logrolling arrangements had never been able to maintain. When the House of Representatives approved the conference report, the extremely low level of sectional stress and the complete isolation of the Philadelphia and Boston trade area delegations in opposition to the proposal reflected the inroads the periphery party had made into the industrial core and the subsequent consensus that emerged on the relief measures of the First Hundred Days.

Throughout the seventeen-year odyssey of the Muscle Shoals complex, southern congressmen consistently pursued a policy of expediency intended to bring economic aid to their region.* At every turn, southern tactics met with solid opposition from members representing the industrial East. Even the midwestern agrarians were often indifferent to southern legislative goals. More than anything else, the politics of the farm crisis was a politics of mutually competitive "belts" (see map 4.2). In the Northeast and metropolitan centers of the Great Lakes, the nation's increasingly vast manufacturing capacity dominated both city and village. The interest of the industrial-commercial cities was clearly bound up in the prosperity of their respective enterprises. The tributary hinterlands, increasingly devoted to truck farming and dairy operations which fed the laboring masses in the cities, were inevitably pulled into the political orbit of their industrialized urban centers. Farmers in the manufacturing belt neither dominated the regional economy nor felt sympathy for the plight of their cash-crop counterparts in the remainder of the nation.

Outside the industrial core, the agrarian periphery cultivated a wide variety of crops and raised livestock for domestic and foreign markets. Three commodities, however, stood out from all the rest in terms of economic importance and political saliency: corn (and its connection to swine production), cotton, and wheat.[71] Though slowly expanding into the western plains of Texas and Oklahoma, cotton remained almost entirely a southern crop, with its primary territory following the contours of the traditional "black belt." Here and in the wheat regions of the Dakotas, Kansas, and the Pacific Northwest the economic imperatives of the rural hinterland controlled the politics of local urban centers and thus the entire region. In the corn belt, commodity cultivation met and intermingled with the fringe territory of the manufacturing belt, but here, too, the imperatives of commodity agriculture prevailed. In sectional terms, these belts were the primary protagonists of farm crisis politics. The congressmen from districts which contained a more diversified economic base and therefore fell outside these great regions were compelled to adjust to the dynamics of the sectional alignment thus thrust upon them.

A stable, comprehensive alliance between the representatives of the three agricultural regions did not develop before the New Deal for several reasons.

*Hubbard, *Origins of the TVA*, p. 114. George Tindall has summarized the successive positions of southern delegations in the dispute: "first, support for governmental operation to produce cheap fertilizer, then for Henry Ford's offer to transform it into a vast industrial complex, then opposition to acquisition by Alabama Power or the American Cyanamid Company, and finally support for the Norris idea of governmental development which seemed to promise the most widespread diffusion of cheap power." *The Emergence of the New South*, p. 241.

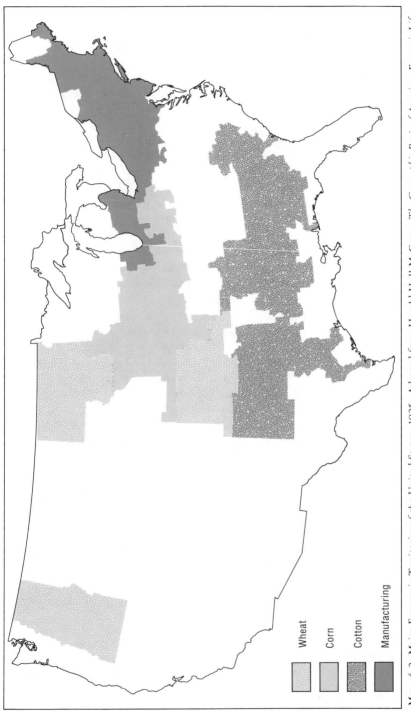

Map. 4.2. Major Economic Territories of the United States, 1925. Adapted from Harold Hull McCarty, *The Geographic Basis of American Economic Life*, Port Washington, N.Y.: Kennikat Press, 1970; original edition, 1940, frontispiece. Wheat areas adapted from C. Langdon White and Edwin J. Foscue, *Regional Geography of Anglo-America*, New York: Prentice-Hall, 1943, p. 544. Economic territories redrawn to fit congressional district boundaries.

Wheat

Corn

Cotton

Manufacturing

The most important difficulty standing in the way of agrarian solidarity was the limited scope of federal policy. The small size of government made logrolling opportunities between the sections relatively rare since legislative situations in which a regional delegation could "reciprocate" were often delayed for months or even years. Then, too, the limited scope of government activity meant, in practical terms, that legislative action which might have any significant impact on the political economy bulked very large in the policy process and therefore was difficult to broker. In addition, the relatively small scope of government encouraged legislative specification. In this period, Congress did not delegate vast discretionary authority to federal departments and agencies, and when farm legislation came to the floor of the House and Senate, the sectional implications were often explicit. Members could not escape the political liabilities of logrolling by creating a bureaucratic policy process removed from the public eye but jealously overseen by legislative committees. That political strategy would come with the New Deal; in the 1920s, political support on each piece of legislation would have to be publicly and separately traded, and the Muscle Shoals controversy illustrates to what extent one factor, the consumption of fertilizer, could divide the potentially dominant farm bloc into regional factions.

In addition, the policy initiatives of the farm bloc were continually frustrated by the different way in which each commodity related to the world-economy. No political conflict better illustrated this problem than the McNary-Haugen movement. McNary-Haugenism was a political response to the increasingly unfavorable terms of trade between agriculture and the remainder of the economy in postwar America.[72] Among the factors underlying the deteriorating economic position of agriculture, the most important involved the growing unmarketability of agricultural products in foreign trade. Some of the causes of declining returns from the export trade have already been examined and might be considered remediable. But at least one factor was intimately linked to a permanent change in the nature of the American economy.

> The natural course of events in an industrializing economy is for exports to become increasingly manufactured products while imports are becoming increasingly of the raw material variety. This follows from the fact that industrialization implies a progressive cheapening of the factors of production most essential to factory production, and a progressive increase in the cost of those factors most needed in raw material producing industries. Artificially to stimulate agricultural exports would unquestionably be tantamount to slowing down this evolution.[73]

In some respects, the McNary-Haugen proposal was intended both to turn agricultural production into a form of industrial manufacturing through the creation of a benign, government-sponsored "trust" and to soften the adjustment of the agrarian sector to its emerging subordinate role in American life.

McNary-Haugen bills were introduced in Congress on five occasions,* but all followed the general form of the original measure. McNary-Haugenites proposed that a government corporation be created and capitalized at 200 million dollars with funds drawn from the federal treasury. This corporation would purchase agricultural commodities on the open market until the domestic price reached a target called the "ratio-price": the price level at which the purchasing power of commodity production relative to the general price level would equal that prevailing prior to World War I. In order to carry out its mission, the corporation would normally purchase more of an eligible commodity than it could resell in the domestic market at the ratio-price. The "surplus" would be exported and sold at the prevailing, ordinarily lower world market price. A tariff-barrier would be erected to prevent this surplus from returning to the United States (and thus re-depressing the domestic market). Normally, the corporation would thus incur a loss when it sold "surplus" commodities abroad. In order to make good its operating deficit, the government marketing agency would, by one means or another, "tax" the farmers producing the commodity according to their annual production.[74] George Soule, hypothetically assuming the perspective of a wheat farmer who has sold a thousand bushels, has provided a lucid example of the McNary-Haugen mechanism:

> Suppose that wheat was selling on the world market at $1 a bushel, that the tariff was 20 cents a bushel, and that one-fifth of the crop was exported. Under ordinary conditions the farmer would receive $1 a bushel, or $1,000 in all. But under this plan he would receive $1.20 a bushel, or $1,200 for a thousand bushels. He would pay back 20 cents a bushel on the two hundred bushels exported, or $40. His net receipts would thus be $1,160.[75]

The effectiveness of the plan in raising farm income was thus directly related to the proportion of the total crop, by commodity, that was normally exported. For crops such as corn or wheat, which generally sold 85 percent or more of production within the domestic market, the marketing plan held significant promise. For cotton producers who normally exported more than half of each harvest, the proposal was much less exciting. †

---

*The first was in the 68th Congress, 1st Session (1924); the second, 68:2 (1925); the third, 69:1 (1926); the fourth, 69:2 (1927); and the fifth, 70:1 (1928). The second bill did not come to a vote. Benedict, *Farm Policies of the United States*, p. 212.

†The major criticism of the plan, at least by disinterested parties, was that it would increase production of eligible commodities, thus increase the surplus, thus depress the world price, thus increase the "tax" which offset the corporation's deficit, and ultimately return the farmer to his previous position. But contemporary economists still preferred McNary-Haugen to the industrial tariff. "The fundamental difference between this plan and the protective system is that this would seem to encourage *a larger production of the right products than is economical*—those in which we have demonstrated our comparative advantage; whereas the protective system promotes *too large a production of the wrong products*—those in which we are at comparative disad-

The originators of the plan, George N. Peek and Hugh Johnson, believed that the major problem confronting agricultural producers was that they sold their commodities in a competitive world market and bought necessary equipment and supplies in a protected industrial economy.* In addition to its protectionist implications, Peek and Johnson intended their proposal to be a marketing device "built on the philosophy that farmers could be helped if they were forced to participate in a great pool or cooperative enterprise. This was to be accomplished by making all the producers of a commodity share the responsibilities of keeping prices up by paying the equalization fee."[76] A third purpose of the plan which became increasingly attractive to agrarian radicals throughout the twenties was to serve as a mechanism for redressing what they conceived to be an imbalance of economic power within the nation. Democrat Ashton Shallenberger of Nebraska reflected that sentiment when he spoke in 1927 on the third version of the proposal to reach the floor: "The dominating power in national politics today is organized wealth. Farm wealth is the Nation's biggest business asset but in the past unorganized as a political power. This bill will give that wealth a Federal organization through which agriculture can makes its voice heard and its power felt."[77] Under any guise, the McNary-Haugen proposal ran into "wild" opposition on Wall Street and hostility from industrial labor.[78] Business condemned the legislation as "socialism," while to workers whose employment was already protected by the tariff the mechanism implied an intolerable rise in the cost of living.

The House of Representatives defeated the first McNary-Haugen bill on June 3, 1924, by a substantial margin (155 to 223). Unsurprisingly, members from districts in the manufacturing belt were almost unanimously opposed to a "tariff for agriculture" (see map 4.3). In this "historic exhibition of geographical division on a legislative issue,"[79] the cotton South voted solidly with the industrial East. Only districts on the fringes of the black belt (along the coast or in the West) abstained or, in a few instances, supported the wheat-corn initiative. Significantly, the congressman from Muscle Shoals, Miles Allgood, voted for the measure and two other north Alabama representatives abstained. Such was the extent of agrarian reciprocity in 1924.

---

vantage . . . no argument is needed to convince economists that the former is the less uneconomical of the two." Black, "The McNary-Haugen Movement," *American Economic Review* 18 (September 1928): 418.

*Peek and Johnson became close friends through their employment on the War Industries Board during World War I. Saloutos and Hicks, *Twentieth Century Populism*, p. 377. When Peek took over the management of the Moline Plow Company after the war ended, he brought Johnson with him. As business at the plow company turned sour during the agricultural depression, Peek noted, "You can't sell a plow to a busted customer." He and Johnson collaborated on a series of pamphlets discussing the plight of the farmer and subsequently embarked on a campaign for governmental relief. General Johnson later went on to head the National Recovery Administration—in many ways the successor to the War Industries Board—and created its memorable insignia, the Blue Eagle. Schriftgiesser, *This Was Normalcy*, p. 223. Peek was to become the father of the Agricultural Adjustment Administration.

The cotton belt delegations were not converted to McNary-Haugenism —at least at first—for a number of reasons. As Grant McConnell has noted, any remedy for the "farm surplus which exploited foreign markets and was built on tariffs ran head on into two stubborn facts: cotton was already exported in larger quantities than most crops, and tariffs were traditionally disliked in the South."[80] But three less fundamental factors influenced southern voting: cotton producers were more interested in federal subsidies for a cooperative marketing system; they considered the equalization fee to be a burdensome tax on their operations; and the price of cotton was substantially above the target levels provided in the legislation when the vote was taken. Furthermore, less than three months earlier most members from the wheat and corn districts had either abstained on the vote or opposed passage of the Ford offer for Muscle Shoals.

The general level of sectional stress elicited by the first McNary-Haugen bill, a moderately high 58.7 (table 4.5), understates the visual impact of the regional pattern (map 4.3). The extremely unusual northeastern core–southern periphery agreement stands out in stark relief to the sweeping expanse of midwestern and mountain support for the relief proposal. Only congressmen from isolated urban centers such as Denver, St. Louis, Indianapolis, Cincinnati, Los Angeles, and coastal districts bordering San Francisco stood against the measure in the West, though a scattering of members from areas like Minneapolis and the two Kansas Cities abstained. When the bill was reintroduced the following year, the proposal expired without coming to a vote.

In preparation for a second attempt to enact the McNary-Haugen proposal, farm leaders from the corn belt met with directors of the Memphis cotton exchange and told them "to write their own ticket."[81] The result was an amended program that provided for the participation, wherever possible, of cooperatives in the actual handling of the surplus and a proviso exempting cotton (and corn) from payment of the equalization fee for three years.[82] These changes plus a sharp decline in cotton prices increased southern support, but on May 21, 1926, this McNary-Haugen proposal was again defeated in the House (167 to 212).[83] Except for the Birmingham trade area delegation (a majority of which now supported the legislation in anticipation of reciprocal backing for their Muscle Shoals plans), new southern support was equally distributed throughout the cotton belt. The overall sectional alignment and level of stress almost replicated the vote recorded two years earlier.*

In following months the price of cotton continued to fall and many southern congressmen reconsidered their positions.[84] Sensing a favorable opening, proponents revised the McNary-Haugen plan once more. The new legislation reported by the House Agriculture Committee in January 1927 pro-

---

*Supporting passage were 98 Republicans, 66 Democrats, and 3 members of the Farmer-Labor party. In opposition were 121 Republicans, 89 Democrats, and 2 Socialists. Benedict, *Farm Policies of the United States*, p. 225.

posed to support prices on five basic commodities (wheat, cotton, corn, rice, and hogs), aid cooperatives in their handling and processing operations, eliminate references to the tariff, and apply the equalization fee to cotton immediately in order to finance the storage of surpluses. In addition, before any commodity could come under the program, a favorable vote must be secured from "representatives of half the product."[85] These changes, though to some extent cosmetic, altered the focus from the tariff-orientation of previous plans to the "orderly" marketing perspective desired by the South.

Even with the now limited reliance on the tariff, however, some southern Democrats were suspicious of the intentions of western agrarian members. Hampton Fulmer of South Carolina noted the long tradition that stood behind a northeastern-midwestern coalition:

> There is one thing I can not understand, and that is why you folks from the West let those birds from New England come down here and propose any kind of class legislation in the interest of their people, and every one of you fellows from the West, like goats going to pasture, march right up and stick your fists on the dotted line.[86]

McNary-Haugenites such as John Robsion, a Kentucky Republican, sought to persuade skeptical southerners that, indeed, they both had a common enemy—the same antagonist that had thrust the First World War upon a reluctant nation:

> The great manufacturing interest of the East and the great cities; the big newspapers of the big cities; the United States Chamber of Commerce, representing the big business of the country; the big Miller's Trust, the Tobacco Trust; grain speculators; the big packers and cotton combines; and many of the Members of the House and Senate representing the big industrial and big city districts. Many of these are very anxious to secure the farmers' products at the smallest price possible.[87]

In spite of lingering suspicion, the farm bloc held together and the McNary-Haugen legislation passed the House on February 17, 1927. The conservative Republican establishment slandered the motives of the farm bill's supporters; Chief Justice William Howard Taft charged that victory was accomplished only by "bribing the cotton people and the tobacco people" with changes in the bill's specifications.[88] On February 25, President Coolidge vetoed the legislation, sending a message that crackled with hostility.[89]

The vote by which the 1927 bill passed the House was one of the ten high-stress, closely contested roll calls in the 69th Congress (1925–27). In many respects, the sectional alignment was similar to that of 1924 (compare maps 4.3 and 4.4). The Northeast was even more solidly opposed to farm relief in 1927 than it had been earlier, and a few members in the West now voted against the bill. (At least one of these, Republican James Tincher of Kansas, had been promised a judgeship by the Administration.) But the plan picked

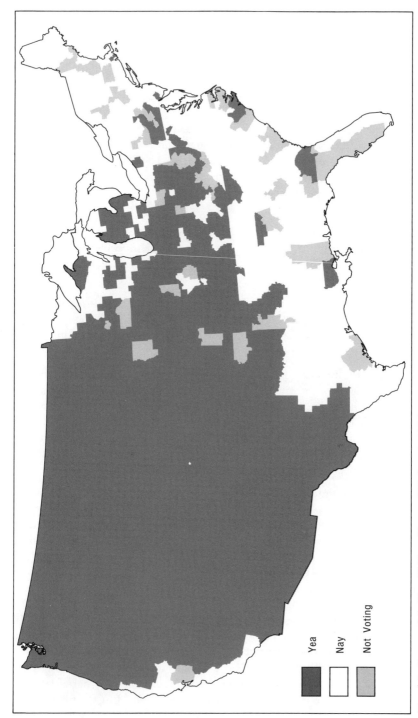

Map 4.3. Passage of the First McNary-Haugen Bill, June 3, 1924

Yea

Nay

Not Voting

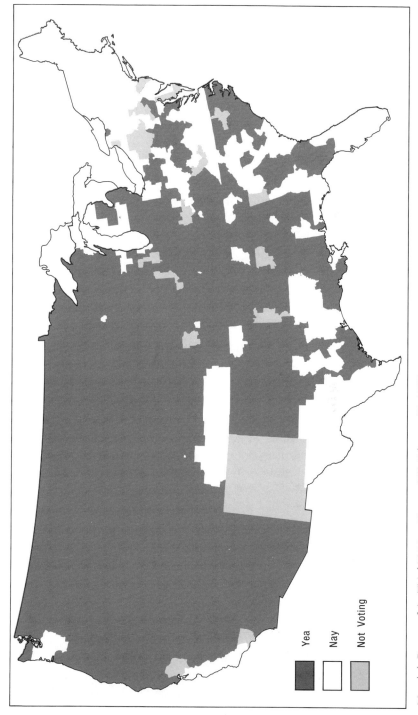

Map 4.4. Passage of the Third McNary-Haugen Bill, February 17, 1927

Yea

Nay

Not Voting

up support in Wisconsin, Minnesota, and—most notably—the cotton belt.

On May 3, 1928, the now well-functioning farm bloc (which would three weeks later pass legislation proposing a public corporation for the Muscle Shoals complex) once more voted up a McNary-Haugen marketing scheme. The voting pattern was almost identical with that of the February 1927 roll call, but a new Republican president, Herbert Hoover, vetoed the bill.

In the following year, however, Hoover reacted to increasing farm discontent and proposed an agricultural relief program that became the Agricultural Marketing Act of 1929. The law appropriated 500 million dollars to a federal farm board which was authorized, in turn, to loan funds to cooperative associations. It was hoped that these cooperatives would follow policies which would ensure the orderly marketing of agricultural commodities.[90] However, before the measure passed the House, the McNary-Haugen forces attempted to resurrect a variation of their plan in the form of an amendment to the president's initiative. The amendment, which had already drawn majority support in the Senate, would have allowed the farm board to implement an "export debenture" program. Briefly described, the debenture plan established a bounty on agricultural exports by creating

> an arrangement whereby exporters of those agricultural products of which we produce a surplus [would] receive from the Treasury Department certificates having a face value established by Congress and intended to represent the differences in costs of production between here and abroad, such certificates being negotiable and good for their face value in the payment of import tariffs on any articles later imported.[91]

While the debenture plan differed from previous agrarian proposals in several respects, the amendment represented the last gasp of McNary-Haugenism. On June 13, 1929, the House of Representatives turned back the debenture substitute (146 to 185) as members from districts that straddled the boundary between the manufacturing and corn belts shifted toward the core opposition (see table 4.5). Southern delegations, on the other hand, moved toward the farm bloc program, and the level of sectional stress rose to a high 62.6 as a result.

The federal program created by the Agricultural Marketing Act turned out to be a dismal failure. Since the administration of the marketing system did not provide restrictive controls on production, agricultural produce continued to flood the marketplace. In fact, production was stimulated by federal reclamation and irrigation projects, improvements in crop yield per acre that arose out of scientific research disseminated by a host of public and private agencies, and the frantic efforts of individual operators to repay mortgages during a period of gradual deflation. The *coup de grace* was delivered by the onset of the Great Depression, which unrelentingly drove market prices lower and before which the farm board was completely helpless.[92]

Table 4.5. Trade Area Delegation Support for McNary-Haugenism, 1924–1929

Trade Area[a]	First McNary-Haugen (June 3, 1924)	Second McNary-Haugen (May 21, 1926)	Third McNary-Haugen (Feb. 17, 1927)	Fourth McNary-Haugen (May 3, 1928)	Federal Farm Board (June 13, 1929)
Philadelphia	Priv[b]	Priv	Priv	Priv	Priv
Boston	Priv	Priv	Priv	Priv	Priv
New York	Priv	Priv	Priv	Priv	Priv
Pittsburgh	Priv	Priv	Priv	Priv	Priv
Buffalo	Priv	Priv	Priv	Priv	Priv
Detroit	Priv	Priv	Gov	Gov	Priv
Louisville	Gov	Priv	Gov	Gov	Priv
San Francisco	*Split*	Priv	Gov	Gov	Gov
Cincinnati	*Split*	Priv	Priv	Priv	Priv
Chicago	Gov	Gov	Gov	Gov	Gov
Minneapolis	Gov	Gov	Gov	Gov	Gov
Denver	Gov	Gov	Gov	Gov	Gov
Cleveland	Priv	Priv	Priv	Priv	Priv
Kansas City	Gov	Gov	Gov	Gov	Gov
Omaha	Gov	Gov	Gov	Gov	Gov
Indianapolis	Gov	Gov	Gov	Gov	Priv
Baltimore	Priv	Priv	*Split*	Gov	Priv
Richmond	Priv	Priv	Priv	Priv	Gov
New Orleans	Priv	Priv	Priv	Gov	Gov
St. Louis	Gov	Gov	Gov	Gov	Priv
Dallas	Priv	Priv	Gov	Gov	Gov
Birmingham	Priv	Gov	Gov	Gov	Gov
Atlanta	Priv	Priv	Gov	Gov	Gov
Memphis	Priv	Priv	Gov	Gov	Gov
Sectional Stress	58.7	58.2	56.8	59.1	62.6

[a]Trade area delegations are ranked in descending order of their support for the core position on the ten high-stress roll calls recorded during the 69th Congress (1925–27); see table 2.5.

[b]"Priv" indicates that a majority of the trade area delegation opposed the McNary-Haugen program (and, thus, supported the "private enterprise" alternative); "Gov" indicates that a majority of the delegation supported the McNary-Haugen program (and, thus, supported "government intervention" in the economy); *Split* indicates that the delegation divided evenly on the roll call.

SOURCE: Computations from roll call data.

The New Deal and the 74th Congress, 1935–1937

Of the ten high-stress, closely contested roll calls recorded in the 74th Congress, eight concerned the distributive benefits related to some aspect of public works policy or industrial subsidization. Specifically, two high-stress votes appeared on legislative consideration of a bill to administer and maintain the

Blue Ridge Parkway in Virginia and North Carolina, two roll calls were taken on the mechanism by which the seafood industry would pay for federal inspection of its products, and one high-stress vote was recorded on passage of public works legislation for the control of floods on the Mississippi River. Additional high-stress votes were registered upon passage of the rivers and harbors authorization bill, an amendment to include potatoes in the list of crops covered by the Agricultural Adjustment Act, and passage of the Merchant Marine Act. Only two of the ten high-stress roll calls had a focus broader than a particular economic sector or government activity. These occurred on a procedural motion related to a suit filed by Randolph Hearst against a Senate committee investigating lobbying activities surrounding passage of the public utility holding company bill and on an amendment to the veterans' bonus bill.

These high-stress roll calls were not confined to a few policy areas with a long political tradition and consistent sectional alignments, as had been the case in previous periods in American history. Instead, the regional implications of New Deal policies were often difficult to discern or predict and congressional alignments were probably more unstable, as a consequence, than at any other period in history. Two immediate results of this political instability were that the typical underlying pattern of sectionalism was less in evidence than in any of the other nine Congresses examined in this study and that the average level of sectional stress, reflecting the regional inconsistency of contemporary political coalitions, was extraordinarily low (see tables 2.5 and 2.6).

In many respects, the New Deal revolutionized the political system by creating an entirely new political economy. Before 1933, most public policies pitted the interests of northeastern capital against the economic imperatives of periphery agriculture and mineral production. Both major political parties represented sectional elites, and congressional politics reflected the incompatible interests of the core and periphery economies. The periphery party (the Democrats) only controlled Congress when it successfully exploited otherwise latent class conflict in the northern core, and, given the policy contradictions inherent in a periphery elite–lower-class core alliance, victory was normally short-lived. By transforming the political economy, the New Deal made possible a pluralistic system in which the core lower class, represented by organized labor, could permanently participate in the councils of the periphery party. As Ellis Hawley noted, this pluralist transformation was the artifact of government intervention in the economy:

> What had been an essentially monolithic economy in 1929, one dominated for the most part by the business-financial element, was being converted into something basically different, an economy of great countervailing forces in which organized groups fought each other for their respective shares of the national income and appealed to political power to aid them in this struggle. For agriculture the government had moved into the marketplace and by the use of public power had given the farm-

ers the advantages of corporate organization without forcing a collectivization of actual operations. For labor governmental intervention in the bargaining process had not been so complete, but labor organization and the growth of labor power were certainly encouraged to the extent that the Administration maintained a friendly attitude, established minimum standards, absorbed surplus labor, required recognition of unions, and restrained a number of employer practices that had been used to break unions in the past.[93]

Not only did federal intervention mold commercial agriculture and organized labor into political forces that could match the strength of high finance and industry, but the *way* in which the central government expanded peeled off one industrial sector after another from the previously monolithic core opposition to economic regulation. Ultimately, the economy of every region came to posess advantages that arose from some aspect of "positive" federal policy.

A major feature of the New Deal political economy was the decentralization of policy control. This decentralization assumed at least three forms:

1. federal-state arrangements in which the central government was often limited to fiscal support, and policy formulation was delegated to the states;
2. the proliferation of independent agencies designed to cater to and arbitrate economic conflict within circumscribed sectors of agriculture or industry with little sensitivity to "outside" pressure; and
3. the delegation of vast amounts of legislative power to executive agencies, which decentralized policy determination away from the floors of Congress and into the discretionary hands of the multitude of newly created or reorganized executive agencies.

"Cooperative federalism," the federal-state arrangement described above, allowed national policies to vary widely in response to differences in regional politics. For example, Section 14(b) of the Taft-Hartley Act allowed states to adopt "right to work" laws prohibiting enforcement of a union-shop contract. In practice, this provision meant that the pursuit of labor's goals in the North, which constituted a kind of class war in industrialized regions, did not spill over and disrupt elite hegemony in the southern periphery. The proliferation of federal agencies decentralized policy into discrete and narrowly defined sectors of the economy. The increasing scope of administrative discretion granted these agencies, as well as their limited missions, produced a regulatory politics of consensus within each policy arena: the purpose of government intervention became the maximization of economic advantage for regulated interests.

The institutional maturity of the congressional committee system provided a political counterpart to executive decentralization. By 1933, the seniority system was firmly entrenched in the assignment processes of both chambers and both political parties, and committee jurisdictions had been codified, once in 1907 by Asher Hinds and again, significantly, in 1936 by Representative Clarence Cannon of Missouri.[94] The heterogeneous interests of the New Deal coalition were filtered through the largely "self-selecting" procedures of committee assignment and ultimately reemerged in the distinct policy orbits of legislative panels. Very early in the New Deal, most committees became dominated by the interests that fell within the regulatory or distributive scopes of their respective jurisdictions. Interests that fell between the boundaries of competing jurisdictions, or were not powerful enough to "capture" a committee's attention, became increasingly "illegitimate" as the committee system developed strong norms of political reciprocity. Reciprocity between committees, which in practice meant that the members of committee majorities supported the position of other committee majorities during floor consideration, institutionalized "logrolling" among the interests represented in the various committees (and, broadly speaking, within the New Deal coalition). The viability of committee reciprocity, in turn, depended on the delegation of legislative authority. Discretionary statutes minimized the direct political costs of logrolling by couching federal policy in broad, ambiguous language which lacked *prima facie* regional implications. The rapid expansion of the federal government during the New Deal supported the development of a strong committee system by increasing the number of legislative opportunities for reciprocation and shortening the time intervening between the striking of a political "deal" and its consummation. By placing on the legislative agenda programs favored by almost every committee in Congress, most legislative panels acquired a stake in the New Deal explosion of governmental activity.

Given the class basis of their electoral support, northern Democrats clearly had an interest in expanding central government powers as a means of controlling "predatory" wealth. In some respects, the southern periphery elite shared labor's resentment of northern wealth, but congressmen from the South also feared a strong central government as a potential agent of intersectional "oppression." In the early years of the New Deal, however, the southern wing of the party supported Franklin Roosevelt's initiatives on the basis of four apparent motives: a desire to retain power as the majority party; the judgment that a political program limited in its benefits to the periphery would lead to defeat; the belief that Roosevelt's measures "represented a giant, nation-wide cornucopia from which federal aid poured into the desperately Depression-ridden South"; and an early belief that FDR's programs resembled Woodrow Wilson's New Freedom.[95]

In Roosevelt's first term, periphery congressmen felt they could control the administrative state being constructed by the New Deal coalition. They anticipated that its worst excesses would be limited to northern districts and directed against their most powerful political opponents, the core industrialists and financiers. As the price of their participation in the New Deal coalition, the southern wing requested a share of the "spoils" (which came to them more or less automatically through the operation of the committee system) and northern tolerance of race segregation in the periphery. Roosevelt himself was largely indifferent to civil rights measures because he felt that the political conflict they would produce would endanger high-priority legislation in other areas. It was also extremely doubtful that such measures could be enacted over a Senate filibuster.* The northern wing of the party, despite periodic and largely symbolic attempts to pass anti−poll tax or anti-lynching legislation, also generally tolerated segregation as a necessary political compromise. Building upon that tolerance, the New Deal coalition retained power until the civil rights movement split the party asunder thirty years later.

Two aspects of the New Deal period were particularly significant for the institutional development of the House of Representatives. The first was the rapid development of a strong committee system built upon "floor reciprocity," which paralleled the vast expansion of central government activity and an enormous increase in executive discretion. Before the Roosevelt era, floor references to congressional committee deliberations and appeals for roll call support for committee leaders were fairly uncommon, although public statements of the committee's "position" increased steadily in the years following the 1910 Cannon Revolt. Beginning in 1933, however, the committee position became a strong cue guiding the voting decisions of individual members. As such, it became a powerful competitor with administration preferences and party policy. In most cases, of course, the committee's position was still a reflection of partisan conflict within the government and nation. However, committee members increasingly deviated from the modal position of their respective parties as self-selection assignment processes altered the composition of individual committees in the direction of interested constituencies. The lengthening average tenure of members and stability of committee procedures encouraged political careers within legislative panels rather than the floor-oriented structure of party organizations. In addition, the rapid decline in party cohesion (under pressure from the heterogeneous constituent base of the New Deal coalition) encouraged the introduction of institutional norms such as floor reciprocity between the respective members of the different committees. During the New Deal these trends were still recent developments, and, as we shall see, the strong committee system that later emerged (particularly between 1947 and 1965) was as yet unfinished.

The second aspect of the New Deal which greatly affected the develop-

---

*Accounts sympathetic to Roosevelt emphasize that New Deal legislation generally had the effect of raising living and education standards for southern blacks and that Eleanor Roosevelt openly campaigned for civil rights legislation. However, ostensibly on constitutional grounds, Roosevelt failed to support even federal anti-lynching legislation which would have required the least federal intervention in southern mores and eliminated the most barbaric aspect of the race code. Friedel, *F.D.R. and the South*, pp. 81, 84−92, 86−97. See also John Frederick Martin, *Civil Rights and the Crisis of Liberalism: The Democratic Party, 1945−1976* (Boulder, Colo.: Westview Press, 1979), pp. 60−61.

ment of the House was the political adjustment of bipolar sectional conflict within the Democratic party. As Howard Odum described the region, the South was "essentially colonial in its economy" and entered the Great Depression possessing "the general status of an agricultural country engaged in trade with industrial countries."[96] George Tindall has elaborated on this theme by implicitly acknowledging the national core-periphery division of labor: "The South produced chiefly raw materials and industrial roughage for the market-oriented industries of the North, and as a primary producer remained in a dependent and tributary status, performing those functions that brought smaller rewards in a modern economy."[97] During the Depression, the "colonial economy" of the South was ravaged far beyond the comprehension of most contemporary northern residents. The prostrate condition of the periphery led its congressmen to support progressive taxation (which raised comparatively more revenue from core industrial regions) and vast relief programs (which, while they favored the North, still redistributed income to the South because they were financed through progressive tax schedules). On these policies, both the plantation elite and northern labor could agree. The opposition came from core elites represented by Republicans or, increasingly, from northeastern Democratic "conservatives."

But the New Deal, particularly after 1935, was also creating a strong central state. It was tying individual sectors of the private economy to government regulatory policy and subsidization and striking down constitutional limitations on federal power.[98] Periphery congressmen, quite rationally given their interests, viewed the rise of a strong central state with great alarm. They anticipated that the southern periphery could not consistently control the political institutions which influenced, if not dominated, the course of the central bureaucracy. In fact, the internal dynamics of the New Deal coalition demanded an ever-increasing scope for executive and bureaucratic discretion. At some point, this discretion reduced the ability of political institutions to influence the bureaucracy even with a strong committee system. Thus, although its congressmen might dominate the majority party, the southern periphery would always find the maintenance of majority status and regional policy influence somewhat contradictory goals. Furthermore, the emerging bureaucracy of the post–New Deal state was predictably recruited from core educational and corporate institutions.[99] The enrollment of Roosevelt appointees in the civil service after 1936 increased core dominance of the central, Washington-based bureaucracy by raising educational standards beyond the reach of the periphery's young adults (who were the product of an impoverished, substandard educational system) and by further reducing bureaucratic sensitivity to political influence.

The inability of the periphery to control national politics meant that this central bureaucracy would either fall under the influence of the northern wing of the Democratic party (the "left"), or pursue the interests of the core elite when Republicans captured the executive branch, or, in a perfectly balanced pluralistic system, remain indifferent to broad sectional alignments and favor narrowly defined special interests that came within the jurisdiction of individual agencies. A central state dominated by the Democratic left would, southern congressmen felt, destabilize the social caste system upon which the economic and political hegemony of the plantation elite was founded. The return of the Republican party to power would mean a renewal of economic exploitation of the southern periphery by the North and the dismantling of regionally redistributive taxation and public works policies. If anything, the party of the core elite would exact a higher tribute than the Democratic left (or so it seemed in 1933). In a balanced, pluralistic system, a professional bureaucracy would still constitute a long-term threat to the southern social system. Even where core working-class and elite interests could be effectively played off against one another, a politically active civil service would still support the elimination of regional diversity in policy implementation and the concentration of power in the hands of the central bureaucracy. The incremental application of national standards and the increasing implementation of public policy by the federal civil service could not avoid undermining the feudal organization of the southern economy; national programs, where they were centrally controlled, usually addressed the problems of an industrial, progressive society and did not mesh well with the agrarian structure of the South. Thus, while the process would take longer under the scenario of a neutral bureaucracy, all three future projections of the New Deal state seemed to imply the end of race segregation and at least some deterioration in the political hegemony of the plantation elite.

The sectional wings of the Democratic party entered the Roosevelt era with very different policy goals, and one of the major tasks of the party leadership was to construct a policy "process" which could satisfy both factions. The southern periphery desperately needed an enormous infusion of federal relief money. Southern congressmen preferred that this regional redistribution of wealth be administered either by temporary executive fiat (e.g., Harry Hopkins's Works Progress Administration) or by decentralized programs that relied on state or local organizations (e.g., the Rural Electrification Administration). By contrast, the northern wing of the party wanted permanent, national programs to protect organized labor and other lower-class core groups and minorities from a resurgent industrial and financial elite. A central bureaucracy located beyond the reach of potentially unsympathetic state governments also allowed core working classes to exploit the national strength of their periphery alliance.

Both factions wished to maintain the majority status of the party in Congress. Given the competing interests of their party colleagues from the North, turning the New Deal coalition into a permanent alliance meant that southern members would have to support at least some of the policy goals of organized labor. However, explicit resort to logrolling and compromise to resolve all policy disagreements between the two wings of the Democratic

Table 4.6. The New Deal, the Committee System, and High Sectional Stress, 1933–1939

Trade area[a]	Amendment— National Industrial Recovery Act (May 26, 1933)	Patman Bonus Bill (Mar. 22, 1935)	Merchant Marine Act (June 27, 1935)	Recommit Wage and Hour Bill (Dec. 17, 1937)	Amendment— Works Progress Administration (Feb. 2, 1939)	Amendment— Agricultural Parity Payments (Mar. 28, 1939)
Philadelphia	Comm	Comm	Comm	Comm	Comm	Comm
Boston	Comm	Comm	Comm	Floor	Comm	Comm
Cincinnati	Comm	Comm	Comm	Comm	Comm	Comm
Detroit	Comm	Comm	Floor	Floor	Comm	Comm
Cleveland	Comm	Comm	Floor	Comm	Comm	Comm
New York	Comm	Comm	Comm	Comm	Comm	Comm
Chicago	Floor	Floor	Floor	Comm	Comm	Comm
Kansas City	Floor	Floor	Floor	Floor	Comm	Floor
Louisville	Floor	Comm	Floor	Floor	Floor	Comm
Indianapolis	Comm	Comm	Floor	Comm	Comm	Comm
Minneapolis	Floor	Floor	Floor	Comm	Comm	Floor
St. Louis	Floor	Comm	Floor	Floor	Comm	Floor
Richmond	Comm	Comm	Comm	Floor	Floor	Floor
San Francisco	Comm	Comm	Comm	Floor	Comm	*Split*
Baltimore	Comm	Floor	Comm	Comm	Comm	Comm
Birmingham	Floor	Comm	Comm	Floor	Floor	Floor
Atlanta	Floor	Floor	Floor	Floor	Floor	Floor
Dallas	Floor	Floor	Floor	Floor	Floor	Floor
Pittsburgh	Comm	Floor	Comm	Comm	Comm	Comm
Denver	Floor	*Split*	Floor	Floor	Comm	Floor
New Orleans	Floor	Floor	Comm	Floor	Floor	Floor
Memphis	Floor	Comm	Floor	Floor	Floor	Floor
Committee Position	Yea	Nay	Yea	Nay	Yea	Nay
Outcome	Yea	Yea	Yea	Yea	Yea	Nay
Sectional Stress	84.0	43.5	59.1	45.5	71.4	61.2

[a] Trade area delegations are ranked in descending order of their support for the core position on the ten high-stress roll calls recorded during the 74th Congress (1935–36); see table 2.5.

[b] "Comm" indicates that a majority of the trade area delegation supported the position taken by a majority of the committee members reporting the legislation to the floor; "Floor" indicates that the delegation opposed the position taken by the committee members; *Split* indicates that the delegation divided evenly on the roll call.

SOURCE: Computations from roll call data.

party would have entailed prohibitive bargaining costs. In effect, a strong committee system reduced the bargaining costs necessary to the maintenance of the New Deal coalition. Combined with decreasing party cohesion and the pluralistic pursuit of legislative goals, the committee system made the emergence of monolithic and uncompromising sectional blocs within the Democratic party much less likely than it would have been otherwise. One of the most interesting aspects of the developing committee system with its emphasis on logrolling and compromise was its demoralizing effect on the Republican minority. While Republicans throughout the period attempted to split the New Deal coalition by exploiting latent sectional divisions, their efforts usually foundered on the shoals of floor reciprocity or executive discretion.

New Deal Roll Call Analysis and Description

In order to demonstrate the interplay of sectional conflict and the dynamics of the committee system during the New Deal period, all roll calls of "high visibility" public policies (unemployment relief, minimum wage legislation, etc.) in which substantial opposition (greater than 40 percent) appeared have been examined. These roll calls were divided into two groups: those possessing the highest and lowest sectional stress scores. With few exceptions, the votes included in tables 4.6 and 4.7 represent the greatest and least sectionally polarized contested roll calls recorded between 1933 and 1939. The few omissions are in the interest of a wider sampling of policy types and an even chronological distribution. Some roll calls, such as those on anti-lynching legislation, are not treated here because they are covered in other chapters. Before generalizing the results of this analysis, some discussion of the individual roll calls is in order, beginning with the six high-stress votes.

On May 26, 1933, the floor manager of what became the National Industrial Recovery Act offered an amendment to the public works portion of the bill. Sponsored by a majority of the committee, the amendment altered the formula under which federal subsidies for state construction of public roads would be allocated. Since 1916, the Federal Bureau of Roads had distributed subsidies to the states in proportion to: (1) their comparative population (one-third of total appropriations); (2) their total land area (one-third); and (3) their total road mileage (also one-third). The committee amendment proposed to alter the formula to one-fourth area, one-fourth mileage, and one-half population. Since the amendment changed no other provision of the bill or existing law, the change suggested by the committee did nothing more than reallocate federal subsidies toward states which possessed greater population density and urbanization.[100] Under the amendment, for example, New York, Pennsylvania, Illinois, and Massachusetts would have gained a total of thirteen million dollars. Montana, Texas, and Nevada would have been the biggest losers.

The roll call which ensued on the amendment produced one of the highest levels of sectional stress in the last century (84.0). The floor supported the

Table 4.7. The New Deal, the Committee System, and Low Sectional Stress, 1933–1939

Trade area[a]	Amendment—Unemployment Relief (April 21, 1933)	Death Sentence—Public Utility Holding Co. Act (Aug. 22, 1935)	Passage—Reconstruction Finance Corp. (Mar. 19, 1936)	Recommit Frazier—Lemke (May 13, 1936)	Amendment—C.C.C. (May 12, 1937)	Amendment—Emergency Relief Appropriations (June 1, 1937)
Philadelphia	Comm	Comm	Floor	Comm	Floor	Floor
Boston	Comm	Comm	Comm	Comm	Comm	Comm
Cincinnati	Split	Comm	Comm	Comm	Split	Floor
Detroit	Floor	Comm	Floor	Floor	Comm	Comm
Cleveland	Comm	Floor	Comm	Split	Comm	Comm
New York	Floor	Comm	Comm	Comm	Floor	Floor
Chicago	Floor	Comm	Comm	Comm	Floor	Floor
Kansas City	Floor	Split	Floor	Floor	Floor	Comm
Louisville	Floor	Split	Comm	Comm	Floor	Floor
Indianapolis	Floor	Floor	Comm	Comm	Floor	Floor
Minneapolis	Comm	Floor	Floor	Floor	Comm	Comm
St. Louis	Floor	Floor	Comm	Comm	Floor	Floor
Richmond	Floor	Floor	Comm	Comm	Floor	Split
San Francisco	Comm	Floor	Comm	Floor	Split	Floor
Baltimore	Floor	Floor	Floor	Comm	Floor	Comm
Birmingham	Floor	Floor	Comm	Comm	Floor	Comm
Atlanta	Floor	Floor	Comm	Comm	Floor	Comm
Dallas	Floor	Floor	Comm	Floor	Floor	Floor
Pittsburgh	Split	Floor	Comm	Split	Floor	Floor
Denver	Floor	Floor	Comm	Split	Floor	Split
New Orleans	Floor	Floor	Comm	Split	Floor	Floor
Memphis	Floor	Floor	Comm	Comm	Floor	Comm
Committee Position	Nay	Nay	Yea	Nay	Nay	Yea
Outcome	Yea	Yea	Yea	Nay	Yea	Nay
Sectional Stress	34.8	33.1	35.4	35.9	30.4	35.7

[a] Trade area delegations are ranked in descending order of their support for the core position on the ten high-stress roll calls recorded during the 74th Congress (1935–36); see table 2.5.

[b] "Comm" indicates that a majority of the trade area delegation supported the position taken by a majority of the committee members reporting the legislation to the floor; "Floor" indicates that the delegation opposed the position taken by the committee members; Split indicates that the delegation divided evenly on the roll call.

SOURCE: Computations from roll call data.

Table 4.8. Voting on the National Industrial Recovery Act: Change in the Road Money Formula, May 26, 1933

Member's State Gains from Change in Formula:

	Total	Trade Area Position	
		Same	Different
Members Voting with State	222 (90.6%)	218 (98.2%)	4 (1.8%)
Members Voting against State	23 (9.4%)	16 (69.6%)	7 (30.4%)

Member's State Loses from Change in Formula:

	Total	Trade Area Position	
		Same	Different
Members Voting with State	158 (100.0%)	143 (90.5%)	15 (9.5%)
Members Voting against State	0	0	0

Summary

	Committee Majority	State's Interest	Trade Area Position
Members Supporting	222 (55.1%)	380 (94.3%)	377 (93.5%)
Members Opposing	181 (44.9%)	23 (5.7%)	26 (6.5%)

SOURCES: Data describing the effect of the formula change taken from the *Congressional Record*, 73:1:4365–66, May 26, 1933. Computations from roll call data.

committee majority (222 to 181) and the amendment passed. Interestingly, a majority of the Ways and Means Committee Democrats opposed the new formula (7 to 8) while the Republicans on the panel supported the change (7 to 2). Almost all members (94 percent of the total membership, 96 percent of the committee) voted according to the interests of their respective states (see table 4.8). The Kentucky and Alabama delegations, whose states stood to gain trivial amounts if the formula were changed but who voted against the amendment, accounted for most of the deviants from this pattern. The deviant Kentucky members seem to have followed the lead of their colleague on the Ways and Means Committee, who also voted against the amendment. Overall, the very high sectional stress score was primarily a by-product of the almost universal loyalty of members to their states' interests in the formula and the fact that high population density was a demographic characteristic shared by core industrial regions to the exclusion of southern and western trade areas. Even though the committee position prevailed, the roll call pattern reveals little evidence of floor reciprocity. Indeed, when members deviated from the interest of their constituents it was to vote for the committee *minority*, not the majority. In this case, the absence of reciprocity seems to have been a product of the extremely high electoral costs of compromise. The regional implications of a voting stand were explicit and undiluted by any other issue. Thus, the committee's victory was due to the calculated design of the formula change, which benefited states containing a majority of the total membership.

On March 22, 1935, the House of Representatives chose between two alternative plans for the immediate payment of a "bonus" to veterans of the First World War. A veterans' bonus had been established in 1924 by legislation which "equalized" the wages of men in uniform with the income of those who remained in civilian life during the war. The bonus was deferred through the creation of a life-insurance policy which was to mature in 1945. During the Depression Congress made several attempts to enact legislation which would convert these insurance policies into an immediate cash payment. On both occasions President Roosevelt vetoed the "bonus" bill, but on the second override attempt the bonus bill's supporters were victorious.[101] The vote included in table 4.6 was one of the ten high-stress, closely contested roll calls recorded in the 74th Congress (1935–37) and involved a choice between a payment scheme sponsored by Representative Wright Patman of Texas (a Democrat who decades later would become chairman of the House Banking and Currency Committee) and a plan supported by the majority of the Ways and Means Committee.

Briefly stated, the Patman scheme would have authorized the printing of new currency in an amount sufficient to immediately pay the veteran the full value of his bonus. Supporters of Patman's alternative favored the "inflationary" impact that the scheme would have had on the national economy and derided the Ways and Means plan as a sop to the nation's bankers. While Patman himself tried to sidestep the inflationary charge, he openly acknowledged his ideological antipathy to the financial community:

> The puppets and hirelings of Wall Street call it an inflationary bill, because they are trying to mislead the people. Our bill does step on the big bankers' toes, I will admit that. It will cause $2,000,000,000 to be placed in circulation, upon which no one will be paying interest, and probably cause the withdrawal of $2,000,000,000 of big bankers' money that has been issued to the bankers free of charge and upon which someone is paying interest every day it is outstanding.[102]

Patman's supporters remembered the nineteenth-century battle over the free coinage of silver and the continuing struggle of the "people" against the "money trust." A pacifist congressman who had served in the prewar Congress and returned with the New Deal, Democrat Finly Gray of Indiana, bridged the historical gap between agrarian populism and Depression-spawned radicalism in his defense of the "printing-press" amendment:

> . . . the money illusion, taking advantage of the power of money, operating, hidden, covered, and concealed, to transfer wealth and property from one class to another, is the most gigantic and colossal fraud which men have ever invented to take from their fellow men.
>
> Some day the people will learn of the truth and the facts of this gigantic and colossal fraud perpetrated and imposed upon them, how the manipulating financiers have been and still are collecting billions from

them as interest for the use of their own money. And then they will rise up in righteous wrath . . . they will throw off the forms of government and ignore the orders of peace and civil life. And they will drive the money changers from the temple by force and fire, and if the misers and Shylocks still stubbornly stand out and resist hiding behind the puppet rulers, as they have been sheltered in the past, they will storm the temples of government and one stone will not lie upon another.*

The legislation sponsored by the Ways and Means Committee, called the Vinson bill after author Fred Vinson of Kentucky, provided for payment of the bonus through the issuance of new debt in the form of interest-bearing bonds. Supporters argued that the committee bill was "fiscally sound" and "noninflationary"; opponents emphasized that interest payments would flow through to the financial community and burden the government with "unnecessary subsidies" to unearned wealth. Since both sides supported immediate payment of the bonus, the only issue decided by the March 22, 1935, roll call was the method of payment and the broader question of federal fiscal policy. Generally speaking, trade area delegations from the industrial and commercial core supported the fiscal conservatism of the committee alternative while the traditionally populist regions of the agrarian periphery held to the inflationary promise of Patman's amendment. The Patman substitute prevailed on a very close vote (207 to 204), but the legislation was lost when the Senate failed to override the first Roosevelt veto of bonus payments.

While inflation and relief programs represented the periphery's response to the Depression, the core increasingly turned to government regulation and subsidies. The Patman substitute was typical of a temporary, nonbureaucratic extension of state power; by contrast, the Merchant Marine Act of 1935 symbolized the permanent, bureaucratic intervention in the economy favored by the industrial regions. The Merchant Marine Act required that three-quarters of all crew members on United States vessels be American citizens. It also prescribed hours and working conditions, and created the U.S. Maritime Commission to distribute operating and construction subsidies to owners of American fleets.[103] On June 27, 1935, the House passed the legislation in a very close contest (194 to 186), even though members of the Merchant Marine Committee favored the bill by a four-to-one margin. This roll call, like the bonus bill, was one of the ten high-stress, closely contested votes recorded in the 74th Congress. However, the sectional alignment clearly deviated from

---

***Congressional Record*, 74:1:4223, March 21, 1935. Representative Glenn Griswold, also from the Indiana delegation, restated Gray's argument later the same day: "Under the Vinson bill you pay to the money changers a premium. You fill the coffers of the bondholders so that they will smile while you pay the obligation of the Nation to the men who gave their lives, their health, and well-being to their country. By the Vinson bill you will plunder the whole taxpaying public and do it in the name of those who sleep in foreign battlefields and toss on the beds of American hospitals." Ibid., p. 4233.

the historical core-periphery pattern. Every trade area delegation which centered on a major seaport supported the bill (Philadelphia, Boston, New York,
San Francisco, Baltimore, and New Orleans), but most interior regions opposed passage. Those interior delegations that supported the maritime program (e.g., Richmond, Birmingham, and Pittsburgh) often followed the lead
of trade area colleagues on the committee. While this roll call reveals some
evidence of reciprocity and the outcome supported the committee position, a
majority of non-committee members voted against the act (182 to 179).

A leading congressional history of the New Deal called the December 17, 1937, roll call to recommit the Wage and Hour bill "the clearest
indication of sectional divisions of any vote to that time."[104] While James
Patterson, the author, perhaps exaggerated the depth of sectional conflict
(compare sectional stress scores on the road formula, bonus bill amendment,
and Merchant Marine Act, for example), the struggle over enactment of the
Wage and Hour bill foreshadowed the development of a conservative coalition
between Republicans and southern Democrats and confirmed some of the
worst apprehensions of the periphery with reference to the permanent expansion of federal regulatory power. The legislation proposed the creation of a Fair
Labor Standards Board with discretionary power over the wages and hours of
labor but which would aim, over a period of years, at a wage "floor" of forty
cents an hour and a limit of forty hours a week. Work beyond the forty-hour
week would be compensated at time and a half. The bill also prohibited child
labor.[105]

Congressmen from the southern periphery opposed the Wage and Hour
bill as a "northern industrialist–inspired attempt to reduce the cost advantages of growing southern competitors."[106] These members offered several justifications for the comparatively low wage scales that prevailed throughout the
South. To begin with, periphery representatives claimed that living costs were
generally lower in the South and workers could therefore live equally well on a
lower wage. In addition, southern spokesmen asserted that discriminatory
freight rates maintained through federal regulation retarded regional industrialization, and a relatively lower wage scale was the only compensating response southern industry could make. Furthermore, given the competitive
situation, artificially higher wages would restrict economic development and
thus prolong and intensify southern poverty. Finally, the historical resentment
felt by the southern periphery for its subordinate position within the national
economy intensified congressional suspicions concerning the purpose and impact of federal regulation. As Paul Mertz has written,

> A corollary of the New South idea in the 1930s was that the region's
> economy was "colonial." Its industries were owned and managed by
> outside capital. Since the promoters of industrialism assumed that plen-
> tiful resources assured economic development, they focused on this con-
> dition to explain why the South's backwardness persisted. At first they

stressed that the section produced mostly raw materials and semi-processed goods which were finished in the North. Thus the profits from manufacturing accrued to outsiders and the South paid high prices to buy items made from its own products. By the late 1930s the concept of a colonial economy expanded as many concluded that national policies hindered the South's industrial progress.[107]

To Democrat Wade Hampton Kitchens of Arkansas, for example, it seemed that there were "lurking and concealed objectives in this bill which to me appear selfish, sectional, dicriminatory, and destructive to small industrial plants and their labor to the great advantage of the large monopolistic plants." He went on to say:

> Nor am I able to forget that the large industries and their labor in certain sections have been fostered and protected by tariffs and cheaper freight rates at the expense of all other labor, farmers, and other consumers, and thereby have been given special privileges and financial favors not enjoyed by others. This bill, as I see it, will operate to create and foster further centralization and monopoly rather than decentralization of industry.[108]

From the other side of the aisle, Republican John M. Robsion of Kentucky, who represented an impoverished Appalachian district, strongly condemned the bill:

> It is born out of sectional feeling and jealousy. The proponents, in some of the sections of the North and East, do not disguise their purpose. They claim it will stop the movement of industries, factories, mills, and shops in the North and East, and force those that have gone South to go out of business or go back to the North and East.[109]

After the Wage and Hour bill was favorably reported by the Committee on Labor (only three members of which represented southern constituencies while nine of twenty-one were drawn from the Northeast), southern congressmen on the Rules Committee refused to permit floor consideration. In response, the Democratic leadership of the House, with strong support from the administration, filed a discharge petition which, when finally signed by 218 members, brought the legislation to the floor over the objections of the Rules Committee.* During the campaign which accompanied the discharge

---

*According to Walter J. Heacock, "One observer called the seventeen-day struggle to secure the necessary 218 signatures 'one of the hardest and hottest behind-the-scenes battles the members had witnessed in years.' With the full support of the President, the leaders used every conceivable means to gain signatures, including committee appointments and 'trades' on the basis of other legislation." "William B. Bankhead and the New Deal," *Journal of Southern History* 31:3 (August 1955): 356. Citing public accounts of political pressure and explicit logrolling, Republican Hamilton Fish of New York urged the House to investigate improper influence

effort, representatives from agrarian districts were urged to sign the Wage and Hour petition in return for labor and urban support for a pending farm bill.[110] But the agrarian-labor bargain lasted only long enough to bring the bill to the floor. In the end, twenty-eight congressmen who had signed the petition subsequently voted to recommit the measure to the Committee on Labor and the bill was killed (216 to 198).*

On the December 17, 1937, recommittal motion, the Committee on Labor opposed recommittal by a three-to-one margin (16 to 5). Partisan divisions dominated the panel, with Republicans supporting the motion (4 to 1) and Democrats in opposition (15 to 1). However, the partisan split was less pronounced in the voting of non-committee members. Congressmen from states with prevailing wages below forty cents an hour for unskilled labor voted to recommit the Wage and Hour bill by a margin of nearly nine to one (89.7 percent; see table 4.9). Only two of the seventy-eight members from these states (Arizona, New Mexico, and the states of the former Confederacy minus Texas) were Republicans. Fifty-four percent of voting congressmen from states with wage scales in the middle range (forty-one to fifty cents an hour) opposed recommittal. Members from periphery areas in the middle range (e.g., Texas) voted to kill the bill, and members from regions bordering the core opposed recommittal. Thus members from districts with an unclear direct interest in the legislation tended to associate with one or two broad poles of the underlying sectional alignment. As a result, 79 percent of these members supported the position taken by a majority of their trade areas delegation.

----

during congressional deliberations. According to Fish, Democrat Martin Dies of Texas publicly claimed "That they have swapped everything today but the Capitol. . . . They promised so much there won't be anything left for the federal government," and Democrat A. Willis Robertson of Virginia was reputed to have said that "reprisals are openly threatened." *Congressional Record*, 75:2:759, December 2, 1937.

*According to James T. Patterson, this was "the most smashing defeat Roosevelt had ever received in the House." *Congressional Conservatism and the New Deal*, p. 195. Democratic Representative John J. O'Connor of New York City, during discussion on a special order for another farm measure, exaggerated the extent of metropolitan-rural cooperation while outlining its history: "We Members from the North and from New York, for instance, from the metropolitan areas, have been fairly consistent in voting in favor of farm bills. As a matter of fact, from the days of the McNary-Haugen bill there have been few farm bills which would have passed this House if it had not been for the support of the Members from the North and especially by getting sufficient votes from New York. For instance, I remember just at the close of the first session of the Congress, when a cotton bill was under consideration and it became necessary to change enough votes to pass that bill. We got enough changes from New York and the surrounding territory to pass the bill. The McNary-Haugen bill was passed by votes from New York, just a handful. The Bankhead cotton bill was passed by just a few votes from New York. Of course, at those times we had certain assurances of reciprocity. For instance, at the time in the closing days of the first session of this Congress when some of us stood at this door to the Speaker's lobby and got the votes necessary to pass the cotton bill, we had pretty definite assurances that we would get considerable help from a certain section of this country on the wage and hour bill. History records the result of that hard and fast agreement." *Congressional Record*, 75:3:1651, February 8, 1938.

Table 4.9. Voting on the Wage and Hour Bill: Motion to Recommit, December 17, 1937

State Entrance Wage for Common Laborers at or below $.40/Hour:

	Total	Trade Area Position	
		Same	Different
Members Voting to Recommit	70 (89.7%)	65 (92.9%)	5 (7.1%)
Members Voting to Consider	8 (10.3%)	3 (37.5%)	5 (62.5%)

State Entrance Wage for Common Laborers between $.41 and .50/Hour:

	Total	Trade Area Position	
		Same	Different
Members Voting to Consider	28 (45.9%)	17 (60.7%)	11 (39.3%)
Members Voting to Recommit	33 (54.1%)	31 (93.9%)	2 (6.1%)

State Entrance Wage for Common Laborers at or above $.51/Hour:

	Total	Trade Area Position	
		Same	Different
Members Voting to Consider	162 (58.9%)	135 (83.3%)	27 (16.7%)
Members Voting to Recommit	113 (41.1%)	51 (45.1%)	62 (54.9%)

Summary

	Committee Majority	State's Interest[a]	Trade Area Position
Members Supporting	198 (47.8%)	260 (62.8%)	302 (72.9%)
Members Opposing	216 (52.2%)	154 (37.2%)	112 (27.1%)

[a] "State's Interest" defined as a vote to recommit for members that represent states with an entrance wage below $.41/hour and as a vote to consider for members from states with an entrance wage above $.40/hour.

SOURCES: Data on prevailing wages taken from "Geographic Classification of Average Hourly Entrance Rates of Adult Male Common Laborers, in 20 Industries, July 1937," compiled by the Bureau of Labor Statistics of the United States Department of Labor and inserted in the *Appendix* to the *Congressional Record*, 75:2:505–6, December 17, 1937. Computations from roll call data.

Wage rates were highest in the Northeast, industrial Midwest, and Pacific Coast states. In states where the prevailing wage exceeded fifty-one cents an hour, 59 percent of the members opposed recommittal. However, in these states, as was true for the Labor Committee, there was a pronounced partisan division which reflected internal class cleavages, and partisanship reduced support for the "state's interest." Though a substantial minority of core Republicans favored the Wage and Hour bill, political conflict over passage in the industrial regions was essentially a contest between labor and capital. Early in the following year, the Democratic leadership again filed a discharge petition to sidestep the Rules Committee, and the bill became law in June 1938.

In their fight against a national minimum wage, periphery congressmen had argued that the lower cost of living in their districts justified a lower wage rate. However, when the House of Representatives considered regional wage

differentials within the Works Progress Administration, these same congressmen argued that variation in the cost of living should not be used as a
benchmark for the allocation of relief funds. Core congressmen, on the other
hand, argued for one national wage standard for private enterprise (the Wage
and Hour bill) but insisted that regional differences in living standards be
reflected in WPA (government) wages. For most of the New Deal, WPA wage
rates varied enormously from one section of the country to another but were
generally far higher in core industrial areas than in the agrarian periphery for
all categories of labor:

> WPA wage rates differed according to classification of workers—un-
> skilled, intermediate, skilled, and professional or technical; according to
> four national regions; and according to the degree of urbanization of the
> particular county within the region . . . after 1935, differentials against
> the South were lessened by the requirement of Congress that distinction
> in wage rates for similar work in various sections of the country should
> not be greater than could be justified by differences in the cost of liv-
> ing. . . . Probably more influential than any scrutiny of relative costs of
> living was the willingness of national relief authorities to take as an
> empirical guide the lower *level* of living in the South.[111]

In 1938, WPA rates for unskilled labor ranged from a low of 23 cents an hour
in South Carolina to a high of 67.5 cents in Indiana.*

---

*David L. Potter, *Congress and the Waning of the New Deal* (Port Washington, N.Y.:
Kennikat Press, 1980), pp. 66, 69. The WPA relief program was also difficult to integrate with
the seasonal demands of the plantation economy of the South: "cotton farmers, and growers of
other crops as well, were 'quite brazen' in their demands for relief curtailment during crop
seasons. Planters frequently complained of labor shortages to their congressmen. . . . The relief
establishment felt constrained to accommodate these demands, especially in the cotton belt."
Mertz, *New Deal Policy and Southern Rural Poverty*, p. 49. WPA administrators attempted to
balance the competing goals of economic relief, on the one hand, and the labor requirements of
the plantation system, on the other (p. 235). See also Patterson, *Congressional Conservatism and
the New Deal*, pp. 144–45.

The roll call pattern reveals little evidence of reciprocity in that only three members from
low-wage states supported the committee but, unlike the road allocation formula of 1933, trade
area cohesion was greater than the loyalty of members to the interests of their individual states.
Almost the entire difference arose from the tendency of congressmen in the middle ranges
(thirty-one to fifty cents an hour) to align with their trade area. Given that the Tarver amendment limited variation to a *range* of wage scales within which, probably, most of these states
already fell, most members in the two middle categories probably represented districts not
directly affected by the amendment. These members tilted toward both their trade area delegations and the committee position. Sectional stress on the roll call was extremely high (71.4) and
followed the normal, bipolar alignment.

These wage rates represent an average of "high" and "low" scales for individual states as
provided in a table, "Average Earnings per Worker per Month on WPA State Programs, September, October, November, 1938," inserted in the *Congressional Record*, 76:1:1084–85, February 2, 1939. Average wages in Arkansas, Florida, Georgia, North Carolina, and Tennessee (in

On February 2, 1939, during consideration of an appropriations bill, Democrat Malcolm C. Tarver of Georgia offered an amendment which would have limited regional variation in WPA wages for the same class of work to a maximum of 25 percent. Because the national WPA average hourly rate was unknown and, in any case, would have varied across different classifications of labor (with varying regional implications), the exact point or threshold at which individual districts would have benefited from the Tarver amendment can not be determined. However, states receiving WPA wages at or below thirty cents an hour clearly would have benefited, and their representatives overwhelmingly supported the limitation (96.7 percent; see table 4.10). States at or above forty-one cents an hour certainly would have lost relief funds; their representatives opposed the amendment by a margin of nearly nine to one (88.9 percent). Congressmen from states falling in the middle range (31 to 40 cents an hour) split on the amendment, although a substantial majority, 80 percent, supported the position adopted by their trade area delegation. The Appropriations Committee opposed the Tarver amendment by a small margin (19 to 14) and the full House supported the committee (252 to 140).

On March 28, 1939, Democrat Clarence Cannon of Missouri proposed an amendment to an agriculture appropriations bill which led to another high-stress roll call (table 4.6). Splitting the Committee on Appropriations evenly (19 to 19) and losing narrowly in the full House (191 to 204), the amendment would have provided 250 million dollars for parity payments to wheat, cotton, corn, rice, and tobacco producers under the Agricultural Adjustment Act of 1938.[112] In many respects (e.g., the list of eligible commodities and the notion of parity) the second Agricultural Adjustment Act resembled the McNary-Haugen proposal of a decade earlier, and the sectional alignment on the parity amendment was remarkably similar. Although the amendment failed, logrolling between urban and rural Democrats reminded contemporary observers of the 1937 farm and Wage and Hour bills. In 1939, many of these same members traded support on parity payments (rural) and relief appropriations (urban-core).[113] Three months later, on June 22, 1939, ten congressmen from New York City, Chicago, and Boston crossed over to support a second attempt to add the Cannon amendment, and the appropriation passed.[114]

Even on the six low-stress roll calls (table 4.7), sectional overtones colored the debate and influenced voting. Two of these low-stress roll calls (an amendment to an unemployment relief measure in 1933 and an amendment to a Civilian Conservation Corps bill in 1937) occurred over the coverage of agency personnel by civil service regulations. In both cases, the legislative committee favored civil service coverage and the floor replaced the committee

---

addition to South Carolina) were all at or below twenty-five cents an hour. Those in Illinois, Massachusetts, Montana, and Wisconsin were all at or above sixty cents an hour.

Table 4.10. Voting on the Works Progress Administration: Striking Amendment to Narrow Regional Wage Differences, February 2, 1939

Average W.P.A. Hourly Wage for Unskilled Labor:
$.30 and under (state average)

		Trade Area Position	
	Total	Same	Different
Members Supporting Amendment	3 (3.3%)	0 (0.0%)	3 (100.0%)
Members Opposing Amendment	87 (96.7%)	84 (96.6%)	3 (3.4%)

$.31 to .40 (state average)

		Trade Area Position	
	Total	Same	Different
Members Supporting Amendment	40 (60.6%)	38 (95.0%)	2 (5.0%)
Members Opposing Amendment	26 (39.4%)	15 (57.7%)	11 (42.3%)

$.41 to .50 (state average)

		Trade Area Position	
	Total	Same	Different
Members Supporting Amendment	100 (84.0%)	99 (99.0%)	1 (1.0%)
Members Opposing Amendment	19 (16.0%)	7 (36.8%)	12 (63.2%)

$.50 and above (state average)

		Trade Area Position	
	Total	Same	Different
Members Supporting Amendment	109 (93.2%)	109 (100.0%)	0 (0.0%)
Members Opposing Amendment	8 (6.8%)	0 (0.0%)	8 (100.0%)

Summary

	Committee Majority	State's Interest[a]	Trade Area Position
Members Supporting	252 (64.3%)	322 (82.1%)	352 (89.8%)
Members Opposing	140 (35.7%)	70 (17.9%)	40 (10.2%)

[a] "State's Interest" defined as a vote for the amendment for members that represented states with an average W.P.A. wage below $.41/hour and as a vote against the amendment for members from states with an average wage above $.40/hour.

SOURCE: State wage rates represent an average of "high" and "low" scales for individual states as provided in "Average Earnings per Worker per Month on W.P.A. State Programs, September, October, November, 1938," *Congressional Record*, 76:1:1084–85, February 2, 1939. Computations from roll call data.

requirement with non–civil service "patronage" employment. Republicans, both on and off the respective committees, almost unanimously opposed patronage. House Democrats were badly split, with a tendency for periphery members to support patronage and core representatives to favor civil service regulations. Partisan considerations, reinforced by the core base of the party, clearly motivated Republicans. The opposition party wanted to minimize the political and administrative resources available to a Democratic president. Core Democrats were influenced by somewhat contradictory motives. Many would have liked to maximize Roosevelt's patronage opportunities (a goal FDR himself supported),* but civil service regulations tended to increase the prospects for permanent retention of New Deal agencies once the economic emergency passed. They also favored the well-educated middle class of the industrial-commercial core over the impoverished periphery.

Although southern congressmen were not unanimously opposed to civil service requirements, most supported the patronage alternative. As Claude Fuller of Arkansas noted when he offered a patronage amendment to the 1933 unemployment relief bill, a politically independent bureaucracy was apt to be manned by "outsiders" and civil service provisions appeared to be sponsored by self-interested federal employees:

> To my amazement and surprise, in a case where it provides for a dole or charity to help the unemployed, the Civil Service employees have inserted a clause here providing that this law shall be administered by them . . . we would have to call in the Civil Service to administer this law back in our county, back in our towns in the State from which we come.†

Southerners tended to agree with Democrat Charles Faddis of Pennsylvania, who emphasized the seemingly "permanent" aspects of civil service employment and a career bureaucracy's indifference to political influence. As Faddis offered the amendment, he noted that it had

---

*These competing considerations were well understood by all major political actors. "The President . . . seldom disapproved congressional exemptions of newly created alphabetical agencies from the classified service. As these exemptions increased, the jobs proliferated and the appointive power of the President was accordingly greatly expanded. In the same manner as Wilson, Roosevelt rewarded and punished to support his social program and to bind together the discordant party he had inherited. The nature of the emergency was probably the essential moving force behind the unusual subservience of Congress in 1933. Nevertheless, the patronage was used for all it was worth to further the President's aims. Its importance can be gauged by the concerted and successful efforts of Congress to prevent the extension of the merit system during the middle thirties." Paul P. Van Riper, *History of the United States Civil Service* (Evanston, Illinois: Row, Peterson, 1958), p. 320.

†*Congressional Record*, 72:1:2121–22, April 21, 1933. Paul Van Riper also emphasized the influence of this factor on periphery attitudes: "A completely competitive and nonpolitical federal or state civil service in which a Negro might reach a place of power and prominence could not be considered. Moreover, a non-political federal bureaucracy, not subject to checks by southern senators and congressmen, might endanger the political stability of the area." *History of the United States Civil Service*, p. 334.

the effect of striking out the civil service provisions in connection with
this act. . . . I am not yet ready to vote to perpetuate a bureaucracy with
the inevitable tendency of bureaucracy to create reasons to continue its
own existence when the emergency has passed. . . . The civil service has
a high disregard and utmost contempt for the provisions of laws passed
by Congress. . . . We must regulate them, or they, instead of the electorate, will govern this nation.[115]

Finally, most southern Democrats, like many of their party colleagues in the
North, favored patronage as a partisan resource and would have supported civil
service provisions if a Republican had occupied the White House. Unlike their
northern counterparts, however, many periphery members much preferred
decentralized relief programs to bureaucracy-intensive, central government
policies.[116] As a result of all these factors, support for civil service coverage was
limited to a few badly divided core delegations and trade areas in traditionally
"progressive" regions (for example, Minneapolis and San Francisco).

Purely partisan considerations also dominated the voting on an amendment to the Emergency Relief Appropriations bill. Supported by a majority of
the Committee on Appropriations, the chairman of the Roads Committee,
Wilburn Cartwright of Oklahoma, proposed to replace a lump-sum appropriation with an amendment which specifically allocated road-relief funds by
category (federal-aid highways, secondary and rural free delivery roads, railroad crossings, etc.). As James T. Patterson has noted, adoption of the amendment "would not only have reduced Roosevelt's potential political power but
would have guaranteed certain sums of money to projects within [the] home
districts" of congressmen.[117] The pork barrel aspect appealed to Democrats
such as John L. McClellan of Arkansas, who also remarked upon the "inso-
lence" of a discretionary bureaucracy:

In most instances we are accorded the best of treatment and very cour-
teous consideration by the various departmental chiefs, but there are
exceptions, and I dislike to see Members of Congress vote appropriations
and sign blank checks, and then have to go beg of some subordinate for a
little bit of money for a work project in his own district. I am tired of
it.[118]

But it was Republican Earl C. Michener of Michigan who best expressed the
motives of the opposition: "I am opposed to giving the President, or any other
individual, the right to spend this vast amount of money without let or hin-
drance on the part of anyone. The bill gives the President practically unlimited
authority."[119] On this amendment, floor voting reflected both partisan and
intraparty opposition to Roosevelt, and no recognizable alignment emerged
(though trade areas containing Republican majorities or benefiting disproportionately from a specified distribution of funds supported the amendment).

The three remaining low-stress roll calls all involved issues which combined partisan and class cleavages. Chronologically, the first was the vote by which the House of Representatives ratified a "modified death sentence" provision in what was to become the Public Utility Holding Company Act. In its original version, the "death sentence" clause passed by the Senate placed the burden of proof on holding companies to either demonstrate valid economic reasons for their continued existence or face dissolution on January 1, 1940. The House replaced the "death sentence" clause with a provision limiting dissolution to instances in which the Securities and Exchange Commission (SEC) could prove divestiture was in the public interest.[120] The conference between the House and Senate produced a third version of the clause which ultimately became law. The conference language permitted the SEC to allow a holding company to control more than one integrated utility if the individual utilities would not be economically viable when operated alone or if the holding company structure was compatible with decentralized, local management, operating efficiency, and effective regulation. In all other cases, holding companies could not own more than one operating company and one subsidiary. The major change from the Senate version was that the conference language modified the "death sentence" clause by allowing the SEC to consider a broader range of factors when granting an exception to enforcement.

The chairman of the Interstate and Foreign Commerce Committee, Sam Rayburn of Texas, supported the Senate compromise. A majority of the full committee and of those members serving in the conference with the Senate supported the more flexible House language. On the floor vote, the sectional pattern was muddled for several reasons. The difference between the two positions taken by the House and Senate involved a disagreement over the amount of discretion to be granted the SEC which might have been more apparent than real given the subsequent history of implementation. Most periphery members strongly supported the Senate death sentence because that version appeared directed against northern economic "royalists," limited bureaucratic discretion, and was strongly supported by a Democratic president. Northern trade area delegations, on the other hand, were deeply divided. Many northern Democrats joined their Republican colleagues in support of the House language which, they hoped, would favor holding company interests. Enough core Democrats opposed their party to produce a striking bipolar alignment even while internal delegation dissension registered a relatively low level of sectional stress (33.1; see table 4.7).

On March 19, 1936, the House of Representatives amended the statutory authority of the Reconstruction Finance Corporation (RFC) by passing legislation relating to the taxation of preferred stock, capital notes, and bank debentures while they were owned by the RFC. The legislation was intended to "exempt from taxation [by state and local governments] that particular class of preferred stock which the Congress authorized the RFC to buy from national banks" and from eligible state banks and to provide that if "the RFC loans money to closed banks at 3½ percent the receivers of those banks must then reduce the interest on notes and other forms of debts owed the banks to a rate not to exceed 4½ percent." The legislation, unanimously supported by the Committee on Banking and Currency, represented a compromise between moderate factions of the left and right.*

The Frazier-Lemke agricultural bill produced an incongruous alliance between agrarian radicals in the Midwest and a minority of urban Democrats. It also produced an exceptionally low level of sectional stress (35.7; see table 4.7). Opposed by a majority of the Committee on Agriculture (12 to 9) and by the Rules Committee, the legislation would have provided three billion dollars for the refinancing of farm mortgages at interest and repayment rates very favorable to participating farm owners (1½ percent a year for both interest and principal, 3 percent total). When the bill came to the floor under a discharge petition, members from districts with a high percentage of mortgaged, owner-operated farms (mostly in the wheat and corn belts) attempted to logroll support with urban and labor members. Although they met with some success on the discharge petition, the American Federation of Labor's opposition to the bill as "inflationary" eroded core Democratic support when a motion was offered to recommit the bill to the Agriculture Committee. Most periphery members from the tenant-farming, sharecropping cotton belt consistently opposed the bill, as did the Roosevelt administration.†

Although this selection of roll calls and issues does not constitute a complete sample of Depression programs and policies, several conclusions can be

*Liberals received a limit on interest rates to minimize "profiteering" at the expense of the public treasury and both factions saw benefits in the exemption from state and local taxes. The exemption was essential to the viability of the agency (otherwise state or local governments could tax the corporation out of existence, in effect, vetoing the program at the local level) and it lowered the tax burden of private financial institutions.

Most opponents (144 members voted against passage) represented ideological extremes. States' rights advocates favored the continued tax liability of the RFC, ostensibly for revenue purposes, and claimed the agency's policies were centralizing the private financial system by subsidizing national banks associated with the Federal Reserve to the competitive disadvantage of state-chartered institutions. These members were joined by midwestern agrarian radicals who, like Wright Patman of Texas, considered the exemption an "evil" subsidy to bondholders. On the right, large numbers of core Republicans and Democrats opposed the bill because they felt the RFC dangerously interfered with the private economy and constituted a threat to political freedom. As a result of these conflicting motives and interpretations, trade area cohesion was extremely low (35.4 on the sectional stress index), and only five major delegations tilted against the bill. *Congressional Record*, 74:2:4055, March 19, 1936. At this time, the Reconstruction Finance Corporation owned about a fifth of the total capital stock of banks belonging to the Federal Reserve System. Mitchell, *Depression Decade*, pp. 167–68.

†For comments by members on internal dissension within the Committee on Agriculture and the necessity (from the agrarian perspective) of maintaining good relations with urban members, see *Congressional Record*, 74:2:7168, 7170–71, May 13, 1936. Other members recited the opposition of the "powerful invisible government." While the legislation captured the attention of the House for almost a month and came onto the floor over the combined opposition of the legislative committee, the Rules Committee, the Democratic leadership, and the administration, no summary of the struggle seems to appear in any secondary source.

drawn from the evidence. At the broadest level of generalization, sectional stress tended to be greatest where the substantive impact of the policy change was well defined and paralleled the underlying, bipolar alignment (for example, the National Industrial Recovery Act [NIRA] formula, the WPA wage standard, and agricultural parity payments). Sectional stress appeared to decline slightly when the substantive impact deviated from the fundamental alignment (as in the stark coastal-interior division of the 1935 Merchant Marine Act) or divided core interests along class lines (the inflationary Patman "bonus" or the Wage and Hour bill). Reflecting the type of policies that made the New Deal coalition possible, sectional stress was lowest on policy questions which primarily involved the scope and quality of executive discretion (civil service coverage for the administrators of relief employment programs, executive authority over the allocation of public works appropriations, and the modified "death sentence" clause). Though decisions involving adminsitrative and executive discretion were almost invariably partisan and raised broader issues such as the prospective lifespan of the central bureaucracy, the inherent ambiguity of future implementation (which could either be more or less favorable to a member's district than a specified outcome) tended to convert these contests into struggles over political capital. Thus, the lower sectional stress score on these votes was a product of their inherent ambiguity, which reduced the electoral cost of logrolling between the two disparate wings of the Democratic party while it raised the partisan incentive to go along. In all four cases, President Roosevelt, who possessed the greatest political resources and who had the most at stake on the outcome, prevailed over the opposition of a committee majority.

While the Roosevelt administration suffered defeat on the Wage and Hour bill, it carried ten other votes on which the president indicated a position. The administration was apparently indifferent to the structure of the NIRA road money formula. More significant, in eleven of the twelve decisions displayed in tables 4.6 and 4.7 (all except the Wage and Hour bill), a majority of the Republicans on the respective panels voted with the committee majority. The Democratic side, however, was predominantly in the committee minority on five votes and split evenly on a sixth. Of all the roll calls analyzed here, only the Wage and Hour bill exhibited something like a "conservative coalition" between Republicans and southern Democrats. Instead, the most common committee cleavage produced a majority composed of a cohesive bloc of core Republicans and a minority of Democrats also drawn predominantly from industrial regions.

Thus, the committee system in the 1930s exhibited a strong tendency to produce policies favored by a bipartisan coalition of core representatives. Floor opposition to committee majorities was largely composed of midwestern agrarians and southern Democrats. For example, the seven major trade area delegations that opposed the position of the committee majority on eight or more of the twelve decisions included Kansas City, St. Louis, Atlanta, Dallas,

Denver, New Orleans, and Memphis. On the other hand, five trade areas supported the committee position on eight or more roll calls: Philadelphia, Boston, Cincinnati, Cleveland, and New York. Dallas and Boston were at the respective extremes of the distribution. One partial explanation for this committee system "tilt" toward core interests appears to be the broad incompatibility between working-class core and periphery elite policy goals. The sectional conflict over the Wage and Hour bill, for example, grew out of the competition between northern and southern labor markets. In the industrial core, labor productivity was enhanced by the higher quality of public education and capital-intensive production. In these regions the working class commanded a greater income than in the labor-intensive economy of the periphery, in which a high percentage of the work force was illiterate and unskilled. Southern labor, in effect, competed with the greater productivity of northern workers by accepting a lower wage. When organized labor proposed a minimum wage throughout the nation, working-class interests were split along sectional lines even when partisan cleavages reflected the existence of a class division within the industrial core.

The dynamics of the committee system itself offer a second explanation. With some clear exceptions (which will be treated in chapter 6), a strong committee system effectively divides up control over the political economy among the members of the respective committees. For example, in order to translate the potential control over the private economy into tangible political power, most committees have sought to expand federal authority within their policy jurisdiction. Individual members discovered that their congressional careers were intimately connected to the committees to which they were assigned and that administrative oversight could be used to manipulate a portion of the political economy. Thus, expansion of the central government in conjunction with the maturing committee system conferred a greater number and variety of political resources than could a decentralized or laissez-faire state. Ideally, the political interests of legislative committees are best served by the creation of permanent central bureaucracies with broad discretionary mandates. During the New Deal, the maturing committee system attempted to turn emergency, temporary programs into permanent bureaucracies. Thus, committees tended to favor civil service provisions over patronage, centrally controlled over federal-state administrative structures, and discretionary language over well-articulated statutes. For reasons that have been suggested, all of these preferences were closer to the political imperatives of the industrial core than to the perceived needs of the southern agricultural economy. Thus, other things being equal, the dynamics of a strong committee system were usually more compatible with the politics of the core than of the periphery. Because of the general bias of the committee system toward activism, core members were usually more successful in attracting marginal support within the committee. In the two instances where the committee majority opposed the activist alternative—parity payments and the Frazier-Lemke bill—the first involved a committee with a unique set of institutional incentives and the second was an exceptional example of convergent core–southern periphery intersts. In both cases, the committee majority favored the core.

With a few prominent and important exceptions such as the Rivers and Harbors, Agriculture, Flood Control, and Post Office committees, southern members found the activist bias of most legislative panels inconsistent with the interests of their section. This circumstance might have encouraged periphery members, to a greater extent than their core colleagues, to seek assignment to those committees whose institutional position and legislative purpose were more compatible with their inclinations. Assignment to the Rules Committee (where political resources are created by holding up legislation) or Appropriations (which is encouraged by its position to cut federal spending) was made attractive by the place of the southern periphery in the national economy, and assignment to these committees was made possible by the greater seniority often possessed by southern Democrats.

Conclusion

Out of the politics of the New Deal emerged a pervasive predisposition in favor of the expansion of central government regulatory and fiscal authority which was to persist for forty years. The collapse of the national economy allowed the periphery-based Democratic party to expand into the industrial core by exploiting hitherto dormant class conflict. The result of this expansion was the New Deal coalition: a combination of core working-class and periphery elite elements within the same party. The core and periphery factions discovered that their interests and political goals were often incompatible and, for that reason, both party cohesion and the effectiveness of central party leadership declined. Replacing political parties as the major programmatic protagonist was the committee system which achieved preeminence in the legislature. The developing strength of the committee system was based on floor reciprocity, a behavioral norm in House voting which itself was supported by the vast expansion of government activity and executive discretion. These last two developments, in turn, created a civil service bureaucracy which would feed designs for ever greater government intervention back into the legislative process. The supporting political ideology of government expansion was "interest-group liberalism"; the fiscal justification was Keynesian economics.[121] One of the ironic keystones of the edifice was tolerance of southern race segregation by the northern, working-class faction of the Democratic party.

The development of a strong, independent committee system covered nearly four decades. It began with the Cannon Revolt in 1910 and did not reach full maturity until 1947 (when the 1946 Reorganization Act was implemented). The destruction of the committee system may also take decades, but appears to have been in progress since the civil rights legislation passed by the 89th Congress (1965–66). However, while a long-term decline in legislative committee influence seems to have begun, and while the previously uninterrupted growth in centralized governmental power has perhaps been halted, the politics of the New Deal and floor reciprocity continue to reduce the intensity of sectional stress in a number of ways that, along with contemporary accounts of sectional conflict, will be discussed in the following chapters.

5

War Mobilization, Farm Legislation, and Civil Rights: 1940–1970

In many respects, the mobilization of the American economy which enabled the United States to prosecute the Second World War was an extension of the New Deal. Both involved a rapid expansion of economic controls by the federal government and a major transfer of authority from Congress to the executive branch. At least two important distinctions must be drawn, however. During the New Deal, the anomalous loss of influence by the core industrial and commercial elite created a national power vacuum which allowed the Roosevelt coalition to grow to extraordinary size. The very size of the coalition, however, left the New Deal somewhat amorphous even as the permanent agencies and bureaus of the modern state were being erected. Part of the genius of the New Deal was the way in which the constantly changing and flexible alignments within the "bloated" Democratic coalition deflected the rejuvenation of the Republican party in the years immediately preceding World War II.

While the resurging influence of the industrial elite never swept away the decentralized committee system which made possible the bipolar Democratic majority, Republican victories did eliminate the marginal Democratic members in the industrial core who had composed a "bridge" between the two poles and had exerted a moderating force on the labor wing of the party. Without the committee system, it is conceivable that the growing success of the Republican party would have led to a formal split in the Democratic party. But the committee system allowed the leadership to prevent divisive policies (e.g., civil rights legislation) from reaching the floor of the House or Senate and provided an institutional structure which automatically generated the necessary political cues and incentives that made the bipolar coalition workable.

The mobilization of the American economy for the war effort reversed the New Deal balance of power. The influence of the industrial elite through the Republican party was now seen as a permanent factor in national politics, while wartime controls were assumed, by most political actors and observers, to be temporary expedients. The legislative struggles over wage-price controls, labor contracts, and the continuation of emergency controls into the postwar era confirmed the role of the core working-class as an equal competitor in the sectional economic conflict between the industrial-commercial and agrarian elites.

During the two decades following the war, the conditions for a bipolar New Deal coalition were tolerance of race segregation in the southern periphery, the relative isolation of class conflict in the industrial core, and a dependence on administrative discretion and legislative decentralization as methods of minimizing intraparty political conflict. Before 1930, the Republican party had continuously exploited sectional conflict as a strategy for retaining national power; in the next thirty-five years, the Democrats sought to minimize regional competition to the same end.

The Second World War

A description of congressional politics during and immediately following the Second World War must begin with a division of the era into two periods. From the attack on Pearl Harbor until the opening of the 79th Congress in January 1945, the outcome of the war was in doubt. The success of the war effort was the primary goal of most congressmen, as it was for most Americans, and political conflict was largely confined to a debate over a narrow range of differences concerning the most effective way of mobilizing the nation's resources. Since congressmen did not believe national mobilization could be guided or set down in statutory language, most political conflict in the Congress occurred over the selection of administrative personnel and the process of decision-making in the executive branch. With the exception of a few clear attempts to overturn administrative orders which damaged or hindered the interests of specific groups, Congress rarely attempted to decisively shape mobilization policies. Most congressional influence over administrative decision-making took the form of symbolic gestures or exhortations. The highly discretionary form of war legislation and the inhibitions placed on the pursuit of direct, narrow political goals either in debate or in legislation combined to restrict the frequency with which political conflict produced contested roll calls and to decrease the level of sectional stress on those roll calls that were recorded.

Military strategy and tactics were almost exclusively controlled by the executive with little or no consultation with Congress, and the most politicized aspect of the American war effort was the massive intervention of the federal government into the domestic economy. Governmental controls on

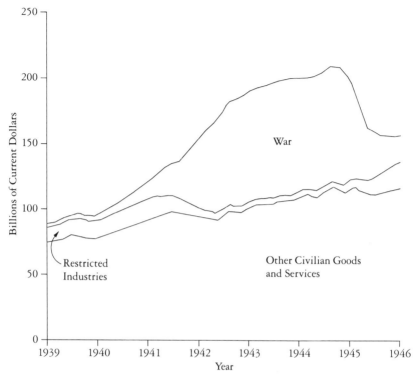

Figure 5.1. Gross National Product, 1939–1946 (Annual Rate in Current Dollars)
SOURCE: *Wartime Production Achievements and the Reconversion Outlook*, War Production Board (Washington: 1945), p. 28.
NOTES: Restricted industries include motor vehicles, consumer durable goods, nonwar construction, and consumer purchases of gasoline. All data after May, 1945 estimated by War Production Board.

production took several forms. As part of the conversion from a peacetime to a war economy, the War Production Board placed restrictions on the use of iron and steel in consumer goods and prohibited new home construction. Every industrial plant constructed, every ton of steel fabricated, and every ingot of aluminum poured during the war years required War Production Board approval.[1] As a result of these federal controls, the prewar production of consumer durable goods was reduced by 29 percent by June 1942.[2] The War Production Board also guided the vast expansion of American industrial capacity; largely under its direction, the gross national product more than doubled between June 1940 and June 1945 (figure 5.1). In constant dollars, 1944 manufacturing volume exceeded 250 percent of 1939 levels, and raw materials production was up some 60 percent (figure 5.2). The size of the labor force,

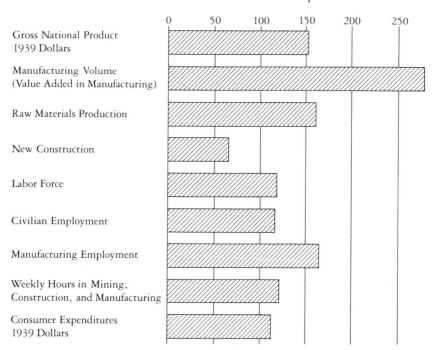

Figure 5.2. Wartime Expansion in the United States, 1939–1944
SOURCE: *Wartime Production Achievements and the Reconversion Outlook*, War Production Board (Washington: 1945), p. 2.

civilian and manufacturing employment, and length of the work week each increased, but federal rationing and price controls reduced corresponding consumer expenditures. In sum, federal intervention completely transformed the economy by blurring the boundary between public and private decision-making, by controlling wages and prices in the private marketplace, by "socializing" nearly half of total output, and by regulating (often indirectly) "the movement of labor from plant to plant, from industry to industry, and from region to region."[3]

For the purposes of mobilizing the domestic economy the most important statutes were the Second War Powers Act of March 1942 and the Emergency Price Control Act of January 1942. By granting the War Production Board nearly unlimited authority to allocate materials or facilities in any manner the board thought necessary, the Second War Powers Act gave statutory legitimacy to an executive agency that had originally been created by presidential order.[4] Similarly, the constitutional standing of the Office of Price Administration was reinforced and its powers expanded by the Emergency Price Control Act. Like most legislation passed during the early years of the war, both acts were highly discretionary and, where they specified any aspect of war policy, tended to describe the process of decision-making that should be followed. The almost complete absence of statutory limits on administrative power and Roosevelt's penchant for filling federal positions with strong personalities combined to produce a unique era in American politics. Policy decisions connected with the mobilization, which could be reversed or nullified at any time, often reflected a struggle for dominance among the chief administrators of the war effort, each policy "becoming identified with specific individuals and changes of policy with attempts to remove key individuals from positions of authority."[5] Congressional attempts to alter the administrative process of a war policy (by, for example, ordering the Secretary of Agriculture to review price controls on agricultural production set by the Office of Price Administration) were normally directed at a particular administrator rather than intended to effect a specific and permanent policy change. Administrators were often viewed as "tendencies" in an administrative process whose course might be changed by the tone of congressional debate; federal policy, in its specifics, was seen as beyond the power of Congress to shape directly. Congressional action thus had an unpredictable impact on the substance of mobilization policy, which operated primarily through the intermediary of bureaucratic personalities and politics.

Of all major areas of domestic control, labor policy emerged as the one most executive in origin. Almost all important federal controls emerged from within the executive branch with little or no congressional consultation. The only major piece of labor legislation to originate in Congress was the War Labor Disputes Act, which passed over a presidential veto in 1943. In contrast, most agricultural controls were heavily influenced by congressional action. Even here, however, Roosevelt frequently challenged Congress on the formula which determined the parity price of agricultural commodities, the sale of surplus production, and related efforts to hold down the price of food. Between these two extremes but somewhat closer to labor policy, restrictions on industrial production, including price controls and allocation orders, were centered in the executive branch but subject to intense scrutiny and possible reversal by statute or congressional investigation.[6]

Each of these three major sectors—labor, agriculture, and industry— had an important stake in the way mobilization and conversion affected their place in the national economy. Most federal policy was based on the concept of the "freeze." When frozen, a specified set of economic relationships which had existed or prevailed in the prewar period were written into an administrative rule or, less frequently, a statute. Because the demands of the war economy vastly and artificially distorted the distribution of resources and income that had prevailed before mobilization, each major sector pressed competing claims for provision of crucial national resources (such as gasoline) and liberalization of price controls on its production. The prewar period was the last "normal" period by which to judge these competing claims which, in effect, divided and redistributed national income. The distortions of the war effort, however, led to ever-increasing demands for interim adjustment, and, in a very tangible sense, any administrative tilt favoring one or another of the three sectors threatened to decisively reshape the distribution of postwar economic and political power.[7]

As an administrative process a war program usually presented three major aspects to congressmen. The broadest aspect encompassed the notion of "equality of sacrifice" which, in spite of many ambiguities, often served as a starting point in political debate. In one sense, "equality of sacrifice implied the continuance of a given relationship. As the war drained the country's wealth, no one would be richer and everyone would be proportionately poorer, having at the end of the war about the same relative economic status as he had at the beginning."[8] This notion went somewhat beyond the concept of a freeze, for it allowed congressmen to contemplate a corrective interim adjustment of prewar relationships. For example, many members used the idea to promote legislation imposing a wartime draft on civilian labor (national service) so that federal authorities could control all employment decisions including a decision not to work.[9] The extent of temporary controls was another feature of wartime administrative power that drew congressional attention. Even though federal controls were nearly always accompanied by enforcement authority in the form of civil and criminal penalities, most administrators preferred to use positive economic incentives to encourage compliance. For example, the federal government underwrote and subsidized much of the cost of industrial expansion, guaranteed that war contracts would be profitable (through cost-plus provisions), and suspended anti-monopoly restrictions if they threatened to hamper production.[10] Still, almost every major economic group argued for less regulation and centralized direction in its own sector. Some groups were extremely apprehensive about the effect of the war effort on economic and political independence. During consideration of amendments to the Emergency Price Control Act in the fall of 1942, for example, a representative of the Congress of Industrial Organizations held that "an attempt to institute wage control could bring in its wake the break-down of voluntary collective bargaining, the establishment of dictatorial controls over labor and industry, and the destruction of a free democratic labor movement."[11]

In its third aspect, the temporary controls of war mobilization were viewed as potential antecedents to national economic planning and, thus, a significant extension of New Deal policy initiatives. From this perspective, Rexford Tugwell compared the approaching conflict to the First World War. World War I, he argued in 1939, had freed Americans from bondage to the free enterprise system and persuaded them to accept a form of "disciplined cooperation." Although war was a terrible thing, Tugwell maintained, "the fact is that only war has up to now proved to be such a transcending objective that [capitalist] doctrine is willingly sacrificed for efficiency in its service."[12] Most congressmen, however, believed that the reform effort of the New Deal and the hitherto growing demand for centralized planning should be suspended for the duration.[13] One reason Congress rarely protested the creation of a new war agency within the executive branch was that war agencies were viewed as temporary expedients and many congressmen feared that an explicit statutory mandate would confer too much permanency on extraordinary war measures. Roosevelt was, in effect, encouraged to increase his own vast discretionary authority during the emergency in order to ensure that such power would not extend into the postwar era.[14] The war itself forced supporters of the New Deal to concede precedence to the overriding imperatives of military objectives and revealed that centralized power, even though lodged in a progressive welfare state, could be turned to illiberal uses.[15]

As the New Deal receded, reformers fought an often unsuccessful rearguard battle to preserve at least token budgetary and statutory authority for many recently created agencies. Among the skirmishes that they lost were struggles over the continued existence of the Civilian Conservation Corps, the Works Progress Administration, and the National Youth Administration.[16] Despite the retreat of the New Deal, the bipolar Democratic coalition remained intact within the war-mobilized Washington bureaucracy and the legislative halls of Congress. But the interests associated with the two great wings of the party did not benefit equally from the changing economic relations imposed by the mobilization.

Compared to southern agriculture, the interests of industrial labor in the North were served very well by the Roosevelt administration's conduct of the war. In order to minimize work stoppages and strikes over the organization of war employees into industrial unions, the War Labor Board instituted a "maintenance of membership" policy. Under "maintenance of membership" no worker could be forced to join a union as a condition of employment, but, if he did not leave the union during an initial fifteen-day withdrawal period, the worker was compelled to maintain his membership for the remainder of the contract period.[17] Industrial representatives on the Board charged that the clause, in practice, "amounted to a camouflaged closed shop."[18] Partly as a result of the Board's policy, individual membership in unions affiliated with the American Federation of Labor climbed from 4.6 million in 1941 to 7.0 million in 1945, and total union membership rose from 10.5 to 14.7 million.[19] The expanding labor organizations used their stronger bargaining position to gain the maximum wage increases allowed under federal controls, and to exceed these limits by negotiating expanded fringe benefits, retirement plans, and job reclassification.[20] Despite the New Deal, the only significant redistribution of national income toward labor between 1919 and 1945 occurred during the years of the Second World War.[21]

With rare exceptions, the southern wing of the Democratic party supported administration policy. One reason for that support was the continuation of New Deal policies that favored the southern periphery (e.g., TVA, agricultural supports, and administration efforts to use the war to dismantle protectionist barriers to free trade). Federal controls on business and heavy war

Table 5.1. Comparison of Pre–World War II Industrial Production and Wartime Facilities Expansion

	Prewar Private Economy		War Expansion	
Region	1939 Value of Production (millions of dollars)	Percentage of Total U.S. Production	Value of Production Added 1940–45 (millions of dollars)	Percentage of Total Added U.S. Production
New England	3,877	9.8	1,101	5.1
Middle Atlantic	11,788	29.8	3,941	18.2
East–North Central	12,461	31.5	6,773	31.4
West–North Central	2,176	5.5	1,688	7.8
South Atlantic	3,600	9.1	1,551	7.2
East–South Central	1,345	3.4	1,248	5.8
West–South Central	1,305	3.3	2,544	11.8
Mountain	435	1.1	818	3.8
Pacific	2,571	6.5	1,938	9.0
Total United States	39,558	100.0	21,602	100.0[a]

[a] 1940–45 total does not include 3,556 in productive capacity that was not distributed among the regional categories.

SOURCE: *Wartime Production Achievements and the Reconversion Outlook* (Washington: War Production Board, 1945), p. 36.

taxes also promised to prevent the enrichment of northern industrial interests that had occurred during the First World War. Finally, the war brought a new kind of prosperity to the periphery and accelerated a secular tendency for industry to relocate from the Northeast into the Far West and South. Although secondary to measures designed to increase war production as rapidly as possible, the War Production Board's attempt to disperse new capacity to "uncongested areas" resulted in a significant shift in industrial location.[22] From 1940 to 1943 the population of Charleston, South Carolina, rose by 37 percent, that of Norfolk, Virginia, by 57 percent, and Mobile, Alabama, by 61 percent as shipbuilding and other war-related industry expanded.[23] The result of the War Production Board's dispersal policy was to permanently enlarge the periphery's share of national industrial capacity (table 5.1). In the West–South Central census division, for example, the region's share of industrial production after the war was three and a half times as large as the corresponding prewar figure (11.8 vs. 3.3 percent).

Roll Call Analysis, 1945–1946

Congressional politics during the 79th Congress (1945–46) at first anticipated the successful conclusion of the war and later reflected the intense struggle for political advantage during demobilization and reconversion. As the favorable outcome of the war became more certain, inhibitions on congressional debate rapidly disappeared, and an increasing preoccupation with narrow economic interests was reflected in the expanding number of contested roll calls and the rising level of sectional stress in congressional voting.

Of all war-related programs, the most contentious involved price control measures and proposed restrictions on organized labor. All three major interests, agriculture, business, and labor, opposed controls on their own activities and products. However, among the three groups there existed significant differences in the nature and intensity of that opposition. Where controls could not be avoided, for example, organized labor tended to favor administrative discretion over statutory specification. Agriculture and business representatives, on the other hand, supported statutory alternatives to administrative rule-making in their own areas.

Agrarian representatives supported expanded wartime controls on both business and labor; those interests returned the favor by supporting more stringent controls on agriculture. Agriculture and business representatives combined to push for greater federal control over labor activities, and labor tended to join agrarian members in favoring expanded restrictions on American business. In these alternating coalition patterns two of the three interests generally supported stronger federal controls on the economic transactions of the third. One significant exception to this trilateral and pluralistic pattern involved the nexus between business and labor activities. Where restrictions and controls on labor spilled over into corporate decision-making prerogatives, business opposition to labor regulation tended to increase. The most common examples of such controls included wage standards, work force ceilings, and job classifications—all of which inhibited management discretion in corporate planning and decision-making. In these cases, representatives who were ordinarily hostile to labor interests tended to oppose the imposition of federal controls. Similarly, federal ceilings on industrial profits were sometimes opposed by labor representatives, who interpreted them as placing an effective lid on wartime wage increases.

In sectional terms, agrarian interests were represented by delegations in the South, Great Plains, and Mountain regions. Business interests, among which industrial concerns loomed as the most relevant and influential, dominated most core delegations, with supporters of organized labor composing a sizeable minority—in some cases, a slim majority—of individual trade areas. Roll calls which provoked the highest levels of sectional stress pitted the interests of the agrarian periphery against the labor interests of core industrial regions in the Northeast and Midwest. These issues fell into two broad categories: measures to specify controls on agricultural production, and measures to regulate the business-labor nexus. Both types of legislation tended to unite labor and business representatives from core regions and, thus, mitigated the internal class conflict that otherwise significantly lowered trade area cohesion in industrial regions. Roll calls on measures that singled out either business or labor organizations without directly implicating the other revealed strikingly low levels of regional polarization.*

During the last year of the war and the first year of the postwar period, Congress considered legislation which was intended to reconvert the nation from the extraordinary measures typical of earlier mobilization controls to the more stable and less interventionist policies that many members considered appropriate to a peacetime economy. Unlike the earlier period, during which the outcome of the war was uncertain and extensive discretionary controls were interpreted as essential to the war effort, reconversion stimulated debate over the scope and functions of the central government in a post–New Deal, post-war economy. This debate produced eight of the high-stress, closely contested roll calls recorded during the 79th Congress (1945–46). (For the regional voting alignment on six of these eight votes, see table 5.2.)†

Of all war-related issues considered during the 79th Congress, perhaps the most important concerned the extension of wartime agencies and controls into the postwar period. Three of the six high-stress, closely contested roll calls raised this question in one form or another, and their regional voting patterns are nearly identical. The first of these was recorded on January 24, 1946, during consideration of a bill making appropriations for the Executive Office of the President and miscellaneous boards. An amendment offered to the bill proposed to eliminate all funding for the Government Information Service. The Service was the last vestige of the Office of War Information which had been the propaganda arm of the government during the war. The Office of War Information had been stripped of its domestic branch in 1943 after repeated public endorsements of New Deal programs provoked congressional hostility. By 1946, the office had eliminated most foreign activities and was limited to the publication of a manual of government organization, the handling of correspondence and phone calls addressed to the "United States Government," and the operation of a clipping service for the president. Although

---

*Examples of such measures and their respective roll call patterns will not be discussed at length here, but a few can be mentioned in passing. The vote on a motion to restore funds for the National Youth Administration, a New Deal agency, exhibited a sectional stress score of 41.5 (*Congressional Record*, 78:1:6969, July 1, 1943). The roll call on an amendment (proposed by business) to further specify administrative controls on prices in wholesale trade scored 41.5 on the index (*Congressional Record*, 79:2:3941, April 17, 1946). A score of 38.3, one of the lowest for any contested roll call during the war period, was produced by the roll call taken on passage of the War Labor Disputes (Smith-Connally) Act (*Congressional Record*, 78:1:5391, June 4, 1943).

†The four high-stress, closely contested roll calls not included in table 5.2 were a vote to close debate on the appointment of House conferees to consider H.R. 1752 (the industrial draft bill described in the text); a vote on the adoption of an open rule for the consideration of a bill to establish penalties for the disclosure of war communications related to national security (H. Res. 367); a vote on an attempt to add funds to the budget of the Grazing Service within the Interior Department (unrelated to the war effort); and a vote on an amendment intended to eliminate funding for the Tennessee-Tombigbee waterway (also unrelated to the war effort).

Table 5.2. Trade Area Delegation Voting on Selected High Stress, Closely Contested Roll Calls, 1945–1946

Trade Area[a]	Extension of Wartime Controls on Industry and Labor					Executive Discretion
	Office of War Information January 24, 1946	Manufacturing and Business Census May 3, 1946	Commerce Department Agencies May 3, 1946	Industrial Draft March 27, 1945	War Labor Disputes Act Repeal December 11, 1945	State Department Commissaries May 11, 1945
Indianapolis	Abol	Abol	Abol	Abol	Ext	Abol
Philadelphia	Abol	Abol	Abol	Abol	Ext	*Split*
Buffalo	Abol	Abol	Abol	Abol	Abol	Abol
Omaha	Abol	Abol	Abol	Abol	Abol	Abol
Cincinnati	Abol	Abol	Abol	Abol	*Split*	*Split*
Minneapolis	Abol	Abol	Abol	Abol	*Split*	Abol
Denver	Abol	Abol	Abol	Abol	Abol	Abol
St. Louis	Abol	Abol	Abol	*Split*	Ext	Abol
Detroit	Abol	Abol	Abol	Abol	Abol	Abol
Pittsburgh	Abol	*Split*	Ext	Abol	Ext	Ext
Kansas City	Abol	Abol	Abol	Abol	Abol	Abol
Boston	Abol	Abol	Abol	Ext	Ext	Abol
New York	Ext	Abol	Abol	Ext	Ext	Abol
Chicago	*Split*	Ext	Ext	Abol	Ext	Ext
San Francisco	*Split*	Ext	Ext	Ext	Ext	Ext
Cleveland	Ext	Ext	Ext	Abol	Ext	Ext
Baltimore	Ext	Ext	Ext	Ext	Abol	Ext
Atlanta	Ext	Ext	Ext	Ext	Abol	Ext
Richmond	Ext	Ext	Ext	Ext	Abol	Ext
New Orleans	Ext	Ext	Ext	Ext	Abol	Ext
Birmingham	Ext	Ext	Ext	Ext	Abol	Ext
Memphis	Ext	Ext	Ext	Ext	Abol	Ext
Dallas	Ext	Ext	Ext	Ext	Abol	Ext
Sectional Stress	54.1	59.9	57.4	62.0	54.4	59.1

[a] Trade area delegations are ranked in descending order of their support for the core position on the ten high-stress roll calls recorded during the 79th Congress (1945–46); see table 2.5.

[b] "Abol" indicates that a majority of the trade area delegation opposed extension of wartime controls into the postwar era; "Ext" indicates that the delegation supported the extension; *Split* indicates that the delegation divided evenly on the roll call.

SOURCE: Computations from roll call data.

the amendment involved a small amount of money and seemingly innocuous government functions, the issues it raised represented a general evaluation of war mobilization policies and their role during reconversion.[24]

Similar motives governed House consideration of an amendment to abolish the Census of Manufacturers and the Census of Business. Offered to the appropriation bill for the Department of State, Justice, and Commerce, the proposal stimulated a vigorous debate over the relevance and purpose of information-gathering by the government. Supporters of the amendment argued that the collection of commercial and industrial data by the Bureau of the Census was duplicated in other federal agencies and constituted an unnecessary government intrusion into business affairs. Opponents claimed that the public availability of economic data allowed small business to compete with the largest corporate firms and that the collected information was necessary for other foreign and domestic government programs as well.[25] The relationship between information-gathering, on the one hand, and the extension of wartime controls into the postwar era, on the other, was probably the major consideration involved in congressional voting decisions. Those members who had favored emergency controls on the industrial economy during the war—primarily congressmen from the agrarian periphery and labor representatives—continued to support government regulation of industry and, thus, opposed the amendment. Conversely, a majority of those members from districts in the industrial core favored abolition of data collection because their interests were frustrated by a large governmental presence in the economy.*

The anti-control sentiment carried over into a third roll call which occurred on an amendment to reduce funds for three agencies which Secretary Henry Wallace wanted to create within the Department of Commerce. In hearings before the Appropriations Committee, Wallace had claimed that these agencies would provide technical and marketing assistance to small businesses. The sponsor of the amendment argued that adoption would result in "less Government interference with business by bureaucratic dreamers and planners."[26] The sectional alignment on this and the preceding two roll calls was virtually identical (see table 5.2). Almost without exception, core delegations supported the abolition of emergency controls on industry and the reduction in scope and size of their respective bureaucracies. Agrarian delegations and northern areas dominated by labor members generally supported the extension of controls and the retention of war agencies.

Another important issue in the closing days of the war involved the extension and retention of controls on industrial labor. Because these controls also tended to implicate business operating decisions, both business and labor representatives overwhelmingly opposed them. Agrarian representatives, on the other hand, supported labor controls because implementation would be largely restricted to core industrial regions and promised to reestablish "equality" between the respective wartime gains of organized labor and periphery agriculture.

Legislation intended to create an "industrial manpower" draft passed the House on a roll call which exhibited the highest level of sectional stress on all closely contested votes recorded in the 79th Congress. The bill was the admin-

---

*While this roll call produced a striking partisan split, a large number of abstentions by labor Democrats in the core delegations and Republicans in the periphery reinforced the underlying sectional polarization of the two parties.

istration's response to disruptions and shortages in the labor market. When the end of hostilities in the European theatre was anticipated in the summer and fall of 1944, the government cut back on military contracts to industrial plants. The Battle of the Bulge in December 1944 forced the United States to resume a relatively high rate of purchasing, but because workers laid off from war industries had quickly found employment unrelated to the war effort and were unwilling to reenter "temporary" employment, many defense plants experienced difficulty rebuilding their work force. Their predicament led President Roosevelt to propose a "national service act" in his state of the union message on January 6, 1945.[27]

During hearings before the House Military Affairs Committee, the industrial draft was endorsed by war-related agencies such as the Selective Service System, the War and Navy Departments, and the War Production Board. Only one major private group, the American Farm Bureau Federation, supported the bill. Representatives of the AFL, CIO, railroad unions, Chamber of Commerce, and the National Association of Manufacturers all testified against a civilian manpower draft.* After passing the House and Senate, the bill went into conference between the two chambers. Their resulting compromise included all workers (regardless of age or sex) and conferred upon the Director of War Mobilization and Reconversion the authority to establish a ceiling on employment within a firm (and, thus, prevent firms from hoarding labor). Under the legislation, the Director would also have been allowed to "freeze" employment at a plant (forcing labor to remain in place regardless of alternative employment opportunities). In theory, the proposed law took the form of an amendment to the Selective Service Act but would have been administered entirely outside the system. Perhaps the most crucial feature of the plan was its selectivity. As the chairman of the Military Affairs Committee, Democrat Andrew J. May of Kentucky, described it: "This bill does not as a blanket cover the whole country and all industry. . . . It merely authorizes the Director of War Mobilization to determine in a certain area, for instance the city of Detroit or the city of Pittsburgh or the city of Cincinnati, what plants are essential to the war effort and what are not."[28] While the legislation was highly discretion-

---

*United States Bureau of the Budget, *The United States at War* (New York: DaCapo Press, 1972), p. 453. During the period between the president's message and the adoption of the conference report by the House, the administration tried to solve the labor problem using existing emergency authority. "In several critical areas an attempt was made during February and March 1945 to compel transference of workers from less essential to more essential plants by reducing the employment ceilings of less essential employers. A basic difficulty was that wages and conditions in the plants to which workers were to be transferred were not sufficiently attractive to make transference palatable to the workers, and the War Manpower Commission had no power to change this situation. Moreover, with the end of the war obviously near, workers were unwilling to move from permanent to temporary jobs. . . . It proved impossible to compel workers to change jobs without a statute providing authority over employers as well as workers and including some guarantee to the transferred workers of reemployment in their previous jobs." Pp. 454–55.

ary, most members clearly anticipated that enforcement authority would be exercised almost exclusively in the larger industrial centers where labor shortages were most acute.

Both the regional nature of administration support and the intensity of the opposition were conveyed in one New York Republican's comments: "The fact that this conference report proposes to enslave free people does not disturb those who are imbued with a philosophy of slavery." [29] Although the House of Representatives adopted the conference report, the Senate rejected the compromise, and congressional support for a manpower draft waned with the increasing pace of reconversion.

With the end of the war, proposals to repeal emergency mobilization controls often passed with little or no opposition. An exception was the repeal of the 1943 War Labor Disputes Act. Labeled the Smith-Connally Act, this legislation had been intended to seriously discourage labor disputes from maturing into work stoppages in critical war industries. Richard Polenberg has sketched an excellent summary of the act and its effect on wartime labor relations:

> Although the AFL and CIO thundered that it was "the worst anti-labor bill passed by Congress in the last hundred years," and denounced it as "the very essence of Fascism," the Act did not seriously weaken trade unions. Ways were discovered to evade the ban on political contributions and, when necessary, leaders could quietly encourage strikes without saying so in public or exposing themselves to indictment. Since criminal penalties applied only to stoppages in plants taken over by the government, and then only to individuals who fomented strikes rather than those who went on strike, most workers were never in jeopardy. Finally, the government was reluctant to press charges against union officials lest they be made martyrs. [30]

Under an earlier executive order based on presidential war power, the National War Labor Board possessed the authority to compel arbitration in labor disputes, and board decisions could be enforced through the seizure of plants by the government. [31] However, labor and management hostility to any government interference in collective bargaining turned that ultimate enforcement power into a somewhat blunt instrument. In addition, the more or less tenuous constitutional basis for this emergency power vanished with the end of hostilities.

By the end of 1945, the War Labor Disputes Act was already an anachronism. Representative Everett Dirksen of Illinois described the act's quaintest feature during the Republican-controlled portion of floor debate: "Hostilities ended nearly four months ago, and yet the NLRB has no choice except to conduct strike votes when strike notices have been filed and still ask the question, 'Do you wish to permit an interruption of war production in wartime as a result of this dispute?'"[32] Although repeal generally enjoyed widespread support, the legislative vehicle that developed provoked strong opposition by introducing extraneous policy considerations and procedural controversies.

The first problem that confronted the repeal proposal was an intense jurisdictional conflict between the Committee on Military Affairs and the Committee on Labor. Since the original War Labor Disputes Act had been referred to Military Affairs in 1943 (because of the bill's relationship to war production), the Speaker had sent the repeal proposal back to Military Affairs and in that way bypassed the Labor Committee. The jealousy thus engendered between the two committees was reinforced by a significant difference in their overall policy orientation: the Labor Committee contained few southern or mountain members and was very sensitive to the political influence of organized labor, while Military Affairs was much less favorably inclined toward union desires and more sympathetic to the subordination of private interests to the needs of national security. Once the military panel received the repeal legislation, it expanded the purpose of the bill without holding public hearings in which the "representatives of the AFL, the CIO, railroad labor organizations, the United Mine Workers, or . . . some of the sane industrialists" could have been heard.[33]

As finally drafted by the committee, the repeal legislation contained three controversial features. On the one hand, it proposed restrictions on the ability of organized labor to impose political levies upon its members. Labor unions had evaded similar restrictions in 1943 when the Attorney General had defined them as nonprofit organizations.[34] Furthermore, if a labor union had signed a contract in which a "no-strike" or "binding arbitration" clause appeared and that labor union had called or encouraged a strike during the life of the contract, the legislation stipulated that the employer would be relieved of any obligation under the agreement and the union would lose its status as a bargaining agent for the following twelve-month period. Finally, if union employees damaged the property of the employer or injured any party as a result of a breach of the labor contract, the union would be subject to suit in the District Court of the United States where the injury occurred. The employer was equally liable if he illegally locked out his employees and deprived them of work. These provisions went far beyond a simple repeal of the 1943 act and, because the legislation might have intensified rather than alleviated labor disruptions, encouraged many core Republicans to oppose the bill.

The roll call pattern displayed in table 5.2 describes the recorded vote on the special order that brought the bill to the floor. For reasons described above, the legislation did not involve simple abolition of wartime controls on organized labor; instead, these controls were to be replaced by much more onerous and permanent regulation of labor-industry relations. For that reason, almost all major industrial trade areas opposed the measure. Detroit was the lone exception. Agrarian areas generally and, more particularly, the southern periphery supported the replacement of wartime controls with permanent federal regulations. Both parties were deeply divided on the vote, and the special order was narrowly defeated (182 to 200).

The last roll call included in table 5.2 was decided by an almost straight party-line vote. Only one Democrat voted with the Republican majority, and no Republican voted with the Democrats. The recorded vote occurred on a motion to concur in a Senate amendment to a State, Justice, and Commerce appropriation bill. The Senate amendment would have allowed the State Department wider discretion and freedom in dispensing and collecting funds for the operation of a commissary service in occupied Europe. As one Democrat described the reason for the program: "with the liberation of areas formerly occupied by the enemy, economic conditions in certain areas made it impossible for the Foreign Service personnel to obtain food and other essential commodities except through the military service or providing its own facilities where the military could not provide them."[35] The question raised by the Senate amendment involved the relative freedom with which the State Department would operate the service. Republicans insisted upon greater congressional control of appropriations. The Democrats, reflecting the southern base of the party and the region's support for executive controls in the recent war, supported the amendment. The relatively high-stress score was a product of the underlying sectional alignment of the two parties reinforced by the pattern of abstentions (of which there were 125).

In some ways, the politics of the 79th Congress (1945–46) were similar to those conflicts that had dominated the New Deal 74th (1935–36). Both Congresses divided over the extent of executive discretion and over disputes concerning the permanency of "temporary" agency authority. During the New Deal, however, it was the northern wing of the Democratic party that had most consistently supported an expanding, permanent federal bureaucracy. The southern wing was more ambivalent—particularly on questions concerning the enrollment of employees in the civil service or centralization of power in Washington. This pattern changed during the war, when federal controls more completely permeated the American economy than at any other time in history. Somewhat incongruously, the general purpose of these controls was to minimize the redistribution of wealth between the major sectors during the mobilization. As the major beneficiary of the war effort, organized labor was the target of increasingly hostile legislation as reconversion to a comparatively deregulated peacetime economy drew near. The northern wing of the party (and many core Republicans) came to oppose the extension of wartime controls for that reason. Southern and western agricultural gains, on the other hand, lagged behind the improved economic positions of both labor and industry. As a result, periphery representatives did not seek the abandonment of emergency authority in the agricultural sector and, instead, sought the expansion of federal production controls, price supports, and subsidization.

Agricultural Supports and Controls, 1955–1956

Of the ten high-stress, closely contested roll calls recorded during the 84th Congress (1955–56), four concerned agricultural supports and controls.* Similar in many ways to wartime measures, these supports and controls were intended to relieve distress in the agricultural economy. The immediate cause of this distress in the years between 1951 and 1960 was a chronic surplus in the production of foodstuffs and fibers during a period of rising productivity and capital intensification in the agricultural sector. Between 1940 and 1964 farm production increased at an annual rate of 2 percent despite the extensive diversion (after 1955) of acreage into conservation programs. In the absence of such cropland diversion, the Department of Agriculture has estimated that the rate of increase would have nearly doubled to 3.5 percent per year.[36] Underlying the rapid expansion of American agricultural capacity was an historic increase in farm productivity, with an annual rate almost twice as high as in any previous period.[†] Measured in output of real product per man-hour, agricultural productivity nearly doubled between 1949 and 1960 and increased at a rate nearly two and a half times as great as that experienced in manufacturing employment.[‡] Increasing productivity was connected to several other changes in the rural economy. While the physical output of the American farm rose by one-quarter between 1950 and 1959, total agricultural employment declined by about 30 percent.[37] These trends reflected a changing economic mix in agricultural investment. While land costs remained fairly constant between 1950 and 1960 (8.9 and 8.5 percent of total operating expenses respectively), labor input decreased from 41.8 to 30.1 percent of total costs and capital

---

*Other topics covered by these high-stress roll calls included an Immigration and Naturalization Service rider to a Department of Justice appropriations bill and the adoption of legislation giving congressional support to the regional dispersion of industrial capacity. Both topics and the political conflict they engendered reflected the regional patterns and concerns of the preceding war period. A seventh roll call occurred on a reclamation bill which provided for federal cooperation in nonfederal water projects. A measure dealing with public transportation in the District of Columbia produced another high-stress, closely contested vote which brought out the latent civil rights implications of federal control of the District. The last two of the ten votes dealt with a school construction bill which would have denied federal aid to any state that failed to comply with Supreme Court integration orders.

†United States Department of Agriculture, *Changes in Farm Production and Efficiency, A Summary Report, 1962*, Statistical Bulletin No. 233 (Washington: September 1962). The average annual increase in agricultural productivity was 1.1 percent between 1870 and 1900, 0 percent (slightly negative) between 1900 and 1925, 1.2 percent between 1925 and 1950, and 2.0 percent between 1950 and 1961.

‡Harold G. Vatter, *The U.S. Economy in the 1950's: An Economic History* (New York: W. W. Norton, 1963), p. 249. During the 1950s, "Not only did the long-run curve for agricultural productivity take a sharp upturn, but the curve was steeper than that for the nonfarm sector. . . . Output per man-hour worked in agriculture rose more than 6 per cent per year over the decade, which in the annals of productivity increase is nothing short of phenomenal."

investment rose from 49.3 to 61.4 percent during the same period.* Two of the more tangible aspects of these changes were a doubling in the number of tractors between 1945 and 1965 and, in order to exploit the economies of scale possible under capital-intensive cultivation, an increase in the size of the average farm from 197 acres in 1950 to 303 acres in 1959.† All of these trends suggested the existence of a "permanent" overcapacity in American agriculture that, in the absence of government intervention, threatened the agrarian economy with immense social and economic hardship.

The political struggle over McNary-Haugenism during the 1920s had foreshadowed the acceptance of government regulation that emerged in the New Deal period. Under the Agricultural Adjustment Act of 1938, centralized decision-making in the form of government price supports and production controls temporarily improved the economic position of the American farmer during the Great Depression.‡ During World War II, price supports and acreage controls were largely superfluous because the war effort greatly expanded the market for agricultural products. In fact, governmental controls during the war years were largely intended to keep prices down and thus to help contain inflation. After the war, the perceived threat of an agricultural depression similar to the one following the First World War and the "success" of interventionist measures during the New Deal and war mobilization periods encouraged a continuation of centralized decision-making. An activist agriculture policy was further encouraged by acceptance in American public life of "the proposition that it was the province of government to underwrite commercial agriculture through price guarantees. . . . This acceptance was of course part of the growing acquiescence in the practice (though by no means yet the principle everywhere) of governmental quasi-planning." The most likely alternative to that policy was "the ruthless expulsion of resources from agriculture that would occur under the unfettered functioning of the private market mechanism."[38]

Postwar agricultural programs continued price supports and (usually weak) production controls on most farm commodities. Support levels were set at a minimum of 90 percent of parity, provided Congress appropriated sufficient funds,§ and were sufficiently high to provide more stimulation to the

---

*Earl O. Heady, Edwin O. Haroldsen, Leo V. Mayer, and Luther G. Tweeten, *Roots of the Farm Problem* (Ames: Iowa State University Press, 1965), p. 12. These changes in the proportional shares of labor and capital in agricultural production represented an acceleration of a secular trend.

†Schlebecker, *Whereby We Thrive*, pp. 279, 288. Largely because of acreage diversion programs, harvested cropland actually declined by nearly 10 percent between 1950 and 1959.

‡Don Paarlberg, *American Farm Policy: A Case Study of Centralized Decision-Making* (New York: John Wiley and Sons, 1964), p. viii. "Centralized decision-making of this kind was justified by the urgency of the times, by the failure of the free system to function in an appropriate manner, and by the lack of agreement on superior alternatives."

§Schlebecker, *Whereby We Thrive*, p. 286. The parity price is the price at which a given quantity of a commodity will buy a "market basket" of other goods equivalent to what it had

agricultural sector than restrictions on production could counterbalance. Increases in demand following the outbreak of the Korean War on June 25, 1950, postponed the realization of the economic implications of the high support levels. However, with the end of the war in 1953, the continuation of 90 percent parity supports was partially responsible for a chronic surplus in basic commodities and the twin problems of reserve disposal and mounting storage costs. Political conflict also emerged over the relative "parity" between the agricultural and industrial sectors of the national economy and between the various producers within the agricultural sector itself.[39]

During the 1950s the most important issues in agricultural policy concerned the level (percentage of parity) at which price supports should be set, the extent and rigor with which production controls should be applied, and alternative methods of disposing of the surplus that continuously flowed into government hands.[40] With the advent of the Eisenhower administration, the executive branch moved away from the high and rigid price support programs that had been the hallmark of war mobilization and postwar policy. In their place, the Republican president suggested the implementation of flexible support prices which could be adjusted in response to changes in agricultural production. Flexible support prices, it was argued, would generally be lower than existing rigid price floors and would force production to more closely approximate "real" demand by reallocating capacity among commodities and forcing marginal producers out of business (and consolidating their acreage with that already held by more efficient operators). To deal with the surplus, Eisenhower's Secretary of Agriculture, Ezra Taft Benson, supported enactment of a Soil Bank program which would allow producers to lease a portion of their acreage to the federal government which would then order its conversion to pasture or alternative soil-conserving uses. In addition, the administration backed a combination foreign aid–surplus disposal program popularly known as PL480 (after its public law number).* The common goal of flexible sup-

---

purchased in a specified base period. The notion of parity is intended to indicate a "fair" price for the commodities produced by American farmers compared to the goods which they must purchase on the open market. F. L. Thomsen and R. J. Foote, "Parity Price," in Vernon W. Ruttan, Arley D. Waldo, and James P. Houck, eds., *Agricultural Policy in an Affluent Society* (New York: W. W. Norton, 1969), pp. 90–95.

*Schlebecker, *Whereby We Thrive*, p. 287. The original Soil Bank program rapidly proved to be a failure. American farmers diverted their worthless or marginal lands into the bank and increased their efforts on acreage that remained in production. The program was divided into two parts: an acreage reserve and a conservation reserve. Eligibility under the acreage reserve section was limited to "allotment" crops subject to stringent production controls and sometimes resembled, at least to those left out of the program, an unjustified pork barrel policy. For example, Democrat Charles H. Brown of Missouri attempted to remain high-minded in spite of the arbitrary distribution of payments: "Now, if we want to be provincial about this, which I do not want to be, I refuse to be a party to any program that is going to continue $42 an acre payments for brush in the Corn Belt when my people cannot get $42 an acre for their brush in south Missouri." *Congressional Record*, 85:1:3588, March 13, 1957.

ports, the Soil Bank, and what became the Food for Peace program was to gradually eliminate marginal producers and ultimately pave the way for the total abandonment of federal controls on prices and production.[41] In 1945 the average parity ratio for agricultural commodities stood at 109 percent of the average purchasing power of similar commodities during the years between 1910 and 1914.[42] By 1950 the parity ratio had declined to 101, and during the Eisenhower years it plummeted to 84 (1955) and 90 (1960).

Secretary Benson, writing after his service in the Eisenhower cabinet, argued that the Republican initiatives were in some sense inevitable: "We could not go on indefinitely under the old programs without piling up mountainous surpluses, losing markets, wasting resources, running up heavy dollar losses and, most important of all, endangering the economic independence of our farm people."[43] The administration was not only concerned with the size of federal expenditures and the reestablishment of a free market in agriculture, however. It also perceived that government intervention in the agricultural sector was rapidly building ties between the agrarian periphery and labor-oriented lower classes of the industrialized core. Government supports and controls built advantages into the national political economy that became increasingly "addicting" as the agricultural sector became further and further removed from competitiveness within the world economy and the "natural" level of real demand for basic commodities in the national market. Increasing numbers of marginal producers had become economically dependent on federal policies and, thus, *politically* dependent on the New Deal coalition which supported government intervention. Republican policy was intended to reduce this political dependence by eliminating, probably at high social cost, the central state apparatus upon which it was based. In a very real sense, the Republican effort was a long-term program to split asunder one of the political supports for the bipolar Democratic coalition. This effort ultimately failed, and government subsidies returned, with a vengeance, under Presidents Kennedy and Johnson.*

While the Republicans, bolstered by the arguments of most agricultural economists, could argue that government intervention was economically counterproductive, the Democrats countered that administration alternatives were harsh and politically motivated. Those who advocated government supports noted the potentially useful aspects of agricultural consumption patterns. In the aggregate, the price elasticity of demand for farm commodities is $-.25$, which means that for every 1 percent increase in the supply of farm commodities on the market, farm prices are depressed 4 percent, gross receipts 3 percent, and net farm income 9 percent in the short run.[44] The relative

---

*As Secretary Benson noted, "Economics, emotions, and party and sectional loyalties had become enormously intertwined with the farm issue, much as they had in the slavery issue just before the Civil War." Benson, *Cross Fire*, p. 157.

inelasticity of the demand curve implies that a relatively small increase or decrease in the total supply can mean the difference between farm prosperity or depression—hence the potential profitability of production controls and the "ever-normal granary" concept. At least three other reasons for government intervention are often cited. First, federal programs stabilize income and eliminate some of the risks inherent in agricultural operations. Second, government programs have eased the social and economic costs associated with the industrialization of the national economy and the transition to capital-intensive agriculture. Finally, government holdings of surplus commodities provide a secure stockpile in the event of a national emergency.[45] To this list can be added a potent political motive for the continuation of commodity programs. According to one authority, if all government intervention had ceased, average farm prices would have plummeted 20 percent, gross receipts 15 percent, and net farm income 45 percent.* Although the most severe impact on the agricultural sector would have been relatively short-lived, the cessation of governmental supports and controls would have meant bankruptcy to hundreds of thousands of marginal producers.

Critics of federal farm programs cited a wide variety of very real and apparently insoluble problems. The most fundamental of these difficulties was the obvious failure of the political system to implement effective domestic controls on production. An agricultural economist who served in the Eisenhower administration subsequently wrote:

> In a country like the United States, with a representative government and with a tradition of freedom, the Congress will not write, the executive branch will not enforce, and the farmers will not accept the degree of production control required to balance supply with available markets at the levels of price support promised by the politicians.[46]

In the absence of effective domestic controls, government price supports had a number of adverse side effects. Among the most important of these effects were the encouragement of expanded production of crops with artificially maintained prices, the freezing of historical (and progressively more inefficient) patterns of production among farms and regions as a result of government allotments, the inflation of land prices, and general overcapitalization of controlled commodity production. Also significant was the creation of new "surpluses" in unsupported crops when acres diverted from regulated commodities were planted with uncontrolled alternatives. For the nation as a whole, government intervention in the agricultural sector restrained overall economic expansion by diverting resources into already glutted markets and

---

*Tweeten, "Commodity Programs for Agriculture," p. 105. This estimate was made in 1967, and, while conditions were somewhat different in the 1950s, the impact of government programs was roughly the same order of magnitude.

rewarding unproductive activity (e.g., soil conservation in excess of normal operating requirements).*

There were also foreign policy implications embedded in a system of federal controls. Any price support mechanism that placed a floor on the domestic (American) price tended to peg that price above world levels in international trade. For that reason, government supports had to be accompanied by import restrictions, which had the unfortunate side-effect of inviting foreign retaliation. In addition, the artificially maintained American price meant that domestic production could only compete in the world market with the aid of export subsidies.[47] Such subsidies, in turn, brought charges of "dumping" by foreign producers and threatened to start a trade war. In the absence of export subsidies, the United States provided a price umbrella in international trade for foreign producers by serving as a high-cost, marginal contributor to world supplies and a storehouse of surplus production.† While the federal government attempted to control the domestic cultivation of cotton, it could obviously do nothing to curtail foreign production. As the competitive position of American cotton weakened, foreign producers expanded cultivation to meet the increasing demands of world trade.‡

In sum, federal price support programs have had three primary effects on American agricultural involvement in the world economy. First, American producers have become much more sympathetic to protectionism as a result of the imposition of import controls. In addition, though American producers are ultimately still dependent on export markets, the proportion of American production sold abroad has declined sharply and government policy has insulated the domestic producer from the short-term effects of changes in international market conditions. Finally, crops such as cotton, which formerly "sold on its merits" in world markets, have become, in effect, "state-traded" commodities.[48] The complex mechanism for marketing surpluses has become an extension of American diplomacy, subject to negotiation and linked to other

---

*Vatter, *The U.S. Economy in the 1950's*, p. 257. During the debate on the 1959 wheat program, Republican Robert Michel of Illinois, later to become leader of his party, maintained that congressmen were generally aware of the economic "futility" of government intervention: "By increasing price supports on wheat and reducing acreage, it [the government's program] will encourage increased production on the remaining acres and decrease consumption. The effect is obvious. It will further build up the wheat carryover and increase Government costs." *Congressional Record*, 86:1:10553, June 11, 1959.

†Marion Clawson has succinctly described the American role in the international cotton market: "When production in other parts of the world is low and/or demand abroad is high, cotton flows out of the United States to help satisfy the demand; when production in other parts of the world is high and/or their demand is low, more United States produced cotton goes into storage under government loan. This regularizing effect is in addition to the price-increasing effect of U.S. cotton programs." *Policy Directions for U.S. Agriculture* (Baltimore: Johns Hopkins Press, 1968), p. 178.

‡Paarlberg, *American Farm Policy*, p. 237. As a result of price supports, the production of synthetic fibers (in competition with cotton) has been artificially stimulated and tobacco has faced a weakening export market (p. 233).

trade agreements on industrial commodities. Unlike the late nineteenth century, when all American producers needed to compete in world markets, the middle twentieth-century farm operator needed a strong, benevolent state to support his prices at home and to dispose of his "surplus" abroad.

Fundamental Conflict between the Core and Periphery

The heart of the American economy in the mid-twentieth century was located in the manufacturing belt of the Northeast and the large and small industrial centers of the Midwest. Aside from the extension of this belt into the southern reaches of Ohio and Indiana and into the central territory of Illinois, the industrial core encompassed roughly the same regions as it had in the 1920s.[49] Spreading outward from the industrial core were concentric zones of agricultural specialization which were the product of several factors associated with a regional division of economic activity. The three most important factors influencing the shape and distribution of these zones were the average wage for manual labor, the price of agricultural acreage, and transportation costs (translated into proximity to metropolitan markets). Closest to the industrial centers of the metropolitan core and in some cases nestled between them was truck gardening specializing in high-value, perishable vegetable crops. Also intermixed within the territory of the manufacturing belt was a zone of specialization in milk and poultry products (Minnesota, Wisconsin, and upstate New York). In the case of milk, the product was bulky, highly perishable, and possessed a highly stable market in the nation's urban centers.[50] Poultry and, to some extent, livestock yards could afford the relatively expensive costs of location in the manufacturing belt because of the economical utilization of land and a comparative reduction in transportation costs. The economic dependence of agricultural producers in the truck garden and dairy zones on the metropolitan markets of the industrial core and on the scope and health of the core consumer market has historically led their political representatives to sympathize with core interests in national politics.

In the third zone of specialization lies the great corn belt of the nation in which the "corn-hog" cycle of livestock production is dominant. The eastern end of this zone reaches into Ohio, Indiana, and central Illinois and is comparatively dedicated to livestock production. This section of the belt is a net importer of corn and other feed grains. The western portion, Iowa, southern Minnesota, Nebraska, and northern Missouri, is, on balance, a net exporter of grain to the eastern portion of the corn belt. The importance of this division will become apparent later in this section. While corn belt producers—like dairy and truck garden operators—are dependent on domestic urban markets, several differences have combined to loosen political ties with the industrial core. For example, corn belt products can be held off the domestic market because they are nonperishable and are more widely involved in international trade.

At the greatest remove from the core and constituting the heart of the agrarian periphery are the fourth (wheat, small grains, and cotton) and fifth (sheep and cattle grazing) concentric zones.[51] These regions have the least direct and immediate involvement with core consumer markets and are almost always found in political opposition to industrial trade area delegations.

Though climate is a decisive factor in the location of agricultural activity where it has any influence at all (e.g., oranges), climatic conditions seem to control only broadly what most farmers choose to grow. Similarly, the nature and quality of the soil seems to be comparatively insignificant in the evolution of regional specialization.[52] Instead the geographical concentration of the various types of production has been stable and consistently arrayed (at least in the twentieth century) because of the persistent dominance of urban, industrial activity in the northeastern and midwestern core. In fact, in many areas agricultural specialization has become even more intensive. For example, in the years between 1937 and 1965 total national acreage devoted to the cultivation of corn dropped from 94 million to 82 million acres. Outside of the corn belt, total acreage declined by 15 million acres. During the same time period the corn belt added 3 million acres.[53] In the case of corn, this geographical intensification has taken place despite the existence of governmental controls which have tended to encourage its dispersal.[54] On the other hand, the historical westward march of cotton cultivation was retarded by government intervention.[55]

Since the major wheat-producing regions cannot, because of climatic conditions, easily shift to the cultivation of alternative crops, they are the least flexible agricultural areas of the nation.* During debate on a proposal to exempt the first fifteen acres of any farm from wheat production controls, Republican William Henry Avery of Kansas suggested the existence of a historical claim to produce wheat:

> I can understand the feeling of my colleagues who come from historical non-wheat-producing States with regard to this 15-acre proposal, and I hope those people can understand our feelings on this matter. If we had the climate and other conditions that were necessary, if we could get into the production of tobacco, and other things that historically belong to the Southern States, it would affect your markets and your economy and we could be taking away from you something that historically belongs to you. So it is with regard to the wheat-producing area in the Middle West.[56]

The exemption would have allowed producers in other sections of the country who, because of production controls, had to reduce the cultivation of supported crops such as cotton to replant diverted acreage with wheat. From the

---

*Clawson, *Policy Directions for U.S. Agriculture*, p. 180. Clawson argues that this inflexibility has made the wheat regions of the nation more dependent than other regions on a stable export market.

perspective of the traditional wheat producer, the provision artifically encouraged wheat cultivation in areas in which it normally would not have been competitive with other crops and, thus, reduced the effectiveness with which the wheat producer's own program would raise net income.

The "terms of trade" between agriculture and the remainder of the national economy, a concept dating back at least to the McNary-Haugen struggle of the 1920s, gradually deteriorated over the half century between 1910 and 1960. By the latter year, twice as much physical output was required to provide the same relative income as prevailed in 1910. In this respect, American agriculture has suffered from a lower-echelon position in the regional division of labor.* As an emerging, world-class industrial and commercial power, the American manufacturing belt had few effective competitors in the world economy. The agrarian periphery, on the other hand, faced unskilled, low-wage competition from many underdeveloped nations. Over the long run the inferior position of American agriculture has been reflected in its decreasing share of the gross national product, on a per capita basis. Many agricultural spokesmen have interpreted the political struggle over price supports and production controls as a movement to reestablish a balance between the industrial and agricultural shares of the national income. Like Mississippi Democrat Jamie Whitten, these spokesmen have decried the comparable forms of government intervention that have propped up the industrial economy:

> Price supports are made necessary by the other laws that we have on our statute books giving labor the right to organize, giving labor the right to strike, giving labor minimum wages, and industry's having the right to make up its own profits through cost-plus and other laws on the statute books. If we are not to wreck our economy, agriculture has got to have the right to meet the changing practices in industry and labor or our whole economy will go down in total collapse.[57]

For core representatives, the clearest answer for the perennial farm crisis has been the reinstatement of "free market" competition. This solution would certainly increase the relative income of the industrial core and erase the inherent contradictions and inefficiencies of government intervention. In the agrarian periphery, however, what the core interprets as "wasteful subsidies" appear to be an eminently reasonable policy of income stabilization.†

---

*"American agriculture is similar to the national economies of many underdeveloped countries, where a larger volume of exports is required to provide the same external purchasing power." Clawson, *Policy Directions for U.S. Agriculture*, pp. 189–90.

†In a sense, the two great sections inhabit totally different worlds. As Representative Wint Smith of Kansas put it: "In this so-called tragedy of surplus crops those who know the least about the facts are the most certain that they know just where to find the guilty party—and strangely enough the Hawkshaws and Ellery Queens who claim they have the solution to the farm problem live in the large cities, and most of these city experts would not know the difference between a Holstein and a Plymouth Rock." *Congressional Record*, 86:1:10523, June 11, 1959.

In some respects, post–New Deal farm programs have been similar to late nineteenth-century industrial tariff policy. Both forms of government intervention have attempted to insulate a particular sector of the national economy from foreign competition. The withdrawal of American manufacturing from the world-economy almost a century ago protected industry from the potentially withering competition of developed western European economies. The withdrawal of American agriculture in the mid-twentieth century has protected the periphery from Third World competition. Behind this superficial similarity, however, lie several important differences. The first and most important is that the industrial tariff propelled the United States into the front ranks of the world system. It was successful in the sense that it did not seem to hinder and actually may have stimulated the pace of economic development. Agricultural withdrawal, on the other hand, only postpones an inevitable shift in production down the rungs of the world-economy toward developing nations of the world. With a total elimination of government supports and controls, American agriculture would not disappear, but the pattern of resource allocation and specialization would be dramatically altered. A second significant difference is that, unlike nineteenth-century industry, agricultural production is subsidized in the domestic market but a sizeable percentage of total output is still exported. Aside from import controls on supported commodities and the emergence of central government control (and subsidization) of the export trade, the disposal of agricultural surpluses abroad has probably increased political support for a return to industrial protectionism. When cotton, for example, is sold abroad at a prevailing world price substantially below the domestic level, it is possible—even likely—that the same cotton will return to the American market as manufactured textile products. By artificially subsidizing the foreign manufacturer at the expense of the American textile producer, the disposal of surplus cotton stocks has naturally increased the clamor for higher trade barriers on "cheap" foreign textiles.[58]

In 1962, only three states contained a farm population in excess of 30 percent of the total residents (North Dakota—32.8; South Dakota—31.9; and Mississippi—31.2). Almost all of the twenty-three states with a farm population greater than a tenth of the total lay outside the manufacturing belt. Vermont and Indiana were the only exceptions. Rhode Island (0.7), Massachusetts (1.0), New Jersey (1.2), and Connecticut (1.4) all contained farm populations smaller than 2 percent of the total.[59] In the country as a whole, then, the American farmer was a distinct and very small minority, and many analysts ascribed his relative political success to an irrational, sympathetic agrarian tradition and, more tangibly, the malapportionment of congressional membership, which over-represented rural, agrarian interests at the expense of urban constituencies.[60]

During the eight years of the Eisenhower administration, the House of Representatives considered four separate price support measures which were general in nature. Each of these deeply divided core and periphery delegations

Table 5.3. Trade Area Delegation Voting on Major Farm Policy Decisions, 1954–1958

Trade Area[a]	Flexible Parity Amendment July 2, 1954	Agricultural Act of 1956 April 18, 1956	Price Support Freeze March 20, 1958	Farm Bill Rule June 26, 1958
Philadelphia	Compet	Compet	Compet	Compet
Boston	Compet	Compet	Compet	Compet
New York	Compet	Compet	Compet	Compet
Buffalo	Compet	Compet	Compet	Compet
San Francisco	Compet	Compet	Compet	Compet
Cleveland	Compet	Compet	Compet	Compet
Chicago	Compet	Compet	Compet	Compet
Baltimore	Compet	Compet	Compet	Compet
Detroit	Compet	Supp	Supp	*Split*
Pittsburgh	Compet	Compet	Compet	Compet
Cincinnati	*Split*	Supp	Compet	*Split*
Indianapolis	Compet	Compet	Compet	Compet
Omaha	Compet	Compet	Supp	Supp
St. Louis	Supp	Supp	Supp	Supp
Denver	Compet	Compet	Supp	Compet
Richmond	Compet	Compet	*Split*	Supp
Kansas City	Supp	Supp	Supp	Supp
Minneapolis	Supp	Supp	Supp	Supp
New Orleans	Supp	Supp	Supp	Supp
Atlanta	Supp	Supp	Supp	Supp
Birmingham	Supp	Supp	Supp	Supp
Memphis	Supp	Supp	Supp	Supp
Dallas	Supp	Supp	Supp	Supp
Sectional Stress	62.9	56.9	63.4	62.0

[a]Trade area delegations are ranked in descending order of their support for the core position on the ten high-stress roll calls recorded during the 84th Congress (1955–56); see table 2.5.

[b]"Supp" (Supports) indicates that a majority of the trade area delegation favored the continuation or expansion of price supports as an integral part of a national farm program; "Compet" (Competition) indicates that a majority of the trade area delegation favored the discontinuation or partial retraction of price supports maintained by the federal government; *Split* indicates that the trade area delegation divided evenly on the roll call.

SOURCE: Computations from roll call data.

(see table 5.3). The first political test occurred on a key amendment to the 1954 farm bill which reduced the minimum level of commodity price supports to 82.5 percent of parity in 1955 and to 75 percent thereafter. Though price supports could still fluctuate between these floors and 90 percent (the ceiling), the Eisenhower administration was dedicated to a gradual lowering of support levels and loosening of production controls until commodity markets again became freely competitive. Only dairy products, for which price supports were

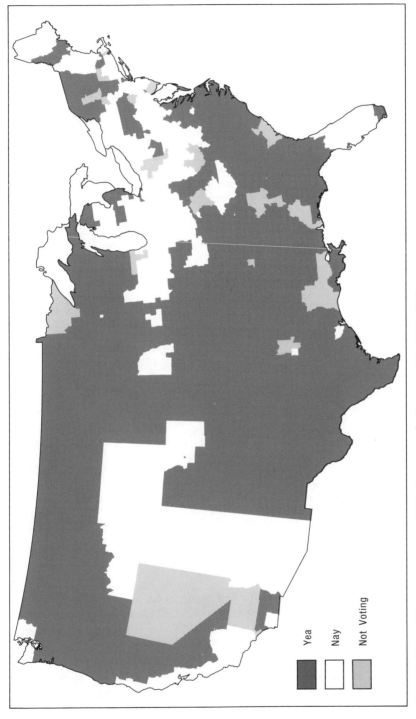

Map 5.1. Proposed Freeze on Agricultural Price Supports and Allotments, March 20, 1958

in fact raised, were exempted from the administration's strategy. The amendment carried, 228 to 170, with 182 Republicans, 45 Democrats, and 1 Independent supporting the "flexible parity" provision. Opposed to the administration (and backing continued high price supports) were 147 Democrats and 23 Republicans. Noting the stiff opposition the plan had encountered in the House, Secretary Benson recounted, "the Administration had bearded the so-called farm bloc lions in their den and had come out carrying their whiskers."[61]

On April 18, 1956, the House of Representatives attempted to enact a second general farm bill over an Eisenhower veto. The override attempt failed (211 to 202) to attract the necessary two-thirds majority, and the Agricultural Act of 1956 was later amended to meet the administration's objections. The vote on the override (table 5.3) and the roll call by which the original bill had passed the House before being sent on to the Senate were among the ten high-stress, closely contested roll calls recorded during the 84th Congress. The bill vetoed by Eisenhower would have returned federal subsidies to what the president termed "a war-time rigid 90 percent of parity supports for the basic commodities."[62]

In early March of 1958, the Senate passed a bill which would have prevented any reduction in the level of commodity price supports that had prevailed during the previous year, and sent the legislation on to the House. In a third classic test between the high-support, interventionist philosophy of the periphery and the free-market orientation of the administration, the House of Representatives adopted the Senate bill, 211 to 172. Eisenhower later vetoed the legislation and no attempt was made to override. The voting pattern on the "freeze" bill revealed a deep sectional split between the industrial core and the agrarian periphery (see map 5.1). The only periphery regions which favored the administration were the citrus areas of Florida and California, which were not covered by federal price supports or allotments (though citrus producers are subject to marketing orders), the wool and sheep-grazing territory of the mountain states (exceptionally favored by Eisenhower administration policy), and subsistence farming districts in the Appalachian Mountains (which had little involvement in the national economy).[63] Opposition to the administration's position in the manufacturing belt was limited to urban constituencies in Boston, Detroit, and New York, coal-producing districts in eastern Pennsylvania and to the southwest of Pittsburgh, and the dairy districts of upstate New York. The political imperatives of the New Deal Democratic coalition explain (as will be shown) the urban and coal producer anomalies. Dairy producers supported the "freeze" because milk products were included in the bill. The corn belt was divided between western producers which were net "sellers" of corn (and would benefit from high price supports) and eastern, industrial core producers who supplemented their own grain supplies with regional imports for livestock feed (and thus would buy at high support levels). In general, this intersectional division reflects the fundamental core-periphery cleavage underlying the American political system, and despite some shifts by discrete producers reflecting temporary political advantage, all major farm legislation provoked a very similar geographical split.

The last roll call displayed in table 5.3 occurred on adoption of an "open rule" which would have allowed floor consideration of a bill to renew, at high price support levels, six separate commodity programs. Opposed by the administration, the rule was defeated, and the legislation was later defeated a second time under an alternative parliamentary procedure called "suspension of the rules." In the table the twenty-three trade area delegations (see table 2.5) are ranked according to the support they gave the "core position" on the ten high-stress, closely contested roll calls in the 84th Congress (it will be remembered that six of the ten dealt not at all or tangentially with agricultural policy). As can be seen, most of the twenty-three delegations consistently assumed either a "free market competition" or "high price support" position (ten and eight delegations, respectively). This pattern corresponds with the fundamental core-periphery cleavage.

The preceding votes occurred during consideration of omnibus farm legislation that included most price support mechanisms and commodity production controls. Though the voting patterns are similar, the politics of individual commodity programs have reflected the narrower regional base directly implicated by each policy and the relationship between that commodity-region and the sectional dynamics of the national political economy (see table 5.4). Government intervention in the agricultural sector has focused on six so-called basic commodities: wheat, corn, cotton, rice, tobacco, and peanuts. Interventionist measures have centered on these crops for two important reasons. First, the nature of the consumer demand curve for these commodities, compared to other crops, has been such that a given reduction in supply would result in a larger market price increase; thus, production controls promised to result in relatively greater increases in net farm income. Second, the six commodities do not deteriorate in storage and require a minimum of special handling. These "basic commodities" together with about a half-dozen minor crops were the only important supported and controlled crops, numbering about 6 percent of the 200 different commodities theoretically eligible for interventionist subsidies. Together, these dozen crops accounted for about 20 percent of total farm income and required about 75 percent of the appropriations expended in support of farm prices.*

Roll call votes on five of the six basic price support programs (all but rice) are displayed in table 5.4. Three of the roll calls occurred upon passage of a

---

*Paarlberg, *American Farm Policy*, pp. 22–23. In 1960, at the end of the period, five commodities (corn, cotton, dairy products, grain sorghums, and wheat) received 91 percent of all federal support payments but represented only 40 percent of the value of all agricultural production. Soth, *An Embarrassment of Plenty*, p. 117.

Table 5.4. Trade Area Delegation Voting on Selected Commodity Programs, 1951–1959

Trade Area[a]	Peanuts March 7, 1951	Upland Cotton May 3, 1956	Corn March 13, 1957	Tobacco June 10, 1959	Wheat June 12, 1959
Philadelphia	Compet	Compet	Supp	Compet	Compet
Boston	Compet	Compet	Compet	*Split*	Compet
New York	Compet	Compet	Compet	Compet	Compet
Buffalo	Compet	Compet	Compet	Compet	Compet
San Francisco	Supp	Compet	Compet	Supp	Supp
Cleveland	Compet	Compet	*Split*	Compet	Compet
Chicago	Compet	Compet	Supp	Compet	Compet
Baltimore	Supp	Compet	Compet	Supp	Compet
Detroit	Compet	*Split*	Supp	Compet	Supp
Pittsburgh	Compet	Supp	Compet	Supp	*Split*
Cincinnati	Supp	*Split*	Supp	Supp	Supp
Indianapolis	Compet	Compet	Supp	*Split*	*Split*
Omaha	Compet	Compet	Supp	Supp	*Split*
St. Louis	*Split*	Supp	Supp	Supp	Supp
Denver	Supp	Supp	Supp	Supp	Supp
Richmond	Supp	Supp	Compet	Supp	Compet
Kansas City	*Split*	Compet	Supp	Supp	Supp
Minneapolis	Supp	Supp	Supp	Supp	Supp
New Orleans	Supp	Supp	Compet	Supp	Supp
Atlanta	Supp	Supp	Compet	Supp	Supp
Birmingham	Supp	Supp	*Split*	Supp	Supp
Memphis	Supp	Supp	Compet	Supp	Supp
Dallas	Supp	Supp	Compet	Supp	Supp
Sectional Stress	52.9	53.8	51.6	40.3	62.7

[a] Trade area delegations are ranked in descending order of their support for the core position on the ten high-stress roll calls recorded during the 84th Congress (1955–56); see table 2.5.

[b] "Supp" (Supports) indicates that a majority of the trade area delegation favored the continuation or expansion of price supports for the respective commodity; "Compet" (Competition) indicates that a majority of the trade area delegation favored the discontinuation or partial retraction of price supports maintained by the federal government; *Split* indicates that the trade area delegation split evenly on the roll call.

SOURCE: Computations from roll call data.

price support policy (corn, tobacco, and wheat), one took place upon a motion to recommit (kill) legislation allowing peanut producers to expand acreage without lowering price supports, and the upland cotton vote occurred on an amendment to the Agricultural Act of 1956 which would have "fixed" a high price support level for cotton. The upland cotton roll call was also one of the ten closely contested, high-stress votes recorded during the 84th Congress. Generally speaking, the voting patterns correspond to the underlying core-periphery cleavage regardless of the commodity under consideration. The one exception is the 1957 vote on passage of the corn bill.

Reciprocity between Commodities

Aside from the primary conflict between the industrial core and the agrarian periphery, the most striking characteristic of agricultural policy has been the strong tradition of reciprocal political support between the representatives of the basic commodity regions. During debate over adoption of a new tobacco program in 1959, Republican Robert Michel of Illinois stressed the durability and pervasiveness of political reciprocity within the agricultural sector:

> I can recall in my 12 years here on the Hill listening to debate on farm legislation up in the gallery and here on the House floor and I have heard it said we have given you wheat boys an opportunity to write your section of the bill, you corn boys have written your section, those interested in cotton have written your section, peanuts, yours, tobacco, rice, and so forth, and it has always made me feel as though it has just been one grand log-rolling operation. To use the same logic in consideration of a labor bill, you would think all that was necessary was to call in Mr. Reuther, Mr. Hoffa, and Mr. Meany and give them precisely what they want.[64]

Underlying political reciprocity between the basic commodities was the economic interdependence of agricultural production. Price support levels and production controls on one regulated commodity often had important consequences for the cultivation and marketing of one or more other crops. The possible conflict of interest between the basic commodities was often softened by compromise or eliminated before farm legislation reached the floor of the House or Senate. In the process of adjusting the various claims of the different crop producers, general policies such as the acreage reserve program (which idled cropland in all the major commodity regions) and rural development legislation served to cement political ties within the farm bloc. The process of adjudication and compromise was furthered by institutional arrangements such as the executive Department of Agriculture and the House and Senate Committees on Agriculture, which insulated farm policy from competing and "outside" political pressures. During the 1950s, for example, the House Committee on Agriculture divided its jurisdiction over agricultural policy into commodity Subcommittees on Cotton, on Peanuts, on Rice, on Tobacco, on Wheat, and on Livestock and Feed Grains (Corn). Congressmen attracted to the committee came predominantly from rural districts in which agricultural activities were a major economic factor, and committee members, once on the full committee, sought assignment to one or more of the subcommittees which best reflected the interests of their districts.[65] The coalition-building, then, of the log-rolling operation began within these separate subcommittees. In them, the representatives of each commodity interest drafted legislation for

Table 5.5. Classification of Trade Areas by Economic Type

Basic Commodity Trade Areas

Corn:	Cotton and Rice:	Cotton and Wheat:	Tobacco:
Des Moines	Memphis	Amarillo	Evansville
St. Louis	Cotton and Peanuts:	Rice:	Knoxville
Sioux City	Birmingham	Houston	Louisville
Corn and Wheat:	Dallas	New Orleans	Nashville
Kansas City	San Antonio	Sacramento	Richmond
Minneapolis	Cotton and Tobacco:	Peanuts and Tobacco:	Wheat:
Omaha	Charlotte	Norfolk	Billings
Cotton:	Cotton, Peanuts, and Tobacco:		Spokane
Little Rock	Atlanta		Wichita
Phoenix			
Shreveport			

Diversified Trade Areas

Charleston, W. V.	Jacksonville	Oklahoma City	Savannah
Denver	Los Angeles	Portland	Seattle
Duluth	Miami	Salt Lake City	Tampa
El Paso	Milwaukee	San Francisco	Tulsa
			Washington, D.C.

Manufacturing Belt Trade Areas

Corn:	Non-corn:	
Chicago	Albany	Harrisburg
Cincinnati	Baltimore	New York
Columbus	Boston	Philadelphia
Dayton	Buffalo	Pittsburgh
Indianapolis	Cleveland	Providence
Peoria	Detroit	Syracuse
Toledo	Grand Rapids	

their particular crop; then, in the full committee, other producer representatives adjusted each proposal in order to minimize any conflict of interest with their own commodities. Finally, the coalition-building process moved to the floor of the House where, as will be shown, negotiations between the farm bloc and industrial labor representatives within the New Deal Democratic coalition produced the marginal support necessary for passage.

Before proceeding to examine some of the broader characteristics of political reciprocity and conflict within the 1950s farm bloc, the sixty-five trade areas which composed the national urban center network during the 1950s must be categorized by their economic position within the industrial core–agrarian periphery division of labor (see table 5.5). Twenty trade areas lay primarily within the nation's manufacturing belt, beginning with Boston in the Northeast, extending south to Baltimore, and west to Chicago. As has been noted, the western reaches of the manufacturing belt overlapped with a portion of the corn producing region. Seven trade areas lay within both the industrial core and the corn belt. Each of the remaining forty-five trade areas fell within one of the basic commodity regions or contained a "diversified" agricultural base in which unsupported crops or livestock production was dominant. The agrarian periphery was composed primarily of those trade areas which produced the basic commodities. Outside the industrial core, six trade areas accounted for a significant portion of the corn belt and six more lay within the main wheat producing regions. The cotton belt extended over important parts of ten periphery trade areas; within the South, cotton producing trade area economies often included the cultivation of rice, tobacco, and peanuts.

Politically located between the core and periphery, fifteen widely separated Pacific, Gulf Coast, and Mountain trade areas contained diversified agricultural activities in which the six basic commodities played an unimportant role. Economically, many of these trade areas were either integrated with or dependent upon the markets of the major core industrial centers. Dairy production in the Chicago milkshed (Duluth and Milwaukee), citrus production in the subtropical areas of Florida and California, and truck farming in the San Francisco and Washington, D.C., trade areas exemplify the often close ties between diversified agriculture and metropolitan markets.* In many cases, these diversified areas were seaports containing some of the industrial and commercial activities that characterize the core economy. In contrast, most of the basic commodity regions were located away from the coast in the nation's vast interior. As Charles O. Jones noted, the Agriculture Committee members who represented these districts were often at odds with their basic commodity colleagues:

> The "diversified" (mainly non-basics) group often find their interests conflicting with those of representatives in the other groups. They complain that their farmers are at a disadvantage since their non-basics either do not receive price supports or receive less support than the basics; the price supports for the few basics grown do not make up for the deprivation of profits attributable to acreage and marketing controls (the complaint of California cotton farmers); and they must pay higher prices for the basics as well as pay higher taxes.[66]

In practice, diversified agriculture was often left out of the intense negotiations and bargaining that typified farm bloc politics.

Each major category (manufacturing belt, basic commodity regions, and

---

*In order to categorize the sixty-five trade areas, their territories were compared to the manufacturing belt depicted in Allan Pred, "Toward a Typology of Manufacturing Flows," in Fred E. Dohrs and Lawrence M. Sommers, eds., *Economic Geography: Selected Readings* (New York: Thomas Y. Crowell, 1970), p. 274; and the commodity regions described in Ladd Haystead and Gilbert C. Fite, *The Agricultural Regions of the United States* (Norman: University of Oklahoma Press, 1955), pp. 86, 106, 123, 124, 142, 184, and in Edward Higbee, *American Agriculture: Geography, Resources, Conservation* (New York: John Wiley and Sons, 1958), pp. 55, 374, 386. The "diversified" grouping contains regions that have specialized in dairy production (e.g., Duluth and Milwaukee) and range livestock (e.g., Salt Lake City and El Paso).

diversified agriculture) occupied a distinctive position in the political economy of agriculture. In the 1920s, immediate self-interest, largely uncomplicated by institutional arrangements or partisan considerations, had dictated the politics of McNary-Haugenism. Though the sectional cleavages of the 1950s were at least as intense, the political dynamics of agricultural policy were more complex. Voting charts on four of the five roll calls treated in table 5.4 are provided in table 5.6.*

In each instance, the basic commodity program considered on the floor favored a continued policy of high price supports and production controls which promised, in the short term at least, to increase the income of participating producers. A vote for each program, therefore, was a vote for continued government intervention in the cultivation and marketing of each commodity. On the basis of immediate self-interest, the representatives of farm constituencies belonging to trade area delegations in which a given basic crop was grown, all other factors aside, should have overwhelmingly favored the program pertaining to that crop. In two cases, upland cotton and tobacco, interested congressmen unanimously backed the corresponding programs. Congressmen from rural wheat producing districts cast nearly 80 percent of their votes in favor of the 1959 wheat bill, and some 90 percent of "farm," corn belt districts (both inside and outside the industrial core) supported their commodity program.

On the basis of economic interdependence between a trade area's commodity-producing hinterland and its urban center, non-farm members belonging to each basic commodity delegation should have both favored adoption of the program and supported passage by a greater percentage than any non-farm category. For example, non-farm congressmen from cotton delegations should have favored adoption of the amendment to the Agricultural Act of 1956 and should have produced a larger supporting percentage than any remaining (other basic, diversified, or manufacturing belt) non-farm category. As it turned out, four out of five non-farm, cotton delegation members backed the amendment. Though the percentage was slightly less than the 84.6 mark chalked up by "non-farm, other basic" members, the 80 percent figure was substantially higher than the remaining non-farm categories. Except for a

---

*The 1951 vote on the peanuts program is not analyzed in table 5.6 because data concerning the percentage of the constituency employed in agriculture were not available. In each table the 435 districts of the House of Representatives have been divided into four general types depending on the categorization of the trade area in which each district falls. The first type is composed of all trade area delegations in which the basic commodity under consideration forms an important part of the economic base of the region. All other basic commodity delegations constitute the second entry in each chart, followed by the diversified trade areas and, finally, by the manufacturing belt members. Manufacturing belt delegations have been separated into those trade areas which overlapped with the eastern portion of the corn belt and those which did not contain important corn producing regions. The voting patterns of each type of trade area have been further subdivided into "farm" and "non-farm" constituencies. All "farm" districts contain an economy in which 5 percent or more of the population was employed in agriculture.

Table 5.6. Voting on Basic Commodity Supports, 1956–1959

Type of Trade Area[a]	Percentage Favoring		Total
	Farm District[b]	Non-farm[b]	
Upland Cotton Supports (1956)			
Upland Cotton	100.0 (53)[c]	80.0 (5)[c]	98.2 (58)[c]
Other Basic	48.6 (72)	84.6 (13)	54.1 (85)
Diversified	44.0 (50)	30.8 (26)	39.5 (76)
Manufacturing Belt:			
Corn	13.6 (22)	41.2 (17)	25.6 (39)
Non-corn	17.4 (46)	38.9 (90)	31.6 (136)
Total	16.2 (68)	39.3 (107)	30.3 (175)
Corn Supports (1957)			
Corn	86.8 (38)	42.9 (7)	80.0 (45)
Other Basic	37.8 (90)	27.3 (11)	36.6 (101)
Diversified	50.0 (54)	30.4 (23)	44.2 (77)
Manufacturing Belt:			
Corn	100.0 (25)	61.1 (18)	83.7 (43)
Non-Corn	60.4 (48)	17.6 (91)	32.4 (139)
Total	74.0 (73)	24.8 (109)	44.5 (182)
Tobacco Supports (1959)			
Tobacco	100.0 (38)	100.0 (5)	100.0 (43)
Other Basic	94.1 (85)	75.0 (12)	91.8 (97)
Diversified	79.2 (53)	45.8 (24)	68.8 (77)
Manufacturing Belt:			
Corn	43.5 (23)	40.0 (20)	41.9 (43)
Non-corn	22.2 (45)	39.4 (94)	33.8 (139)
Total	29.4 (68)	39.5 (114)	35.7 (182)
Wheat Supports (1959)			
Wheat	77.8 (27)	50.0 (2)	75.9 (29)
Other Basic	82.8 (93)	86.7 (15)	83.3 (108)
Diversified	64.0 (50)	50.0 (24)	59.5 (74)
Manufacturing Belt:			
Corn	33.3 (21)	33.3 (18)	33.3 (39)
Non-corn	22.7 (44)	13.9 (72)	17.2 (116)
Total	26.2 (65)	17.8 (90)	21.3 (155)

[a] For the classification of trade areas, see table 5.5.

[b] Districts were classified into "farm" and "non-farm" categories on the basis of the 1954 Census of Agriculture. All "farm" districts contained an economy in which 5 percent or more of the population was employed in agriculture (see *Congressional Quarterly Almanac: 85th Congress, 1st Session . . . 1957*, vol. 13 (Washington: Congressional Quarterly, 1957), pp. 326–27.

[c] Figures in parentheses are the number of congressmen who voted within each category.

SOURCE: Computations from roll call data.

similar anomaly in the wheat program chart, the other three votes generally followed the expected pattern.

Aside from the basic commodity trade area delegations, the greatest amount of political support should have come from the other commodity members who were not directly interested in the program under consideration. In all cases except the corn program, this pattern held. On the corn bill, other basic commodity delegations did not support passage. The roll call voting on this bill, if viewed in conjunction with roll call behavior on the cotton amendment, strongly indicates antagonism between the cotton and corn members. Only 31.5 percent of the members from farm districts in cotton growing areas supported the corn bill, and only 30.8 percent of the farm congressmen from corn delegations outside the manufacturing belt favored adoption of the upland cotton amendment. Both figures are substantially lower than those for all "other commodity" members.

In almost every respect the diversified delegations also behaved as would be expected: less support for each program than the basic commodity members but more than the manufacturing belt congressmen. The only significant exception was, once more, voting on the corn bill, which found farm congressmen from diversified districts less supportive than their manufacturing belt counterparts. Before discussing the behavior of industrial core delegations, two policy aspects of inter-commodity reciprocity should be analyzed.

The wheat bill considered by the House in the 1959 vote combined a 20 percent acreage reduction with a price support level set at 80 percent of parity. The administration urged a larger reduction in acreage allotments and firmly opposed an increase in the support level.* These aspects of the wheat program were also broadly typical of the other three commodity votes. Each commodity's representatives attempted to expand the income of their constituent producers, while the Republican administration attempted to "scale back" the size of national acreage allotments, the parity price floor, or both. A major difference in the politics of the wheat program, however, was the statutory provision that allowed any farmer to plant and market fifteen acres without an allotment. While some large wheat producers in "traditional" growth regions (e.g., North Dakota and Kansas) opposed the exemption, many producers viewed the fifteen-acre exemption as a political necessity. By the late 1950s, 600,000 farmers had planted wheat under this provision, and the "loophole," which originally had been created to lessen the burden of administrative enforcement, now drew political support for a high allotment–high support policy from many areas in the corn belt and dairy regions of the nation. With-

---

*Secretary Benson called the proposed reduction in acreage "meaningless" because the higher support price would inevitably increase yields on the remaining acres and ultimately fail to reduce (and perhaps enlarge) the annual surplus. President Eisenhower later vetoed an amended bill which cut allotments by one-quarter but raised the price floor to 90 percent of parity. Benson, *Cross Fire*, pp. 459–62.

out the exception, one analyst felt, "farmers in these areas would . . . have been apathetic or even hostile."* The fifteen-acre exemption became, in effect, an interregional side payment which expanded the political constituency of the wheat program by "artificially" encouraging small-scale production in non-traditional regions.

The characteristics of corn production placed this commodity in a position within the national political economy very different from that of other "basics." Most important, the cultivation of corn was intimately linked to livestock—particularly hog production. Less than one in every ten bushels was processed directly into feed; instead, over 60 percent of all production was fed to livestock on the same farm on which the corn was grown. After deducting direct consumer uses, the remainder marketed off the farm was also ultimately used as livestock feed.† Because most corn was produced and converted into livestock on the same farm, production controls were voluntary and limited to producers who marketed most or all of their crop.‡ For a number of reasons, including administrative difficulties, noncompliance, and selective diversion of acreage, even these voluntary controls did not significantly reduce corn production. But diverted acreage under any "control" program (includ-

---

*Paarlberg, *American Farm Policy*, pp. 214–15. Normally, farm congressmen in the industrial core tended to remain aloof from the reciprocity network that involved other commodity members. "For many Northeastern Republicans . . . a distaste for price support programs was reinforced by the possession of a number of poultry and dairy farmer constituents interested in purchasing cheap feed grains." David R. Mayhew, *Party Loyalty among Congressmen* (Cambridge: Harvard University Press, 1966), p. 39.

†Paarlberg, *American Farm Policy*, p. 197. One aspect of the corn program not discussed here was that manipulation of the price level and production controls could be used to indirectly influence livestock markets.

‡"If controls were made mandatory, these things would happen:

"Farmers who had never been in the program would have to come in. They would include livestock farmers who have fewer incentives for a control program than do sellers of cash corn and who are opposed, many of them, on ideological grounds.

"Farmers who overplanted their allotments and fed the excess to their own livestock would have to be taken into court and fined. This is vastly different from enforcing compliance for other crops. Wheat and tobacco are sold directly, with the help of a marketing card, after acreage controls have been checked and verified. There is a ready method of preventing sales from acreage in excess of quotas and a ready procedure for assessing penalities. But how could government officials police the livestockman who exceeded his corn acreage allotment? This fellow feeds all his corn; the excess corn becomes an unidentified part of his many hogs and cattle, which may move to market through any of a dozen channels on any day of the year.

"With many farmers unfavorably disposed toward the program and with regulatory procedures difficult to enforce, the courts might soon become clogged with cases brought by government against farm people whose only offense was to grow corn on their own land, feed it to their own pigs, and sell their pigs in a competitive market. They would have asked no help from the government and would have gotten none. Would juries fine or imprison such farmers? The Congress has never been willing to put this question to the test. General Eisenhower, livestock farmer from Pennsylvania, said that if corn controls were made mandatory and if he were found to have violated such a law, he would go to jail and continue his protests from behind the bars." Ibid., p. 206 (italics removed).

ing corn, wheat, and cotton) could be replanted with uncontrolled crops. The most significant of the "replacement" crops were non-corn feed grains such as sorghum, barley, and oats. During the 1950s about 7 percent of the nation's harvested cropland was diverted out of wheat and cotton and into feed grains which directly competed with corn as an intermediary in livestock production. As a result, even with voluntary controls on corn, the total production of feed grains expanded by 10 percent during the decade and created a direct and intense policy conflict between corn producers and those cultivating cotton and, to a lesser extent, wheat as a primary crop.[67]

Since passage of the first McNary-Haugen bills in the second half of the 1920s, the basic alliance or "power axis" within the congressional farm bloc had always been between corn and cotton. By the late 1950s that alliance was rapidly deteriorating, and more than any other single factor, the growing cleavage between corn and cotton belt members could be traced to the problem of feed grain surpluses.[68] Policy-makers were unable to develop remedies for the surplus which both recognized the interdependence between controls on different crops and the production of feed grains and promised to reduce total production without disrupting historical patterns of cultivation. Every suggestion seemed to tilt farm income toward one region to the disadvantage of the other.*

*During floor consideration of the 1957 corn bill, one possible remedy proposed by cotton belt members was an amendment which would have made southern feed grains eligible for participation in the Soil Bank program. The proposal would have both reduced southern acreage cultivated in supplementary feed grains and increased farm income in the South. The range of reactions among corn belt congressmen indicated the intense desire for compromise while at the same time highlighting the seeming impossibility of a solution. Republican Ralph Harvey of Indiana pointed out to his colleagues that the "reason corn as a commodity is having difficulty is because of the surplus feed grains that have been brought into the pattern of production and have thereby displaced corn from its normal pattern of use" (*Congressional Record*, 85:1:3586, March 13, 1957). For some corn belt members, this development implied that the South should be "written into" the corn program and permitted to share in the benefits.

Other midwestern congressmen, particularly those whose districts overlapped into the manufacturing belt, believed that the corn program (a legitimate claim by traditional producers) was being held hostage as a political tactic to further "illegitimate" claims on the national treasury. The interests of such members in passage of a corn bill were somewhat compromised by the often substantial industrial populations in their districts and the tendency for their agricultural sectors to be net purchasers of corn on the open market. Consequently, these eastern corn belt representatives were often impatient with southern claims. Republican Clare Hoffman of Michigan put their position best when he said, "the corn boys complain and apparently they are not going to get any relief unless our friends from the South are permitted to put the feed grains into competition with our corn and get paid for so doing." *Congressional Record*, 85:1:3585, March 13, 1957. Harvey pointed out that the cotton program was also very expensive and (somewhat inaccurately) that "we in the North have had to pay year after year millions of dollars not to the little man of the South with whom we all sympathize and wish to aid but to these big, rich corporations."

For these members, the obvious solution to the feed grains surplus was to prohibit the diversion of idled cotton acreage into crops grown in competition with corn. As one Appalachian Republican (who did not have strong interests on either side) summarized the conflict, "the

Though the dissolution of the corn-cotton alliance appears to have been the natural result of an irresolvable policy conflict (given that the agriculture budget could not infinitely expand), the Eisenhower administration aggravated the political cleavage by playing the two groups off against one another.* After a southern amendment to include feed grains lost on an unrecorded teller vote in the Committee of the Whole in 1957 (defeated, in part, by corn belt members), southern trade area delegations withdrew support for the legislation (see table 5.4) and the entire corn bill went down in flames, 188 to 217. The *Congressional Quarterly Almanac* for 1957 has provided a summary of that vote.[69] Corn, wheat, and dairy congressmen—about three-quarters of whom were Republicans—favored the corn bill without southern feed grain eligibility for soil bank payments. Rice members split almost evenly, and the representatives of the major southern commodities (cotton, tobacco, and peanuts) opposed adoption of the program containing the feed grain exclusion. Over 90 percent of these members were Democrats. The politics of the 1957 corn bill indicated that reciprocity between the representatives of the different commodities was not automatic and was complicated by conditions and situations created by the very programs benefiting the individual producer groups.

	Total	Farm	Non-farm
Democrats	63–156	52–80	11–76
Republicians	125–61	95–25	30–36

Even given the tendency for major commodity regions to become one-party regions and the tendency for producers to favor high support prices for their own commodity regardless of party allegiance, the two parties have nevertheless played a significant role in farm legislation aside from the representation of constituency self-interest. The willingness of congressmen to reciprocate support across commodity programs, for example, was strongly influenced by the class structure of American agriculture. Class competition within agriculture was primarily expressed through partisan politics. Republican farmers tended to be upper- and middle-income producers, whose interests were often reflected in the anti-interventionist policy orientation of the American Farm Bureau Federation.† These producers favored high price sup-

---

debate on this corn bill has developed a clear pattern of antagonism of the wheat and corn growers of the Central and Western States against the producers of other basics in the Southern States" (Representative Will E. Neal of West Virginia, *Congressional Record*, 85:1:3591, March 13, 1957).

*Ezra Taft Benson, for example, saw favorable signs in the breakdown of reciprocity between cotton and corn members. "The farm bloc apparently had split wide open, with the cotton, peanut and tobacco South in general beginning to take sides with us against the high-price-support-minded wheat and corn North." *Cross Fire*, p. 351.

†Benson described the American Farm Bureau Federation as "consistently wary of government controls, . . . opposed to government price fixing, farm income grounded in Federal subsidies, and government production controls as a means of 'stabilizing' the farm economy."

ports on their own commodities but generally opposed corresponding treatment for other crops. Though their congressmen were more likely to support other farm programs, these (usually) Republican members often stood outside the New Deal coalition of periphery agriculture and core industrial labor which provided the larger political framework for government support programs.

Lower-income, marginal producers tended to join the National Farmers Union and have their interests represented within the Democratic party. The poorest farm operators resided in the cotton, tobacco, rice, and peanut producing areas of the southern periphery. Almost totally dependent on federal intervention, these farmers formed the backbone of the farm bloc by encouraging their congressmen to seek unity within the agricultural sector and by tolerating strong political ties with the interests of industrial labor. Democrats also tended to represent high-risk agricultural regions such as the wheat areas of the nation in the Dakotas, Kansas, Nebraska, and the Pacific Northwest. Operators in these regions often interpreted government intervention as a necessary socialization of an unacceptably high level of risk because they usually could not convert to other crops and because the semi-arid climate and variable rainfall had an unpredictable, often decisive impact on the quantity and quality of the harvest. In general, Democratic producers were disproportionately drawn from these high-risk agricultural regions, the lower-income ranks of American agriculture, and from a shrinking cohort of younger debt-ridden farmers who tended to favor inflationary policies. High price support programs kept many marginal operators in business and, thus, tended to tie these farmers to the political process of reciprocity within the farm bloc and the New Deal Democratic coalition that made high supports possible. Given the sectional distribution of farm income and operating risk, interventionist policies and the political relationships that such programs entailed were more popular in the South and plains states than they were in the immediate agricultural hinterland of the industrial core.

Agricultural producers within the manufacturing belt or on its borders—in contrast to those in the periphery—were relatively prosperous. Most operators of corn/livestock, dairy, or poultry units fell within the top 40 percent of all producers in terms of average annual income.[70] These Republican operators came in greater numbers from areas of relatively stable harvests and reliable income, often thought of themselves as "scientific farmers" interested in the long-term future of the agricultural sector, and were disproportionately drawn from the population of older, successful operators who had repaid their mortgage and no longer had an interest in "inflationary" government policies.[71]

The Eisenhower administration and almost all Republicans representing

---

The National Farmers Union, on the other hand, held to "the theory that farm prices are, and should be 'made in Washington,'—that the agricultural economy must depend on Federal subsidies to give farmers their 'share' of the national income." *Cross Fire*, p. 156.

metropolitan constituencies in the manufacturing belt supported lower minimum price support levels and a flexible parity policy. The party of the core elite anticipated that such changes in the farm program would enlarge the share of the national income retained in the heavy industrial regions. Furthermore, a flexible, low-parity program was less expensive than the Democratic alternative. In addition, the Republican administration and its congressional allies felt that only a gradual return to world market conditions and the reestablishment of a domestic free market in the major commodities could be a real and permanent "solution" to the problem of surpluses. This economic solution required a massive reallocation of productive resources out of the agricultural sector and implied bankruptcy for thousands of marginal operators who would subsequently be forced into sectors which were more competitive within the world-economy.[72] High price supports and production controls only postponed and retarded what critics saw as an inevitable restructuring of American agriculture. Finally, the Republicans wished to split apart the New Deal coalition which had been forged out of the economic dependence of the marginal operator on interventionist controls and price supports. Even with the steady exodus of low-income farmers into the industrial economy (which took place despite government subsidies), a significant portion of the agricultural sector threatened to become permanently dependent on federal aid and, by implication, on the political alliances with organized labor which made that aid possible.*

The Farm Program and the New Deal Coalition

The least support for each commodity policy, based on immediate economic self-interest, should have come from "non-farm" manufacturing belt congress-

---

*Writing in 1964, former Benson aide Don Paarlberg described one form which this economic dependence could assume: "The limitation on tobacco production is the acreage allotment. Since tobacco production is very profitable, the value of an acre of production rights is very high. An acre of tobacco allotment, independent of the land and buildings associated with it, was estimated to add $1,673 to the sale value of tobacco farms in Pittsylvania County, Virginia, during 1957. This is many times the value of the figure has increased further. It is said that in some sections of North Carolina an acre of tobacco allotment is worth $5,000" (*American Farm Policy*, p. 234). For the producer who owned the acreage when the allotment program went into effect, the capitalization of government-supported income into land values can be considered a "windfall profit," but to all future purchasers the allotment program represented a fixed (and politically vulnerable) capital investment. Tobacco allotments dramatically altered land values because production controls were singularly effective in increasing producer income. That effectiveness could be traced to the absence of any directly competing crop or synthetic substitute (which could potentially sabotage production controls on tobacco) and a very inelastic consumer demand curve (based on nicotine addiction). Still, production controls and price supports were slowly strangling the American export market for the crop (ibid., pp. 233–34). Other basic commodities were not as favorably placed in the national economy (e.g., corn), but all experienced "over-capitalization" in land and equipment as a result of government intervention. Recognizing the political implications of

Table 5.7. Percentage of Urban Core Party Members Supporting Basic Commodity Support Programs

Commodity	Democrats	Republicans
Corn	10.0 (50)	26.8 (41)
Wheat	21.7 (46)	0.0 (26)
Cotton	70.0 (50)	0.0 (40)
Tobacco	59.3 (59)	5.7 (35)

men who represented districts outside the corn belt. In the voting on two programs, for wheat and for corn, these were in fact the least supportive members. Only 13.9 percent backed the 1959 wheat bill and only 17.6 percent voted for the 1957 corn program. On the other two commodity roll calls, however, the same group provided support comparable to or exceeding that of members in the other categories. In the case of tobacco and cotton, nearly two out of every five members from industrial core constituencies backed policies which favored the agrarian periphery. The explanation for this core support for agrarian policies is, of course, the New Deal coalition between industrial labor and the southern periphery.

If the voting behavior of non-farm, industrial core members from outside the corn belt is divided by party, the pattern and direction of reciprocity becomes more distinct. In table 5.7, the four commodities are ranked by the proportion of the representatives from their respective areas of greatest production who belong to the Republican party. Corn belt members almost always heavily favored the GOP; congressmen from wheat districts joined the Republican caucus with somewhat less frequency; and cotton and tobacco areas almost never strayed from the Democratic party. As can be seen, the direction of political support tended to follow party ties. For the Republicans, urban core members provided only lukewarm support for even the one commodity that penetrated the manufacturing belt; they solidly opposed programs that lay entirely in the agrarian periphery. Industrial core Democrats, on the other hand, provided some votes for all four commodities and even a large majority for the two "Democratic" crops. Clearly, these votes could not have been motivated by the direct self-interest of Democratic constituents; commodity programs were intended, albeit indirectly, to raise the cost of food to the urban consumer.* Instead, the political alliance that they implied was based on often

---

continued economic dependence, the Eisenhower administration strove mightily to reimpose free market competition upon the "basics."

*At times, the Democratic party leadership would have liked their colleagues to ignore the retail price implications of government supports. In an attempt to increase support for the 1959 wheat bill, Majority Leader John McCormack from Boston baldly argued in floor debate, "Anyone from the cities who votes against any bill because he thinks it is going to increase the cost of living to the consumers in the city is making a very serious mistake." *Congressional Record*, 86:1:10539, June 11, 1959.

explicit trades between congressmen tied to organized labor and those who represented one of the major agricultural commodity belts.

Logrolling between the two sectional wings of the Democratic party was facilitated by three features of the contemporary political system. The most amorphous of the three was the development of an interventionist "public philosophy" that could be used to defend votes which, on their face, ran against the immediate interest of coalition members. During floor debate on the 1959 wheat bill, Democrat Quentin Burdick of North Dakota made such a justification for wheat support, stating, "Just as I support measures directly affecting the urban areas as being in the national interest, I ask my city friends to support this legislation in the national interest." [73] The philosophical cover for similar notions of the "national interest" was sometimes quite thin and was always frustrating to those Republicans who watched from the sidelines. As one such member noted during the debate,

> Recently, certain Members of the House who have city districts openly appealed to rural Members of the House to support public housing, slum clearance and subsidy programs for big cities. Reciprocal support on measures for the farmer such as this wheat bill was promised. Some back scratching arrangements are not in the public interest and, for one, I will not have any part in them. [74]

Thus, Republican members, usually representing either upper-class core constituencies or relatively prosperous agricultural districts closely tied to core consumer markets, tended to vote in accordance with the immediate interest of their electorates. This tendency reinforced an ideological predisposition that favored less government intervention in all aspects of American life.

For the Democrats the problem was more complicated and became intertwined with a second institutional arrangement that provided essential support for the New Deal coalition. The committee system, in effect, divided up control of the national political economy between the two polar factions of the majority party. Of the two most crucial committees in the labor–farm bloc logroll, the Committee on Agriculture held jurisdiction over all major farm programs and was dominated by members from the major commodity regions. On the Democratic side, cotton, tobacco, and rice members held a large majority of the seats. [75] For those members who represented labor districts, the focus of legislative attention was the Committee on Education and Labor, a panel ultimately dominated by representatives from urban, industrial districts. Subject to arbitration by the party leadership and, independently, by the Committee on Rules (which often controlled access to the floor), the two wings of the party pursued their most important legislative goals (i.e., farm subsidies and labor law) with relatively little input from the opposition party. One of the necessary conditions for the strength and effectiveness of this political decentralization of legislative power was the generation of "public interest" arguments favoring the passage of legislation by the reporting committees. In hearings, committee reports, and floor debates, leaders of the party, allied bureaucrats, and private interest groups would forge a political justification which could bridge the sectional cleavage. Though many observers might argue that the sum total of such explanations verged on logical incoherence (e.g., tobacco price supports and funding for lung cancer research), the general ideological thrust was toward greater government intervention in the economy.

The last institutional feature of the New Deal coalition was the arbitrating and unifying role of the party leadership. Considered individually, labor and farm initiatives embodied clearly conflicting sectional implications. Even considered as explicit, one-time trades (votes on a specific labor bill for a particular commodity program), the "free-rider" problems were enormous. How many urban industrial Democrats, for example, could vote against the cotton bill before reciprocity with the periphery unraveled? As David Mayhew has observed,

> The public exhortations engaged in by the Democratic leadership in winning urban and industrial votes were most often appeals to party unity or homilies on the expertise of the Agriculture Committee. The debates were punctuated with references to the mutual obligations of sections of the party to each other on matters of concern to each.*

The efforts of the party leadership were, of course, not limited to farm legislation, and the broad effect of party loyalty appeals was to mildly coerce potential "free riders" back into the confines of the bipolar coalition.

One of the primary requirements for the efficient operation of the New Deal coalition was the suppression of intraparty dissent. By making routine support for the legislative products of the committee system a major test of party loyalty, the committee and floor leaders encouraged legislative panels to develop easily defended policy justifications (for the campaign use of all members). They also supported the decentralization of fratricidal conflict into the discreet corridors of the committee labyrinth. Criticism of committee proposals on the House floor was considered unseemly by many committee chairmen—for example, Harold C. Cooley of North Carolina, chairman of the Agriculture Committee, who entered the debate on the 1951 peanut bill:

> I would like to say to gentlemen from New York and to gentlemen from metropolitan districts in this House that we will welcome an expression of your views at any time legislation is being considered. I think it would be in the interest of the welfare of the country if some of the people from

*Mayhew, *Party Loyalty among Congressmen*, p. 51. Mayhew provides extensive roll call evidence of reciprocal political ties and notes that "machine" Democrats were more likely to logroll than politically independent members (pp. 49–50).

city districts would come to the Committee on Agriculture and express their views rather than wait until the last minute when legislation is being considered on the floor of the House.[76]

There were two reasons for preventing a public airing of intraparty dissent. First, public opposition increased the potential electoral costs for those who remained loyal to the party by raising very appealing (at least to one or the other poles of the party) objections to the committee's handiwork. In addition, bargaining on the floor of the House tended to reveal the more pragmatic and less idealistic foundations of party policy.

One of the rare public revelations of the often intense negotiations within the party took place during debate on a 1952 Republican amendment which proposed to remove peanuts from the list of "basic" commodities.[77] The amendment would have made peanut producers ineligible for price supports and was intended, by the Republicans, to drive a wedge between the labor and agrarian wings of the majority party. Representative Daniel Flood, a Pennsylvania Democrat from a coal mining district, used the tactical situation created by the Republicans to press for party support for a mine-safety bill which was stalled before the Committee on Rules. This remarkable speech bears quoting at some length; it begins with Flood's discussion of the peanut amendment.

> I bow to the opinion and the experience and awareness of the subject [of] the members of this committee [Agriculture]. This is their problem, and because of the procedure of this House and the way we operate here and because the work is left to the committee, perforce we must follow their advice.
>
> Now the number of bales of cotton yield per acre in my district is very, very, very small, believe me. The number of peanuts, the pounds of tobacco that we get from my coal mines would not fill your hat. Yet I come here year after year baring my breast to the slings and arrows of the outraged farm districts, and vote for them. But it is a one-way street, it is a one-way street . . .
>
> Why do you otherwise charming, gracious, intelligent, patriotic, and learned gentlemen tell us how to run the coal mines, tell us how to house our poor, our starving in our cities? Why do you not reciprocate and take our advice on matters affecting our areas which at least are equally as important to the general welfare as your farm areas—for we are the consumers—we must also live.
>
> You point to me in the great debates on the control bill for years and you get down and thunder at me that I am a Socialist if I support liberal legislation. Daniel John Francis Joseph Flood a Socialist. What double-barreled nonsense. I would never vote for any Socialist legislation, and you know it. Housing for the poor in great cities. That is not socialism— that is Americanism. . . . We need your help badly for work and safety.

My friends have gone through this aisle shoulder to shoulder for you year after year. We ask you for bread, you farmers, and you give us stone.

To these remarks, Democrat Price H. Preston of Savannah, Georgia, whose district bordered on a major peanut-producing region, replied,

> he [Flood] made some slight, very courteous reference to the fact that certain Members from the South sometimes do not vote on measures that are important to his area in a manner that would be pleasing to his people, but may I say that the majority of the Members of the House of Representatives from the South have supported public housing. . . . We feel for you and your problems, and hope to reciprocate for the generosity you have shown.

At this stage in the debate, Flood decided to press his point home.

> I have just come from testifying before the Committee on Rules with many of your Members on both sides of the aisle in behalf of that vital and important legislation, the mine safety bill. Now will you look into your hearts and vote, and will the gentleman from Georgia preach the gospel in the ears of all our friends from the South to support that mine-safety legislation when it comes on this floor as we are going to support you today? Now this is a ball game—let us play it.[78]

Following Flood's exhortation, both Graham A. Barden of North Carolina, Chairman of the Education and Labor Committee, and Edward Cox of Georgia, Chairman of the Rules Committee, rose to assure their colleagues from the coal districts that due and proper consideration was being given to the mine safety bill. Since Cox himself represented one of the most important peanut producing regions of the nation (in southwest Georgia), the Republican amendment to exclude peanuts from the list of "basics" presented an effective opportunity to spring loose the safety legislation. In order to bring this frank exchange to a close on a harmonious note, the Democratic Majority Leader John McCormack of Massachusetts took responsibility for both policies. After urging defeat of the peanut exclusion amendment, McCormack committed the party leadership to prompt passage of the mine safety bill: "I consider this 'must' legislation and I hope the Rules Committee will report a rule."[79]

Since the Second World War, several other explicit bargains between the agrarian and labor wings of the Democratic party have come to light. In the early weeks of the 84th Congress (1955–56), the president of the Congress of Industrial Organizations, Walter Reuther, testified before the Committee on Agriculture *in favor* of 90 percent parity. His counterpart in the American Federation of Labor, George Meany, wrote a letter to the committee supporting the goal of high (90 percent) price support on basic commodities and reiterating labor's solidarity with America's agricultural producers. In return for organized labor's backing, the southern members promised to vote for legislation which would establish a higher national minimum wage. After setting the stage for this gigantic logroll, both sides delivered on their commitments.[80] A less formal agreement between labor supporters of food stamp legislation and agrarian members interested in passage of a combination wheat-cotton commodity bill was reached in April 1964. The trade was arranged by representatives of the Department of Agriculture in the executive branch and the House Democratic leadership. The bills passed within one hour of each other in a trade that has been called "82 percent successful."[81] In 1973, the industrial labor–agrarian periphery coalition was resurrected over the opposition of a Republican presidential administration. The 1973 farm bill involved a logroll between passage of the cotton section of the measure and defeat of an amendment to a minimum wage bill which would have established a lower wage floor for students and persons under eighteen years of age. On this occasion, Representative William R. Poage of Texas, chairman of the full Agriculture Committee, hurried the farm bill to the floor so as "to limit the time span between floor action on the minimum-wage and farm bills, in order to facilitate vote trading between the two issues." By 1973, however, the civil rights movement had weakened the bonds that tied the two wings of the Democratic party together, and both the complexity of bargaining arrangements for logrolling and the number and effectiveness of floor assaults on Democratic unity had dramatically increased.*

Race Relations, 1965–1966

During the 89th Congress (1965–66), federal legislation in the area of race relations and civil rights produced five of the ten high-stress, closely contested roll calls and clearly dominated sectional conflict. Three of the roll calls were taken on the proposed Civil Rights Act of 1966, including approval of the special order which brought the legislation to the floor, an amendment that would have limited the ability of the Attorney General to file desegregation suits, and a motion to delete the open-housing title of the bill. The two remaining votes were recorded on a motion to discharge the Rules Committee of a special order which eventually brought to the floor legislation providing for

---

*Agriculture Chairman Poage's relations with congressional lobbyists representing organized labor and with members of his own party from labor constituencies were so bad that he asked northern members of the committee to conduct a "dry run" before he himself met with them. Weldon V. Barton, "Coalition-Building in the United States House of Representatives: Agricultural Legislation in 1973" (paper delivered at the 1974 Annual Meeting of American Political Science Association, Palmer House, Chicago, Illinois, August 29–September 2, 1974). David R. Mayhew believes "that the Democratic approach to agriculture [described in the text] helped to preserve the sometimes tenuous connection between the Northern and Southern wings of the party. So long as the South, or most of it, remained predominantly agricultural, there was good reason for it to remain Democratic." *Party Loyalty among Congressmen*, pp. 52–54.

"home rule" in the District of Columbia, and on an amendment which specified driver's insurance requirements in the District. Both votes were significant for their impact on race relations in that they determined how much political autonomy the federal district (containing a black population majority) would possess and the extent to which governmental actions in the capital would serve as precedents for federal legislation elsewhere. Although this was not the first time that civil rights measures had surfaced among the top ten high-stress, closely contested roll calls in the twentieth century, race relations clearly dominated sectional conflict in the 1965–66 period to an extent not experienced since the late nineteenth century.*

The 1893 abandonment of federal measures to protect black suffrage rights in the South had coincided with the rapid extension of voting restrictions across the section. Beginning with the 1890 constitutional convention in Mississippi, which coincided with congressional defeat of the Force Bill, all southern and many northern states adopted one or more elements of the Mississippi Plan. These measures included the inauguration of stringent residency requirements, poll taxes which were often cumulative and paid months in advance of an election, and literacy tests accompanied by a requirement that the prospective voter "understand" the state and federal constitutions. As a result of these new suffrage restrictions, nearly all southern blacks and many poor whites were effectively disfranchised.[82] The new voting restrictions were the political counterparts of the "race codes" which first took form as strong social norms and were later embodied in state laws dealing with education, public accommodations, and marriage. The immediate political motives for the disfranchising measures were quite diverse, however. In Georgia and South Carolina, for example, agrarian radicals viewed the black vote as under the control of the "Bourbon" plantation elite and supported disfranchising restrictions as a means of removing the black vote from political competition. In other states such as Alabama, Louisiana, North Carolina, and Virginia, more conservative political elements enacted voting barriers in order to give whites control of local governments in black majority counties and as a means of tilting the balance of electoral power toward the plantation regions of the black belt and away from lower-class upland whites. In these efforts, the black and, less often, the poor mountain white were seen as sources of alien political beliefs—a kind of northern-oriented "fifth column" that threatened purely southern interests and, more particularly, the political goals of the plantation

---

*Two of the high-stress, closely contested roll calls recorded in the 84th Congress (1955–56) had also touched upon federal intervention in race relations. Both occurred on legislation which would have provided federal aid for the construction of local schools. Other high-stress, closely contested roll calls in the 89th Congress included a special order for legislation increasing the salary of Supreme Court justices (with symbolic civil rights implications), passage of a bill to repeal Section 14(b) of the Taft-Hartley Act, two votes on the creation of a new federal program to increase cotton consumption, and adoption of the conference report on the Demonstration Cities and Metropolitan Development Act of 1966.

elite. The result was a political system based on a small, upper-class, white minority which justified its control by defending segregationist institutions against real or imagined attacks by federal authorities, as well as by ostensibly promoting the section's interests within the national political economy.

The durability of this system was repeatedly demonstrated as the Supreme Court sporadically and ineffectively struck down separate elements of the electoral system as incompatible with the federal constitution. In 1915, the Court invalidated the so-called "grandfather clause" which had exempted from the literacy qualification voters who had been entitled to vote prior to 1867 or were the sons or grandsons of those who had been so entitled. A Louisiana addition to the "Mississippi Plan," the grandfather clause had, in effect, made the literacy test apply only to blacks. By 1915, when the Court finally acted, the clause applied to only a small fraction of the southern electorate. In six decisions between 1927 and 1948 the Supreme Court invalidated various versions of the "white primary" which had prevented blacks from participating in elections which chose Democratic party nominees.[83] Even when combined with the Civil Rights Acts of 1957 and 1960, these decisions did little to threaten plantation elite hegemony in the South.

Major Civil Rights/Race Relations Legislation in the Twentieth Century

In the remainder of this section, legislative action on thirty-three separate civil rights measures is analyzed in order to illustrate: (1) the intense sectional conflict over federal intervention in race relations; (2) the role of the party leadership and the committee system in obstructing passage of such measures; (3) the importance of national "detente" on civil rights to the maintenance of a bipolar Democratic coalition; and (4) the rapid decline of sectional stress in civil rights decisions after 1965. These measures were selected because they all came to a vote in the House of Representatives and comprise six distinct and overlapping series of civil rights efforts. Together they compose the large majority of federal civil rights bills seriously considered during the twentieth century.* The analyzed legislation includes:

1. Three anti-lynching bills (1922–40);
2. Six anti–poll tax measures (1942–62);
3. Six omnibus civil rights proposals (1956–67);

*Some important omissions should be noted: the Fair Employment Practices Commission proposals of the Truman administration, the amendments offered in 1956 and 1961 by Representative Adam Clayton Powell to education aid bills (the amendments made conformance to Supreme Court decisions a precondition of federal aid), and diverse efforts to amend various authorizing bills to block the implementation and enforcement of busing orders (e.g., from the Departments of Education and Justice). Omitted civil rights measures either duplicated legislation included in the analysis or did not emerge from the legislative process frequently enough to comprise a series.

4. Six bills related to the Civil Rights Commission (1958–72);
5. Four voting rights measures (1965–81);
6. Seven anti-busing amendments to appropriations bills (1968–77) and one proposed anti-busing amendment to the U.S. Constitution (1979).

For each of the thirty-three measures, the vote selected for analysis was recorded the first time the House passed the legislation (for an account of twenty-five of these measures see table 5.9).

There is some overlap between these series; for example, proposals for or extensions of the Civil Rights Commission appeared in the Civil Rights bills of 1956, 1957, and 1964, and authority to institute a constitutional challenge to the poll tax was given to the Justice Department by the 1964 Civil Rights Act. The latter act also conferred authority upon the Justice Department to prosecute lynching cases. Aside from this overlap, each series (e.g., the three anti-lynching votes) is quite distinct, and in most cases the specific content of legislative proposals changed very little over the life of the series.

Between 1922 and 1965 civil rights bills produced more consistent regional alignment patterns and provoked higher levels of sectional stress than any comparable federal policy. This consistency is illustrated by the trade area alignments displayed in table 5.8. Each of the six series is represented by the roll call recorded upon the first occasion the House considered the topic, and in all but two cases (the civil rights bill of 1956 and the 1958 roll call on Civil Rights Commission funding) these votes were also those which exhibited the highest levels of sectional stress in each series. Aside from the San Francisco delegation's opposition to federal anti-lynching authority in 1922 and voting on the 1968 anti-busing amendment to education appropriations, the only deviation from the prevailing alignment was the behavior of the Louisville delegation. The map depicting the voting on passage of the 1965 Voting Rights Act demonstrates the sectional alignment in a different perspective (map 5.2). In the 1965 vote some dissension within the South emerged as many urban members of the region supported the bill (e.g., from the cities of Memphis, Atlanta, Jacksonville, New Orleans, and St. Petersburg–Tampa). Otherwise, the stark regional cleavage evident on the 1965 Voting Rights Act was typical of the historical division over civil rights measures in general.

No civil rights legislation was voted on in the House of Representatives between the 1890 Force Bill and the 1922 anti-lynching proposal introduced by Republican Leonidas Dyer of St. Louis, Missouri.* In 1922, anti-lynching legislation was politically attractive to the Republicans for several reasons. The party was still consolidating its national position following the reestablishment of congressional dominance in the 1918 off-year elections and Harding's victory in the 1920 presidential contest. At the same time, House

---

*This excludes repeal of Reconstruction statutes in 1893, efforts to segregate federal bureaucracies and veterans' homes during the Wilson administration, and contested election cases.

Table 5.8. Trade Area Delegation Voting on Major Civil Rights Bills, 1922–1968

Trade Area[a]	Civil Rights Measure					
	1922 Anti– Lynching	1942 Anti–Poll Tax	1956 Civil Rights Bill	1958 Civil Rights Commission	1965 Voting Rights	1968 Busing
New York	Fed[b]	Fed	Fed	Fed	Fed	Fed
Philadelphia	Fed	Fed	Fed	Fed	Fed	State
Boston	Fed	Fed	Fed	Fed	Fed	Fed
Chicago	Fed	Fed	Fed	Fed	Fed	Fed
Detroit	Fed	Fed	Fed	Fed	Fed	Fed
Buffalo	Fed	Fed	Fed	Fed	Fed	Fed
Pittsburgh	Fed	Fed	Fed	Fed	Fed	Fed
San Francisco	State	Fed	Fed	Fed	Fed	Fed
Denver	Fed	Fed	Fed	Fed	Fed	State
St. Louis	Fed	Fed	Fed	Fed	Fed	State
Cleveland	Fed	Fed	Fed	Fed	Fed	Fed
Omaha	Fed	Fed	Fed	Fed	Fed	Fed
Cincinnati	Fed	Fed	Fed	Fed	Fed	Fed
Indianapolis	Fed	Fed	Fed	Fed	Fed	*Split*
Minneapolis	Fed	Fed	Fed	Fed	Fed	Fed
Kansas City	Fed	Fed	Fed	Fed	Fed	State
New Orleans	State	State	State	State	State	State
Louisville	*Split*	Fed	*Split*	Fed	Fed	State
Birmingham	State	State	State	State	State	State
Richmond	State	State	State	State	State	State
Memphis	State	State	State	State	State	State
Atlanta	State	State	State	State	State	State
Dallas	State	State	State	State	State	State
Sectional Stress	78.2	83.2	79.4	78.6	71.8	62.9

[a] Trade area delegations are ranked in descending order of their support for the core positic on the ten high-stress roll calls recorded during the 89th Congress (1965–66); see Table 2.

[b] "Fed" (Federal) indicates that a majority of the trade area delegation supported passage of th respective measure; "State" indicates that the trade area delegation opposed passage (reservin such authority to the state governments); *Split* indicates that the delegation divided evenly c the legislation. In the 1968 vote, opposition to an anti-busing amendment was labele "federal."

SOURCE: Computations from roll call data.

Republicans enjoyed the largest majority in their history (302 members). With the Democratic opposition almost exclusively confined to the southern periphery, resurrection of the race issue promised to make the Democracy even more unattractive to northern constituencies and thus to further secure Republican power. With few northern members to water down the southern cast of the Democratic caucus, the party would appear monolithically tied to the forces of racial oppression. In the House itself, the prosecution of an anti-lynching proposal would drive a wedge between the southern and western regions of the agrarian periphery and would yield, as it turned out, immediate

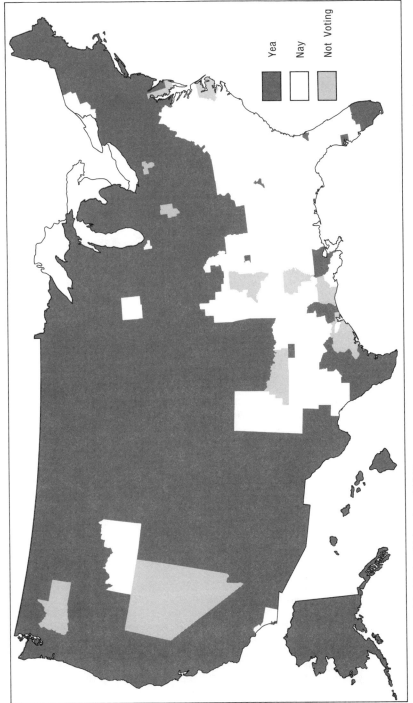

Map 5.2. Passage of the Voting Rights Act of 1965

dividends in the form of the protectionist Fordney-McCumber Tariff and the temporary frustration of the slowly developing farm bloc which later ripened into McNary-Haugenism.

Since 1892, when over two hundred and fifty persons were put to death by mobs in the United States, the number of lynchings had been in steep decline.* Although a significant minority occurred in the West and a few in the North, most lynchings had always taken place in the South. By the close of World War I, lynchings numbered about fifty a year, almost all occurred in the South, and, in that region at least, the overwhelming majority of the victims were black. The regional concentration of lynchings in the South was one of the attractive features—to the Republicans—of the federal remedy proposed in the Dyer bill, because a clear connection could be established between lynchings and the maintenance of the southern race code. In addition, lynchings offered some of the most morally repugnant incidents in American history—incidents which made opposition to a legislative remedy almost impossible for northern Democrats.† The Dyer bill thus posed a dilemma for the

*Many southern congressmen argued that this decline vitiated the rationale supporting federal legislation. For example, Democratic Representative Hatton Sumners of Texas, a high-ranking minority member of the Judiciary Committee which reported the Dyer bill, maintained that the respective state governments were adequately coping with the problem and noted that "We have reduced lynching, not withstanding the increase in population, from an average of 112 a year to 63 last year." *Congressional Record*, 67:2:1743, January 25, 1922. On the two other occasions (1937 and 1940) when the House passed anti-lynching bills, Sumners chaired the Judiciary Committee and used his position to frustrate, successfully in 1937, committee consideration of the measures. The *Literary Digest* reported the occurrence of sixty-one lynchings in 1920 distributed as follows: "Texas, 10; Georgia, 9; Alabama, Florida, Mississippi, each 7; California, Minnesota, North Carolina, Oklahoma, each 3; Arkansas, Illinois, Kansas, Kentucky, Missouri, Ohio, South Carolina, Virginia, West Virginia, each 1, covering 18 states." *Congressional Record*, 67:1:544, December 19, 1921. For data on the number and frequency of incidents, see *Lynchings and What They Mean*, Southern Commission on the Study of Lynching (Atlanta: The Commission, 1931). The frequency of mob execution (as a percentage of the total black population) varied inversely with county population size, urbanization, and black tenancy, and positively with interracial social contact during the months between planting and harvest, the rate at which blacks owned their own land, the percentage of whites in the county population, and political/social unrest. Thus, the modal lynching occurred during the summer months in a poor, white county with a high degree of black land-ownership (and, consequently, relatively intense black-white economic competition). Though in almost all cases the commission of a crime was alleged as the reason for the action, lynching served to enforce the more subjective aspects of the race code—particularly those social norms governing relations between black men and white women and those which demanded black social deference in situations where the races occupied the same economic strata. Rarely were the perpetrators even indicted for their participation, and the implication of large parts of the white community in the act served to galvanize race solidarity while terrorizing the black population into submission.

†One example cited during floor debate involved a man who had been charged with murder in the state of Arkansas. Captured weeks later in El Paso, Texas, the alleged murderer was being returned to Arkansas when he was seized by a mob in Mississippi, driven back to Arkansas by automobile, and there killed. The following account was taken from the *Memphis Press*, Thursday, January 27, 1921: "More than 500 persons stood by and looked on while the

small northern wing of the Democratic party; these members were forced to choose between loyalty to their southern leaders and compliance with constituency opinion. Few, however, voiced their dissent from their party's position as openly as Representative Anthony Griffin of New York:

> To make opposition to this legislation the test of loyalty to Democratic principles would be "the most unkindest cut of all," and perhaps the most futile and ill-considered act of party leadership in the past 30 years. I warn you that Democrats of the North can not be dragooned into such policies.
>
> Democracy need make no compromise with race prejudice. If you want to destroy the Democratic Party in the North just hitch up with such reactionary policies and the deed is done.[84]

Finally, the Dyer bill was an attractive civil rights vehicle precisely because the legislation implicitly charged periphery communities with lawlessness. For decades southern congressmen had defended social segregation and political disfranchisement as a constitutionally protected exercise of state "police powers" and condemned federal legislation as a usurpation of state sovereignty. The failure of southern peace officers to protect criminal defendants, even as their congressmen engaged in a condemnation of federal remedies, seemed to transform the southern conception of political "liberty" into a constitutional right protecting barbarism.*

Many Republicans felt that the anti-lynching bill was unconstitutional because it allowed the federal government to levy a fine on county governments. The likelihood that this provision, at least, would be invalidated by

---

Negro was slowly burned to a crisp. A few women were scattered among the crowd of Arkansas planters, who directed the gruesome work of avenging the death of O. T. Craig and his daughter, Mrs. C. O. Williamson.

"Not once did the slayer beg for mercy despite the fact that he suffered one of the most horrible deaths imaginable. With the Negro chained to a log, members of the mob placed a small pile of leaves around his feet. Gasoline was then poured on the leaves and the carrying [out] of the death sentence was underway.

"Inch by inch the Negro was fairly cooked to death. Every few minutes fresh leaves were tossed on the funeral pyre until the blaze had passed the Negro's waist. As the flames were eating away his abdomen, a member of the mob stepped forward and saturated the body with gasoline. It was then only a few minutes until the Negro had been reduced to ashes." *Congressional Record*, 67:1:547, December 19, 1921.

*One of the provisions contained in the Dyer bill held that any county in which a lynching took place or through which the victim was transported would be subject to a $10,000 fine payable to the victim's relatives, or, if none existed, the federal government. Other sections defined a "mob" as a group of five or more persons in riotous assemblage acting together outside the authority of law to execute a person as punishment for a real or imagined crime, asserted that any state or subdivision which failed to prevent a lynching thereby denied "equal protection" under the law, proposed imprisonment for up to five years and a $5,000 fine for any peace officer responsible for the protection of the victim, and made participation in a lynch mob by anyone a federal crime punishable by imprisonment of five years to life.

the Supreme Court was viewed as a calculated risk by those who wished to see the legislation implemented. For those who did not, the Supreme Court was seen as a fail-safe mechanism in case the Republican political advantage was pressed too far and the bill was actually enacted.*

The ambivalence of Republican supporters of anti-lynching legislation later hardened into a fairly consistent pattern. The Republicans, representing the core industrial and commercial elite, pushed civil rights measures such as the Dyer bill at least partly in order to split the bipolar alliance of core lower-class and periphery plantation interests. But many members of the Republican party were very reluctant to see legislation enacted which promised to expand central government power, and this reluctance grew as the New Deal coalition seemed to take on the trappings of a permanent political arrangement. A consistently lower proportion of Republicans favored civil rights legislation in the four decades following 1922 (see figure 5.3), the greatest difference between the parties occurring over the Dyer bill, when only 7.8 percent of all Democrats and 92.7 percent of Republicans supported passage. Differences between the parties gradually narrowed until the late 1960s, when the center of civil rights opposition moved decisively into the Republican party. Until that time, leading party members could be counted on to raise the "race issue" whenever it promised to disrupt majority party unity, but rarely pressed the resulting initiatives with any vigor.[85]

Those members of the Democratic party who represented industrial working-class constituencies did not fear the development of a strong central government and, in fact, favored the expansion of federal power in many areas. Moderates within the northern wing of the party, however, were unenthusiastic about civil rights because the issue threatened to dissolve the bipolar coalition and, thus, the attainment of a wide range of legislative goals. Nothing better illustrates the wariness with which New Deal Democrats approached civil rights than Roosevelt's attitude in 1938 toward the second unsuccessful attempt to enact an anti-lynching bill. As described by the *Christian Century*:

> In the midst of the filibuster President Roosevelt was asked at his press conference on January 14 whether he favored the bill. He refused to be committed. His evasive reply took the form of an observation that probably enough talk on the question was going on in Congress without his

---

*The *Literary Digest*, for instance, reported that "many Northern editors" believed the fine to be unconstitutional (June 10, 1922, p. 14). As one Texas Democrat noted, many members of the House on both sides of the issue doubted the sincerity of the bill's sponsors: "You will pass it in the House, and possibly in the Senate, though I doubt it, but either in the other end of this Capitol or in conference it is going to die a natural death, and that death was intended by the very men who have been speaking in its favor for several weeks." Representative Thomas Blanton, *Congressional Record*, 67:2:1787, January 26, 1922. Even though the Dyer bill might be considered a largely symbolic political vehicle, the high level of sectional conflict it engendered gave rise to some of the most bitter and "unparliamentary" debate ever witnessed in the House. See, for example, the *Congressional Record*, 67:2:1721, January 25, 1922.

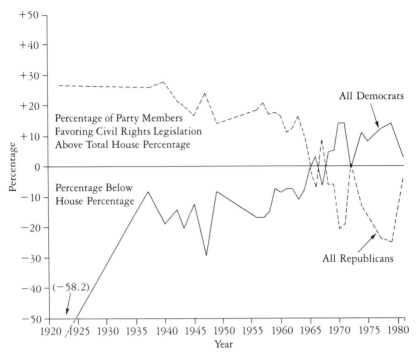

Figure 5.3. Relative Percentages of the Two Major Party Memberships Favoring Civil Rights Legislation, 1922–1981

saying anything on the subject. Emboldened orators against the bill broadened and sharpened their assertions that the anti-lynching measure was not a part of the President's program, that it did not command his support. On that point, Senate majority leadership and sponsors of the bill attempted no refutation. A forthright White House expression might have cut through the welter of filibuster fustian to save the bill.[86]

During floor debate, Democratic Senator Claude Pepper of Florida "contended that a federal anti-lynching bill is out of harmony with the New Deal. It runs counter to 'progressive democracy as it has been given expression and application in later days by the great humanitarian of our generation, Franklin D. Roosevelt.'" Noted Arthur Krock of the *New York Times*, "The President realizes . . . how his signing such a bill 'would be resented [in] the South.'" * The

Christian Century 55 (February 23, 1938): 238–40. Explaining his neutrality to Walter White of the National Association for the Advancement of Colored People, FDR said southerners were "chairmen or occupy strategic places on most of the Senate and House committees. If I come out for the anti-lynching bill now, they will block every bill I ask Congress to pass to keep America from collapsing. I just can't take that risk." John Frederick Martin, *Civil Rights and*

problem facing the party leadership was to set up a legislative system which, while decentralizing control over the development of most federal programs to the various wings of the party, would provide a means for preventing "sensitive" issues such as civil rights from surfacing on the floor of the House or Senate.

To this end, the party leadership viewed a strong committee system as the basis of the New Deal coalition and used the institutional structures thus created to naturally suppress civil rights legislation. However, the more ideologically committed elements of the northern wing supported federal legislation as a strategy for building a national working-class party which, ultimately, would not depend on the elite of the southern periphery for its majority. While the party leadership and northern moderates were unwilling to risk their national majority for the enactment of civil rights legislation, many core members welcomed the gamble and lamented the political opportunities that would be lost through continued toleration of southern segregationist institutions. As one of but many voices decrying the costs of compromise, the *New Republic* anticipated the twenty-year struggle over the poll tax which was to begin in 1942:

> . . . a solid phalanx, Democratic in name, reactionary in principle, and with an influence far beyond that of the states it represents, has been constructed in the halls of Congress. There may have been a time when the poll tax was the special and particular problem of the inhabitants of eight states south of the Mason-Dixon line. But if ever democracy was such a localized issue, it can no longer be so regarded. For national economic and social reform is being hampered by a narrow, undemocratic clique of politicos from the poll tax states, permanently vested in office by spoon-fed machines.*

---

the Crisis of Liberalism: The Democratic Party, 1945–1976 (Boulder, Col.: Westview Press, 1979), p. 61.

New Republic 102 (May 20, 1940): 664–66. The *Nation* repeated these sentiments nearly two years later as an anti–poll tax bill neared a vote in the House of Representatives: "Like the fight against slavery before it, the fight against the poll tax is a fight to save the North and the rest of the country from the power wielded in Congress by a small and reactionary Southern oligarchy.

"Ten of the thirty-three standing committees in the Senate are headed by men from the eight poll-tax states, most of them men of the extreme right.

"In the House twelve of the forty-four standing committees have chairmen from the poll-tax states. A few of these occasionally turn up on the progressive side of an issue, but most of them are thoroughly reactionary.

"The poll tax, by cutting down the number of voters, gives these men a permanence in Congress that men from other districts can rarely achieve." (Vol. 154, March 21, 1942, p. 329).

In 1939, the *Christian Century* had remarked on the class (not race) basis of the poll tax, "this archaic tax keeps the poor from the polls and allows cliques of economic royalists to dominate the south and head off progressive legislation. . . . the main effect is to disfranchise

While almost all northern congressmen voted for civil rights legislation when the bills confronted them on the floor of the House, only those members of the Democratic party from industrial labor constituencies seemed sincerely enthusiastic about enactment.*

Southern opposition to civil rights legislation was monolithic and implacable between Reconstruction and the 1965 Voting Rights Act. During this period congressmen from the southern periphery sought to preserve the cheap and captive labor pool that segregationist institutions provided for rural plantation owners and low-skill manufacturing industries. Southern congressmen routinely supported the legislative goals of the labor wing of the party as long as their effects were limited to the industrial core. For this reason, agriculture and most seasonal activities such as canning and cotton ginning were exempted from minimum wage and union legislation; the two clear conditions for southern participation in the New Deal coalition were northern tolerance of race segregation and the confinement of class competition to the political economy of the industrialized core. Even though the South benefited from the intersectional redistribution of wealth that a larger federal government made possible, the increasing strength of central state bureaucracies—in combination with consolidation of the economic and political power of core industrial unions—ultimately created a favorable environment for the civil rights measures of the 1960s.

Until 1964, most civil rights measures were exploited for symbolic advantage by all political factions. For example, Senate debate on a federal anti–poll tax bill in 1944 drew these observations from *Time*:

> . . . a cynical Senate had quietly made an election-year deal, arranged everything backstage in advance. There would be 1) no filibuster, 2) no cloture, 3) no Marcantonio bill.
>
> By the terms of the deal, Southerners would be allowed to protest at length and get themselves on record as favoring the poll tax and "white

---

the poor white, since the Negro would still be kept from the ballot box by other means." (Vol. 56, September 20, 1939, pp. 1135–36.) The other means referred to included the literacy test, the "understanding the Constitution" requirement, and, of course, outright intimidation. In 1942 eight states (Alabama, Arkansas, Georgia, Mississippi, South Carolina, Tennessee, Texas, and Virginia) maintained a poll tax of one to two dollars a year with, in some cases, cumulative tax provisions that could increase the levy to a maximum of fifty dollars if the tax was not paid for a period of many years.

*Irrefutable evidence of the "true" motivations of congressmen is, of course, notoriously difficult to gather. The most convincing evidence of the ambivalence of most northern Republicans and machine Democrats is the discrepancy between their inclination to sign discharge petitions and their public support of civil rights initiatives, but the same conclusion might be drawn from congressional debate and, more generally, platform contests in contemporary presidential nominating conventions. After 1957, the linkage between civil rights and institutional reform became increasingly explicit and strengthened the political interest of labor Democrats in civil rights measures.

supremacy." Republicans and Northern Democrats, prodded by church, liberal, labor and Negro organizations, would pass around a petition to impose cloture and force a vote. When cloture failed . . . the bill would be quietly shelved.[87]

This, indeed, was the bill's fate. Twelve years later, an omnibus civil rights bill backed by the Eisenhower administration moved down the same path toward certain oblivion.* After 1956, however, civil rights legislation became an increasingly serious threat to segregationist institutions, and every year thereafter congressional consideration of such measures became less of a charade.

In the twentieth century, no major civil rights initiative has ever been defeated in a straight up-or-down vote on the floor of the House or Senate. Instead, defeat has come at the hands of the committee system or has been due to the norms which, in the past, supported the senate filibuster. Table 5.9 describes the procedural decisions which arose upon consideration of twenty-six of the thirty-three bills analyzed in this section. The twenty-six measures share two characteristics: each ultimately came to a vote on the House floor, and all but three fell under the jurisdiction of the House and Senate Judiciary Committees. The only civil rights legislation omitted from the table were the seven anti-busing riders to education appropriation bills (1968 to 1977). Twenty-five of the twenty-six bills in the table—the sole exception being an attempt to pass an anti-busing constitutional amendment in 1979—cleared the House of Representatives.

Normally, legislation introduced into the House or Senate is first referred to a permanent, "standing" committee which then deliberates on the bill's merits. Ordinarily, if the legislative committee refuses to report the measure to the full chamber, the bill will die without further action. If it is reported, the Rules Committee or, less frequently, the Speaker, controls the decision whether to bring the bill to the floor of the House. In the much less centralized proceedings of the Senate, floor consideration is a more or less consensual decision worked out by the majority and minority party leaders in the form of a "unanimous consent agreement." The primary purpose of such an agreement is to limit floor debate and thus avoid a filibuster. A filibuster can be ended by "cloture," which required the agreement of two-thirds of those Senators voting on the motion between 1917 and 1949, two-thirds of all Senators between 1949 and 1959, back to two-thirds of those voting between 1959 and 1975,

---

*On this occasion, the *New Republic* condemned the political farce played out on the floor of the House of Representatives: "All were aware the Senate's Southern bloc stood by to administer the kiss of death to the total legislation, amendments and all.

"So a great and funny time was had by all—hoots of laughter ringing out from the floor as amendments such as this [adding "sex" discrimination to the list of infractions that the proposed Civil Rights Commission would investigate] were successfully proposed. It was not happy laughter. It was rather derisive and sardonic. It was the kind that is heard when the joke is one that the joker feels is a little shameful" (Vol. 135, July 30, 1956, p. 7). *Time* said that this debate was carried on "in a spirit of good, dirty, cynical fun" (July 30, 1956, p. 9).

and three-fifths of the entire membership thereafter. Largely because the filibuster posed the greatest threat to civil rights legislation, twenty-two of the
twenty-six bills described in the table were first considered in the House. Only
the 1959, 1962, 1963, and 1965 initiatives started in the Senate.

The committee system, which was ordinarily utilized by the bipolar
Democratic coalition to distribute tangible benefits to its members, was so
hostile to civil rights initiatives that not one of the twenty-six bills followed a
normal legislative path.* The nearest approximations to a normal routine
came in 1967 and 1972, when passage of extensions of the Civil Rights Commission occurred under "suspension of the rules." At that point, use of the
suspension procedure was solely a parliamentary convenience and did not necessarily imply that the Rules Committee was hostile to the bill.†

Under the rules of the House of Representatives, there exist a number of
ways by which a majority of all members may circumvent their own Judiciary
Committee if that panel refuses to report a bill that the majority favors. The
most important of these procedures is a "discharge petition" which, when
signed by 218 members (a bare majority), discharges a committee from further
consideration and can bring a bill to floor over the objections of the Speaker
and the Rules Committee. On five of the twenty-three bills referred to the
panel, the House Judiciary Committee was discharged by such a petition. In
four of these cases (1937, 1942, 1943, and 1945) a special order from the
Rules Committee was discharged at the same time. In 1979, the discharge
procedure was used to bring an anti-busing constitutional amendment to the
floor over the objections of the Judiciary Committee.

On the first four discharge petitions, it seems clear that the committee
bottled up the legislation for purely political, not programmatic, reasons. The
immigration and economic (e.g., bankruptcy, antitrust, and injunction) aspects of the panel's jurisdiction made the Judiciary Committee exceptionally
attractive to the northern wings of both parties. Largely as a result, members
of the committee usually provided a higher floor support percentage for civil
rights bills than the House as a whole.‡ And, in fact, when the House finally
voted to pass the 1937 anti-lynching bill, support for the legislation was
significantly greater from the committee than from the remainder of the House
(see table 5.10).

Texas Democrat Halton Sumners chaired the committee in all four years,
and his opposition almost certainly made favorable consideration more difficult. But fewer than a third of all committee members signed the discharge

---

*The normal consideration of civil rights legislation would have included a favorable
report by both Judiciary Committees, adoption of a special order reported by the House Rules
Committee, the absence of a filibuster or a cloture motion in the Senate, and floor approval by
both chambers.

†The 1981 Voting Rights Act also came very close to the normal path of successfully
enacted legislation.

‡This was, in fact, the case in fifteen of the twenty-six votes in table 5.9.

Table 5.9. Legislative Consideration of Civil Rights Bills, 1922–1981

Year Passed by the House	Type of Bill	House of Representatives			Senate		
		Judiciary Committee	Rules Committee	Floor Passage	Judiciary Committee	Floor Debate	Floor Passage
1922	Anti-Lynching	Reported	Reported	Yes	Reported	Yes	No Vote
1937	Anti-Lynching	Discharged		Yes	Reported	Cloture Failed	No Vote
1940	Anti-Lynching	Reported	Reported	Yes	Reported	No	No Vote
1942	Anti–Poll Tax	Discharged	Discharged	Yes	Reported	Cloture Failed	No Vote
1943	Anti–Poll Tax	Discharged	Discharged	Yes	Reported	Cloture Failed	No Vote
1945	Anti–Poll Tax	Discharged	Discharged	Yes	Reported	Cloture Failed	No Vote
1947	Anti–Poll Tax	Reported[a]	Suspension[a]	Yes	Reported[a]	Yes	No Vote
1949	Anti–Poll Tax	Reported[a]	Reported	Yes	No Action[a]	No	No Vote
1956	Civil Rights Bill	Reported	Reported	Yes	No Action[a]	No	No Vote
1957	Civil Rights Act	Reported	Reported	Yes	Calendar[a]	Yes	Yes
1958	Civil Rights Commission[a]	Not Applicable		Yes	Not Applicable	Yes	Yes
1959	Civil Rights Commission[a]	No Action	Reported	Yes	No Action	Yes	Yes
1960	Civil Rights Act	Reported	Reported[a]	Yes	Reported[a]	Yes	Yes[a]
1961	Civil Rights Commission[a]	No Action	Reported	Yes	No Action[a]	Yes	Yes
1962	Anti–Poll Tax	Reported	Suspension[a]	Yes	No Action[a]	Yes	Yes
1963	Civil Rights Commission[a]	No Action	Suspension[a]	Yes	No Action[a]	Yes	Yes
1964	Civil Rights Act	Reported	Reported[a]	Yes	Calendar[a]	Cloture Invoked	Yes
1965	Voting Rights Act	Reported	Reported	Yes	Reported[a]	Cloture Invoked	Yes
1966	Civil Rights Bill	Reported	21 Day Rule[a]	Yes	Calendar[a]	Cloture Failed	No Vote
1967	Civil Rights Act	Reported	Reported	Yes	Reported[a]	Cloture Invoked[a]	Yes
1967	Civil Rights Comission[a]	Reported	Suspension[a]	Yes	Reported[a]	Yes	Yes
1969	Voting Rights Act	Reported	Reported	Yes	Reported[a]	Yes	Yes
1972	Civil Rights Commission[a]	Reported	Suspension[a]	Yes	Reported[a]	Yes	Yes
1975	Voting Rights Act	Reported	Reported	Yes	Calendar[a]	Cloture Invoked	Yes
1979	Busing	Discharged	Not Applicable	No	Not Applicable	Not Applicable	Not Applicable
1981	Voting Rights Act	Reported	Reported	Yes	Calendar[a]	Yes	Yes

ᵃNOTES: In 1947 and 1949, anti–poll tax bills were considered in the House Administration and Senate Rules and Administration Committees. In 1947, 1962, 1963, 1967, and 1972, civil rights bills passed the House under a procedure known as "suspension of the rules," which is controlled by the Speaker and does not require action by the Rules Committee. In 1957, 1964, 1966, 1975, and 1981, legislation passed by the House was placed directly on the Senate Calendar, thereby bypassing the Senate Judiciary Committee. In 1958 funding for the Civil Rights Commission was added to the annual appropriations bill for the Executive Office of the President and did not involve either the Judiciary Committee or Rules. In 1959 and 1961 legislation extending the Civil Rights Commission was added to appropriation bills, thereby bypassing legislative committees in both chambers. In 1960, 1965, 1967, and 1969, bills were referred to the Senate Judiciary Committee with a fixed deadline for their report; action by the committee cannot, therefore, be considered "voluntary" (in 1969, for example, the committee chose to make no formal report). In 1960 and 1967, efforts to invoke cloture failed prior to passage. In 1960 and 1964, the House Rules Committee reported legislation only under serious pressure from a hostile discharge petition. In 1966 legislation was brought to the floor under the twenty-one day rule after the Rules Committee failed to report a special order. In 1963, extension of the Civil Rights Commission was added to a private bill and thus bypassed both Judiciary Committees. In 1962 and 1963, the anti–poll tax constitutional amendment was tacked onto another piece of legislation, effectively bypassing the Senate Judiciary Committee.

Table 5.10. Percentage of Members Supporting Passage of Discharged Civil Rights Legislation, 1937–1945

Bill	Democrats		Republicans		All Parties	
	Judiciary Committee	All	Judiciary Committee	All	Judiciary Committee	All
1937 (Anti-lynching)	72.2	62.0	100.0	96.0	79.2	69.8
1942 (Anti–poll tax)	61.5	61.0	100.0	96.9	76.2	75.1
1943 (Anti–poll tax)	57.1	50.5	100.0	90.9	73.9	70.7
1945 (Anti–poll tax)	63.6	57.8	100.0	87.3	76.5	70.5

petition in 1937: 31.6 percent of panel Democrats and 33.3 percent of Republicans. And in the three remaining petitions, fewer than half of Judiciary Committee members supported the discharge of anti–poll tax legislation. Even though breached successfully on these four occasions, the panel's Democratic contingent composed the first line of defense for the New Deal coalition's civil rights "policy" of non-intervention. During the halcyon years of the bipolar alliance, literally hundreds of civil rights proposals languished under the watchful eye of the committee.*

The most important barrier, however, was the Rules Committee. Often considered the most powerful committee in the House, the Rules Committee's principal power is the responsibility for "special orders" which, in effect, confer parliamentary privilege upon legislation and pave the way for consideration on the floor. Normally, the adoption of a special order is the only way a controversial bill may move to the floor, though the Speaker may recognize a motion to "suspend the rules and pass" a bill. While the adoption of a special order and subsequent passage of the legislation require only a simple majority of those voting, suspension requires a two-thirds majority. Thus, the Speaker may supplant the Rules Committee only when the legislation already enjoys extraordinary support. Of the twenty-six bills described in table 5.9, twenty-one passed the House with a majority greater than two-thirds, and the suspension procedure was used five times. In the first three cases (1947, 1962, and 1963), suspension was clearly used as a means of bypassing a hostile Rules Committee. In the four early discharge petition measures (1937–45), each of which enjoyed support on the floor greater than two-thirds, the absence of a suspension motion is a strong indication of the Speaker's indifference or hostility.† Indeed, during consideration of the 1937 anti-lynching bill, Democratic Speaker William Bankhead of Alabama warned that "what Fort Sumter started will only be a picnic" after enactment of a federal statute.‡

With only two exceptions (in 1956 and 1958), Democratic members of the Rules Committee were consistently less favorable to civil rights legislation than the remainder of their party over the period 1922 through 1965 (see figure 5.4). During these four and a half decades, the committee was dis-

---

*During the 74th Congress, for example, the Judiciary Committee brooded silently over thirty-two anti-lynching bills.

†It must be remembered, however, that a motion to suspend would not only have bypassed the Rules Committee but also, in effect, would have discharged the Judiciary Committee. The Speaker's reluctance to thus use his authority could, at least theoretically, be ascribed to his party's stake in the efficient functioning and prerogatives of the committee system itself and a consequent hesitancy to transgress legislative norms which buttressed the system. For more on the motion to suspend, see *Rules of the House of Representatives* (Washington: Government Printing Office, 1967), Rule XXVII.

‡Richard Polenberg, *One Nation Divisible: Class, Race, and Ethnicity in the United States Since 1938* (New York: Penguin Books, 1980), p. 32. While Bankhead voted against the 1937 bill, most Speakers do not vote on measures that come before the House unless their vote is decisive.

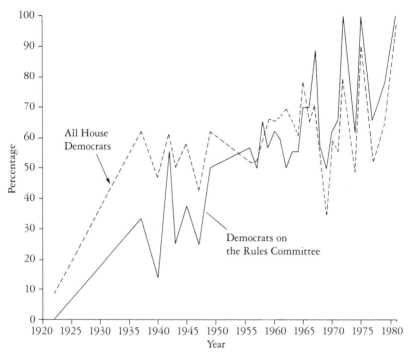

Figure 5.4. Percentage of Rules Committee and House Democrats Favoring Major Civil Rights Legislation, 1922–1981

charged four times and was bypassed by suspension procedures on three occasions. In other cases, it sent a rule to the floor only after a discharge petition had been signed by a near majority of the House membership (211 signatures in 1960 and 173 in 1964), and "voluntarily" reported special orders for civil rights legislation in only eight of the eighteen bills analyzed. In every case except the 1965 Voting Rights Act, a greater percentage of committee Republicans than Democrats supported passage during this period. Even in 1966, when Rules Democrats began to disproportionately favor civil rights measures over their Republican counterparts and the remainder of the Democratic party, a special order was involuntarily reported under the "twenty-one day" rule.*

*The "twenty-one day rule" allowed the chairman of the legislative committee that favorably reported a bill to call up a special order for the bill's consideration if, after twenty-one calendar days following introduction and referral of the special order, the Rules Committee failed to approve the order. The rule applied only during the 81st Congress (1949–50), when the Speaker had to recognize the committee chairman, and the 89th Congress (1965–66), when the Speaker retained discretion over recognition. It is significant that this rule has been adopted only when the northern wing of the Democratic party has dominated the House. For more on the rule and its history, see *Guide to the Congress of the United States* (Washington: Congressional

Table 5.11. Signers of Discharge Petitions on Civil Rights Legislation, 1937 and 1960

Category of Congressmen	1937		1960[a]	
	Number of Members	Percentage Signing	Number of Members	Percentage Signing
Democrats:				
Members of the Discharged Committee(s)	29	27.6	8	50.0
Chairmen	47	25.5	20	20.0
All Members	331	44.1	283	57.6
Republicans:				
Members of the Discharged Committee(s)	10	50.0	4	0.0
Ranking Members	47	74.5	20	5.0
All Members	89	73.0	153	28.8
Both Parties:				
Members of the Discharged Committee(s)	39	35.9	12	33.3
Chairmen/Ranking Members	94	50.0	40	12.5
All Members	435	50.1	436	48.0

[a] Only 209 of the 211 members who signed the 1960 petition are actually known.
SOURCES: *Congressional Record*, 75:1:2856, March 29, 1937; and *1960 Congressional Quarterly Almanac* (Washington: Congressional Quarterly Service, 1961).

As an illustration of the defensive reaction of the committee system to civil rights legislation and the implied threat to the bipolar Democratic coalition, the pattern of support for two discharge petitions—separated by nearly a quarter of a century—has been analyzed (see table 5.11). The 1937 petition successfully discharged both the Rules and Judiciary Committee and led to passage of the anti-lynching bill of that year. Twenty-three years later a peti-

---

Quarterly Service, 1971). The four discharge petitions adopted between 1937 and 1945 were unusual in several respects. First of all, petitions that receive 218 signatures are quite rare in and of themselves—only twenty-two were successful in that respect between 1933 and 1971. Thus, civil rights legislation composed a much higher proportion of discharge motions than of the hundreds of bills which passed the House every year over the same period. In addition, these petitions combined into one action the discharge of the Judiciary Committee (and the anti-lynching or anti–poll tax bill) with the discharge of the Rules Committee (and the special order). By discharging the special order, the civil rights measure was brought to the floor regardless of whether the Judiciary Committee had reported it. For that reason, these four petitions violated the "prerogatives" of both committees and were, to a disproportionate extent, opposed by members of both panels and generally by high-ranking committee members of both parties.

During debate on the 1937 discharge motion, Rules Chairman John O'Connor of New York first indicated his support for anti-lynching legislation in principle but then said, "I would like to have seen this bill brought before the House in the proper orderly way so as to give us an opportunity to vote upon it in the regular parliamentary procedure." O'Connor then voted against the special order and, when it passed anyway, supported the anti-lynching bill. *Congressional Record*, 75:1:3383–84, April 12, 1937.

tion was filed in order to dislodge from the Rules Committee what became the Civil Rights Act of 1960. In this instance the Judiciary Committee had favorably reported the bill, and the Rules Committee, after 211 members had signed the discharge petition (eight short of the required majority),* "voluntarily" relinquished a special order which brought the bill to the floor. As can be seen, members of the discharged committees from both parties were more reluctant to sign the petitions than were their colleagues. Because the party was in the majority both years, all committee chairmen were Democrats. In 1937, nearly three-quarters of the forty-seven chairmen, including members from California (2), Illinois (2), Indiana, Michigan, New York, and Ohio, refused to sign the petition.† Reflecting the even stronger institutional position and role of the committee system in 1960, the percentage of chairmen supporting discharge had dropped to one in five, and on this occasion failed to include northern committee leaders from Colorado, Missouri, and Pennsylvania. As was the case in 1937, these high-ranking members who refused to sign the petition later supported passage of the legislation when it came to the floor, indicating that they supported civil rights for personal (or constituency) reasons, but opposed it out of larger political concerns. With a different set of long-term political motives, the large majority of Republicans also voted for passage: 96.0 percent in 1937 and 89.8 percent in 1960. Corresponding Democratic figures were 62.0 percent and 65.6 percent.

Because support for civil rights legislation based on its *merits* seems to have been fairly stable in both parties between 1937 and 1960, the dramatic decrease in Republican willingness to violate the *procedural* prerogatives of the committee system and the slightly less significant increase on the Democratic side deserve close inspection. From the evidence, members of the Republican party seem to have been more hostile to the prerogatives of the committee system in 1937 than were the Democrats. The situation was reversed in 1960. While the changing attitudes of the rank and file were not always reflected in the behavior of Democratic chairmen, the increasing willingness of the industrial labor wing of the party to violate committee privileges presaged the more formal assaults on the committee system which came in the form of the Rules Committee expansion of 1961, adoption of a twenty-one day rule in 1965, and the deposition of committee chairmen in 1975. Intertwined with these efforts to "reform" the organization of the House and the distribution of political power within the party were the 1960s civil rights movement and an apparent desire on the part of many northern members to risk their majority status within the country in order to create an ideologically consistent working-class

---

*Following the admission of Alaska and Hawaii as new states, the House temporarily possessed 437 members.

†Deep South constituencies were over-represented within the Democratic party and even more concentrated in the higher seniority ranks of the separate committees. In the Republican party a similar pattern held for midwestern and, to a lesser extent, northeastern districts. See Barbara Hinckley, *The Seniority System in Congress* (Bloomington: Indiana University Press, 1971).

party. As was true in the last decade of the nineteenth century, the civil rights legislation of the 1960s was also intended to destabilize the political position of the plantation elite.

While this shift in political strategy by the core working-class wing was not, by its very nature, the result of publicly concerted action in which all the motives of the different actors were manifest, several related trends and events seem consistent with the destabilization theme. First, the data on comparative party support for civil rights legislation indicate a decisive and persistent switch in 1965 (see figure 5.3)—the year in which the Voting Rights Act passed. In institutional terms, the Democratic party's new civil rights policy was confirmed by the disproportionate support given by members of the formerly obstructive Rules Committee. The new policy has also included efforts by the party leadership to keep anti-busing legislation off the floor. Nothing better illustrates this change than the 1979 effort to discharge the Judiciary Committee of a constitutional amendment to ban court-ordered busing. This effort during the 96th Congress (1979–80) was led by renegade Democratic Representative Ronald M. Mottl, whose district lay in the white, working-class suburbs of Cleveland, Ohio.

> Mottl had also led the drive to bring the amendment to a vote via a discharge petition in the 95th Congress. But whenever the number of signers neared 200, the House leadership put pressure on members to withdraw their names.
>
> This time, Mottl and L. A. "Skip" Bafalis, R-Fla., reached the magic number by pulling off a dramatic midnight coup. Late June 27, with no advance warning, they got the final 18 members to march down the aisle of the House together to sign the petition, bringing the total to 218. The House leadership, taken by surprise, had no chance to counteract the move.*

The shift on civil rights was supported by the centralizing effect of the expanding power of the Democratic Caucus and by the Speaker's new influence over the assignment of party members to the Rules Committee. There were also other attacks on traditional institutional norms and organization. As a result, the Democrats have suffered increasing losses in both the southern and western periphery, as the new programmatic imperatives of the party have radically shifted policy-making and political incentives in line with the demands of the

---

*Signing the petition were 86 Democrats and 132 Republicans. Southern congressmen numbered 78, divided between 43 Democrats and 35 Republicans. Some signatures were added only because members thought the leadership's opposition would continue to prevent the legislation from reaching the floor, and thirty-one members who signed the petition ultimately voted against the proposed amendment. *1979 Congressional Quarterly Almanac* (Washington: Congressional Quarterly Service, 1980), p. 483. Representative Mottl accused the Judiciary Committee of frustrating "the majority will despite overwhelming evidence that the public is fed up with social engineering by an imperial judiciary, while Congress stands idly by."

industrial core. The behavior of a large number of Democratic congressmen suggests that many members would have liked to preserve the decentralizing policy-making norms of the committee system while awaiting the political revolution that enfranchisement of the southern lower classes was intended to spark, and the reforms which have progressively weakened the role played by the committee system in the House do not mean that the institution has lost all political value to the industrial labor wing of the party. As the 1979 discharge petition account illustrates, there are still some policy proposals that these members would like to see "bottled up."

Senate Consideration of Civil Rights Bills

In the Senate, the Judiciary Committee had been a persistent barrier to civil rights legislation since 1956, largely under the leadership of Democrat James Eastland of Mississippi, who retired in 1979. Of the twenty-two civil rights bills referred to the Judiciary Committee, only eight were voluntarily reported back to the Senate (see table 5.9). Six of these measures were considered before the end of World War II, when non-southerners chaired the committee. After 1945, the Senate panel reported only two bills without duress (1967 and 1972).*

The consistent hostility of the Senate panel was only one of two reasons that most civil rights bills began in the House of Representatives. The other was the Senate filibuster. Although it is not always easy to distinguish a lengthy discussion of the merits of a bill and extended debate intended to kill legislation, filibusters occurred on the great majority of the twenty-two measures that reached the Senate floor (see table 5.9).† Of the twenty-seven votes

---

*In the twenty-two applicable cases (excluding 1947, 1949, 1958, and 1981), the committee only reported eight bills voluntarily. Six of these measures were considered before the end of World War II, when the House Judiciary Committee was more or less hostile to civil rights initiatives. Since 1945, the Senate committee has only reported two bills without duress (1967 and 1972). In five instances (1957, 1964, 1966, 1975, and 1981) the Judiciary Committee was bypassed altogether when bills passed by the House were placed directly on the Senate Calendar. From the calendar, the legislation could be brought to the floor without the committee's consent. In two cases (1959 and 1961), legislation extending the Civil Rights Commission was added to otherwise unrelated appropriation bills and in that way bypassed both the House and Senate Judiciary Committees. In 1962 and 1963, similar strategies added the anti–poll tax constitutional amendment and another extension of the Civil Rights Commission to unrelated legislation and thereby avoided the Senate Committee. On four occasions (1960, 1965, 1967, and 1969), civil rights bills were referred to the committee with the stipulation that they be reported back to the Senate within a stipulated length of time. These reports cannot be considered "voluntary" actions by the committee. In only one case (1956) was the Senate Judiciary Committee allowed "to sit" on a civil rights bill until the legislation died at the end of the session.

†One of the reasons the Judiciary Committee was allowed to scuttle the 1956 omnibus civil rights bill was the threat of a filibuster. Similar threats prevented the Senate from considering legislation on the floor in 1940 and 1949. In 1922 and 1947, Senate filibusters stopped

on cloture motions that were recorded between 1933 and the end of 1966, sixteen (59.3 percent) occurred on civil rights legislation. At times, in fact, the sole purpose of Rule 22 seemed to be to prevent federal intervention in the race relations of the South.[88]

In the absence of a strong committee system, a hostile Rules Committee, an often indifferent Speaker, and the Senate filibuster, Congress would have enacted many more and much stronger civil rights measures between 1922 and 1966. This can be concluded from the general pattern of decision-making (described in table 5.9) without ascribing the fate of any particular bill to any particular rule or legislative norm. It is a little more difficult to estimate which feature of the institution was the most effective in squelching civil rights measures. In sheer volume, the House Judiciary Committee, particularly before 1950, probably pigeon-holed the greatest number of bills. On the other hand, because the Senate filibuster was so intimidating, most civil rights measures—at least those that were debated on the floor of either chamber—were first introduced and seriously pursued in the House. After 1950, when the House committee became comparatively favorable to civil rights legislation, the Senate Judiciary Committee became, coincidentally, hostile.* This analysis is, of course, biased toward successful efforts to dislodge bills from the House Judiciary and Rules Committees, since it includes only bills that were voted on in the House and automatically omits all legislation successfully blocked by those two panels. For this reason, the House committees must be deemed even more hostile and more effective in their hostility than they appear here.

In every instance, procedures that violate important committee prerogatives or override significant legislative norms have been disproportionately applied to civil rights legislation. Tabulated in the form of discharge petitions, use of the twenty-one day rule, and the direct placement of legislation on the Senate calendar, the evidence indicates that the committee system under Democratic stewardship was far more hostile to civil rights than to any other policy that enjoyed majority support in the Congress.† This was because civil

---

legislation without a cloture vote. Attempts to end debate failed in 1937, 1942, 1943, 1945, and 1966 when cloture motions were defeated. In these ten cases, the filibuster rule prevented the passage of legislation that otherwise, on an up-or-down vote, probably would have been approved. In two cases (1960 and 1967), cloture motions initially failed before the legislation passed. In 1957, a filibuster took up thirty-seven legislative days before a compromise worked out by the Democratic Majority Leader, Senator Lyndon Johnson of Texas watered down the 1957 Civil Rights Act and induced southern orators to quit their posts. John Frederick Martin has provided an account of that compromise in which he describes Johnson's efforts to impose "moderation" as increasingly unsuccessful after the resurgence of the northern wing following the landslide 1958 election. *Civil Rights and the Crisis of Liberalism*, pp. 162–67.

*In 1964, Senator Hubert Humphrey, a Minnesota Democrat, claimed that 121 civil rights measures were referred to the Senate Judiciary Committee between 1953 and 1963 and that of those bills, only one (in 1960, under an imposed deadline) was ever reported.

†In 1922 and 1947, when Republicans controlled the Congress, no part of the commit-

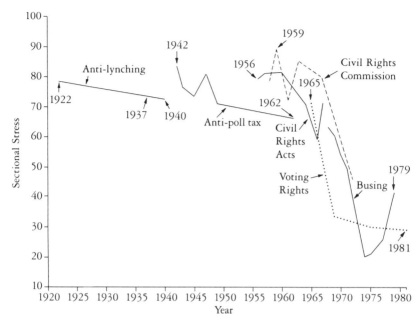

Figure 5.5. Sectional Stress and Civil Rights Legislation, 1922–1981

rights legislation disrupted the always fragile cohesion of the New Deal coalition. Had the enactment of the major civil rights measures of 1964 and 1965 taken place earlier, they would have spelled the (premature) destruction of that coalition. By implication, the Democratic party tolerated race segregation through support for the committee system and other traditional legislative norms, and it is reasonable to assume that the strong committee system and respect for the legislative norms supporting the Senate filibuster were essential preconditions for maintenance of the bipolar Democratic majority.

Historical Pattern of Sectional Stress

From 1922 to 1965, consideration of civil rights legislation produced the most stable regional alignments in American history (see table 5.8) and the highest levels of sectional stress the political system has ever experienced (figure 5.5). The precipitous decline in sectional competition that began following passage of the Voting Rights Act of 1965 will be discussed shortly. First, it should be noted that sectional stress scores for each civil rights series tended to decline

tee system presented an obstacle to civil rights legislation, though the filibuster remained effective.

over time. In all six, the level of sectional stress on the original legislative initiative was higher than that of the last measure in the series, although regional polarization declined much more gradually in the anti-lynching and anti—poll tax series than in the last four.

Since the highest sectional stress level was not recorded until 1959 (on an extension of the Civil Rights Commission) and since regional polarization on civil rights measures was at least as great from 1956 to 1965 as it had been earlier, the moderate downward trends in the first two series should probably not be interpreted as evidence of a secular decline in sectional conflict over race relations between 1922 and 1965. These two trends seem to be partially the result of the "maturation" of each policy proposal over time. When, for example, anti-lynching legislation was first seriously considered, the proposal triggered a broad response to *all* the policy differences that had separated the industrial core and southern periphery. The symbolic content of the legislation was very high at this stage. Later, as the policy proposal began to be weighed more on its own merits and practical prospects for implementation, some members outside the South found reasons to oppose the measure. On the other hand, in the periphery regions that have exhibited some of the characteristics of the core economy (e.g., St. Louis), a dawning realization that policy implementation would not necessarily lead to a general disruption of segregationist institutions resulted in new support for these measures. The "individualization" of a proposal over time, then, tended to split those delegations that bordered the periphery and, thus, reduce regional polarization. "Individualization" probably also increased the ability of southern congressmen to trade votes with northern members in isolated cases, because the availability of "constitutional" objections and other arguments would have widened, to some extent, the freedom of action of northern members.

The precipitous decline in regional polarization that has taken place since 1965 is due to very different factors. One of the most important developments has been an expansion of the southern electorate after 1965 which, at the national level, has significantly reduced the formerly monolithic opposition of southern trade area delegations to civil rights legislation.[89] For what have become the more "traditional" programs, such as the Civil Rights Commission and the Voting Rights Act, the reduction of southern opposition has allowed the emergence of a truly national consensus. In 1972, for instance, only sixty-six congressmen voted against an extension of the commission (under 20 percent of those voting). In 1978, the commission was extended on only a voice vote in the House, the first time in at least a century that either chamber had approved a civil rights measure without formally recording the names of opponents. In 1981, only twenty-four House members voted against an extension of the Voting Rights Act. Richmond, Virginia, was the only trade area delegation to oppose passage; all seven members, six Republicans and one Democrat, voted no.

But more important than the development of a national consensus on traditional objectives has been the "nationalization" of federal intervention in race relations. The first anti-lynching bills were not proposed until mob execution had almost become a purely southern phenomenon. The poll tax had always been limited to southern electoral systems, and the early civil rights acts were solely intended to either enfranchise southern blacks or aid the federal courts in dismantling school systems which had been segregated under the authority of state law. Even the original Voting Rights Act of 1965 was limited to the South by the definition of "targeted areas." Targeted areas were those states or political subdivisions in which the Attorney General determined that a literacy test or similar device had been used as a qualification for voting on November 1, 1964, *and* the Director of the Census determined that fewer than 50 percent of the persons of voting age residing in the area were registered to vote or actually voted in the November 1, 1964, presidential election. Since information on which constituencies fell within these categories was freely available to congressmen during consideration of the act, the regional impact of this triggering formula was well-known. Areas targeted by the act included the entire states of Alabama, Georgia, Louisiana, Mississippi, South Carolina, and Virginia, plus twenty-eight counties in North Carolina, three in Arizona, and one in Idaho.* However, later extensions of the Voting Rights Act expanded the prohibition of literacy tests to the entire country and added language that required bilingual election materials in areas containing both relatively significant numbers of non–English speaking voters and a low rate of electoral participation. The 1970 bill also contained a section which attempted, through federal law, to set a national voting age standard of eighteen years.† Other proposed, but unsuccessful, amendments to these extensions of the 1965 act have reflected both the increasing "consensus" characteristics of the program and the effects of "nationalization." In 1975, the nine amendments which came to a vote in the House of Representatives averaged 25.9 on the sectional stress index. In 1981, the average on five amendments dropped to a remarkably low 19.3.

No civil rights issue has had a greater nationalizing impact than the court-ordered busing of school children that has taken place in the last fifteen years. At first, busing orders seemed directed primarily at southern school districts which attempted to implement "freedom-of-choice" plans and, thus, effectively evade racial integration of the former dual school systems. The federal Department of Health, Education, and Welfare provided some assistance to the courts in striking down these plans under the authority granted the department in Title VI of the 1964 Civil Rights Act. As busing orders, both bureaucratic and judicial, moved outside the South, they took the form of

---

*In these targeted areas, literacy tests and similar voting qualifications were automatically suspended, and the Attorney General enjoyed very broad discretionary power to install federal examiners to enroll disfranchised voters and to review proposed changes in election law.

†With respect to state and local elections, the Supreme Court later ruled this attempt unconstitutional.

Table 5.12. Congressional Voting on Anti-Busing Riders to Appropriations Bills (1968–1977) and the Proposed Constitutional Amendment to Ban Busing (1979)

Type of Trade Area	Percentage of Congressmen Opposing Busing							
	1968	1969	1970	1971	1974	1975	1977	1979
Dual School Systems	85.5	83.5	87.0	88.8	83.2	83.7	72.9	63.2
No State Law or Local Option	28.4	24.8	36.4	40.9	51.5	52.1	51.2	41.4
No Court-Ordered Busing	29.1	23.7	34.5	39.5	49.4	48.6	50.0	38.0
Court-Ordered Busing	27.0	27.0	40.3	43.5	55.7	59.5	53.7	48.3
After Busing Order	—	—	—	—	53.8	61.4	52.5	48.3
Before Busing Order	27.0	27.0	40.3	43.5	57.5	57.5	57.1	—
Total (All Categories)	48.7	45.6	54.9	58.0	62.8	63.5	58.9	49.2
Sectional Stress	62.9	60.8	54.1	49.3	20.4	21.9	26.3	41.6

SOURCE: Computations from roll call data.

"remedies" for most administrative acts which were intended to result in race segregation but did not explicitly mention race. Their application in the North created increasing opposition to busing orders outside the South. As a means of documenting the growing "nationalization" of school integration efforts, congressional voting is analyzed here on seven anti-busing riders to appropriation bills and on the 1979 attempt to pass a constitutional amendment to ban busing. The seven riders were chosen because these amendments were offered on a more or less annual basis for almost a decade and because the formal language of the "limitation on appropriations" was in each case quite similar. The 1979 proposed constitutional amendment was included because of its clear symbolic and substantive importance.

The fifty trade area delegations can be divided into two broad groups (table 5.12). The first group contains those trade areas in which state law mandated the segregation of the races into "dual school systems" or allowed local school districts the option of instituting such a policy. In 1954 when the Supreme Court invalidated the "separate but equal" constitutional justification for segregation and began to impose integration orders, twenty-one states maintained dual school systems.* In these states, court-ordered or bureaucratic busing orders were usually intended to complete the dismantling of historically segregated systems, and the districts were *prima facie* more vulnerable to busing decisions. Throughout the period between 1968 and 1979, a large majority of the trade area delegations from these states supported anti-busing legislation. Opposition peaked in 1971 when almost 90 percent of the members in this category favored restrictions on the imposition of bureaucratic busing orders as a precondition for the receipt of federal aid. In that year,

*In 1954, seventeen states imposed dual school systems state-wide (Alabama, Arkansas, Delaware, Florida, Georgia, Kentucky, Louisiana, Maryland, Mississippi, Missouri, North Carolina, Oklahoma, South Carolina, Tennessee, Texas, Virginia and West Virginia). Four states allowed local districts to segregate but did not require separate schools (Arizona, Kansas, New Mexico, and Wyoming).

all but one of the formerly segregationist trade area delegations backed the appropriation rider and the single exception, Charleston, West Virginia, divided evenly.* Opposition to anti-busing proposals climbed dramatically in 1977 and again in 1979. In the latter year, eight of the twenty-seven delegations refused to support the proposed constitutional amendment. This group included members from the Charlotte, Houston, Little Rock, and Tulsa trade areas. As with civil rights legislation generally, this acceptance of busing as a tool for school integration seems due to the electoral influence of newly enfranchised blacks and to the relative absence of new integration orders or expanded implementation in recent years.

The second group contains the trade area delegations from the twenty-nine states in which there were no mandated or local option dual school systems at the time of the Brown decision. With the exception of the 1979 vote, congressmen in this category have exhibited a steadily increasing inclination to oppose busing. In 1969, more than three of every four members in these delegations opposed an anti-busing rider; by 1974, a majority supported a very similar restriction on federal spending for busing. As a result of the increasing hostilty of northern members to busing orders, the marginal difference in support for anti-busing legislation between the two broadly defined groups declined from 58.7 percent in 1969 to 21.8 in 1979.† This "nationalization" of the busing issue has been accompanied by a corresponding decrease in regional polarization from a level of sectional stress of 62.9 (1968) to a low of 20.4 (1974).

With a few qualifications, the second group can be divided between those trade areas in which the urban center was ordered by a federal court to implement a busing plan and those in which such an order was never imposed. The trade area delegations in the first class (and the year in which the court order became effective) are: Denver (1973), Detroit (1974), Boston (1974), Buffalo (1976), Cleveland (1976), Milwaukee (1977), Omaha (1978), Minneapolis (1978), and Columbus, Ohio (1979).[90] Trade areas in which the urban center was not the target of a busing order imposed by a federal court include Chicago, Cincinnati, Des Moines, Honolulu, Los Angeles, New York, Philadelphia, Pittsburgh, Portland, Salt Lake City, San Francisco, Seattle, and Spokane. Before referring to the data in table 5.12, a number of observations should be made. First, the division of trade areas into those in which the urban center was the object of a federal court-order and those in which the urban center was not such a target does not quite square with the legislative initiatives analyzed in the table. The seven riders offered to appropriation bills, for

---

*Trade area delegations that delivered a significant number of *pro-busing* votes over the decade included Charleston (West Virginia), Washington, D.C., Miami, and St. Louis. On most occasions, the remaining twenty-three delegations unanimously supported anti-busing legislation. The total number of voting members in this category ranged from 120 (1968) to 152 (1979).

†The number of voting members in this category ranged from 222 (1968) to 273 (1979).

example, restricted *bureaucratic* (HEW), not court-ordered, busing, and thus would not have had any direct effect on the federal courts. Busing plans originating with HEW could not be used to categorize trade area delegations because the federal bureaucracy was much more reluctant to enforce desegregation plans which might result in a busing order and also because cases of noncompliance ultimately ended up in the federal courts anyway; federal court orders were much more clearly defined than pressure applied by the federal bureaucracy. In one sense, then, congressional support for anti-busing riders can be interpreted as an attempt to prevent bureaucratic pressure from evolving into litigation and, more to the point, a reaction to busing as an integration tool (because the courts were perceived to be beyond the range of a legislative remedy). It should be noted that some of the trade area urban centers in the "no court-ordered busing" category were compelled to implement busing plans by state court orders (e.g., Los Angeles, Philadelphia, and Pittsburgh). In these delegations support for anti-busing riders was as great as or greater than anti-busing sentiment in those ordered to bus by federal courts.*

Only in 1968, long before busing orders became common in the North, did members from court-ordered trade area delegations provide more support for busing than those in the "no court-ordered" category. After 1968, court-ordered delegations rapidly increased their backing for anti-busing riders, gradually expanding their margin over the remainder of the North until they delivered support 10.9 percent greater in 1975 and 10.3 percent greater on the 1979 proposal to amend the U.S. Constitution.†

*A number of other distinctions could be drawn which would make the differences in the table between the "court-ordered" and "no court-ordered" categories somewhat greater. In addition to moving trade areas subjected to state court orders from the latter to the former category, subdividing each class by the minority proportion of the school population would also more starkly contrast the rapid increase in opposition to busing by congressmen from metropolitan areas containing large minority populations.

†Probably because the implementation of federal court orders was anticipated years in advance during the extended litigation which preceded the physical transfer of students, the level of legislative opposition seems to have been the same before and after the court order became effective. The largely decentralized and idiosyncratic process in which busing has been implemented in the North seems to have placed these trade area urban centers onto a number of different "tracks." Some led to massive and publicly resisted busing-orders handed down by federal courts (e.g., Boston), others led to extended and inconclusive negotiations between the school district and the federal bureaucracy (e.g., Chicago), still others resulted in busing plans ordered by state judicial authorities (e.g., Pittsburgh), and in a few, busing plans were voluntarily developed by the school districts themselves (e.g., Seattle and Portland). Whether an urban center found itself on one "track" or another was often unrelated to the gravity of constitutional violation (and thus the degree of underlying societal discrimination which the trade area had exhibited historically). But the most radical remedies for constitutional violations (and thus the greatest public resistance to implementation) arose from federal and state court-ordered busing. For that reason, at the beginning of the decade no differences were observed between those delegations representing trade areas in which a major federal court order was later implemented and those trade areas in which the urban center ended up on a different track.

As the decade wore on, those congressmen whose constituencies were in or near an urban center that was headed for a federal court order gradually moved into opposition to busing as an integration policy. The most dramatic transformations were to be seen in the Boston delegation, where none of the sixteen members voting in 1970 supported an anti-busing rider and where half of the eighteen voting members did so in 1975. In the Cleveland delegation, support for the rider increased from 29 percent to 62 percent over the same years. The most consistently pro-busing delegation represented the New York City trade area. In 1971, the forty-nine voting members of this delegation provided 27 percent of all the pro-busing votes cast in the House of Representatives.*

Politically, the most remarkable result of court-ordered busing has been (in conjunction with desegregation and black enfranchisement in the South) the elimination of civil rights as an intensely sectional issue. The regional pattern of voting on the 1979 proposed constitutional amendment illustrates this depolarization (see map 5.3). Surprising opposition to the amendment developed in the South, while a majority of the congressmen from the cities of Boston, Philadelphia, Pittsburgh, Cleveland, and Detroit supported passage. The most regionally cohesive pro-busing sentiment was found in the largely white regions of the Pacific Northwest, the upper Mississippi River Valley, and rural portions of the Northeast. This pattern is almost certain to undergo significant change in the future as unanticipated judicial and adminsitrative decisions are handed down and as "white flight" completes the residential resegregation of northern metropolitan areas. In the South, the political cohesion of regional delegations has become dependent upon the effective representation of black political demands.[91] This development alone suggests that civil rights will never again be used as a weapon in national politics by either the industrial core or the southern periphery. Thus, the precipitous decline in sectional competition charted in figure 5.5 would appear to be a permanent development.

Conclusion

In 1949, one of the most astute observers of American politics, Harvard political scientist V. O. Key, wrote:

> Southern political regionalism derives basically from the influence of the Negro. Other factors, to be sure, contribute to sectional character, but in the final analysis the peculiarities of southern white politics come from the impact of the black race. Common concern with the problems of a cotton economy forms a foundation for regional unity, although perhaps

---

*The forty-nine members made up 13.7 percent of the total number of votes cast on the appropriations rider.

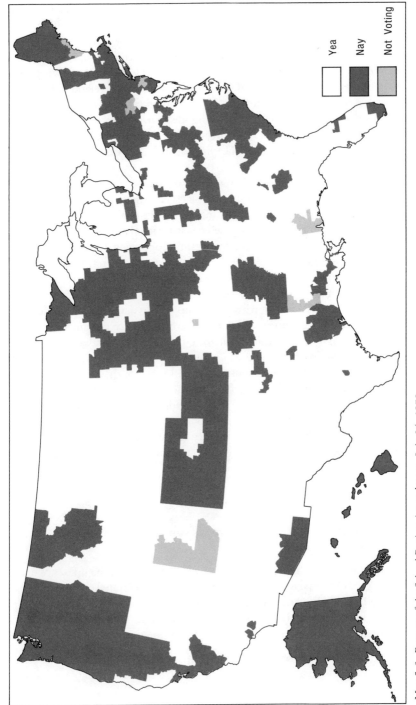

Map 5.3. Passage of the School Busing Amendment, July 24, 1979

to a lesser extent than several decades ago. A white population that is predominantly native-born, Anglo-Saxon is bound together by a sentiment of unity against those sections whose people include many recent immigrants. A rural, agricultural people views with distrust the urban, laboring classes of the North. The almost indelible memories of occupation by a conqueror create a sense of hostility toward the outsider. . . . Southern sectionalism and the special character of southern political institutions have to be attributed in the main to the Negro.[92]

At the end of his monumental study, *Southern Politics in State and Nation*, Key argued that the most important sources of southern political unity were the suffrage restrictions which prevented a working-class party from emerging and creating a two-party system that would mirror developments in the industrial North. Enfranchisement would, he argued, allow the "natural" political and economic trends taking place in the region to erode the distinctive character of southern political imperatives. These trends included the emergence of an indigenous and Republican-inclined industrial and commercial elite, the northward migration of rural black populations, urbanization, and the decreasing dominance of the plantation economy.[93] As Key noted, civil rights legislation, including measures to expand the southern electorate, have provoked the highest levels of sectional competition ever recorded in American history.[94] The civil rights legislation passed in the 1960s has effectively and permanently removed the "race question" as the primary basis of sectional conflict. The lower classes have been enfranchised, and regional urbanization and industrialization have proceeded apace. Yet sectionalism on economic issues, as we shall see in the next chapter, has not dissipated.

The causes for the failure of Key's predictions seem to lie in three areas. First, Key (and other commentators throughout the twentieth century) only saw a monolithic South with respect to race relations. The North also exhibited a broad consensus on this issue that should probably have been attributed to much more complex motives than simple altruism or sense of justice. In this chapter, some of these motives have been suggested. They include Republican attempts to divide the New Deal coalition in order to exploit a temporary political advantage, and efforts by the northern industrial labor wing of the Democrats to create a national working-class party. Clearly the Republicans would not cease their attempts to divide the New Deal coalition even when civil rights did not provide an effective means of achieving that goal. Furthermore, the now-dominant labor wing of the Democratic party has rediscovered what many New Deal congressmen recognized fifty years ago, that class conflict was as much an intersectional phenomenon as a characteristic of northern, urban center politics. A United Auto Worker in Detroit takes home an annual salary greater than all but a small percentage of the population in Mississippi, and efforts to "nationalize" labor legislation, ironically, have tended to divide the projected members of the new working-class party. For example, it is significant that repeal of Section 14(b) of the Taft-Hartley Act was considered in the 89th Congress along with the Voting Rights Act and also provoked one of the most regionally polarized alignments in that Congress. While the representatives of industrial labor maintained that the repeal of "right to work" exemptions would project economic justice into the southern periphery, most congressmen from the South interpreted the effort as an attempt to suppress regional economic growth by eliminating the wage scale advantage of the periphery and extending the influence of core organizations into the section.

In addition, Key's failure seems partially due to the irrational paranoia of southern politicians. Their extravagant rhetorical defense of segregation appears to have confirmed the widely held northern belief that integration and enfranchising measures would destabilize the hegemony of the plantation elite and lead to the development of a much more "pluralistic" political environment. Upon passage of the 1964 Civil Rights Act, for example, the Chairman of the House Rules Committee, Howard Smith of Virginia, shouted, "The second invasion of the Southland has begun—Hordes of beatniks, misfits and agitators from the North, with the admitted aid of the Communists, are streaming into the Southland mischief-bent, backed and defended by other hordes of federal marshals, federal agents and federal power." * Though the southern periphery is now more pluralistic than before 1965, on issues other than race southern trade area delegations have maintained virtually the same level of cohesion that previously existed with a much more restricted electorate. The emergent pluralism of the South has been largely an aspect of state and local politics, with little noticeable impact on the form of core-periphery political competition.[95] As it turned out, the stridency of the southern defense of race segregation convinced all political actors—including the agrarian periphery of the South—that more was at stake in civil rights legislation than in fact was the case.

Finally, Key may have underestimated both the breadth of the effort to destabilize the southern plantation elite and the persistence of institutional arrangements and behavioral norms even after the reasons for their existence have been fatally undermined. The civil rights effort of the 1960s was accompanied and followed by attacks on the Rules Committee, northern-inspired violations of the seniority system, and a reduction in the deference exhibited to

---

*As it turned out, Smith himself was a political casualty of the civil rights "wars," although his defeat in a 1966 Democratic party primary was due neither to the Voting Rights Act nor to the activities of "Communist beatniks" but came about as a consequence of the expansion of the federal bureaucracy into the Washington, D.C., suburbs and the increasing frequency with which Virginians registered in the Republican party. Government bureaucrats interpreted Smith's views on race as both obnoxious and incompatible with their own interests in a stronger central state, and the GOP drained off those voters who might have otherwise tolerated segregationist attitudes as a price of Smith's economic conservatism.

legislative committees on the floors of both chambers. While each of these features of congressional organization have been weakened to an extent that probably makes the growth of a strong, centralized party alternative inevitable, the latter development is probably still at least a decade away. When it arrives, the two parties will almost certainly resemble the homogeneous sectional bastions that characterized American politics at the turn of the century.

6

The Decline of the Core
Economy, 1970–1980

The end of the civil rights era marked the beginning of an entirely new and unanticipated period in American political development, one brought on by the precipitous decline in the heavy industrial base of the core economy. In several respects, the persistence of intense sectional competition in the post–civil rights era was just as surprising as the rapid deterioration in the vitality of American industry. The success of the civil rights movement during the 1960s had resolved, albeit in the core's favor, the oldest and most persistent regional dispute in American history. As a result of this resolution, many political observers expected that the South would be finally integrated into the cultural and political norms that typified the remainder of the nation.[1]

The "nationalization" of the southern periphery was expected for several reasons. Among the most significant was the dismantling of segregationist institutions. It was argued that the maintenance of these institutions in the face of northern hostility had required an enormous diversion of political energy and resources that otherwise would have been devoted to the economic development of the region. Southern congressmen were often reluctant to support the creation of a strong central state which could subsidize regional development because a powerful federal government could also restructure race relations. At the local level, industrialization was often discouraged because the interests associated with the plantation economy believed the movement of new plants into the region would disrupt racial norms.

The success of the civil rights movement eliminated or, at least, dramatically reduced the significance of these political and economic "perversions" of southern society. The defense of segregationist institutions was now a hopeless task because the expansion of the southern electorate under the Voting Rights Act brought both blacks and lower-class whites into the mainstream of the political process. Not only would federal enforcement of voting rights bring on a normalization of political life, but many observers felt that suffrage expansion would also inevitably liberalize political institutions in the South and

256

provide a largely indigenous protection against the reemergence of segregation. The elimination of elite-dominated structures would allow the expression of the natural pluralism of American society throughout the region. In areas where the historical remnants of segregation continued to divert indigenous political forces in unnatural directions, the exercise of federal power would continue to remake southern political institutions and social relations in accordance with national norms.*

In the process of integrating the southern periphery into the dominant national political and social norms, the civil rights effort would benefit the industrial core in a number of ways. Both directly through the expansion of the electorate and indirectly by raising the cost of agricultural labor, the nationalization of the South weakened the hegemony of the plantation elite.† Of all interests in American society, none had opposed the interests of the industrial core with more vehemence than had the mandarins of cotton culture.‡ In a related development, northern industrial unions expected to absorb the southern workforce into their ranks. This absorption would eliminate a union-free refuge for low-wage firms, establish a national floor for industrial wages, and, as a consequence, expand the national political and economic strength of organized labor. In turn, the political destabilization of the plantation elite and the unionization of southern labor would undermine the decentralized committee system in Congress (upon which, it was felt, inordinate periphery influence over national affairs rested). Restructuring the committee system would further the development of centralized, cohesive party organizations heavily influenced by the class-based interests which had characterized political conflict within the industrial core since the New Deal.

Political events between 1966 and 1982 disappointed each of these expectations to some degree. The civil rights movement hastened the mechanization of southern agriculture and a subsequent urbanization of southern society. These trends, as expected, destabilized the political hegemony of the plantation elite. Surprisingly, however, they did not reduce the national cohe-

---

*This extension of federal power was not without its ironical aspects. In the North, for example, white metropolitan suburbs were seen as a racist refuge from the growing minority populations of the central city. A dismantling of these artificial barriers to social integration was often suggested as the only long-term solution to race discrimination and hostility. In the South, however, the Justice Department overturned numerous annexation proposals, preventing southern cities from absorbing their white suburbs because such plans might have diluted the voting power of minority groups. Thus, the nationalization of southern institutions meant the imposition, in some cases, of segregationist northern racial arrangements.

†Implementation of civil rights measures coincided with reapportionment decisions handed down by the federal courts which reinforced this shift in the distribution of political power away from the rural, Bourbon elite toward the (often urbanized) lower classes.

‡The political decline of the plantation elite was reinforced by the expanding cultural influence of the northeastern centers of New York, Boston, and Philadelphia. This expansion took place after World War II as a result of the growing exposure of Americans to national television network programming. See Daniel J. Elazar, "Megalopolis and the New Sectionalism," *Public Interest*, No. 11 (Spring 1968): 67–85.

sion of southern congressional delegations. Only on civil rights issues themselves were southern representatives less united after the political revolution of the 1960s. Furthermore, the political expectations of organized labor have been sorely disappointed on every front; the region remains a right-to-work bastion in which union political influence is normally viewed as a form of northern economic imperialism.

The declining influence of the congressional committee system has nominally conformed to expectations, but the deposition of southern chairmen and the associated "democratization" of procedure has not produced a strong party system that can bridge the regional divide. While the decentralized legislative process of the past facilitated compromise and muted regional strife, the new centralization of political competition on the congressional floor has yet to develop mechanisms which would deflect sectional conflict into ongoing logrolling arrangements between core and periphery delegations. Ironically, the civil rights movement may have increased the intensity and breadth of sectional competition by removing the political inhibitions imposed on southern congressmen by the maintenance of segregation and eliminating the racial overtones that made the accommodation of southern interests politically expensive for northern Republicans.

The most sectionally divisive policies in the years following the civil rights era have been those that either directly channeled federal funds to the industrial core or retarded the shift of population and economic activity to the periphery. The context of this new round of sectional competition has been the precipitous and seemingly permanent economic decline of the industrial core. Many explanations have been given for the deteriorating health of heavy industry in the United States, but only two stand out as primary. Of these, the more important has been the spiraling cost of energy. In addition to rising energy prices, both the relatively high wages and rigid work rules associated with unionization have contributed to economic decline.*

---

*Among the reasons most often cited to explain the relative decline of the industrial core compared to the southern and western periphery are the much greater social welfare burdens carried by the North; federal policies which discriminate against the North and are the heritage of historical southern domination of the congressional committee system; the "negative" business climate of the North; the widespread use of air conditioning in the periphery, which made the climate there more congenial; the lack of an indigenous resource base in the industrial core; and the secular decline in transportation costs which has allowed industrial production to migrate away from primary markets and opened up the previously unexploited labor pools of the agrarian interior. For a discussion of these factors, see Michael J. McManus, "In the Face of Dire Economic Necessity," *Empire State Report*, October–November, 1976; and "Why Migration Became a Flood Tide," *Business Week*, May 17, 1976, pp. 95–97. Energy costs and unionization are emphasized in the text because they seem to account for the timing and direction of the northern economic decline and because most political conflict between the regions has presumed their primary role in recent economic developments. For an extensive discussion of all these factors, see Bernard L. Weinstein and Robert E. Firestine, *Regional Growth and Decline in the United States* (New York: Praeger, 1978), esp. ch. 2. The authors believe the more favorable

The rapidly increasing price of all forms of energy since the oil embargo of 1973 has produced a number of persistent dislocations in both the domestic and world economies.* In the domestic economy, the increase in energy prices has reversed the "terms of trade" between the sectional poles by revaluing upward energy-related, periphery resources. This revaluation has produced a massive transfer of income from the northern industrial core to the resource-rich mountain West and Southwest. The Northeast in particular has been devastated; in 1972, the region transferred $7 billion to the remainder of the world economy in order to import fuel. Three years later the energy trade deficit of the region had risen to $20.7 billion—$17.3 billion for petroleum products and $3.4 billion for natural gas.† Furthermore, the rising cost of energy has made that factor of production more important as a determinant of the location of economic activity, and widening differentials developed in regional energy costs during the 1970s, even within the context of overall price increases.[2] Thus, not only did the resource-related sectors of the periphery expand to meet the increasing demand for energy, but those sectors of the economy for which energy is an important factor in production costs tended to shift in the 1970s toward domestic sources of supply (for which costs have been generally lower).‡

"business climate" in the South explains much of the apparent reversal in long-term regional growth rates.

*The Director of the New England Research Office, an organization supported by the region's congressional delegation, emphasized the importance of energy: "There is probably no single factor which has hurt the regional economy as much over the past six years as the rapid increase in oil prices relative to the price of natural gas in the Sunbelt." Michael J. McManus, "In the Face of Dire Economic Necessity," *Empire State Report*, October–November 1976, pp. 344–45. One contemporary example of the effect of energy costs was cited by Richard Corrigan: "New York State steam electric plants paid $1.90 to generate one million BTU's of energy from oil last year, according to the Federal Power Commission; New England paid $1.84. Arkansas, Louisiana, Oklahoma, and Texas, however, paid only 91 cents to generate the same amount of power from natural gas." "The Search for Energy: Endless and Costly," *Empire State Report*, October–November 1976, p. 383.

†These figures are not adjusted for corporate ownership of energy producing firms, and include payments made to foreign producers. Neal R. Pierce, "The Northeast Maps Battle Plan for Economic Revival," *Empire State Report*, December 1976.

‡Walt W. Rostow has suggested that the world economy has entered an early phase of a fifth Kondratieff upswing: "The period since the end of 1972 is the fifth time in the past 200 years that a rise in the relative prices of basic commodities has occurred; and on each of the other four occasions it has been accompanied by manifestations similar to those we have experienced over the past five years: an accelerated general inflation, an extremely high range of interest rates, pressure on the real wages of industrial labor, pressure on those with relatively fixed incomes, and shifts of income favorable to producers of food as well as energy. The other four occasions occurred in the 1790s, the early 1850s, the second half of the 1890s, and the late 1930s. On each occasion, food and raw material prices then fluctuated in a relatively high range for about 25 years. Approximately another 25 years followed in which the trends reversed; that is, the prices of basic commodities were relatively cheap, as they were from 1951 to 1972. Each of these periods was, in an important sense, unique, and the trends did not unfold smoothly; but

Though it broadened the regional export base of the periphery economy, this redistribution of national wealth has not, for the most part, assumed the form of higher corporate profits for the major oil and gas producers. Because many if not most of the shareholders to whom these profits are ultimately distributed do not live in the resource-producing areas of the nation, the major impact of higher energy prices in the energy-producing states has been felt in higher rents, royalty payments, increased state and local tax revenue, and general economic development associated with an expanding export base.[3] The redistribution of income toward the periphery, in effect, has allowed that section to displace some of the costs of economic development onto the consuming regions of the industrial core. Out of the clearest forms of displacement has been the severance tax.*

The surge in energy prices did not take place in the United States alone. All the major industrial powers experienced a severe drain on their economies as a result of the increase in the cost of energy, and few of these nations possessed an indigenous energy source that could ameliorate the consequent impact on their international trade balance. In the years following the 1973 embargo, competition in foreign trade between each of these industrialized nations and the United States has intensified as each has attempted to offset the spiraling cost of petroleum imports with an increased exportation of manufactured goods.[4] For the most part, this competition has centered in well-established, mature industrial sectors in which technological innovation has not compensated for the higher costs of American labor. As a result, the heavy industrial centers that have typified the core economy of the United States have experienced a low or even negative return on invested capital over the last decade. The two most important lagging heavy industries have been automobile manufacturing and steel production.[5] Relatively little new capital has been invested in these sectors, and their increasing obsolescence—reflected in stagnating or even declining productivity—has intensified the economic pressure to either shut down or relocate those plants which continue to operate.

The relocation of heavy industry and manufacturing out of the Northeast and Midwest has occurred in two directions. The major flow has been to sites

---

the fact is that the world economy for almost two centuries has been subject to a rough and irregular pattern of long cycles in which periods of about 20 to 25 years of high relative prices for food and raw materials gave way to approximately equal phases of relatively cheap food and raw materials." "Regional Change in the Fifth Kondratieff Upswing," in David C. Perry and Alfred J. Watkins, eds., *The Rise of the Sunbelt Cities* (Beverly Hills: Sage, 1977), pp. 88–89.

*Toby Moffett, a Connecticut Democrat, noted this effect during House floor debate on a change in the revenue sharing formula: "We have some regions that are quite depressed compared to those oil-producing regions. What are we going to do . . . when these bloated treasuries from State severance taxes in [Louisiana] and Texas and Oklahoma and Alaska lead those States to then say, 'Come on down here Connecticut, New York, New Jersey, Illinois, and Michigan industries, come on down here. We will forgive your taxes for 5 years. We have got so much money in our treasuries we do not know what to do.'" *Congressional Record*, 96:2:H10605, September 13, 1980.

outside of the United States where wage differentials and lower tax burdens can be fully exploited. Relocation outside the United States has occurred both through reinvestment of capital abroad by American firms and through the preemption of American markets by foreign producers when domestic plants are shut down.*

The second trend has been relocation to the domestic periphery. Though the migration of mature industrial processes from the domestic core to the southern and western periphery has been of major historical importance to the development of the American South and West, the character of economic growth in the periphery has changed in recent years.

> Industrial growth in the nonmetropolitan South has contributed significantly to a reversal of the historical trend. Most southern industry before the 1960's was of the so-called old age stage in a process by which industries tend to filter down from areas of (greater) industrial development as such industries undergo a maturation process. These industries are characterized by low wages and a labor force consisting primarily of semiskilled and unskilled workers. The presence of these industries would not, however, guarantee economic and population growth in a given area, as they tended neither to stimulate in-migration nor to assist the younger, better educated, and more highly skilled workers who would be more likely to leave the area. Recently, however, these old age industries have in some areas been supplanted by others requiring greater capital investment and higher employee skill levels, including machinery and chemical activities.[6]

In the past, a significant portion of all low-wage, low-skill manufacturing moved to the southern periphery once the technology supporting their industrial processes had fully matured. This interregional flow was most pronounced for those industries whose raw materials originated in the periphery (such as textiles). But this earlier migration hardly constituted solid economic growth, since the move to the southern periphery was often but a stage leading to permanent relocation abroad.

The rapid expansion of the periphery economies in the last two decades, however, has differed from the earlier period of industrial diffusion in two primary ways. First, relocating northern production has not been the most significant contributor to growth.[7] Instead, perhaps because the periphery does not have the resource base for auto and steel production and because smaller interregional wage differences have narrowed the advantages of domestic relocation, heavy industrial production has moved to points outside the

---

*Many of these plants are not closed permanently but, instead, only operate during a general economic expansion when increasing demand makes them marginally profitable. Thus, these plants tend to be the first to be closed during a recession and the last to open during an upturn. Advisory Commission on Intergovernmental Relations, *Regional Growth: Historical Perspective* (Washington: 1980), p. 58.

national economy.* Second, the economic expansion of the periphery has been stimulated by the diffusion of large-scale, high-technology production. Although research and development activity continues to be centered in the core, the mass production of high-technology goods has often bypassed northern industrial centers to locate in the periphery.[8] For the most part, these new trends in economic development are an unplanned and unanticipated response to market forces.†

The decline of the core economy has been commonly attributed to the economic maturity of the major industrial sectors and of the larger, supporting infrastructure. Both factors are associated with the chronological economic age of the industrial base, declining rates of improvement in labor productivity, and generally low rates of economic growth. As the industrial base of a regional economy ages, the historical heritage of past expansions and manufacturing processes presents an increasingly serious obstacle to future growth. Over time, the originally vibrant industries have occupied most of the prime locations within the region, drawn most of the fixed capital investment into their plants, and trained an increasingly specialized and expensive work force. New technological developments and access to new pools of low-cost labor render these old industrial plants and their workers "obsolete"—nonviable in a market economy.[9] In Ohio, for example, over a fifth of total industrial capacity has been classified as obsolescent, compared to a national average of 12 percent. In the older primary metals and non-electrical machinery sectors, 40 percent of industrial capacity is now estimated to be obsolete.[10]

The supporting economic infrastructure exhibits similar problems. The historical heritage of nineteenth- and early twentieth-century industrialization includes a high level of unionization, which has tended to retard the adaptation of the work force to new technological processes, and an increasingly large dependent population on the welfare, unemployment, or old-age assistance rolls. Political conflict originating in disputes over industrialization has also left a number of residual constraints on regional economic growth in the form of zoning ordinances, construction codes, and environmental regulations. Though designed to protect the citizenry from the ravages of industrialization, this legislative heritage also retards the adaptation of the manufactur-

---

*For a lengthy treatment of the convergence of regional income trends and wage patterns, see Advisory Commission on Intergovernmental Relations, *Regional Growth*. That report concludes: "despite the overall convergence in regional wages, the differences may still be large enough (whether adjusted for industrial structure or not) to be consistent with further competitive shifts. The narrowing in these wage differentials over time is also consistent with the historical diminution in competitive shifts" (p. 47).

† "Unlike the experience of other Western nations, these changes appear to have reflected a private response to economic forces, rather than being the result of conscious government intervention to achieve regional balance. Indeed, the speed and relative ease with which these considerable regional changes have occurred may explain why the U.S. has established, in contrast with Western European nations, so few mechanisms for dealing with regional disparities." Advisory Commission on Intergovernmental Relations, *Regional Growth*, p. 26.

ing belt to economic change. In addition to all of the above, the transportation network in the industrial core comprises

> very substantial capital and operating costs but, given the decline in usage, becomes much more a hindrance than a positive asset. The mass transit facilities of New York are prototypical, operating at a deficit of several hundred million dollars a year largely borne by the general taxpayer; they cannot be substantially abrogated without completely shaking the city's ecology. Furthermore, although they represent a high level of essentially fixed expenditure, they cannot be made financially viable without virtually doubling the number of consumers.[11]

The industrial core, of course, has possessed these liabilities for several decades. The event which drove the heavy industrial sectors into precipitous (as opposed to gradual) decline was the explosion in energy costs. Following the oil embargo, the sharp increase in the relative price of energy rendered a large percentage of existing industrial capacity obsolete as energy costs became a primary determinant of industrial location.* In mature industrial sectors, technologial innovation became necessary just to *maintain* existing levels of productivity. Given the other obstacles presented by unionization, intensified foreign competition, and a collapsing infrastructure, many firms chose to shut down or relocate old facilities rather than rehabilitate them.†

One national financial weekly compared the decline of the industrial core to Joseph Schumpeter's explanation of the dynamics of capitalist economic growth—a process of "creative destruction" in which newly emerging industries must, of necessity, inflict pain and hardship upon those in relative decline. *Business Week* went on to say:

> As long as this process takes place within a given region, labor and capital thrown out of employment in the declining sectors can easily be reemployed in the rising sector, so growth creates no real problems. But when this process causes some political jurisdictions to decline and oth-

---

*Before 1973 only a few industries, such as aluminum reduction plants and chemical and glass factories, were significantly influenced by energy costs. See Miernyk, "Rising Energy Prices and Regional Economic Development."

†Some observers have seen a certain irony in the apparent reversal of fortunes between the core and periphery. "Not only have the Northeastern cities lost their position as the preeminent national urban centers, but their role at the top has been usurped by a region which has overcome the deeply embedded subordination built up during two epochs [mercantile and industrial] of carefully crafted institutional and economic barriers. The Northeastern cities, once the recipients of the benefits of these barriers, found themselves trapped by their elimination. While they were saddled with an old, slowly growing industrial foundation, the Sunbelt cities, because they had previously been blocked from adopting these same activities, were in a more flexible position to shift with the changing needs of the economy. In a sense, they presented the economy with a *tabula rasa*, uncluttered with the outmoded infrastructure and habits characteristic of past eras." Watkins and Perry, "Regional Change and the Impact of Uneven Urban Development," p. 41.

ers to rise, trouble is bound to ensue. . . . As long as the migration of industry and population was gradual from what was a relatively rich Northeast to what was a relatively impoverished South and Southwest, it helped to unify the nation. But within the past five years the process has burst beyond the bounds that can be accommodated by existing political institutions.[12]

The acclerating migration of displaced industrial workers into the periphery almost immediately provoked a political response among core congressmen.*

The decline of the industrial core since the onset of the energy crisis has spawned a number of explicitly regional political organizations. The emergence of these new organizations can be directly connected to the dramatic divergence in regional growth rates since 1973.[13] In order to illustrate this connection, the historical growth rates of those states which have, hypothetically, been most affected by the post-embargo rise in energy prices must first be compared with those states which have been the least affected. In the preparation of figure 6.1, the fifty states were first ranked on a composite scale that included both the relative cost of energy provided to gas and electric utilities and the proportion of total fossil fuel consumption imported from outside the state. The cost factor indicates the relative impact of energy price increases on the geographical location of those firms not involved in energy production or distribution. The importation data give equal weight to alteration in the interstate "terms of trade." Since most observers believe that the full effect of the energy crisis on regional economic development was reinforced by unionization, the states were further divided into those that are union shop (allowing collective bargaining agreements to require union membership as a condition of employment) and those that prohibit union shop provisions (right-to-work).[14]

As might be expected, the union shop/right-to-work dichotomy closely coincided with relative energy disadvantage.† In figure 6.1, the yearly change in total population for both the ten most energy-disadvantaged (high-cost and large imports), union-shop states and the ten most energy-rich, right-to-work states was calculated as a percentage of total national growth. For example, from July 1, 1974, to July 1, 1975, nine-tenths of 1 percent of the increase in national population occurred in the energy-disadvantaged, union-shop

---

*Adding in some ways to the economic distress of the industrial core has been what Brian Berry has termed a feeling "deeply embedded in the culture" that the aging industrial metropolis "is an effluent, an inevitable discard with no enduring value." Cited in Sternlieb and Hughes, *Post-Industrial America*, p. 162.

†The ten energy-disadvantaged, union-shop states (Connecticut, Delaware, Maine, Massachusetts, Michigan, New Jersey, New York, Oregon, Rhode Island, and Vermont) held an average rank of 5.5 on the energy scale (1 = the most disadvantaged). The ten energy-advantaged, right-to-work states (Arizona, Arkansas, Kansas, Louisiana, Mississippi, North and South Dakota, Texas, Utah, and Wyoming) averaged 35.2 on the same scale. The scale was constructed by Shirley P. Burggraf, "Energy: The New Economic Wildcard," pp. 838–40.

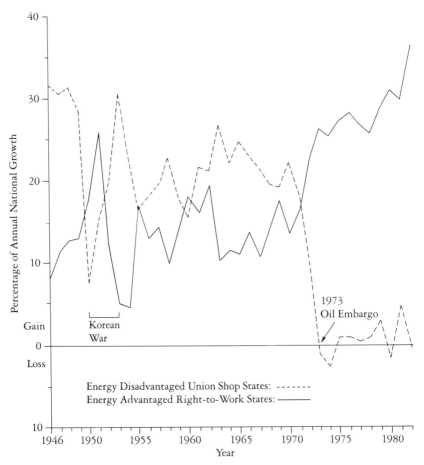

Figure 6.1. Union Shop Status, Energy Advantage, and Population Change as a Percentage of Annual National Growth, 1946–1982

states.[15] The 1975 figure for energy-advantaged, right-to-work states was 27 percent of national growth.

This relationship between energy costs and unionization, on the one hand, and economic growth, on the other, is a comparatively recent development. Until 1973, the only significant period in which the energy-rich, union-free states outstripped their union shop competitors was during the first two years of the Korean War. Until the 1973 embargo, the energy-disadvantaged states grew *faster*, in absolute terms, than the low-cost, energy-rich states. Because of this earlier, comparatively rapid expansion, the national population share of the ten union-shop states experienced little overall change in the postwar era in spite of the post-embargo decline. In 1946, these states contained 33.8 million people or 24.2 percent of the national population. By 1982, the absolute total had risen to 49.0 million, but the percentage had declined to 21.2. In 1946, the right-to-work states held a population of 17.3 million (13.1 percent of the national total). Thirty-six years later, 33.2 million (14.3 percent) resided in the same states.* Given the 1946–72 pre-embargo expansion, the collapse of the unionized, industrial economy after 1973 came as a brutal surprise that had profound political repercussions. †

In fact, there was a close chronological connection between the collapse of the industrial core, the oil embargo, and the formation of regional political coalitions intended to retard or even reverse the apparent trend of the market economy.‡ In the House of Representatives, the largest of these new organiza-

---

*Though a number of changes in relative energy costs and right-to-work status occurred over these years, none of the ten union shop states enacted a right-to-work law. It should be noted, however, that significant levels of energy production have only recently occurred in states like Utah and Wyoming.

†Carol L. Jusenius and Larry C. Ledebur conclude that "with the exception of the decade 1910–20, the rate of employment growth in [New England] has lagged behind that of the United States since the turn of the century." *Where Have All the Firms Gone?* p. 3. The exceptional decade coincided with the military expansion which led to United States involvement in World War I (see chapter 4).

‡The first professionally staffed congressional office serving a national region was the New England Congressional Caucus and Research Office, formed in 1972. Timothy B. Clark, "The Frostbelt Fights for a New Future," *Empire State Report*, October–November 1976. See also Jusenius and Ledebur, *Where Have All the Firms Gone?* p. 3; and Neal R. Pierce, Jerry Hagstrom, and Sarah Warren, "The New Congressional Politics: Single-Issue Caucuses," *Empire State Report*, October–November 1978, pp. 28–32. In 1980, the Advisory Commission on Intergovernmental Relations advised that "those who view faster rates of growth in relatively poorer regions with alarm implicitly accept the desirability of the perpetuation of the initial disparities," but noted, "if recent differences in rates of regional growth are extrapolated into the future, it is possible that the Northeast will become substantially poorer than the Southeast and Southwest and that the Northeast's relatively slow growth may become absolute decline. It is this type of extrapolation that lies behind the concern about 'a new war between the states' and the increasing number of regional organizations and coalitions studying the questions of regional differential growth and urging changes in federal policy to compensate for these differences." *Regional Growth: Historic Perspective*, pp. 12, 1. Historically there has been a high inverse correlation between per capita income and energy employment within the producing states (Miernyk, "Rising Energy Prices and Regional Economic Development," p. 3). This inverse correlation, however, seems to be significantly changing under the employment shifts induced by the upward revaluation of periphery reserves. Having analyzed six business cycles between 1948 and 1975, Richard F. Syron noted that both the New England and East North Central regions exhibited the greatest dependence on cyclical durable goods manufacturing while the mountain and West South Central states were nearly immune to economic downturns. He concluded that because these regions "are becoming more varied in their response to national economic patterns, the debate over regional impacts seems likely to escalate." Somewhat prophetically, he pointed out that this "widening of differences in regional economic behavior would also call into question the ability of macro policy alone to bring about satisfactory economic conditions in all parts of the country," while "the debate over who gets what share of national output [might become] so fractious that the various regions are left fighting over the

tions was the Northeast-Midwest Economic Advancement Coalition, which arose, according to its executive director, "out of a common perception that the entire urban, industrial tier from New England through the Middle West shared fundamental economic circumstances."[16] At the time of its formation on September 1, 1976, the coalition included sixteen state delegations with a potential membership of over two hundred.*

Summarized in general terms, there were several justifications for the new aggressiveness of the industrial core. By the first line of reasoning, the core regions took a paternalistic pride in the economic development of the periphery while pointing out that the historic subsidization of periphery growth had created an obligation on the part of newly developing regions to reciprocate now that the manufacturing belt had lost its vitality. In a more jaundiced view, the benefits of federal largesse, strewn so generously upon the South and West, had given those regions unjustified advantages in the now intensified competition for industry and population growth. As the Director of the New England Research Office put it,

> For years, it was equitable for the more affluent North to be taxed heavily through the progressive personal income tax, with the funds used in large measure to finance the development of the South and West. What has happened, beginning with the New Deal, is a massive redistribution of income from northern earnings to underwrite the TVA's economic development, the construction of a galaxy of military bases, defense plants and aerospace facilities, the irrigation of the Southwest, the digging of canals hundreds of miles long to make ports out of various inland cities of the South, the electrification of rural areas, and the construction of super-highways which opened up vast new areas for development.[17]

The most significant contemporary evidence of the historical subsidization of periphery growth was the continuing flow (one commentator called it a "hemorrhage") of federal spending out of the industrial core.

The earliest and most widely cited data on the regional impact of federal revenue and spending patterns were published by the *National Journal* in June 1976.[18] In brief, these figures revealed a net "loss" of $29.4 billion by the fourteen leading industrial states and a net "gain" of $26.6 billion by twenty-nine southern and western states in 1975. The heaviest burden was carried by the five Great Lakes states of Ohio, Indiana, Michigan, Illinois, and Wiscon-

---

pieces of a diminished national pie." Richard F. Syron, "Regional Experience during Business Cycles—Are We Becoming More or Less Alike?" *New England Economic Review*, November–December 1978, pp. 25–34.

*The sixteen states included six in New England, and New York, New Jersey, Pennsylvania, Ohio, Indiana, Michigan, Illinois, Wisconsin, Minnesota, and Iowa. Michael J. Harrington, "In Congress, An Effort to Reverse the Tide," *Empire State Report*, October–November 1976. See also Michael J. McManus, "The Northeast Coalition Begins to Move," *Empire State Report*, January 1977, pp. 31–34.

sin, which together paid $18.6 billion dollars more into the federal treasury than they received back in the form of federal grants, contracts, or payments to individuals.[19] While congressional efforts to soften the impact of the energy crisis on the industrial tier predated 1976, the widespread publication of these revenue and spending patterns provided a rationale for further political action.[20] Twelve months later, the *National Journal* again published evidence of regional "discrimination" by the federal government by analyzing the new 1976 data and outlining recent efforts to redirect spending patterns.[21] Since then, regional spending and revenue figures have been extensively analyzed and reported, although many analysts were unconvinced by these findings or the policy implications that were drawn from them.*

Roll Call and Policy Analysis

In order to discuss the political characteristics of sectional economic competition between 1971 and 1980, two types of roll calls and their associated policy aspects are analyzed in this chapter. In the first category fall nine of the ten high–sectional stress, closely contested roll calls recorded during the 94th Congress (1975–76) which determined the policy themes of the period (see chapter 2). Four of these represented contests between the core and periphery over the direction of federal spending patterns (for three of these, see table 6.1, roll calls 6, 12, and 18). These included two attempts to block the relocation of the National Oceanographic Office from Suitland, Maryland, to Bay St. Louis, Mississippi, passage of a bill authorizing $2.3 billion in federal loans to New York City, and an amendment that would have redirected federal spending under the Comprehensive Employment and Training Act (CETA) by manipulating the allocation formula. Five high-stress, closely contested roll calls occurred on legislation which extended or maintained federal regulatory authority which tended to benefit the political economy interests of the indus-

---

*Walt W. Rostow, for example, has maintained that "major regional changes in the country have been only marginally determined by the balance of federal tax and expenditure flows." "Regional Change in the Fifth Kondratieff Upswing," p. 96. One of the most extensive treatments was published in ch. 4, "The Federal Government and Regional Economic Activity," of Advisory Commission on Intergovernmental Relations *Regional Growth*. Justifying its interest in this area, the Commission cited "a belief that the federal government's share of total economic activity has grown so large and its laws and regulatory activities have become so pervasive that it influences in important ways what happens in the private sector of the economy. In this view, regional disparities (in growth rates or levels of well-being) are not unadulterated market phenomena, the result of the pure working out of the regional economic efficiency calculus, but to a major extent they are related to the regional impact of federal activity" (p. 50). There are many serious problems with treating this type of data in summary form. For examples, see the qualifications attending the conclusions contained in George Roniger's "The Impact of Federal Expenditures on the Northeast Coast," published in the *Congressional Record*, 94:2: 29590–91, September 9, 1976.

trial core (the effects will be discussed presently). Taken on a wide variety of topics (see roll calls 11, 15, 16, 17, and 19 in table 6.1), these included tallies concerning the withdrawal of federal lands in the West from mineral production and the mandatory extension of the federal unemployment compensation program to state governments which had not voluntarily included their employees in the past. Of the other three, one occurred upon passage of the proposed Consumer Credit Protection Act (which, in effect, nationalized regulations concerning the collection of consumer debts); one hampered the ability of the Federal Energy Administration to decontrol the allocation and pricing of petroleum products; and one blocked the Interstate Commerce Commission from permitting freight forwarders to enter into unregulated contracts with railroad lines. The one roll call which does not fall neatly into either the federal spending or nationalization themes, though it approaches the form of a regional subsidy, is on an amendment which proposed the deletion of a $3 million appropriation to fund the promotional and research activities of Cotton, Incorporated. This decision and the second vote on relocation of the National Oceanographic Office were not included in table 6.1.

The second category of policy conflicts analyzed is composed of additional roll calls which extend the nationalization and federal spending themes of the ten high-stress, closely contested votes of the 94th Congress. Roll calls in this category occurred within the 1971–80 period and were not subject to the "closely contested" criterion (majorities smaller than 55 percent). Almost all legislative decisions in this group exhibited sectional stress scores greater than fifty; all roll calls which exhibited low sectional stress scores or occurred on policy decisions that fell outside the federal spending or nationalization themes (e.g., foreign aid, agriculture, and school prayer) were excluded. Among roll calls on closely related policy decisions, the vote exhibiting the highest level of sectional stress was always included.

The roll calls contained in table 6.1 thus constitute a representative sample of high-stress decisions on the regional redistribution of national wealth and the nationalization of the social welfare state. Together, these votes also outline the broad characteristics of the most regionally divisive contests recorded during the 1971–80 decade. Sectional conflict on policies that fell within these themes increased for much of the decade (additional evidence for this apparent trend will be presented later). The twenty-two votes in table 6.1 can be divided into two groups. The nine votes possessing the highest stress scores all dealt directly with the allocation or targeting of federal spending. Eight of these concerned the manipulation of grant-in-aid formulas. In most of these contests, sectional political sentiments heavily colored the debate. For example, during House discussion of the public works job formula in February 1977, Representative Silvio Conte, a veteran Republican from Massachusetts, aggressively pressed the claims of the industrial core in language that revealed the saliency of local economic concerns:

Table 6.1. High-Stress Legislative Decisions Concerning the Redistribution of National Wealth and Nationalization of Social Welfare Programs, 1971–1980

Date	Subject	Characteristic Dividing Core and Periphery	Sectional Stress Index	Support for the Core Position (percentage):[a] Democrats	Republicans	Committee Holding Jurisdiction	Position of Committee Majority	Floor Outcome
1: Aug. 27, 1980	Formula allocating fuel subsidies for the poor.	Heating degree days.	82.9	48.1	58.3	Appropriations	Core	Core
2: May 10, 1977	Formula allocating community block grants.	Age of housing stock.	72.5	62.3	66.4	Banking	Core	Core
3: Feb. 24, 1977	Formula allocating public works jobs.	Unemployment rates.	71.6	45.2	32.0	Public Works	Per.	Per.
4: July 12, 1978	Formula allocating federal education funds (ESEA).	AFDC children from families above the poverty level.	69.6	62.9	38.9	Education	Core	Core
5: Sept. 16, 1980	Targeting of defense contracts (Maybank amendment).	Unemployment rates.	68.7	60.9	45.2	Appropriations	Core	Core
6: Feb. 10, 1976	Formula allocating CETA grants.	Unemployment rates.	65.6	51.5	53.5	Education	Core	Core
7: May 5, 1976	Formula allocating Land and Water Conservation grants.	State population size.	64.5	46.5	40.6	Interior	Per.	Per.
8: Nov. 13, 1980	Formula allocating revenue sharing funds.	State severance taxes on energy production.	62.4	49.4	33.6	Gov't Operations	Per.	Per.
9: May 13, 1977	Formula allocating countercyclical assistance funds.	Unemployment rates and state/local tax effort.	59.1	69.3	50.0	Gov't Operations	Per.	Core
10: Sept. 18, 1975	Discretionary federal authority to ban the use of natural gas as a boiler fuel.	Natural gas production and use as a boiler fuel.	55.9	77.4	74.2	Commerce	Core	Core
11: July 22, 1976	Legislative veto for decisions withdrawing public lands from mineral production.	Federal land ownership.	55.0	60.2	28.9	Interior	Per.	Per.
12: Oct. 1, 1975	Location of National Oceanographic Office.	Siting in Maryland or Mississippi.	54.9	62.2	35.9	Appropriations	Per.	Core

13: Sept. 9, 1976	"Prevention of significant deterioration" section of Clean Air Act.	Regional air quality.	54.8	74.2	47.5	Commerce	Core	Core
14: Aug. 1, 1979	Rationing plan for gasoline: set aside for heating oil.	Residential heating oil use.	54.0	54.1	57.8	Commerce	Core	Core
15: July 20, 1976	Coverage of employees in federal unemployment program.	Current participation of state and local employees.	52.2	68.4	23.7	Ways and Means	Core	Core
16: July 19, 1976	Passage of the Consumer Protection Act.	Differences in state regulation of debt collection activity.	52.0	59.5	41.1	Banking	Core	Per.
17: June 1, 1976	Mandatory separation of changes in petroleum allocation and price decontrol regulations.	Oil production and regional differences in energy costs.	52.0	74.0	14.0	Commerce	Per.	Core
18: Dec. 2, 1975	Federal loans to New York City.	New York City and state fiscal liability.	51.7	62.9	27.5	Banking	Core	Core
19: Dec. 17, 1975	Permission to allow freight forwarders to enter into contracts with railroads.	Location of freight forwarders in largest urban centers.	51.0	54.2	32.6	Commerce	Per.	Per.
20: Apr. 19, 1973	Use of federal Highway Trust Funds for mass transit projects.	Reliance on mass transit systems.	50.5	54.3	38.0	Public Works	Per.	Per.
21: Feb. 5, 1976	Deregulation of natural gas prices.	Natural gas production and consumption patterns.	50.2	69.0	11.7	Commerce	Split	Core
22: Sept. 19, 1972	Exemption of small firms from compliance with the Occupational Safety and Health Act.	Effectiveness of alternative state regulation and labor contract provisions.	50.0	65.1	26.6	Appropriations	Per.	Per.

^aThe core position is defined as the vote supported by a majority of congressmen in the Boston, New York, and Philadelphia trade area delegations, and the periphery position is defined as the vote supported by the Atlanta, Birmingham, Dallas, Memphis, and New Orleans delegations. In every instance the core and periphery positions were antithetical.

SOURCE: Compiled by author. Table includes eight of the ten high-stress, closely contested roll calls recorded during the 94th Congress (1975–76) and a representative sample of all high-stress decisions concerning the redistribution of national wealth and nationalization of social welfare programs recorded between 1971 and 1980.

Recently, as you know, much attention has been focused on the economic erosion of the Northeast and Midwest regions compared to the economic standing of the Sunbelt States. As cochairman of the New England Congressional Caucus and a member of the Northeast-Midwest Economic Advancement Coalition, I am seriously concerned over the high unemployment and economic stagnation of the Northeast.

I believe it is imperative to initiate policies to reverse this regional decline and to take remedial action by determining more equitable Federal allocation formulas. Certainly unemployment is one of the major areas in need of infusion of Federal funds, since the Northeast has the highest unemployment and business failure rate in the nation.[22]

In this instance, debate turned on whether public works jobs should be distributed to the states wholly on the basis of the absolute number of unemployed persons or whether 35 percent of the funding should be reserved solely for states with unemployment rates in excess of 6.5 percent.

Lists describing the impact of the formula change on the shares for individual states openly circulated on the House floor in this and the other formula struggles. Most votes were ultimately cast according to the relative advantage to be gained by the constituencies represented by the individual members. In the case of an amendment offered by Democratic Representative Andrew Maguire of New Jersey to the formula allocating the Land and Water Conservation Fund (vote 7 in table 6.1), 83.2 percent of those voting supported the formula alternative that benefited their respective states. Members from the states that would have smaller allocation shares under the amendment formula cast 156 of their 163 votes (95.7 percent) against the change. Congressmen from the states that would gain higher shares voted 170 to 59 (74.2 percent) in support of its adoption.*

Manipulation of aid distribution by formula change was encouraged by the large number and variety of grant-in-aid programs and the existence of detailed information about the consequences of different federal aid formulas. However, the manipulation of allocation formulas is at least as old as the New

---

*The eleven states which would have benefited under the amendment were California, Florida, Illinois, Massachusetts, Michigan, Missouri, New Jersey, New York, Ohio, Pennsylvania, and Texas. The impact of the amendment can be seen by comparing the 1978 column under "New formula, fiscal year" in the table titled "36 States Lose; 14 States Gain under H.R. 12234 Formula Change" with the 1978 column in the table "State Receipts from Land and Water Conservation Fund under H.R. 12234 with Maguire Amendment," *Congressional Record*, 94:2:12547–48 and 12537–38 respectively, May 5, 1976. Among both groups, congressmen tilted toward the larger interests of their regions. Of the seven 'yea' votes cast by members whose states were disadvantaged by the amendment, five came from Connecticut, Indiana, Rhode Island, and Wisconsin. Of the fifty-nine negative votes cast by congressmen whose states gained under the Maguire proposal, thirty-seven were tallied in the California, Florida, and Texas delegations. As a result of these defections, the Maguire amendment lost even though the states which would have gained under the change contained 251 congressmen—well over half the membership of the House.

Deal, and even relatively "primitive" census data and hand calculations could have suggested alternative proposals for federal highway appropriations, public works projects, welfare aid under AFDC, or hospital construction.[23] The fact that federal grant-in-aid formulas became the focus of regional contention in the 1970s must be seen as a political manifestation of the deteriorating economic and fiscal vitality of the industrial core. Taken as a whole, these grant programs allowed the manufacturing belt to expand their social welfare systems without aggravating local tax differentials (and, thus, increasing the competitive advantage of the periphery in the contest for new firms). In addition, the increasing number of formula fights in the 1970s reflected a deployment of political resources away from a focus on the more subtle mechanics of the political economy.

The second natural grouping of roll calls in table 6.1 (roll calls 10–22) primarily involves the use of federal regulatory authority in the maintenance and promotion of sectional interests. The 1971–80 decade was noteworthy in the extent to which environmental, energy, and labor measures were explicitly put to the service of regional economic interests.[24] Even so, the substantial class implications of many of these initiatives reduced the internal cohesion of both core and, to a lesser degree, periphery delegations and so resulted in moderately lower levels of sectional stress. Ten of the thirteen roll calls in the second grouping relate to alternative proposals for the expansion or contraction of federal regulatory authority.

The primary characteristics dividing the respective interests of core and periphery delegations on these votes comprise a litany of problems associated with the decline of the industrial core: an aging stock of residential housing, welfare populations supported at levels far above the national median, polluted air basins, dependence on high-priced heating oil, deteriorating fiscal health of the largest metropolitan centers, and a reliance on massively subsidized urban mass transit systems (see the fourth column of table 6.1). The economic characteristics that most commonly divided the sections politically were the geographical distribution of energy resources (particularly natural gas) and wide differentials in unemployment rates. While New England and the Far West have exhibited rates of unemployment above the national average for most of the past thirty years, it was only in the last decade that these regions were joined by the remainder of the Northeast and Great Lakes states.[25] This recent convergence of regional unemployment levels has made the use of unemployment figures in federal spending formulas very attractive, even when their accuracy or policy relevance might be doubted.*

* *Congressional Record*, 95:1:14611, May 13, 1977. Democrat Les Aspin of Wisconsin observed, "As the Bureau of Labor Statistics has testified before our subcommittee [concerning] unemployment statistics for small communities, anything less than 50,000 is almost a random number." *Congressional Record*, 95:1:14604–5, May 13, 1977. The floor debate is summarized in a front-page story in the *New York Times*, May 14, 1977. During floor debate on the Intergovernmental Anti-Recession Assistance Act formula (Countercyclical Assistance, vote 9, table

As can be seen, the two major parties were badly divided on almost all of the twenty-two roll calls. Low party cohesion on high-stress roll calls underlines the vulnerability of the present two-party system to a reemergence of uncompromising sectional conflict; neither party can successfully span the bipolar structure underlying the American political system without a serious deterioration in party unity. Furthermore, although both parties are badly divided, the center of gravity of the Republican party has apparently shifted into the periphery, and that of the Democratic party toward the core. While some evidence for such a shift in the respective roles of the two major parties could be seen in civil rights voting during the late 1960s and early 1970s (see chapter 5), the fact that Republicans showed greater support for the periphery position on eighteen of these recent twenty-two high-stress roll calls confirms an historic reversal within the party system. In each of the nine periods studied from 1880 through 1970, the Republican majority position was the core position. Now, for the first time, as the old manufacturing base that gave impetus to its ascent was rapidly decaying, the party of the nation's industrial and commercial elite shifted to the opposite pole. On the twelve recorded votes which determined the direction of federal spending patterns, the Republicans gave the periphery position an average of 57.5 percent of their votes compared to the Democrats' 43.7 percent. Significantly, this tilt toward the periphery was much greater on the broader regulatory or nationalizing decisions; on those ten votes, the periphery position drew an average of 64.2 percent of all Republican and 34.4 percent of all Democratic votes. It must be borne in mind that the Democrats controlled many delegations in the western periphery and all the delegations in the South, and the numerical center of gravity of the party—compared to the Republicans—still resided in the periphery if measured solely in raw number of seats. Clearly, many Republicans in core delegations were tilting heavily toward the periphery in their voting decisions and many Democrats in the periphery were leaning toward the position of their colleagues in the core. What these averages suggest, then, is that the dynamics of national party competition have accelerated a reversal and deepening shift in the sectional poles of the two parties. Furthermore, many of the Republican seats in the industrial core and Democratic members in the devel-

---

7.1), Representative Blouin of Iowa deplored the use of county level unemployment estimates: "when we get into that can of worms, our eyes are opened pretty quickly. They are the most inaccurate and in many cases totally unacceptable ways of determining hurt that anyone could possibly devise." The use of unemployment data in allocation formulas has also encountered severe criticism from the Advisory Commission on Intergovernmental Relations, in *Counter-cyclical Aid and Economic Stabilization* (Washington: Government Printing Office, 1978) (see the section titled "Unemployment Data as a Guide for Economic Policy"). This publication also contains a summary of the major features of the public works jobs, the Comprehensive Employment and Training Act, and the Anti-Recession Assistance programs. For skepticism about unemployment figures generally, see "Why the Unemployment Rate Is Out of Touch with the Real World," *Fortune*, May 8, 1978, pp. 136–46.

oping periphery must be considered marginal (if and when a repolarization of the party system takes place). Given the decline of the committee system as a mediating institution in sectional conflict and the historical pattern of bipolar political competition, it is difficult to believe that partisan centers of gravity on policy decisions and the geographical distribution of party members can remain inconsistent. In this sense, the position of the two parties on policy decisions might be viewed as the leading indicator of partisan change, and the present distribution of party members could be considered an historical artifact or lagging indicator of past party allegiance within the electorate.

Over half of the legislative decisions described in table 6.1 originated in only three of the twenty-one standing committees in the House (see column 7): six in Interstate and Foreign Commerce, four in Appropriations, and three in Banking. The committees on Education and Labor, Government Operations, Interior, and Public Works each produced two high-stress roll calls and the Ways and Means Committee produced the last. The significance of this pattern as an indication of the failure of institutional "reform" efforts and classic floor reciprocity patterns is discussed in chapter 7. The Banking and Education and Labor panels generated policy decisions favoring the industrial core, while Government Operations, Interior, and Public Works tilted toward the periphery (see column 8). The position of the other committees was mixed. Almost all of the policy decisions described in the table had been high in the priorities of the Northeast-Midwest Economic Advancement Coalition.* The political conflict that anticipated in many ways the coalition's formation and subsequent activity was the struggle over aid to New York City.

New York City Aid

On December 2, 1975, the House of Representatives approved legislation authorizing $2.3 billion dollars in federal loans to be made available to the city of New York. The margin of victory for the city was a scant ten votes (213 to 203). The decision was important to the study of the American political system for several reasons. Perhaps most significant, the fact that the nation's premier urban center faced imminent default on its debt payments and possible bankruptcy dramatically symbolized the economic problems of the industrial core in a way that no other national event has done. As many observers noted, New York, along with many other governmental bodies located in the manufacturing belt, had embarked upon a general expansion of public services

---

*One description of these goals went: "The coalition is now battling for a change in the school aid formula and is ready to fight for a better break on a broad range of national grant programs, including the Comprehensive Employment and Training Act, countercyclical revenue sharing, federal highway and mass transit programs, housing assistance and the medicaid formula for reimbursing the states." Neal R. Pierce and Jerry Hagstrom, "Regional Groups Talk about Cooperation but They Continue to Feud," *National Journal*, May 27, 1978, pp. 844–45.

and welfare programs just as the region fell into the precipitous economic decline of the 1970s.* In the Northeast, the regional economy revolved around one city to an extent unparalleled in any other area of the nation, and for the industrial core the prostration of the Empire City implied similar trends for nearby major urban centers and their hinterlands.[26]

The New York City aid bill was also significant in that it typified the kind of narrowly distributive policy that could trigger immense national cleavages around the two great sectional poles.† In terms of direct impact, the New York City loans benefited only residents of the urban center itself and, by removing possible state liability for the city's debts, citizens in the upstate counties. While politicians and analysts argued that default would jeopardize the "national interest" by disrupting private financial markets, the link was tenuous and, in any event, only held appeal for those who were already predisposed to support New York because of historical political alliances and a close coincidence of interest with the city on unrelated portions of the political economy. As Mark Shields put it, "New York's sanctimonious and self-righteous grovel with a tin cup was a spectacle most non–New Yorkers secretly relished."[27]

Of the trade area delegations in which nine or more members cast ballots on the New York aid legislation, the most cohesive represented the city and its tributary hinterland. New York State congressmen unanimously supported the bill and the giant New York trade area contingent provided a favorable fifty-vote margin (51 to 1; see table 6.2). Outside New York and its immediate hinterland a large majority (55.5 percent) of the nation's representatives actually opposed passage. Among the largest trade area delegations, however, only St. Louis, Atlanta, Dallas, and Charlotte voted to deny assistance. Though Democrats were more favorably inclined than Republicans within nearly every delegation, New York aid cannot be said to have been a partisan issue. Instead, the difference between the two parties was largely a function of constituency composition. Like New York City itself (all seventeen of its representatives

---

*See, for example, Rostow, "Regional Change in the Fifth Kondratieff Upswing," p. 95: "Somewhat like slow-moving Great Britain in the 1960s, the high-income North had committed itself to enlarged public and private services at a time when its manufacturing base, with high obsolescence in certain sectors, was waning, its rate of population increase was slowing down, and population was actually declining in some major urban areas. The unfavorable shift in the region's terms of trade, as in Britain, reduced real income at just the time it confronted unemployment rates about 2% higher than those in the South and Southwest. The fiscal problems posed for state and local government were only in degree less acute than for New York City." Other analysts felt that the plight of northern industrial centers could, in equal or larger part, be traced to the failure of their central cities to annex surrounding territory and thereby avoid ruinous revenue competition with suburban governments. See Lynn E. Browne and Richard F. Syron, "Cities, Suburbs and Regions," *New England Economic Review*, January–February 1979, pp. 41–57.

†The controversy over the location of the National Oceanographic Office is another example of this phenomenon.

Table 6.2. Trade Area Delegation Voting on Passage of the New York City Aid Bill, December 2, 1975

Trade Area[a]	Favoring Passage					
	All Members		Democrats		Republicans	
	%	(N)	%	(N)	%	(N)
New York City	98.1	(52)	100.0	(38)	92.9	(14)
San Francisco	82.4	(17)	92.9	(14)	33.3	(3)
Pittsburgh	80.0	(10)	85.7	(7)	66.7	(3)
Detroit	76.2	(21)	100.0	(13)	37.5	(8)
Boston	72.2	(18)	84.6	(13)	40.0	(5)
Cleveland	66.7	(9)	80.0	(5)	50.0	(4)
Philadelphia	55.6	(18)	88.9	(9)	22.2	(9)
Chicago	55.6	(27)	86.7	(15)	16.7	(12)
Minneapolis	54.5	(11)	83.3	(6)	20.0	(5)
Los Angeles	52.0	(25)	80.0	(15)	10.0	(10)
Washington, D.C.	50.0	(10)	57.1	(7)	33.3	(3)
St. Louis	44.4	(9)	50.0	(8)	0.0	(1)
Atlanta	9.1	(11)	9.1	(11)	—	—
Dallas	8.3	(12)	9.1	(11)	0.0	(1)
Charlotte	0.0	(16)	0.0	(13)	0.0	(3)

[a] Trade areas listed are those of which nine or more delegation members cast ballots on the bill.

SOURCE: Computations from roll call data.

were Democrats), the center city districts of each trade area tended to be represented by Democrats. Since the fiscal position of many of these highly urbanized areas within the national political economy was not dissimilar to New York's, the coincident voting patterns simply reflected corresponding constituent interests. Where the urban center did not share the fiscal distress or industrial and commercial characteristics of the nation's largest city (e.g., Atlanta, Charlotte, and Dallas), partisan loyalty could not bridge the sectional cleavage.

Republicans, on the other hand, nearly always represented hinterland districts at some remove from the urban center. Except in the New York trade area, where economic interdependence linked the hinterland directly to the city's fate, Republicans generally showed little sympathy for New York's difficulty. In this connection, we might note that one of the typical aspects of a high-stress core-periphery dispute is a tendency for rural districts in the manufacturing belt to favor the periphery position somewhat more strongly than their metropolitan counterparts, and a much fainter tendency for urban members in the periphery to favor the core. For this reason, intense bipolar disputes are sometimes characterized as "rural-urban cleavages," but it should be noted that a true split between city and hinterland would internally divide every trade area delegation and, thus, result in a low level of sectional stress. On highly polarized issues, then, these intra-delegation tendencies are relatively insignificant.

Following enactment of the aid legislation, any policy that appeared to favor New York City in the allocation of federal funds quickly reopened the controversy over the extent of national responsibility for the urban center's difficulties. In many instances, members found it politically advantageous to single out the city for attack during floor debate. For example, Republican Mickey Edwards of Oklahoma, in support of his amendment to change the federal aid to education formula, noted:

> Twice in the last 4 years we have been asked to use the money or credit of our constituents to bail out New York City. At [this] time, I am standing up here wearing a necktie sent to every Member of Congress by the mayor. . . . in recognition of what this Congress had done to bail out that city, and yet tonight we find a bill that has been changed to take again from our children in the rest of these States to give to New York City.

Immediately, Democratic Representative William D. Ford of Detroit rose to chastise the Oklahoman.

> I might suggest to the gentleman that I intend to be fighting to give equity to his schools in Oklahoma in a little while when they [New York members] try to cut the impact aid. If he wants to play a cannibalistic game. . . . , he will find Oklahoma is on the short end of the stick. It is very shortsighted for him to shortchange New York in order to try to prejudice the Members.

To this and other comments, Edwards replied, "It does not make sense to weight so heavily the AFDC recipients, because an area like New York that goes overboard in giving away AFDC will naturally qualify more for that kind of aid." At this point, a congressman from the city, Theodore Weiss, rose in New York's defense.

> When the gentleman from Oklahoma first decided to offer this amendment and sent out a "Dear Colleague" letter, the gentleman focused not on New York City and its AFDC recipients but the gentleman focused on Wayne County, Michigan, and Detroit, Michigan. Apparently since then the gentleman has had occasion to rethink which location would be more vulnerable and decided it would be the better part, if not wisdom, but pragmatism, to level his attack on New York City.*

---

*Congressional Record, 95:2:H6580–82, July 12, 1978. On another occasion, during debate on the amendment offered by Democrat Les Aspin of Wisconsin which would have changed the countercyclical assistance formula (vote 9 in table 6.1), Ronald Dellums of Oakland, California, complained, "many of the more conservative Members of Congress over the

Even politicians who represented districts within the industrial core were not always immune to suspicions concerning the altruism or ulterior motivations of the Empire City's requests. After formation of the Coalition of Northeast Governors on July 23, 1976, Timothy Clark noted, "Interviews with officials in states around the region . . . revealed a deep fear among some that New York somehow wants to use the Coalition to help bail out New York City."[28] In Congress, however, these suspicions were largely laid aside by the natural allies of the metropolis. Furthermore, after original passage of the aid package, a friendly Democratic party leadership could concentrate its efforts on attempts to resurrect the bipolar alliance, persuading "southern politicians [to] trade votes for federal aid to New York City in exchange for New York votes on programs that would benefit the South."[29] While the leadership was partially successful in these efforts—reflected in wider victory margins and lower stress scores when the loan authorization came up for renewal—the political cost to New York incurred by the city's fiscal problems was very high, and the metropolis remained the most visible symbol of sectional competition in the 1970s (much as Birmingham, Alabama, had been during the civil rights period).*

Defense Expenditures and the Maybank Amendment

Of all federal spending patterns, the one produced by military procurement for the Department of Defense has provoked the greatest recent controversy and criticism among core representatives. One analyst estimated that the defense portion of the federal budget alone produced in 1977 a net "loss" of more than $10 billion for the Northeast and $15 billion for the Great Lakes states.[30] Without these "inequitable" burdens, it was calculated that the Northeast and Midwest would about hold their own in the remainder of the federal budget. Asked about the recent shift of defense spending into the South, Speaker "Tip" O'Neill of Massachusetts claimed that the process "was a political vendetta by the Nixon Administration, no question about it. We lost all these shipyards because Nixon hated the Northeast, he hated Massachusetts. There's no question about that. But I think that that was because Nixon was at heart a hater."[31] When Nixon left the White House and even

---

last 2 or 3 years have beaten New York to death. And to see my liberal colleague taking on New York and making it another whipping boy on the floor of this House greatly saddens me." Later, Democrat Adam Benjamin of Gary, Indiana, added, "I do not enjoy these fratricidal debates and I do not care to characterize this as another New York versus the Nation epic." *Congressional Record*, 95:1:14610 and 14618, May 13, 1977.

*The original aid package had provoked one of the ten high-stress, closely contested roll calls recorded during the 94th Congress (vote 18 in table 6.1). Reauthorization, passing the House on June 8, 1978, with 61.4 percent of all votes cast, produced a much lower sectional stress score of 35.5.

after Jimmy Carter was inaugurated as president, however, the tilt toward the southern and western periphery persisted, and pressure to redirect federal defense spending toward the manufacturing belt began to build.

The object of this political pressure became the reinstitution of "Defense Manpower Policy No. 4-B," a presidential directive that had been issued by President Truman in 1952. Under the order, the Department of Defense was directed to set aside a portion of its procurement contracts for "labor surplus areas" and give preference to bids from firms in such areas. The order brought the Defense Department into conformance with the purchasing practices of most civilian agencies of the federal government. In 1953, however, Congress attached a rider to the Defense Appropriations bill that read: "no funds herein appropriated shall be used for the payment of a price differential on contracts hereafter made for the purpose of relieving economic dislocations." Known as the "Maybank amendment" after the South Carolina Senator who sponsored it, the rider was the product of a contest between New England and Carolina textile manufacturers. By adopting the provision, Congress effectively prevented the Department of Defense from favoring high-cost New England mills at the expense of their low-cost southern competitors.[32]

The Maybank amendment was attached to every annual appropriations bill for the next twenty-six years (through 1979). In 1980 alone, deletion of the amendment was estimated to result in the redirection of between $10 billion and $15 billion in defense contracts not directly related to the national security.[33] The firms favored by removal of the limitation were located in labor markets with unemployment rates 20 percent higher than the national level, with a floor of 6 percent (the local unemployment rate below which no area would qualify) and a ceiling of 10 percent (above which all areas would be eligible). Deletion of the amendment was called the Northeast-Midwest Economic Advancement Coalition's "greatest" victory during 1980.[34]

For the first eight years in which it operated, the Maybank rider was not exposed to an open floor struggle or recorded vote. But on June 28, 1961, a Pennsylvania Republican, John Saylor, offered a proposal to strike the limitation, provoking a floor debate with overtones anticipating the 1970s. In the debate, one southern California congressman noted pointedly that the defense effort "is not a WPA project. It is not a welfare program." This was to become a common theme among future supporters of the Maybank amendment. As an argument in favor of repeal, Daniel Flood of Pennsylvania emphasized that the limitation effectively restricted the political influence of congressmen: "this pernicious language . . . is being used by the Defense Procurement people against you and me every hour of this day because no matter where you go down there . . . they will dust off this dead horse and parade it in front of you."[35] Nearly twenty years later, William

Table 6.3. Voting on Maybank Amendment Repeal, 1961–1980

	Members Supporting Repeal							
	1961		1978		1979		1980	
Category	%	(N)	%	(N)	%	(N)	%	(N)
Appropriations Committee Members	27.7	(47)	37.5	(48)	50.0	(48)	58.3	(48)
Delegations in the Manufacturing Belt	60.8	(186)	77.8	(153)	90.1	(142)	92.6	(162)
All Other Delegations	26.5	(226)	20.4	(225)	21.0	(219)	29.7	(236)
Entire House	42.0	(412)	43.7	(378)	48.2	(361)	55.3	(398)
Sectional Stress Index	48.0		59.1		67.8		68.7	

SOURCE: Compiled from roll call data.

Chappell of Florida cited this prospect as just the reason the Maybank proviso should be retained: "If you want to start a real, sure-enough political animal, if you want to turn him loose on military procurement, you will do just what you are talking about, because the Secretary of Defense will have every pressure in the world to designate all kinds of areas to lower the standards of competition and all the rest."[36]

By the late seventies, the accelerating decline in the core economy and the associated concentration of high unemployment rates in the Northeast had raised the political stakes accompanying the Maybank amendment. Henry Gonzalez of San Antonio said in 1979 that the repeal proposal "should be labelled 'the biggest New York buck for the bang,' because it really is an amendment prepared by the Northeast corridor lobby. . . . It is a geographical effort on the part of the Northeast corridor to foist special favor legislation for that section, and not anything else."[37] A year earlier one New York City member had rather naively maintained, "the Maybank amendment belongs to an outdated time when one section of the Nation looked with deep suspicion at other sections of the Nation. It belongs to a time when Federal spending was a small tool which a shrewd Congressman could utilize to give his area a leg up over some other section of the Nation."[*] Few congressmen could afford to be neutral in this contest over reallocation of the largest single item in the federal budget, and the debate reveals the increasing difficulty of bridging the chasm between the sections.

By 1980, four recorded votes on the Maybank amendment had been taken in the House of Representatives (table 6.3). These roll calls exhibited an incremental increase in regional polarization, starting with the moderately

[*]*Congressional Record*, 95:2:H8085, August 8, 1978. The New York Democrat, Joseph Addabbo, cited a "survey" conducted by the Northeast-Midwest Coalition which showed "that Maybank discriminates against 270 congressional districts around the Nation." The Coalition was often mentioned in the floor debates on repeal between 1978 and 1980.

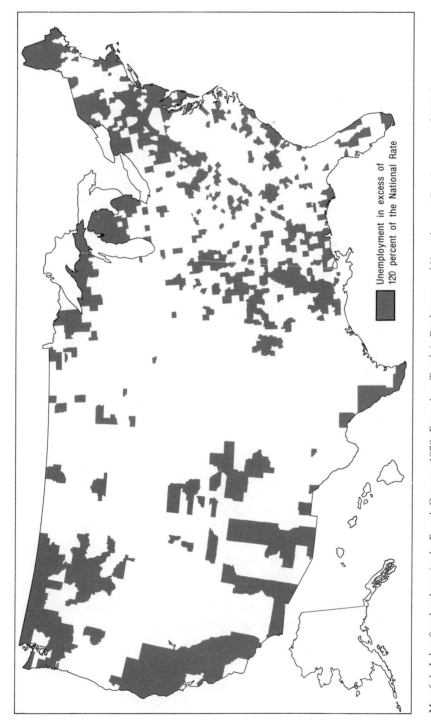

Map 6.1. Labor Surplus Areas in the Fourth Quarter, 1978. From *Area Trends in Employment and Unemployment*, Employment and Training Administration, U.S. Department of Labor.

Unemployment in excess of 120 percent of the National Rate

high level notched in the initial repeal attempt in 1961 and ending with the extremely high mark set in 1980.* Independent, parallel increases also occurred in the percentage of Appropriations Committee and House members supporting repeal. In 1961 and 1978, the committee was significantly more hostile to repeal than the full House. The 1979 floor vote by Appropriations members clashed with a 27 to 14 (65.9 percent) tally in favor of the Maybank proviso recorded during committee deliberations.† By 1980, the floor positions of the committee members were markedly more favorable to repeal. A major factor in the 1980 victory, compared to the 1979 defeat, was the floor attendance of thirteen formerly abstaining New York trade area delegation congressmen who converted a 38 positive vote margin in 1979 into a 51-vote plurality in 1980. No negative votes were cast within the delegation in either year.

In determining whether a particular constituency would have benefited from deletion of the Maybank amendment, a major consideration would have been whether or not the congressman's district contained "labor surplus areas" as determined by the Secretary of Labor. As core representatives constantly pointed out, these areas of extraordinarily high unemployment were scattered throughout the country (see map 6.1). However, labor surplus areas in the South and West were much less likely to draw a greater share of defense spending after repeal of Maybank than their counterparts in the industrial core. In the South and West, high unemployment was a characteristic of rural and small-town labor markets in which firms potentially interested in defense procurement either did not exist or were not oriented toward the national market in which the federal government made its purchases. Of all major southern metropolitan areas, for example, only Atlanta and Miami were eligible in 1978. In the manufacturing belt, however, the great metropolitan centers of Boston, New York, Philadelphia, Baltimore, Buffalo, Pittsburgh, and Detroit all shared "labor surplus" status. Furthermore, in southern and western counties that were eligible and contained firms that could bid for defense contracts, lower labor costs (associated with a non-unionized work force) and reduced overhead costs (in the form of relatively advantageous tax rates) often meant that these firms could submit competitive bids even without repeal of the Maybank proviso. In fact, everything considered, such producers might come out *worse* after the amendment was deleted because the terms of competition would be equalized with depressed northern regions. While the precise line

---

*In 1961, 1979, and 1980 the struggle was over simple repeal of the Maybank amendment. In 1978, core members supported substitute language that read: "No more than 10 percent of the funds appropriated in this Act shall be used for payments under contracts hereafter made for the purpose of relieving economic dislocations." In practice, this amendment would have differed little from simple repeal.

†Reported by Republican Kenneth Robinson of Virginia during floor debate, *Congressional Record*, 96:1:H8691, September 28, 1979. The most likely explanation for the inconsistency between tallies in the committee and on the floor would appear to be abstention by core members during proceedings in the committee.

separating those districts which would benefit from repeal from those that would suffer would have been hard to draw, a fairly close approximation was the boundary which divided the old manufacturing belt from the rest of the nation (see table 5.6).

By and large, the increasing level of regional polarization and floor support for repeal efforts between 1961 and 1980 was the product of the increasing economic difficulties experienced within the manufacturing belt and a consequent heightening in the cohesion of the respective trade area delegations. Outside the manufacturing belt, only about one-fifth to one-quarter of all congressmen supported repeal, and there was little indication of a trend in any direction. Within the manufacturing belt, however, opposition to the Maybank amendment grew significantly —from 60.8 percent in 1961 to 92.6 percent in 1980. By 1980, the level of political cohesion within the industrial core was not only indicative of the high level of unemployment and economic decline in that section, but also represented a growing consensus that, in this as in many other areas, a competitive marketplace had become a detrimental feature of the national political economy for the Northeast and Midwest.*

Distribution Formulas and Sectional Stress

Unemployment rates also entered into another regionally polarized roll call recorded during the 94th Congress (1975–76). This policy decision involved a choice between two formulas governing the distribution of federal funds under the Comprehensive Employment and Training Act. The Education and Labor Committee formula concentrated CETA Emergency Employment expenditures (Title VI, Part B of the Act) in areas of "substantial" unemployment (see below). An amendment offered from the floor by Representative Michael Blouin of Iowa proposed to lower the definition of "substantial" unemployment to 4.5 percent and to increase the proportion of funds distributed on a per capita basis. Under the committee formula, labor areas with unemployment rates above 6.5 percent would have received substantially greater funding per unemployed person than would areas below that threshold; under the Blouin formula, since almost all labor areas would have qualified at 4.5 percent, expenditures under Part B would have been much more evenly distributed and based largely on the absolute number of unemployed within the area compared to the national total.†

For the most part, congressmen chose between the two formula alternatives on the basis of constituency interest, and almost all deviations from that pattern were toward the larger interest of the core or periphery (see table 6.5

---

*Many members, of course, switched positions over the twenty-year period. One of the most symbolic of these switches was the change in position by Silvio Conte, a Massachusetts Republican. Later to become one of the leaders of the New England Caucus and the Northeast-Midwest Coalition, in 1961 Conte had voted *for* the Maybank amendment.

† Even under the Blouin formula, however, the greater part of distributed funding would

Table 6.4. Alternative Formulas under Title VI, Part B of the Comprehensive Employment and Training Act

Education and Labor Committee	Blouin Amendment
25% of expenditures distributed to all areas on the basis of the number of unemployed located in each area relative to the total number of unemployed in the entire nation;	50% of expenditures distributed to all areas on the basis of the number of unemployed located in each area relative to the total number of unemployed in the entire nation;
75% of expenditures distributed to those areas where unemployment exceeds 6.5% on the basis of the number of "excess" unemployed in an area relative to the total excess unemployment in all such areas ("excess" unemployment equals the number of unemployed minus 6.5% of the area labor force).	50% of expenditures distributed to those areas where unemployment exceeds 4.5% on the basis of the number of "excess" unemployed in an area relative to the total excess unemployment in all such areas ("excess" unemployment equals the number of unemployed minus 4.5% of the area labor force).

Table 6.5. Unemployment Rates in Major Metropolitan Areas and Voting on the Blouin Amendment

Metropolitan Area	Unemployment Rate (%)[a]	Vote on Blouin Amendment		
		Yea	Abstention	Nay
Detroit	12.7	0	1	6
Boston	11.0	0	0	4
New York	10.5	1	1	21
Newark	10.1	0	0	8
San Diego	10.1	0	0	2
Chicago	9.9	1	0	12
San Francisco	9.6	0	3	5
Philadelphia	9.4	1	2	4
Los Angeles	9.0	2	2	12
Pittsburgh	8.8	0	1	2
St. Louis	8.4	1	0	2
Cleveland	7.2	0	0	8
Minneapolis	6.3	1	0	2
Dallas	5.1	4	0	0
Houston	4.6	3	0	0

[a] Metropolitan areas included are those too small to be shown on map 6.2 and those representing the extreme ends of the national distribution. Unemployment rates of other selected labor areas in December 1975: New Bedford, Mass., 13.7 percent; Lawrence, Mass., 13.3; Buffalo, N.Y., 12.8; Tampa–St. Petersburg, Fla., 12.4; Waterbury, Conn., 12.1; El Paso, Tex., 10.1; Harrisburg, Penn., 5.7; Manchester, N.H., 5.5; Charleston, W.V., 5.5; Raleigh-Durham, N.C., 5.5; Denver, Col., 5.5; Tulsa, Okla., 5.5; Cedar Rapids, Ia., 5.4; Jackson, Miss., 4.9; Chattanooga, Tenn., 4.9; Madison, Wis., 4.6; and Richmond, Va., 4.2.

SOURCE: Unemployment rates (December 1975) from Employment and Training Administration, Department of Labor, *Area Trends in Employment and Unemployment* (Washington: January–February 1976).

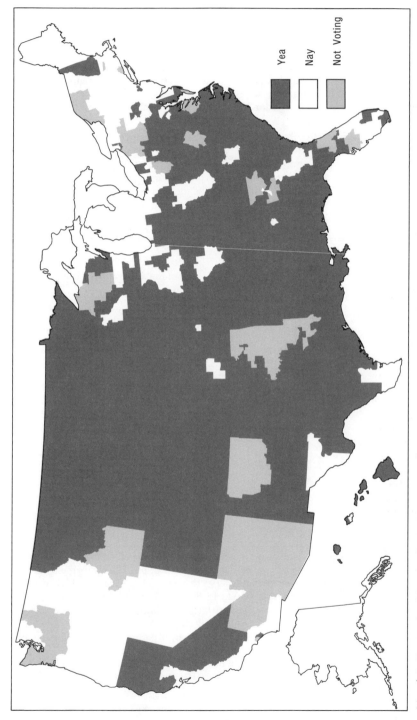

Map 6.2. Congressional Support for the Blouin Amendment to the CETA Formula, February 10, 1976

Table 6.6. Analysis of Voting on the Blouin Amendment

Classification	Yea %	(N)	Nay %	(N)
Districts with Unemployment Rates in Excess of 6.5%	33.0	(94)	67.0	(191)
Districts with Unemployment Rates at or under 6.5%	86.4	(95)	13.6	(15)
			Yule's Q = .86	
Republicans	46.5	(60)	53.5	(69)
Democrats	48.5	(129)	51.5	(137)
			Yule's Q = .04	
Liberals[a]	29.0	(54)	71.0	(132)
Conservatives[a]	65.2	(135)	34.8	(72)
			Yule's Q = .64	
Manufacturing Belt Trade Area Delegations[b]	20.6	(35)	79.4	(135)
Non–Manufacturing Belt Trade Area Delegations[b]	68.4	(154)	31.6	(71)
			Yule's Q = .79	
Northeast[c]	20.4	(22)	79.6	(86)
Midwest[c]	44.1	(52)	55.9	(66)
South[c]	87.0	(94)	13.0	(14)
West	34.4	(21)	65.6	(40)

[a] "Liberals" were those congressmen who scored fifty or more on the 1976 rating scale published by the Americans for Democratic Action. "Conservatives" are those who scored under fifty on the scale.

[b] See chapter 5 for the designation of manufacturing belt delegations.

[c] The boundaries of these sections are conventional: Deleware, Maryland, and West Virginia are included in the Northeast, Kentucky and Oklahoma in the South, and Missouri in the Midwest.

SOURCE: Computations from roll call data.

and map 6.2). When the vote is analyzed for four criteria—unemployment rate, party membership, ideological tendencies, and location with respect to the historical manufacturing belt (see table 6.6)—the factors showing the closest tie to the roll call pattern are the unemployment rate and the location with respect to the old manufacturing belt. Since the policy decision itself revolved around the use of unemployment rates as a central term in an allocation formula, the high association with relative unemployment levels is not surprising. During this period, the unemployment rate in most regions of the country was generally declining, and one explanation for the fact that many of

have gone to the industrial core, where unemployment rates tend to be higher under conditions of relatively equal economic distress. The more generous unemployment benefits provided in these older industrial regions, both in size of payment and length of coverage, encourage a greater percentage of the unemployed workforce to report to unemployment offices over a longer period of time. While the Department of Labor does not rely exclusively on filed claims in computing area rates (adjusting them for seasonal variation, short-term or temporary job loss, etc.), these differences in state program characteristics still influence the overall reported rate.

those districts with rates above 6.5 percent still supported Blouin is that these members expected their areas to slip under the target percentage in the near future. Many of those members whose constituency interest was unclear seem to have gravitated toward the sectional pole with which they were most frequently allied on other issues.

In contrast, party membership seems to have had little or no effect on the outcome; the two parties divided almost identically on the amendment. On the other hand, ideological orientation was moderately associated with positions on the roll call. Members with scores below fifty ("Conservatives") on the rating scale published in 1976 by the Americans for Democratic Action were more likely to vote for the amendment than were members who scored fifty or above ("Liberals"). As will be suggested in chapter 8, the coincidence of ideological and sectional cleavages strongly suggests that the former are but an epiphenomenon of the latter.

On May 10, 1977, the Northeast-Midwest Coalition scored a major legislative victory when the House of Representatives turned back an attempt by Democrat Mark Hannaford of California to amend the allocation formula for the community development block grant program.[38] The Banking, Finance, and Urban Affairs Committee had previously changed the then current formula (based on population, amount of overcrowded housing, and poverty—the last weighted twice) by allowing cities to choose to use an alternative formula which weighted the amount of pre-1940 housing 2½ times, poverty 1½ times, and growth lag once (the extent to which a locality's growth rate fell below the national average for all metropolitan areas). Since metropolitan centers in the manufacturing belt were wealthier, contained a much older housing stock, and grew much more slowly than many cities in the South and West, the net effect of the new alternative formula was to drastically shift federal funding toward northern areas.* The floor manager for the bill, Democrat Stanley Lundine of upstate New York, claimed that the new formula "was designed expressly to favor the demographic characteristics which best measured need in the Northeast and Midwest central cities and was expressly designed to compensate those cities for the bias inherent in the old community development formula."† Hannaford's amendment would have eliminated the

---

*As Hannaford noted, the "new formula is heavily biased against the West. It is heavily biased against the South, and it is heavily biased against the suburbs. . . . I cannot accept that the suburbs in my district in Los Angeles and Orange Counties, California, some of them with many low-income people, should be taxed to support the revitalization of Detroit or Newark." He added, "This bill looks at old buildings, regardless of their state of repair, as a measure of need; and it mindlessly and arbitrarily passes out money on that basis." "Additional Views of Representative Mark H. Hannaford on H.R. 6655," *The Housing and Community Development Act of 1977*, House Report 95-236.

†*Congressional Record*, 95:1:4137, May 6, 1977. Southern and western members remained unconvinced. In the words of Arkansas congressman Bill Alexander, "Instead of helping abate and remove and arrest the regional biases and the regional prejudices that are so much a

Table 6.7. Voting on the Community Development Block Grant Formula

	Position on the New Committee Alternative			
	Yea		Nay	
Category	%	(N)	%	(N)
Members Whose States Would Gain under the New Formula	96.3	(208)	3.7	(8)
Members Whose States Would Lose Funding under the New Formula	27.3	(53)	72.7	(141)
Loss under 10% of Previous Funding Level	71.0	(22)	29.0	(9)
Loss over 10% of Previous Funding Level	19.0	(31)	81.0	(132)
Manufacturing Belt Trade Area Delegations	98.2	(168)	1.8	(3)
Non-Manufacturing Belt Trade Area Delegations	38.9	(93)	61.1	(146)

SOURCE: Computations from roll call data. State allocations with and without the new committee formula are described in the *Congressional Record*, 95:1:4137–38, May 6, 1977.

committee formula alternative and reverted the allocation pattern to the previous distribution. As was true of all other formula fights during the 1970s, the voting on the House floor closely followed the interests of individual constituencies (see table 6.7). Here, too, the roll call pattern paralleled the prevailing core-periphery cleavage.

Federal Aid to Education

During the 1970s, the House of Representatives voted on five different manipulations of the allocation formula for distributing federal education aid.* Since its inception, the allocation formula for Title I funds under the Elementary and Secondary Education Act (ESEA) has been heavily weighted toward children from families with incomes below the national poverty line. While there has

---

part of this institution, this bill, I believe, has intensified those prejudices." *Congressional Record*, 95:1:4238, May 10, 1977.

*Under Title I of the Elementary and Secondary Education Act, the federal government provides aid to local education agencies. The allocation formula determines the allotment each school district is entitled to receive if the district submits an application proposing programs to meet the needs of educationally deprived children within their jurisdiction. These applications are reviewed and approved by state educational agencies. Several features of this program should be noted. The federal government provides few guidelines that would regulate state review, and, since funds are not transferable between districts, each state agency has a strong incentive to approve every application it receives (otherwise that part of the state's share is lost). For these reasons, the primary role of the act is as a fiscal device for the distribution of taxes collected at the national level to local school districts (via the self-interested cooperation of state agencies). See the *Education and Labor Committee Report on H.R. 69* (House Report 93-805); and Joel Berke and Michael Kirst, *Federal Aid to Education* (Lexington, Mass.: Lexington Books, 1972).

been much debate over the precise definition of poverty (for example, whether it should be adjusted for regional differences in the cost of living), most political conflict over the formula has been focused on a second factor: the number of pupils from families receiving Aid to Families with Dependent Children (AFDC) whose combined welfare payments place them above the national poverty line. Because of the far more generous and extensive welfare programs in the manufacturing belt and Pacific Coast states, AFDC caseloads heavily skew aid distribution toward the industrial core. In 1973, for example, 70.4 percent of the ESEA eligible children in California had qualified under the "AFDC above poverty" provision. Figures for other core states were: New York, 69.7 percent; Connecticut, 65.9 percent; Illinois, 62.9 percent; Michigan, 59.4 percent; Maryland, 49.2 percent; and Ohio, 45.7 percent. In the developing periphery, the AFDC provision was almost useless because of the tighter restrictions placed on eligibility and lower average payments. Representative percentages were: North Carolina, 10.6 percent; South Carolina, 2.2 percent; and in Tennessee, Arkansas and Mississippi, no qualifying children.[39] As a result, congressmen from the manufacturing belt have supported and periphery members have opposed an expansion of the influence of the "AFDC above poverty" factor within the education formula.

Children from families below the national poverty line, on the other hand, are heavily concentrated in the rural South, particularly in the old, heavily black plantation counties in which cotton culture historically flourished. In the basic ESEA formula, pupils from families below the poverty line are counted regardless of whether their families receive AFDC payments. Political support for expanding the influence of this factor in the allocation formula has been the mirror image of backing for the AFDC provision.

On several occasions, northern congressmen have proposed a heavy reliance on the absolute numbers of schoolchildren. This apparently simple scheme would, compared to the historical distribution pattern, tilt federal aid even more sharply toward the industrial core.*

Before 1975, floor amendments which proposed changes in the education formula consistently sought to increase the influence of the "AFDC Above Poverty" or "Absolute Number of Pupils" factors at the expense of "Pupils Below Poverty Line" (see table 6.8).[40] The Green amendment weighted the absolute number of pupils by directly including them in the formula and indirectly favored AFDC children through a "hold harmless" provision that guaranteed that no district would receive less in fiscal year 1974 than it had in fiscal year 1973. The Quie amendment allowed the commitee amendment to stand but substituted an 85 percent "hold harmless" clause for the 100 percent funding (identical to Green) urged by the committee. Without the per pupil provision in the Green amendment, a 100 percent "hold harmless" provision

---

*An additional, common element in these formulas is a factor which adjusts a state's proportional share up or down if the state average per pupil expenditure is greater or lower than the national average.

Table 6.8. Effect of Floor Amendments on Education Formulas Contained in Bills Reported by the Education and Labor Committee, 1973–1978

Amendment Sponsor (Year)	AFDC above Poverty	Pupils below Poverty Line	Absolute No. of Pupils
Edith Green—Ore. (1973)	More	Much less	More
Albert Quie—Minn. (1973)	More	Less	More
Peter Peyser—N.Y. (1974)	Much more	Less	More
James O'Hara—Mich. (1974)	More	Much less	Much more
Mickey Edwards—Okla. (1978)	Less	More	Minimal

Table 6.9. 1978 Aid Formula Proposed by the Education and Labor Committee

State Proportional Entitlement $= (P + AFDC + NDF) \times .4$ (SAPPE)

Factors:
- $P =$ Number of children from families with incomes below the poverty line.
- $AFDC =$ Number of children from families receiving AFDC with incomes above the poverty line.
- $NDF =$ Number of children in institutions for the neglected and delinquent and in publicly supported foster homes (relatively insignificant).
- $SAPPE =$ State average per pupil expenditure; cannot be below 80 percent or above 120 percent of the national average (floor and ceiling respectively).

tended to retard the otherwise dramatic increase in the influence of the AFDC factor. The number of pupils from AFDC families above the old poverty level rapidly expanded with the raising of welfare payment levels during the inflation of the 1960s and this expansion was entering into the calculations of the formula with use of the new 1970 census data.*

In 1974, the Education and Labor Committee recommended that all children below a new (Orshansky) definition of poverty and two-thirds of the AFDC pupils above that line be counted in the formula. The Peyser amendment would have made several changes that moved the formula toward the absolute number of pupils but primarily raised the AFDC factor from two-thirds to 100 percent of all pupils. The O'Hara amendment dropped the AFDC factor altogether and replaced it (and the state average expenditure element) with a double-weighted emphasis on the absolute number of pupils. Paradoxically, the combination of these changes with a 90 percent "hold harmless" provision actually increased the influence of the distribution of AFDC pupils even as the factor itself was eliminated.

In 1978, the Education and Labor Committee proposed several changes in the federal aid formula (see table 6.9). The most important of these pro-

---

*For a discussion of the effect of inflation on the "Pupils Below Poverty Line" factor and the consequent increasing influence of the AFDC element in the formula, see Richard F. Bensel,

Table 6.10. Voting on Floor Amendments to Federal Education Formulas, 1973–1978

	"Yea" Votes (Percentage): Members from States That Would Benefit		"Yea" Votes (Percentage): Members from States That Would Lose Funds		Percentage of Votes Reflecting States' Interests ("Yea" and "Nay")		"Yea" Votes (Percentage): Manufacturing Belt Trade Area Delegations		"Yea" Votes (Percentage): Non-Manufacturing Belt Trade Area Delegations		Sectional Stress
Amendment	%	(N)	%	(N)	%	(N)	%	(N)	%	(N)	
Green (Oreg.) Sept. 25, 1973	—		—		—		65.2	(158)	36.2	(224)	44.0
Quie (Minn.) Sept. 25, 1973	92.4	(264)	36.2	(116)	83.7	(380)	96.2	(158)	60.4	(222)	55.3
Peyser (N.Y.) Mar. 26, 1974	59.7	(77)	12.2	(336)	82.6	(413)	45.3	(172)	3.7	(241)	52.9
O'Hara (Mich.) Mar. 26, 1974	41.3	(242)	1.7	(173)	65.1	(415)	45.6	(171)	10.2	(244)	40.6
Edwards (Okla.) July 12, 1978	81.2	(202)	5.9	(185)	87.3	(387)	20.1	(164)	63.7	(223)	69.6

SOURCE: Computations from roll call data. For information on the impact of formula amendments, see the *Congressional Record*, 93:1:3:1210–12 (Quie formula); 93:2:H2136 (Peyser formula); 93:2:H2140 (O'Hara formula); and 95:2:6533, 6580–82 (Edwards formula). Complete data on the Green amendment are unavailable; its impact would have been similar to that of the O'Hara proposal.

posed changes were to switch the definition of poverty from the Orshansky index to 50 percent of the national median income for a family of four and to count all AFDC eligibles in place of the then current two-thirds. The only change in this formula proposed by the Edwards amendment was to count only two-thirds of the pupils otherwise eligible under the AFDC factor. Thus, this was the only one of the five floor amendments that threatened the interests of the industrial core.*

The roll call voting on the five formula amendments provides several important insights into the changing structure of the House of Representatives and the intensity of sectional competition (see table 6.10). As has been noted, only the Edwards amendment proposed a change in the formula that would have been hostile to the interests of the manufacturing belt. In this respect, the series of votes on the education formula, like the Maybank series on defense purchases, indicated that the balance of power on at least a few committees had shifted toward the industrial core.

There are three ways in which such a shift can occur in the committee membership base: the awarding of more assignments to northern congressmen relative to southern colleagues, a shift in the distribution of northern congressmen among the various committees, and an increase in the relative cohesion of members from the industrial core. The general role of the committee system will be discussed in chapter 7; at this point, it can be noted that the first of these changes can be dismissed out of hand, the second occurs very slowly (i.e., over a decade or more at least), and the third seems to coincide most closely with the pattern of voting on the floor. For example, during the same period when the Education and Labor Committee was becoming more favorable to core political interests, there was a growing divergence in floor fights between trade area delegations in and outside the manufacturing belt. This trend coincided with a very irregular increase in the level of sectional stress. (In these comparisons, the O'Hara-Peyser and Quie-Green pairs of votes should be considered together since each pair occurred on the same day.)

The close relationship between the tendency of members to vote their constituency interest and the resulting level of sectional stress should be noted. All of these trends indicate an increasing level of regional competition over formula alternatives which divide the states along the dominant core-periphery cleavage in American politics. Since all of the floor amendments discussed here were contested within the committee before being offered again from the floor, the floor votes can be viewed as a continuation of the struggle within the

---

"Reciprocal Behavior and the Rules of the House of Representatives," ch. 6. In 1966, 89.1 percent of the nation's eligible children qualified under the poverty section and only 10.9 percent under AFDC. By 1974, after the 1970 census, only 41.9 percent qualified under poverty and 58.1 percent, a majority, under AFDC.

*Under the Edwards formula, California, Connecticut, Hawaii, Illinois, Massachusetts, Michigan, New Jersey, New York, Oregon, Pennsylvania, Washington, and Wisconsin would have lost funding.

committee.* Thus, the redesign of the formulas, their impact on floor voting and sectional stress, and the necessity for periphery representatives to take their case to the floor in 1978 (having lost in the committee) all indicate the increasing cohesion and political influence of core congressmen. The growing tendency for members to support their states' interests in the formula fight, to the seeming exclusion of other considerations, further suggests the weakening of institutional constraints (such as committee reciprocity norms), party loyalty, and other traditional political arrangements in the modern House of Representatives.

Energy Policy

In 1976, the leader of the Northeast-Midwest Economic Advancement Coalition, Michael Harrington, stated that the two most important goals of the organization were the regional equalization of energy costs and the nationalization of the welfare system.[41] For a number of reasons, primarily the distribution of energy resources and differences in climate, there are wide regional variations in energy expenditures that operate to the disadvantage of the Midwest and, particularly, the Northeast. Following the spiraling cost of energy after the 1973 embargo, reliance on free market forces would have resulted in a radical redistribution of wealth from the industrial core to the resource-rich periphery. Efforts to reduce the regional impact of rising energy prices could take either of two forms: direct subsidy by the central state of energy use in the core or government regulation of energy pricing and distribution. Core and periphery delegations have radically diverged in their choices between unregulated "market" and government-controlled "subsidy" responses to the energy crisis (table 6.11).

Perhaps the most hoary of all energy policies is the federal regulation of interstate transportation and sale of natural gas. Begun during the New Deal as a relatively consensual policy, federal regulation has been contested in the federal courts and the halls of Congress since the 1940s. It has been a struggle in which, in the words of Elizabeth Sanders, "The combatants tend to view their opponents in exaggerated terms: they are either the minions of the devilish oil lobby or northern socialists bent on pillaging southwestern colonies of their natural resources."[42] By 1974, federal regulation of natural gas prices in the interstate market held down the cost of this major source of energy (about one-quarter of all national energy consumption) to a small fraction of the world price of an equivalent amount of oil. Since this interstate network of regulated pipelines serviced, primarily, the largest metropolitan centers of the Northeast and Midwest, federal control resulted in a direct transfer of billions of dollars from the periphery to the core—even as the unregulated

---

*Though the Quie and Green amendments were offered to a continuing appropriations bill, the legislative situation did not differ markedly from the other formula alternatives.

Table 6.11. Trade Area Delegation Response to the Regional Redistribution of Wealth Produced by Rising Energy Prices, 1976–1980

Trade Area[a]	Natural Gas Deregulation Feb. 5, 1976	Heating Oil Set Aside Aug. 1, 1979	Formula for Fuel Subsidies for the Poor Aug. 27, 1980	Energy Severance Taxes in Revenue Sharing Nov. 13, 1980
Philadelphia	Subsidy	Subsidy	Subsidy	Subsidy[b]
Boston	Subsidy	Subsidy	Subsidy	Subsidy
New York	Subsidy	Subsidy	Subsidy	Subsidy
San Francisco	Subsidy	Subsidy	Market	Market
Detroit	Subsidy	Subsidy	Subsidy	Subsidy
Chicago	Subsidy	Subsidy	Subsidy	*Split*
Indianapolis	Subsidy	Market	Market	Subsidy
Cleveland	Subsidy	Subsidy	Market	Subsidy
Buffalo	Market	Subsidy	Subsidy	Subsidy
Pittsburgh	Subsidy	Subsidy	Subsidy	Subsidy
Minneapolis	Market	Subsidy	Subsidy	Subsidy
St. Louis	Subsidy	Market	Market	*Split*
Cincinnati	Market	Subsidy	*Split*	Market
Kansas City	Subsidy	Market	Market	Market
Denver	Market	Market	Subsidy	Market
Louisville	*Split*	*Split*	Market	Market
Richmond	Market	Market	Subsidy	Market
New Orleans	Market	Market	Market	Market
Birmingham	*Split*	Market	Market	Market
Atlanta	Market	Market	Market	Market
Memphis	Market	Subsidy	Market	Market
Dallas	Market	Market	Market	Market
Sectional Stress	50.2	54.0	82.9	62.4

[a] Trade area delegations are ranked in descending order of their support for the core position on the ten high-stress, closely contested roll calls recorded during the 94th Congress (1975–76); see table 2.5.

[b] "Subsidy" indicates a trade area position favoring direct federal subsidies or regulation to reduce the impact of rising energy prices; "Market" indicates a position tending to favor the unhampered action of market forces on regional economies; *Split* indicates that the delegation divided evenly on the roll call.

SOURCE: Computations from roll call data.

intrastate markets of the producer states reflected the spiraling cost of energy in the form of wellhead prices several multiples higher than those paid by the northeastern-bound interstate carriers. In one of the clearest political tests of natural gas regulation since the federal government took up that task in 1938, the outcome was a narrow defeat for the forces supporting an end to federal controls (see table 6.11).[43]

The second roll call occurred on an amendment offered by Representative Toby Moffett of Connecticut to legislation providing for emergency gasoline

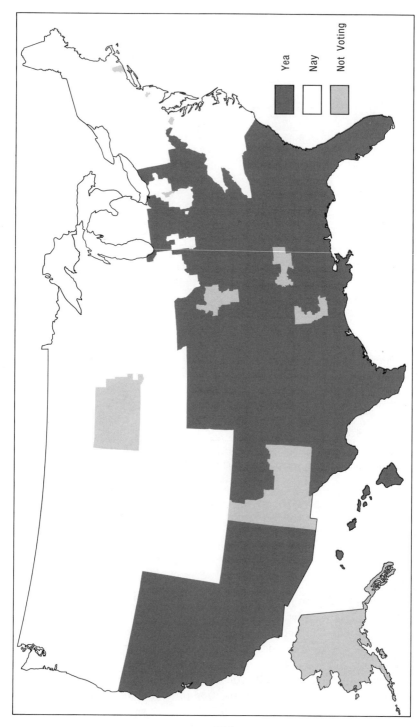

Map 6.3. Congressional Support for the Roybal Amendment to Change the Formula Allocating Fuel Subsidies for the Poor, August 27, 1980

Yea

Nay

Not Voting

rationing during a period of supply shortages. Moffett's proposal would have set aside 1 percent of all "middle distillate" production for use as home heating oil for residential consumption. Since the use of home heating oil is almost exclusively concentrated in the Northeast (particularly New England), where it is an extremely important source of energy, the amendment would have guaranteed the region a supply of this product at the expense of a small decrease in the national supplies of gasoline. By and large, voting on the floor reflected the regional impact of the measure, although industrial delegations outside the Northeast did tend to support the efforts of the Northeast.

Beginning in 1973, the Community Services Administration provided some assistance to low-income people to help pay fuel bills. Four years later, Congress appropriated funds for a special emergency energy program to pay "excessive" home heating expenses. In 1980, the Appropriations Committee allocated $1.6 billion for this program and devised a new formula for distributing funds among the various states. The new formula was based on two factors: the number of low-income residents and, by far the more important element, the square of the number of "heating degree days" recorded by a state. As defined by the National Weather Bureau, heating degree days are the difference between a constant (65 degrees Fahrenheit) and the mean daily temperature.* Since the committee formula heavily favored the northern tier of the nation (by squaring the number of heating degree days and ignoring "cooling" costs), an appeal from the floor was inevitable. The sponsor of the floor amendment was Democratic Representative Edward Roybal of Los Angeles, who sought to tie the allocation of funds to a formula previously approved for use in the Crude Oil Windfall Profits Tax of 1980. Roybal's alternative would have redirected funding toward the southern (and warmer) tier. The ensuing debate culminated in the most regionally polarized voting pattern recorded between 1971 and 1980 (see map 6.3).

Of all the rhetoric accompanying the choice between these two formulas, perhaps the most impassioned and, thus, enlightening was Silvio Conte's speech made in opposition to the Roybal amendment. It is worth quoting at length.

> Florida—my good friend, the gentleman from Florida [Claude Pepper], I was surprised at him, because I bled with him for the poor—that rich State and that great rich district of his, Miami, will get 147 percent more, more than they did last year. This is unconscionable. People are driving down to Florida by the thousands. Why? To pick the oranges and the grapefruits and live in that sunny climate, and they want to come

---

*For example, a mean daily temperature of 45 degrees represents 20 heating degree days; and a mean temperature of 65 degrees or higher represents no heating degree days. The unit is used in the gas industry for predicting local fuel consumption. Monthly and annual figures are reported in the July issue of *Climatological Data*, published by the U.S. Department of Commerce (National Weather Bureau). See also Carl W. Spurlock, "Forecasting Regional Demand for Heating Fuel," *Growth and Change* 9:2 (April 1978): 29–34.

up here and grab this money away from those freezing people in New England. I am surprised.

My good friend, the gentleman from California, Ed Roybal, I was surprised at him. I stood side by side with him, shoulder to shoulder, fighting for the poor people, fighting for bilingual education, because he needed it, he needed it. And now my people need it. They are desperate. Why, they cannot take any more people in his State. Everybody has gone to California. How many more Congressmen are they going to get? Five? Six? Everybody is going to California. California, here I come. Why? Why? Because of the beautiful climate in California.

My population is going down because you have to go out there and chop the wood to keep your stove going, and huddle up there by the stove, because you cannot afford any oil; and you want to take this small morsel away from us.

I say to the gentleman from California (Mr. Roybal) I am surprised at him, because there is a man with the milk of human kindness in his veins—up until this point. I hope nobody will object when he asks unanimous consent to withdraw this amendment.[44]

The Massachusetts Republican's appeal to liberal ideological unity fell on deaf ears in the South and Southwest. Instead, Conte was immediately followed by Texas Democrat Phil Gramm, an arch-conservative, who made his own plea in support of Roybal's proposal: "We are not asking for justice here. . . . All we are saying is, having already been cheated, let us not make it rape." *

The roll call revealed an extremely high level of sectional stress (a score of 82.9) as 94.4 percent of the members' votes were consistent with the interests of their individual states. All 192 voting congressmen whose states benefited from the committee formula opposed the Roybal amendment, while 199 of 222 (89.6 percent) of the members who gained shares backed it. The division closely paralleled the core-periphery split, with 80.8 percent of the members from the manufacturing belt voting for the committee allocation and 67.6 percent of the remaining delegations casting ballots the other way. In a front-page story, the *New York Times* praised the result. The lead sentence read, "The Frost Belt prevailed over the Sun Belt in the House of Representatives today."

---

*Congressional Record, 96:2:H7981, August 27, 1980. Gramm belonged to a sizeable contingent of southern Democratic conservatives who called themselves "Boll Weevils." After Reagan's election, a similar group of liberal northern Republicans formed under the name "Gypsy Moths." During negotiations over the 1982 budget resolution, Conte represented the "moths" at a news conference and mixed metaphors in his account of the bargaining: "Those Boll Weevils. . . . It's like being in a snake pit with those people." Gramm was also a primary antagonist in the budget deliberations. *Congressional Quarterly Weekly Report*, May 22, 1982, p. 1173. Toby Moffett said, "when you have lists circulating on the floor of States that win and States that lose, it brings out the worst in all of us in this body." *Congressional Record*, 96:2:H7983–86, August 27, 1980.

Some Congressmen expressed concern that the outcome presaged increasingly close contests along regional lines for diminishing resources. . . . Sponsors of the proposal pointed to the 1200 deaths that resulted from the heat wave in the Southwest this summer and urged that all forms of home energy use, not merely heating, be considered in the disbursement of funds to reimburse the poor and elderly for spiraling costs.

The chairman of the Northeast-Midwest Coalition, Pennsylvania Democrat Robert Edgar, said the decision was just "the precursor of more intense struggles" yet to come.[45]

The last contentious roll call in table 6.11 occurred on an amendment offered by Andrew Maguire of New Jersey which would have altered the formula under which revenue sharing funds are distributed to the states. As Maguire noted, the five-factor formula allocated 17 percent of all revenue sharing dollars ($900 million in fiscal year 1980) on the basis of "state tax effort"—the extent to which a state taxes the combined income of its residents and firms. Maguire proposed to exclude from the calculation of a state's tax effort a portion of severance, production, and sales taxes levied on petroleum, natural gas, or coal production. The portion to be excluded would have been equivalent to the share of all "mineral resources" that left the state as energy "exports." The Congressional Research Service estimated that eleven states would have lost revenue sharing funds with adoption of the amendment: Alaska, California, Kentucky, Louisiana, Montana, New Mexico, North Dakota, Oklahoma, Texas, West Virginia, and Wyoming.[46] Opponents pointed out numerous examples of manufactured goods exported to the periphery—Michigan's value-added levy on automobiles was a favorite—upon which taxes were levied by industrial states; these taxes would have remained eligible under the revised revenue sharing formula. Vigorous opposition by members from energy producing regions led to an attempt to reassure these colleagues that this proposal was not a "sectional" issue.[47] Instead, proponents held that the amendment was necessary in order to partially offset the $127.7 billion estimated increase in revenue that would accrue to the energy-exporting states as a result of the decontrol of domestic oil prices. The voting pattern on this amendment paralleled that of the other formula fights that have been surveyed: members tended to cast their ballots in line with the interests of their respective states and divided along the old manufacturing belt boundary (table 6.12). A clear difference emerges here, however. Members from the energy-importing areas of the periphery who apparently had the same interests as similar regions in the manufacturing belt opposed the Maguire proposal and thus supported their energy-exporting neighbors. The sectional cleavage dominated all other legislative interests—even, in this case, the direct interests of the individual states.

Table 6.12. Voting on the Maguire Amendment to the Revenue Sharing Formula

Constituencies	Yea %	(N)	Nay %	(N)
Energy-Exporting States	10.7	(9)	89.3	(75)
Energy-Consuming States	53.6	(150)	46.4	(130)
Manufacturing Belt Delegations	75.3	(113)	24.7	(37)
Delegations Outside				
Manufacturing Belt	21.5	(46)	78.5	(168)
Energy-Consuming	27.3	(36)	72.7	(96)
Energy-Producing	12.2	(10)	87.8	(72)

The Nationalization of Labor Policy

In 1977, Congressman Robert H. Michel of Illinois, then the Republican Whip and later Minority Leader in the House of Representatives, surprised many political observers when he maintained that "right to work" laws were helping the South steal industry from the North. He went on to say that the time may have come for the Republican party to end its traditional support for Section 14(b) of the Taft-Hartley Act. Section 14(b) permits the states to prohibit union shop labor agreements and thus block compulsory union membership. Michel's heretical suggestion underlined the growing desperation with which the industrial core sought to nationalize wage standards and working conditions in order to undercut the apparent competitive advantages of the periphery.[48]

By far the most important of these advantages is the Section 14(b) exemption. By 1976, twenty states had passed the necessary legislation blocking a union shop contract within their boundaries. The effect of the "right to work" clause on the political and economic power of organized labor has been dramatic.* Union shop states in the industrial core have a much higher percentage of their work force organized into unions than do "right-to-work" states in the periphery.[49] The chasm between the unorganized textile industry in the Carolinas and the high-wage, unionized automobile industry in Michigan is particularly striking (table 6.13).

The political impact of Section 14(b) on efforts to nationalize labor regulations is suggested by the roll call analysis in table 6.14. For comparative purposes, the last attempt to repeal the "right-to-work" clause in 1965 is included in the table.† The other votes occurred on a 1972 amendment to exclude striking workers from eligibility for food stamp subsidies, an exemp-

---

*Alabama, Arizona, Arkansas, Florida, Georgia, Iowa, Kansas, Mississippi, Nebraska, Nevada, North Carolina, North Dakota, South Carolina, South Dakota, Tennessee, Texas, Utah, Virginia, Wyoming, and, in 1976, Louisiana.

†This contest was one of the ten high-stress, closely contested roll calls recorded during the 89th Congress (1965–66).

tion of firms with fewer than fifteen employees from inspection by officials of the Occupational Safety and Health Administration (OSHA), and a motion to enter into a conference with the Senate over revision of federal minimum wage standards.

The OSHA limitation was probably the most controversial of these roll calls. The most important economic sectors excluded from the regulatory scope of OSHA would have been agriculture and forestry, but opponents of the agency also claimed that enforcement tended to favor large industrial firms that could afford to contest the findings and orders of federal inspectors. In addition to the "economies of scale" that applied to private resistance to government standards and the regional distribution of agricultural and forestry activities, opponents were extremely sensitive to the centralization of power represented by effective enforcement of the Occupational Safety and Health Act. As Keith Sebelius of Kansas described his constituency's attitude: "every morning businessmen and farmers get together in small communities through the 57 counties in my district and equate OSHA and our Federal Government with some totalitarian police state." [50] Finally, since the effectiveness of alternative state regulations or labor contracts as a substitute for federal controls was largely dependent on the local strength of organized labor, "right-to-work" states generally had the most to gain and union shop states the most to lose from enactment of the OSHA exemption.

The roll call on common-site picketing legislation was taken on the conference report reconciling House-Senate differences over the bill. Briefly put, the legislation was intended to reverse a several-decades-old federal court decision that prevented picketing at a construction site if the labor dispute did not involve all the workers on the project. Since most construction involves more than one type of labor and, often, several subcontractors who engage that labor in separate agreements, the court decision had effectively ended picketing at most important construction sites. Enactment of the legislative remedy supported by organized labor would have reversed the court decision and allowed any dispute involving a portion of the employees to shut down the entire

Table 6.13. Percentage of Labor Force Belonging to Unions in Selected States

Right-to-Work States		Union Shop States	
North Carolina	6.9	Michigan	38.4
South Carolina	8.0	New York	38.0
Mississippi	12.0	Pennsylvania	37.5
Florida	12.5	Illinois	34.9
Texas	13.0	Indiana	33.2
Virginia	13.8	Ohio	33.2
New Mexico	14.1	Missouri	32.3
Georgia	14.5	Wisconsin	28.7
Arizona	16.0	New Jersey	28.2
Arkansas	16.8	Rhode Island	27.3

Table 6.14. Congressional Support for Organized Labor: Selected Decisions, 1965–1976

Decision	Trade Area Delegations		State Delegations		Full House	Sectional Stress Index
	Right-to-Work % (N)	Union Shop % (N)	Right-to-Work % (N)	Union Shop % (N)	% (N)	Index
Repeal of Section 14(b) July 28, 1965	15.1 (119)	66.6 (305)	13.4 (119)	67.2 (305)	52.1 (424)	46.3
Food Stamps for Strikers June 29, 1972	27.1 (107)	62.5 (272)	28.8 (111)	62.3 (268)	52.5 (379)	45.0
OSHA Inspection Sept. 19, 1972	14.3 (105)	62.3 (268)	12.0 (108)	63.8 (265)	48.8 (373)	50.0
Minimum Wage Oct. 3, 1972	21.2 (104)	59.3 (280)	22.0 (109)	60.0 (275)	49.0 (384)	45.7
Common Site Picketing Dec. 11, 1975	20.0 (115)	68.0 (303)	19.1 (115)	68.3 (303)	54.8 (418)	47.6
Unemployment Compensation July 20, 1976	19.0 (121)	68.2 (277)	20.3 (123)	68.0 (275)	53.3 (398)	52.2

SOURCE: Computations from roll call data.

site. Opponents believed that the bill would unduly strengthen labor's bargaining position at the site and force contractors to substitute, under threat of a work stoppage, union labor for unorganized employees. If this interpretation were correct, the impact of the bill would fall most heavily on freewheeling construction practices within the right-to-work states. The last roll call was recorded on an amendment to remove a requirement forcing all states and local governments that had not already and voluntarily done so to include their employees in the federal unemployment compensation system. This requirement represented another phase in the gradual nationalization of the unemployment system.

All of these measures deeply divided the House of Representatives along the industrial core (union shop) and developing periphery (right-to-work) cleavage (see table 6.14). In every case, periphery delegations opposed and core delegations supported federal standardization of bargaining agreements, wages, and working conditions.

Environmental Policy and the Clean Air Act

The nationalization of labor regulations has tended to provoke sectional conflict because it reduces the competitive wage and work rule flexibility advantages of the periphery economy. Many environmental policies have regionally polarized the political system for substantially the same reason: they reduce the ability of the periphery economy to compete for new firms or the relocation of existing companies. For example, most major environmental policies directly retard the development of natural resources in the West and, thus, indirectly stimulate the exploitation of similar resources (where they exist) in the East. Strip-mining restrictions, leasing for off-shore drilling on the continental shelf, and legislated prohibitions on the private use of western land in the public domain all fall into this category. The classic example of this kind of policy has been the scrubber requirement imposed by the Environmental Protection Agency on low-sulphur, western coal (for which scrubbing is unnecessary under most standards) in order to stimulate the processing of high-sulphur eastern coal. Since the cost of installing scrubbers for "dirty" eastern coal would otherwise force utilities to abandon its use, the EPA requirement has rescued an otherwise moribund energy source, albeit at a substantial cost in economic efficiency.[51]

But the most massive restriction on economic development in the periphery has resulted from enforcement of another section of the 1970 Clear Air Act. That section states that one of the purposes of the measure is ". . . to protect and enhance the quality of the nation's air resources so as to promote the public health and welfare and the productive capacity of its population . . ." In 1972 this passage was interpreted by a U.S. district judge to mean that federal policy should be the "prevention of significant deterioration" (PSD) in air quality in those areas which were already cleaner than the national standards mandated by the law. On June 11, 1973, the Supreme Court divided 4-4 on this question and thus let the lower court decision stand (*Sierra Club v. Ruckelshaus*).[52] During reauthorization of the Clean Air Act in 1976 (which ultimately did not pass), the Interstate and Foreign Commerce Committee asked the House to give legislative approval to the court's interpretation with a few relatively unimportant administrative provisions. A dissenting member of the committee, David Satterfield of Virginia, charged that, through legislative approval, "we are establishing a policy of locking industry into those areas where there is the greatest amount of pollution and the least room for growth and locking them out of those areas that are relatively clean where there is the greatest room to grow."[53] When legislative approval for the PSD standard was proposed again in 1977, David Stockman of Michigan, later to be the head of the Office of Management and Budget in the Reagan administration, said the policy

> gives EPA and its associated air quality bureaucrats a major new opportunity to exercise authority, and to exert far-reaching management control over those basic national resources—economic, energy, and land— that are inextricably intertwined with air quality . . . it is absolutely clear that no large-scale industrial growth will be permitted in any PSD area (which includes most of the nation for at least one pollutant) without the guidance, technical direction, and stamp of approval of Federal and State air quality bureaucrats.[54]

Several years later, Stockman returned to this feature of the Clean Air Act: "The PSD standard . . . really is a tertiary standard and it has nothing to do with the public health because it is below the primary standard and is there primarily to prevent the dispersion of industrial locations and economic growth in the country."[55] The clearest political test of the PSD requirement came on an amendment offered by Representative Tim Carter of Kentucky on September 9, 1976. Carter's amendment would have replaced stringent EPA controls in designated clean air areas with a pollution "ceiling" of 90 percent of the national primary standard (see table 6.1).[56]

The Nationalization of Welfare

Most interpretations of the politics of AFDC have attributed growth of a social welfare system to the process of industrialization and the resulting political struggle over the scope and role of AFDC in local economies. However, due to the precipitous decline in the industrial core economy and a tremendous increase in the size and fiscal expense of welfare dependency in the major metropolitan centers of the North, the politics of AFDC has largely turned into a politics of subsidization. The major determinants of this struggle have been the regional distribution of the poor in the United States and the varying characteristics of individual state programs. In effect, recent proposals to nationalize AFDC have attempted to impose the characteristics of the core welfare system upon the periphery. Furthermore, the politics of subsidization has been expanded and reinforced by the emergence of formal statutory connections between AFDC dependency and other federal programs. In this respect, the politics of subsidization has turned the welfare recipient into a "fiscal object" whose existence in local economies automatically triggers redistributive, regionally targeted federal spending.

AFDC dependency has been marked by two radically different concentrations within the United States. In the formerly labor-intensive extractive economies of the black belt, Appalachia, and the cut-over districts, AFDC supports a displaced and technically obsolescent labor force. In many of these counties, the population is largely black. In the large urban centers, AFDC dependency is in part related to immigration from rural areas of high unemployment and in part to structural unemployment in capital-intensive heavy industrial sectors (see map 6.4).[57] Although the national AFDC caseload remained basically unchanged between 1971 and 1980 (see table 6.15), AFDC rolls increased substantially in Chicago (Cook County), Detroit (Wayne County), Los Angeles (Los Angeles County), New York (five boroughs), and Philadelphia (see figure 6.2). Altogether, the share of the total AFDC population contained in the nation's five largest cities and their counties remained constant (21.0 percent in 1971 and 20.8 percent in 1980) even as their total population declined by 4.9 percent over the decade.

Reflecting the increasing fiscal distress of the industrial core, the "number one" legislative goal identified by the Northeast-Midwest Coalition became the nationalization of the welfare system and an indexing of federal assistance programs to reflect the local cost of living (which is generally far higher in the industrial core than in the periphery).[58] For decades, Aid to Families with Dependent Children has been a cooperative, mixed federal-state

Table 6.15. National AFDC Caseloads, 1971–1980

Year	AFDC Recipients (December)	Resident Population (July 1)	Percentage of Resident Population Receiving AFDC
1971	10,653[a]	206,827[a]	5.2
1972	11,069	209,284	5.3
1973	10,815	211,357	5.1
1974	11,022	213,342	5.2
1975	11,401	215,465	5.3
1976	11,203	217,563	5.1
1977	10,780	219,760	4.9
1978	10,325	222,095	4.6
1979	10,379	224,567	4.6
1980	11,102	226,505	4.9

[a] Figures are in thousands of persons.
SOURCE: *Statistical Abstract of the United States*, 1981 and 1976.

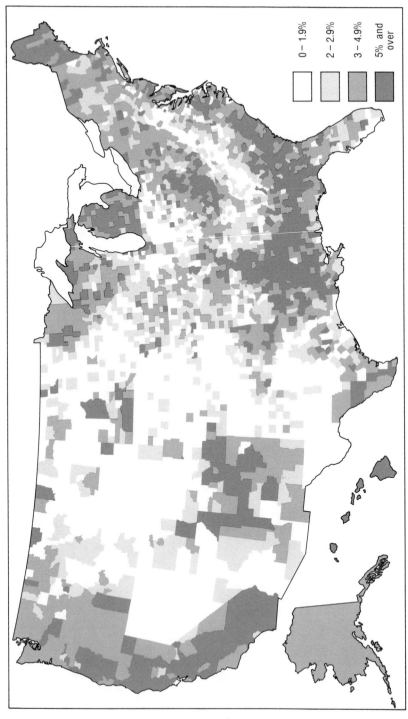

Map 6.4. AFDC Recipients as a Percentage of the Total Population by County, 1978. Calculated from data provided by Rand McNally, *1979 Commercial Atlas and Marketing Guide*, 110th Edition, Chicago: 1979, and by *AFDC Recipients February 1978*, Social Security Administration, 1979.

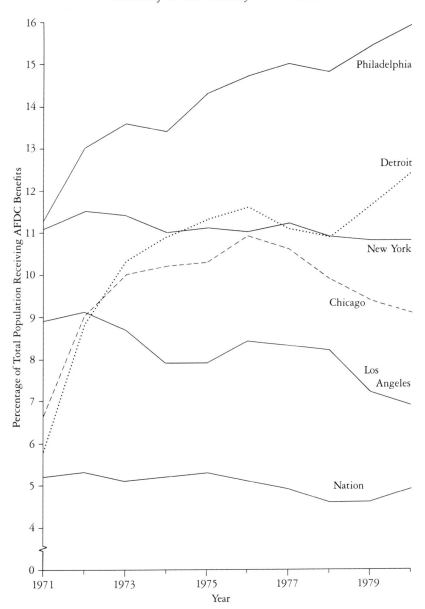

Figure 6.2. Changes in AFDC Dependency in Five Selected Cities and the Nation, 1971–1980

program in which the national government assumes the burden of a portion of the total expenditures and, in return, requires that the program administered by the individual states possess certain characteristics of eligibility and implementation. As a result, AFDC policy varies enormously from state to state.*

In November of 1979, the House of Representatives passed H.R. 4904, the most significant welfare reform in a decade. In general, the legislation proposed a standardization of a wide variety of eligibility and benefit criteria by requiring that the states adopt the new standards as a necessary condition for receiving further federal aid. Though some changes in the Supplemental Security Income program were included, the political significance of the bill was restricted to the AFDC provisions. The most important changes that H.R. 4904 proposed to make in AFDC were to establish a floor under state benefits which, in combination with food stamps, would equal 65 percent of the official poverty income level; to require that eligibility under state programs be extended to two-parent families in which the principal wage-earner was unemployed; and to increase substantially the federal share of total AFDC expenditures. The House of Representatives passed the bill by a recorded vote of 222 to 194. The roll call can most appropriately be analyzed in terms of the compatibility of state programs with the proposed federal criteria (e.g., whether or not benefits were above the 65 percent floor and two-parent families were eligible), the AFDC enrollment level in individual constituencies, and party allegiance.†

---

*Under existing law, the federal government provides a portion of total state AFDC expenditures based on the formula

$$.45 \times \frac{\text{(state's per capita income)}^2}{\text{(U.S. per capita income)}^2}$$

The formula determines the state's share of AFDC expenditures, and the federal government provides the remainder of the program's costs. The ceiling on the federal share of total expenditures is 83 percent and the floor is 50 percent. The greatest federal participation in a state program currently occurs in Mississippi (78 percent) and Alabama (73 percent). Eleven states receive the minimum rate of federal aid. The law actually provides a choice between the formula in the text (which applies to states with an approved Medicaid plan) and the AFDC matching formula which relates the square of the state's per capita income to the square of the national per capita income. Only four states (Arizona, Mississippi, South Carolina, and Texas) use the AFDC alternative to the formula. See Committee on Ways and Means, House of Representatives, House Report 96-451, *Social Welfare Reform Amendments of 1979* (Washington: 1979); Committee on Ways and Means, House of Representatives, *Welfare Reform Legislation* (Washington: 1979); and *Characteristics of State Plans for Aid to Families with Dependent Children* (Washington: Social Security Administration, 1978).

†In order to calculate the level of AFDC dependency within each congressional district, 1978 county recipient data were aggregated for districts containing more than one county. For metropolitan counties which contained more than one congressional district, all districts received identical percentages based on the county level. Where districts divided counties into two or more parts, AFDC recipients were pro-rated among the districts.

The procedure used to determine district AFDC dependency introduces some distortions into the final figures. For example, the percentage of the total population of Los Angeles County

Table 6.16. Welfare Dependency in Democratic and Republican Constituencies, 1978

AFDC Percentage of Population within District	Members from States Meeting Both Criteria (AFDC-U and 65% Threshold)		Members from States Failing to Meet at Least One Criterion		All Members (percentage)	
	Democrats	Republicans	Democrats	Republicans	Democrats	Republicans
	% (N)	% (N)	% (N)	% (N)	% (N)	% (N)
6.5 +	83.0 (78)	17.0 (16)	80.0 (8)	20.0 (2)	82.7 (86)	17.3 (18)
4.5–6.4	65.6 (42)	34.4 (22)	60.6 (20)	39.4 (13)	63.9 (62)	36.1 (35)
3.0–4.4	47.9 (35)	52.1 (38)	67.5 (27)	32.5 (13)	54.9 (62)	45.1 (51)
0.0–2.9	40.7 (22)	59.3 (32)	64.2 (43)	35.8 (24)	53.7 (65)	46.3 (56)

SOURCES: State AFDC-U characteristics taken from Social Security Administration, *Characteristics of State Plans for Aid to Families with Dependent Children* (Washington: Government Printing Office, 1978). State benefit levels relative to the poverty level for a family of four taken from Committee on Ways and Means, House of Representatives, House Report 96-451, *Social Welfare Reform Amendments of 1979* (Washington: Government Printing Office, 1979).

Within each of the other categories, party allegiance seems to have played an important role in determining members' positions on final passage and was strongly correlated with AFDC dependency within the individual districts. Democrats held the vast majority (83 percent) of the seats in districts containing the highest AFDC percentages whether or not the state met the proposed federal criteria (table 6.16). In the states with programs compatible with H.R. 4904, the Democratic percentage declines with AFDC dependency. However, in non-compatible states the Democratic percentage within each quartile of AFDC dependency reveals no pattern after an initial drop between the first (6.5 percent or more) and the second (4.5–6.4 percent) quartiles.

Those states which met neither the AFDC-U criterion nor the 65 percent threshold were overwhelmingly southern (eleven of thirteen), and within every one of these states AFDC dependency was largely associated with labor-intensive extractive economies (usually plantation agriculture).* Another eleven states, largely western and plains states, met the 65 percent of

---

receiving AFDC benefits in 1978 was 8.1 percent. However, within the county, dependency was probably much higher in the inner city districts and far lower in the surrounding suburban constituencies. Given the available data, intra-county apportionment of AFDC recipients was impossible to determine, though reasonable inferences are fairly easy to make. In most metropolitan counties with large congressional delegations, the county shared in the total costs of the welfare burden (in Los Angeles, 16 percent of total expenditures). In these cases, the overall county percentage would be relevant to the determination of legislative attitudes on nationalization and a shift of welfare costs onto the federal government. For raw data, see *Public Assistance Recipients and Cash Payments by State and County (1978)* (Washington: Social Security Administration); and, for population estimates, *1979 Commercial Atlas and Marketing Guide* (Chicago: Rand McNally).

*The thirteen states which met neither criterion are Alabama, Arkansas, Arizona, Florida, Georgia, Kentucky, Mississippi, Louisiana, New Mexico, North Carolina, South Carolina, Tennessee, and Texas. On the other hand, Alaska, Idaho, Maine, Nevada, New Hampshire, North Dakota, Oklahoma, South Dakota, Virginia, and Wyoming met the poverty level criterion but did not provide AFDC-U benefits. The remaining twenty-six states met both criteria.

Table 6.17. Analysis of Voting on the 1979 Welfare Reform Bill

AFDC Percentage of Population within District	"Yea" Votes:					
	of Members from States Meeting Both Criteria		of Members from States Failing to Meet at Least One Criterion		of All Members	
	%	(N)	%	(N)	%	(N)
Over 6.5	86.7	(83)	50.0	(10)	82.8	(93)
Democrats	97.1	(70)	62.5	(8)	93.6	(78)
Republicans	30.8	(13)	0.0	(2)	26.7	(15)
4.5–6.4	74.2	(62)	25.8	(31)	58.1	(93)
Democrats	97.6	(42)	33.3	(18)	78.3	(60)
Republicans	25.0	(20)	15.4	(13)	21.2	(33)
3.0–4.4	60.6	(71)	20.6	(34)	47.6	(105)
Democrats	91.2	(34)	29.2	(24)	65.5	(58)
Republicans	32.4	(37)	0.0	(10)	25.5	(47)
0.0–2.9	45.3	(53)	27.4	(62)	35.7	(115)
Democrats	81.8	(22)	42.5	(40)	56.5	(62)
Republicans	19.4	(31)	0.0	(22)	11.3	(53)
Total	68.8	(269)	27.0	(137)	54.7	(406)
Democrats	94.0	(168)	38.9	(90)	67.8	(258)
Republicans	26.7	(101)	4.3	(47)	19.6	(148)

SOURCE: Computations from roll call data.

poverty income threshold but did not have AFDC-U programs. The remaining twenty-six states, representing nearly all of the major industrial regions of the country, met both criteria. Thus, a categorization of the states into program compatibility with H.R. 4904 in effect divides them into those regions where AFDC was either insignificant (as in the case of the plains and mountain states) or played an important role in rural, agricultural economies, and those areas where AFDC dependency was linked to industrialized urban systems. In the first group, the politics of welfare was not related to national partisan alignments; in the second, AFDC dependency within the districts does appear to have been associated with partisan allegiance.

The positions taken on passage of H.R. 4904 reflected the characteristics of the individual state programs and the partisan loyalties of the district representatives (see table 6.17). Democrats in industrialized states with comparatively generous AFDC programs voted almost unanimously (94 percent) in favor of a further nationalization of eligibility and benefit standards. Republicans from rural states with comparatively restrictive eligibility standards and lower benefit levels voted just as overwhelmingly (96 percent) against the bill. In general, where state programs constructed in response to local political and economic conditions differed from proposed national standards, congressmen in both parties were more likely to oppose the legislation.

District welfare dependency levels, in conjunction with party allegiance and state program compatibility, were strongly associated with support for a nationalized AFDC program (table 6.17). In states with compatible AFDC programs, support for H.R. 4904 ranged from 87 percent in the highest quartile to 45 percent in the lowest. Since the behavior of party members in compatible states did not differ substantially by quartile, these support percentages are largely the product of differences in party representation within each of the quartiles (see table 6.16). In compatible states, support for nationalization significantly differed only between the highest AFDC quartile (50 percent of the members favoring the reform) and the remaining three (about 25 percent supporting the bill). Thus, higher AFDC dependency seems to have favorably influenced positions on H.R. 4904 in those states whose AFDC programs were compatible with the reform. However, that influence was felt primarily through the Democratic party and was reflected through the variation in the partisan composition of the members within each of the quartiles. The behavior of members from states with incompatible programs revealed much narrower differences in partisan support for the reform and much less general sensitivity to AFDC dependency within the district. Thus, a politics of welfare—at least with respect to the setting of national standards—seems to have been far more important to partisan electoral competition in the northern industrialized states than it was in the largely rural states of the South and West.

AFDC is connected both politically and programmatically to other social welfare policies such as unemployment insurance, food stamp allocation and eligibility, Medicaid and Medicare, public housing, and manpower training programs. For example, the relationship between AFDC and federal aid to education is contained in the statutory formula used to apportion federal aid among the various local school districts under Title I of the Elementary and Secondary Education Act of 1965. The aid formula in effect between 1974 and 1979 counted all children from families below the official poverty level plus two-thirds of all children from AFDC families with benefits (including food stamps) which placed them above the poverty line. Programmatic changes which alter the number and distribution of high-income AFDC recipients automatically reshape the allocation of federal education aid. In a similar manner, alteration in unemployment insurance coverage or eligibility indirectly affects the number of people on AFDC rolls (particularly in those states where two-parent families are eligible); more generous unemployment benefits reduce welfare dependency. Unemployment rates also trigger, as we have seen, the targeting of defense spending and public works programs. In each of these areas, the modern welfare state satisfies the needs of the aging industrial core.

The Political and Economic Future of the Industrial Core

The Northeast and Great Lakes regions have played the dominant role in American political development because they have contained three historically necessary aspects of a core economy: money center institutions and corporate headquarters, industrial activities employing the most technologically advanced and productive processes, and advantageous sea lane connections with the world economy. The southern and western periphery, on the other hand, has played a subordinant, almost neocolonial part in the national economic system. Recent events suggest that industrial production in the nation's manufacturing belt will, in the future, no longer possess "core" characteristics. This trend raises several questions concerning the future political and economic relations of the American core and periphery.

The most important of these questions is whether or not the dominant activities of the regional division of labor will remain in the old manufacturing belt. On this point, the weight of informed opinion is that higher-level functions will remain in their historical locations. Daniel Elazar, for example, has argued that improvements in transportation and information since the end of World War II have allowed the development of a new round of "colonialism" even as manufacturing activity has migrated from the core to the periphery. By making long-distance control of branch plant managers and production schedules feasible, Elazar argues, technological change has wiped out what little indigenous control the periphery formerly exercised over its own development and, thus, "paradoxically . . . [has given] the newly emerging sectionalism other sources of strength than those which draw their vitality from mere provincialism."* Robert Cohen similarly argues that "the rise of the Sunbelt, like the development of a third world nation, can be viewed as a new region's integration into the world as well as the national economy. And like a dependent nation, much of the Sunbelt's industry and a significant portion of its finances remain under the control of outside economic actors."[59]

Media accounts, on the other hand, predict an increasingly dreary future for the manufacturing belt. *Business Week*, for example, has argued that the development of the interstate highway system, the subsidization of airport and canal construction, and the development of communications networks have so

---

*Elazar continues, "At the End of World War II, prevailing opinion called for decentralization of America's industrial plant, a reversal of the pattern of industrial concentration which had relegated both the trans-Mississippi West and the ex-Confederate South to colonial status in the national economy for eighty years or more. There was a substantial movement of industry from the Northeastern industrial belt to the West and South in the 1940's and early 1950's. This represented a decentralization of economic activity—but not of economic power. It consisted mainly of the establishment of branch plants in new communities or the purchase of locally owned small industries by major national concerns. Capital and control continued to be concentrated in the great Northeastern cities, from New York to Chicago. The concentration of control in the New York area was even intensified, as companies which had previously maintained their headquarters in other cities of the Northeast and Great Lakes area, in order to be near their plants, found that they could relocate in or near the 'Empire City' and rely on modern communications facilities to maintain contact with an even wider network of field operations." "Megalopolis and the New Sectionalism," pp. 68–69. See also Carol Jusenius and Larry Ledebur, Economic Development Administration, Department of Commerce, *A Myth in the Making: The Southern Economic Challenge and Northern Economic Decline* (Washington: Government Printing Office, November 1976).

altered the "calculus of location strategy" that the Northeast will soon "be stripped of many of the 'export' functions it once sold to other regions, including both manufactured goods and business services."[60] Core congressmen and other political officials have lent rhetorical support to this prognosis.

One essential fact acknowledged in all regional economic forecasts is that firms headquartered in the leading cities of the historical core continue to dominate the nation's corporate and financial decisions. These cities also control a large portion of current investment in the periphery and have a large stake in the continued "agglomeration" of supporting activities (media, advertising, capital markets, export-import services, etc.) in northern metropolitan centers.[61] Recent evidence seems to confirm that "the concentration of decision-making functions proximate to clusters of financial, information, and analytical resources and expertise" may even *increase* simultaneously with the exodus of manufacturing employment.[62]

On the other hand, the distribution of command sectors in the national economy will not be unaffected by the dislocations of the last decade. Historically, the American core has exhibited four characteristics: preeminence in banking and capital markets, comparative dominance over the export-import trade and international investment, possession of sites for most of the largest corporate headquarters, and a disproportionate share of national manufacturing and heavy industrial capacity. With the declining importance of the last-mentioned characteristic, at least three cities display features which might ultimately lead to their entry into "core" status later in the post-industrial era. The most advanced of these centers is San Francisco, which possesses all the characteristics of eastern metropolitan centers and is clearly integrated into the Pacific Basin of the world-economy. The primary difference between San Francisco and eastern core cities has been its dependence on an agricultural and mineral producing hinterland. But the growing significance of nearby satellite cities on the peninsula, across the bay, and in San Jose has reduced the importance of rural portions of the tributary area. Two other candidates for senior status in the urban hierarchy are Houston and Miami. Both still lack the extensive financial resources of other leading urban centers. Miami will never serve as a major port of entry because of its geographical location. Houston, on the other hand, is still primarily dependent on one resource industry (petroleum) and lacks the diversified trade and manufacturing base typical of core centers. Both cities are oriented toward Latin American markets, though Houston also possesses significant links with the Middle East and other oil producing regions. If these two nascent candidates do emerge in the coming decades, their ascent will underscore important (though slowly evolving) changes in the interregional division of labor.

The decline of heavy industry, particularly steel and automobile production, in the manufacturing belt is probably irreversible. At least in part, this decline is the inevitable outgrowth of routinization of production and technological maturity in these sectors. No longer at the top of the economic order in terms of skilled labor requirements or the rapidity of innovation, heavy industry is also not basic to the emerging "high tech" areas of the post-industrial economy. Thus, heavy manufacturing has moved down the ladder of the world economy, and this movement has encouraged a migration of heavy industry and manufacturing out of the United States and into less-developed economies. This migation may not continue, however; it is possible that the United States could return to a high tariff policy that would insulate these sectors from foreign competition. Unlike the protectionist strategy of the nineteenth and early twentieth centuries, which nurtured the rise of the American economy, the erection of a high tariff barrier today would allow the United States to descend gracefully into Wallerstein's "semi-peripheral" status through the subsidization of new low-skill, low-return sectors at the expense of high-technology industries characteristic of the modern core economy (e.g., computers). At this point, however, it must be assumed that the United States will not abandon its free trade posture.

In three metropolitan regions there are increasing indications that a high-technology post-industrial renaissance will maintain the economic dominance of the historical core. In the past, the New York metropolitan area served as the incubator for new industries and production methods, nursing them into adulthood, and then spinning them off into the remainder of the nation while retaining their headquarters units. For a number of reasons, including the city's fiscal difficulties and the severity of the economic dislocations of the seventies, the New York area faltered badly in the post-embargo era. However, the present construction boom in office space indicates that New York will retain its attractiveness for the command sectors of the national economy.[63]

Several analysts report that New England and the San Francisco Bay area have emerged as the dominant regions in the new, post-industrial sectors. For New England this successful transition has made possible the retention and birth of "firms with a relatively large amount of scientific or engineering input in their work, and it encompasses firms that use highly specialized production processes which are not highly diffused."[64] This newly emerging division of labor has allocated the design and development of large-frame computers to the Northeast, while the rest of the manufacturing belt and the South have become the location for subassembly and component plants.[65] In industries for which research and innovation are important parts of the production process but which do not rely on mass production in manufacturing, New England and other core regions have increased their dominance. Production of highly specialized medical instruments, for example, has become increasingly concentrated in Boston, the New York metropolitan area, Chicago, and California.[66] These trends in computer and medical instruments production have been paralleled in electronics and advanced defense systems. In all these sectors, the end product has a relatively high value-to-weight ratio that allows firms to defy the "normal" imperatives of industrial location: transportation costs, proximity of markets, natural resource deposits, and energy supplies.[67] Furthermore, relatively high return on investment allows these sectors to endure labor costs that, in more mature industries, would force relocation into the periphery.

A major advantage of New England and San Francisco in the competition for post-industrial firms is the synergistic effect of an economic "agglomeration" which makes a wide variety of goods, materials, labor, and services available on relatively short notice. In New England, the beneficial aspects of this agglomeration on technological innovation are reinforced by the close proximity of investment centers specializing in venture or risk capital. These centers have arisen out of the "interrelations of old wealth"—the heritage of historical economic dominance—and personal contact with the inventors/enterpreneurs of the new technology.[68] For all these reasons, the northeastern and California seaboards should continue to lead the expansion of high-technology manufacturing, professional services, and export-oriented consulting firms in business, engineering, and finance.[69]

If these economic trends continue, at least two political consequences should ensue. The most important on an historical scale would be a growing divergence of interests between the low-technology, heavy industrial regions of the Midwest and the advanced research and finance centers of the Northeast and San Francisco. While it is far too early to project the political form this divergence will assume, intense struggles over tariff barriers and other types of protectionist measures (e.g., "buy America" requirements) are likely, given the distress of the downwardly mobile, heavy industrial regions. In these struggles, the chairman of the Northeast-Midwest Economic Advancement Coalition in 1980 expressed the belief that the industrial core would face three significant political liabilities during the 1980s: the reapportionment of House seats from the core to the periphery in 1982, the "increasing disparity" in wealth between the Northeast and the Southwest (in favor of the latter— e.g., Louisiana, Oklahoma, and Texas), and the retirement of Speaker O'Neill who, the chairman predicted, would be replaced by a less congenial leader from the South or West.[70]

In the short run, the cohesion of the manufacturing belt delegations should remain high. This cohesion is a reflection of the common interests of the Northeast and Midwest in redirecting federal spending and subsidizing heavy industry. In these efforts, political unity is furthered by the remarkable, if temporary, meshing of interests between capital and labor in the industrial core. Both capital and labor wish to retard, if not reverse, industrial decline, and from this common endeavor has come a significant diminution of class conflict within the core. Industrial decline would be retarded by federal subsidies whose costs would be displaced onto the southern and western periphery (as were the political and economic costs of industrialization originally). Labor's interest in retarding industrial decline, however, is permanent; loss of industrial employment often means the sacrifice of carefully nurtured investments in residential housing, union seniority, and work-related skills, and forces a radical shift in residence. The industrial elite, on the other hand, have shorter-term interests in retarding decline. Not only are their skills less dependent on specific manufacturing processes, but their investments, composing a significant portion of their total income, can be shifted out of the declining sectors of the core economy without a change in residence. Reading the handwriting on the wall, the elite hope only to retard industrial decline long enough to depreciate their capital investments—for example, long enough for U.S. Steel to pay for Marathon Oil and DuPont to reduce its debt from purchase of Conoco. Once this shift has progressed to a certain point, the temporary coincidence of interest between capital and labor will have ended.

In contrast to the permanent decline of heavy industry, the upward revaluation of periphery energy resources by the world economy is probably a temporary phenomenon. While parts of the periphery will doubtless be better off than the industrial Midwest, most parts of the South and West will still occupy a subordinate place in the post-industrial economy.

Conclusion

The economic projections presented here are based on several implicit assumptions. The most important assumption concerns the failure of current efforts to significantly redistribute the national income through a radical redirection of federal spending into the industrial core. As the Advisory Commission on Intergovernmental Relations has noted, these efforts "exacerbate political conflict and sectionalism . . . hamper the necessary adjustments within, and between regional economies and, thus, reduce overall economic efficiency . . . [and] ignore some of the important natural correctives already built into the nation's economy, e.g., the progressive tax system . . . their potential payoff is uncertain at best."[71] A successful redistribution of the national income would indefinitely prolong the contemporary sectional cleavage and, like trade protectionism, ultimately drive the nation into permanent economic decline. Since most efforts to nationalize welfare programs and labor law reflect similar redistributive intentions, political success in these areas would also prolong the contemporary cleavage and encourage continued periphery opposition to a strong central state. In these respects the decentralization of domestic policy and the budgetary stringency of the Reagan administration have furthered the realignment of sectional interests.

7

The Bipolar Democratic Coalition and the Rise and Decline of the Congressional Committee System

In the course of this book several primary connections have been drawn between sectional stress, party composition and organization, and the congressional committee system. The connection between a relatively strong party system and the underlying or fundamental structure of sectional stress will be discussed in chapter 8. The relationship between a strong committee system and the contemporary decline of sectional stress in congressional voting is covered in this chapter and linked to the political imperatives of the Democratic New Deal coalition.

A strong committee system like the one that developed in the United States Congress would be inconceivable in a legislature dominated by strong, disciplined party organizations. Almost by definition, such political parties would exclude minority party members from committee deliberations and coerce recalcitrant majority party colleagues. For this reason alone, the development of the contemporary committee system has implied a concomitant decline in the legislative influence of national party organizations. The incompatibility between a strong committee system and a cohesive, disciplined party structure can also be viewed from another perspective. The goals of the American core and periphery within the national political economy are so antithetical and are pursued so relentlessly that the emergence of strong disciplined parties would mean the steady gravitation of each major party toward one or the other of the two great poles. Disciplined, programmatic parties would compel reluctant members to choose between expulsion for defying party directives or electoral defeat if they complied with them. Over time, the expulsion and electoral defeat of deviant members would steadily move a party's center of gravity toward one of the two great sectional poles and reduce its ability to win elections in the opposite section. The reemergence of disciplined parties would thus re-create the sectionally polarized coalitions of the early twentieth century (with the important distinction that the Republicans would now constitute the periphery party and the Democrats, the core—see chapters 6 and 8).

In a legislature with a strong committee system and weak party organizations, however, members from both the core and periphery can coexist in the same caucus. The decentralization of legislative power and the absence of programmatic discipline allow each congressman to personally tailor his positions to reflect the place and needs of his constituency within the national political economy. Over time, the programmatic independence of individual congressmen increases their general competitiveness in very diverse electoral environments and, by comparison with the alternative of strong party discipline, reduces the homogeneity of constituency interests represented within the party caucus. In this way, a strong committee system *allows* the membership base of each party to become detached from the fundamental bipolar sectional structure of political competition.

A strong committee system *encourages* nationalized party competition by assigning members from both parties to the various committees and subcommittees in Congress. Bipartisan committee assignments provide an incentive for a region to elect members of both parties to Congress and, thus, to dominate those parts of the legislative system that control federal policies important to the trade area's economic base. By electing both Democrats and Republicans to the House, for example, representatives of the Charlotte trade area can theoretically fill every position on the tobacco panel of the full Agriculture Committee. Nationalized party competition based on such incentives only implies that there will be bipartisan representation within trade area delegations (not that individual districts will be politically competitive). The seniority system encourages the district to reelect incumbents, and most members can make themselves politically secure by pursuing the narrowly circumscribed interests of their districts. For that reason, the nationalized party competition fostered by a strong committee system has been associated with a decline in electoral competition generally.[1] Only districts in which no incumbent is standing for election would be expected to produce narrow electoral margins. In summary, then, a strong committee system allows nationalized party competition to develop by providing an institutional structure that is incompatible with disciplined, programmatic parties, and encourages nationalized party competition by rewarding bipartisan representation within each trade area delegation.

The relationship between the emergence of a strong committee system and the evolving political requirements of the New Deal Democratic coalition is a complex one. On the one hand, the institutional dynamics of the committee system are largely self-contained features of Congress. These features include seniority norms, reciprocity between the members of the several committees, and strong reelection proclivities. While they can be more or less related to sectional conflict within the external political environment, these aspects of the committee system can also be considered quite apart from the political imperatives of the Democratic coalition. On the other hand, the evolution of the Democratic party over the last half-century would be inexplicable without reference to the committee system. It was through this system that policy conflicts within the party were methodically resolved through a relentless decentralization of power. It was during the reign of the standing committee that the party system first became regionally depolarized, and subsequently the center of gravity within the Democratic party shifted into the industrial core.

The primary focus in the following sections will be on the relationship between committee recruitment, control of the national economy, and historical political support for a decentralization of legislative activity. Emphasis will be placed on the necessary institutional requirements for a strong committee system. A historic conjunction of these requirements during the "classic" phase of committee dominance reinforced the decentralizing tendency of the New Deal coalition between 1947 and 1965. The chapter concludes with a description of the contemporary decline of the committee system and its probable replacement by a recentralization of power within strong party organizations.

The Committee System and Control of the National Political Economy

The committee system of the House of Representatives is composed of two basic types of units: the standing or full committee and the subcommittee. Of the two, the standing committee is the older and, until the last decade or so, clearly the more important. While the seniority ladders and policy jurisdictions of full committees were well defined and historically stable, until recently subcommittees were often the somewhat arbitrary and fluid result of the changing political goals of standing committee chairmen.

Both full committees and their institutional offspring, subcommittees, divide the national political economy into specific areas which are then controlled by the members assigned to them. Because the economic imperatives of each region relate in different ways to the various parts of the national political economy, an individual member will tend to be attracted to some committees more than others. Generally speaking, members seek assignment to those committees that either affect the economic position of the major export activities of their regions or provide a very broad vantage point over the legislative process which can be brokered into influence over federal policies relating to those key district economic interests. The major federal policy interests of a region assume two forms: those connected with products or services which one

Table 7.1. Manufacturing Belt Members as a Percentage of 1981 Standing
Committee Assignments

Standing Committee	Democrats %	(N)	Republicans %	(N)	Total %	(N)
Agriculture	8.3	(24)	5.3	(19)	7.0	(43)
Armed Services	20.8	(24)	36.8	(19)	27.9	(43)
Veterans' Affairs	23.5	(17)	66.7	(12)	41.4	(29)
District of Columbia	25.0	(8)	33.3	(3)	27.3	(11)
Budget	27.8	(18)	41.7	(12)	33.3	(30)
Appropriations	33.3	(33)	50.0	(22)	40.0	(55)
Standards of Official Conduct	33.3	(6)	50.0	(6)	41.7	(12)
Interior and Insular Affairs	34.8	(23)	6.2	(16)	23.1	(39)
Merchant Marine and Fisheries	35.0	(20)	53.3	(15)	42.9	(35)
Judiciary	37.5	(16)	58.3	(12)	46.4	(28)
Science and Technology	39.1	(23)	58.8	(17)	47.5	(40)
Small Business	43.5	(23)	62.5	(16)	51.3	(39)
Rules	45.5	(11)	20.0	(5)	37.5	(16)
Energy and Commerce	45.8	(24)	50.0	(18)	47.6	(42)
Foreign Affairs	47.6	(21)	53.3	(15)	50.0	(36)
Ways and Means	47.8	(23)	41.7	(12)	45.7	(35)
Government Operations	47.8	(23)	64.7	(17)	55.0	(40)
Public Works and Transportation	48.0	(25)	31.6	(19)	40.9	(44)
House Administration	50.0	(12)	37.5	(8)	45.0	(20)
Education and Labor	52.6	(19)	50.0	(14)	51.5	(33)
Post Office and Civil Service	53.8	(13)	50.0	(10)	52.2	(23)
Banking, Finance, and Urban Affairs	54.2	(24)	55.6	(18)	54.8	(42)
House of Representatives	39.3	(244)	44.5	(191)	41.6	(435)

SOURCE: Joint Committee on Printing, U.S. Congress, *Congressional Directory for the
97th Congress* (Washington: Government Printing Office, 1981). See chapter 5,
above, for definition of Manufacturing Belt Trade Areas.

region "sells" to other areas within the domestic private sector (or world-
economy) and those characteristics of the population or physical environment
of a region which produce federal revenue for the area. In the second category
fall the most "political" portions of the national political economy—those
which are largely removed from the dynamics of the private marketplace (e.g.,
social security benefits, urban renewal, federal aid to education, and veterans'
hospitals).

At the level of the full or standing committee, many different federal
policies are collected into each separate jurisdiction. In most cases at least some
policies have divergent implications with reference to regional economic interests, and as a result, recruitment onto most committees tends to reflect the
range of interests within the House at large. Still, the disparate interests of the
core and periphery within the national political economy can be traced
through committee assignment patterns (see table 7.1). Manufacturing belt
members have been drawn disproportionately toward those committees which

control federal financial and urban policy (Banking), the civilian side of the central state bureaucracy (Post Office and Civil Service), federal regulation of collective bargaining and education subsidies (Education and Labor), and international relations (Foreign Affairs). The Agriculture, Armed Services, and Appropriations Committees have most attracted representatives outside the manufacturing belt. A few committees pull members in patterns which are obliquely related to the core-periphery alignment. For example, the District of Columbia jurisdiction draws congressmen from the immediately surrounding metropolitan area in Maryland and Virginia, while most Merchant Marine members represent port districts located in both the core and periphery.

The basic arenas of policy formation in the House of Representatives are the nearly 150 subcommittees. These subcommittees usually contain between seven and twenty members, and since 1975 each one has held a unique and formally defined jurisdiction.[2] Taken together, the subcommittee network divides the national political economy into small, narrowly circumscribed areas which attract more homogeneous subsets of the House membership than do the broader jurisdictions of their parent committees.

In order to demonstrate the connection between legislative control of the national political economy and constituency interests, recruitment onto these subcommittees can be analyzed from two perspectives. From the first, members are classified by the extent to which their districts contain the beneficiaries of specific federal programs and the resulting distribution of recipients is then traced to recruitment patterns within the subcommittee system. An analysis of the impact of welfare dependency on subcommittee membership (below) uses this perspective. The second perspective emphasizes the electoral connection between committee recruitment and district interest. In this case, campaign contributions from what might well be the largest and most cohesive class of interest groups in America, organized labor, are traced through individual members to subcommittee control of the political economy. In both analyses, it is assumed that the vast majority of subcommittee assignments are the result of self-selection by individual members. Although this assumption has been the subject of some debate, it has generally been supported in other contexts.[3]

For purposes of demonstrating the connection between the distribution of federal beneficiaries and subcommittee recruitment, welfare dependency is an attractive subject because the Aid to Families with Dependent Children program is politically mutable in ways that most geographic, economic, and social characteristics are not (see chapter 6). In the following analysis, both median and mean AFDC dependency levels were calculated for members of 129 of the 148 subcommittees in the 96th Congress (1979–80).* The sub-

---

*All subcommittees with six or more members were included in this investigation. This limitation, which excluded the nineteen subcommittees to which fewer than six members belonged, was imposed because, while it allows the inclusion of all of the subcommittees of the relatively important Appropriations Committee, it still excludes those subcommittees which were too small or too insignificant for analysis. Both median and mean dependency scores were

Table 7.2. Subcommittees Containing Constituencies with the Highest Median and Mean AFDC Populations, 1979

Full Committee	Subcommittee	Median AFDC Percentage	Mean AFDC Percentage
Ways and Means	Public Assistance and Unemployment Compensation	8.1	7.4
Interstate and Foreign Commerce	Transportation and Commerce	7.7	7.6
Ways and Means	Select Revenue Measures	6.8	7.4
Post Office	Postal Operations and Service	6.7	6.9
Ways and Means	Health	6.3	7.3
Judiciary	Courts, Civil Liberties, and the Administration of Justice	6.3	6.0
Small Business	General Oversight and Minority Enterprise	6.2	7.5
House Administration	Personnel and Police	6.2	6.9
Merchant Marine	Merchant Marine	6.1	7.7
Foreign Affairs	Africa	6.0	7.2
House Administration	Accounts	5.7	6.0
House Administration	Libraries	5.7	6.0
Judiciary	Civil and Constitutional Rights	5.7	5.7
Education and Labor	Labor-Management Relations	5.5	6.5
Banking	Consumer Affairs	5.4	7.1
Banking	International Development, Institutions and Finance	5.4	6.0
Government Operations	Manpower and Housing	5.4	6.0
Education and Labor	Elementary, Secondary, and Vocational Education	5.3	6.1
Education and Labor	Postsecondary Education	5.3	6.1
Education and Labor	Labor Standards	5.3	5.7
Government Operations	Commerce, Consumer, and Monetary Affairs	5.2	5.9
Budget	Human and Community Resources	5.1	6.8
Judiciary	Criminal Justice	5.1	5.8

committees were then ranked along both AFDC measures and divided into quartiles. The subcommittees that ranked in the highest quartile on both median *and* mean AFDC dependency are shown in table 7.2. The twenty

---

calculated in order to eliminate subcommittees in which the distribution of district dependency levels was inconsistent (e.g., an extremely low mean score was combined with a relatively high median percentage). For example, the Interstate and Foreign Commerce subcommittee on Health and the Environment had a mean AFDC dependency percentage of 5.5 and a median of 5.2 percent. While the median fell in the highest quartile of all subcommittees, the mean did not, and the subcommittee was not included in table 7.2.

Table 7.3. Subcommittees Containing Constituencies with the Lowest Median and Mean AFDC Populations, 1979

Full Committee	Subcommittee	Median AFDC Percentage	Mean AFDC Percentage
Agriculture	Livestock and Grains	2.2	2.7
Interstate and Foreign Commerce	Oversight and Investigations	2.3	3.5
Government Operations	Legislation and National Security	2.7	3.3
Government Operations	Environment, Energy and Natural Resources	2.8	3.5
Small Business	Antitrust and Restraint of Trade Activities Affecting Small Business	2.8	3.5
Appropriations	Foreign Operations	2.8	3.9
Budget	Legislative Savings	3.0	3.1
Interior	Public Lands	3.0	3.9
Budget	Regulations and Spending Limitations	3.1	4.1
Veterans' Affairs	Education, Training, and Employment	3.1	4.1
Science and Technology	Investigations and Oversight	3.2	3.6
Government Operations	Government Information and Individual Rights	3.2	3.6
Budget	Inflation	3.2	4.1
Science and Technology	Science, Research, and Technology	3.3	4.1
Agriculture	Department Investigations, Oversight, and Research	3.4	3.6
Science and Technology	Energy Development and Applications	3.4	3.9
Banking	International Trade, Investment, and Monetary Policy	3.4	4.0
Appropriations	District of Columbia	3.4	4.0
Appropriations	Agriculture, Rural Development, and Related Agencies	3.4	4.1

subcommittees which fell in both the lowest median and the lowest mean quartiles are listed in table 7.3.

AFDC constitutes the central program around which other social welfare policies revolve and, as such, is both politically and programmatically linked to the other federal functions which together compose the American welfare state. For this reason alone, members representing districts with high AFDC dependency levels should find their way onto those subcommittees which control food stamp eligibilty and distribution, job training programs, aid to elementary and secondary schools (see chapter 6), and programs tailored for or particularly relevant to minority groups. Members from areas of high welfare dependency are in fact attracted to these committees (see table 7.2). Of the 129 subcommittees analyzed, the Ways and Means Subcommittee on Public Assistance and Unemployment Compensation had the highest median AFDC dependency level and the fourth highest mean AFDC percentage. The formal rules adopted by the Committee on Ways and Means specify that the jurisdiction of the subcommittee includes:

> those provisions of the Social Security Act relating to welfare matters; i.e., welfare reform, supplemental security income, aid to families with dependent children, social services and child support, and eligibility of welfare recipients for food stamps. . . . The jurisdiction . . . will also include . . . the Federal-State system of unemployment compensation, and the financing thereof, including the programs for extended and emergency benefits.[4]

Not only is the subcommittee that controls the shape of the AFDC program dominated by members from districts with high dependency levels, but the institutional structure of the House also combines control over unemployment insurance eligibility and benefits, food stamps, and other related programs under the same subcommittee. The subcommittee held jurisdiction over the proposed 1979 welfare reform bill (see chapter 6) and managed that legislation on the House floor.*

The second highest ranking panel on median AFDC dependency was the Subcommittee on Transportation and Commerce organized under the Committee on Interstate and Foreign Commerce. This subcommittee is primarily concerned with regulation of the nation's railroads and in recent years has concentrated its attention largely on federal subsidization of the Conrail system, the maintenance of local rail service, the development of Amtrak and the high-density rail corridor between Boston and Washington, D.C., and bulk railroad rates (particularly those applying to coal).[5] Since most of these policies hold the greatest significance for northeastern and midwestern industrial centers and since these areas contain the highest concentrations of welfare recipients in the nation, the high ranking of this subcommittee in table 7.2 appar-

---

*This combination has a number of unexpected consequences. For example, at this time the unemployment insurance program for some state accounts (particularly Pennsylvania, Illinois, New Jersey, Michigan, Connecticut, and New York) was deeply in the red. As a result, these states, in effect, owed the federal government hundreds of millions of dollars (*Congressional Record*, 96:1:H10280–84, November 7, 1979). Since four of the nine representatives on the subcommittee were drawn from these states, the members could coordinate a solution to the unemployment account deficit by decreasing long-term eligibility for unemployment benefits and increasing federal participation in AFDC-U benefits (see chapter 6). It is significant, in this respect, that passage of a bill granting a temporary extension on repayment of state unemployment account deficits (H.R. 4007) immediately preceded floor consideration of H.R. 4904 (the welfare reform bill).

ently stems from overlapping sets of constituency characteristics and, as will be shown, the deep interest in the activities of this panel exhibited by the political arm of organized labor (see table 7.4). Parallel explanations are indicated for the subcommittees on Postal Operations and Service, the Merchant Marine, Labor-Management Relations (which includes a Task Force on Welfare and Pension Plans), Consumer Affairs, International Development, Labor Standards (which includes workmen's compensation), and Commerce, Consumer, and Monetary Affairs. In each case, the subcommittees control a set of government programs which are of particular significance to organized labor and other interests located primarily in larger metropolitan and older industrial regions of the country.*

As a group, then, the members representing districts in which AFDC dependency is very high have placed themselves in advantageous positions for coordinating the programs that characterize the American welfare state. This distribution of members throughout the subcommittee system suggests the wide variety of possible political and programmatic linkages which take place between diverse federal policies.

The nineteen subcommittees whose constituencies have the lowest levels of AFDC dependency also share a number of common characteristics. Nine of them (including the Government Operations and Budget subcommittee) have jurisdiction over investigations, oversight, and/or budgetary limitations. An additional three subcommittees control appropriations for agriculture and related agencies, for foreign aid and the State Department, and for the District of Columbia. The common thread running through these twelve subcommittees is control over federal expenditures through oversight, budgetary restraint, and appropriations decisions. The other seven subcommittee jurisdictions target constituencies in which welfare dependency is relatively rare.†

*The Ways and Means Subcommittee on Health shares control over the Medicare and Medicaid programs with a similar unit under Interstate and Foreign Commerce. Medicaid is tied directly to AFDC policy both in a substantive way (eligibility of recipients for health benefits) and through common use of the Medicaid formula to calculate federal participation in state-administered health care programs. The subcommittees on Manpower and Housing (including CETA) and Human and Community Resources (welfare policies generally) are additional examples of jurisdictions closely related to the AFDC programs. The subcommittee on Elementary, Secondary, and Vocational Education controls federal aid to elementary and secondary schools, which, as was shown in the previous chapter, is partially allocated on the basis of AFDC dependency. The subcommittees on General Oversight and Minority Enterprise and on Africa are of substantive and symbolic importance to black constituencies, which heavily overlap with constituencies exhibiting high levels of AFDC dependency. The Judiciary and House Administration subcommittees have little or no significance to the overall shape of the American welfare state. The Judiciary panels are important to federal civil rights policies and tend to attract northern liberals from both parties who often represent areas of high AFDC dependency. The House Administration subcommittees are largely institutional service positions with little general policy significance.

†The lowest subcommittee, Livestock and Grains, is of direct relevance to wheat-producing districts in the plains states, where AFDC dependency is remarkably low (see map

Table 7.4. 1976 Campaign Contributions by Organized Labor to Subcommittee Members in the House of Representatives (Average Contribution per Member, in Thousands of Dollars)

Subcommittees with the Highest Contributions		Subcommittees with the Lowest Contributions	
Transportation and Commerce (IFC)	26.0	Standards of Official Conduct [a]	2.5
Employee Ethics and Utilization (PO)	24.9	Military Personnel #1 (AS)	2.3
Consumer Protection and Finance (IFC)	24.4	International Security and Scientific Affairs (IR)	2.9
International Trade, Investment and Monetary Policy (BF)	22.1	Military Construction (App)	3.4
Domestic Marketing, Consumer Relations, and Nutrition (Ag)	21.7	Cotton (Ag)	4.1
		Military Installations and Facilities (AS)	4.1
Housing and Community Development (BF)	21.0	Investigations (AS)	4.2
Space Science and Applications (ST)	20.8	Treasury—Postal Service—General Government (App)	4.3
Postsecondary Education (EL)	20.2	Inter-American Affairs (IR)	4.9
Energy and Power (IFC)	20.2	Tobacco (Ag)	5.0
Economic Stabilization (BF)	20.0	Compensation, Pension, and Insurance (VA)	5.2
Communications (IFC)	19.4	International Economic Policy and Trade (IR)	5.2
Compensation, Health, and Safety (EL)	19.4	Oilseeds and Rice (Ag)	5.5
Water and Power Resources (Int)	19.2	Legislation and National Security (GO)	5.7
Compensation and Employee Benefits (PO)	19.0	State, Justice, Commerce, and Judiciary (App)	5.8
Merchant Marine (MM)	18.9	Miscellaneous Revenue Measures (WM)	6.2
Labor Standards (EL)	18.9	Defense (App)	6.5
Government Activities and Transportation (GO)	18.8	Military Personnel #2 (AS)	6.5
General Oversight and Alaskan Lands (Int)	18.3	Intelligence and Military Application of Nuclear Energy (AS)	6.6
Postal Operations and Services (PO)	18.0	Crime (J)	6.7
The City (BF)	17.7		

[a] Standards of Official Conduct is a full committee with no subcommittees. Only subcommittees with seven or more members (there were 135 in 1977) and full committees with no subcommittees were eligible for this table. Abbreviations: Ag = Agriculture, App = Appropriations, AS = Armed Services, BF = Banking, Finance, and Urban Affairs, EL = Education and Labor, GO = Government Operations, IFC = Interstate and Foreign Commerce, Int = Interior and Insular Affairs, IR = International Relations, J = Judiciary, MM = Merchant Marine and Fisheries, PO = Post Office and Civil Service, ST = Science and Technology, VA = Veterans' Affairs, WM = Ways and Means.
SOURCE: Calculated from data in 1976 *Federal Campaign Finances* (Washington, D.C.: Common Cause, 1977).

An alternative way of analyzing the subcommittee network is to investigate the active expression of political support by constituency interests. A major indicator of that support is campaign contributions to individual congressmen. Because labor unions are probably the single largest force in campaign financing, contributions by organized labor were chosen as the focus for this analysis. By a procedure very similar to that in the preceding AFDC example, monetary contributions by organized labor to the successful 1976 campaigns of congressmen were related to the membership on individual subcommittees. Taken together, organized labor concentrated its resources on subcommittees which controlled those parts of the political economy directly related to its interests in economic regulation or the broader urban, industrial environment in which its members lived. Significantly, five of the subcommittees which received the greatest attention from organized labor also appeared on the list of panels whose members represented districts with relatively high levels of AFDC dependency (Transportation and Commerce, Postal Operations and Services, Merchant Marine, Postsecondary Education, and Labor Standards). By contrast, members of the subcommittee on Legislation and National Security received little campaign support from organized labor and represented constituencies containing comparatively few AFDC recipients. Reflecting the regional coincidence of welfare dependency and the political strength of organized labor, no subcommittee appeared on the low side of one list and the high side of the other.

Those subcommittees which controlled portions of the political economy with little direct economic relevance to trade unions generally received little attention from organized labor. Thus, the Cotton, Tobacco, and Oilseed and Rice subcommittee memberships fell on the low side of table 7.4, and since unionization is prohibited in Defense Department employment, the subcommittees on Military Personnel, Installations and Facilities, Investigations, and Intelligence and Military Application of Nuclear Energy also received little campaign support from organized labor. In contrast, the disproportionate attention paid to members of the Transportation and Commerce Subcommittee by railroad unions helped to push that committee to the top rank in average campaign contributions (see table 7.5). Maritime unions concentrated their support on the Merchant Marine and Labor Standards subcommittees, while the national political arm of the AFL-CIO and the construction unions contributed heavily to the Housing and Community Development panel. In the legislative session immediately following the 1976 election, this subcommittee rewrote the community development block grant formula in order to redirect federal assistance into the manufacturing belt (see chapter 6). In all, four

---

6.4). The same is true of Public Lands. The remaining Banking, Small Business, Science and Technology, and Veterans' Affairs subcommittees contain jurisdictions which might be interpreted as being related to conservative ideological goals (monetary policy, government regulation of small business, commercial applications of government-sponsored research and development, and military service).

Table 7.5. 1976 Campaign Contributions by Individual Labor Unions to Selected Subcommittees in the House of Representatives

		Average Dollar Contribution by Union	
Subcommittee	Labor Union	Subcommit-tee Members	All House Members
Transportation and Commerce (IFC)[a]	Maintenance of Way Employees	318	63
	Railway Clerks	1,755	266
	Railway Labor Executive Association	309	61
	Transit Union	136	51
	Transportation Union	2,036	520
Housing and Community Development (BF)	Building and Construction	228	116
	Carpenters	433	245
	AFL-CIO	1,883	1,021
Merchant Marine (MM)	Longshoremen	288	28
	Marine Engineers	1,277	486
	Maritime	355	127
	Masters' Mates	714	94
	Seafarers	1,143	283
Labor Standards (EL)	Longshoremen	534	28
	Marine Engineers	2,050	486
	Maritime	390	127
	Masters' Mates	600	94
	Seafarers	1,610	283
Postal Operations and Services (PO)	Government Employees (AFGE)	430	48
	Air Controllers (PATCO)	745	84
	Postal Workers	414	53

[a] For full committee names, see note at table 7.4.
SOURCE: Calculated from data in *1976 Federal Campaign Finances* (Washington: Common Cause, 1977).

Banking subcommittees appeared among those ranking high in labor contributions. The combined contributions by the three most politically active organizations of federal civilian employees, the American Federation of Government Employees, the Professional Air Traffic Controllers Organization, and postal workers, placed three Post Office and Civil Service subcommittees in the upper ranks (Employee Ethics and Utilization, Compensation and Employee Benefits, and Postal Operations and Services).

The AFDC and organized labor examples illustrate several facets of the committee system's relationship to the national political economy. The most important of these is the way in which committee and subcommittee jurisdictions carve up control over the political economy and, thus, decentralize influence over the legislative process. These legislative jurisdictions in turn attract those members whose districts have a direct interest in their respective collections of federal policies. The AFDC analysis demonstrates that even a relatively unorganized economic interest, such as welfare dependency, can influence the assignment preferences of congressmen and the consequent distribution of political power. Finally, comparison of the results suggests a few of the ways in which the political interests of seemingly disparate groups such as AFDC recipients and union members coincide both geographically (e.g., in large industrial centers), politically (in subcommittee jurisdictions), and in the political economy (e.g., the relationship between AFDC and eligibility for unemployment compensation). Over time, the dynamics of the seniority system and the gradual development of federal regulatory structures and interventionist mechanisms have given almost every major economic interest a stake in the prevailing decentralization of legislative activity.

Centralization and Fragmentation in the House of Representatives

Since 1880, two broad patterns have characterized much of the historical development of the modern House. The first pattern was a steady, almost ruthless, concentration of power in the hands of the Speaker at the end of the nineteenth and the beginning of the twentieth centuries.[6] This period came to an end with the Cannon revolt in 1910 and the beginning of an equally steady decentralization of legislative influence into the committee system—a process which seems to have been reversed in the mid-sixties.

Over the eight and a half decades which encompass both periods, the House of Representatives established major precedents with reference to the internal distribution of power on six occasions (see table 7.6). Generally speaking, these six precedents can be divided into those that further concentrated power in the hands of the majority party leadership and those that limited majority party control of the legislative process. While members from the industrial core generally supported centralization and periphery members tended to support the "fragmenting" alternative, each precedent was established in a unique political setting and deserves individual treatment.

The growing concentration of power in the office of the Speaker between 1880 and 1910 came at the expense of the privileges of individual members—particularly minority members—on the House floor. The most important single event in this process occurred near the end of the First Session of the 51st Congress, when Speaker Thomas B. Reed of Maine ruled from the chair that members who refused to vote on a question even though they were present could be counted in a quorum. Prior to this ruling, the Republican majority in a closely divided House had been bedeviled by the refusal of the Democratic minority to vote (and thus record their presence) on substantive legislative decisions. Because of the quorum requirement embedded in the Constitution, the Democratic tactic often delayed and sometimes denied House approval of

Table 7.6. Trade Area Delegation Voting on Six Major Precedents in the House of Representatives, 1890–1965

Trade Area[a]	Speaker Reed's Counting of a Quorum (1890)	Cannon Revolt (1910)	Discharge Rule (1925)	Twenty-one Day Rule (1951)	Expansion of Rules (1961)	Twenty-one Day Rule (1965)
Philadelphia	Cent[b]	Cent	Cent	*Split*	Fragm	Cent
Boston	Cent	Cent	Cent	Cent	Cent	Cent
Buffalo	Cent	Cent	Cent	Fragm	Fragm	*Split*
Chicago	Cent	Cent	Cent	Fragm	Fragm	Cent
New York	Fragm	Cent	Cent	Cent	Cent	Cent
Detroit	Cent	Cent	Cent	Fragm	Fragm	Cent
Pittsburgh	Cent	Cent	Cent	Cent	Cent	Cent
San Francisco	Cent	Cent	Cent	Fragm	Cent	Cent
Cleveland	Cent	Fragm	*Split*	Cent	Cent	*Split*
Omaha	Cent	Fragm	Fragm	Fragm	Fragm	*Split*
Cincinnati	*Split*	Cent	Fragm	Fragm	Fragm	Fragm
Minneapolis	Cent	Fragm	Cent	Cent	Fragm	*Split*
Indianapolis	Fragm	—	*Split*	Fragm	Fragm	Fragm
Kansas City	Fragm	Cent	Fragm	Cent	Fragm	Fragm
Denver	—	—	Cent	Fragm	Cent	Cent
St. Louis	Fragm	Fragm	Fragm	*Split*	Cent	Cent
Baltimore	*Split*	Cent	Fragm	*Split*	—	—
Louisville	Fragm	Fragm	Cent	—	Cent	Fragm
Richmond	Fragm	Fragm	Fragm	Fragm	Fragm	Fragm
New Orleans	Fragm	Fragm	Fragm	Fragm	Cent	*Split*
Birmingham	—	Fragm	Fragm	Fragm	*Split*	Fragm
Atlanta	Fragm	Fragm	Fragm	Fragm	Fragm	Fragm
Memphis	Fragm	Fragm	Fragm	Fragm	Fragm	Fragm
Dallas	—	Fragm	Fragm	Fragm	Cent	Fragm
Sectional Stress	55.6	46.9	55.3	38.9	41.0	40.2

Support for Centralization (%)						
Republicans:						
Manufacturing Belt	100.0	85.9	91.2	28.7	17.5	17.1
Outside Belt	100.0	76.3	87.0	18.8	6.3	3.2
Democrats:						
Manufacturing Belt	0.0	0.0	0.0	97.4	98.8	100.0
Outside Belt	0.0	0.0	0.0	40.4	61.9	55.8

[a] Trade area delegations are ranked in descending order of their historical support for the core political position on high-stress roll calls (see table 2.5).

[b] "Cent" (Centralized) indicates that a majority of the delegation supported more concentration of power in the hands of the majority party leadership; "Fragm" (Fragmented) indicates that the delegation opposed such a concentration of power; *Split* indicates that the delegation divided evenly.

[c] See chapter 5 for a definition of Manufacturing Belt Trade Area Delegations.

measures that otherwise had sufficient support in the chamber. In support of his ruling, Speaker Reed argued during the third day of debate,

> There is no possible way by which the orderly methods of parliamentary procedure can be used to stop legislation. The object of a parliamentary body is action, and not stoppage of action. Hence, if any member or set of members undertakes to oppose the orderly progress of business, even by the use of the ordinarily recognized parliamentary motions, it is the right of the majority to refuse to have those motions entertained, and to cause the public business to proceed . . .[7]

By ruling that at least some minority appeals of chair decisions could be considered dilatory on their face, Reed finally brought to an end "a century of warfare over minority obstruction."[8]

The vote included in table 7.6 arose on a motion to lay on the table (kill) an appeal of a Speaker's decision to include abstaining minority members in a quorum necessary to approve the *Journal* account of the previous day's proceedings (January 29, 1890). In appealing the Speaker's decision, the minority hoped to test once again the original quorum ruling and, if that test failed, to follow with a motion to strike that portion of the previous day's *Journal* containing the names of abstaining minority members. This roll call on the motion to table was selected because it followed the most formal presentation of parliamentary arguments for and against the Speaker's ruling.* The tabling motion carried (162 to 0) with 167 abstentions. All "aye" votes have been considered as supporting legislative centralization and all abstentions by the minority have been interpreted as "fragmenting."†

Little more than two weeks after the clash over the disappearing

---

*These arguments were presented amidst scenes of unprecedented chaos and disorder. Hubert Bruce Fuller relates that as the morning of January 30 wore on, "the physical presence but constructive absence theory gave way to the idea of corporeal absence. Members dodged under their desks, behind screens, and bolted for the doors. In the mad rush for the exits members lost all sense of personal and official dignity and some incurred physical injuries. Upon the order of the Chair the doors were bolted and with each test of the quorum count the defiant minority spent their anger in madly raving about the chamber,—pictures of furious inefficiency. . . . This was the most notable parliamentary scene ever enacted upon the American legislative stage." *The Speakers of the House* (Boston: Little Brown, 1909), p. 221. It should be remembered that the House can order the attendance of members through their arrest; Speaker Reed's decision extended that constitutional power to encompass the refusal of the minority to vocally confirm their presence.

†Some Republicans were also absent for various reasons, primarily illness. While their motives cannot be completely ascertained, it seems very likely that none of the majority members intended opposition to the Speaker. For example, William A. Robinson related that on January 29, "161 Republican members were in their places, several of these so ill that they were actually there at the risk of their lives. Of the absentees, several were dangerously sick, and another had been summoned to the bedside of his dying wife." *Thomas B. Reed: Parliamentarian*, p. 207.

quorum, the House of Representatives adopted what became known as "Reed's Rules." Among the most important changes were:

1. Every member must vote unless he has a pecuniary interest in the question before the house.
2. The dignity of the House and the rights of members have precedence over every question but a motion to adjourn.
3. A quorum in the Committee of the Whole, in which bills are debated and amended but not passed, was set at one hundred.
4. Members present but not voting may be counted as a part of a quorum.
5. No dilatory motion shall be entertained by the Speaker.[9]

When he ascended to the speakership in 1903, Joseph Cannon of Illinois enthusiastically embraced and extended these powers, and by 1909, "Uncle Joe" had brought about a "quasi-dictatorship" based on Reed's innovations, the power to make committee assignments and appoint chairmen, absolute authority to grant or withhold parliamentary recognition from the chair, and his own chairmanship of the Rules Committee.

Cannon's reign and the period of centralized authority under the Speaker both came to an end on March 19, 1910, when the House of Representatives voted to remove the Speaker from the Rules Committee and, though not explicitly, to strip from the office the power to make committee assignments. Following this action, the Speaker offered to resign, noting:

> This is a government by the people acting through the representatives of a majority of the people. Results can not be had except by a majority, and in the House of Representatives a majority, being responsible, should have full power and should exercise that power; otherwise the majority is inefficient and does not perform its function. . . . the assault upon the Speaker of the House by the minority, supplemented by the efforts of the so-called insurgents, shows . . . that the Speaker of the House is not in harmony with the actual majority of the House, as evidenced by the vote just taken.[10]

The critical test in the revolt arose after Cannon initially attempted to rule the proposed change in the rules out of order. The author of the resolution containing the change, Republican insurgent George Norris of Nebraska, immediately appealed the Speaker's ruling, and the regular Republican leadership moved to table the appeal. On the ensuing roll call (included in table 7.6), 164 members supported the tabling motion (and the Speaker), 182 voted to keep the appeal before the House, 6 answered "present," and 37 did not vote.[11]

The decentralizing trend that began with the Cannon revolt was interrupted by one significant attempt to reconcentrate legislative power in the majority party leadership. The 1924 election returned thirteen Republican congressmen who had bolted their party in order to support the Progressive presidential candidacy of Senator Robert LaFollette of Wisconsin. At the beginning of the 69th Congress (1925–27), these members were denied invitations to join the Republican caucus and were ultimately stripped of their accrued seniority within the committee system. In addition to this punishment for party disloyalty, the Republican leadership generally restructured the membership of the most important legislative panels and, in conjunction with this reduction in committee autonomy, sought to replace the comparatively liberal discharge rule used in the previous Congress. While the new discharge rule still hypothetically permitted the House to bring a bill to the floor against the wishes of a committee membership, in practice the Republican leadership proposal was so complex and hedged in with restrictive contingencies that successful utilization was extremely unlikely. As one contemporary Democrat, Charles Crisp of Georgia, described the new procedure, "they have proposed a rule which hermetically seals the door against any bill ever coming out of a committee when the Steering Committee or the majority leaders desire to kill the bill." [12] In order to encourage majority party loyalty on the adoption of the new rule, the Republican leadership help up committee assignments until after the roll call had been taken. Despite this implicit leadership threat, twenty-two Republicans opposed their party on the vote (table 7.6). [13] This contest marked a deviant period in the consolidation of committee autonomy and dominance over the legislative process after the Cannon Revolt. While a vote in support of a liberal discharge rule in 1925 was a vote against a strong party leadership, subsequent attempts to assert floor control over the committee system favored leadership influence within the House.* Once the growth of seniority norms reduced the ability of the party leadership to directly affect committee decision-making, a reassertion of authority by the parent chamber became the most appealing method of ensuring party influence over recalcitrant legislative panels.

The first major reassertion of House authority occurred in 1949 when the chamber adopted a "twenty-one day rule" for special orders held up by the Committee on Rules. The rule allowed the chairman of a legislative committee to bypass the Rules Committee and bring a special order to the floor if Rules acted unfavorably or refused to act on the order within twenty-one days of its introduction. Since a special order was almost always necessary for floor consideration of controversial legislation, the 1949 rule both reduced the possible roadblocks that could be placed in the way of important administration measures and dramatically narrowed the legislative prominence of the Rules Committee. In 1951, the House of Representatives again considered the twenty-one day rule, and the Democratic leadership, through Adolph Sabath of Chicago, again argued that the party possessed "only a paper majority" because three members from Georgia, Mississippi, and Virginia preferred to form an "unholy alliance" with the Republican side of the committee. On this

---

*The roll call on the 1925 discharge rule was one of the ten high-stress, closely contested votes recorded during the 69th Congress (1925–27).

vote (included in table 7.6), the House repealed the twenty-one day rule and thus restored the autonomy of the Rules Committee. Eighty-nine Democrats and 158 Republicans supported repeal and 141 Democrats and 37 Republicans backed the twenty-one day provision.

The Rules Committee retained its dominant place in the committee system until the beginning of the 87th Congress (1961–62), when Speaker Sam Rayburn of Texas led a drive to enlarge the membership. The proposal backed by Rayburn and the in-coming Kennedy administration added two party loyalists to the Democratic side and one Republican. As a result of the expansion, the leadership hoped to enjoy a dependable eight-to-seven vote margin on most legislation. One hundred and ninety-five Democrats and 22 Republicans supported the expansion; 64 Democrats and 148 Republicans opposed it. As George Galloway noted, "The split in the Democratic vote on enlarging the Rules Committee presumably indicates why the Democratic caucus could not be effective in the preceding two decades, especially when dissident members held most of the committee chairmanships."[14] Rayburn's strong backing for the expansion and the ascent of fellow Texan Lyndon Johnson into the vice-presidency drew the crucial support of the Texas contingent in the House. Without their votes, the proposal, which was adopted narrowly (217-212), would have failed.[15]

Following the northern Democratic gains in the House which accompanied the 1964 Goldwater debacle, the majority party leadership again proposed and won adoption of a twenty-one day rule for special orders held up by the Committee on Rules. The provision was used eight times during the 89th Congress (1965–66) before it was repealed in 1967. The twenty-one day rule has not been a part of House procedure since that time.

In the first three of these six precedents in the institutional development of the House, the Republicans were in the majority; in the most recent votes, the Democrats have organized the House. Before analyzing the roll calls, it should be noted that on all six the majority party leadership supported a position which expanded their own influence within the institution. For that reason and because procedural rules play an important role in maintaining party unity and party-centered coalition building, clashes over parliamentary procedure are usually among the most strongly partisan questions to come before the House.* Even so, these six contests reveal a fairly consistent sectional pattern. In four cases (1890, 1910, 1925, and 1965), the industrial core supported a centralization of legislative power in the hands of the majority party leadership while the agrarian periphery backed fragmentation on the floor or within the committee system. During the "classic" period of committee system dominance and the bipolar Democratic coalition, the most important procedural questions produced a less polarized regional pattern (1951 and

---

*Currently, there exist only two preconditions for membership in the Democratic caucus: party loyalty on the election of a Speaker and on the adoption of the rules of the House.

1961). Also, under the bipolar Democratic reign, the level of sectional stress has declined—a partial, though less dramatic, reflection of the declining polarization of the national party system (see chapter 8).

The overall core preference for centralized legislative power is reflected within the membership voting patterns of both parties (see table 7.6).* In four of the twelve cases, all members of a party voted the same way and no sectional differences were noted. But in eight cases, party members of trade area delegations located within the manufacturing belt exhibited greater support for centralization. Beginning in 1951, the differences for the Democratic party have been particularly striking. The broad tendency for core congressmen to back centralizing procedures seems to be connected to a greater preference for a stronger national state. Since this preference and its roots have been extensively treated in earlier chapters, it will only be noted here that the administrative apparatus of a centralized state can only be as effective as the political institutions upon which it rests.

A second observation, to which we shall return, is that the original developments in the rise of the committee system came about as a result of a sectional split in the Republican (not the Democratic) party. The middle-western insurgents who broke with their party's leadership in 1910 and 1925 demonstrated their belief that the military pension–protectionist tariff logroll had become irrelevant to agrarian imperatives within the political economy. By 1951 these dissident members of the Republican periphery and deviant southern representatives in the Democratic party made common cause in support for an autonomous Committee on Rules. By 1965 the intensification of another sectional division within the Democratic party was rapidly maturing into a broad, core-led institutional assault on the entire length and breadth of the committee system.

The Historical Development of a Strong Committee System

The strength of the committee system in its relations with the House floor can be defined as the extent of each constituent committee's control over the policy decisions which lay within its jurisdiction. Each committee's degree of policy control is a combination of negative and positive legislative discretion (respectively, the power to block action and the power to enact legislation unaltered by hostile amendments).† Committee integrity depends on the existence of floor reciprocity between the membership of the various committees—a strong propensity to accept and support the policy decisions of committee majorities as the decision of the House itself. The incentives which underlie

---

*For simplicity, the nation has been divided into two exclusive categories, inside and outside the manufacturing belt as it was defined in chapter 5.

†The imposition of the twenty-one day rule, for example, was an attack on the negative discretionary prerogatives of the Rules Committee.

this supportive floor behavior primarily depend on five institutional and membership characteristics: 1) a career orientation toward service in the House of Representatives; 2) firm jurisdictional boundaries and the exclusive referral of each species of legislation to just one committee; 3) freedom of choice by individual members in the awarding of committee assignments; 4) strict limitations on the number and type of multiple committee assignments distributed to the membership; and 5) a strong seniority system separate from other career ladders (e.g., the party leadership). Taken together, these characteristics or conditions channel the legislative energy of congressmen away from the floor into committee chambers.

From 1881 to about 1965 each of these characteristics of the membership and institutional structure grew in strength, encouraging the development of a strong committee system in the House of Representatives (and in the Senate) and a steadily growing decentralization of legislative power. These trends were largely the outcome of unplanned but self-reinforcing exogenous political developments (e.g., longer congressional careers and agrarian and progressive insurgency within the Republican party) and institutional feedback into the electoral arena (e.g., the institutionalization of the bipolar Democratic coalition and the nationalization of party competition). However, before these developments and the contemporary decline of the committee system are examined, the evolution and role of each of the five characteristics should be reviewed.[16]

Career Orientation

Over the last one hundred years, the career orientation of the average member of the House of Representatives has undergone a dramatic transformation (see figures 7.1 and 7.2). In the late decades of the nineteenth century, about 40 percent of the members had no prior experience in the House when they took the oath of office following their election. The highest percentage of first-term members was reached in 1883, when over half (51.5 percent) of the House were sworn in for the first time. With a few exceptions—most notably the electorally turbulent progressive and New Deal periods—the proportion of first-term members steadily declined until the late 1960s. In 1969, less than one-twelfth (8.3 percent) of all members possessed no prior service in the institution. During the last century the proportion of members who have viewed the House as a temporary stage in the development of their private legal practice or business interests has steadily dropped, and the amateur, part-time politician of the last century has been replaced by a full-time professional. The coincident increase in the average length of prior service has been even more steady and equally dramatic. Before 1890, the typical member had served less than three years in the House when he was sworn into a new Congress. By the late 1960s and early seventies, the average congressmen had served over nine years. At the high point in 1971, the typical representative

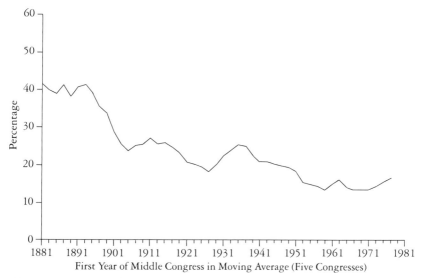

Figure 7.1. Percentage of First-Term Members in the House of Representatives, 1881–1977

SOURCES: Before 1965, adapted from data in Nelson W. Polsby, "The Institutionalization of the U.S. House of Representatives," *American Political Science Review* 62:1 (March 1968); after 1965, compiled from the respective editions of the *Congressional Directory*.

NOTE: In this figure and figures 7.2, 7.6, and 7.8, each point represents the average for five consecutive Congresses. In each case, the average is assigned to the middle year of the decade covered by the five Congresses.

carried nearly a decade of legislative experience (4.92 terms) into the new session, over four times the experience of an average member in 1883 (1.22 terms).

The increasing length of prior service and decreasing percentage of freshman members marked a growing inclination by congressmen to pursue a career within the House to the exclusion of other possible occupational paths. This career orientation within the institution has been important to the development of a strong committee system for several reasons. Most important, the incentives underlying floor reciprocity depend on the pursuit of electoral resources within the committee system. This electoral drive, the desire to produce tangible benefits for the member's district in order to secure reelection, depends upon the reelection proclivities of the member. The structured incentives which support reciprocity, such as targeted committee jurisdictions and seniority rules, are irrelevant or imperfectly related to the more diffuse interests of incumbents who do not intend to run again. Not only is the legislative horizon narrowed dramatically by a decision to retire (which, for example, prevents the trading of votes or influence between Congresses), but most other

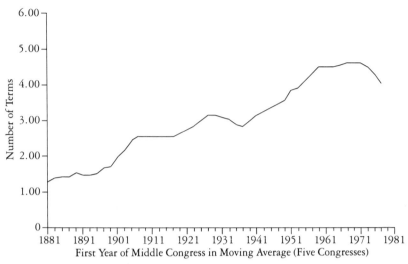

Figure 7.2. Prior Service of Members of the House of Representatives, 1881–1977
SOURCES: Before 1965, adapted from data in Nelson W. Polsby, "The Institutionalization of the U.S. House of Representatives," *American Political Science Review* 62:1 (March 1968); after 1965, compiled from the respective editions of the *Congressional Directory*.

legislative goals (e.g., those stemming from altruism, desire for a place in history, and financial gain) cannot replace the narrow and concrete goals of the electoral drive.[17]

A widely held career orientation also reinforces the role of the seniority system by making committee seniority ladders much steeper than otherwise would be the case, and by making the seniority rules themselves relevant to the electoral drive of the membership. A widely held career orientation lengthens the average period of service in the House. Longer service, in turn, increases the seniority distinctions between adjacent ranks on a committee ladder by raising the average number of terms needed to attain a commitee chairmanship. Both the steeper seniority ladder and the greater prior service for chairmanships are the result of a reduction in the amount of membership turnover on a typical committee. Both effects reduce the significance and frequency of the initial assignment decision controlled by the individual member's party by reducing the number of vacancies to be filled at the base of the committee seniority ladder. Thus, they reduce partisan influence over the committee system. In addition, steeper seniority ladders increase the effectiveness of institutional "socialization" into the norms of legislative behavior.[18]

Under a widely held career orientation, the seniority system abets the reelection designs of congressmen by providing every incumbent with an automatic electoral advantage and by setting several consecutive terms as a necessary condition for significant influence within the House. The seniority system provides all incumbents with a seniority advantage over all challengers, and thus, other things being equal, incumbents are automatically more desirable as candidates. This advantage clearly increases with the service gradient of seniority ladders, which raises the political cost—in terms of lost legislative influence—of replacing an incumbent. This built-in seniority advantage over challengers is the most efficient allocation of an electoral resource to incumbents ever developed and accrues to all members regardless of party and irrespective of meritorious behavior. Finally, by setting several consecutive terms as a precondition for legislative influence, the seniority system discourages those potential candidates who do not intend to pursue a legislative career. Thus, not only does the seniority system reward all incumbents who run again, but it also tends to screen out those challengers who seek only a two- or four-year stint.

Targeted and Exclusive Committee Jurisdictions

One of the most important institutional features supporting a strong committee system is the close connection between the design of committee jurisdictions and the long-term electoral needs of the membership. As was illustrated in the analysis of AFDC dependency and labor campaign contributions, committee jurisdictions divide up the national political economy into collections of federal policies which often coincide with collections of geographically concentrated, overlapping constituency interests. Each jurisdiction is uniquely "targeted" in that it is most relevant to the constituent interests of a more or less well-defined subset of the entire membership (e.g., the subcommittee on the Merchant Marine to major port districts). Thus, "targeted" committee jurisdictions encourage committee reciprocity on the floor by capitalizing upon the diversity of regional interests. When combined with freedom of choice in assignments, targeted jurisdictions promote a decentralization of legislative influence toward individual committees composed of electorally self-interested members.

To assure that this legislative decentralization is compatible with the seniority system and a long-term career orientation, jurisdictional boundaries must be both firm and exclusive. If a member is to commit his political future to service on a particular committee, he must know what parts of the political economy are covered by its jurisdiction both in the next two years and in the far future. A reliance on referral precedents satisfies both conditions. If bill referrals are used to establish precedents interpreting the clauses of a formal jurisdiction, clearly defined jurisdictional boundaries come to depend on a consistent procedural history which, in practice, also guarantees a stable allocation of policies over time. When the formal jurisdiction is disturbed, the supporting role of referral precedents is damaged because the written rules upon which they were based has changed. In addition, members initially attracted to a committee assignment because of the policies under its control are left stranded in posts that have, because of the realignment of jurisdictional boundaries, become less relevant to their electoral interests. The steeper the service gradient on committee ladders, the more costly becomes an attempt by a senior member to follow a wandering jurisdiction through committee reassignment.* Thus, stable and well-defined jurisdictions are necessary conditions for a strong committee system.

Furthermore, committee jurisdictions should be exclusive; no two committees should share competing claims on any area of legislation. This condition ensures that every committee will constitute a necessary stage in the consideration of all policy decisions falling under its jurisdiction and that the majority party leadership, through the Speaker's referral power, cannot play one legislative panel off against another.[19] The only reform of the committee system which has satisfied all three conditions was the 1946 Reorganization (see below). Not surprisingly, the classic phase of committee prerogatives and legislative decentralization ensued in the 1947–65 period.

Freedom of Choice in Committee Assignments

Freedom of choice in committee assignments or a pattern approaching that ideal effectively guarantees that no committee assignment becomes so attractive that reciprocity in floor deliberations is not extended to that committee by other members. If the electoral resources to be gained through committee membership in a decentralized legislature did not outweigh those to be gained through a violation of reciprocal norms on the floor, one of the most important supports for a strong committee system would be lost. By maintaining self-selection as the dominant mode in the assignment process, the majority party leadership has ensured a relative equality in electoral importance between service on the various committees, and thus encouraged reciprocity.

Perhaps the most important single consideration in the maintenance of a self-selecting assignment process is the concept of well-ordered choices. During the 1949–79 period (which overlaps most of the "classic" era of committee system dominance), the majority party leadership regularly manipulated the assignment options available to congressmen in order to preserve freedom of choice in the face of changing demand for specific committee posts.† In order

---

*Since any transfer involving electorally significant jurisdiction (policies which had originally attracted members to the committee) would take away control of these policies from previously interested members, the first result of a transfer is a decrease in the correspondence between jurisdictional definitions and the electoral needs of individual members.

†The following discussion assumes that the majority party leadership pursues two main goals: the retention of the support of their party colleagues (i.e., reelection as Speaker or Majority Leader), and the retention of their party's majority status in the House. For more on this topic, see Robert L. Peabody, *Leadership in Congress* (Boston: Little, Brown, 1976). These goals are directly related. The majority party leadership, by abetting the reelection designs of incum-

to manipulate assignment options, the leadership regularly altered three committee characteristics: the jurisdictional definition, the number of members, and the opportunities for outside, additional assignments. For example, if the demand for assignment to committee X increased beyond the number of available vacancies, the attractiveness of committee X could be manipulated by removing to another committee a portion of the jurisdiction (thus decreasing demand), by increasing the number of members (thus increasing availability and decreasing demand), and/or by restricting the allowable choices for dual assignment (thus decreasing demand). Any or all of these measures could be taken in order to match assignment availability with demand. In practice, however, characteristics inherent in the nature of committee jurisdictions forced reliance on the manipulation of the latter two characteristics.

Limitations on Multiple Committee Assignments

Three main periods between 1949 and 1979 can be identified in the evolution of committee assignment options (see table 7.7). All committees which either were created by or survived the 1946 Reorganization (first implemented in 1947) have been divided into four groups. During the first post-Reorganization period, all members of the committees contained in Group I were eligible for cross-assignments either within Group I or across one of the three other groups (e.g., a member of the House Administration Committee could also be appointed to either Government Operations, Interior, Agriculture, or Rules). All other combinations (such as a Post Office and Armed Services assignment set) were prohibited. The first period lasted from 1949 through 1952.*

In the second period, lasting from 1953 through 1968, cross-assignments between Groups I, II, and III were permitted as well as within Groups I and II. During this period, the Committee on Science and Astronautics was created. From its inception in 1958 until 1971, this committee was included in Group III (all dual assignments on the committee included committees in either Group I or II). Following the start of the 92nd Congress, however, the committee was demoted to Group II, and dual assignments with Group III committees were allowed. Immediately, ten members (58.8 percent) of the majority party opted for those pairs. This change is the only such demotion or promotion between groups during the 1949–79 era.

The third post-Reorganization period is now in progress. Since 1969, triple assignment sets have appeared, Group IV committee members have begun to receive cross-assignments, and the creation of three new standing

---

bent members, retain the support of party colleagues and increase the probability of retaining majority party status.

*This study relies throughout on Democratic party assignments. Since, under any theory of leadership strategy, majority status is a necessary condition for the manipulation of House rules, this study restricts the analysis to periods when the Democratic party was in the majority. Consequently, the analysis begins with 1949 (instead of 1947).

Table 7.7. Growth of Committee Assignments, 1949–1979

Committee	Number of Democratic Members		Number of Exclusive Assignments	
	1949	1979	1949	1979
Group I:				
District of Columbia	15	8	0	0
Government Operations	17	25	10	0
House Administration	15	16	7	0
Internal Security[a]	5	–	0	–
	52	49	17	0
	Change: −5.8 percent		(32.7)[b]	(0)
Group II:				
Interior	15	26	13	0
Merchant Marine	15	25	13	0
Post Office	15	13	13	0
Veterans Affairs	17	19	13	0
	62	83	52	0
	Change: +33.9 percent		(83.9)	(0)
Group III:				
Agriculture	17	27	12	2
Armed Services	19	28	19	7
Banking	16	27	15	4
Education and Labor	16	23	14	3
Foreign Affairs	14	22	13	2
Commerce	17	27	13	2
Judiciary	17	20	16	1
Public Works	16	30	11	3
	132	204	113	24
	Change: +54.5 percent		(85.6)	(11.8)
Group IV:				
Appropriations	27	36	27	28
Rules	8	11	6	10
Ways and Means	15	24	15	18
	50	71	48	56
	Change: +42.0 percent		(96.0)	(78.9)

[a] The Committee on Internal Security (formerly Un-American Activities) was abolished in 1975.

[b] Parenthesized figures are the percentages of members within each group holding exclusive assignments.

SOURCE: Assignments from *1949 Congressional Directory* and *Congressional Quarterly Weekly Report* (April 14, 1979).

committees (Budget, Small Business, and Standards of Official Conduct) has accompanied a rapid degeneration in the previous assignment system. As of 1979, for example, the Democratic membership of the Appropriations Committee held a total of eight cross-assignments (three on the Committee on the Budget, three on Small Business, and two on Standards of Official Conduct).

Table 7.8. Cross-Assignments Allowed During Each Post-Reorganization Period

First Period 1949–52	Second Period 1953–68	Third Period 1969–79[a]
I and I	I and I	I and I
I and II	I and II	I and II
I and III	I and III	I and III
I and IV	I and IV	I and IV
	II and II	II and II
	II and III	II and III
		III and III
		III and IV

[a] In addition to the combinations listed, triple assignment sets began to appear in the third period.

During each of these periods the Democratic party followed a distinct assignment system (see table 7.8). In each system, a maximum set of cross-assignment options was established and, while not all members received the maximum allowable number and type of cross-assignments, no members received cross-assignments which exceeded these options.

Within each period, the number of cross-assignments increased until nearly all the additional options that had been created at the beginning of the period were taken up. At that point (1953 and 1969), a new assignment system was created which expanded both the number and type of permissible cross-assignment options. Table 7.9 describes this steady expansion in cross-assignment options and the number of members holding cross-assignments within each period.

As a result of this evolution in assignment systems, the number and percentage of Democratic members receiving exclusive assignments steadily decreased (see table 7.10). During the first two periods, the expansion in the number of cross-assignments was largely confined to an improvement in the number and type of cross-assignments available to members of Group I and II committees. These cross-assignments were compensation or an equalizer for service on the less attractive committees that make up those groups.*

While the primary impetus behind the first transformation (between the first and second assignment systems) seems to have been the persistent inability of the committees in Groups I and II to attract new members, the second transformation (between the second and third systems) seems to have

---

*During most of the post-reorganization period, Group I and II committees were referred to as "non-exclusive," Group III as "semi-exclusive," and Group IV as "exclusive." In general, most rankings of committee attractiveness have paralleled these divisions. For example, see George Goodwin, Jr., *The Little Legislatures* (Amherst: University of Massachusetts Press, 1970).

Table 7.9. Cross-Assignment Patterns by Group, 1949–1979

Year	Number of Members	Percentage of Exclusive Assignments	Percentage of Cross-Assignments With:			
			I	II	III	IV
			Group I			
1949[a]	55	40.0	3.6	18.2	34.5	3.6
1955	50	6.0	2.0	28.0	62.0	2.0
1961	54	5.6	1.9	14.8	74.1	1.9
1967	53	7.5	1.9	3.8	77.4	1.9
1973	56	0.0	0.0	0.0	94.6	1.8
1979	49	0.0	8.2	6.1	91.8	2.0
			Group II			
1949	62	83.9	16.1	0.0	0.0	0.0
1955	59	30.5	23.7	20.3	25.4	0.0
1961	66	31.8	12.1	12.1	31.8	0.0
1967	67	16.4	3.0	11.9	59.7	0.0
1973	73	2.7	0.0	4.1	89.0	0.0
1979	83	0.0	3.6	2.4	98.8	0.0
			Group III			
1949	132	85.6	14.4	0.0	0.0	0.0
1955	154	70.1	20.1	9.7	0.0	0.0
1961	160	61.9	25.0	13.1	0.0	0.0
1967	160	49.4	25.6	25.0	0.0	0.0
1973	177	23.7	29.9	36.7	0.0	1.1
1979	204	11.8	21.6	40.2	4.9	.5

[a] Cross-assignments with standing committees created since 1947 (Budget, Science and Technology, Small Business, and Standards of Official Conduct) are not included in any group but lower the percentage of members holding exclusive assignments. Where members hold more than two assignments, each assignment is treated individually. For these reasons, horizontal totals after 1955 may be either above or below one hundred percent.

resulted from the creation of three new standing committees since 1967.* These three committees (Budget, Small Business, and Standards of Official Conduct) broke down the second assignment system by becoming an important source of triple assignments (providing the first examples of such options) and cross-assignments with previously exclusive Group IV committees. These precedents were made in part as a temporary accommodation for senior members who had held positions on the former Select Committee on Small Business and as measures to increase the influence and success of the other two committees. However, they have rapidly come to be applied to other committees that

*As mentioned before, the Committee on Science and Technology (formerly Science and Astronautics) was merged into the second assignment system as a Group III committee. Since members who possessed cross-assignments before the committee was created were forced to resign from one of their former positions before taking an assignment on Science and Astronautics, the committee did not destabilize the prevailing assignment system.

Table 7.10. Number of Exclusive and Cross-Assignments among Democratic Congressmen, 1949–1979

Congress	No. of Members	Exclusive Assignments	Dual Assignments	Triple Assignments	Percentage of Democrats Holding Exclusive Assignments
81st	263	230	33	0	87.5
82nd	233	183	50	0	78.5
84th	231	157	74	0	68.0
85th	232	155	77	0	66.8
86th	279	195	84	0	69.9
87th	258	170	88	0	65.9
88th	258	163	95	0	63.2
89th	296	185	111	0	62.5
90th	246	143	103	0	58.1
91st	241	124	114	3	51.5
92nd	254	112	140	2	44.1
93rd	241	97	142	2	40.2
94th	288	87	189	12	30.2
95th	288	82	184	22	28.5
96th	275	81	182	12	29.5

are rapidly declining in prestige and attractiveness (Foreign Affairs and Judiciary are perhaps the most important examples).

Exclusive committee assignments promote a strong committee system in several ways. On the one hand, exclusive assignment options present very well-ordered choices to the membership and thus figure strongly in perceptions of relative "equality" between competing opportunities. Given the experience of the last three decades, any other assignment pattern would appear to be unstable and tend to aggravate expansionary pressures.*

On the other hand, exclusive assignments encourage a clear identification of particular members with specific committees and prevent members only marginally interested in a specific jurisdiction from seeking assignment.

*The most immediate reason for this expansionary tendency is the "automatic" reassignment portion of the seniority rules. Once a committee has been expanded or a dual assignment allowed, those alterations become permanent additions to the choice sets available; because reelected members continue, in the future, to hold such assignments, such choice sets become the minimum expectation for future members of that committee. Because these alterations are nearly always irrevocable, the manipulation of committee characteristics through time can be generalized as a gradual and continual expansion in the number and type of permissible cross-assignments. This expansion is accompanied by an increase in the size of certain committees (a necessary condition for an increase in cross-assignments). Thus, the corrective manipulation when a committee is too attractive is an increase in the size of that committee (diluting the average member's influence and increasing availability). On the other hand, when a committee is not attractive enough, the set of committees on which cross-assignment is allowed is expanded and the size of the committee is either held constant or contracted slightly through attrition.

With dual or even triple assignment patterns, members find it increasingly difficult to hold a particular committee responsible for the failure of some of its members to reciprocate on the floor. The unarticulated perceptions upon which committee reciprocity ultimately depends become hopelessly confused by the intricate net of cross-assignments between almost all possible combinations of committees. Furthermore, an overall expansion in the average size of committees (which accompanies an increase in the proportion of dual or triple assignments) implies that increasingly marginal members have successfully sought assignments. For example, it is not surprising that an Agriculture Committee with seventeen Democratic members in 1947 contained proportionally more members from predominantly rural and cash-crop dependent districts than the same panel with twenty-seven members in 1979.* Similarly, over the same period the Education and Labor Committee became less oriented toward organized labor and the Banking panel's urban tilt moderated. Since these new and marginal members have a smaller stake in the integrity of their committee's decisions (because they have other assignments, and their own districts' interests are less relevant to the committee's jurisdiction), it should be expected that committee reciprocity on the floor would suffer as a result of assignment inflation. That, indeed, has been the result.

The most important single achievement of the 1946 Reorganization was that it imposed exclusive assignment options on a committee system that suffered through nearly half a century of multiple panel membership (see figure 7.3). In 1945, just before Reorganization, the average number of assignments held by a member was 2.17; in 1947, the typical congressmen held but one position (an average of 1.11 assignments). Since then the increasing number of dual assignments, as described above, has again raised the number of posts to about 1.74 (the average of the last four Congresses).[20] This contemporary trend weakens one of the supporting legs of a strong committee system and, thus, the institutional structure that has made an enduring, bipolar coalition within the Democratic party possible.

The Seniority System

The seniority system is a set of behavioral norms that have determined the ranking of party members within each committee (see table 7.11). The criteria upon which the system is based are predictable, objectively determined characteristics of congressmen and their service in the House. Seniority rankings are predictable in that length of service is a relative, not an absolute, property. The relative position of any two members on a committee, for example, is completely predictable over time. If they both remain on the committee and do not change parties, their relative position on the panel will remain un-

---

*This observation holds true even if allowance is made for urbanization, reapportionment decisions, and changes in the political complexion of the party.

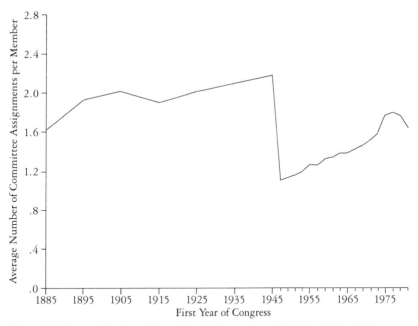

Figure 7.3. Average Number of Committee Assignments per Member, 1885–1981
SOURCE: Compiled from data in the respective editions of the *Congressional Directory*. Before 1945, averages are calculated for every fifth Congress; after 1945, every Congress has been included.

Table 7.11. The Four Basic Rules of Seniority

Rule I: Of any two members on any committee, the member with the greater length of continuous service on that committee has the greater seniority.

Rule II: Of any two members with equal continuous committee service, the member with the greater length of "floor" or "full-house" continuous service has the greater seniority.

Rule III: Of any two members with equal continuous committee service and equal continuous floor service, the member with prior discontinuous floor service has the greater seniority.

Rule IV: If a returning member so wishes, he will be reassigned to the committee posts he held during the last Congress.

SOURCE: Bensel, "Reciprocal Behavior and the Rules of House of Representatives."

changed. While no member can anticipate all the retirements, electoral defeats, deaths, or off-committee transfers of members senior to himself, the effect of these events on his own rise within the committee can be exactly calculated. This feature of the seniority system, more than any other single factor, has been responsible for the secular increase in the career orientation of House members.

Seniority rankings are objectively determined in that all the data necessary to calculate rankings are available in the *Congressional Record* or *House Journal* as information on the oath of office when a member is sworn in and when he is first elected to his current committee assignments.* The significance of this objectivity is that it has effectively ruled out political control over committee rankings and thus placed a major obstacle in the way of efforts to impose programmatic or party loyalty. This feature of the seniority system bears major responsibility for the maintenance of a bipolar coalition within the Democratic party.

The political roots of the seniority system lie in the persistent inability of congressional parties to encompass sectional competition during two periods in American history: the middle-western agrarian insurgency within the Republican party at the beginning of the twentiety century, and the rise of lower-class, labor interests within the Bourbon-dominated Democratic party during the New Deal period (see figure 7.4). Both movements produced a drastic weakening of the respective party caucuses, a decline in the influence of the Speaker and other party leaders, and an overall deterioration in party unity and programmatic loyalty.

By the time World War II had begun, the seniority system was self-maintaining (see figure 7.5). In combination with the autonomous committee system which it helped to produce, the reliance on seniority norms had promoted both the electoral security of congressmen and the detachment of the membership base of congressional parties from the fundamental, bipolar sectional alignment in American politics (see chapter 8). The two developments helped to produce a bipolar Democratic coalition in which the center of political gravity slowly shifted toward the industrial core. They also increased cross-party cooperation—particularly between the southern wing of the Democratic party and the main body of "regular" Republicans outside the Northeast.

At the peak of the seniority system between 1939 and 1973, the most senior member always either retained or was promoted to the highest rank on

*Seniority is universally exemplified in that all members possess the characteristics upon which it is based. While freshmen members are often tied on length of service because they have been elected to the House for the first time and their first seniority ranks are usually determined by some arbitrary means (e.g., by lot), seniority becomes increasingly effective in distinguishing the surviving members as each membership class ages. By the time the members of a class are in line for a chairmanship, they are usually separated from the next highest rung by two or more terms. See Barbara Hinckley, *The Seniority System in Congress* (Bloomington: Indiana University Press, 1971).

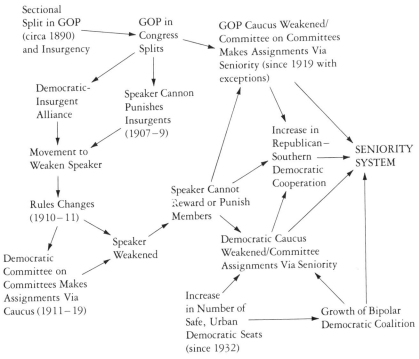

Figure 7.4. Political Roots of the Seniority System, 1880–1965

SOURCE: Adapted, with numerous changes and omissions, from Nelson Polsby, Miriam Gallagher, and Barry Rundquist, "The Growth of the Seniority System in the U.S. House of Representatives," *American Political Science Review* (September 1969).

the Democratic party list for the ten important committees in the House (figure 7.6). By confining the analysis to the most important committees, most situations in which members were forced to choose between two or more chairmanships (for which they were equally eligible) are ruled out of the analysis and the influence of differences between the pre- and post-1946 Reorganization committee systems is minimized.* On the average, about two-thirds of

---

*These committees were selected because a majority of their members held no outside assignment in the 79th Congress—just before the 1946 Reorganization. Historically, exclusive assignment has been a distinguishing characteristic of the most important panels. The eleven committees were: Ways and Means (95.8 percent of the members held no other assignments), Appropriations (92.9 percent), Foreign Affairs (88.0 percent), Agriculture (82.8 percent), Banking and Currency (77.8 percent), Military Affairs (81.5 percent), Naval Affairs (76.9 percent), Interstate and Foreign Commerce (67.9 percent), Judiciary (64.1 percent), Rules (58.3 percent), and Post Office (56.0 percent). After 1946, the Military Affairs and Naval Affairs committees were combined into one panel (Armed Services). Thus, the data in figure 7.6

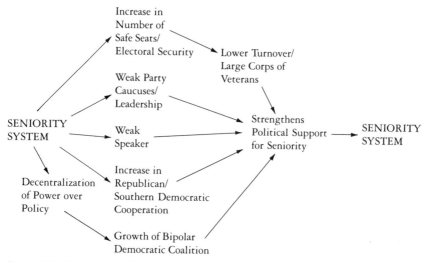

Figure 7.5. How Seniority Was Maintained

SOURCE: Adapted, with numerous changes and omissions, from Nelson Polsby, Miriam Gallagher, and Barry Rundquist, "The Growth of the Seniority System in the U.S. House of Representatives," *American Political Science Review* (September 1969).

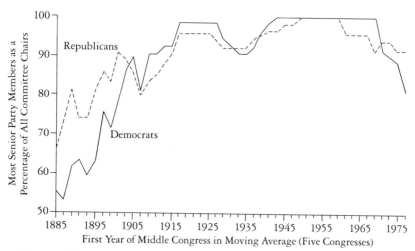

Figure 7.6. Retention or Promotion of Most Senior Member to Highest Rank on Committee Party List, 1885–1977

SOURCE: Compiled from data in the respective editions of the *Congressional Directory*.

the entire House membership held an assignment to one of these committees (67 percent in 1945); the trend lines in figure 7.6 indicate the extent to which a single seniority ladder was the only route to influence within the chamber for these members. By 1939, even the recruitment of members into the Democratic floor leadership—a potential source of distraction from a single-minded pursuit of electoral resources within committee chambers—had become separated from the committee system. During the ensuing "classic" period of committee dominance, most legislative careers were played out within the four walls of but one committee. One of the most important supporting events during the rise of the exclusive committee career was the 1946 reformulation of the committee system.

The 1946 Legislative Reorganization

The 1946 Legislative Reorganization streamlined and modernized the pre-1947 committee system. This modernization, which reduced the number of standing committees from forty-eight to nineteen in the House, was, in the words of George Galloway, the "keystone in the arch of Congressional 're-form.'"* Measured by the sheer number of changes that it made in the committee system, the 1946 Reorganization was the most sweeping reform of the

---

are based on eleven committees before 1947 and ten afterwards. For a discussion of some of the problems of incomparability and of determining member or leadership motivations, see Nelson Polsby, Miriam Gallagher, and Barry Rundquist, "The Growth of the Seniority System in the U.S. House of Representatives," *American Political Science Review* 63:3 (September 1969). The most senior member might not hold the highest rank on one of these committees for one of four reasons: the member might have requested a transfer to another committee (and properly, under the rules, been placed at the foot of the party list), the leadership of his party might have denied him his post for disciplinary reasons, the member might have chosen another chairmanship instead, or the member might have been promoted into the leadership of his party. The first reason probably explains no deviation from seniority norms over the last century for the ten most important committees. Punishment by the leadership was the most common reason for deviations prior to 1915. Competing eligibility for chairmanships explains relatively few deviations, and those few appear after 1975. For example, the declining relative importance of the Post Office and Civil Service Committee led to Representative Morris Udall's rejection of that chairmanship in favor of the Interior and Insular Affairs Committee chair in three successive Congresses beginning in 1977. Between 1915 and 1975 the most common source of deviations was promotion into the party leadership.

*George B. Galloway, *History of the House of Representatives* (New York: Thomas Y. Crowell, 1961). See also Richard Bolling, *House Out of Order* (New York: E. P. Dutton, 1965). Bolling, unlike Galloway, maintained that the 1946 Reorganization did not really "reform" the House because of the "mistaken notion of its supporters that institutional change can be achieved by altering the outward form of the Congress while leaving untouched the substance of the internal 'power structure.'" In *Power in the House* (New York: E. P. Dutton, 1968), Bolling again criticized the reorganization, claiming that "the act touched nothing" because, "if it had done more, it would have trod on the toes of the members of the power structure of the Democratic party."

legislative process in the House of Representatives to occur in the twentieth century. Though the Reorganization expanded congressional staffs, raised members' salaries, and eliminated certain categories of legislation, its most important and difficult changes dealt with the rearrangement of committee jurisdictions and the overall reduction in the number of committees.

However, the 1946 Reorganization was extremely conservative in at least two respects. First, the main thrust of the reform was to strengthen the committee system *vis-à-vis* the floor and the executive branch. By bolstering the resources available to standing committees (e.g., staff and research) and reducing the fragmentation in the pre-1947 system, the reorganization reinforced the dominant role of committees in the Congress. Second, the implementation of the act in 1947 disturbed little of the prevailing distribution of power. Preservation of the two most prominent features of the committee system, seniority and jurisdictions, determined to a large extent the shape of the reorganization and the method chosen to implement it.

The rule changes that took effect in 1947 altered three characteristics of the committee system: jurisdictional definitions, the size of committee memberships, and outside assignment options (membership on more than one committee). In implementing these changes, seniority comparisons were used to allocate assignments on the new committees and arbitrate competing claims where they arose. The nearly complete dependence on seniority for determining the assignments of the continuing membership significantly reduced the uncertainty and potential for disruption that otherwise would have attended the reform. The changes in committee jurisdictions were also carried out in a way that preserved the viability of precedents that had been created under the old system.*

In 1947, the Democratic party created a system which, to a large extent, allowed members to select their new assignment and yet maintain seniority ranks on the new committees. In order to provide continuity in membership assignments (and thus reduce opposition to the reorganization), committee seniority was made transferable from a committee of the pre-1947 system to the corresponding jurisdiction of the merged post-1946 system. The details of the merger were explicitly covered in the standing rules of the 80th Congress and, thus, indicated to which committees a member could, if he chose, transfer seniority. The system of rules governing the allocation of assignments combined committee seniority, automatic eligibility on merged committees, a "trickle-down" method of recording choices (with the most senior members

---

*Committee referral precedents were conserved during the reorganization by combining entire jurisdictions together in order to form new committees (rather than carrying out a piece-meal rearrangement of jurisdictions). For more, see Rule X (1) of the *Rules of the House of Representatives*, 80:1. Each of the jurisdictional definitions under this rule was followed by an interpretive paragraph which listed the names of the merged committees and referred to the major precedents that had gathered under each of these names. See also *Congressional Record*, 79:2:10057, July 25, 1946.

making their choices first), and certain auxiliary rules which protected the rank of members on pre-1947 exclusive committees.*

The primary purpose of the 1946 Reorganization was to strengthen Congress by strengthening the committee system. In the House of Representatives, the reform won approval largely because it left intact the integrity of committee jurisdictions and protected the seniority of the senior membership. Thus, the 1946 Reorganization was both a massive overhaul of the institution and an extremely conservative reinstatement of the existing power structure.

Deterioration in Seniority Norms and Committee Autonomy

The committee system has been placed under severe strain in recent years. High turnover in recent elections has caused seniority ladders to flatten out. In addition, widely publicized violations of seniority norms have probably both decreased the value of high seniority as an electoral resource and increased, for that reason, turnover in membership (by decreasing reelection proclivities). In addition, rule changes during this period have damaged jurisdictional integrity by giving wider discretion to the Speaker. Finally, the third assignment system has rapidly expanded the number of permissible assignment options in a rather haphazard fashion.

The most important cause of the decline in the strength of the committee

---

*Combining committee jurisdictions together protected the viability of historic precedents, but wholesale merger created an entirely new problem relating to membership assignment. Given the great reduction in the number of committees and the number of assignments, scores of members held competing and sometimes contradictory claims on assignments in the new 1947 committee system. During the debate on adoption of the rule changes, there occurred several oblique references to the system for assignment allocation. James Wadsworth of New York: "I cannot stand here at this time and say exactly what is going to happen to every Member of this Congress when he comes back upon being reelected to the next Congress. We will all be treated alike at least" (p. 10042). Emanuel Cellar of New York: "What about the question of seniority? For instance, the Committee on the Judiciary, of which I am the ranking Democratic member, assumes the duties and prerogatives of the Committee on Claims, the Committee on Revision of the Laws, and the Committee on Immigration and Naturalization. I presume that some Members of these committees will try to get membership on the Committee on the Judiciary. What will be their status in reference to seniority?" The vice-chairman of the Joint Committee on Congressional Organization, A. S. Mike Monroney, declined to comment on what he considered strictly partisan decisions (p. 10054); in another context, Monroney speculated, "We have changed the name of the committee from the Civil Service Committee to the Post Office and Civil Service Committee. We make that a major committee. The Civil Service Committee is now composed of 21 Members. Many of those Members enjoy high seniority on other committees, and they will choose their committees. . . . [Members of the Post Office Committee] surely will be eligible for membership on this merged committee and they will be able to enjoy and exercise this learning that they have. . . ." (p. 10070). All passages from the *Congressional Record*, 79:2, July 25, 1946. For a description of the "trickle-down" assignment process actually used in 1947, see Bensel, "Reciprocal Behavior and the Rules of the House of Representatives," Appendix.

system has been the accelerating shift of the center of gravity of the Democratic party toward the industrial core (see figure 7.7 and chapter 8). This shift led to the widening split between the two great, polar factions of the party that ultimately produced the civil rights successes of the 1960s and contemporary attacks on the seniority system. These events, in turn, accelerated the retirement of senior southern members—who have, with increasing frequency, been replaced by Republicans. By a direct feedback effect, these developments have hastened the Democratic shift toward the core.

The increase in membership turnover caused by attacks on the seniority system have, in turn, reduced political support for the system itself and, combined with a stronger party caucus, produced a remarkable democratization of the House rules and a further decentralization of power into the subcommittee network (see tables 7.12 and 7.13).[21] The increasing role of subcommittees in the House and the growing influence of relatively junior members in the party caucus and on the House floor have dissipated the former power of the standing committee system so that many subcommittees possess only a pale shadow of the authority their parent panels once wielded on the House floor. When this

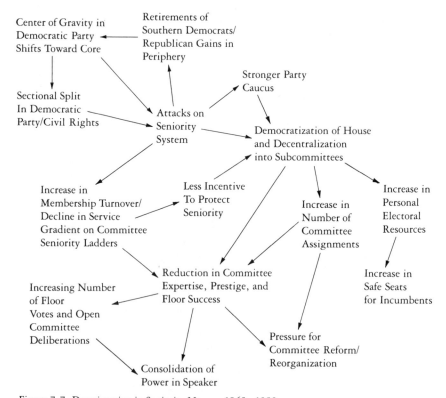

Figure 7.7. Deterioration in Seniority Norms, 1965–1982

Table 7.12. Major Restrictions on Committee Autonomy, 1965–1981

Year	Restriction
1965	The House adopts a twenty-one day rule for special orders (repealed in 1967).
1970	The House orders the publication of committee roll calls and the filing of committee reports with the Clerk within seven days after approval, and allows the Speaker to recognize any member of the Rules Committee to bring up a special order if the committee has previously reported the order.
1973	The Democratic caucus orders the creation of subcommittee jurisdictions to be formally defined under committee rules.
	The House orders open committee meetings except when they are closed by a public vote of the members, when internal budgetary or personnel matters are considered, or when testimony relating to "national security" is heard.
1975	The House orders committees with more than fifteen members to establish at least four subcommittees, authorizes the Speaker to make joint, sequential, or split referral of legislation to committees, and makes numerous changes in committee jurisdiction.
1981	The Democratic caucus places limits on the number of subcommittees the parent panels may establish: Rules and Ways and Means are allowed a maximum of six; Appropriations, a maximum of thirteen; all others, a maximum of eight or whatever they had January 1, 1981, if that the number is less than eight; and all committees with more than thirty-five members are permitted a minimum of six subcommittees if they wish that many.

loss of authority is combined with increasing membership turnover (which prevents the development of stable legislative roles and reputations), there follows a general reduction in committee expertise, prestige, and floor success. The drive toward democratization has produced a rapid increase in the number of committee assignments, an exposure of committee proposals to more frequent roll call challenges, and demands for public access to committee deliberations.

In recent years, the inability of the Democratic party caucus to impose programmatic unity through attacks on the seniority of conservative or even moderate members, and the sometimes chaotic course of deliberations on the floor, have led to a reconcentration of power in the hands of the Speaker. Reminiscent of "Cannonism" at the turn of the century, the Speaker has been given decisive power over the composition of the Rules Committee and, through the Democratic Steering Committee, committee assignments and chairmanships generally.* Another critical blow to committee autonomy was delivered in 1975 when the Speaker was given unprecedented authority to refer legislation to more than one committee, either jointly or sequentially, or to divide a bill

*The Steering Committee is made up of twenty-four members chaired by the Speaker, including the majority leader, the caucus chairman, twelve regionally elected representatives, and nine members appointed by the Speaker.

Table 7.13. Major Changes in Democratic Party Rules Governing Committee Assignments, 1965–1979

Year	Change or Action
1965	Caucus strips John Bell Williams (Mississippi) and Albert W. Watson (South Carolina) of their seniority for supporting Goldwater in the 1964 presidential campaign. (First party punishment for disloyalty since 1911.)
1967	Caucus removes Adam Clayton Powell (New York) from chairmanship of the Education and Labor Committee for misconduct.
1971	Caucus orders Ways and Means Democrats (the Democratic panel controlling committee assignments) to nominate chairmen separately and allows any ten members to demand a public vote on any nomination. If a nomination is rejected, Ways and Means is to make another recommendation.
	Caucus permits members to chair only one legislative subcommittee.
1973	Caucus allows one-fifth of all caucus members to demand a secret ballot on any nomination for a committee chair.
	Caucus orders the election of subcommittee chairs by the Democrats assigned to the respective full committees.
	Democratic rules contain a formal statement of committee assignment options for the first time.
1975	Control over Committee assignments is taken from Ways and Means Democrats and given to the Democratic Steering Committee.
	A secret caucus vote on committee chairs is made automatic and extended to subcommittee chairs on Appropriations.
	If the original Steering Committee recommendation is rejected, competitive nominations can be made from the floor of the caucus.
	Caucus authorizes the Speaker to select Democratic members of the Rules Committee subject to caucus approval.
	Caucus permits returning members of the House to protect only two subcommittee posts at the beginning of a new Congress.
	Caucus strips three committee chairmen of their posts: Hebert of Louisiana in favor of Price of Illinois on Armed Services; Patman of Texas in favor of Reuss of Wisconsin on Banking; and Poage of Texas in favor of Foley of Washington on Agriculture. (See table 7.15.)
1979	Caucus changes three rules governing subcommittees: members are permitted to serve on five subcommittees at most; all subcommittees must allow any member of the parent committee to bid for the chair (Appropriations exempted); and all full committees must allow each member to choose one subcommittee post before any member can choose a second post (Appropriations again exempted).

into sections and refer the parts to separate panels. In conjunction with the other developments that have weakened committee autonomy, these new prerogatives probably endow the Speaker, on paper, with almost as much formal power over the legislative process as Joseph Cannon exercised before 1910. However, the diffuse geographical base of the majority party that was the crowning achievement of the "classic" period of committee dominance now prevents the programmatic unification of the party. Loyalty to any set of broadly conceived policy goals would mean practical political suicide for a substantial portion (principally southerners) of the contemporary caucus.

One ironic product of recent developments has been the increasing electoral security of incumbent congressmen. The democratization of the House has meant not only a dramatic leveling of power within the subcommittee system, but also a rapid increase in the number of personal and committee staff employees, franking privileges, and other institutional benefits relevant to reelection campaigns. With the institution in transition between a strong committee system and a reassertion of party government, the average member works in an extremely individualistic environment. The decline in the committee system has reduced the incentives to reciprocate on the House floor, and the party caucus cannot yet impose effective discipline. Thus, democratization has produced an interim "window" in which personally tailored electoral strategies flourish with great effectiveness.[22]

The Decline in Committee Reciprocity on the Floor

The single most important key to a strong committee system is, of course, floor reciprocity—the tendency of members to support committee decisions when they come to a vote. All the other supporting characteristics of the membership (e.g., career orientation) and institutional structure (e.g., firm jurisdictional boundaries) have the maintenance of floor reciprocity as their ultimate purpose. For nearly a century scholars have concluded that respect for committee deliberations within the House was so high that the committee system was clearly the central feature of the legislative process.[23] Longitudinal evidence of the floor success of committee proposals is, however, sparse.[24] This section presents some contemporary evidence of floor reciprocity patterns and their relation to sectional stress and the party system, and introduces a variety of measures which suggest a deterioration in floor reciprocity.

During the 93rd Congress (1973–74), floor voting patterns revealed a significant differentiation in the regional orientation of legislative committees (see table 7.14). Those committees with a disproportionate number of periphery members, such as Agriculture, Armed Services, and Appropriations, drew heavy support for their proposals from the Atlanta, Charlotte, and Dallas trade area delegations, while core regions were much less enthusiastic about their recommendations. For example, the Boston trade area cast a bare majority of its votes (50.1 percent) in favor of Agriculture positions on the floor, while the Charlotte delegation gave the committee more than six out of every seven of its votes (86.6 percent). On the other hand, committees on which core members were comparatively overrepresented attracted much more floor support from the Boston, New York, Philadelphia, and San Francisco delegations than they received from the periphery. On both Education and Banking Committee policy decisions, for example, the Boston delegation gave a higher percentage of

Table 7.14. Floor Reciprocity in the 93rd Congress (1973–1974)

Trade Area [a]	Percentage of All Votes Cast in Support of Committee Majority [b]							Total: All 21 Committees
	Agriculture	Armed Services	Appro-priations	Commerce	Foreign Affairs	Education and Labor	Banking	
Philadelphia	54.7	71.3	71.2	79.8	68.8	71.0	74.5	73.1
Boston	50.1	57.2	67.8	82.7	81.1	86.0	79.6	77.1
New York	51.5	66.3	70.4	82.8	80.6	81.9	78.6	76.9
San Francisco	65.7	60.2	68.3	82.6	82.9	80.8	76.0	77.1
Detroit	61.1	69.6	71.0	77.9	74.8	72.2	71.8	73.8
Washington, D.C.	59.8	72.3	70.8	74.6	64.4	62.8	64.9	70.1
Chicago	57.1	78.7	72.1	75.4	73.1	70.6	69.5	72.4
Cleveland	55.2	59.7	68.1	80.2	74.6	80.6	72.2	73.7
Los Angeles	58.3	74.0	69.6	77.1	67.7	65.1	65.2	70.9
Pittsburgh	65.7	79.2	76.9	85.9	74.4	84.6	71.6	80.2
Minneapolis	75.5	71.1	73.7	79.8	75.4	74.5	71.7	75.7
St. Louis	72.9	62.9	72.4	80.9	64.4	77.8	66.6	75.8
Louisville	69.8	81.0	76.8	80.4	57.9	71.6	65.0	75.0
Charlotte	86.6	92.4	79.3	75.6	56.3	56.1	60.6	72.8
Atlanta	82.7	78.6	72.1	73.6	48.7	58.2	57.1	70.1
Dallas	80.6	93.2	76.2	66.2	54.6	54.2	56.7	69.6

[a] Only trade area delegations containing nine or more members are included in the table. Delegations are in descending order of their support for the core position on the ten high-stress, closely contested roll calls recorded during the 94th Congress: see table 2.5.

[b] All roll calls recorded on legislation reported by one of the permanent, standing committees during the 93rd Congress are covered, regardless of the margin by which they were decided. Votes counted in computing percentages do not include those of the particular committee under consideration. E.g., the votes of Agriculture members from the Dallas trade area are excluded from the calculation of that trade area's support for the committee. Committees were selected for their general importance, the number of recorded roll calls on legislation reported by each of them (in each case, over thirty), and the comparative imbalance in sectional representation (see table 7.1).

SOURCE: Compiled from raw data summarized in Bensel, "Reciprocal Behavior and the Rules of the House of Representatives."

Table 7.15. A Comparison of the Voting Records of Members Deposed from and Promoted to Chairmanships by the Democratic Caucus in 1975

Committee	Members	Trade Area Delegation	Core: 1975–76	Party Unity	Southern Wing in Party Splits
			Percentage of Support for:[a]		
Agriculture	Deposed: Poage—Texas	Dallas	0.0	27.6	95.4
	Promoted: Foley—Washington	Spokane	80.0	89.9	21.9
Armed Services	Deposed: Hebert—Louisiana	New Orleans	0.0	34.9	87.0
	Promoted: Price—Illinois	St. Louis	70.0	88.9	28.0
Banking	Deposed: Patman—Texas	Dallas	10.0	71.8	49.3
	Promoted: Reuss—Wisconsin	Milwaukee	100.0	88.4	4.1

[a]Data include the percentage of votes cast in support: for the core position on the ten closely contested, high-stress roll calls recorded in the 94th Congress (1975–76); for the Democratic party position on roll calls in which the two parties backed opposite sides; and for the southern wing of the party when the northern and southern wings assumed opposing positions. The last two percentages are calculated for 1974 only.

SOURCES: Core support calculated from roll call data. Party unity and southern wing support recomputed from data in the *1974 Congressional Quarterly Almanac.*

its votes in favor of the committee position than did any other large trade area in the nation. In both instances, the Dallas delegation provided the lowest percentage. On roll calls involving the Foreign Affairs Committee, the Atlanta delegation actually cast a majority of its votes *against* the committee's recommendations. When trade area delegation support for all committees is computed, regional differences in support for individual committees tend to cancel out and only minimal differences in overall floor reciprocity are apparent. On the 1,031 roll calls analyzed in table 7.14, core delegations led by Pittsburgh, Boston, and San Francisco gave marginally greater floor support than periphery areas led by Dallas and Atlanta.

In 1975, when the Democratic caucus deposed three committee chairmen and replaced them with less senior members, the targets of that action were three of the most sectionally polarized committees in the House of Representatives (see table 7.15). In each case the caucus removed a southern committee chairman and replaced him with a colleague who more frequently supported core positions and the northern wing of the party. In all cases, the challenger also supported the Democratic party position (determined by a majority of party members) more often than the incumbent chairman. Subse-

Table 7.16. Intra-Committee Success and Party Affiliation, 93rd Congress
(1973–1974)

	Percentage of Pairs in Which:[a]		
Committee	Democrat Was More Successful Than Republican	Republican Was More Successful Than Democrat	Republican and Democrat Tied
Rules	100.0	0.0	0.0
House Administration	100.0	0.0	0.0
Post Office	99.3	0.0	.7
Education and Labor	89.4	10.6	0.0
Public Works	87.5	11.6	.9
Government Operations	81.3	15.4	3.3
Commerce	79.4	19.9	.7
Ways and Means	77.9	19.3	2.9
Agriculture	77.0	22.3	.7
District of Columbia	75.0	18.3	6.7
Foreign Affairs	71.4	28.3	.3
Banking	69.6	29.9	.5
Judiciary	69.5	27.6	2.9
Merchant Marine	68.5	11.4	20.2
Appropriations	61.3	38.6	.2
Atomic Energy	60.0	35.0	5.0
Science and Technology	59.8	33.8	6.4
Interior	58.8	40.9	.3
Armed Services	27.8	53.7	18.5
Veterans' Affairs	0.0	6.7	93.3

[a] Each committee is divided into two groups: Democrats and Republicans. Each Democrat's intra-committee success score is then compared to each Republican's. For example, on the Rules Committee, which has ten Democrats and five Republicans, fifty (10 × 5) comparisons are made. For the Rules Committee, since each of the ten Democrats has a higher success score than each of the five Republicans, 100 percent of the comparisons fall in the first column.

quent purges of both standing committee and subcommittee chairmen have followed the same pattern.

When the partisan composition of committee majorities is analyzed, a fairly clear tendency toward bipartisanship emerges in committees whose membership and floor voting patterns are tilted toward the periphery (table 7.16). In this analysis each committee member is given an "intra-committee success score" which reflects the percentage of all roll call votes in which he finds himself in the committee majority. These individual success scores are then compared by party (see the note to table 7.16). The Education, Commerce, Foreign Affairs, and Banking committees are all significantly more partisan (in the sense of excluding Republicans from the majority coalition which appears on the floor) than the Appropriations and Armed Services panels. While the Agriculture Committee deviates slightly from the general pattern, Armed Services is the only panel on which a majority of the Republicans are more successful than most Democrats.

Reflecting the close integration between the committee system and partisan legislative goals, the Democratic majority leader (at that time, "Tip" O'Neill of Massachusetts) cast 87.8 percent of his votes in support of the committee majority position during the 93rd Congress (see table 7.17). The tendency of the majority leadership to support exclusive Democratic commit-

Table 7.17. Majority Leader Support and the Success of Democratic Committee Members, 93rd Congress (1973–1974)

Committee	Roll Calls in Which Majority of Democrats Were in Committee Minority		Majority Leader[a] Supported:			
			Committee Majority When Majority of Democrats Were in Committee Minority		Committee Majority When Majority of Democrats Were in Committee Majority or Split Evenly[b]	
	%	(N)	%	(margin)	%	(margin)
Interior	13.0	(6)	20.0	(1/5)	97.2	(35/36)
Government Operations	11.1	(3)	0.0	(0/1)	100.0	(16/16)
Agriculture	9.4	(5)	0.0	(0/3)	88.1	(37/42)
Commerce	8.9	(10)	12.5	(1/8)	94.4	(84/89)
Appropriations	8.8	(16)	6.3	(1/16)	87.1	(135/155)
Banking	7.1	(5)	0.0	(0/5)	92.9	(52/56)
Education and Labor	6.8	(7)	28.6	(2/7)	97.7	(84/86)
Judiciary	6.7	(2)	50.0	(1/2)	100.0	(25/25)
Science and Technology	5.9	(1)	100.0	(1/1)	93.8	(15/16)
House Administration	4.3	(1)	100.0	(1/1)	89.5	(17/19)
Rules	4.0	(5)	0.0	(0/5)	97.4	(112/115)
Foreign Affairs	3.8	(2)	0.0	(0/2)	94.0	(47/50)
Public Works	3.0	(1)	0.0	(0/1)	78.6	(22/28)
Armed Services	0.0	(0)	—	—	77.1	(27/35)
Ways and Means	0.0	(0)	—	—	92.6	(25/27)
Post Office	0.0	(0)	—	—	100.0	(14/14)
District of Columbia	0.0	(0)	—	—	100.0	(22/22)
Merchant Marine	0.0	(0)	—	—	100.0	(11/11)
Veterans' Affairs	0.0	(0)	—	—	100.0	(11/11)
Atomic Energy	0.0	(0)	—	—	100.0	(9/9)
Library	0.0	(0)	—	—	0.0	(0/1)
Total		(64)	14.0	(8/57)	92.7	(800/863)

[a] Since the Speaker normally does not vote on roll calls, the majority leader must be relied upon to represent the position of both leaders.

[b] Democrats split evenly on two roll calls concerning legislation originating with the Education and Labor Committee and on one each for the Committees on Agriculture, Appropriations, Armed Services, Banking and Currency, District of Columbia, Government Operations, and House Administration.

tee majorities is revealed by O'Neill's 14.0 percent support when most Democrats were in the minority and 92.7 percent support when most Democrats were in the majority. Overall, O'Neill supported the committee position of the three periphery committees (discussed above) on 79.7 percent of their recorded votes, while favoring the four core committees on nearly nine out of every ten (89.1 percent).

The data in tables 7.14, 7.16, and 7.17 suggest several conclusions. First, the regional composition of the various committees tends to translate—through internal coalition-building within the panels—into a corresponding pattern of sectional support on the floor.* The extent and content of regional differences within the committee system suggest the way in which different points of the national political economy are relevant to the political goals of congressmen from the great polar sections, and which policy areas are likely to generate sectionally divisive decisions in the future.

The data on partisanship reflect trends that were noted earlier: the center of gravity within the Democratic party has shifted toward the core and, as a consequence, many Democratic periphery members find the Republican minority more compatible as coalition partners than congressmen from the opposite wing of their own party. Considering these developments and the majority leadership's apparent preference for purely Democratic majority coalitions, the deposition of periphery committee chairmen from their posts by the caucus in 1975 is consistent with the sectional shift within the party and the consequent decline of the committee system. For those committees which tilt toward the industrial core, a strong party role in policy decisions is compatible with a decentralization of legislative power. The periphery committees, on the other hand, probably find their interests and political inclinations at odds with those of the contemporary majority party leadership.

Of the general measures of decentralization of the legislative process into the committee system, the number of roll calls is one of the best (see figure 7.8). From 1885 until 1929—just before the onset of the Great Depression and the rise of the New Deal coalition—the frequency of roll calls declined steadily from about one daily to one every three days. From 1929 to 1959, roll call frequency remained at about one vote for every three days the House was in session, with the 1939–48 decade setting an all-time historic low of .29 votes per day. As late as the 88th Congress (1963–64), only .37 roll calls were recorded on an average day. However, the post-1965 period has seen an explosion in roll call activity.

As has been suggested here, floor reciprocity flourishes under two conditions: ambiguity and anonymity. Ambiguity has been incorporated into modern legislative drafts through bureaucratic or executive branch discretion and

---

*In this respect, compare table 7.1 with table 6.1. High-stress policy decisions favoring the core tend to develop in those committees dominated by members who represent the manufacturing belt and vice-versa.

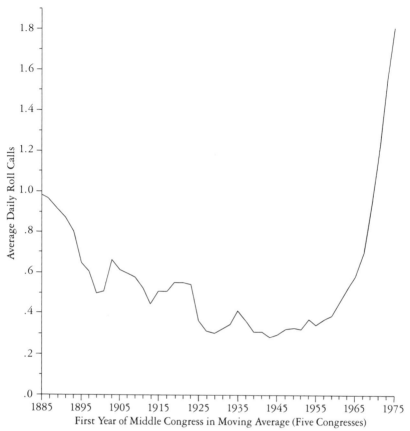

Figure 7.8. Roll Calls per Legislative Day, 1885–1975

SOURCES: Compiled from data in the respective editions of the *House Journal* and the *Congressional Quarterly Almanac*.

has allowed congressmen to support federal policies which, if they had been explicitly stated, would have clearly carried negative implications for their individual districts. Even where clear legislative alternatives were presented on the floor, a reluctance to invoke a recorded vote and the existence of procedural barriers to roll calls during the amending stage of floor deliberations in the Committee of the Whole preserved anonymity. Supporting the committee position on the floor was a simple matter, regardless of the policy implications, if the member's constituency would never discover their congressman's position. Furthermore, when there was no recorded vote, the members attending floor deliberations on a piece of legislation tended to be those assigned to the committee that had reported the bill. Without a roll call, floor consideration was often just an extension of the committee deliberations that had preceded it. In sum, a roll call has often had three purposes hostile to the integrity of committee decision-making: a recorded vote represents an "appeal" to the House to overturn the position of a committee majority, significantly expands the number of non-committee members who participate in a legislative decision, and often forces congressmen to choose between opposition to the committee majority or a public repudiation of their districts' interests.* While there are numerous instances in which congressmen desire to go "on record" or are constitutionally required to cast a public ballot (e.g., social security increases and veto overrides), most roll calls carry negative implications for the strength of committee autonomy.

Coinciding with the steep increase in roll call activity has been a rapid rise in the number of floor amendments to appropriations bills (see figure 7.9). During the 88th Congress (1963–64)—just before the first attacks by the Democratic caucus on the seniority system—only seventy-four amendments were offered to bills reported by the Committee on Appropriations, and of those amendments only about a third (twenty-four) were adopted by the House. By the 94th Congress (1975–76), the number of floor amendments had risen to 228, and over half (120) were accepted by the House. For the Rules Committee, floor success on the adoption of special orders has followed a parallel course (see table 7.18). On the average, 2.2 special orders reported by the Rules Committee were defeated on the floor in every Congress between 1929 and 1968. In the last six Congresses, that average has nearly tripled (to 5.7 defeats).

Table 7.19 summarizes the most important membership characteristics and institutional supports for a strong committee system. As can be seen, under the strong party organization of the House during the late nineteenth and early twentieth centuries, members seldom stood for reelection, often lacked prior legislative experience, held nearly two committee assignments each, ascended to important committee chairmanships through routes other than seniority in nearly a third of all cases, and fairly frequently recorded their votes publicly during floor proceedings. During the "classic" phase of the committee system's development, membership turnover and roll call activity were cut in half (compared to the era of strong party organization). Average prior service more than doubled, and the average number of committee assign-

---

*For more on these points, see Lewis A. Froman, Jr., *The Congressional Process: Strategies, Rules, and Procedures* (Boston: Little, Brown, 1967), pp. 70–89. In 1971, the House of Representatives began recording votes taken in the Committee of the Whole (the amendment stage of the floor deliberations). This change in procedure was symptomatic of the growing support for a recentralization of the legislative process and probably accounts for about one-third to one-half of the increase in roll call activity from 1970 to 1979. In 1979, the House increased the number of members who must request a recorded vote in the Committee of the Whole from twenty to twenty-five. This rule change has decreased the number and frequency of recorded roll calls.

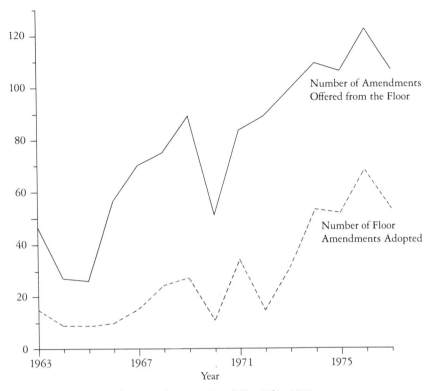

Figure 7.9. Floor Amendments to Appropriations Bills, 1963–1977

SOURCE: Adapted from data in the *Final Report of the Select Committee on Committees*, House Report 96-866 (Washington: 1980), p. 86.

Table 7.18. Number of Rules Committee Defeats on Special Orders, 1929–1980

71st through 75th Congresses (1929–38): 1.8 (average)
76th through 80th Congresses (1939–48): 2.2 (average)
81st through 85th Congresses (1949–58): 3.2 (average)
86th through 90th Congresses (1959–68): 1.6 (average)
91st through 95th Congresses (1969–78): 5.8 (average)
96th Congress   (1979–80): 5.0

SOURCES: Data for the 94th through 96th Congresses gathered by author. Other data from *Congressional Quarterly Weekly Report*, March 30, 1974, p. 808; and Spark M. Matsunaga and Ping Chen, *Rulemakers of the House* (Urbana: University of Illinois Press, 1976), pp. 151–52.

Table 7.19. Membership Characteristics and Institutional Supports for a Strong Committee System in Five Legislative Periods

Characteristic or Support	Strong Party (1881–1909)	Developing Committee System (1911–31)	Emergence of Bipolar Coalition (1933–45)	Classic Committee System (1947–63)	Decline of Bipolar Coalition (1965–81)	Latest (1981)
Percentage of First Term Members	34.2	22.5	23.5	16.5	15.1	16.6
Average Prior Service of Members (Terms)	1.8	2.8	3.0	4.1	4.3	3.7
Committee Assignments per Member	1.9	2.0	2.1	1.2	1.6	1.6
Promotion or Retention of Senior Democratic Party Member on Committee (%)	69.1	95.0	94.8	100.0	90.0	70.0
Average Roll Calls per Legislative Day	.8	.4	.4	.4	1.4	1.8[a]

[a] Figure based on 1979 and 1980 data.
SOURCES: See sources for figures 7.1, 7.2, 7.3, 7.6, and 7.8.

ments was lower by a third. Furthermore, the most senior member held the committee chairmanship in all instances. Though the first two indicators (turnover and prior service) lagged behind this reversal in trends, by 1981 all five had significantly deteriorated from "classic" phase levels. The most dramatic changes have occurred in the roll call activity and seniority indicators.* The Appropriations and Rules committee data presented above demonstrate the consequent deterioration in membership and institutional supports for a strong committee system.

Conclusion

Several efforts have been made to correct the declining effectiveness of the committee system through institutional reform. All have failed largely because they have met resistance from members who benefit from the prevailing distribution of power.[25] Unlike the 1946 Reorganization plan, none of the recent proposals have had as their sole purpose an institutional strengthening of the committee system, nor have they suggested a method by which the power and seniority of individual members might be retained through a

---

*In 1981, Thomas Foley of Washington chose the post of Democratic party whip over the Agriculture chairmanship, Henry Reuss chose to head the Joint Economic Committee over leadership of the Banking panel, and Morris Udall opted for Interior over the Post Office Committee. In none of these cases was the member forced to make the indicated choice. However, their actions do indicate the relative attractiveness and existence of competing career ladders and opportunities.

wholesale reform of committee jurisdictions. Indeed, the 1974 committee reform effort that originated in the Democratic caucus and the 1977 Obey Commission recommendations both supported strong party controls over policy formulation in almost all cases where that goal conflicted with that of an autonomous committee system. Though sectional stress has been quite low in all of these efforts, core delegations have generally supported reform while periphery areas have preferred the status quo.* Given the relative compatibility between a decentralization of legislative influence and a strong party leadership for those committees dominated by core Democrats, it is not surprising that core representatives have backed both subcommittee decentralization and a revival of caucus power.

The data and argument presented in this chapter should be viewed from a broad historical perspective. The development of a strong committee system took at least three and half decades (from 1911 to 1947). The classic phase from the 1946 Reorganization to the first attacks on seniority consumed another eighteen years (1947 to 1964). The relationship of recent events (such as attacks on seniority) to the internal logic of the institution and the measurable decline in various indicators of floor reciprocity suggests the start of an irreversible decline of the committee system and movement toward a strong party organization of the House. However, the recentralization of legislative influence may take decades to mature. While the willingness of the House to establish panels to suggest internal reforms has been repeatedly demonstrated, every major reform proposal over the last decade has either been replaced by a less radical substitute or rejected outright. In this sense, the projected decline of committee system dominance still lacks a single critical event which would mark its onset (such as the Cannon Revolt) or an institutional reorganization that consistently recognizes the new era's most important imperatives (such as the 1946 Reorganization). Instead, the contemporary decline of the committee system has been ushered in by a myriad of distantly related events which may have the sectional repolarization of the congressional party system as their most important result.

*The sectional stress scores on four major reform contests were as follows: on a choice between the reorganization plan recommended by a bipartisan panel headed by Richard Bolling of Missouri and a counterproposal composed by Julia Hansen of Washington and backed by the Democratic caucus, 23.2 (October 8, 1974); on the special order which would have provided for floor consideration of the Obey Commission recommendations, 14.3 (October 12, 1977); on a proposal to establish a new Select Committee on Committees to suggest further reforms, 29.5 (March 20, 1979); and on a motion to create an entirely new Committee on Energy, 12.8 (March 25, 1980). The Boston trade area was the only large delegation to support all four reforms (Bolling over Hansen and "Yea" on the rest), while Dallas was the only delegation to oppose all four.

8

The Changing Sectional Base of the Congressional Party System and American Ideology

The American party system of the late nineteenth and early twentieth centuries was firmly rooted in economic competition between the metropolitan-industrial North and the rural-agrarian South. Until the Great Depression, the most stable electoral periods produced very similar distributions of party strength: the Democrats dominated the eleven states of the old Confederacy and scattered border regions while the Republicans held sway in the remainder of the nation. Between the end of Reconstruction and the New Deal, the party system returned repeatedly to this sectional alignment following periodic expansions of Democratic strength into the North.

The Democratic party was able to expand outside its base in the southern periphery only by exploiting previously latent contradictions or inconsistencies within the policy goals of the Republican coalition. The most important of these normally latent contradictions divided the interests of agricultural producers or the urban lower classes from those of the dominant industrial elite. These class or sector divisions within the industrial North did not often follow well-defined regional boundaries. Furthermore, because the northern working class and agrarian radicals had even more serious long-term problems with the policy goals of the southern plantation elite than they had with the industrial leaders of the metropolitan core, Democratic gains outside the South were usually short-lived. In the years following the 1912 presidential election, for example, many Progressive party members who had cast ballots for Theodore Roosevelt and northern voters who had supported Woodrow Wilson returned to the Republican party. In his endorsement of Charles Evan Hughes, the Republican nominee in 1916, the chairman of the National Progressive Convention described the sentiments of many of these voters when he condemned the alternative.

368

The fixed southern control of the Democratic Party is individualistic in its thinking, sectional in its sympathies, and inherits a tradition against common labor as servile. The social organization is still semi-patriarchal in the rural communities, and the southern environment presents the maximum of natural and cultural resistance to necessary social and industrial standardization.

In contrast, he felt that:

The primary voter mass control of the Republican Party is in the rural communities of the Central, Western, and New England States. This group represents the highest literacy in America, is freest from severe social and economic pressure, is in the zone of the greatest natural tendency to industrial standardization and equality of opportunity, and inherits the tradition of Lincoln and the men who saved the Union.*

During election periods, such as the progressive era, when class divisions in the North destabilized traditional partisan allegiances, the sectional polarization of the two major parties decreased markedly. During periods of relative electoral stability, the fundamental competition between the southern periphery and metropolitan core reemerged within the electoral process. As a consequence, sectional stress within the party system dramatically increased. This regional polarization of party membership and electoral strength represented the "normal" political outcome in all elections until the New Deal.

Before 1932, Democratic appeals to the working class and agrarian radicals of the North were unsuccessful attempts to establish an enduring "bipolar" coalition. The prospect of an alliance which could bridge economic competition between the agrarian periphery and industrial core was attractive to the Democrats for several reasons. On the one hand, their political base in the South was relatively secure after the disfranchisement of blacks and lower-class whites in the late nineteenth and early twentieth centuries. Within the South, the Democratic party was much less vulnerable to Republican exploitation of latent class divisions than the Republicans were in their northern political base. For that reason, the Democrats could exploit class divisions in the North without threatening the political dominance of the plantation elite in the southern periphery. On the other hand, the normal outcome of purely sectional conflict was a national victory for the Republican party. The sectional

---

*The chairman was Raymond Robins, and his comments were inserted into the *Appendix* to the *Congressional Record* (64:2:1803–4, August 11, 1916) by a Republican congressman from Washington, Albert Johnson. Johnson added, "the success of the Democratic Party involves, indeed necessitates, the imposition of southern thought upon northern action"—a form of bondage to "a party whose dominant faction is almost feudal in its treatment of the laboring man." For a general examination of southern influence within the Wilson administration, see George B. Tindall, *The Emergence of the New South: 1913–1945* (Baton Rouge: Louisiana State University Press, 1967), ch. 1.

breadth of the Republican coalition forced the Democrats to exploit class divisions in order to achieve even temporary national success.

With the onset of the Great Depression, several necessary elements of an enduring bipolar coalition between the southern plantation elite and northern working class fell into place. The most obvious was the economic and political prostration of the metropolitan-industrial elite. The extended duration of the industrial collapse purchased time for the construction of political and institutional arrangements which would allow the bipolar coalition to endure. In addition, the economic crisis permitted the Democratic party to shift attention to "economic royalists" within the Republican party—and away from the latent contradictions within their own coalition. The vast increase in executive and bureaucratic discretion during the New Deal permitted the Democrats to divide political spoils between the separate factions without exposing or aggravating the policy contradictions within the party. Finally, the maturation of the congressional committee system produced a legislative decentralization that paralleled the New Deal bureaucratic expansion and even allowed the bipolar coalition to survive the loss of executive or congressional leadership when the Republicans won an election.

Between 1932 and 1964 the New Deal alliance survived more or less intact. At the end of that period the policy foundation of the coalition began to erode with the passage of civil rights legislation, the expansion of southern electorates, and the decline of the industrial core economy. Recent restrictions on committee autonomy and violations of seniority norms have also undermined the coalition, and as the American political system enters the 1980s, the level of sectional stress in the electoral bases of the two parties seems certain to rise.

For various reasons, the evolving structure of American ideological competition also seems to herald the reemergence of a sectionally polarized party system. Since 1932 American ideological belief-systems have become increasingly salient factors in coalition-building within the United States Congress. Both "liberalism" and "conservatism" have comprised proto-coalitions in the form of potential political alliances between otherwise unrelated groups, and these proto-coalitions have more and more frequently replaced party loyalty and institutional norms as the major determinants of congressional voting. As the membership base of the congressional party system has become increasingly detached from the fundamental sectional alignment since World War II, American ideological belief-systems have moved in the opposite direction; "liberalism" has become the ideology of the industrial core, and "conservatism" now provides a theoretical rationale for the political goals of the developing periphery. This evolutionary change in the nature of American ideology has been a response to the declining viability of the bipolar Democratic coalition.

Historical Overview of Sectionalism in the Party System

For most of the last century the two major parties in the House of Representatives have revolved around and serviced the interests of regional elites. The American party system followed a "profoundly sectional alignment" in which extreme regional differences in Republican and Democratic strength persisted from one election to the next.[1] In describing the impact of this alignment on Pennsylvania politics, Walter Dean Burnham has provided an excellent outline of the American political system between 1896 and the New Deal.

> The political simplicity which had thus emerged in this industrial heartland of the Northeast by the 1920's was the more extraordinary in that it occurred in an area whose socioeconomic division of labor was as complex and its level of development as high as any in the world. In most other regions of advanced industrialization the emergence of corporate capitalism was associated with the development of mass political parties with high structural cohesion and explicit collective purposes with respect to the control of policy and government. . . . It is no exaggeration to say that the political response to the collectivizing thrust of industrialism in this American state was the elimination of organized partisan combat, an extremely severe decline in electoral participation, the emergence of a Republican "coalition of the whole" and—by no means coincidentally—a highly efficient insulation of the controlling industrial-financial elite from effective or sustained countervailing pressures.*

Outside of their respective sectional bastions, the two parties sought—and normally failed—to destabilize the opposing party organization by exploiting latent or supressed class conflict. While the Republican party was the handmaiden of industrial and financial wealth in the core regions of the North, the same party represented impoverished blacks and hill country whites in the southern periphery. Similarly, the Bourbon-controlled Democratic party exploited ethnic, labor, and agrarian disaffection with core elite (Republican) policies in the North.

Section	Republican Party	Democratic Party
Industrial Core (North)	Industrial and financial elite, and allied interests	Large minority of working class, ethnic groups, and agrarian radicals
Agrarian Periphery (South)	Poor, upcountry whites and blacks (largely disfranchised after 1900)	Plantation elite and allied interests

*Burnham continues, "the only kinds of attacks that could be made effective on a *nationwide* basis against the emergent industrial hegemony—the only attacks that, given the ethnic

In the most general terms, the salient domestic issue in American politics between the end of the Civil War and the Great Depression was the issue of economic colonialism.[2] The most important aspect of the colonial relationship between the agrarian periphery and industrial core was the process of industrialization itself. In its earliest stages the process heightened sectional differences and regional antipathy between an "industrializing and economically ascendent Northeast and a vast rural hinterland."[3] The high tariff, imperialism, and other anti-agrarian policies upon which American industrialization was based effectively prevented any permanent alliance between the agrarian periphery and the lower classes of the core.[*] The Republicans, representing the interests of the newly emerging industrial centers, were the "nationalist" party and sought to expand both the internal and foreign markets for manufactured goods. For much of the same period, the Democratic party was far more favorable to a weak central government and, at times, was almost separatist in its orientation. The process of industrialization in the end consumed the very political system that had nurtured it, and the northern industrial elite never regained the political dominance that it held prior to the Great Depression.

While the Great Depression made the New Deal possible, several other factors made the bipolar coalition of southern plantation interests and northern labor an attractive political arrangement. The vast expansion of American industry had made domestic manufacturing the most productive and efficient in the world-economy. For that reason, the traditional Democratic endorsement of free trade and a low tariff had become compatible with the employment of northern labor in industrial occupations. Even though the New Deal coalition has been described as "the democratic class struggle,"[4] class conflict was almost entirely confined to the North and was at the expense of the industrial elite. For the life of the New Deal coalition, one of the underpinnings of Democratic party unity was the exclusion of the southern periphery from most provisions of federal labor law (e.g., no minimum wage for agricultural labor, the Section 14[b] exemption from the Taft-Hartley Act, and decentralization of unemployment and relief policies). The northern wing acquiesced in this limitation, while the southern wing agreed to support a vast increase in American involvement in world affairs and the protection of U.S. foreign investment and trade ties.

The principal compromise among the policy positions assumed by the New Deal alliance, however, centered on race. For most of the 1932–64 period, the "marriage . . . remained tolerable to each partner on rather expedi-

---

heterogeneity and extremely rudimentary political socialization of much of the country's industrial labor, could come within striking distance of achieving a popular majority—came out of these colonial areas." "The End of American Party Politics," *Transaction* 7:2 (December 1969): 12–22.

[*]Ladd, *American Political Parties*, 131. Ladd continues, "The politics of industrialization was a sectional politics, with the separate regions perhaps further separated in basic political concerns than at any other point in American history" (p. 132).

ent grounds, such as easy presidential votes for the northern wing and congressional seniority for the southern."[5] As a leader of a southern delegation to
the 1952 Democratic convention pointed out, under this arrangement the
northern wing implicitly tolerated southern racism as the price of participation in a majority coalition.

> We've been Democrats too long to let any hotheads drive us out of the
> party. . . . We are probably going to get a terrible platform plank on
> civil rights. But we've had planks we didn't like before, and our repre-
> sentatives and senators have been able to beat them off in Congress. . . .
> After all, so long as we can hold powerful places in Congress, the presi-
> dent can recommend all he wants to, but he still can't get his bills
> through if our fellows won't help him.[6]

While the northern wing of the party chafed under the coalition's implicit
toleration of race segregation, the southern wing threatened repeatedly to bolt
over the increasingly liberal attitude of the national party on the same issue.
By the mid-1960s, the "national democratic party . . . moved from a position
of occasional flashes of embarrassment about southern Democrats to a position
of increasing intransigence" on the question of race segregation in the southern
periphery.[7] At the same time, middle- and upper-class white southerners were
leaving the party in droves.

The commonly perceived connection between a strong committee system, reliance on seniority rules, and political support for segregation made it
logical to combine the nearly complete dismemberment of segregationist institutions with a recentralization of legislative decision-making. When combined with efforts to expand and nationalize federal social welfare policies, this
upheaval in the foundations of the bipolar alliance represents an attempt to
form a truly national working-class party. In 1932, this attempt almost certainly would have failed.

Sectional Stress in the Congressional
Party System: 1881–1984

The sectional stress index can easily be adapted in order to measure regional
polarization within the congressional party system if party affiliation is considered as analogous to "yea" and "nay" votes.* If one party controls almost all of

---

*When adapted, the index indicates the extent to which the membership base of the
respective parties divides the nation into two or more sectional bastions. The sectional stress
index formula (see Appendix) is

$$\left(\frac{a}{b} - c\right) \cdot \frac{1}{d}$$

In order to measure stress in the party system, new factors must be substituted. When altered:
a = total number of members in all trade area party majorities; b = total number of members

Table 8.1. Sectional Stress in the Membership Base of Congressional Parties, 1881–1984

Congress (Years)	Sectional Stress in the Party System	Congress (Years)	Sectional Stress in the Party System
47th (1881–83)	54.1	73rd (1933–34)	26.1
48th (1883–85)	29.3	74th (1935–36)	16.6
49th (1885–87)	55.6	75th (1937–38)	18.7
50th (1887–89)	47.8	76th (1939–40)	40.5
51st (1889–91)	54.7	77th (1941–42)	41.0
52nd (1891–93)	19.5	78th (1943–44)	55.0
53rd (1893–95)	39.2	79th (1945–46)	46.9
54th (1895–97)	60.9	80th (1947–48)	61.3
55th (1897–99)	53.6	81st (1949–50)	36.6
56th (1899–1901)	58.7	82nd (1951–52)	49.0
57th (1901–3)	62.4	83rd (1953–54)	52.1
58th (1903–5)	61.9	84th (1955–56)	44.4
59th (1905–7)	69.1	85th (1957–58)	44.3
60th (1907–9)	61.1	86th (1959–60)	22.2
61st (1909–11)	57.0	87th (1961–62)	27.9
62nd (1911–13)	48.8	88th (1963–64)	28.3
63rd (1913–15)	26.4	89th (1965–66)	10.6
64th (1915–17)	48.8	90th (1967–68)	31.6
65th (1917–19)	60.5	91st (1969–70)	31.7
66th (1919–21)	52.8	92nd (1971–72)	26.1
67th (1921–23)	70.7	93rd (1973–74)	25.4
68th (1923–25)	57.6	94th (1975–76)	14.6
69th (1925–27)	59.9	95th (1977–78)	13.9
70th (1927–29)	60.6	96th (1979–80)	15.1
71st (1929–31)	59.1	97th (1981–82)	20.2
72nd (1931–33)	64.1	98th (1983–84)	15.3

SOURCE: Calculated from data on party membership contained in the *Congressional Directory* for each Congress.

the seats within one region and if another party holds similar sway in a second region, the membership distribution will produce a high sectional stress score. If the parties are represented on a roughly equal basis throughout the country, then the stress score will be correspondingly low.

Of the fifty-one Congresses that convened between 1881 and 1984, the parties were the most regionally polarized in the 67th Congress (1921–23), which met following Warren Harding's landslide election in 1920. Harding carried into office 302 Republicans who were opposed in the House by 132

---

in the chamber; c = percentage of total members belonging to the majority party; and d = percentage of total members belonging to the minority party. Where there exist more than two parties, the factors in the formula must be changed slightly: a = total number of members in all trade area party *pluralities*; b = total number of members in the chamber; c = percentage of total members belonging to the *plurality* party; and d = percentage of total members belonging to *all non-plurality parties*.

Democrats and one Socialist. The geographical distribution of the two parties produced a sectional stress score of 70.7. The Democrats held every district in Alabama, Arkansas, Florida, Georgia, Louisiana, Mississippi, North Carolina, and South Carolina. The party also picked up all but one seat in both the Texas and Virginia delegations. The Republicans swept all but one of the rural seats in the Midwest. The Democrats did not carry a majority of the districts in any large metropolitan delegation in the North and, outside of the largest cities, scored victories only in Albany and Buffalo, New York. The most significant northern Democratic delegation lay entirely within the corporate boundaries of New York City (see map 8.1 and table 8.2). In general outline, the distribution of the two parties in the 67th Congress was typical of the Republican-dominated House of the late nineteenth and early twentieth centuries.

The 1964 election produced the least polarized party distribution in the last hundred years. Lyndon Johnson brought 295 Democrats into the 89th Congress, more than double the 140 Republicans elected, and the resulting geographical distribution produced a stress score of only 10.6. Only nine of the fifty trade area delegations sent a majority of Republicans to Washington, and only one of these delegations (Minneapolis) was over ten members in size. In all but one trade area delegation (Wichita, with two congressmen), the Democrats were able to elect at least a quarter of the members. (See map 8.2.)

Since the Democrats tended to hold the great majority of urban districts too small to be illustrated on the map, Republican dominance in the rural regions of the Northeast and Midwest gives a misleading impression of sectional polarization (see table 8.2). Throughout the twentieth century, Repub-

Table 8.2. Sectional Base of the Party System, Metropolitan Districts,[a] 67th and 89th Congresses

	Republicans in:			
	67th Congress		89th Congress	
Metropolitan Delegation	%	(N)	%	(N)
Los Angeles			35.3	(17)
San Diego			50.0	(2)
San Francisco	100.0	(2)	40.0	(5)
Chicago	66.7	(9)	25.0	(12)
Baltimore	50.0	(2)	0.0	(3)
Boston	75.0	(8)	0.0	(5)
Detroit	100.0	(2)	14.3	(7)
St. Louis	50.0	(2)	33.3	(3)
Northeastern New Jersey	85.7	(7)	20.0	(10)
New York City	66.7	(24)	12.0	(25)
Philadelphia	100.0	(7)	28.6	(7)
Pittsburgh	80.0	(5)	50.0	(4)

[a] Metropolitan districts listed are those with areas too small to be shown on maps 8.1 and 8.2.

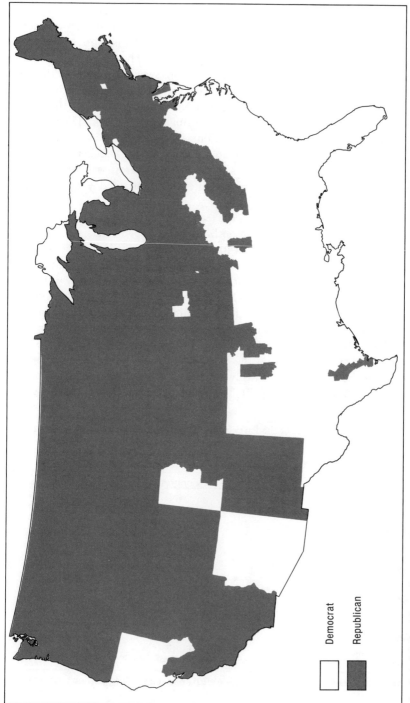

Map 8.1. Sectional Base of the Party System: 67th Congress (1921–1923)

Democrat

Republican

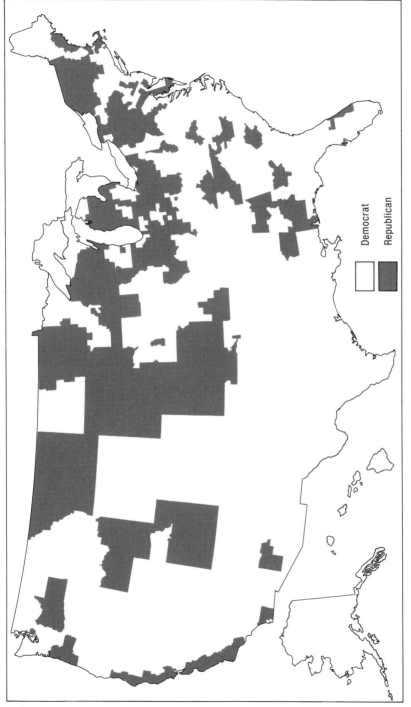

Map 8.2. Sectional Base of the Party System: 89th Congress (1965–1966)

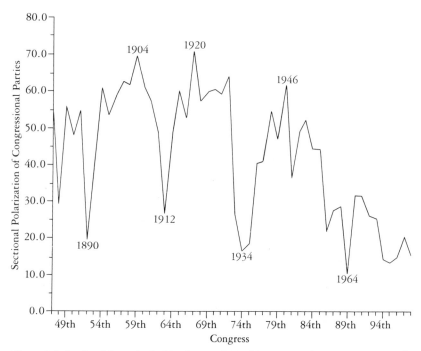

Figure 8.1. Sectional Stress in the Membership Base of Congressional Parties, 1881–1984
SOURCE: Calculated from data on party membership in the *Congressional Directory* for each Congress.

lican strength in the major metropolitan centers of the nation has declined, and, since 1960, the GOP has become increasingly competitive in southern congressional races. Allowing for these two trends, the party distribution in the 89th Congress was typical of periods of Democratic dominance in the last half of the twentieth century. The two periods illustrate both the type of geographical distribution that produces very high or low sectional stress scores and the pattern resulting from the increasing "nationalization" of the party system that has taken place since 1932.

On the whole, the last century has been punctuated by a cyclical pattern of sharp, short declines in sectional stress followed by a strong resurgence in polarization (see table 8.1 and figure 8.1). The three most prominent peaks in congressional party polarization occurred as a result of the 1904, 1920, and 1946 elections. The deepest troughs came immediately following the 1890, 1912, 1934, and 1964 congressional elections. However, the peaks have been less high and the troughs have been deeper and more prolonged in recent years than at any time in the past. In addition, the level of sectional stress in the congressional party system has been generally declining since the New Deal began in 1933. Since 1958, and particularly in the years after 1974, the level of polarization has been more or less consistently low.

In addition to this longitudinal decline, two factors seem to be historically associated with decreasing regional polarization in the party system: electoral instability and the size of the Republican party. Sectional stress in the party composition of the House declines during periods of electoral instability only to resurge during the more stable periods between critical elections. In addition, sectional stress has been positively associated with the size of the Republican party in the House over the last century. Generally speaking, the greater the Republican majority in the House of Representatives, the greater the regional polarization of the party system. On the other hand, when the Democratic party has enjoyed a broad national following, the level of sectional stress in the party system has been low.

The connection between electoral stability and regional polarization can be clearly demonstrated by comparing sectional stress in the composition of congressional parties with Gerald Pomper's classification of presidential elections.[8] There have been seventeen congressional elections since 1880 which have either coincided with, or occurred between, "maintaining" presidential elections. "Maintaining" elections are those in which the cleavage in the electorate presents a high level of continuity with previous elections and the majority party for that historical period is victorious. The average sectional stress index for the seventeen "maintaining election" Congresses is 53.4. "Deviating" elections preserve the existing electoral cleavage but temporarily depress the majority party's vote enough to elect a president from the minority party. In Congresses associated with deviating elections, the polarization of the two parties produced an average sectional stress score of 44.2. Thirteen congressional contests have coincided with or taken place within two years of either a "realigning" or "converting" election. In a "realigning" election, previously stable electoral cleavages undergo a great deal of change, and as a result, the dominant party in the previous period goes down to defeat. In a "converting" election, major voting blocs shift between the two parties but the dominant party is still able to win the presidency. In the Congresses associated with these two types of elections, the level of sectional stress has declined significantly. (See table 8.3.) Because Pomper's classification ends with the 1964 election (a "converting" contest), this analysis only runs to 1966. The association between increasing electoral instability and decreasing regional polarization in the congressional party system will be discussed in connection with the size of the Republican party.

When the Republicans controlled over 60 percent of the House, as they have in only four of the last fifty-two Congresses, the average sectional stress score (65.6) reflected an extreme polarization of the party system. When the party organized the House but held fewer than 60 percent of the seats, the level of sectional stress usually declined moderately (an average score of 57.5). In

Table 8.3. Sectional Stress in the Congressional Party System and Critical Presidential Elections, 1880–1966

Congressional Election	Average Sectional Stress Index	Number of Elections
Coincides with or Occurs between Two Maintaining Presidential Elections	53.4	17
Coincides with a Deviating Election or Occurs between a Deviating and a Maintaining Election	44.2	14
Coincides with or Occurs Adjacent to at Least One Realigning or Converting Election	40.0	13

SOURCES: Categorization of presidential elections: Gerald Pomper, "Classification of Presidential Elections," *Journal of Politics* 29 (1967): 535–66. Averages calculated from data presented in table 8.1.

Table 8.4. Sectional Stress in the Congressional Party System and the Size of the Republican Party in the House, 1881–1984

Republicans as Percentage of Total Membership	Number of Congresses	Average Score on the Index	Percentage of Congresses within Five Index Points of Mean	Average Score	
				1881–1930	1931–84
60.0 +	4	65.6	75.0	65.6 (4)	—
50.0–59.9	14	57.9	92.9	57.6 (12)	59.4 (2)
40.0–49.9	18	41.4	16.7	49.8 (5)	38.1 (13)
0.0–39.9	16	24.1	25.0	28.6 (4)	22.6 (12)

SOURCE: Calculated from data presented in table 8.1.

general, when the Republicans have controlled the House, the regional polarization of the party system has been consistently high and remarkably stable (see table 8.4). In contrast, sectional stress has plummeted when the Democrats have won the election. This relationship between the size of the Republican party and sectional stress persists even when the last century is divided into pre– and post–New Deal periods (though the secular decline in polarization is evident).

Both the size of the Republican party and electoral stability appear to contribute to sectional stress in the congressional party system. Analysis of the forty-four Congresses elected between 1880 and 1966 (see table 8.5) reveals that these two factors were, with remarkable consistency, mutually reinforcing.* Placed in historical context, partisan strife between the Republican and

*On the horizontal axis of Table 8.5, the forty-four Congresses are categorized into four columns corresponding to the increasing size of the Republican party in the House. On the vertical axis, the elections are divided into three rows according to increasing electoral instability. If the two factors, size of Republican party and electoral instability, reinforce each other, the average polarization should increase for all rows when read left to right and should

Table 8.5. Sectional Stress in the Congressional Party System, Critical Elections, and the Size of the Republican Party in the House, 1880–1966

Type of Congressional Election[a]	Average Sectional Stress Index by Size of Republican Party in the House of Representatives			
	0–39%	40–49%	50–59%	60–100%
Maintaining	34.2 (4)	50.9 (2)	58.9 (9)	69.9 (2)
Deviating	28.6 (4)	49.9 (8)	52.4 (2)	—
Realigning or Converting	18.9 (4)	38.0 (4)	57.6 (3)	61.3 (2)

[a]Congressional election categories are those described in table 8.3. The number of elections in each cell is given in parentheses.

SOURCE: Pomper, "Classification of Presidential Elections." Averages calculated from data presented in table 8.1.

Democratic parties overlay bipolar economic competition between the industrialized, metropolitan core and the agrarian, southern periphery. In this bipolar alignment, the South has been significantly more isolated from the mainstream of national politics than has the North. Since, until recently, the Republican party has been unable to penetrate the region even during its most successful electoral periods, southern delegations in Congress have also been more internally cohesive than their northern counterparts. The areas of greatest partisan competition (the agrarian plains and the border regions) share some of the political interests that characterize both sectional poles, but, on balance, they have been significantly more compatible with a northern industrial-commercial coalition led by the Republican party than with the southern, agrarian, and race-conscious Democratic alternative. As a result, the natural sectional cleavage to which the party system returned time and time again was one in which the Democratic party totally dominated the southern sectional pole with almost no representation either in the North or in the border regions. (For the geographical form of this natural cleavage, see map 8.1.) When the Democratic party penetrated the North, the party temporarily exploited latent inconsistencies within the Republican coalition by introducing political issues which cut across the dominant bipolar system.

The Democratic Party and the South

The historically close connection between the Democratic party and the expression of southern political interests requires a brief elaboration. In every Congress convened between 1877 and 1983, Democrats have occupied a ma-

decrease for all columns when read top to bottom. With one exception (the cell containing two deviating elections resulting in Republican majorities of less than 60 percent), this appears to be true. In addition, if the two factors are reinforcing, we should expect the score in the upper right-hand cell to be higher and the score in the lower left-hand cell to be lower than all other entries. This, indeed, is the case.

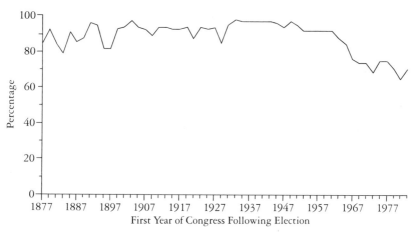

Figure 8.2. Percentage of Southern House Seats Held by Democrats, 1877–1984
SOURCE: Compiled from information contained in the respective editions of the *Congressional Directory*.
NOTE: Includes all eleven states that once composed the Confederacy plus Kentucky and Oklahoma.

jority of southern seats in the House of Representatives.* In fact, for most of the last century, over 80 percent of southern districts have been represented by Democrats. In the three decades between 1931 and 1961 the percentage never fell below 90 percent (figure 8.2). Beginning with the national Republican resurgence in 1966, however, the Democratic proportion of all southern districts has fallen below 80 percent in nine consecutive elections and, in 1981, registered a post-Reconstruction low of 65.3 percent. In these years, Republican inroads in the South account for a substantial portion of the national depolarization of the party system.

In addition, the percentage of southern members within the Democratic caucus in the House has been a fairly accurate marker for sectional stress in the membership base of congressional parties (figure 8.3). Over the last century four temporal peaks in southern dominance of the House caucus stand out (1895, 1905, 1921, and 1947) and coincide exactly with the four most prominent peaks in sectional stress (following the 1894, 1904, 1920, and 1946 elections—see figure 8.1). Similarly, the three deepest troughs in southern

---

*The beginning date, 1877, was chosen because it is the date conventionally given for the end of Reconstruction.

dominance (1891, 1913, and 1937) almost exactly match the three low points in sectional stress prior to the civil rights era (following the 1890, 1912, and 1934 elections). Over the entire century, the level of sectional stress in the congressional party system was highly and inversely associated with the electoral success of Democratic congressional candidates outside the South. The correlation between the level of sectional stress and southern Democrats as a percentage of the national party is a remarkably high .893 between 1881 and 1984 (see table 8.6). When the century is divided into four twenty-five-year periods, the closest association between the two factors roughly coincides with the most vital years of the bipolar, New Deal coalition and the "classic" phase of the committee system in Congress (1933–58). In these years, the Democrats expanded their political base in the industrial North while retaining almost exclusive control of the agrarian South. The correlation in these thirteen Congresses was a near unity .965.

The breakup of the New Deal coalition dramatically reduced the connection between sectional stress and the presence of southern Democrats in the party caucus; in the twelve Congresses since 1958, the correlation between the two has been .666. During these years, growing Democratic penetration of the industrial core has been associated with increasing Republican success in the South. Regional polarization in the party system has also been positively associated with the role of the Democratic party as the exclusive vehicle for southern influence in the House of Representatives (see figure 8.4 and table

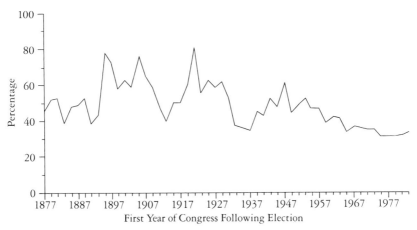

Figure 8.3. Southern Democrats as a Percentage of All Democratic House Seats, 1877–1984
SOURCE: Compiled from information contained in the respective editions of the *Congressional Directory*.

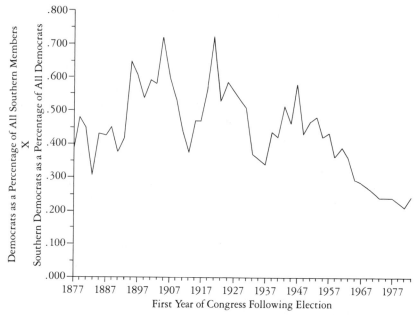

Figure 8.4. The Democratic Party as a Vehicle for Southern Influence in National Politics, 1877–1984
SOURCE: Compiled from data used in constructing the previous two figures.

Table 8.6. Sectional Stress in the Congressional Party System and the Role of the Democratic Party as the Vehicle of Southern Political Influence, 1881–1984

		Correlation between Sectional Stress and:	
Period	Number of Congresses	Southern Democrats as a Percentage of the National Party in House of Representatives	Democratic Party as an Exclusive Vehicle of Southern Influence[a]
1881–1907	13	.781	.825
1907–33	13	.771	.788
1933–58	13	.965	.954
1959–84	13	.666	.425
1881–1984	52	.893	.907

[a] Determined by the formula: (percentage of all southern seats held by Democrats) × (percentage of southerners in the national Democratic caucus) (see figure 8.4).

8.6).* Here the disintegration of the New Deal coalition produces an even starker deviation from the historical pattern; in the last twenty-four years, the correlation between sectional stress and the role of the Democratic party as the political vehicle of southern influence has plummeted to .425. Since the historical dominance of the South by the Democratic party was, until recently, uniformly high, most of the fluctuation in the role of the party as the political vehicle for southern interests can be traced to the expansion of party strength in the North and West (compare figure 8.4 with figure 8.3). Until the early 1960s, southern influence within the party declined in direct proportion to Democratic success outside the region. Since 1961, the declining importance of the Democratic party as a vehicle for southern influence can, for the first time, be partially attributed to declining party strength within the South itself. In addition, the role of the party as the exclusive vehicle of southern interests and the level of sectional stress in the congressional party system are now less closely associated. This recent dissociation reflects the fact that regional polarization outside the South has increased even as Democratic hegemony within the South decays.

Sectional Stress in Presidential Elections

The recent decline in sectional stress in the party system and in Democratic dominance in the South has coincided with a steady deterioration in the cohesion and political importance of national party organizations. Among the most important indicators of national party weakness and decline have been the increasing frequency of split-ticket voting, the persistence of congressional Democratic strength in the South (even as Democratic presidential candidates have become increasingly unpopular in the region), the increasing amplitude of partisan swings between elections, and the erosion of traditional party allegiances. This progressive deterioration in the primacy of party has been termed "dealignment" and partisan "decomposition."[9]

Though it has become increasingly common throughout the twentieth century, split-ticket voting can be described as a fairly recent phenomenon (see table 8.7). In national politics, perhaps the most important result of split-ticket voting has been the increasing divergence between outcomes in presidential and congressional races. Until 1924, an average of fewer than 10 percent of all congressional districts revealed a discrepancy between the party of

---

*Multiplying together the two percentages (Democrats as a proportion of all southern members and southern Democrats as a proportion of all Democrats) is a somewhat arbitrary decision, although the resulting data have several attractive properties. At unity, Democrats would control all southern districts but occupy none of the northern and western seats. At zero, the Democrats would not control a single southern district and party strength would lie entirely in the North and West. In addition, multiplication tends to accentuate the amplitude of southern influence—further emphasizing the peaks and troughs.

the winning congressional candidate and the prevailing presidential nominee. From 1924 through the Roosevelt years, the proportion of congressional districts with split results remained steady at about 14 percent. Beginning with the Dixiecrat revolt in 1948, the divergence between presidential and congressional contests has reached staggering proportions. In 1972, for example, nearly four out of every ten congressional districts were carried by the nominee of one party at the presidential level and by the nominee of the other party in the congressional race. Many political analysts have accounted for the rise in split-ticket voting by citing the persistence of Democratic strength in southern congressional races even as the region deserts the presidential nominee.

Table 8.7. Congressional Districts with Split Election Results: Districts Carried by a Presidential Nominee of One Party and by a House Nominee of Another Party, 1920–1980

Presidential Election	Number of Districts Analyzed	Number of Districts with Split Results	Percentage of All Districts with Split Results	Percentage of Splits Involving Minor Party
1900 (McKinley)	295	10	3.4	0
1904 (Roosevelt)	310	5	1.6	0
1908 (Roosevelt)	314	21	6.8	0
1912 (Wilson)	333	84	25.2	50.0
1916 (Wilson)	333	35	10.5	0
1920 (Harding)	344	11	3.2	0
1924 (Coolidge)	356	42	11.8	28.6
1928 (Hoover)	359	68	18.9	1.5
1932 (Roosevelt)	355	50	14.1	10.0
1936 (Roosevelt)	361	51	14.1	19.6
1940 (Roosevelt)	362	53	14.6	9.4
1944 (Roosevelt)	367	41	11.2	2.4
1948 (Truman)	435	92	21.1	33.7
1952 (Eisenhower)	435	84	19.3	1.2
1956 (Eisenhower)	435	130	29.9	1.5
1960 (Kennedy)	437	114	26.1	2.6
1964 (Johnson)	435	145	33.3	0
1968 (Nixon)	435	137	31.5	35.0
1972 (Nixon)	435	190	43.7	0
1976 (Carter)	435	124	28.5	0
1980 (Reagan)	435	147	33.8	0

SOURCES: Data on elections from 1900 through 1916 and on minor party results from Walter Dean Burnham, *Critical Elections and the Mainsprings of American Politics* (New York: W. W. Norton, 1970), p. 109. 1948 election figures from data in Edward Franklin Cox, "Voting in Postwar Federal Elections: A Statistical Analysis of Party Strengths Since 1945" (diss., Wright State University, 1966). Figures for other elections from 1920 to 1964 from Milton C. Cummings, Jr., *Congressmen and the Electorate: Elections for the U.S. House and the President, 1920–1964* (New York: Free Press, 1966), p. 32. Figures for the last four presidential elections from data in the *Congressional Quarterly Weekly Report*.

Table 8.8. Comparison of Sectional Stress in the Membership Base of Congressional Parties and Presidential Elections, 1920–1980

Election Year	Congressional Parties	Presidential Election	Winning Presidential Candidate	Losing Presidential Candidate	Third Party[a]
1920	70.7	86.5	324 (R)	111 (D)	—
1924	59.9	73.5	299 (R)	121 (D)	15 (LF)
1928	59.1	46.4	323 (R)	112 (D)	—
1932	26.1	48.3	348 (D)	87 (R)	—
1936	18.7	25.6	392 (D)	43 (R)	—
1940	41.0	36.2	308 (D)	127 (R)	—
1944	46.9	38.1	280 (D)	155 (R)	—
1948	36.6	35.6	244 (D)	160 (R)	31 (ST)
1952	52.1	38.4	297 (R)	138 (D)	—
1956	44.3	26.2	328 (R)	107 (D)	—
1960	27.9	34.0	209 (D)	228 (R)	—
1964	10.6	36.7	375 (D)	60 (R)	—
1968	31.7	37.5	227 (R)	160 (D)	48 (GW)
1972	25.4	7.0	378 (R)	57 (D)	—
1976	13.9	41.5	223 (D)	212 (R)	—
1980	20.2	15.1	309 (R)	126 (D)	—

[a] LF = Robert LaFollette; ST = Strom Thurmond; GW = George Wallace.
SOURCES: Congressional sectional stress scores: see table 8.1. Pre-1948 presidential election returns by congressional district have been estimated using the procedure described in the text. 1948 presidential election returns by congressional district from Cox, "Voting in Postwar Federal Elections: A Statistical Analysis of Party Strengths Since 1945." Presidential scores from 1952 forward calculated from data in the *Congressional Quarterly Weekly Report* and the *Almanac of American Politics*.

But, as the results of Jimmy Carter's presidential campaign in 1976 demonstrate, the rise of split-ticket voting has become a truly national phenomenon. Even while both Carter and congressional Democrats swept the South, 124 of the contests for seats in the House diverged from their respective presidential returns.

A comparison of sectional stress in presidential and congressional elections over the last sixty years reveals an apparently growing divergence in the respective regional polarization of presidential races and the congressional party system (see table 8.8).* In three of the last five elections (1964, 1972, and 1980), the discrepancy between sectional stress in congressional and presi-

*For the period before 1948, the presidential result in the individual congressional districts was calculated from raw election data where such information was available for entire counties. In cases where more than one congressman was elected from a single county, the winning presidential nominee in that county was assumed to prevail in every congressional district. This fairly strong assumption probably artificially inflated sectional stress scores in presidential races in both 1920 and 1924. For contests after Al Smith's candidacy in 1928, the assumption probably deflated the stress score. After 1944 in presidential contests and in all congressional races from 1920 to 1960, complete electoral data by district were available and utilized.

dential races has established twentieth-century highs. In four of the last six contests sectional stress in presidential races has exceeded regional polarization in the congressional party system. This recent pattern is somewhat surprising given the volatility of partisan swings and the tremendous instability of regional strength in recent presidential contests. For example, the stress scores for the 1964 and 1976 presidential contests—which are fairly close in magnitude—are based on extremely different regional distributions of party strength. Aside from the relative lack of a regional pattern in the 1972 and 1980 returns, sectional stress in presidential contests has remained relatively constant since the beginning of the New Deal.

Sectional Stress and the Party System in the 1980s

In 1960, E. E. Schattsneider described the 1930 election—the first of the Great Depression—as heralding the substitution of a "national political alignment for an extreme sectional alignment everywhere . . . except the South." [10] Six years later, Philip Converse predicted that regional convergence toward a nationalized party system would *not* include "widespread party competition in portions of the South which remain rural" and that the "rural southern hinterland will remain largely a fief of the Democratic party" because of an accident of "history." [11] But one by one the elements that held the bipolar New Deal coalition together have been eaten away. Civil rights legislation and the expansion of the southern electorate have removed two of the most onerous restrictions on the freedom of movement by southern congressmen between competing political coalitions. Institutional attacks on the seniority system and the committee system in general have further decreased the incentive to remain within the party increasingly dominated by members representing the industrial-commercial core. Finally, the precipitous decline in the competitive position of heavy industry in the world-economy threatens the interregional detente on protectionism.

All these recent trends suggest the final dissolution of the New Deal coalition and a probable return to a regionally polarized party system. Two of the most recent third-party campaigns indicate the most significant centrifugal forces pulling apart the Democratic coalition. The George Wallace vote in 1968 revealed the southern periphery's dissatisfaction with the pro-labor and civil rights position of the northern wing of the party. The regions in which Wallace ran strongly exactly coincide with the periphery end of the American political alignment. In 1980, John Anderson's race provided an outlet for the frustrations felt by industrial and commercial seaport electorates—a frustration engendered by the Carter administration's unsuccessful attempts to bridge the sectional divide (see maps 8.3 and 8.4). But the repolarization of the party system needs a triggering event which would lead to an unambiguous commitment by one of the parties to the interests of one or the other of

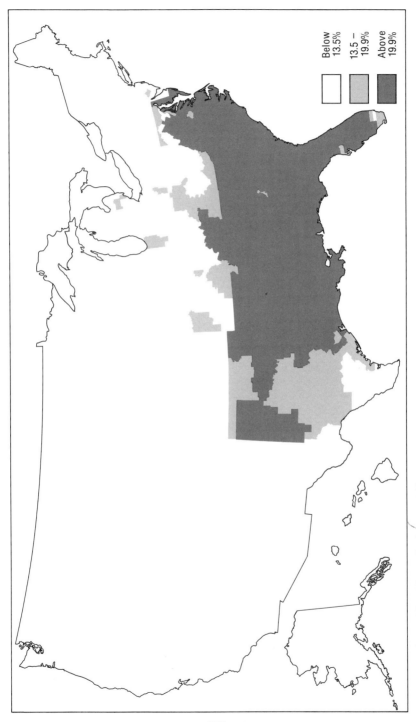

Map 8.3. 1968 Presidential vote for George Wallace

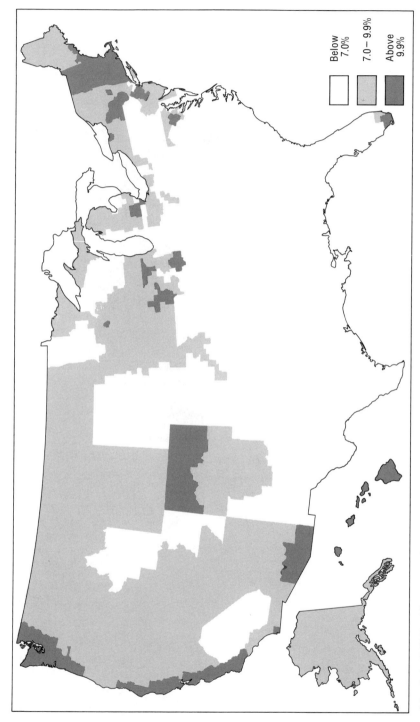

Map 8.4. 1980 Presidential vote for John Anderson

the two great polar sections.* Such a revival of sectional loyalties would lead in both parties to the atrophy of the excluded sectional wing. Burnham, while acknowledging the regional diversity that has existed within both major parties, has suggested that Ronald Reagan's rise to power may represent such a triggering event.

> Regional battles are likely to become major features of national political conflict, inside and outside Congress, irrespective of which president or party is in power. But under a conservative administration, the decline of the old industrial heartland will become more and more explicit. In particular, the vast increase in military consumption expenditures which is projected through mid-decade will considerably accelerate the transfer of wealth and power toward the South and West.[12]

If this scenario unfolds, the end of the fifty-year hiatus of sectional stress in the party system will witness a reversal in party roles. In the regional "shakedown" that would accompany increased party cohesion, the Republicans, the former handmaidens of industrialization, would be transformed into the party of the periphery. The Democrats, formerly the representatives of the "conquered provinces,"[13] would probably consolidate their strength in the old industrial core.

American Ideology, the Party System, and Sectional Stress

The sectional depolarization of the congressional party system was the ultimate result of those events and institutions which made a stable, bipolar, New Deal coalition possible: a strong committee system, increasing bureaucratic and executive discretion, and an almost total absence of formal party discipline. As the depolarization of the party system has progressed—particularly after the end of the Eisenhower administration—the alignment of ideological proto-coalitions has moved toward the historical axis of sectional competition. In order to understand why these diametrically opposed trends have occurred during the same, post–World War II decades, American ideologies must be viewed as the primary alternatives to party-based coalitions within their respective political eras. The belief-systems which support ideological proto-coalitions are largely unarticulated and often logically incoherent. The one characteristic that gives these beliefs a role in the political system is that they bind together sets of public policy stands. These bundles of policy positions represent a lowest common denominator for an alternative proto-coalition whose most likely membership cuts obliquely across the alignment undergirding the party system.

*Burnham, "American Politics in the 1970's: Beyond Party?" p. 334. Burnham speculates that if party decomposition continues (an unlikely event, he believes), "under these conditions of pervasive public discontent, democracy will be progressively emptied of any operational meaning as executive-bureaucratic imperatives came to dominate the political system" (p. 340).

Several corollaries follow from this interpretation of the role of ideology in the American political system. The first is that ideological proto-coalitions are normally less viable than their party-based alternatives and thus represent minor faultlines in contemporary politics. In those cases where the proto-coalitions based on ideological belief-systems came to represent major cleavages in the United States, party organizations moved toward the same ideological alignment. In most instances where such movement occurred, the party organization first merged with representatives of the leading ideological associations and, afterwards, these ideological groups lost most of their significance apart from the parties that absorbed them.

Thus, the ultimate destiny of most important ideological movements is annihilation through absorption into one of the two major parties. The two clearest examples of this process in American history were the absorption of the Populist party into the Democratic coalition of 1896 and the merger between the progressive movement and the Democratic party during the Wilson years.

Since the beginning of the New Deal, the two most important American ideologies have been "liberalism" and "conservatism." To an extent unparalleled in history, these belief-systems have been empirically, though not philosophically, well defined. On the left, the hearth of liberalism has been tended by the Americans for Democratic Action (ADA) since the organization's founding in 1947. For over three decades the ADA has decisively settled disputes over the relationship between liberalism and contemporary policy choices. In addition, the organization has published annual ratings of congressional voting behavior which provide a practical and indispensable guide to the ideological orientation of individual senators and representatives. Without these ratings—which are now mimicked by numerous groups at all points of the political compass—much of the descriptive utility of ideological labels would be lost. The ADA voting scores allow analysts to describe political actors as "liberals" or "conservatives" without reference to a well-developed political philosophy. In fact, the avoidance of a rigid philosophical emphasis has probably been one of the necessary elements of the ADA's long existence in competition with party organizations.

From its creation, the ADA has primarily represented an alliance of organized labor and the intelligentsia on the moderate American left. As a consequence, the organization has always been very closely associated with the northern industrial wing of the Democratic party and has endorsed the candidacy of every Democratic presidential candidate from Truman through Carter.* It should be noted, however, that the ADA endorsed pre-nomination

---

*Clifton Brock believes that this consistent affection for the party's choice has been a by-product of the structure of the electoral system: "Presidential candidates must appeal first of all to the urban masses of the large and doubtful states. This is especially true of Democratic candidates. . . . ADA's short-term political goals—such as public housing, civil rights, social security, increased unemployment compensation, aid to depressed areas, federal aid to education and other welfare measures—are generally the same policy objectives apparently desired by the

challenges to the only two southern presidents, backing Eugene McCarthy of Minnesota in 1969 and Edward Kennedy of Massachusetts in 1979.*

In Senate races between 1947 and 1962, the ADA endorsed twenty Democrats for every Republican who also found favor with the organization.[14] The ratio has probably not changed much in subsequent elections. In some respects, however, relations between the ADA and congressional Democrats have not been close. After its first general election campaign in 1948, the ADA called for a weakened Rules Committee and the expulsion of Dixiecrats from the congressional caucus.[15] Since then the organization has regularly called for the abandonment of seniority norms, a stronger caucus, and other institutional reforms intended to either impose party loyalty on the dissident southern wing or centralize parliamentary authority in the hands of the northern majority. Even so, many congressmen and senators have been drawn from the ranks of the ADA; as early as 1950, there were forty ADA members in the House and seven in the Senate.[16] Almost all of these members belonged to the northern wing of the party and were closely allied with organized labor. Many of them—including Hubert Humphrey of Minnesota, Don Edwards of California, Allard Lowenstein of New York, Donald Fraser of Minnesota, George McGovern of South Dakota, Patsy Mink of Hawaii, and Father Drinan of Massachusetts—have gone on to lead the ADA as the organization's national chair. This close association with the northern wing carries over into day-to-day lobbying within Congress. In 1965, the ADA described the Democratic Study Group as a very effective liberal force with which it worked "very closely."[17] On another occasion, an ADA lobbyist stated that the ADA worked "almost 100 percent of the time" with the political arm of the United Auto Workers and the Democratic Study Group.†

The close association of the ADA with the northern industrial wing of the Democratic party is reinforced by the regional distribution of the organization's membership (see table 8.9). The ADA started as a "relatively small New York movement," and although membership has expanded to all parts of the nation, nearly 20 percent of the membership was still drawn from New York State almost a quarter of a century after the organization's founding.[18] Over half of the national membership resided in the Northeast, with members con-

---

majority of urban voters." *Americans for Democratic Action: Its Role in National Politics* (Washington: Public Affairs Press, 1962), p. 26.

*The ADA national board endorsed McCarthy by a rather close vote of 64 to 47. The endorsement led to a deepening split between the labor and intelligentsia factions of the organization and a mass exodus of union representatives from the ADA. "Liberal Split: ADA and LBJ," *Commonweal*, March 1, 1968, p. 643–44; *Time*, February 23, 1968, p. 19; *Newsweek*, February 26, 1968, p. 25. In 1979, the national convention endorsed Kennedy over incumbent Carter by a vote of 500 to 0. *Commonweal*, August 3, 1979, pp. 420–22.

†John L. Moore, "Washington Pressures/Weakened ADA Seeks 'Silent Majority' Support," *National Journal*, September 5, 1970, p. 1930. Between 80 and 90 percent of nonsouthern Democratic members of the House of Representatives have belonged to the Democratic Study Group since it was organized in the late 1950s.

Table 8.9. 1970 Membership of the Americans for Democratic Action, by State and Region

State	Number	Percentage of National Total
New York	8,300	19.7
California	6,700	15.9
Illinois	4,950	11.7
Pennsylvania	4,400	10.4
Massachusetts	3,300	7.8
Greater Washington, D.C.	2,400	5.7
Michigan	1,800	4.3
Ohio	1,800	4.3
New Jersey	1,600	3.8
Connecticut	1,000	2.4
Northeast	21,100	50.1
Midwest	10,950	26.0
West	8,300	19.7
South	1,800	4.3
National	42,150	100.0

SOURCE: John L. Moore, "Washington Pressures/Weakened ADA Seeks 'Silent Majority' Support," *National Journal,* September 5, 1970, p. 1933. Membership of Greater Washington, D.C., area included in northeastern total. Table does not include 8,175 members listed as "At Large."

centrated in Boston, Philadelphia, and Washington, D.C.—as well as the New York metropolitan area. Another quarter of the national total belonged to chapters in the Midwest. These members were primarily concentrated in the large Chicago, Detroit, and Cleveland branches. The San Francisco (Northern California) division probably composed two-third or more of the total membership in the West. These figures illustrate the extremely close association between ADA affiliation and residence in the industrial core.

Perhaps the most important way that the ADA affects the course of American politics is through the publication of its annual ratings of congressmen on a "liberal–conservative" spectrum. Many groups—including the northern wing of the Democratic party and organized labor—have a stake in the empirical definition of "liberalism." To the extent that the assignment of labels to political actors is a pragmatic recognition of the interests represented in the liberal coalition, the ratings reflect the sometimes logically inconsistent political demands of individual groups while preserving the symbolic value of the term "liberalism." Once published, these ratings of individual representatives and senators strongly influence the ideological labeling of government policies in the press and in common political discourse. In the absence of logically consistent and well-developed philosophical systems, government policies are labeled "conservative" if conservative congressmen support (and liberals oppose) their implementation and "liberal" if the situation is reversed.

Because an explicit and common referent is so much more powerful than an abstract and diffuse set of principles (upon which there would be little agreement), continuity in American ideology resides in the present preferences of last year's adherents (and not in any consistent application of a belief system to individual government actions). The empirical "political" content of contemporary ideological labels is further increased by the close involvement of congressmen in the construction of the ratings.*

Liberalism and Bipolar Sectionalism

The northern wing of the Democratic party and the Americans for Democratic Action thus have common political bases in the industrial core, overlapping leadership, and similar policy goals. Because of these common interests, the ADA ratings have consistently identified labor-oriented, northern Democrats as the leading exponents of liberalism.† However, in the selection of votes that compose the ratings, there has been significant variation in the degree to which liberalism has been attributed to the ADA's major political rivals: the Republicans and the southern wing of the Democratic party. During the early years of the organization's existence, the ratings revealed an affinity for southern Democrats compared to the Republican party. In the last two decades, however, ADA positions have moved closer to the northern wing of the Republican party. (See table 8.10. In this analysis, ratings published by the *New*

---

*According to an interview with John Isaacs, a legislative staff member, "the ADA vote selection process involves three steps: first, two staff members prepare a broad list of votes from all those taken during the session; then, from 20 to 25 congressional aides select the key votes and present them for final approval to the ADA executive committee, chaired by a member of Congress—Rep. Donald M. Fraser (D-Minn.).

"Four criteria are used to select the votes, Isaacs explained: 1) The vote must be on an important issue; 2) procedural votes generally are chosen because they reveal basic liberal and conservative positions that often are obscured in a vote on final passage; 3) votes that are reasonably close are selected because they show a distinction in position, a clash between sides on an issue; and 4) votes are chosen for issues on which the ADA has taken a stand or committed its resources and manpower.

"ADA officials are aware that a high ADA rating actually can be a political albatross for some incumbents at election time. Isaacs noted that 'some members don't like the ratings because they are open to attack by opponents for having high scores.'" *Congressional Quarterly Weekly Report*, July 6, 1974, pp. 1750–51.

† In some cases the ADA has explicitly abandoned objective principles when a policy goal threatened these members. In 1978, for example, the ADA proposed altering the revenue sharing formula in order to target funds toward the absolute number of poor individuals in state and local governmental units. Because of regional differences in the cost of living, the change would have meant a substantial shift in funding from the Northeast and Midwest to the South. When computer projections confirmed this shift, the ADA backed away from the proposal. As lobbyist Leon Shull put it, "Too damn many people were going to be hurt." Rochelle L. Stanfield, "Playing Computer Politics with Local Aid Formulas," *National Journal*, December 9, 1979, p. 1980.

Table 8.10. Average ADA Scores for Democrats in Leading Periphery Delegations
and for Republicans in Leading Core Delegations, 1945–1976

	79th Congress (1945–46)		84th Congress (1955–56)		89th Congress (1965–66)		94th Congress (1975–76)	
	%	(N)	%	(N)	%	(N)	%	(N)
Periphery Delegations[a]	Average Democratic Liberalism Score							
Atlanta	38.9	(6)	41.9	(8)	21.9	(9)	19.7	(10)
Birmingham	37.1	(7)	61.0	(8)	11.1	(3)	15.4	(4)
Dallas	28.0	(7)	26.8	(9)	20.8	(12)	13.1	(9)
Memphis	29.2	(8)	47.9	(7)	15.7	(6)	28.2	(5)
Total	33.0	(28)	43.8	(32)	19.2	(30)	18.5	(28)
Core Delegations[a]	Average Republican Liberalism Score							
Boston	24.4	(9)	55.3	(10)	32.5	(7)	53.8	(5)
Detroit	14.4	(6)	24.7	(5)	6.7	(7)	7.7	(5)
New York	30.0	(18)	51.2	(24)	31.7	(12)	42.1	(14)
Philadelphia	25.9	(9)	37.5	(8)	12.5	(8)	29.5	(8)
Total	25.7	(42)	46.9	(47)	22.2	(34)	35.4	(32)
Difference between Periphery Democrats and Core Republicans	+7.3		−3.1		−3.0		−16.9	

[a]The major polar delegations represent the extreme ends of the sectional alignment
since the end of World War II (see table 2.5).

SOURCES: Scores for the 79th Congress compiled from ratings published by the *New
Republic*, September 23, 1946, pp. 368–72. Ratings for the 84th Congress from the
ADA World. Scores for the 89th and 94th Congresses from the *Congressional Quarterly
Weekly Report*, February 25, 1966, pp. 472–73; February 5, 1977, pp. 229–35; May
22, 1976, pp. 1301–7; and the *Congressional Quarterly Almanac*, 1966, pp. 1412–13.

Republic served as a surrogate for ADA scores in the 79th Congress (1945–46);
the ADA was founded a year later.[19])

The apparent ideological movement of southern Democrats and northern Republicans between 1945 and 1975 would be difficult to explain without reference to the changing political goals of the ADA and northern Democrats.
In fact, a good case can be made that an objective measure of ideology—if one
had been possible—would have revealed diametrically opposed trends. Southern Democrats should have become more liberal as Republicans replaced party
members in the most conservative districts and as blacks and poor whites
entered the electorate. Northern Republicans should have become more conservative as Democrats replaced members in the urban industrial districts and
the center of gravity of the party shifted into the South and West.

Instead, early liberalism ratings revealed a Republican party that was
more conservative than the southern Democratic wing. In the early post–
World War II years, the Republicans were viewed, not surprisingly, as the
most important opponents of the northern wing of the Democratic party.
Republicans still held, in normal years, a substantial majority of the districts

in the northern industrial core. This fact forced the northern Democrats to concentrate on intraregional class conflict within the Republican party and, for that reason, draw stark ideological distinctions between the political program of organized labor and a GOP heavily influenced by the industrial elite. Furthermore, northern Democrats depended on southern votes for their participation in party control of the national government. Consequently, *New Republic* and *ADA* ratings constituted a mild affirmation of the pragmatic policy basis of the New Deal coalition. Finally, the party system was still fairly polarized along sectional lines (see table 8.1), and the affiliation of liberal organizations with the relatively small northern Democratic wing allowed "liberalism" to be a political program very distinct from mainstream Republican or Democratic alternatives.

Votes selected by the *New Republic* during the 79th Congress included a Republican motion to recommit an extension of the Reciprocal Trade Agreement Act (the liberal position was "nay"), a Republican amendment that would have allowed price control ceilings to reflect "the cost of production" and a "reasonable profit" on every item ("nay"), and an amendment to abolish federal livestock subsidies ("nay"). Other roll calls in the ratings which effectively discriminated between northern Republicans and southern Democrats involved a Republican amendment to prohibit federal funds for United Nations aid to Russia and Eastern Europe ("nay") and a multi-billion dollar loan to Great Britain ("yea"). Votes on atomic energy, the employment service, labor legislation, and price control also tended to raise southern Democratic and lower northern Republican scores.[20]

As the center of gravity of the Democratic party moved into the industrial core, members of the southern wing became the most important opponents of the alliance between industrial labor and the intelligentsia. This transformation was partially the result of Democratic success in the North, which, on the one hand, made stark ideological contrasts with Republican electoral opponents a secondary political priority, and, on the other hand, held out the promise of release from the burdens and compromises of southern participation in the New Deal coalition. As a purely political program, the civil rights legislation of the 1960s was a more or less calculated gamble on the future of a labor–lower class party (see chapters 5–7). In this gamble, strong ideological distinctions between the new working-class center of the party and the now "reactionary" periphery elements became more important than competition with the apparently defeated Republicans. In addition, as the new "establishment" party in the industrial core, the northern wing now embraced a political program some parts of which could be supported by northern Republicans. With the easing of intraregional class conflict, both northern Democrats and Republicans could join in supporting civil rights, extending some aspects of labor regulation to the South, and attempting to reverse the decline of the core economy. Furthermore, during the last two decades the party system became detached from the underlying sectional alignment as the center of the Democratic party moved into the old industrial core and the Republican party shifted to the periphery. This consistent but gradual trans-mutation of the two parties, combined with the depolarizing influence of the committee system, produced a dispersion of major party strength throughout the nation. In this environment, the ADA could propose an explicitly sectional policy agenda and remain distinct from and independent of the two major parties.

This new sectional agenda is illustrated by the legislative decisions in-cluded in the liberalism ratings for the 94th Congress (1975–76). The ADA included an amendment to continue federal price regulation of major natural gas producers ("yea" was the liberal position), an amendment to repeal the oil and gas depletion allowance ("yea"), and a resolution to disapprove of Presi-dent Ford's plan for the gradual decontrol of domestic oil prices ("yea"). Sev-eral roll calls on civil rights or anti–sex discrimination measures also tilted the ratings toward northern Republicans. The inclusion of recorded votes on mili-tary spending (e.g., procurement of the B-1 bomber) and foreign policy tended to produce a similar effect. The most sectionally divisive contest in-cluded in the ratings was the vote on authorization of federal loans to New York City ("yea" was the liberal position).[21]

Within the Democratic party, the relationship between liberalism (as defined by the ADA and *New Republic*) and support for the industrial core (as defined by the ten high-stress, closely contested roll calls in each period) has always been high, ranging from .58 to .88 when votes that enter into both scores are included and from .37 to .85 when these votes are excluded from the calculation of core support (see table 8.11). The correlation is somewhat lower for the first postwar decades because of the northern Democratic emphasis on direct electoral competition with Republicans and a consequent, albeit luke-warm, endorsement of the bipolar New Deal coalition. The adoption of an explicitly sectional political program by the northern wing and the implicit gamble on the formation of a viable, national working-class party are reflected in the extremely high correlations of the 1960s and 1970s.

Within the Republican party, this pattern is repeated: during the early Congresses, Republicans *outside the core* (with lower core support scores) re-ceived slightly higher liberalism ratings than the direct electoral competitors of the northern Democrats inside the manufacturing belt. The resulting nega-tive correlation between liberalism (on ADA votes) and core support (on the ten high-stress, closely contested roll calls) within the Republican party thus reflects early northern Democratic attention to political competition in the core and reliance on the New Deal coalition. As the northern Democratic wing expanded and grew more confident, the ADA turned its attention toward the southern bloc within the party. Republican correlations rose to levels similar to those within the Democratic party as liberals adopted an explicitly sectional political program.

When the memberships of both parties are included together in the

Table 8.11. Correlation between Liberalism[a] and Support for the Industrial Core,[b] 1945–1976

Congress[c]	Party	Liberalism and:	
		Core I	Core II
1945–46	Democrats	.58	.37
1955–56	"	.59	.51
1965–66	"	.88	.79
1975–76	"	.87	.85
1945–46	Republicans	−.07	−.25
1955–56	"	.38	.23
1965–66	"	.76	.64
1975–76	"	.81	.79
1945–46	All Members	−.49	−.57
1955–56	"	−.02	−.14
1965–66	"	.83	.70
1975–76	"	.84	.82

[a] According to ADA and *New Republic* ratings.
[b] On high-stress, closely contested roll calls.
[c] In all four Congresses, the ratings published by the *New Republic* or the ADA included at least one (1945–46, 1955–56, and 1975–76) and at most three (1965–66) of the ten high-stress, closely contested roll calls recorded during the Congress. Core I scores included these overlapping votes and calculated individual support for the industrial core position on these high-stress, closely contested decisions. Core II scores were calculated in the same manner but excluded those votes used in the liberalism ratings.

analysis, the basic pattern is even more striking. Since southern Democrats scored somewhat higher in the liberalism ratings than did northern, core Republicans, the correlations between ideology and support for the core were strongly negative in the 79th Congress (1945–46) and slightly negative ten years later. This basic pattern is reinforced by the fact that Republicans held the majority of core districts in these Congresses and, thus, composed the establishment or mainstream political vehicle for industrial interests in the national political system. In the last two decades, the correlations have been strongly positive, reflecting the selection of rating votes that draw sharp distinctions between the two wings of the Democratic party and mute policy differences with the dwindling number of core Republicans.

By the middle of the 1970s, the empirical definition of liberalism was securely tied to the political imperatives of the industrial core in the national political economy. At the same time, the northern wing of the Democratic party had become the major and increasingly dominant partner in what remained of the New Deal coalition. The coincidence of these trends seems to imply two future events: the exhaustion and possible dissolution of the Americans for Democratic Action as an important political force, and a radical repolarization of the party system along the fundamental sectional alignment. Historical experience strongly suggests that victory for the northern wing within the Democratic party and a consequent unequivocal embracement of the political programs supported by the liberal coalition will undercut the independent role of the ADA as an alternative proto-coalition. In some states in the North, this process is already well advanced.*

Historical experience suggests that ideological coalitions—when they become influential forces in the contemporary political system—reveal the future of American party competition. The populist, progressive, and now the liberal movements all suggest this pattern. By emphasizing the bipolar New Deal coalition in the late 1940s and 1950s, liberals anticipated the depolarization of the party system in the 1960s and 1970s. The present posture of the ADA, from this perspective, heralds a return to a highly polarized party system and, incidentally, its own organizational demise.

Conclusion

Before the New Deal, the successful exploitation of cross-cutting sectional issues by the Democratic party usually increased the instability of the electoral system. At the presidential level, the Democratic appeal to western agrarian radicalism produced the converting election of 1896. The Wilson progressive response to industrialization led to the deviating elections of 1912 and 1916, and the Al Smith and Franklin Roosevelt association with class, ethnic, and urban interests brought on the converting election of 1928 and the realigning 1932 election. In all these elections, the Democratic party was able to penetrate northern districts normally dominated by the Republicans. However, because the party system during these periods had deviated from its "natural" sectional cleavage and because the cross-cutting issues exploited by the Democratic party increased electoral instability, the success of Democratic candidates outside the South did not—until 1932—produce a new bipolar partisan arrangement; few northern trade area delegations were moved en bloc into the party.

The dominant sectional cleavage between the parties reflected the distribution of core and periphery elites. Periods of electoral stability (in which traditional allegiances held party lines intact) ensued when neither party attempted to exploit latent class or other cross-cutting cleavages in the other party's native section. Electoral instability occurred when one party, usually the Democrats, attempted to forge an alliance between the economic elite of one region and disaffected, lower-class minorities in the opposing party's bastion. When led by the Democrats, such coalitions imposed a heavy price on northern labor and agrarian radicals (as in, for example, race policy, free trade,

---

*In "both these states [Michigan and Minnesota], ironically, success was fatal to ADA's own organization. Once a liberal party was in safe control in Minnesota, ADA's members either lost interest or disappeared into the party organization itself. . . . some of its leaders question Humphrey's assertion that there is no need for ADA in Minnesota. . . ." Brock, *Americans for Democratic Action*, p. 28.

and redistributive programs benefitting the periphery). These pre–New Deal coalitions were usually short-lived because they lacked the necessary institutional arrangements for the minimization of intraparty sectional conflict.

During maintaining elections, the party system returned to the natural, elite-dominated sectional alignment. Until 1932, this reversion to electoral stability meant that the Republican party regained those seats that had been temporarily captured by the Democrats or third-party members. This return to the Republican coalition did not eliminate inconsistencies in political interest between the border regions (e.g., the plains states and Ohio Valley) and the industrialized core. Instead, the border trade areas elected Republicans who, depending on the historical environment, practiced "fusion," "progressive," "insurgent," or "farm bloc" forms of political deviance from party regularity.

Since 1932, sectional conflict has been complicated by the increasing importance of political competition between the largest urban centers and their dependent hinterlands. The Roosevelt coalition exploited this new cleavage by forging an alliance between the agrarian interior regions of the South and northern urban blocs of workers, ethnics, and racial minorities. This coalition almost immediately uncovered inconsistencies of interest at least as large as those that had existed within the urban and rural parts of the previous Republican combination.

The New Deal coalition survived, however, for three reasons. First, the northern wing, for nearly three decades, tolerated race segregation inside the South as the price of participation within a majority party. Second, Congress, and particularly the House of Representatives, created an institutional arrangement that decentralized control over federal policy. Finally, the post–New Deal congressional Democratic parties were willing to tolerate a much higher level of policy deviance than their predecessors.

Historically, the size of the Republican party was positively associated with the level of sectional stress in the congressional party system because the prevailing bipolar alignment implied a core-dominated majority party and a minority party confined mainly to the periphery. When regional polarization reached its highest levels, the core-dominated party controlled between 65 and 70 percent of the seats of the House, and the political system was characterized by great electoral stability. When the core party has controlled less than two-thirds of the membership, that has been because the periphery has successfully introduced "cross-cutting" cleavages which exploit latent class divisions in the industrial-commercial pole and, thus, reduce core political cohesion. Had the number of Republicans ever exceeded two-thirds of the House, the attendant penetration of the southern periphery by the GOP would have entailed a similar exploitation of cross-cutting issues in the Democratic bastion. For most of the last century, however, periphery elites made such an exploitation of class conflict impossible by denying suffrage to blacks and many hill-country whites. This interpretation expands upon the position of E. E. Schattsneider and others, who viewed the post-Reconstruction regional alignment of the parties as the conscious and conspiratorial design of sectional political elites (i.e., northern industrial magnates and southern planters).[22] These elites undoubtedly supported the creation of a sectionally based party system, but the evidence suggests that *they could not have prevented the regional polarization of the parties.* They succeeded in building a regionally structured party system because they supported the inevitable.

Both the historical evolution of the congressional party system and the contemporary posture of the major American ideological organizations suggest a radical restructuring of American politics along regional lines that are strongly reminiscent of the late nineteenth–early twentieth centuries. The roles of the two parties, however, are reversed: the Democrats are now the representatives of the industrial core and the Republicans are becoming the party of the developing periphery. The most likely policy issue which will precipitate a sectional repolarization of party strength is economic "protectionism" implemented by the erection of tariff barriers, the setting of import quotas, and the informal allocation of international markets among the major industrial nations.

9

Conclusion

In the last one hundred years of sectional conflict in American politics, six dates stand out: 1893, 1910, 1933, 1947, 1964, and 1973. The first date marked repeal of the last Reconstruction acts and a tacit commitment by the industrial North not to interfere with southern resubordination of the black man. After 1893 the southern plantation elite openly conspired to disfranchise both blacks and poor whites for seven decades, all the while protected by northern indifference and a thin facade of constitutional interpretation.

The Cannon Revolt of 1910 heralded the onset of a slow but persistent decline in the strength of national party organizations. Provoked by a sectional split within the Republican party between the agrarian Midwest and the industrial East, the fall of Speaker Cannon underlined the weakening appeal of the traditional Republican positions on military pensions and imperialism to rural electorates in the midwestern plains. Ultimately, the Cannon episode laid the foundation for a strong congressional committee system. With the inauguration of Franklin Roosevelt in 1933, the bipolar New Deal coalition was born. Because of the extraordinary potential incompatibility within this alliance between the southern plantation elite and the northern industrial lower classes, the Democratic party increasingly exploited the conflict-reducing arrangements built into congressional seniority norms, the committee system, and large grants of legislative authority to the executive branch bureaucracy. This political and governmental design was greatly reinforced by implementation of the 1946 Reorganization Act. The ensuring eighteen years comprised the classic phase of committee dominance and ultimately released the congressional party system from its historically close ties to the fundamental, underlying sectional alignment.

Passage of the 1964 Civil Rights Act brought the classic phase of the committee system to an end and irreparably divided the New Deal coalition. The oil embargo of 1973 accelerated the hitherto gradual deterioration in the industrial base of the American manufacturing belt. The comparatively explosive growth of the southern and western periphery renewed open sectional competition between the trade areas of the core and periphery. However, for the first time in over a century the agenda of regional conflict did not include civil rights legislation. For this reason alone, 1973 may turn out to be one of the most significant dates in American political development.

Summary of the Evidence

Most of the analysis and interpretation in this study has been confined to the chapters (3–6) which present data on sectional conflict within the House of Representatives in ten historical periods. Within each period, regional competition was focused on a different set of policy issues involving the use of federal power to shape the national political economy. In some instances, the primary issue was the internal redistribution of wealth. In others, cleavages developed over measures to reduce the political autonomy of the American periphery. The largest category of policy decisions producing sectional schism involved the relation of the United States to the larger world-economy.

In the 49th Congress (1885–87), the most contentious political issue facing the nation concerned the eligibility of Union veterans of the American Civil War for military pensions. The pension issue was intimately intertwined with the protective tariff on industrial goods, and it was the tariff, not pensions *per se*, which produced the intense sectional conflict of the 1880s. The military pension/protective tariff "engine of industrial development" persisted in American politics until the onset of the First World War, and even though the political saliency of Civil War pensions declined after the turn of the century, tariff battles continued until the beginning of the New Deal.

The "redemption" of southern politics by the plantation elite after the end of Reconstruction led to the dramatic emergence of contested elections as the most intense sectional issue dominating the 54th Congress (1895–97). Like military pensions in the preceding decade, the unseating of southern Democrats in favor of Republican challengers was closely connected to the Civil War and subsequent military occupation of the South.

American imperialism at the turn of the century produced levels of sectional stress in congressional voting which—with the exception of civil rights legislation—have never been matched in the last century. The growing empire presided over by the 59th Congress (1905–7) was supported by a political coalition that included the metropolitan East and the grain-producing regions of the Midwest.

The overlapping political coalitions that had previously supported military pensions, attempts to destabilize the plantation elite in the southern periphery, and imperial expansion all started to unravel with the beginning of World War I. The deteriorating effectiveness of these coalitions was due to the growing incompatibility between the interests of the agrarian Midwest and plains states and the economic goals of the metropolitan, industrial core.

This divergence became evident in the military preparations of the 64th Congress (1915–17), which preceded American entry into the First World

War. The South and much of the West opposed the belligerent policy advocated by the industrial East, and this alignment did not disappear until after Congress had formally approved a Declaration of War. Following the Armistice in 1918, the regional alliance between the South and West reemerged in the form of McNary-Haugenism and other proposals to use the federal government to alleviate the acute agricultural depression of the 1920s. Agriculture policy dominated the political agenda of the 69th Congress (1925–27) and, indeed, much of the entire interwar period.

By institutionalizing a bipolar political alliance between the plantation elite of the southern periphery and the working class of the industrial North, the New Deal permanently reshaped the American political system. The high-stress policy decisions of the 74th Congress (1935–36) illustrated the institutional basis of the New Deal coalition: a strong committee system, a reliance on executive and bureaucratic discretion, and broad tolerance for policy differences within the Democratic party.

During World War II, the mobilization of the American economy was effected by the imposition of strict federal controls on prices and production in the private economy. The political and economic environment within which these controls were established divided the country into three broad interests: organized labor, the business community, and agricultural producers. As the war effort came to a close, these interests struggled over the extension of emergency measures into the postwar period. The policy conflicts of the 79th Congress (1945–46) reflected the widespread gains in membership and improvement in working conditions that had accrued to organized labor during the war. These gains subsequently sparked support by agricultural and some business representatives for comparatively harsh measures to retract the new advantages.

The emergency price guarantees and controls on agricultural commodities during the war made for a comparatively easy transition into widespread federal involvement in the agricultural economy in the postwar era. By the 84th Congress (1955–56), government intervention relied upon an intricate but viable alliance between the urban and agrarian wings of the Democratic party. Despite the existence of this bipolar, partisan alliance, intense sectional competition between the manufacturing belt and the southern periphery was a major and consistent feature of federal agriculture policy throughout the 1950s.

The 89th Congress (1965–66) marked the end of New Deal coalition effectiveness and the termination of the classic period of committee system supremacy within the legislative branch. The immediate cause of both events was the enactment of major civil rights legislation which destabilized the political hegemony of the plantation elite within the South and signaled a more or less explicit campaign to turn the Democratic party into a truly national working-class organization.

The breakup of the New Deal alliance over federal civil rights measures pointedly indicated the changing sectional base of the Democratic party. As the center of gravity within the party moved toward and into the industrial core, the Republicans declined in the manufacturing belt and expanded in the southern and western periphery. These trends produced the partisan cleavages that accompanied attempts to halt or retard the precipitous decline of the core economy during the 94th Congress (1975–76). These attempts were focused primarily in three policy areas: the reorientation of federal spending away from the developing periphery and toward the decaying industrial core; a national-ization of labor and other regulatory policies which would reduce the competi-tive economic advantages of areas outside the industrial East; and the expan-sion of price and production controls on oil and natural gas. While most of the ten high-stress, closely contested roll calls recorded during the 94th Congress reflected these policy goals, the best individual example of core-periphery conflict during the 1970s was the extension of federal aid to New York City in 1975.

From 1880 to about 1930, the membership base of the congressional party system followed the fundamental, underlying sectional alignment of American politics. During these decades, sectional stress on major policy deci-sions usually assumed the form of intense partisan conflict in which the Demo-crats represented the southern periphery and the Republican party was the political vehicle for the interests of the industrial core. In this period, ideo-logical belief-systems such as populism and progressivism outlined proto-coalitions which cut across the sectional alignment and, thus, across the party system.

The maturation of the committee system during and after the New Deal decade institutionalized the bipolar Democratic coalition and encouraged a secular depolarization of congressional party membership during the next half-century. The gradual movement of the Democratic party out of the South and of the Republican party out of the East and Midwest could not have taken place without the relentless decentralization of legislative decision-making during the classic phase of the committee system (roughly 1947–65). The major concern of American liberalism at the onset of the classic phase was the direct electoral competition between northern Democrats and their Republi-can opponents. Ideological ratings in this period emphasized policy differences between the northern members of both parties and downplayed political con-flict between the sectional wings of the Democratic party. When, by the end of the classic phase, Democratic membership had shifted radically toward the industrial core and electoral competition with the declining core Republican party became less urgent, ideological ratings by the leading liberal organiza-tion—the Americans for Democratic Action—painted an increasingly stark contrast between the two great regional wings of the Democratic party. At the same time, ideological differences between northern members of the major parties seemed to narrow. By the decade of the seventies, the correlation be-tween liberal ideological beliefs (as measured by the ADA) and support for the political imperatives of the industrial core (as exhibited on high-stress roll calls) approached unity and seemed to presage a radical repolarization of the congressional party system.

Geopolitical Change

The fundamental sectional alignment in the American political system has remained unchanged for more than a century. During these years, however, the economic base of the different regions has undergone, in each case, a complete transformation. In order to explain both continuity and change, the sources—they might well be called wellsprings—of geopolitical interests should be reviewed.

By far the most important of all these sources is the changing nature of the world-economy. From one perspective, changes in the world-economy are largely beyond the control of the United States. For example, the rapid rise of the international price of crude oil and the growing competition of foreign textile and automobile producers were both events that the United States government could not directly suppress. In that sense, such trends are exogenous to the domestic political system even though they have important political consequences within the nation.

While the United States must more or less react to changes in world trade patterns rather than control them, the nation can determine the relationship between the domestic economy and the world-system through tariffs, subsidies, import quotas, etc. Of the ten periods that have been analyzed, political conflict over the relationship between the domestic and world economies has been central in four: the reinforcing policy coalitions which supported military pensions and the tariff; turn-of-the-century imperialism; McNary-Haugenism; and the farm legislation of the 1950s. Each of these periods represented a different stage in the nation's development as the country progressed from an agrarian, periphery economy located near the lower rungs of the world-system to a dominant industrial power at the center of the global core.

Immanuel Wallerstein's theoretical description of the structure of the world-economy offers at least three conclusions concerning the destiny of individual nations within the world order. First, Wallerstein considers the autonomy of most societies in the periphery to be hopelessly compromised by their inferior position in the global system. In contrast, nations in the advanced core of the world-economy are much more able to control their fate than societies which occupy the lower rungs of the international division of labor. Second, core nations universally prefer to maintain their high-ranking role in the world-economy to the primary alternative—relative economic decline—and energetically resist any move down the ranks of the international division of labor. Finally, as a derivative of the first two generalizations, the world-system should be very stable through history. Underdeveloped societies are unable, for the most part, to move up the international economic hierarchy, and advanced nations are unwilling to move down.

The United States is, of course, an exception to the first of these conclusions. The withdrawal of the American economy behind the protective tariff enabled the nation, eventually, to rise within the world system. Any interpretation of this historical period, from 1880 to 1930, most concede the relative autonomy of the then underdeveloped American nation. Furthermore, the internal politics of the tariff and imperialism suggest a second deviation from Wallerstein's theory. The model suggests that movement up the international division of labor will be the consensual goal of most national populations; in most countries, political opposition to economic advance would either be insignificant or dependent on established core economies abroad (i.e., friendly native elites under colonial rule). In the United States, however, political opposition was as implacable and powerful as it was independent of foreign political manipulation and control. Put very simply, the southern plantation elite preferred that the United States remain a periphery nation within the world system, and it vigorously opposed tariff walls and the imperial designs of the industrial core. The emerging industrial elite of the North was viewed as more threatening to the interests of the southern plantation economy than foreign exploitation. While it is true that the United States pursued a development strategy despite southern opposition, the massive political cleavages associated with American industrialization emphasize the absence of a national consensus on this policy. Thus, it is quite possible that an autonomous, underdeveloped nation might prefer periphery status in the world system. In the United States, for example, history might have been forever altered if civil war pensions had not extended the pro-development coalition into the western prairie and mountains (and thus co-opted a national majority).

If, as appears likely, the representatives of the old manufacturing belt come to advocate a full program of economic protectionism for the now declining industrial core, the United States will once more face a developmental choice. A protectionist strategy for the heavy industrial products of the Midwest and parts of the Northeast would ensure relative economic decline for the United States in the world economic hierarchy. Protectionism is no longer a developmental strategy but, instead, a program by which relatively primitive modes of production can be retained in an otherwise advanced core economy. Retention of these modes significantly decreases the long-term competitive position of the technologically advanced sectors of the American economy. Thus, the old industrial core would prefer relative national decline in the world system to relative sectional decline within the national economy. Once more, the United States lacks a national consensus on the attractiveness of core status in the world-system and might choose to forfeit its favored place at the top of the hierarchy.

Regardless of the choice finally made by the nation, some change in the internal core-periphery division of labor is inevitable. The United States is one of the few countries in the world-system which is large and varied enough to maintain an intersectional division of labor comparable to the divisions which exist between nations. This domestic order, characterized by a fundamental sectional cleavage between the northeastern seaboard and the southern interior, has exhibited great historical continuity. However, the precipitous decline of the midwestern extension of the national core suggests an impending, unprecedented alteration in the internal order. One of two trends might develop. On the one hand, sectional economies might converge and thus eliminate the more significant aspects of the historic core-periphery division. This hypothetical projection is consistent with the view that sectionalism has been in continuous decline since the Civil War and has largely become an anachronism as cultural differences have eroded away. As we have seen, the average level of sectional stress on roll call decisions in the House of Representatives has declined since the beginning of the Great Depression. While this decline in sectional stress in roll call voting is consistent with a decline in the general influence of sectionalism, the roll call patterns after 1930 can also be explained by other events: the rise of the New Deal coalition; a temporary increase in class conflict within the industrial core (which has now apparently abated); the influence of a strong committee system in Congress; and a radical depolarization of the membership base of the congressional parties. All of these factors are reversible and, in fact, seem to be reverting to a pre-Depression pattern.

The second alternative is the renewal of regional economic differences. At the broadest developmental level, sectional differences can be renewed through the redistribution of national wealth from the periphery to the core and through the reinforcing influence of agglomeration in the most important research and trade centers. Intersectional redistribution will occur because the historic core areas of the national economy control a disproportionate amount of the nation's productive capacity. Most corporate profits, even if earned through operations in the periphery, will be redistributed to individuals within the core. Furthermore, the location of the highest orders of economic activity—international finance and capital markets, corporate headquarters, export-import trade, communications and publishing, and research and development—are all strongly influenced by the efficiencies of agglomeration. The high value placed on the interchange of information, ideas, and relatively scarce technical resources encourages firms and institutions engaged in these activities to "clump" together in a small number of major metropolitan centers. The current location of these agglomerations and the incentives which encourage new firms to locate within these centers strongly indicate a self-renewing commercial, financial, and technological specialization in the core.

From another perspective, the very way in which regional economic and social infrastructures have been constructed argues for the continuation of sectionalism. The massive, high-density urban complexes of the industrial core, for example, encourage a regional demand for subsidized, fixed-rail mass transit systems. The spatial diffusion and relatively small size of centers in the modern periphery, on the other hand, predispose a policy emphasis on freeway construction. These differences in economic and social organization are reinforced by the contemporary pattern of regional growth. The rapid expansion of cities and small towns in the South and West further contributes to the urban and suburban sprawl which already distinguishes them. The stagnation of northern centers, in contrast, has accentuated their relative age and spatial density.

The renewal of regional polarization is reinforced by the well-advanced and probably irreversible decline of those political institutions which have moderated the political expression of sectional economic imperatives. The disappearance of the New Deal coalition eliminates one of the most effective restraints on sectional political cleavages within the Democratic party. The corresponding weakening of the congressional committee system also encourages a relatively uninhibited pursuit of a regional interests. To these events can be added the continuing creation and maintenance of established regulatory and subsidy mechanisms in the national political economy. Some of the oldest regulatory structures in the United States, such as the administrative apparatus that subsidized air service to small and medium-sized cities, are currently being dismantled. Others, in some instances much larger in scope, are expanding in influence. The Environmental Protection Agency's implementation of the Clean Air Act is but one example.* If, as seems likely, tariff barriers for the deteriorating heavy industries of the old manufacturing belt emerge over the next decade, the sectional alignment on protectionism could dominate all other regionally divisive policy conflicts. Those policies whose sectional interests do not coincide with the protectionist pattern might then, as was true at the turn of the century, be subordinated to the tariff alignment. If anything, the absence of either strong congressional parties or a relatively effective committee system suggests that the creation of a stable protectionist coalition will occupy much of the political energy and attention of future Congresses. At present, no political organization exists which could impose tariff barriers as a party program, and no institutional arrangement seems sufficiently influential to create a stable cross-party coalition through logrolling.

Sectional Stress in American Political Development

Two primary claims have been advanced in these pages. The first is that regional competition has been "fundamental" within the American political

---

*On the regional implications of regulatory initiatives in the 1970s, see Elizabeth Sanders, "The Roots of Regulation: Economies and Politics before and during the 1970's" (paper presented to the annual meeting of the American Political Science Association, Denver, Colorado, September 3, 1982).

system—fundamental in the sense that other perspectives from which development might be interpreted are of secondary, transient importance. As the most fundamental influence in national development, sectional conflict decisively shaped the institutional structures, political parties, and ideological belief-systems of American political life. These, in turn, have partially determined the intensity with which sectional imperatives have been expressed within the political system. Recognition of the immutable alignment of sectional conflict shaped the New Deal coalition, encouraged the rise of the committee system within Congress, and led American liberalism to pragmatically advance the political interests of the northern wing of the Democratic party.

Evidence has also been presented in support of the second primary hypothesis: that the fundamental, underlying sectional alignment has assumed the same pattern in every political period for the last century. In fact, the persistent, unchanging pattern of the sectional alignment—compared to the great changes that have taken place in the membership base of congressional parties, the institutional organization and structure of Congress, and the empirical aspect of American ideology—reinforces the claim of fundamentality. In brief, sectional competition within the American political system is bipolar in nature. At one end of the primary alignment, several sub-regions compose what has been called the industrial core. The trade delegations most commonly associated with this pole have been Boston, Chicago, New York, Philadelphia, and San Francisco. At the other end, several trade areas occupy what has been termed the agrarian periphery: Atlanta, Dallas, Denver, Memphis, and Richmond. This core-periphery alignment has reemerged within each historical period and within very different policy contexts; the cumulative evidence strongly suggests that the fundamental structure of regional competition has been consistent since the political reintegration of the South after Reconstruction.

American social scientists have been notably reluctant to portray political conflict in sectional terms. To a certain extent, this reluctance stems from the post–World War II behavioral revolution which made available electoral and survey data on both a national and international scale. The structure of questions included in a national survey, for example, compels the respondent to assume a national rather than localistic focus. The underdeveloped philosophical framework of contemporary American ideologies, to cite another example, has led analysts to rely on organized interest groups in the assignment of ideological ratings to congressmen. In order to support the utilization of these group scores, scholars inadvertently convey the impression that widely held belief-systems, rather than regional economic interests, dominate congressional debate. The notion that legislators coalesce to defend regional imperatives in the national political economy has long been subordinated to the conception of political conflict as the promotion of ideals or even broad class interests (on the European model). The sectional stress interpretation, however, is compatible with rational choice theories of politics which assume economic interest as the most powerful single motive in political action. The sectional stress approach differs from rational choice theories in viewing politics on a macro, as opposed to micro, level and in attempting to trace long-lasting regional imperatives in both the national political economy and the world system. However interpreted, sectional conflict is undeniably persistent and deeply rooted—a "massive fact" of American political development.

Appendix/Notes/Index

Appendix: Methodology

The primary units of analysis in this study are regional trade area delegations in the House of Representatives. While the use of trade areas effectively eliminates many of the problems associated with traditional notions of American regionalism, the theory and principles upon which trade area systems are founded will probably be unfamiliar to most readers. The following discussion of the trade area concept and the trade area boundaries used in this study prepares the way for presentation of the sectional stress index near the end of the Appendix. The concept of sectionalism upon which the statistical formula of the index is based, the empirical connection to trade area delegations in Congress, and a demonstration of the calculations of "sectional stress" entailed by the index are elaborated here.

Traditional Notions of Section

Traditional notions of section have three major deficiencies. First, sectional divisions tend to be a static product of historical experience. For example, a critical watershed in American history—the Civil War—is the primary basis for the traditional designation of the eleven states of the Confederacy as a separate region. Though this designation has been of great political and social relevance in the nineteenth and twentieth centuries, the historical experience in which it is rooted has made it increasingly anachronistic. Because they lack an independent theoretical foundation, traditional sectional concepts (e.g., "North" and "South") remain static until a new critical watershed reshapes our commonly shared conceptions of salient regional differences.

Furthermore, the nature of the "historical" section inhibits the recognition of a new critical watershed. Because no alternative sectional distinction is as commonly accepted as the North-South dichotomy, gradual or incremental realignments of sectional stress are largely reinterpreted in terms of the one over-arching North-South division. When these traditional regional definitions are used in the contemporary analysis of the direction and strength of sectional stress, they filter political events into conventional and possibly irrelevant geographical categories. Political analysis and interpretation based on the historical section are often thus transformed into an explanation of deviating cases. Since these cases are generated by the application of an historically rooted scheme to the contemporary political system, the possibility that the sectional alignment of the nation has shifted, and that a new set of regional boundaries would capture or resolve these deviating cases, is analytically precluded. Similarly, when static boundaries based on historical experience alone are used to analyze sectional stress in the past, the resulting sections presuppose the events they are intended to help explain. In order to avoid these deficiencies, a conceptualization of sectional stress must permit the strength, alignment, and direction of regional competition to vary and evolve over time. Otherwise, as is the case with traditional regional concepts, any claim that the lines of sectional stress have not shifted cannot amount to more than unsupported assertion.

Finally, traditionally defined sections carry little or no cross-national theoretical meaning. When reduced to a set of geographical lines, the historical foundation for the traditional American section does not permit extrapolation even to those nations with similar historical experiences and political institutions (such as Canada or Australia). Without a clear and general formulation of what a section or region is, corresponding territories in other nations cannot be identified. Similarly, the historical section precludes or inhibits extrapolation into the future.

In order to develop a meaningful theory of sectional stress, something must replace the traditional American section as the major unit of analysis. The replacement must satisfy several conditions. First, the new unit of analysis must have a theoretical foundation that is grounded in an ahistorical experience. The theoretical basis for the regional unit must rely on social characteristics and phenomena which are common to a wide variety of—if not all—societies. Only then can an ecological theory of sectional stress be developed and tested cross-nationally. Second, reflecting an ever-changing social and economic reality, the unit of analysis should evolve naturally over time. Without the potential for change, the theoretical justification for a set of regional boundaries would rapidly become anachronistic. Finally, the new unit of analysis should be much smaller in size than the traditional American sections. Both cross-national and historical analysis require that the basic unit be something similar to a "building block" in the coalition processes that characterize sectional stress. As a theory of sectional stress develops, the unit of analysis will come to have a much closer connection to the explanatory scheme than it will have at the outset. In the beginning, however, the sectional scheme must be grounded in the most universal systems of social life, permit the widest application both cross-nationally and historically, and preclude the fewest possible regional alignments. "Trade areas" satisfy all of the above conditions.

Trade Areas in Theory and History

In theory, a trade area is composed of two interdependent parts: an urban center and a surrounding hinterland made up of rural areas and subordinate cities. The trade area is that territory within which the influence of the urban center is dominant over that of competing cities. That territory has also been called the urban center's tributary area, market area, sphere of influence, and urban field.[1] The urban center is a gathering and refining point for the products of the hinterland and distributes finished goods throughout its tributary area. In addition, the urban center services the hinterland by providing for the cultural and financial needs of the region.

> The major trade center of each trade area should dominate the retail and wholesale trade activity. It should be the transportation, banking, and insurance center for the area, headquarters for numerous federal offices, and play a dominant role in area politics. It should be the major marketing center for the area's products. It may be the headquarters of big manufacturing concerns with factories in smaller trade centers. It should be the major convention city of its area and often the recreational, music, art, literary, religious, educational and medical center. Its newspapers and radio stations should blanket the area and most of the beer consumed in the area should be manufactured in the major trade center.[2]

The trade area concept grew out of the "central place theory" of urban settlement first developed by Walter Christaller and later refined by August Losch and Brian Berry.[3] The theory presumes the existence of a hierarchy of urban centers. A town or city at the lowest level or order of urban center services a largely rural population with daily needs such as food, transportation, and mail delivery. Assuming that these lowest-order cities occupy an uninterrupted plain with no significant geographical barriers, it is postulated that each will be at the center of a hexagon-shaped hinterland. The range of each of these non-overlapping hinterlands is determined by the "range of a good" (the distance which people will travel to obtain a particular service) and the "threshold" (the minimum amount of purchasing power sufficient to support the supply of a particular good from a central point).*

---

*James H. Johnson, *Urban Geography* (London: Pergamon Press, 1967), p. 98. Raymond Murphy also discusses range and threshold (*The American City*, p. 75): "Threshold population has been defined as the minimum population size of an urban center which will support an urban function. Thus in a certain locality barber shops may be rare in villages with less than 300 inhabitants. This, therefore, marks the approximate threshold population for barber shops in the locality.

"The range of a good marks out the zone or tributary area around a central place from which persons travel to the center to purchase the good (service or merchandise) offered at the place. Theoretically, the upper limit of this range is the maximum possible radius of sales. Beyond this limit the price of the good is too high for it to be sold, either because the distance

Higher-order centers provide increasingly specialized services to nested hinterlands. For instance, the second-order urban center would include in its hinterland all of its immediate (first-order) tributary area and additional territory drawn from smaller first-order centers. At the highest level, a large regional capital provides extremely specialized services and products to a vast hinterland. Throughout much of the regional tributary area, the distance involved in making a journey to the regional capital is so great that personal trips are fairly rare.

Central place theory is based on a number of assumptions which, taken together, have made empirical testing of its implications difficult. The theory assumes that the region throughout which the urban centers are located is a plain without significant topographical relief, having a homogeneous ecological environment and a uniform distribution of rural population. Furthermore, transportation services must be equally provided in all directions and must not be influenced by technological advances (which would significantly increase the "range of a good").[4] Because the theory is based on marketing principles, the location and size of urban centers relative to their service functions is assumed to be unrelated to their industrial, mining, or political functions. In application, the theory works best in small territories containing low-order urban centers and functions.

James Vance, in developing a spatial theory to explain the location of wholesaling activity, has suggested several reasons for the failure of "central place" theory to account for the rise of national metropolitan centers.[5] The most important reason for the failure of central place theory at the regional and national level is that its principles are present-centered, static, and nonevolutionary. Once the central place hierarchy of cities and spatial distribution of urban centers have been determined, the principles of central place theory cannot explain the relative growth and decline of individual cities, the expansion and contraction of their spheres of influence, or the distorting impact of specialized functions (e.g., in resort or retirement cities) or public policy decisions (e.g., in university towns or state capitals).

In his attempt to revitalize central place theory, Vance argues that cities constitute "man's largest and most durable artifact" and any settlement pattern largely reflects "the massive inheritance of the furniture of the past."[6] In order to explain the rise of "merchant" cities or wholesale trade centers, Vance maintains that transportation modes and settlement patterns must be viewed in an historical evolutionary context.

---

results in too high a price, or because of the greater proximity of consumers to an alternate center (the real limit). The lower limit of the range is the radius that encloses the minimum number of consumers necessary to provide a sale volume adequate for the good to be supplied profitably from the central place. In the case mentioned, the population of the serving urban center is the threshold population for barber shops."

> The pattern of wholesale trade conforms . . . to distinct *regional structures* which are the physical expression of historical-geographical forces. . . . Unlike the concept of regions and regionalism, these regional structures are not ideographic. Their nature is explained by a few general dynamics that have application to all regions and times basically because they are fully able to comprehend changes wrought in time.[7]

Although he intends to develop a general theory, Vance's analysis is largely restricted to the United States. The "general dynamics" of wholesale trade center development depend on four factors: "points of attachment," "breaks in transport mode," the concept of an "entrepôt," and "unraveling points of trade." The growth of trade centers in America began with and was fundamentally affected by the colonial economic relationship with Europe. The first trade centers were "points of attachment" through which goods were moved and exchanged between the home country and the colonies. These urban centers were located on the eastern littoral of the American continent, where natural "breaks in transport mode" between wind-driven sailing vessels and overland carriage or inland waterways occurred. The seaboard cities became "entrepôts," each a premier center for the gathering of extractive produce and the distribution of finished goods for its upriver hinterland. As the country was settled, new urban centers rose up at additional "unraveling points of trade" in the interior. Each unraveling point was "the last point common to a sufficient number of supply lines to the frontier to assure a reasonable institutional income to the trader."[8] As the interior of the country was settled, wholesale centers developed that cannot be explained in terms of their export-import functions. These inland junctions, built to facilitate railroad and inland waterway transportation, became "the first internally determined" distribution centers. After the country passed out of the frontier period (about 1880–1900), the national trade center system was largely fixed and resistant to change.[9] The emphasis on historical settlement patterns, prevailing transportation modes, external political and economic attachments, and contemporary resistance to alterations in the trade center network distinguishes Vance's explanation of American metropolitan development from the implications inherent in Christaller's central place theory.

While the theoretical foundation for the trade area concept is well developed and most analysts generally agree on the broad form of the American urban system, different methods of identifying regional or national urban centers and their respective hinterlands will produce slightly different results. For example, an urban hierarchy based on population size will differ slightly from an alternative utilizing wholesale trade figures or private financial activity. Even when the urban hierarchy has been identified, the choice of a measure of urban center dominance will influence the determination of trade area boundaries. For example, an analysis of newspaper circulation will produce trade area limits that need not coincide exactly with those developed from data on railroad freight traffic or the flow of telephone messages.* However, as will be shown below, trade areas based on somewhat different economic indicators for different periods exhibit remarkable continuity over time.

In general, trade areas are characterized by two different urban center– hinterland relationships. In the first, hinterland boundaries define the outer reaches of urban center penetration of non-metropolitan territory. Within this relationship, the urban center is clearly the dominant partner, much larger in population than its tributary territory and largely independent of the separate economic interests of the immediate hinterland. The hinterland, on the other hand, performs service functions (truck-farming, industrial subsidiary production, etc.) for the center and is thus dependent on the success and prosperity of the urban economy. Urban center dominance over hinterland activity is typical of advanced core industrial regions. In the periphery, the metropolitan economy services the collection and distribution needs of rural production, and the extractive, raw material base of the hinterland controls the prosperity of the relatively less populous urban center. Cities in the American South have historically followed this pattern.†

---

*See Chauncy D. Harris, *Salt Lake City: A Regional Capital* (Chicago: University of Chicago Press, 1940); Howard L. Green, "Hinterland Boundaries of New York City and Boston in Southern New England," *Economic Geography* 31 (October 1955): 283–300; Edward L. Ullman: "Mobile: Industrial Seaport and Trade Center" (Ph.D. diss., University of Chicago, 1943); Robert E. Dickinson, *City and Region: A Geographical Interpretation* (London: Routledge and Kegan Paul, 1964), ch. 11. "Even though a single index should prove usable, it will remain that community boundaries are zones rather than lines. They are formed where the territories of neighboring communities converge and overlap, where the integrating influences emanating from different centers meet in competition, and where, in consequence, the communal attachments of the local residents are not only divided but in a state of flux. The dynamics of the modern community is, in fact, largely responsible for the diffuseness of its boundaries. Every relative change in the time and cost of transportation and every relative shift in market conditions has immediate repercussions in the expansion or contraction of the community.

"A second factor involved in the indistinctness of boundaries is the interpenetration of dependent communities. . . . The introduction and rapid improvement of mechanically powered transport facilities together with their stimulation to specialization have enabled each local population to participate in the affairs of remote as well as neighboring communal groups." Amos H. Hawley, *Human Ecology: A Theory of Community Structure* (New York: Ronald Press, 1950), pp. 249–55.

†The indicators that have been selected to define trade area boundaries measure only the relative amount of economic interaction between the urban center and hinterland. Thus defined, the number of trade areas is sensitive to the level of interaction analyzed. For example, retail shopping patterns will describe far smaller and more numerous areas than do wholesale distribution networks. While the latter are more useful in the analysis of regional voting patterns, it should be remembered not only that these units of analysis change over time but also that they are not rigidly delineated in any particular period. For example, the New York trade area does not possess the analytically distinct qualities of, say, the political boundaries of New York State. At the level of political analysis that will be undertaken here, this potential deficiency does not pose any difficulty, nor should it pose problems for cross-national comparison. At this stage, conventionally defined and commonly accepted trade area divisions have been relied upon even

Summary of Trade Areas, 1881–1981

Four sources were used for deriving trade area boundaries: for 1881–1901, data on railway networks, which were the dominant transport mode during those two decades; for 1901–21, the national financial system, highlighted by the Federal Reserve System; for 1921–41, two sets of wholesale trade distribution areas developed and published by the federal government; and for 1941–81, three different Rand McNally divisions, each a composite guide for marketing decisions by Rand McNally's corporate clientele. The last three of these trade area systems, covering the period between 1901 and 1981, were selected from several plausible alternatives. Each system was selected partly because it was the result of extensive research into national trade patterns and urban center–hinterland linkages. Furthermore, each set of trade area boundaries was based on a wide variety of data (even though the primary indicators were relatively narrow), and each trade area scheme was published by a prominent authority (either the government or Rand McNally) which intended it for broad, practical use as a marketing aid or to provide an effective regional structure for a major federal agency.

The more detailed descriptions of trade areas that follow are essential to the specialist, but the general reader may wish to skim this section and move on to the discussion of the sectional stress index which closes the Appendix.

Trade Area Boundaries, 1881–1901

Unlike the corresponding periods after the turn of the century, usable trade area boundaries for the years 1881–1901 were not discovered in any published source. In order to increase the likelihood of replicability, the urban center–hinterland network developed here relies on a "central place" interpretation of the contemporary railroad system.[10] Emerging as the dominant transportation mode during the latter part of the nineteenth century, railroads liberated the metropolitan system from its prior dependence on navigable waterways. While the impact of rail expansion probably had not been fully expressed in the shape of the metropolitan system before 1900, railroads had already become the major urban center–hinterland link in many if not most parts of the country.

For 1881–1901, trade area urban centers were designated by three criteria. Each city, in order to qualify as an urban center, had to be served by at least

---

though their separate theoretical bases vary slightly. In a more advanced study (for example, a comparison of trade area cohesion between core and periphery centers over time), the trade area unit would necessarily require more consistent and rigorous definition. Finally, though the indicators that have been chosen to delineate trade area boundaries do not indicate the direction or degree of dependency between urban center and hinterland, trade areas—once defined—can be roughly divided into those dominated by the urban center or hinterland on the basis of population, industrial production, or any of a number of other measures.

three railroad trunk lines connecting it to other major centers. This threshold was low enough to allow port cities such as Charleston to qualify and, as it turned out, did not eliminate any candidate city that met the other two criteria. Population thresholds of 30,000 in the 1880 and 50,000 in the 1890 census returns were set for the 1881–91 and 1891–1901 urban center designations, respectively. The explosive, late nineteenth-century growth of the nation's cities required the use of different population thresholds in the two decades. In both periods, subordinate cities—those which lay within seventy-five miles of a larger urban center—were "suppressed" or disqualified. For example, Brooklyn, Jersey City, Newark, New Haven, and Paterson were located within a seventy-five-mile radius of New York City, the nation's largest urban center in both periods. Even though these five cities met the other two criteria (rail service and size), they were disqualified by their proximity to New York and, thus, omitted from the contemporary urban hierarchy.

Once urban centers had been designated, trade areas were drawn according to relative proximity to rail lines serving each of the qualified cities. Territory was allocated by county to the urban center nearest to it by rail, and the "reach" of any urban center was considered to be equal to that of any other center regardless of relative size. The resulting trade area boundaries for the two decades are shown in maps A.1 and A.2.*

Many of the cities designated as urban centers in 1880 and 1890 were also chosen as "reserve cities" by the Comptroller of the Currency during the late nineteenth century (see table A.1). † Only one 1883 reserve city, Washing-

---

*The procedure developed for use in these two periods roughly follows that originally suggested by Daniel Bogue, *The Structure of the Metropolitan Community* (Ann Arbor: University of Michigan Press, 1949). With some refinement, such as setting a minimum distance between urban centers and a higher threshold in the northeastern states, Bogue defined sixty-seven urban centers in the United States as all those possessing a population in excess of 100,000. Hinterlands were delimited by assuming that: "A metropolis can dominate all of the area which lies closer to it than to any other similar city, even if the other metropolis is larger. The boundaries of metropolitan areas, therefore, pass through the points bisecting the airline distance between adjacent metropolitan centers."

While the criteria used in this volume have the dual advantages of cross-national replicability and fair representation of the historical urban-hinterland environment, they have a number of shortcomings. The first of these is the utilization of a central place framework at the regional and national level (see the discussion in the previous section). The assumption of "equal reach" for all cities is also unrealistic. Larger cities naturally "suppress" the trading range of competing cities at a greater distance than would smaller centers. Finally, the determination of hinterland boundaries at the local level inevitably requires some subjective decisions. The method is not entirely "automatic." However, it should be noted that these boundaries are ultimately used to fix the location of congressional district membership in the various trade area delegations. At that level, most subjective decisions are neutralized.

†The reserve system in the late nineteenth century was, of course, very different from what it is today. "For the general run of national banks throughout the country, specie and lawful money reserves had to equal at least fifteen per cent of their deposits and note issues; funds deposited with national banks located in the 'reserve' cities could be counted in with those reserves up to three-fifths of the required total. Leading financial centers of the country were

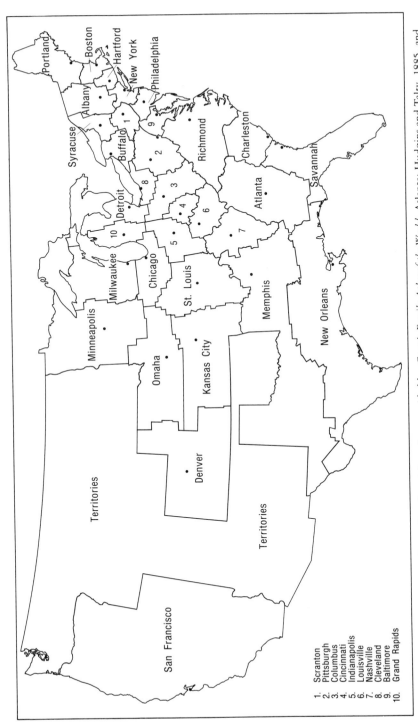

Map A.1. 1885 Trade Area Boundaries. Developed from data provided by *Gram's Family Atlas of the World*, Atlanta: Hudgins and Talty, 1885, and *Compendium of the Eleventh Census: 1890*, Census Office, Department of the Interior, V. I, 1891, pp. 434–35.

1. Scranton
2. Pittsburgh
3. Columbus
4. Cincinnati
5. Indianapolis
6. Louisville
7. Nashville
8. Cleveland
9. Baltimore
10. Grand Rapids

Map A.2. 1895 Trade Area Boundaries. Developed from data provided by *Atlas of the World*, New York: Rand McNally and Co., 1895, and *Compendium of the Eleventh Census: 1890*, Census Office, Department of the Interior, V. I, 1891, pp. 434–35.

Boston
Hartford
New York
Philadelphia
Albany
Syracuse
Buffalo
Richmond
Charleston
Atlanta
Detroit
Milwaukee
Chicago
Des Moines
St. Louis
Memphis
New Orleans
Kansas City
Omaha
Minneapolis
Denver
Territories
San Francisco
Los Angeles

1. Scranton
2. Baltimore
3. Pittsburgh
4. Cleveland
5. Columbus
6. Cincinnati
7. Indianapolis
8. Louisville
9. Evansville
10. Nashville
11. Grand Rapids

Table A.1. Population (1880, 1890) and Reserve Status (1883, 1900) of Leading Trade Area Urban Centers

Trade Area Urban Center	Population		Reserve City in:
	1880	1890	
New York, N.Y.	1,206,299	1,515,301	1883 and 1900
Chicago, Ill.	503,185	1,099,850	1883 and 1900
Philadelphia, Pa.	847,170	1,046,964	1883 and 1900
St. Louis, Mo.	350,518	451,770	1883 and 1900
Boston, Mass.	362,839	448,477	1883 and 1900
Baltimore, Md.	332,313	434,439	1883 and 1900
San Francisco, Calif.	233,959	298,997	1883 and 1900
Cincinnati, Ohio	255,139	296,908	1883 and 1900
Cleveland, Ohio	160,146	261,353	1883 and 1900
Buffalo, N.Y.	155,134	255,664	
New Orleans, La.	216,090	242,039	1883 and 1900
Pittsburgh, Pa.	156,389	238,617	1883 and 1900
Detroit, Mich.	116,340	205,876	1883 and 1900
Milwaukee, Wis.	115,587	204,468	1883 and 1900
Minneapolis, Minn.[a]	46,887	164,738	1883 and 1900
Louisville, Ky.	123,758	161,129	1883 and 1900
Omaha, Neb.	30,518	140,452	1900 only
Kansas City, Mo.	55,785	132,716	1900 only
Denver, Colo.	35,629	106,713	1900 only
Indianapolis, Ind.	75,056	105,436	1900 only
Albany, N.Y.	90,758	94,923	1883 and 1900
Columbus, Ohio	51,647	88,150	1900 only
Syracuse, N.Y.	51,792	88,143	
Richmond, Va.	63,600	81,388	
Nashville, Tenn.	43,350	76,168	
Scranton, Pa.	45,850	75,215	
Atlanta, Ga.	37,409	65,533	
Memphis, Tenn.	33,592	64,495	
Grand Rapids, Mich.	32,016	60,278	
Charleston, S.C.	49,984	54,955	
Hartford, Conn.	42,015	53,230	
Evansville, Ind.[a]	29,280	50,756	
Los Angeles, Calif.[a]	11,183	50,395	1900 only
Des Moines, Ia.[a]	22,408	50,093	1900 only
Savannah, Ga.[a]	30,709	43,189	1900 only
Portland, Me.[a]	33,810	36,425	

[a] In 1883, only St. Paul held reserve status; in 1900, both Minneapolis and St. Paul were reserve cities. Evansville, Los Angeles, and Des Moines were trade area urban centers in 1895–96 but not in 1885–86. Savannah and Portland (Me.) were trade area centers in 1885–86 but not in 1895–96.

SOURCES: Population figures for 1880 and 1890 from *Compendium of the Eleventh Census: 1890* (Washington: Census Office, Department of the Interior, 1891), 1:434–35. Reserve city designations for 1883 from *Report of the Comptroller of the Currency, 1883* (Washington: Government Printing Office, 1883), pp. 169–213. Reserve city designations for 1900 from *Annual Report of the Comptroller of the Currency* (Washington: Government Printing Office, 1900), pp. 685–741.

ton, D.C., was not included in the designated centers for 1881–91. Washington lies within a seventy-five-mile radius of Baltimore. For the second period (1891–1901), Washington (which was again overshadowed by Baltimore), Brooklyn (subordinate to New York City), St. Joseph (subordinate to Kansas City), and Lincoln (subordinate to Omaha) were the four 1900 reserve cities excluded from the list of leading trade area centers by the distance criterion. Portland (Oregon) and Houston, both reserve cities in 1900, did not meet the population threshold of 50,000 and thus were not designated urban centers for the 1891–1901 decade.

The rail-based trade areas were subsequently used to locate congressional delegations. A plurality of the population of each congressional district determined its placement within one of the thirty-three trade area delegations between 1881 and 1891 and the thirty-four delegations between 1891 and 1901. In both cases, population figures were taken from the 1890 census. In the other eight decades, the same procedure, utilizing revised trade area boundaries and contemporary census data, was used to identify congressional delegations within the respective periods.

Trade Area Boundaries, 1901–1921

Under the Federal Reserve Act of 1913, a newly created Reserve Bank Organization Committee made up of the Secretary of the Treasury, Secretary of Agriculture, and Comptroller of the Currency was instructed to "designate not less than 8 nor more than 12 cities to be known as Federal Reserve cities." By dividing the United States into separate districts, each centered on one Federal Reserve city, the committee was to apportion territory between districts "with due regard to the convenience and customary course of business."[11] The committee's decisions, as they were subsequently refined by the Federal Reserve Board through 1921, provide the trade area boundaries for the third and fourth decades of analysis (1901–11 and 1911–21).

---

designated 'reserve' cities. In these cities national banks had to maintain twenty-five percent reserves, but could count deposits with New York banks as part of these reserves up to half of the required total. New York was established as [a] 'central reserve' city. National banks in New York had also to maintain twenty-five per cent reserves. Such reserves, however, had to be held *in toto* in the vaults of the individual banks." William J. Schultz and M. R. Caine, *Financial Development of the United States* (New York: Prentice-Hall, 1937), p. 317. "In another respect, a step toward territorial decentralization of the country's banking structure was taken during the 1880's. An amendment to the National Banking Act in 1887 authorized cities with populations over 200,000 to become central reserve cities: such action was made dependent upon the application of three-quarters of the national banks in any city with the necessary population. Chicago and St. Louis banks hastened to have their cities qualified as central reserve centers. Redeposits of western banks, instead of going exclusively to New York, to some extent came to center upon these cities" (ibid., p. 388). "Similarly a request from three-fourths of the National banks in any city of fifty thousand inhabitants would authorize the Comptroller to make that city a reserve city of the second-class." John Jay Knox, *A History of Banking in the United States* (New York: Bradford Rhodes, 1903), p. 285.

As the committee viewed its task, the most important and complex decisions concerned the apportionment of territory among the several districts. The selection of reserve cities, by comparison, was relatively simple. * In carrying out their assignment, the members were influenced by several factors, including:

> First. The ability of the member banks within the district to provide the minimum capital of $4,000,000 required for the Federal reserve bank, on the basis of 6 per cent of the capital stock and surplus of member banks within the district.
>
> Second. The mercantile, industrial, and financial connections existing in each district and the relations between the various portions of the district and the city selected for the location of the Federal reserve bank.
>
> Third. The probable ability of the Federal reserve bank in each district, after organization and after the provisions of the Federal reserve act shall have gone into effect, to meet the legitimate demands of business, whether normal or abnormal, in accordance with the spirit and provisions of the Federal reserve act.
>
> Fourth. The fair and equitable division of the available capital for the Federal reserve banks among the districts created.
>
> Fifth. The general geographical situation of the district, transportation lines, and the facilities for speedy communication between the Federal reserve bank and all portions of the district.
>
> Sixth. The population, area, and prevalent business activities of the district, whether agricultural, manufacturing, mining, or commercial, its record of growth and development in the past and its prospects for the future.
>
> In determining the several districts the committee has endeavored to follow State lines as closely as practicable, and whereever it has been found necessary to deviate the division has been along lines which are believed to be most convenient and advantageous for the district affected.[12]

Three of these were directly related to the operating requirements of the reserve system itself. The first set a capitalization threshold for member banks within a proposed district. The third factor apparently set a ceiling or limit on the scale of operations within any one reserve bank. And the fourth distributed the capital provided by the government evenly throughout the nation. Two other considerations also influenced the board: the statutory limit on the number of reserve cities that could be designated, and a "tilt" toward boundaries which coincided with state lines. Taken together, these can be classed as five

---

Senate Documents, p. 367. The committee chose Boston, New York, Philadelphia, Cleveland, Richmond, Atlanta, Chicago, St. Louis, Minneapolis, Kansas City, Dallas, and San Francisco as reserve cities.

"administrative" goals which were tangential to a consideration of the economic integration or interdependence of urban/hinterland territories.

The remaining three factors explicitly enumerated by the organization committee emphasized trade and communication patterns: the economic ties between the designated reserve city and the delineated hinterland, the ease and frequency of communication between that city and surrounding territory, and the composition of the economic base in relation to future growth. Of all the factors that the Reserve Bank Organization Committee considered, however, the most important to its final decision was a poll of private banks. Each of the 7,471 national banks which agreed to join the proposed Federal Reserve System was asked to indicate which city should receive the reserve bank with which it (the national bank) would be connected.[13]

The ballot that each bank received asked two separate questions. The banks were first asked to rank-order the three possible reserve center cities with which they most preferred to be connected within the new reserve system. Each bank was then asked to name the proper location of from eight to twelve federal reserve banks such as to form a national network. Of the 7,471 ballots distributed, the organization committee received 6,724 indications of most-preferred (first-order) reserve bank locations. On many ballots, second- and third-order preferences were not listed by responding banks.

The committee received formal applications from thirty-seven cities (see table A.2) which presented detailed arguments to support their designation as district reserve bank centers.* No city which did not submit a brief in support of its claims was given reserve bank status. The two most important criteria for designation seemed to have been the total capital and surplus held in national banks located within each applicant city and the percentage of first-place ballots naming that city from prospective member banks within the immediate area. All twelve federal reserve bank cities were ranked in the top twenty-five cities in the nation in terms of capital held in national banks (see table A.3).† Of these twenty-five, twelve cities received first-place votes from over 35 percent of the responding banks in their federal reserve district as the boundaries were ultimately defined. Eleven of these twelve (New York, Chicago, Philadelphia, Boston, San Francisco, St. Louis, Minneapolis, Kansas City, Richmond, Atlanta, and Dallas) were designated as district reserve bank centers. The one exception, Cleveland, was awarded reserve bank status in spite of the

---

*Several of these applications anticipated the type of data that were ultimately used by the committee. See "Greater Kansas City's Natural Banking Territory" (p. 175), "Geographical Representation of Interbanking Relations of Minneapolis and Outside Points" (p. 235), and "Map Showing Location of Banks Carrying Accounts with Richmond Banks and Trust Companies" (p. 305), *Senate Documents*.

†Twin cities such as Minneapolis–St. Paul, Dallas–Fort Worth, and the two Kansas Cities are combined in table A.2 because their respective applications were in direct competition and individual bank respondents often did not discriminate between them.

Table A.2. Amount of Capital and Surplus in Cities Considered for Federal Reserve Center Status and Tabulated Vote on Designation

City	Capital and Surplus (Thousands of Dollars)	First-Place Votes in District (Percentage)	Votes Received Nationally (Percentage)	1921 Reserve City Designation[a]
New York	249,305	90.4 (420)[c]	86.1	bank
Chicago	69,050	81.8 (861)	86.9	bank
Philadelphia	62,065	71.2 (708)	29.7	bank
Boston	48,081	72.8 (394)	64.6	bank
Pittsburgh	48,514	42.9 (685)	16.5	branch
San Francisco	44,880	55.7 (460)	79.1	bank
St. Louis	29,140	50.2 (414)	72.4	bank
Cincinnati	20,350	28.3 (685)	16.0	branch
Baltimore	19,760	29.7 (431)	16.3	branch
Cleveland	14,400	16.1 (685)	6.9	bank
Minneapolis	13,710	56.6 (645)	29.9	bank
(incl. St. Paul)	(23,310)	(77.5)	(40.5)	
Kansas City, Mo.	11,650	46.2 (769)	20.8	bank
(incl. Kansas City, Kans.)	(12,450)	(48.4)	—	
Washington, D.C.	11,165	5.8 (431)	17.1	
Richmond	9,484	38.7 (431)	5.4	bank
Atlanta	8,600	38.9 (319)	50.1	bank
New Orleans	8,230	9.7 (319)	68.1	branch
Louisville	8,225	18.6 (414)	3.5	branch
Denver	7,538	17.2 (769)	60.9	branch
Houston	7,050	15.7 (618)	5.7	branch
Portland, Oreg.	6,675	16.3 (460)	10.4	branch
Omaha	6,560	24.8 (769)	8.3	branch
Dallas	5,900	37.5 (618)	9.4	bank
(incl. Ft. Worth)	(9,850)	(52.3)	(11.8)	
Seattle	5,560	8.7 (460)	27.3	branch
Columbus	4,673	5.3 (685)	—	
Spokane	4,172	5.7 (460)	1.5	branch
Birmingham	3,114	16.9 (319)	—	branch
Charlotte	1,850	4.4 (431)	—	
Columbia, S.C.	1,825	6.5 (431)	—	
Savannah	1,600	7.5 (319)	—	
Memphis	1,590	3.4 (414)	2.2	branch
Lincoln, Neb.	1,330	2.9 (769)	—	

Cities Not Requesting Reserve Status in 1914				
Buffalo	—	3.1 (420)	—	branch
Des Moines	3,055	2.0 (861)	—	
Detroit	—	2.6 (861)	—	branch
Helena	—	— (645)	—	branch
Indianapolis	9,410	1.6 (861)	—	
Jacksonville	—	4.4 (319)	—	branch
Little Rock	—	0.0 (414)	—	branch

Table A.2. (continued)

City	Capital and Surplus (Thousands of Dollars)	First-Place Votes in District (Percentage)[c]	Votes Received Nationally (Percentage)	1921 Reserve City Designation[a]
Los Angeles	—	5.7 (460)	3.4	branch
Nashville	4,198	6.9 (319)	—	branch
Salt Lake City	—	5.9 (460)	2.5	branch

[a] A blank indicates that the city was not the location of either a federal reserve bank or branch.

[b] Three cities that requested reserve bank status are excluded from this table: Wheeling, Montgomery, and Chattanooga.

[c] Parenthesized figures in this column are the total number of votes cast in each reserve district.

SOURCES: Data on capital and surplus: United States Senate, "Location of Reserve Districts in the United States," *Senate Documents* 16:485 (Washington: Government Printing Office, 1914), p. 365, table B. First-place votes within districts: adapted from ibid., pp. 349–50. Votes received nationally: adapted from ibid., pp. 356–57. 1921 reserve city designations: *Eighth Annual Report of the Board of Governors of the Federal Reserve System, 1921* (Washington: 1922), pp. 693–99.

Table A.3. Size and Wealth of Federal Reserve Districts as of March 4, 1914

District Number and Federal Reserve City	Land Area (sq. miles)	Population (1910)	National Banks		
			Number	Capital and Surplus (thousands of dollars)	6 Percent Subscription (thousands of dollars)
1 Boston	61,976	6,552,681	445	165,409	9,925
2 New York	47,654	9,113,614	477	343,693	20,622
3 Philadelphia	40,449	7,932,065	757	208,136	12,488
4 Cleveland	72,693	8,326,668	767	200,123	12,007
5 Richmond	152,931	8,519,310	475	105,055	6,303
6 Atlanta	233,821	8,677,288	372	77,353	4,641
7 Chicago	171,306	12,348,767	952	207,998	12,480
8 St. Louis	194,767	8,747,662	458	83,179	4,991
9 Minneapolis	433,281	5,195,886	687	78,382	4,703
10 Kansas City	450,831	5,671,051	836	93,167	5,590
11 Dallas	430,329	5,797,970	731	92,334	5,540
12 San Francisco	683,852	5,089,304	514	130,423	7,825
Total	2,973,890	91,972,266	7,471	1,785,252	107,115

Note: Data include all national banks in each reserve district.

SOURCE: United States Senate, "Location of Reserve Districts in the United States," *Senate Documents* 16:485 (Washington: Government Printing Office, 1914), p. 364, table A, part 1.

fact that both Pittsburgh and Cincinnati held more total capital in national banks and were more popular choices within the fourth Federal Reserve District.*

The percentage of first-place votes within each city's reserve district is not an entirely unbiased indicator of regional dominance. The committee, after deciding which twelve cities would be designated reserve centers, designed the district boundaries largely on the basis of these ballots. Districts designed around competing but unsuccessful applicant cities would have similar improved the percentage of first-place ballots that they received. However, if total first-place ballots regardless of the ultimate location of member banks are considered, a pattern very similar to the one designated by the committee emerges. Eighteen cities received one hundred or more first-place ballots in the Treasury Department survey. Ten of these received more than 235 ballots, and only two of these (Pittsburgh and Cincinnati) were not designated reserve bank cities. Of the remaining eight cities, Dallas (with 233 first-place votes), Richmond (170), Atlanta (124), and Cleveland (110) prevailed over Omaha (218), Baltimore (141), Denver (136), and Louisville (116) in the committee's decisions. In three of these cases (Dallas, Richmond, and Atlanta), the committee clearly compensated for the relatively underdeveloped financial system in the South (with its consequent small number of banking institutions) and sought a regional balance in the distribution of districts.[14]

Between 1914 and 1921, the Federal Reserve board modified district boundaries in response to petitions from local banks and created reserve branches in order to relieve congestion in central banks and to respond to coninuing political friction produced by the original selection procedure. In all, twenty-three branch banks were created, and their designation and the delimitation of their territories generally followed the organization committee's principles (see table A.2 and map A.3). These twenty-three financial regions, together with the original twelve reserve bank cities, provide the trade area boundaries used in this study for 1901–21.†

*The organization board made no comment on this choice. However, it might be noted that the committee designated the maximum number of reserve districts and attempted to distribute reserve centers evenly throughout the country. Cleveland linked two equally important nearby financial centers, Pittsburgh and Cincinnati. Cleveland, thus, may have been a compromise choice between the competing claims of the other two cities and that compromise would explain the lack of public opposition to Cleveland's designation.

†The closing paragraph of the Reserve Bank Organization Committee's decision indicates that the survey data collected by the Treasury Department were transferred to the district banks for this purpose: "It is no part of the duty of the organization committee to locate branches of the Federal reserve banks. The law specifically provides that 'each Federal reserve bank shall establish branch banks within the Federal reserve district in which it is located.' All the material collected by the committee will be placed at the disposal of the Federal reserve banks and the Federal reserve board when they are organized and ready to consider the establishment of branch banks." *Senate Documents*, p. 363.

For appeals and consequent modification of district boundaries, see "Exhibit I: Appeals from Decisions of the Reserve Bank Organization Committee," *1914 Annual Report of the Federal*

Map A.3. 1921 Federal Reserve Branch Bank Territories. From *Eighth Annual Report of the Board of Governors of the Federal Reserve, 1921*, Washington, D.C.: 1922, pp. 693–99. For boundaries within the Eighth Federal Reserve District only, see the *Twenty-Fourth Annual Report, 1938*, Washington, D.C.: 1938, p. 292.

1. Pittsburgh
2. Cincinnati
3. Louisville
4. Nashville
5. Birmingham
6. Memphis

Trade Area Boundaries, 1921–1941

A Department of Commerce publication, *Market Data Handbook of the United States*, was the source of trade area information for the 1921–31 period.[15] In several folding maps which accompanied the handbook, the Department provided several alternative trade area schemes, including one drawn by the marketing division of the International Magazine Company and another by the J. Walter Thompson Company. The first map described consumer trading areas and the second outlined retail shopping areas. Both of these contained too many trade areas for use in this analysis. Instead, a third delineation, also included in the *Handbook*, was utilized. Batten, Barton, Durstine, and Osborn, the private firm that developed the areas, explained them in this way.

> In an effort to obtain flexibility of distribution effort, to control costs, and to eliminate waste in distribution, this company, in 1923, decided to segregate counties into groups that would fit the various distribution efforts that are usually employed. Newspaper circulation was taken as the basis for defining the areas, and analysis showed that there were 745 areas that could be delineated. The areas contained one or more counties, each of which received more than half of its daily newspaper circulation from one of the 745 points of publication.
>
> During the succeeding five years these 745 areas were worked into larger areas in order to lessen sales cost accounting and to conform to trade conditions. The effort has been to draw a boundary around the activities of local jobbers, retailers, and chains, out of a given warehouse point, rather than to define the limits of each one's influence. The result was the 187 local area divisions shown here. The heavier black outlines show these areas grouped as they are covered by Sunday newspaper circulation out of major centers.*

In the end, the company identified fifty major trading areas (map A.4). With one exception (Helena, Montana), every city serving as the site of a district reserve or reserve branch bank in 1921 was designated a trading center in

---

Reserve Board, pp. 192–93; "Exhibit M: Changes in Federal Reserve Districts," *1915 Annual Report of the Federal Reserve Board*, pp. 114–20; and "Exhibit H: Changes in Federal Reserve Districts," *1916 Annual Report of the Federal Reserve Board*, pp. 122–33 (see also pp. 21–22).

El Paso was not large enough to control a congressional district in either 1905 or 1915. In both cases, the El Paso region was merged into the Dallas area. Oklahoma (1907), Arizona (1912), and New Mexico (1912) did not become states until after the 59th Congress (1905–7).

*These maps were provided with one caveat: "The Department of Commerce assumes no responsibility for the accuracy of these three . . . maps, but presents them as suggestions of possible groupings of counties around trade centers and it is believed they will be of some help to the individual sales manager in laying out his own sales and operating territories and allocating his advertising and sales expense." Stewart, *Market Data Handbook of the United States*, p. 2, accompanying map.

1929. However, many more centers were added (including Albuquerque, Columbus, Fort Worth, Indianapolis, and Knoxville).

In 1941, the Bureau of Foreign and Domestic Commerce published an *Atlas of Wholesale Dry Goods Trading Areas* (which was intended "to be of particular assistance to dry goods wholesalers, and manufacturers of dry goods and other products selling through wholesale dry goods houses, who may use it in a critical analysis of their existing territories, and also when planning to open up new territory.").[16] Beyond its use here as the source for trade area boundaries in the 74th Congress, the *Atlas* is noteworthy in that the procedure used to delineate trade patterns was both theoretically informed and drew upon direct correspondence with regional wholesalers through a blanket questionnaire.

Elma Moulton of the Marketing Research Division of the Bureau, author of the *Atlas*, distinguished the marketing characteristics of "dry goods" from the subjects of two similar studies produced by the National Wholesale Druggists' Association (*Distribution through Drug Channels in the 84 Wholesale Trading Areas*) and the Bureau of Foreign and Domestic Commerce (*Atlas of Wholesale Grocery Territories*).[17] In those two studies, particularly the wholesale grocery trade delineation, "convenience goods of daily consumption" which are distributed to a large number of retailers within a relatively small radius and at fairly frequent and regular intervals were analyzed. In contrast, dry goods possess "shopping" characteristics in that "consumption extends over a longer period and replenishment is less frequent," although, like grocery items, they are "staple goods of constant consumer use." As a result, wholesale dry goods marketing centers were spaced further apart than their grocery counterparts and, thus, Moulton arrived at only 46 major trading areas for dry goods distribution compared to the 184 suggested for the grocery trade.

In 1941, the wholesale dry goods trade was carried on by three types of economic units: manufacturers' sales branches and offices, agents and brokers, and full service and limited function wholesalers.[18] Since each type of distributor would have, even within the industry, a different relation to the market, Moulton isolated the full service and limited function wholesalers for the construction of regional trade boundaries. It should be noted that the wider range of goods distributed by full service wholesalers corresponds more closely to trade area marketing theory than the national distribution of goods from manufacturers' sales branches or brokers.

In March 1939, the Bureau mailed questionnaires to 600 general line dry goods wholesalers whose names and addresses had been supplied by the Wholesale Dry Goods Institute. The list provided by the Institute included, by report, all general line wholesalers in the nation, and 54 percent replied to the inquiry. The most important feature of the questionnaire was a map of the United States upon which each firm was asked to sketch the boundaries of its regularly served trading area(s). Primary dry goods wholesaling centers were designated on the basis of information provided by the questionnaire, the 1935 Census of Business, and an analysis of available transportation routes.

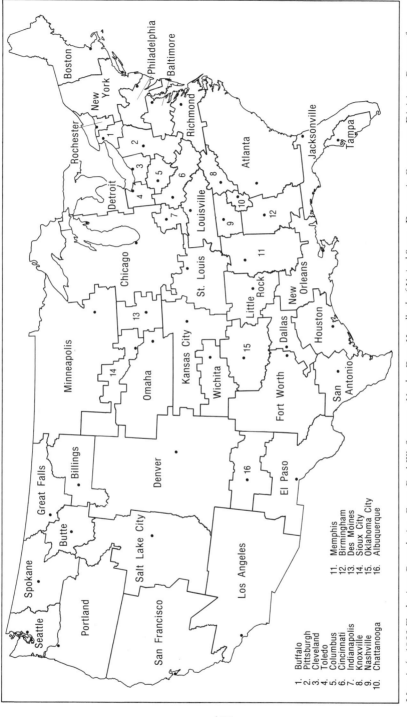

Map A.4. 1925 Trade Area Boundaries. From Paul W. Stewart, *Market Data Handbook of United States*, Domestic Commerce Division, Bureau of Foreign and Domestic Commerce, United States Department of Commerce, Washington, D.C.: Government Printing Office, 1929, accompanying map.

1. Buffalo
2. Pittsburgh
3. Cleveland
4. Toledo
5. Columbus
6. Cincinnati
7. Indianapolis
8. Knoxville
9. Nashville
10. Chattanooga
11. Memphis
12. Birmingham
13. Des Moines
14. Sioux City
15. Oklahoma City
16. Albuquerque

Map. A.5. 1935 Trade Area Boundaries. From Elma S. Moulton, *Atlas of Wholesale Dry Goods Trading Areas*, Marketing Research Division, Bureau of Foreign and Domestic Commerce, United States Department of Commerce, Washington, D.C.: Government Printing Office, 1941, accompanying map.

The Bureau identified both "primary" trading areas which, taken together, completely covered the country with exclusive territories, and "secondary" trading areas which extended the wholesale center's hinterland into adjoining primary areas and, thus, established overlapping trade territories. The primary trade areas were relied upon in the present study.

In many respects, the 1941 delineation of wholesale trade area boundaries corresponds to the divisions suggested by the Bureau in 1929. A comparison of maps A.4 and A.5 reveals a consolidation of trade areas in the West and Great Plains; the 1941 delineation eliminated territories based in Spokane, Butte, Great Falls, Billings, Albuquerque, Omaha, El Paso, and Fort Worth. On the eastern seaboard, however, the wholesale dry goods study added Portland (Maine), Troy, Syracuse, Hartford, Providence, Charleston (West Virginia), Savannah, Winston-Salem, Augusta (Georgia), and Charleston (South Carolina).

Trade Area Boundaries, 1941–1981

The annual editions of the Rand McNally *Commercial Atlas and Marketing Guide* first included a map of "Major Trading Areas" in 1946. Since 1946, Rand McNally's trading area boundaries have undergone four revisions (in 1948, 1954, 1955, and 1960). The original delineation of trade areas and urban centers was the basis for analysis of congressional activity between 1941 and 1951. The third revision, current in the 1955–59 editions inclusive, provided the trade area system for the 1951–61 decade. For the last two decades (1961–81), the congressional trade area delegations were based on the fourth revision, which has remained unchanged since 1960.* (See maps A.6–A.8.)

Rand McNally's Major Trading Areas are constructed out of smaller "Basic Trading Areas."

The selection of Basic Trading Centers is based mainly on their importance as centers for the purchase of *shopping goods*—those retail items, such as clothing, for which the shopper is willing to travel some distance in order to compare quality, style, and price from store to store. Department stores and apparel stores account for most sales of shopping goods. In contrast, *convenience goods* are the items which most shoppers do not travel far to purchase. Typical convenience goods businesses are food stores, drug stores, and automobile service stations. Shopping goods represent the best means for distinguishing the towns to which people travel to make purchases. These towns are also natural centers for other

Commercial Atlas and Marketing Guide (Chicago: Rand McNally). From 1946 to 1947, Rand McNally set up 60 major trading areas composed of 366 basic trading areas; from 1948 through 1953, 63 major and 368 basic areas; for 1954, 63 and 451; from 1955 through 1959, 65 and 459; and from 1960 to the present, 50 and 494.

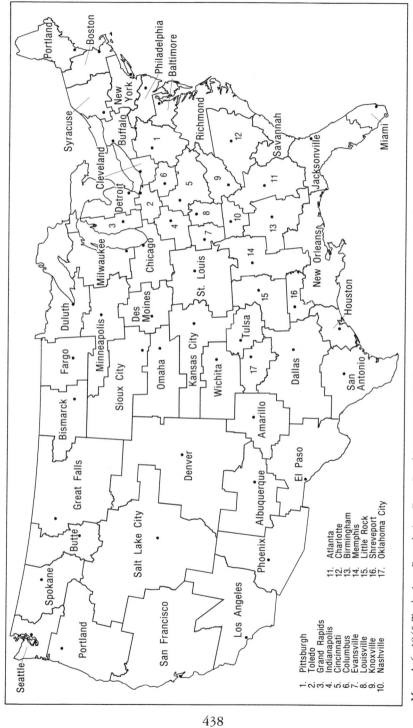

Map. A.6. 1945 Trade Area Boundaries. From Rand McNally, *1946 Commercial Atlas and Marketing Guide*, 77th Edition, Chicago: 1946, accompanying map.

1. Pittsburgh
2. Toledo
3. Grand Rapids
4. Indianapolis
5. Cincinnati
6. Columbus
7. Evansville
8. Louisville
9. Knoxville
10. Nashville
11. Atlanta
12. Charlotte
13. Birmingham
14. Memphis
15. Little Rock
16. Shreveport
17. Oklahoma City

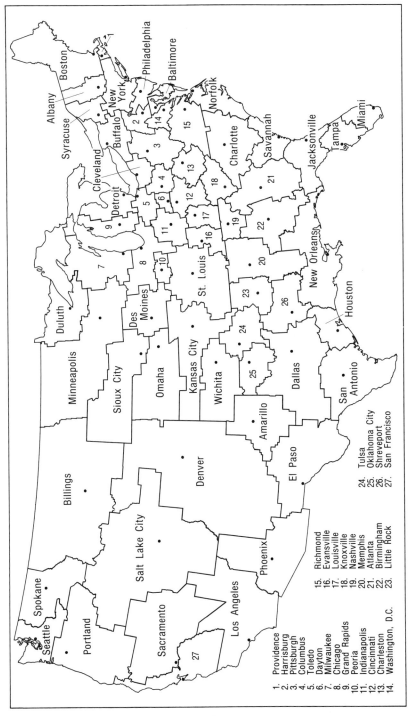

Map A.7. 1955 Trade Area Boundaries. From Rand McNally, *1957 Commercial Atlas and Marketing Guide*, 88th Edition, Chicago: 1957, pp. 50–51.

1. Providence
2. Harrisburg
3. Pittsburgh
4. Columbus
5. Toledo
6. Dayton
7. Milwaukee
8. Chicago
9. Grand Rapids
10. Peoria
11. Indianapolis
12. Cincinnati
13. Charleston
14. Washington, D.C.
15. Richmond
16. Evansville
17. Louisville
18. Knoxville
19. Nashville
20. Memphis
21. Atlanta
22. Birmingham
23. Little Rock
24. Tulsa
25. Oklahoma City
26. Shreveport
27. San Francisco

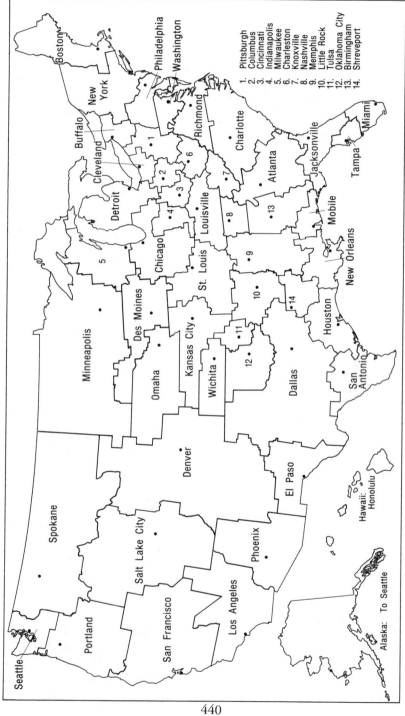

Map A.8. 1965–1975 Trade Area Boundaries. From Rand McNally, *1978 Commercial Atlas and Marketing Guide*, 109th Edition, Chicago: 1978, pp. 64–65.

1. Pittsburgh
2. Columbus
3. Cincinnati
4. Indianapolis
5. Milwaukee
6. Charleston
7. Knoxville
8. Nashville
9. Memphis
10. Little Rock
11. Tulsa
12. Oklahoma City
13. Birmingham
14. Shreveport

specialized services, including entertainment, education, and medical care.[19]

Basic Trading Area boundaries follow county lines and are assigned according to three criteria: accessibility, relative location, and historical cultural ties.

1. Accessibility: Usually people shop in the most accessible Basic Trading Center, which may not be the nearest because of such factors as terrain, highway and railway facilities, bridges, etc.
2. Relative location: People may pass up one trading center in favor of another that is only slightly more difficult to reach and offers a much larger selection of goods and services. For example, in southern Utah most of the counties are assigned to the Salt Lake City Basic Trading Area even though another Basic Trading Center, Provo, lies directly between these counties and Salt Lake City. For people who have made the long trip from southern Utah, the much more extensive shopping facilities of Salt Lake City make up for the short extra distance they must travel beyond Provo.
3. Historical and cultural ties: In some areas, counties have maintained a connection with a given Trading Center even though another center is now equally accessible, reflecting such factors as historical development, early cultural and economic ties, former transportation routes, and even State lines. Often such ties are evidenced by data on daily newspaper circulation by county, which are significant because few people buy more than one daily paper regularly, and naturally tend to buy a paper published in the city to which they generally go for shopping.[20]

In the construction of both Basic and Major Trading Areas, the company utilizes both the notion of "trading centers" and the concept of a "tributary area" for which the trading center serves as a focal point. Each Major Trading Area is focused on a large city of national or regional prominence which provides specialized wholesaling, advertising, and banking services to the territory contained in surrounding Basic Trading Areas. These tributary Basic Areas are combined into the Major Trading Area with the constraint that no Basic Area is partitioned between two competing Major Trading territories.

Between sixty-three and sixty-five trade areas were included in the first three versions of Rand's major trading territories, and the number of areas represented a significant increase over Moulton's 1941 scheme. In part, the Rand system chronicled the emergence of many similar regional centers. These newer regional trading centers were primarily located in the West (Spokane, Phoenix, El Paso, etc.) and the Midwest (Omaha, Tulsa, Oklahoma City, Des Moines, Grand Rapids, Toledo, etc.). Along the eastern seaboard and in the Northeast, the number of trade areas remained static or actually declined as the result of consolidation into territories focused on a larger city (Hartford into New York, Charleston into Savannah, etc.).

The most interesting comparison, however, is between the 1935 trade area boundaries and those for the 1961–81 period. These involve roughly the same number of trade centers (forty-six in 1931–41 and fifty in 1961–81) and, thus, the changing designations more accurately reflect changes in the urban hierarchy. In the West, the rise of new regional centers to prominence between 1935 and 1965 was reflected by the inclusion of Spokane, Phoenix, and El Paso with their respective tributary areas. Hawaii was added in the survey for the first time as an independent trading area focused on Honolulu; the new state of Alaska was assigned to Seattle. In the relatively mature urban network of the Midwest, minor changes occurred, with Omaha, Des Moines, and Milwaukee replacing Sioux City in the list of designated centers. Some shifting also occurred in the western portion of the South (Oklahoma City, Tulsa, Shreveport, Little Rock, and Mobile replaced Fort Smith). With the exception of the new retirement centers of Miami and Tampa, the eastern seaboard continued to undergo consolidation. Providence and Portland (Maine) merged into Boston's tributary area. Upstate New York (Troy and Syracuse) were captured by New York City. The Charlotte trade area (formerly centered on Winston-Salem) came to include Charleston (South Carolina) and Wilmington. The city of Atlanta absorbed Augusta, Georgia, into its trading hinterland.

The historical development of these trade area systems confirms Vance's argument about the historical movement away from the colonial entrepôts of the eastern seaboard. The development of internal markets and national transportation systems, the rise of domestic manufacturing, the exploitation of natural resource deposits, and the contemporary shift toward regions offering significant amenities such as mild climate and recreation have all culminated in this evolutionary trend. While the influence of history can be read into the contemporary urban network, the evolution of the trade area system has no ultimate solution or state of rest. The country cannot be interpreted as "settled" and the urban hierarchy as stable except in terms of the current state of social and economic development. Predicting the emergence of future trade centers requires either the extension of contemporary trends into the far future or the accurate forecast of new and currently unknown developmental factors. Thus, the urban network may evolve in fairly unpredictable directions, and technological change makes any notion of entropy analytically untenable.

Summary of Trade Area Delegations, 1881–1981

Over the century from 1885 to 1981, the number of congressmen in the House of Representatives rose from 325 to 435, an increase of 48 percent. Table A.4 presents a summary list of congressional trade area delegations and their sizes for the middle year of each decade. Just over half of the overall increase in the size of the House, 56 of the 110 members, occurred in the American West. Corresponding with the settlement of the West, the number of trade areas in this region expanded rapidly from two (Denver and San Francisco) in 1885 to nine in 1975.*

In the mature commercial and industrial regions of the Northeast and the Midwest, both the number of trade areas and the number of congressmen remained relatively constant. In 1885 the two regions encompassed a total of 23 trade areas and 222 congressmen. In 1975, the corresponding figures were 20 and 239. Aside from the West, the American South was the only region to show marked change in its urban network during the last century. The number of trade centers of regional importance increased from 8 to 21 and the number of congressmen rose from 94 to 121.

The Sectional Stress Index

Though many types of materials are utilized here, the primary source of data for the analysis of sectional conflict is roll calls taken in the House of Representatives. In connecting roll call behavior to the existence and intensity of sectional stress, the most important analytical tool will be the sectional stress index. A careful explanation of the index formula is therefore in order.

Because some legislative policy decisions divide the nation's representatives into more geographically homogeneous coalitions than others, sectional stress does not occur to the same degree on all roll calls. An index used to measure the relative amount of sectional stress associated with different policy decisions should meet two requirements. First, the conceptual basis of the index should correspond to a natural and commonly held notion of "sectionalism." From this perspective, the formula should calculate the relative degree to which regional delegations are internally cohesive and externally opposed to each other. Second, the simplicity and generality of the measure should allow its use in very diverse political environments. As an approach to the study of national political institutions, the concept of sectional stress should facilitate cross-national application.

$$\text{Index of Sectional Stress} = \left(\frac{a}{b} - c \right) \cdot \frac{1}{d}$$

where: a = The total number of members in all trade area majorities;
b = The total number of votes cast;
c = The percentage of total votes cast on the winning side of the roll call; and
d = The percentage of total votes cast on the losing side of the roll call.

---

*In addition to inclusion of the El Paso trade area in the Dallas congressional delegation in both 1905 and 1915, Spokane was included in the Seattle delegation in 1905, Billings in the Great Falls delegation in 1925, and Bismarck in the Fargo, North Dakota, delegation in 1945. In all cases, the reason for the combination was that the first named trade area did not have enough people to support a congressman.

Table A.4a. Identity of Major Trade Centers and Size of Congressional Trade Area Delegations, 1885–1975: The Northeast

Trade Area	Delegation Size									
	1885	1895	1905	1915	1925	1935	1945	1955	1965	1975
Portland, Me.	4	—	—	—	—	4	3	—	—	—
Boston	14	19	28	31	28	17	19	18	18	18
Providence	5	5	—	—	—	2	—	4	—	—
Hartford	—	—	—	—	—	5	—	—	—	—
Troy	—	—	—	—	—	3	—	—	—	—
Albany	8	7	—	—	—	—	—	3	—	—
New York	22	25	40	47	53	41	54	51	57	54
Syracuse	5	5	—	—	2	6	6	3	—	—
Rochester	—	—	—	—	—	8	—	—	—	—
Buffalo	8	7	5	6	5	—	9	8	6	6
Philadelphia	15	16	26	30	22	25	18	15	18	18
Scranton	5	7	—	—	—	—	—	—	—	—
Harrisburg	—	—	—	—	—	—	—	5	—	—
Pittsburgh	11	11	11	11	18	14	16	13	13	12
Charleston, W.V.	—	—	—	—	—	7	—	4	4	3
Baltimore	7	7	8	8	9	8	6	5	—	—
Washington, D.C.	—	—	—	—	—	—	—	3	10	10
Number of Trade Areas in Section	11	10	6	6	7	12	8	12	7	7
Number of Congressmen in Delegations	104	109	118	133	137	140	131	132	126	121

Table A.4b. Identity of Major Trade Centers and Size of Congressional Trade Area Delegations, 1885–1975: The Midwest

Trade Area	Delegation Size									
	1885	1895	1905	1915	1925	1935	1945	1955	1965	1975
Cleveland	6	7	14	16	6	9	7	9	10	10
Columbus	11	10	—	—	6	5	6	5	4	3
Cincinnati	8	7	12	11	9	8	12	6	6	6
Dayton	—	—	—	—	—	—	—	3	—	—
Toledo	—	—	—	—	5	—	5	3	—	—
Detroit	7	7	5	6	9	16	12	13	20	21
Grand Rapids	4	5	—	—	—	—	4	3	7	—
Indianapolis	10	8	—	—	6	9	6	6	7	4
Evansville	—	4	—	—	—	—	3	3	—	—
Chicago	13	16	56	58	48	43	21	21	27	29
Milwaukee	9	10	—	—	—	—	8	8	9	7
Peoria	—	—	—	—	—	—	—	1	—	—
St. Louis	17	13	21	21	12	17	14	14	9	9
Des Moines	—	9	—	—	4	—	6	6	6	6
Minneapolis	9	12	16	19	15	16	9	12	13	12
Duluth	—	—	—	—	—	—	2	2	—	—
Fargo	—	—	—	—	—	—	3	—	—	—
Sioux City	—	—	—	—	3	2	3	3	—	—
Omaha	9	8	7	7	7	—	5	5	4	3
Kansas City	15	16	11	11	13	13	9	7	6	7
Wichita	—	—	—	—	3	5	3	2	2	1
Number of Trade Areas in Section	12	14	8	8	14	11	19	20	13	13
Number of Congressmen in Delegations	118	132	142	149	146	143	138	132	123	118

445

Table A.4c. Identity of Major Trade Centers and Size of Congressional Trade Area Delegations, 1885–1975: The South

Trade Area	Delegation Size									
	1885	1895	1905	1915	1925	1935	1945	1955	1965	1975
Richmond	17	17	29	30	7	11	11	6	7	7
Norfolk	—	—	—	—	—	—	—	5	—	—
Wilmington	—	—	—	—	—	2	—	—	—	—
Winston-Salem	—	—	—	—	—	6	—	—	—	—
Charlotte	—	—	—	—	—	—	14	14	17	17
Augusta, Ga.	6	9	—	—	—	1	—	—	—	—
Charleston, S.C.	3	—	—	—	—	3	—	—	—	—
Savannah	—	—	—	—	—	—	3	3	—	—
Atlanta	19	21	12	13	29	10	8	8	11	11
Jacksonville	—	—	3	4	3	4	4	3	5	5
Tampa	—	—	—	—	—	—	—	3	3	3
Miami	—	—	—	—	1	—	2	2	3	6
Chattanooga	—	—	—	—	—	—	—	—	—	—
Knoxville	—	—	—	—	3	4	5	4	4	3
Louisville	7	7	7	7	10	5	2	2	6	8

Nashville	7	8	7	7	4	4	4	3	3	3
Memphis	19	20	8	8	10	11	9	8	8	7
Little Rock	—	—	5	5	6	—	5	3	3	3
Birmingham	—	—	8	9	9	10	9	8	7	6
Mobile	—	—	—	—	—	—	—	—	2	2
New Orleans	16	17	9	9	11	10	10	10	5	7
Shreveport	—	—	—	—	—	—	2	4	3	2
Houston	—	—	5	5	6	4	3	3	6	6
San Antonio	—	—	—	—	2	5	4	4	3	4
El Paso	—	—	—	—	1	—	1	1	1	2
Ft. Worth	—	—	—	17	4	—	—	—	—	—
Dallas	—	—	13	—	5	15	10	11	14	13
Amarillo	—	—	—	8	—	—	2	2	—	—
Oklahoma City	—	—	—	—	7	—	4	3	4	4
Tulsa	—	—	—	—	—	—	5	4	2	2
Ft. Smith	—	—	—	—	—	5	—	—	—	—
Number of Trade Areas in Section	8	7	11	12	18	17	21	23	21	21
Number of Congressmen in Delegations	94	99	106	122	119	110	117	114	117	121

Table A. 4d. Identity of Major Trade Centers and Size of Congressional Trade Area Delegations, 1885–1975: The West

Trade Area	Delegation Size									
	1885	1895	1905	1915	1925	1935	1945	1955	1965	1975
Billings	—	—	—	—	—	—	—	2	—	—
Great Falls	—	—	—	—	—	—	—	—	—	—
Helena	—	—	1	2	1	—	1	—	—	—
Butte	—	—	—	—	—	—	1	—	—	—
Spokane	—	—	—	2	3	—	2	2	5	4
Seattle	—	—	3	3	3	8	5	6	5	6
Portland	—	—	2	3	3	3	4	4	5	4
Salt Lake City	—	4	2	4	3	3	3	3	3	4
Denver	1	—	3	4	5	6	5	7	7	7
Albuquerque	—	—	—	—	1	—	2	—	—	—
Phoenix	—	—	—	—	—	—	2	2	3	4
Los Angeles	—	2	2	4	4	12	14	18	24	27
San Francisco	8	11	7	9	9	10	10	10	15	17
Sacramento	—	—	—	—	—	—	—	3	—	—
Honolulu	—	—	—	—	—	—	—	—	2	2
Number of Trade Areas in Section	2	3	7	8	10	6	11	10	9	9
Number of Congressmen in Delegations	9	17	20	31	33	42	49	57	69	75
Number of Trade Areas in Nation	33	34	32	34	49	46	59	65	50	50
Number of Congressmen in Delegations	325	357	386	435	435	435	435	435	435	435

The formula used in calculating the relative sectional stress on individual roll calls, in brief, compares the cohesion of trade area delegations to the winning margin on the roll call as a whole. Variable *a* is the total number of members in all of the separate trade area delegation majorities. When *a* is divided by *b*, the resulting fraction is the level of trade area or sectional cohesion on the roll call. Subtracting *c* yields the percentage improvement over random voting. For example, if 75 percent of all members vote in line with their trade area majorities and the winning margin is 60 percent, the index reveals a 15 percent improvement over random voting; the total number of members in all trade area majorities (*a*) divided by the total number of votes

			Number of Members Voting on Roll Call		
Trade Area	Yea	Nay	Trade Area Majority	Trade Area Minority	N
Metropolis	0	15	15	0	15
Union City	30	13	30	13	43
Springdale	30	12	30	12	42
Total	60	40	75	25	100

cast (*b*) could not be less than the winning margin of 60 percent and, in fact, is 15 percent greater. Dividing the improvement over random voting (here 15 percent) by the percentage of total votes cast on the losing side of the roll call converts the index to a 100-percent point scale. At 100, the trade area delegations are perfectly polarized on the roll call; at zero, the policy decision provokes no regional alignment whatsoever. The resulting score in this particular calculation is 37.5.[21] Sectional Stress in the party system can be measured in much the same way as on individual roll calls (see chapter 8).

Conclusion

The methodology proposed here promises two major advantages over plausible alternatives. First, the use of trade areas, congressional delegations, and analysis of roll call voting in the House of Representatives assures great continuity of results over time. Two similar sectional stress scores should represent similar degrees of spatial polarization even if they are calculated for congressional votes temporally separated by a century or more. This longitudinal continuity is a product of the conjunction of the units analyzed, statistical formula, and data base.

Second, the trade area approach, though based on an entirely independent theoretical foundation, interacts in a very fertile way with a "core-periphery" interpretative framework. Major urban centers clearly play an extraordinarily important organizing role in an interregional division of labor. By gathering and refining the production of its hinterland and exporting the region's goods to other sections, the major urban center is the gateway through which the world-economy touches the entire region. In the core sections of the United States, the major urban center dominates the hinterland and determines the policy imperatives of the region. In the periphery, the hinterland with its dependence on a cash crop or extractive economy dominates the urban center gateway and imposes its own political imperatives upon the city. In both cases, economic interdependence has forced political homogeneity upon the entire trade area delegation. Interdependence within the trade area, combined with the inevitable incompatibility between the political economy requirements of the core and periphery, has resulted in the "massive fact" of sectional stress.

Notes

Chapter 1: Introduction

1 The following discussion is largely based on two of Frederick Jackson Turner's works: *Sections in American History* (New York: Henry Holt, 1932); and a post-humously edited collection of his unpublished manuscripts, *America's Great Frontiers and Sections*, ed. Wilbur R. Jacobs (Lincoln: University of Nebraska Press, 1969).

2 Turner, *Sections in American History*, p. 183.

3 Ibid., p. 37.

4 Ray Allen Billington, *Frederick Jackson Turner: Historian, Scholar, Teacher* (New York: Oxford University Press, 1973), p. 467.

5 Turner, *Sections in American History*, p. 205.

6 Ibid., p. 47.

7 Frederick Jackson Turner, "Sections and Nation," *Yale Review* 12 (October 1922):7.

8 Turner, *America's Great Frontiers and Sections*, p. 67.

9 Ibid., p. 67.

10 V. O. Key, *Politics, Parties, and Pressure Groups* (New York: Thomas Y. Crowell, 1964), p. 238.

11 Ibid., p. 229. Key's description implicitly follows Frederick Jackson Turner's frontier thesis on this point.

12 Ibid., p. 234.

13 Key, *Politics, Parties, and Pressure Groups*, pp. 224–25.

14 Ibid., p. 248.

15 Julius Turner, *Party and Constituency: Pressures on Congress*, rev. ed. (Baltimore: Johns Hopkins Press, 1970), ed. Edward Schneier. In the following discussion, all references will be to the revised edition.

16 Ibid., pp. 165–66.

17 Ibid., p. 166.

18 Ibid., p. 206.

19 For examples of the cross-cultural use of trade area theory, see Carol A. Smith, *Regional Analysis: Economic System*, vol. 1 (New York: Academic Press, 1976).

20 Immanuel Wallerstein, *The Capitalist World-Economy* (Cambridge: University Press, 1979), p. 271.

451

21 Immanuel Wallerstein, *The Modern World-System: Capitalist Agriculture and the Origins of the European World-Economy in the Sixteenth Century* (New York: Academic Press, 1974), p. 347.
22 Wallerstein, *The Capitalist World-Economy*, p. 158.
23 Ibid., p. 159.
24 Ibid., p. 160.
25 Ibid., p. 37.
26 Ibid., pp. 71, 162.
27 Ibid., p. 38.
28 Ibid., pp. 37–38.

Chapter 2: Overview

1 Richard F. Bensel, "The Origins of the Discretionary State: Political Insurgency and Statutory Articulation, 1895–1917" (paper presented to the annual meeting of the American Political Science Association, New York, 1981). See also Elizabeth Sanders, "Business, Bureaucracy and the Bourgeoisie: The New Deal Legacy," in Alan Stone and Edward J. Harpham, eds., *The Political Economy of Public Policy* (Beverly Hills: Sage Publications, 1982).
2 Richard F. Bensel, "Creating the Statutory State: The Implications of a Rule of Law Standard in American Politics," *American Political Science Review* 74:3 (September 1980): 734–44.

Chapter 3: Tariffs, Elections, and Imperialism: 1880–1910

1 Immanuel Wallerstein, *The Capitalist World-Economy* (Cambridge: Cambridge University Press, 1979), p. 31. See also pp. 29, 84–85.
2 Walter Dean Burnham, "The End of American Party Politics" (Transaction) *Society* 7:2 (December 1969): 16.
3 The literature on the American tariff system and its effect is both vast and contentious. Frank W. Taussig, in his *Protection to Young Industries as Applied in the United States* (Cambridge, Mass.: Moses King, 1883), and *Some Aspects of the Tariff Question* (Cambridge, Mass.: Harvard University Press, 1915) was the most respected contemporary critic of protectionist doctrine. Both Tom E. Terrill, *The Tariff, Politics, and American Foreign Policy, 1874–1901* (Westport, Conn.: Greenwood Press, 1973) and Festus P. Summers, *William L. Wilson and Tariff Reform* (New Brunswick, N.J.: Rutgers University Press, 1953) provide detailed accounts of the politics of the nineteenth-century tariff.
4 Allan Nevins, *Grover Cleveland: A Study in Courage* (New York: Dodd, Mead, 1944), p. 326.
5 Robert McElroy, *Grover Cleveland: The Man and the Statesman* (New York: Harper and Brothers, 1923), p. 190.
6 Nevins, *Grover Cleveland: A Study in Courage*, p. 172; John William Oliver, *History of the Civil War Military Pensions, 1861–85* (Bulletin of the University of Wisconsin, No. 844, Madison: 1917), pp. 77, 108–9.
7 William H. Glasson, *Federal Military Pensions in the United States* (New York: Oxford University Press, 1918), p. 238; Herbert Agar, *The Price of Union* (Boston:

Houghton Mifflin, 1966), p. 582; James Ford Rhodes, *History of the United States*, 8 vols. (New York: MacMillan, 1928), 8:298–99.

8 Nevins, *Grover Cleveland: A Study in Courage*, p. 326. For an account of the Pension Bureau, see Leonard D. White, *The Republican Era: 1869–1901* (New York: Macmillan, 1958), pp. 208–21.

9 David R. Dewey, *National Problems*, vol. 24 of *The American Nation: A History*, ed. A. B. Hart (New York: Harper and Brothers, 1907), p. 85.

10 Nevins, *Grover Cleveland: A Study in Courage*, p. 328.

11 Ibid., pp. 327–28.

12 *Congressional Record*, 49:1:7053, July 16, 1886.

13 Ibid., 49:1:7051, July 16, 1886.

14 McElroy, *Grover Cleveland: The Man and the Statesman*, pp. 195–96.

15 Nevins, *Grover Cleveland: A Study in Courage*, p. 332.

16 Henry Jones Ford, *The Cleveland Era* (New Haven: Yale University Press, 1919).

17 Edwin Sparks, *National Development*, vol. 23 of *The American Nation: A History*, ed. A. B. Hart (New York: Harper and Brothers, 1935), p. 289. A total of eight billion dollars was paid out in Civil War pensions, of which Walter Prescott Webb estimated that seven billion went to the North while one billion was distributed to the South and West. Agar, *The Price of Union*, p. 583.

18 Glasson, *Federal Military Pensions*, p. 267.

19 Summers, *William L. Wilson and Tariff Reform*, pp. 48–49.

20 Agar, *The Price of Union*, p. 583–86, 590.

21 Harry N. Scheiber et al., *American Economic History* (New York: Harper and Row, 1976), p. 284.

22 Ford, *The Cleveland Era*, pp. 152–56. See also Charles H. Hession and Hyman Sardy, *Ascent to Affluence* (Boston: Allyn and Bacon, 1969), pp. 493–95.

23 Oliver, *History of the Civil War Military Pensions, 1861–85*, p. 97; Glasson, *Federal Military Pensions*, p. 220.

24 *Congressional Record*, 50:1:1637, March 1, 1888.

25 Ibid., 50:1:1627, March 1, 1888.

26 Glasson, *Federal Military Pensions*, p. 218; also see pp. 221, 256–57.

27 Ibid., p. 263.

28 Ibid., p. 266.

29 For a description of the tariff bills, including their probable effects, see F. W. Taussig, *The Tariff History of the United States* (New York: Augustus M. Kelley, 1967); and Edward Stanwood, *American Tariff Controversies in the Nineteenth Century* (Boston: Houghton Mifflin, 1903). Congressional district maps of House voting on the McKinley tariff of 1890 and the Wilson tariff of 1894 can be found on pp. 172 and 274 respectively of Dewey, *National Problems*. Similar maps displaying House voting on the 1909 Payne-Adlrich tariff and the 1913 Underwood tariff are provided in John D. Hicks, *The American Nation* (Cambridge, Mass.: Houghton Mifflin, 1941), p. 447.

30 See, for example, C. Vann Woodward, *Origins of the New South: 1877–1913* (Baton Rouge: Louisiana State University Press, 1951), ch. 11, "The Colonial Economy." William Hesseltine maintained that "Reconstruction was the method by which the 'Masters of Capital' sought to secure their victory over the vanquished 'Lords of the Manor,' and through which they expected to exploit the resources of the South-

ern states." *Sections and Politics: Selected Essays by William B. Hesseltine*, ed. Richard N. Current (Madison: State Historical Society of Wisconsin, 1968), p. 46.

31 *Congressional Record*, 51:1:6497, June 25, 1890.

32 For an account of the Hayes-Tilden presidential election, see C. Vann Woodward, *Reunion and Reaction* (Boston: Little, Brown, 1951).

33 Agar, *The Price of Union*, pp. 496–98.

34 Stanley P. Hirshson, *Farewell to the Bloody Shirt: Northern Republicans and the Southern Negro, 1877–1893* (Bloomington: Indiana University Press, 1962), p. 203.

35 Vincent P. DeSantis, *Republicans Face the Southern Question* (Baltimore: Johns Hopkins Press, 1959), p. 198; Lawrence Grossman, *The Democratic Party and the Negro: Northern and National Politics, 1868–1892* (Urbana: University of Illinois Press, 1976), p. 146.

36 This description draws on DeSantis, *Republicans Face the Southern Question*, pp. 198–99, and Hirshson, *Farewell to the Bloody Shirt*, pp. 204–5.

37 Hirshson, *Farewell to the Bloody Shirt*, p. 202.

38 *Congressional Record*, 51:1:6773, June 30, 1890.

39 Ibid., 51:1:6706, June 28, 1890.

40 Grossman, *The Democratic Party and the Negro*, p. 146. See also DeSantis, *Republicans Face the Southern Question*, p. 211.

41 George H. Mayer, *The Republican Party: 1854–1966* (New York: Oxford University Press, 1967), p. 230.

42 Ibid., pp. 227–28. See also Ellis Paxson Oberholtzer, *A History of the United States Since the Civil War*, vol. 5 (New York: MacMillan, 1937), p. 117.

43 Grossman, *The Democratic Party and the Negro*, p. 150.

44 Ibid., pp. 158–61.

45 Almost all accounts emphasize the prominent role of northern commerce in arranging the ultimate demise of the Lodge bill. Agar, *The Price of Union*, p. 498; DeSantis, *Republicans Face the Southern Question*, pp. 199, 213; David R. Dewey, *National Problems* (New York: Harper and Brothers, 1907), p. 169–70; Hirshson, *Farewell to the Bloody Shirt*, pp. 216–18, 222–23, 234, 243; Mayer, *The Republican Party: 1854–1966*, p. 229–30; Rhodes, *History of the United States*, vol. 8, p. 361. See also Current, ed., *Sections and Politics*, "Economic Factors in the Abandonment of Reconstruction."

46 Hirshson, *Farewell to the Bloody Shirt*, p. 219.

47 *Congressional Record*, 51:1:6773, June 30, 1890.

48 Grossman, *The Democratic Party and the Negro*, p. 147. See also pp. 143, 156.

49 Ibid., pp. 154–55; Hirshson, *Farewell to the Bloody Shirt*, p. 248.

50 Grossman, *The Democratic Party and the Negro*, p. 150.

51 Hirshson, *Farewell to the Bloody Shirt*, p. 244. See also Grossman, *The Democratic Party and the Negro*, pp. 158–61.

52 Dewey, *National Problems*, p. 171.

53 J. Morgan Kousser, *The Shaping of Southern Politics: Suffrage Restriction and the Establishment of the One-Party South, 1880–1910* (New Haven: Yale University Press, 1975). See also Mayer, *The Republican Party: 1854–1966*, p. 230.

54 *Congressional Record*, 53:1:2293, October 7, 1893.

55 Ibid., p. 2304.

56 Ibid., 53:1:2343, October 9, 1893.

57 For a summary of the case, see Chester H. Rowell, *Digest of Contested Elections in the House of Representatives: 1789–1901*, pp. 547–52. For discussion of improperly marked ballots, see *Congressional Record*, 54:2:981–82, January 20, 1897.

58 *Congressional Record*, 54:2:987, January 20, 1897.

59 Ibid., p. 1032–34.

60 Hirshson, *Farewell to the Bloody Shirt*, pp. 236, 251–52; Mayer, *The Republican Party: 1854–1966*, p. 230.

61 Agar, *The Price of Union*, p. 500.

62 Rhodes, *History of the United States*, vol. 7, p. 363.

63 Hession and Sardy, *Ascent to Affluence*, p. 501. For a review of the literature on this point, see Philip S. Foner, *The Spanish-Cuban-American War and the Birth of American Imperialism: 1895–1902*, vol. 1, *1895–1898* (New York: Monthly Review Press, 1972), ch. 14.

64 Goram Rystad, *Ambiguous Imperialism: American Foreign Policy and Domestic Policy at the Turn of the Century* (Stockholm: Scandinavian University Books, 1975), pp. 34–35.

65 Ibid., p. 55.

66 For an example of this perspective involving Hawaii, see Walter LaFeber, *The New Empire: An Interpretation of U.S. Expansion, 1860–1898* (Ithaca: Cornell University Press, 1963), p. 368.

67 William Appleman Williams, *Americans in a Changing World: A History of the United States in the Twentieth Century* (New York: Harper and Row, 1978), pp. 46–47.

68 Mahan's interpretation appeared in his *The Influence of Sea Power upon History: 1660–1783* (Boston: Little, Brown, 1890). For a discussion of the contemporary influence of the maritime-mercantilist viewpoint, see Foner, *The Spanish-Cuban-American War*, 1:301–2; LaFeber, *The New Empire*, p. 383; Julius W. Pratt et al., *A History of United States Foreign Policy* (Englewood Cliffs, N.J.: Prentice-Hall, 1980), pp. 169–71; Rystad, *Ambiguous Imperialism*, pp. 40–41; and Williams, *American in a Changing World*, pp. 37–38.

69 Howard R. Smith, *Economic History of the United States* (New York: Ronald Press, 1955), p. 426.

70 Foster Rhea Dulles, *America's Rise to World Power* (New York: Harper, 1955), p. 52.

71 *Congressional Record*, 55:2:3816, April 13, 1898. The text of the joint resolution appeared on p. 3810 and the Democratic substitute was inserted on p. 3815.

72 Ibid., 55:2:5967, June 15, 1898. Fitzgerald subsequently charged that American annexation would serve the interests of English imperial policy.

73 Ibid., p. 5983.

74 Ibid., p. 5974. At one point in the debate, the hula dance was discussed.

75 Ibid., p. 6014.

76 This summary of the amendment appears in Hicks, *The American Nation*, pp. 340–41.

77 Ibid., p. 341.

78 Ibid., p. 342.

79 *Congressional Record*, 56:2:3380, March 1, 1901.

80 Ibid., p. 3381.

81 Ellis Paxson Oberholtzer, *A History of the United States*, vol. 5 (New York: MacMillan, 1937), pp. 590–97, 644–48, 666–69.

82 *Congressional Record*, 57:1:7479, June 26, 1902.

83 Republican Frank Mondell of Wyoming, *Congressional Record*, 59:1:1547, January 25, 1906.

84 Charles Reid of Arkansas, *Congressional Record*, 58:2:5139, April 19, 1904. Reid asked western Republicans, "Are you content to remain forever in a state of colonial vassalage to New England?" (p. 5140).

85 Hicks, *The American Nation*, p. 349; Williams, *Americans in a Changing World*, p. 46.

86 Pratt, *A History of United States Foreign Policy*, p. 363.

87 Cited in Agar, *The Price of Union*, p. 622.

Chapter 4: War, Agricultural Depression, and the New Deal: 1910–1940

1 *Congressional Record*, 64:1:8868, May 29, 1916.

2 Foster Rhea Dulles, *America's Rise to World Power: 1898–1954* (New York: Harper and Row, 1955), p. 104.

3 Warren I. Cohen, *The American Revisionists* (Chicago: University of Chicago Press, 1967), p. 50.

4 Daniel M. Smith, "National Interest and American Intervention, 1917: An Historiographical Appraisal," in John Milton Cooper, Jr., ed., *Causes and Consequences of World War I* (New York: Quadrangle Books, 1972), pp. 53–56.

5 Harry N. Scheiber et al., *American Economic History* (New York: Harper and Row, 1976), pp. 317–20.

6 Ibid., p. 319.

7 George Soule, *Prosperity Decade: From War to Depression, 1917–1929* (New York: Harper Torchbooks, Harper and Row, 1968), pp. 253–55. See also Hal B. Lary et al., *The United States in the World Economy*, U.S. Department of Commerce, Bureau of Foreign and Domestic Commerce, Economic Series No. 23 (Washington: Government Printing Office, 1943), selections reprinted in *American Economic Development since 1860*, ed. William Greenleaf (Columbia: University of South Carolina Press, 1968), pp. 357–77.

8 Soule, *Prosperity Decade*, p. 253.

9 Arthur S. Link, *Wilson the Diplomatist: A Look at His Major Foreign Policies* (Baltimore: Johns Hopkins Press, 1957), p. 36.

10 For a summary of the studies which promote such interpretations, see Smith, "National Interest and American Intervention, 1917," pp. 53–70.

11 Dulles, *America's Rise to World Power*, p. 99.

12 Harley Notter, *The Origins of the Foreign Policy of Woodrow Wilson* (Baltimore: Johns Hopkins Press, 1937), p. 635.

13 Ibid., p. 635. Notter goes on to say, "The opinion that the Allies' condition weighed in the decision of *when* to go to war is here accepted as justified; there would have been no advantage in delaying our entrance into the war until the Allies had collapsed."

14 Soule, *Prosperity Decade*, p. 8.

15 *Appendix* to the *Congressional Record*, 64:1:384, February 21, 1916.

16 John Milton Cooper, *The Vanity of Power: American Isolationism and the First World War, 1914–1917* (Westport, Conn.: Greenwood, 1969), p. 90.

17 Ibid., p. 96. See also George C. Herring, Jr., "James Hay and the Preparedness Controversy, 1915–1916," *Journal of Southern History* 30:4 (November 1964): 383–404.

18 Arthur S. Link, *Woodrow Wilson and the Progressive Era: 1910–1917* (New York: Harper Torchbooks, Harper and Row, 1963), p. 213.

19 Cooper, *The Vanity of Power*, p. 92.

20 Alex Mathews Arnett, *Claude Kitchin and the Wilson War Policies* (Boston: Little, Brown, 1937), p. 161.

21 *Appendix* to the *Congressional Record*, 64:1:1313–14, May 29, 1916.

22 *Congressional Record*, 64:1:8971, May 31, 1916.

23 Charles Tansill, *America Goes to War* (Boston: Little, Brown, 1938), pp. 37–38. He adds later, "The industrial East would have fought vigorously against an embargo, but there was strong pacifist sentiment in many sections of the United States which would have quickly rallied to the support of a restrictive policy" (p. 64).

24 Murray Rothbard, "War Collectivism in World War I," in Ronald Radosh and Murray Rothbard, eds., *A New History of Leviathan* (New York: Dutton, 1972), pp. 66–111.

25 Ray Allen Billington, "The Origins of Middle Western Isolationism," *Political Science Quarterly* 60:1 (March 1945): 51.

26 Ibid., p. 52.

27 Reported in Billington, "The Origins of Middle Western Isolationism," p. 54.

28 *Appendix* to the *Congressional Record*, 64:1:41, December 16, 1915.

29 Ibid., 64:2:900, January 30, 1917.

30 H. C. Peterson and Gilbert C. Fite, *Opponents of War: 1917–1918* (Madison: University of Wisconsin Press, 1957), p. 43.

31 George B. Tindall, *The Emergence of the New South: 1913–1945* (Baton Rouge: Louisiana State University Press, 1967), p. 33.

32 Arthur S. Link, "The Cotton Crisis, the South, and Anglo-American Diplomacy, 1914–1915," in J. Carlyle Sitterson, ed., *Studies in Southern History* (Chapel Hill: University of North Carolina Press, 1957), p. 122.

33 Ibid., p. 130.

34 Ibid., p. 135. More generally, see Alexander De Conde, "The South and Isolationism," *Journal of Southern History* 24:3 (August 1958): 337–39; and Tindall, *The Emergence of the New South*, ch. 2.

35 *Appendix* to the *Congressional Record*, 64:2:398–402, February 19, 1917. For similar complaints voiced by a congressman representing a tobacco district, see the comments of Byrns of Tennessee, *Congressional Record*, 64:1:13938–40, September 6, 1916.

36 Arthur S. Link, *Wilson: Confusion and Crises, 1915–1916* (Princeton: Princeton University Press, 1964), pp. 27–28.

37 Arthur S. Link, *Wilson the Diplomatist: A Look at His Major Foreign Policies* (Baltimore: Johns Hopkins Press, 1957), p. 28.

38 Link, *Woodrow Wilson and the Progressive Era*, p. 211.

39 Ross Gregory, *The Origins of American Intervention in the First World War* (New York: W. W. Norton, 1971), p. 88.

40 Link, *Wilson: Confusion and Crises, 1915–1916*, pp. 175–76.

41 Cooper, *The Vanity of Power*, p. 113.

42 Link, *Wilson: Confusion and Crises, 1915–1916*, p. 193.

43 Richard L. Watson, *The Development of National Power: The United States, 1900–1919* (Boston: Houghton Mifflin, 1976), p. 192.

44 For an analysis of the vote, see Cooper, *The Vanity of Power*, pp. 226–27.

45 Link, *Wilson: Confusion and Crises, 1915–1916*, pp. 331–32.

46 Ibid., p. 334.

47 For an analysis of this roll call by party and region, see Cooper, *The Vanity of Power*, pp. 226–28.

48 Link, *Wilson: Confusion and Crises, 1915–1916*, p. 337.

49 A sampling of these sentiments would include the following insertions in the *Appendix* to the *Congressional Record*: 64:1:40–43, 247–49, 266–68, 365–68, 384–87, 665–67, 932–34, 1194–96, 1218–19, 1280–83, 1313–14, 1592–93, 1700–8, 1725–30, 1687–89, 1811–12, 1837–45, 1878–79, 1884–85, 1893; and 64:2:112–15, 398–402, 545–52, 747–49, 801–6, 817–19, 889–93, 899–912.

50 Harold C. Halcrow, *Agricultural Policy of the United States* (Englewood Cliffs, N.J.: Prentice-Hall, 1953), p. 249.

51 Murray R. Benedict, *Farm Policies of the United States: 1790–1950* (New York: Twentieth Century Fund, 1953), pp. 236–37.

52 Harold Barger and Hans H. Landsberg, *American Agriculture: 1899–1939* (New York: National Bureau of Economic Research, 1942), pp. 79–83.

53 Scheiber et al., *American Economic History*, p. 345.

54 Gilbert C. Fite, *George N. Peek and the Fight for Farm Parity* (Norman: University of Oklahoma Press, 1954), pp. 5, 7.

55 Ibid., pp. 8–11.

56 Ibid., p. 4. For a concise description of declining farm income in the postwar period, see Scheiber et al., *American Economic History*, pp. 345–46; and Henry C. Wallace, "The Wheat Situation," *Yearbook of the Department of Agriculture, 1923* (Washington: Government Printing Office, 1924), selections reprinted in Greenleaf, ed., *American Economic Development Since 1860*, pp. 309–23.

57 Campbell, *The Farm Bureau and the New Deal*, p. 37; Grant McConnell, *The Decline of Agrarian Democracy* (Berkeley: University of California Press, 1953), p. 63.

58 Theodore Saloutos and John D. Hicks, *Twentieth Century Populism: Agricultural Discontent in the Middle West, 1900–1939* (Lincoln: University of Nebraska Press, 1951), p. 372.

59 The best general source is Preston J. Hubbard, *Origins of the TVA: The Muscle Shoals Controversy, 1920–1932* (Nashville: Vanderbilt University Press, 1961). See also Stephen K. Bailey and Howard D. Samuel, *Congress at Work* (New York: Henry Holt, 1952), ch. 8.

60 Hubbard, *Origins of the TVA*, pp. 2–3.

61 *Congressional Record*, 64:2:4611, April 4, 1918.

62 Ibid., p. 4612.

63 Hubbard, *Origins of the TVA*, chs. 2–3.

64 Ibid., ch. 3.

65 Ibid.

66 *Congressional Record*, 68:1:3904, March 10, 1924.

67 C. Landon White and Edwin J. Foscue, *Regional Geography of Anglo-America*, pp. 113–14.

68 Hubbard, *Origins of the TVA*, pp. 227–35.

69 Ibid., pp. 272–75.

70 *Congressional Record*, 71:2:9758, May 28, 1930.

71 The specialization of all agriculture regions in single-crop cultivation increased throughout the 1920s. Soule, *Prosperity Decade*, p. 235.

72 Earl O. Heady, *Agricultural Policy under Economic Development* (Ames: Iowa State University Press, 1962), p. 28.

73 Howard R. Smith, *Economic History of the United States* (New York: Ronald Press, 1955), p. 547.

74 Benedict, *Farm Policies of the United States*, pp. 212–13.

75 Soule, *Prosperity Decade*, p. 247.

76 Fite, *George N. Peek*, p. 61.

77 *Congressional Record*, 69:2:3690, February 14, 1927.

78 Karl Schriftgiesser, *This Was Normalcy* (Boston: Little, Brown, 1948), p. 173; Smith, *Economic History of the United States*, p. 547.

79 James H. Shideler, *Farm Crisis: 1919–1923* (Berkeley: University of California Press, 1957), p. 279.

80 McConnell, *The Decline of Agrarian Democracy*, p. 61.

81 Fite, *George N. Peek*, p. 152. Also see ch. 10, "The Marriage of Corn and Cotton."

82 John D. Black, "The McNary-Haugen Movement," *American Economic Review* 18 (September 1928): 407–9; Saloutos and Hicks, *Twentieth Century Populism*, p. 391.

83 Fite, *George N. Peek*, p. 152; Christiana McFadyen Campbell, *The Farm Bureau and the New Deal* (Urbana: University of Illinois Press, 1962), p. 40.

84 Fite, *George N. Peek*, p. 170.

85 Benedict, *Farm Policies of the United States*, pp. 226–27; Black, "The McNary-Haugen Movement," pp. 409–10; Saloutos and Hicks, *Twentieth Century Populism*, p. 399.

86 *Congressional Record*, 69:2:3549, February 11, 1927. John D. Black pointed out that the legislation would probably have had little impact on the price of cotton in any event. "The McNary-Haugen Movement," pp. 416, 420.

87 *Congressional Record*, 69:2:3544, February 11, 1927. Democrat Thomas Rubey of Missouri echoed that sentiment. *Congressional Record*, 69:2:3620, February 12, 1927.

88 William Allen White, *A Puritan in Babylon: The Story of Calvin Coolidge* (New York: MacMillan, 1938), p. 350. A. B. Genung reports that "shrewd trading on a coal bill" also produced new support from Pennsylvania members. *The Agricultural Depression Following World War I and Its Political Consequences* (Ithaca, N.Y.: Northeast Farm Foundation, 1954), p. 50.

89 White, *A Puritan in Babylon*, p. 262.

90 Scheiber et al., *American Economic History*, p. 347.

91 Saloutos and Hicks, *Twentieth Century Populism*, pp. 390, 406–7.

92 Harris Gaylord Warren, *Herbert Hoover and the Great Depression* (New York: W. W. Norton, 1967), pp. 168–76.

93 Ellis Hawley, *The New Deal and the Problem of Monopoly* (Princeton: Princeton University Press, 1966), p. 197.

94 Asher C. Hinds, *Hinds' Precedents of the House of Representatives* (Washington: Government Printing Office, 1907); Clarence Cannon, *Cannon's Precedents of the House of Representatives* (Washington: Government Printing Office, 1935).

95 Frank Friedel, *F.D.R. and the South* (Baton Rouge: Louisiana State University Press, 1965), p. 48.

96 Howard Odum, *Southern Regions of the United States* (Chapel Hill: University of North Carolina Press, 1936), p. 353.

97 Tindall, *The Emergence of the New South*, pp. 594–95. See also pp. 594–606; and Rupert Vance, *Human Geography of the South* (Chapel Hill: University of North Carolina Press, 1932), pp. 442–81.

98 Tindall, *The Emergence of the New South*, p. 621.

99 Elizabeth Sanders, "Business, Bureaucracy, and the Bourgeoisie: The New Deal Legacy," in Alan Stone and Edward Harpham, eds., *The Political Economy of Public Policy* (Beverly Hills, Calif.: Sage Press, 1982).

100 For a table illustrating the effect of the amendment, see *Congressional Record*, 73:1:4365–66, May 26, 1933.

101 See Basil Rauch, *The History of the New Deal: 1933–1938* (New York: Creative Age Press, 1944), p. 227; Arthur M. Schlesinger, Jr., *The Politics of Upheaval* (Cambridge, Mass.: Houghton Mifflin, 1960), pp. 10–11.

102 *Congressional Record*, 74:1:5467, April 11, 1935.

103 Rauch, *The History of the New Deal*, p. 231; Scheiber et al., *American Economic History*, p. 379; Hawley, *The New Deal and the Problem of Monopoly*, pp. 235–38.

104 James T. Patterson, *Congressional Conservatism and the New Deal* (Lexington: University of Kentucky Press, 1967), p. 196.

105 Rauch, *The History of the New Deal*, pp. 288, 305–6. Paul E. Mertz adds that the final bill "set a minimum wage of forty cents an hour, but provided that pay scales in low wage industries would reach the national level by 1945. . . . Otherwise the measure allowed no regional differentials." *New Deal Policy and Southern Rural Poverty* (Baton Rouge: Louisiana State University Press, 1978), p. 230.

106 Mertz, *New Deal Policy and Southern Rural Poverty*, pp. 222–23.

107 Ibid., pp. 228, 222–23. See also Rauch, *The History of the New Deal*, p. 284; and George W. Stocking, *Basing Point Pricing and Regional Development: A Case Study of the Iron and Steel Industry* (Chapel Hill: University of North Carolina Press, 1954), pp. 149–51.

108 *Congressional Record*, 75:2:1830, December 17, 1937. For other references to sectional impact, see pp. 1811, 1818, and 1831.

109 Ibid., pp. 1794–95.

110 Ibid., 75:2:759, December 2, 1937; Patterson, *Congressional Conservatism and the New Deal*, p. 194. See also pp. 179, 182–83, 193–98; and Tindall, *The Emergence of the New South*, pp. 434–44, 533–35.

111 Broadus Mitchell, *Depression Decade: From New Era to New Deal, 1929–1941* (New York: Holt, Rinehart, and Winston, 1947), pp. 321–23; Sanders, "Business, Bureaucracy, and the Bourgeoisie."

112 For a description of the second Agricultural Adjustment Act of 1938 and the operations of the Commodity Credit Corporation, see Rauch, *The History of the*

New Deal, pp. 302–4. See also Benedict, *Farm Policies of the United States*, pp. 375–80.

113 Patterson, *Congressional Conservatism and the New Deal*, p. 303.

114 Campbell, *The Farm Bureau and the New Deal*, pp. 115–21.

115 *Congressional Record*, 75:1:4390, May 11, 1937.

116 Sanders, "Business, Bureaucracy, and the Bourgeoisie."

117 Patterson, *Congressional Conservatism and the New Deal*, pp. 173–74.

118 *Congressional Record*, 75:1:5028, May 25, 1937.

119 Ibid., p. 5029.

120 For a summary of the legal structure of public utility holding companies, the "death sentence" clause, and the Securities and Exchange Commission, see Mitchell, *Depression Decade*, pp. 174–76; Rauch, *The History of the New Deal*, p. 180; Hawley, *The New Deal and the Problem of Monopoly*, pp. 329–37. For an account of congressional deliberations on the act, see Patterson, *Congressional Conservatism and the New Deal*, pp. 51–58.

121 Theodore J. Lowi, *The End of Liberalism: The Second Republic of the United States*, 2nd ed. (New York: W. W. Norton, 1979).

Chapter 5: War Mobilization, Farm Legislation, and Civil Rights: 1940–1970

1 *Wartime Production Achievements and the Reconversion Outlook* (Washington: War Production Board, 1945), p. 5. For a comparative analysis of the American war effort, see Alan S. Milward, *War, Economy, and Society: 1939–1945* (Berkeley: University of California Press, 1979).

2 Richard Polenberg, *War and Society: The United States, 1941–1945* (Philadelphia: J. B. Lippincott, 1972), p. 11.

3 *Wartime Production Achievements and the Reconversion Outlook*, p. 5.

4 Polenberg, *War and Society*, pp. 8–9.

5 Roland Young, *Congressional Politics in the Second World War* (New York: Columbia University Press, 1956), p. 40.

6 Ibid., p. 5.

7 Ibid., pp. 7–8.

8 Ibid., p. 6.

9 *Congressional Record*, 79:1:2856, March 27, 1945.

10 Polenberg, *War and Society*, pp. 12–13.

11 United States Bureau of the Budget, *The United States at War* (New York: DeCapo Press, 1972), p. 240.

12 Polenberg, *War and Society*, p. 74.

13 Young, *Congressional Politics in the Second World War*, p. 9.

14 Ibid., p. 32.

15 Polenberg, *War and Society*, p. 75.

16 Ibid., p. 80.

17 Ibid., p. 58–59.

18 Ibid., p. 158. Polenberg adds, "in large part they were right."

19 John R. Craf, *A Survey of the American Economy: 1940–1946* (New York: North River Press, 1947), p. 49.

20 John Morton Blum, *V Was for Victory: Politics and American Culture During World War II* (New York: Harcourt Brace Jovanovich, 1976), pp. 140–41.

21 Ibid., p. 141.

22 *Wartime Production Achievements and the Reconversion Outlook*, pp. 35–36.

23 Polenberg, *War and Society*, p. 139.

24 *Congressional Record*, 79:2:368, January 24, 1946. The roll call produced a perfect party-line split: 151 Republicans favoring and 177 Democrats opposed to the amendment.

25 *Congressional Record*, 79:2:4417, May 3, 1946.

26 Republican Thomas D. Winter of Kansas, *Congressional Record*, 79:2:4427, May 3, 1946.

27 *The United States at War*, pp. 452–53.

28 *Congressional Record*, 79:1:2841, March 27, 1945.

29 Ibid., 79:1:2845, March 27, 1945.

30 Polenberg, *War and Society*, p. 169.

31 *The United States at War*, pp. 193–94.

32 *Congressional Record*, 79:1:11825, December 11, 1945.

33 Ibid., 79:1:11821, December 11, 1945.

34 Ibid., 79:1:11823, December 11, 1945.

35 Ibid., 79:1:4471, May 11, 1945.

36 Lauren Soth, *An Embarrassment of Plenty* (New York: Thomas Y. Crowell, 1965), p. 180.

37 Harold G. Vatter, *The U.S. Economy in the 1950's: An Economic History* (New York: W. W. Norton, 1963), p. 249. See also John T. Schlebecker, *Whereby We Thrive: A History of American Farming, 1607–1972* (Ames: Iowa State University Press, 1975), p. 279.

38 Vatter, *The U.S. Economy in the 1950's*, p. 248.

39 Don Paarlberg, *American Farm Policy: A Case Study of Centralized Decision-Making* (New York: John Wiley and Sons, 1964), p. ix.

40 Vatter, *The U.S. Economy in the 1950's*, p. 250.

41 A good, but not unprejudiced, contemporary account of Eisenhower administration policy is Ezra Taft Benson's *Cross Fire: The Eight Years with Eisenhower* (Garden City, N.Y.: Doubleday, 1962).

42 These were "the so-called best years for U.S. farming." Schlebecker, *Whereby We Thrive*, p. 286. Parity averages are on page 293.

43 Benson, *Cross Fire*, p. 157.

44 Luther G. Tweeten, "Commodity Programs for Agriculture," in Vernon W. Ruttan et al., eds., *Agricultural Policy in an Affluent Society* (New York: W. W. Norton, 1969), p. 105.

45 Ibid., p. 107.

46 Paarlberg, *American Farm Policy*, p. ix.

47 Trudy Huskamp Peterson, *Agricultural Exports, Farm Income, and the Eisenhower Administration* (Lincoln: University of Nebraska Press, 1979), p. 35.

48 Ibid., p. 242.

49 Compare Map 4.2 with Allan Pred, "Toward a Typology of Manufacturing Flows," in Fred E. Dohrs and Lawrence M. Sommers, eds., *Economic Geography: Selected Readings* (New York: Thomas Y. Crowell, 1970), p. 274.

50 For a good study of the locational imperatives of dairy farming in the Great Lake states and New England, see Ronald L. Mighell and John D. Black, *Interregional Competition in Agriculture* (Cambridge: Harvard University Press, 1951), esp. ch. 5, "The Geography and Trends of the Dairy Industry."

51 John T. Schlebecker, "The World Metropolis and the History of American Agriculture," *Journal of Economic History* 20:2 (June 1960): 187–208. Schlebecker postulates a sixth and last zone composed of frontier products such as "fur, spices, and gold."

52 Ibid., p. 192. Regional concentration and specialization in agricultural production has been steadily increasing during the twentieth century; see Morton D. Winsberg, "Concentration and Specialization in United States Agriculture, 1939–1978," *Economic Geography* 56:3 (July 1980).

53 Soth, *An Embarrassment of Plenty*, p. 180.

54 Paarlberg, *American Farm Policy*, p. 209.

55 Marion Clawson, *Policy Directions for U.S. Agriculture* (Baltimore: Johns Hopkins Press, 1968), p. 214.

56 *Congressional Record*, 86:1:10553, June 11, 1959.

57 *Congressional Record*, 86:1:10425, June 10, 1959.

58 On the diverging interests of cotton producers and American textile manufacturers, see Peterson, *Agricultural Exports, Farm Income, and the Eisenhower Administration*, p. 102.

59 Ross B. Talbot and Don F. Hadwiger, *The Policy Process in American Agriculture* (San Francisco: Chandler, 1968), p. 73.

60 See, for example, Edward Higbee, *Farms and Farmers in an Urban Age* (New York: Twentieth Century Fund, 1963), pp. 119–20.

61 Benson, *Cross Fire*, p. 206. As long as marketing quotas for the crop remained in effect, tobacco price supports would remain at 90 percent of parity. See Stanley Andrews, *The Farmer's Dilemma* (Washington: Public Affairs Press, 1961), pp. 96–98, for a comparison of the 1954 vote with 1927 passage of the McNary-Haugen plan.

62 Benson, *Cross Fire*, p. 319.

63 For a succinct description of marketing orders, see Paarlberg, *American Farm Policy*, pp. 320–24. On administration attitudes toward wool production, see Benson, *Cross Fire*, p. 188.

64 *Congressional Record*, 86:1:10423, June 10, 1959.

65 For an excellent analytical description of the 1950s Committee on Agriculture, see Charles O. Jones, "Representation in Congress: The Case of the House Agriculture Committee," *American Political Science Review* 55:2 (June 1961): 358–67.

66 Jones, "Representation in Congress," pp. 359–60.

67 Paarlberg, *American Farm Policy*, pp. 207–9.

68 David R. Mayhew, *Party Loyalty among Congressmen* (Cambridge: Harvard University Press, 1966), pp. 36–37.

69 *1957 Congressional Quarterly Almanac*, pp. 637–38.

70 See, for example, the income map provided by Clawson, *Policy Directions for U.S. Agriculture*, p. 83.

71 Talbot and Hadwiger, *The Policy Process in American Agriculture*, pp. 14–16.

72 Schlebecker, *Whereby We Thrive*, p. 287; Peterson, *Agricultural Exports, Farm Income, and the Eisenhower Administration*, pp. 18–19.

73 *Congressional Record*, 86:1:10534, June 11, 1959.

74 Thomas Pelly of Washington State, *Congressional Record*, 86:1:10533, June 11, 1959. Pelly, it should be noted, represented the city of Seattle and often voted for urban aid programs.

75 Jones, "Representation in Congress," p. 360.

76 *Congressional Record*, 82:1:2110, March 7, 1951.

77 J. Roland Pennock cited this floor exchange in his "Party and Constituency in Postwar Agricultural Price-Support Legislation," *Journal of Politics* 18:2 (May 1956): 182.

78 *Congressional Record*, 82:2:8652, June 30, 1952.

79 Ibid., 82:2:8654, June 30, 1952.

80 Pennock, "Party and Constituency in Postwar Agricultural Price-Support Legislation," pp. 202–9.

81 Randall B. Ripley, *Party Leaders in the House of Representatives* (Washington: Brookings Institution, 1967), pp. 132–36.

82 For example, see C. Vann Woodward, *The Origins of the New South: 1877–1913* (Baton Roue: Louisiana State University Press, 1967), pp. 342–43; and Paul Lewinson, *Race, Class, and Party: A History of Negro Suffrage and White Politics in the South* (New York: Grosset and Dunlap, 1965), pp. 218–19.

83 The Supreme Court decisions referred to here were *Guinn v. United States* (1915), *Nixon v. Herndon* (1927), *Nixon v. Condon* (1932), *Grovey v. Townsend* (1935), *United States v. Classic* (1941), *Smith v. Allwright* (1944), and *Rice v. Ellmore* (1948).

84 *Congressional Record*, 67:2:1716–17, January 25, 1922.

85 For an example of skillful manipulation of the civil rights issue, see Ripley, *Party Leaders in the House of Representatives*, p. 134.

86 *Christian Century* 55 (February 23, 1938): 238–40.

87 *Time*, May 22, 1944, p. 19.

88 For a complete list, see *Guide to the Congress of the United States* (Washington: Congressional Quarterly Service, 1971), p. 85.

89 For an extended discussion of the change in behavior of southern local and congressional officials, see M. Elizabeth Sanders, "Electorate Expansion and Public Policy: A Decade of Political Change in the South" (Ph.D. diss., Cornell University, 1978).

90 A complete list of busing decisions handed down by federal and state courts or by the Department of Health, Education, and Welfare does not seem to exist. While many materials were consulted in the construction of this category in table 5.12, the most important sources were *Desegregation of the Nation's Public Schools: A Status Report* (Washington: Commission on Civil Rights, Government Printing Office, 1979) and *The Unfinished Business: Twenty Years Later* (Washington: Commission on Civil Rights, Government Printing Office, 1977).

91 See Sanders, "Electorate Expansion and Public Policy: A Decade of Political Change in the South."

92 V. O. Key, Jr., *Southern Politics in State and Nation* (New York: Vintage Books, 1949), p. 665.

93 Ibid., ch. 31, "Is There a Way Out?" pp. 664–75.

94 A superficial survey of pre–Civil War congressional voting seems to confirm this observation. See, for example, Charles S. Sydnor, *The Development of Southern Sec-*

tionalism: 1819–1848 (Baton Rouge: Louisiana State University Press, 1948); and Frederick Jackson Turner, *The United States, 1830–1850: The Nation and Its Sections* (New York: Holt, Rinehart, and Winston, 1935).

95 For a somewhat similar argument, see Sanders, "Electorate Expansion and Public Policy: A Decade of Political Change in the South."

Chapter 6: The Decline of the Core Economy: 1970–1980

1 A few influential political observers dissented from this view. For example, see Kevin Phillips, *The Emerging Republican Majority* (New Rochelle, N.Y.: Arlington House, 1969), ch. 3.

2 Shirley P. Burggraf, "Energy: The New Economic Development Wildcard," in *The White House Conference on Balanced National Growth and Economic Development*, Final Report, July 1978, Appendix (vol. 6), pp. 795–845.

3 William H. Miernyk, "Rising Energy Prices and Regional Economic Development," *Growth and Change* 8:3 (July 1977): 1–7. See also Walt W. Rostow, "Regional Change in the Fifth Kondratieff Upswing," in David C. Perry and Alfred J. Watkins, eds., *The Rise of the Sunbelt Cities* (Beverly Hills: Sage, 1977), pp. 83–103.

4 David Gisselquist, *Oil Prices and Trade Deficits: U.S. Conflicts with Japan and West Germany* (New York: Praeger, 1979).

5 For a description of the dependence of the core economy on these two industries, see R. R. Widner, *The Future of the Industrial Midwest: A Time for Action* (Columbus: Academy for Contemporary Problems, 1976).

6 Fred M. Shelley and Curtis C. Roseman, "Migration Patterns Leading to Population Change in the Nonmetropolitan South," *Growth and Change* 9:2 (April 1978): 14–23. See also Wilbur Thompson, "The Economic Base of Urban Problems," in Neil W. Chamberlain, ed., *Contemporary Economic Issues* (Homewood, Ill.: Richard D. Irwin, 1973); and Niles M. Hansen, *Location Preferences, Migration, and Regional Growth* (New York: Praeger, 1973).

7 On this point generally, see Alfred J. Watkins and David C. Perry, "Regional Change and the Impact of Uneven Urban Development" in David C. Perry and Alfred J. Watkins, eds., *The Rise of the Sunbelt Cities* (Beverly Hills: Sage, 1971); and Carol L. Jusenius and Larry C. Ledebur, Economic Development Administration, Department of Commerce, *Where Have All the Firms Gone?: An Analysis of the New England Economy* (Washington: Government Printing Office, 1977).

8 See, for example, John S. Hekman, "The Future of High Technology Industry in New England: A Case Study of Computers," *New England Economic Review*, January–February 1980, pp. 5–17.

9 Advisory Commission on Intergovernmental Relations, *Regional Growth: Historical Perspective* (Washington: 1980), pp. 31–32.

10 R. R. Widner, *National Shifts and the Future of Ohio's Economy* (Columbus: Academy for Contemporary Problems, n.d.), cited in Rostow, "Regional Change in the Fifth Kondratieff Upswing."

11 George Sternlieb and James Hughes, eds., *Post-Industrial America: Metropolitan Decline and Interregional Job Shifts* (New Brunswick, N.J.: Rutgers University, Center for Urban Policy Research, 1975), p. 2.

12 "The Second War between the States," *Business Week*, May 17, 1976, p. 92.

13 In addition to the discussion in the text, see Advisory Commission on Intergovernmental Relations, *Regional Growth*, pp. 5, 20.

14 Lynn E. Browne with Peter Mieszkowski and Richard F. Syron, "Regional Investment Patterns," *New England Economic Review*, July–August 1980, pp. 5–23. The authors conclude that energy costs and labor environments exhibit the only significant effects on the interregional flow of investment.

15 The yearly estimates are from the *Statistical Abstract of the United States* (Washington: Bureau of the Census), and are for July 1 in all years except 1980 (April 1 official census). July 1, 1981, figures are from *Provisional Estimates of the Resident and Civilian Population of States* (Washington: Bureau of the Census, 1982).

16 Neal R. Pierce, Jerry Hagstrom, and Sarah Warren, "The New Congressional Politics: Single-Issue Caucuses," *Empire State Report*, October–November 1978.

17 Michael J. McManus, "In the Face of Dire Economic Necessity," *Empire State Report*, October–November 1976, p. 345.

18 *National Journal*, June 26, 1976, pp. 878–91.

19 Ibid. See also Michael J. McManus, "How the Northeast Finances Southern Prosperity," *Empire State Report*, October–November 1976. In a series of articles published between February 8 and 12, 1976, the *New York Times* also attributed southern and western expansion to federal spending.

20 See, for example, Neal R. Pierce, "Northeast Governors Map Battle Plan for Fight over Federal Funds Flow," *National Journal*, November 27, 1976, pp. 1695–1703.

21 Joel Havemann and Rochelle L. Stanfield, "A Year Later, the Frostbelt Strikes Back," *National Journal*, July 2, 1977, pp. 1028–32.

22 *Congressional Record*, 95:1:5305, February 24, 1977.

23 See, for example, the formula dispute over the distribution of "road money" described in chapter 2 (also see table 4.8). For a discussion of the contemporary impact of the factors listed earlier, see Rochelle L. Stanfield, "Playing Computer Politics with Local Aid Formulas," *National Journal*, December 9, 1978, pp. 1977–81. See also "Regionalism in Congress: Formulas Debated," *Congressional Quarterly Weekly Report*, August 20, 1977, pp. 1747–52.

24 See, for example, David Stockman, "The Social Pork Barrel," *Public Interest*, Fall 1978.

25 Advisory Commission on Intergovernmental Relations, *Regional Growth*, pp. 26–29.

26 Juan de Torres, "The Decline of the East," *Across the Board* (New York: The National Industrial Conference Board, April 1977). By early 1975, the "accelerated relative decline" of the Northeast had affected the New York region to an extent "beyond the capability of the current political system to effect repairs in the near future." See also Michael R. Greenberg and Nicholas Valente, "Recent Economic Trends in the Major Northeastern Metropolises," in Sternlieb and Hughes, *Post-Industrial America*, p. 97.

27 Mark Shields, "The Northeast: Patronizing Panhandler," *Empire State Report*, October–November 1976, p. 355. For an interpretation of the "national interest" implications of New York City default, see Daniel P. Moynihan, "The Politics and Economics of Regional Growth," *Public Interest*, No. 51 (Spring 1978): 3–21.

28 Timothy B. Clark, "The Frostbelt Fights for a New Future," *Empire State Report*, October–November 1976, p. 337.

29 Neal R. Pierce and Jerry Hagstrom, "Regional Groups Talk about Cooperation, but They Continue to Feud," *National Journal*, May 27, 1978, p. 844.

30 James R. Anderson, "The State and Regional Impact of the Military Budget," printed in the *Congressional Record*, 94:2:24274, July 28, 1976. While these figures are subject to considerable and unpredictable error, most northern members believed the "true" picture of military spending would reveal even more stark regional imbalances.

31 Martin Nolan, "The Northeast—Our New Appalachia?" *Boston Globe*, July 11, 1976, reprinted in the *Congressional Record*.

32 Ibid., 87:1:11504, June 28, 1961; 96:1:H8694, September 28, 1979; and 96:2:H8881, September 16, 1980.

33 For a list of these goods, see ibid., 96:2:H8888–89.

34 Robert S. Marcus, "Playing Coalition Politics for Big Bucks," *Empire State Report*, November 16–30, 1980, pp. 398–401. Other "victories" cited by the director were the allocation formula in the Community Development Block Grant Program of 1977, the Food Stamp Act Amendments of 1980, and the Low-Income Energy Assistance Appropriation of 1980.

35 *Congressional Record*, 87:1:11504 and 11505, June 28, 1961.

36 Ibid., 96:2:H8882, September 16, 1980.

37 Ibid., 96:1:H8697, September 28, 1979.

38 An extended account of this legislative decision appears in Havemann and Stanfield, "A Year Later, the Frostbelt Strikes Back." See also the front-page story in the *New York Times*, May 11, 1977; and "House Boosts Aid Share for Older Cities," *Congressional Quarterly Weekly Report*, May 14, 1977, pp. 891–92, 906–8.

39 For data on the AFDC factor's impact on state allocation shares, see House Report 93–805, p. 10.

40 For the specific formula alternatives, see the *Congressional Record*, 93:1:31210–12, September 14, 1973 (Quie amendment); *Part 19: Title I Funds Allocation*, Hearings before the Subcommittee on Elementary, Secondary, and Vocational Education, of the Committee on Education and Labor, House of Representatives, November 1–10, 1977 (Washington: Government Printing Office, 1978) (Edwards amendment); and Richard F. Bensel, "Reciprocal Behavior and the Rules of the House of Representatives" (Ph.D. diss., Cornell University, 1978), ch. 6 ("The Political Economy of Congressmen"), pp. 226–41 (Peyser and O'Hara amendments).

41 Nolan, "The Northeast—Our New Appalachia?"

42 M. Elizabeth Sanders, *The Regulation of Natural Gas: Policy and Politics, 1938–1978* (Philadelphia: Temple University Press, 1981), p. xiii.

43 The roll call was recorded on a recommittal motion offered by Clarence Brown of Ohio. For an extensive account of this amendment and a close analysis of the voting pattern, see Sanders, *The Regulation of Natural Gas*, pp. 155–61.

44 *Congressional Record*, 96:2:H7980, August 27, 1980.

45 *New York Times*, August 28, 1980.

46 *Congressional Record*, 96:2:H10601–2, November 13, 1980.

47 Toby Moffett of Connecticut, ibid., H10605, November 13, 1980.

48 *New York Times*, March 1, 1977, p. 22.

49 "No Welcome Mat for Unions in the Sunbelt," *Business Week*, May 17, 1976, p. 109 (see table 6.13).

50 *Congressional Record*, 92:2:31316, September 19, 1972. The district represented by Sebelius grows more wheat than any other in the nation.

51 See Bruce A. Ackerman and William T. Hassler, *Clean Coal, Dirty Air* (New Haven: Yale University Press, 1981).

52 Committee on Interstate and Foreign Commerce, House of Representatives, *Clean Air Act Amendments of 1976* (Washington: Goverment Printing Office, 1976). I am indebted to B. Peter Pashigian for providing me with the general account of the economic impact of PSD contained in his "Environmental Regulation: Whose Self Interests Are Being Protected?" (unpublished manuscript).

53 *Congressional Record*, 94:2:29245, September 8, 1976. On general aspects of the policy, see Roger D. Blair, James M. Fesmire, and David L. Kaserman, "Regional Considerations of the Clean Air Act," *Growth and Change* 7:4 (October 1976).

54 Committee on Interstate and Foreign Commerce, House of Representatives, "Additional Views of Representative Dave Stockman," *Clean Air Act Amendments of 1977* (Washington: Government Printing Office, 1977), pp. 537–38.

55 Subcommittee on Health and the Environment, Committee on Interstate and Foreign Commerce, House of Representatives, *Oversight–Clean Air Act Amendment of 1977*, July 30–November 28, 1979 (Washington: Government Printing Office, 1980), p. 84.

56 For other examples of federal regulatory policies which have retarded the shift of economic activity to the periphery, see Donald W. Lief, "The Regional Impact of the Regulators," *Empire State Report*, October–November 1976, pp. 391–92.

57 Larry Long, *International Migration of the Poor: Some Recent Changes* (Washington: Bureau of the Census, 1978). For a concise description of the sectional distribution of AFDC recipients, see Richard F. Bensel, "The Regional Distribution of Aid to Families with Dependent Children," *Texas Business Review* 54 (November–December 1980).

58 Marcus, "Playing Coalition Politics for Big Bucks"; and Neal R. Pierce, Jerry Hagstrom, and Sarah Warren, "The New Congressional Politics: Single-Issue Caucuses," *Empire State Report*, October–November 1978, pp. 28–32.

59 Robert B. Cohen, "Multinational Corporations, International Finance, and the Sunbelt," in Perry and Watkins, eds., *The Rise of the Sunbelt Cities*, pp. 211–25.

60 "Why Migration Became a Flood Tide," *Business Week*, May 17, 1976.

61 Cohen, "Multinational Corporations, International Finance, and the Sunbelt."

62 Jusenius and Ledebur, *Where Have All the Firms Gone? An Analysis of the New England Economy*.

63 For a slightly more pessimistic view, see Sternlieb and Hughes, *Post-Industrial America*, pp. 164–65.

64 John S. Hekman, "Can New England Hold onto Its High Technology Industry?" *New England Economic Review*, March–April 1980, pp. 35–44.

65 Ibid.

66 Ibid.

67 John S. Hekman, "The Future of High Technology Industry in New England."

68 John S. Hekman and John S. Strong, "The Evolution of New England Industry," *New England Economic Review*, March–April 1981, pp. 35–46.

69 Lynn E. Browne and John S. Hekman, "New England's Economy in the 1980's," *New England Economic Review*, January–February 1981, pp. 5–16.

70 Representative Robert Edgar of Pennsylvania, *New York Times*, August 28, 1980, p. 1. Michael Harrington, the founder of the coalition, relished a continuation of sectional strife: "Regionalism has played a significant part in American history since the beginning. . . . And it's not reasonable to expect it to go away." Pierce and Hagstrom, "Regional Groups Talk about Cooperation, but They Continue to Feud," p. 845.

71 Advisory Commission on Intergovernmental Relations, *Regional Growth*, p. 91.

Chapter 7: The Bipolar Democratic Coalition and the Rise and Decline of the Congressional Committee System

1 See, for example, Morris P. Fiorina, *Congress: Keystone to the Washington Establishment* (New Haven: Yale University Press, 1977); John A. Ferejohn, "On the Decline of Competition in Congressional Elections," *American Political Science Review* 71:1 (March 1977): 166–76; and Melissa P. Collie, "Incumbency, Electoral Safety, and Turnover in the House of Representatives, 1952–1976," *American Political Science Review* 75:1 (March 1981): 119–31. On the decline of party voting, see Jerome M. Clubb and Santa A. Travgott, "Partisan Cleavage and Cohesion in the House of Representatives, 1861–1974," *Journal of Interdisciplinary History* 7:3 (Winter 1977).

2 For more on recent developments in subcommittee organization, see Lawrence Dodd and Bruce Oppenheimer, *Congress Reconsidered* (New York: Praeger, 1977).

3 On the committee assignment process in general, see Kenneth Shepsle, *The Giant Jigsaw Puzzle* (Chicago: University of Chicago Press, 1978).

4 *Congressional Record*, 96:1:H542, February 8, 1979.

5 For an analysis of the regional politics of transportation regulation, see Elizabeth Sanders, "The Roots of Regulation" (paper presented to the 1982 annual meeting of the American Political Science Association, Denver, Colorado).

6 On this topic generally see M. P. Follett, *The Speaker of the House of Representatives* (New York: Longmans Green, 1896); George B. Galloway, *History of the House of Representatives*, 2nd ed. (New York: Thomas Y. Crowell, 1976); Chang wei Chiu, *The Speaker of the House of Representatives since 1896* (New York: Columbia University Press, 1928); and Randall B. Ripley, *Majority Party Leadership in Congress* (Boston: Little, Brown, 1969).

7 William A. Robinson, *Thomas B. Reed: Parliamentarian* (New York: Dodd Mead, 1930), p. 215.

8 Galloway, *History of the House of Representatives*, p. 56.

9 Herbert Bruce Fuller, *The Speakers of the House* (Boston: Little, Brown, 1909), p. 228.

10 *Congressional Record*, 63:1:3436–37, March 19, 1910.

11 There are several excellent accounts of this struggle. See, for example, Kenneth Hechler, *Insurgency* (New York: Columbia University Press, 1940); William R. Gwinn, *Uncle Joe Cannon, Arch-foe of Insurgency* (New York: Bookman Associates, 1957); and C. R. Atkinson, "The Committee on Rules and the Overthrow of Speaker Cannon" (Ph.D. diss., Columbia University, 1911).

12 *Congressional Record*, 69:1:388, December 7, 1925.

13 Paul DeWitt Hasbrouck, *Party Government in the House of Representatives* (New York:

MacMillan, 1927). See pp. 163–65 for a description of the new discharge rule and pp. 26, 35–37, and 53 for a brief account of the leadership actions and strategies.

14 Galloway, *History of the House of Representatives*, p. 187.

15 This clash has been termed "the most critical fight" of Rayburn's seventeen-year career as Speaker between 1940 and his death in 1961. For a complete account of the politics behind the expansion and a close analysis of the vote, see Milton C. Cummings, Jr., and Robert L. Peabody, "The Decision to Enlarge the Committee on Rules: An Analysis of the 1961 Vote," in Robert L. Peabody and Nelson W. Polsby, eds., *New Perspectives on the House of Representatives* (Chicago: Rand McNally, 1963), pp. 167–94.

16 For more on the theoretical considerations which support the following discussion, see Richard F. Bensel, "Reciprocal Behavior and the Rules of the House of Representatives" (Ph.D. diss., Cornell University, 1978).

17 David R. Mayhew, *Congress: The Electoral Connection* (New Haven: Yale University Press, 1974).

18 See Richard F. Fenno, Jr., *The Power of the Purse* (Boston: Little, Brown, 1966).

19 For an extension of this discussion, see Richard F. Bensel, "The Integrity of Committee Jurisdictions and the 1975 Reorganization" (paper delivered to the 1979 Annual Meeting of the Southern Political Science Association, Atlanta, Georgia).

20 For more on self-selection in the assignment process, see Irwin Gertzog, "The Routinization of Committee Assignments in the U.S. House of Representatives," *American Journal of Political Science* 20:4 (November 1976): 693–712; and Shepsle, *The Giant Jigsaw Puzzle*.

21 For more on these reforms, see Larry C. Dodd and Bruce I. Oppenheimer, "The House in Transition: Change and Consolidation," in *Congress Reconsidered*, 2nd ed. (Washington: Congressional Quarterly Press, 1981), pp. 31–61.

22 See Fiorina, *Congress: Keystone to the Washington Establishment*.

23 See Woodrow Wilson, *Congressional Government* (Cleveland: World Publishing Company, 1956); Lauros G. McConachie, *Congressional Committees: A Study of the Development of Our National and Local Legislative Committees* (Boston: Thomas Y. Crowell, 1893); and George Goodwin, Jr., *The Little Legislatures: Committees of Congress* (Amherst: University of Massachusetts Press, 1970).

24 See Anne L. Lewis, "Floor Success as a Measure of Committee Performance in the House," *Journal of Politics* 40:2: 460–67.

25 For a detailed account of the Bolling reorganization plan of 1974 and the Hansen proposals which ultimately replaced the Bolling panel's suggestions on the House floor, see Roger H. Davidson and Walter J. Oleszek, *Congress against Itself* (Bloomington: Indiana University Press, 1977).

Chapter 8: The Changing Sectional Base of the Congressional Party System and American Ideology

1 Everett Carll Ladd, Jr., *American Political Parties: Social Change and Political Response* (New York: W. W. Norton, 1970), p. 5.

2 Herbert Agar, *The Price of Union* (Boston: Houghton Mifflin, 1950), p. 444.

3 Ladd, *American Political Parties*, p. 130.

4 Seymour Martin Lipset, cited in Walter Dean Burnham, "Toward Confrontation?"

in Seymour Martin Lipset, ed., *Party Coalitions in the 1980s* (San Francisco: Institute for Contemporary Studies, 1981), p. 380.

5 Philip E. Converse, "On the Possibility of a Major Political Realignment in the South," in Angus Campbell, Philip E. Converse, Warren E. Miller, and Donald E. Stokes, *Elections and the Political Order* (New York: John Wiley and Sons, 1966).

6 Quoted in Allan P. Sindler, *Political Parties in the United States* (New York: St. Martin's Press, 1966), pp. 86–87. For an account of the nascent New Deal coalition's attitude toward southern segregation, see James T. Patterson, "The Failure of Party Realignment in the South, 1937–1939," *Journal of Politics* 27:3 (August 1965): 602–17.

7 Converse, "On the Possibility of a Major Political Realignment in the South," p. 240.

8 The categorization of presidential elections used in this chapter has been adapted from Gerald Pomper, "Classification of Presidential Elections," *The Journal of Politics* 29 (August 1967): 535–66.

9 Respectively, Martin P. Wattenberg and Arthur H. Miller, "Decay in Regional Party Coalitions," in Lipset, ed., *Party Coalitions in the 1980s*, pp. 349–50; and Walter Dean Burnham, "American Politics in the 1970's: Beyond Party?" in Jeff Fishel, ed., *Parties and Elections in an Anti-Party Age* (Bloomington: Indiana University Press, 1978), pp. 333–41.

10 E. E. Schattsneider, *The Semi-Sovereign People* (New York: Holt, Rinehart, and Winston, 1960), p. 89.

11 Converse, "On the Possibility of a Major Political Realignment in the South," p. 242.

12 Burnham, "Toward Confrontation?" p. 381.

13 Ladd, *American Political Parties*, p. 132.

14 Clifton Brock, *Americans for Democratic Action: Its Role in National Politics* (Washington: Public Affairs Press, 1962), p. 18.

15 *New Republic*, December 20, 1948, p. 7.

16 Ibid., April 17, 1950, p. 15.

17 *ADA World* 20:7 (November 1965).

18 Brock, *Americans for Democratic Action*, p. 58. In one of the few commercial advertisements ever published in the *ADA World*, the *New York Post* offered mail subscriptions in a 1958 issue.

19 For the close organization links between the *New Republic* and the Americans for Democratic Action and a description of the role of the former as the leading liberal organ, see Brock, *Americans for Democratic Action*, pp. 46–49 and *passim*.

20 For a complete description and list of these votes, see *New Republic*, September 23, 1946, pp. 368–72.

21 *Congressional Quarterly Weekly Report*, February 5, 1977, pp. 229–35, and May 22, 1976, pp. 1301–7.

22 Schattsneider, *The Semi-Sovereign People*, ch. 5.

Appendix: Methodology

1 Raymond E. Murphy, *The American City* (New York: McGraw-Hill, 1966), p. 52.

2 Lewis F. Thomas and Robert M. Crisler, *A Manual of the Economic Geography of the*

United States Based on Trade Areas and Geographical Regions (St. Louis: Educational Publishers, 1953).

3 See the discussion of Christaller's work in Edward Ullman, "A Theory of Location for Cities," *American Journal of Sociology* 46 (1941): 853–64. See also August Losch, *The Economics of Location* (New Haven: Yale Press, 1954); Brian Berry, *Geography of Market Centers and Retail Distribution* (Englewood Cliffs, N.J.: Prentice-Hall, 1967). For a general discussion of the entire approach, see Ray M. Northam, *Urban Geography* (New York: John Wiley and Sons, 1975), pp. 120–41.

4 Northam, *Urban Geography*, pp. 128–29.

5 Vance provides an outline of the theoretical assumptions underlying Christaller's central place theory in *The Merchant's World: The Geography of Wholesaling* (Englewood Cliffs, N.J.: Prentice-Hall, 1970), pp. 140–42.

6 Ibid., p. 144.

7 Ibid., p. 96.

8 Ibid., p. 81. See also p. 97: "the specific location of these unraveling points will depend largely on the particular type of transportation in use."

9 Ibid., p. 103. Vance's account is generally compatible with John R. Borchert, "American Metropolitan Evolution," *Geographical Review* 57:3 (July 1967): 301–32. See particularly Borchert's discussions subtitled "Sail-Wagon Epoch, 1790–1830" and "Steel-Rail Epoch, 1870–1920."

10 As previously noted, Borchert calls this period the "Steel-Rail Epoch." During the half century 1870–1920, the nation was "knit together by a standardized nationwide system of rail lines, and the modern pattern of major urban centers was beginning to emerge." Borchert, "American Metropolitan Evolution," p. 316. See also Michael P. Conzen, "A Transport Interpretation of the Growth of Urban Regions," *Journal of Historical Geography* 1:4 (1975): 361–82.

11 United States Senate, "Location of Reserve Districts in the United States," *Senate Documents* 16:485 (Washington: Government Printing Office, 1914), p. 361.

12 Ibid., p. 361.

13 Ibid.

14 Ibid., pp. 350–51.

15 Paul W. Stewart, Domestic Commerce Division, Bureau of Foreign and Domestic Commerce, Department of Commerce, *Market Data Handbook of the United States* (Washington: Government Printing Office, 1929).

16 Elma S. Moulton, Marketing Research Division, Bureau of Foreign and Domestic Commerce, Department of Commerce, *Atlas of Wholesale Dry Goods Trading Areas* (Washington: Government Printing Office, 1941), p. 8.

17 Bureau of Foreign and Domestic Commerce, U.S. Department of Commerce, Domestic Commerce Series No. 7, *Atlas of Wholesale Grocery Territories* (Washington: Government Printing Office, 1927); National Wholesale Druggists' Association, *Distribution through Drug Channels in the 84 Wholesale Trading Areas* (New York: 1935).

18 *Atlas of Wholesale Dry Goods Trading Areas*, p. 2. These units divided up the total dollar volume of wholesale dry goods in the following proportions: manufacturer's sales branches and offices, 16.7 percent; agents and brokers, 42.7 percent; and full service and limited function wholesalers, 40.6 percent.

19 *Trading Area Manual*, (Chicago: Rand McNally, 1973), p. 2.

20 Ibid., p. 2.

21 For a discussion of an earlier version of this formula, see Richard F. Bensel, "Sectional Stress and Ideology in the U.S. House of Representatives," *Polity* 14:4 (Summer 1982): 657–75.

Index

Addabbo, Joseph, 281n

Advisory Commission on Intergovernmental Relations: on the decline of the industrial core, 261n; on regional convergence of wages, 262n; on regional growth, 262n, 266n; on federal spending and regional development, 268n, 316; on unemployment data in federal spending formulas, 274n

Agar, Herbert, 113n

Agricultural Act of 1956, 203, 205, 209

Agricultural Adjustment Act: foreshadowed by McNary-Haugen plan, 105; roll call on, 148; and political conflict on parity payments, 165, 171

Agricultural Adjustment Act of 1938, 192

Agricultural legislation, 50

Agricultural Marketing Act of 1929, 146

Agricultural supports and controls: sectional stress on roll calls concerning, 190, 203–5, 209; and market forces, 192, 200, 216; and the world economy, 194, 196–200, 216, 407; economic justification for, 194–95; economic criticism of, 195, 212n; and basic commodities, 204; and the committee system, 206–7; and political reciprocity between commodities, 206–14; and tobacco allotments, 216n

Agriculture: position of in the national economy, 130, 139, 191; regional specialization in, 197, 207–8

Aid to Families with Dependent Children: and New York City, 278; and ESEA formula, 289–93, 311; welfare dependency and the decline of the industrial core, 304–11; regional distribution of recipients, 305; 1979 welfare reform bill, 308, 324; federal aid formula, 308n; welfare dependency in congressional districts, 308–9n; and unemployment insurance, 311, 324n; welfare dependency and the com-

mittee system, 321–29; programmatic linkages, 324–25; welfare dependency and labor contributions, 327–29; welfare dependency and wheat production, 325n

Alabama: restricts suffrage, 81, 223; and naval appropriations, 127; and road subsidy formula, 157; lynchings in, 228n; poll tax in, 233n; and the 1965 Voting Rights Act, 247; dual school system in, 248n; a right-to-work state, 300n; and AFDC formula, 308n; welfare program in, 309n

Alabama Power Company, 131, 134–35

Alaska: construction of railway in, 128; and regional redistribution of income, 260n; and revenue sharing formula, 299; welfare program in, 309n; in Seattle trade area, 442

Albany, New York, 375

Albuquerque, New Mexico, 50, 433, 437

Alexander, Bill, 288–89n

Allgood, Niles, 136, 141

American Farm Bureau: and formation of farm bloc, 135; and draft for industrial labor, 187; and agricultural supports, 214–15

American Federation of Government Employees, 328

American Federation of Labor: and Frazier-Lemke bill, 170; and WW II, 181, 189; and draft for industrial labor, 187–88; and agricultural supports, 221–22

American Federation of Labor-Congress of Industrial Organizations, 327

Americans for Democratic Action: and voting on New York City aid, 26, 28; and political economy of liberalism, 28; and ratings of liberalism, 30, 288, 392, 394–400, 406–7; endorses Kennedy, 393n; endorses McCarthy, 393n; and revenue sharing formula, 395n; and party system, 399–400

475

Amtrak, 324
Anderson, John, 388
Appalachian Mountains, 203
Arizona: statehood, 88, 100–101; and the Wage and Hour bill, 162; and the 1965 Voting Rights Act, 247; dual school system in, 248n; an energy-advantaged, right-to-work state, 264n, 300n; and AFDC formula, 308n; welfare program in, 309n; and the Federal Reserve System, 433n
Arkansas: and WPA wage rates, 164–65n; lynchings in, 228–29; poll tax in, 233n; dual school system in, 248n; electricity generation costs in, 259n; an energy-advantaged, right-to-work state, 264n, 300n; AFDC and ESEA formula, 290; welfare program in, 309n
Aspin, Les, 273n, 278n
Atlanta, Georgia: and 1920 value-added in manufacturing, 56n; supports free trade, 70; and New Deal committee system, 171–72; and the 1965 Voting Rights Act, 225; and New York City aid, 276–77; and Maybank amendment, 283; and floor reciprocity, 357; sectional alignment of, 411; Federal Reserve city, 427n, 428, 431; trade area territory, 442
Atlas of Wholesale Dry Goods Trading Areas, 434, 437
Atlas of Wholesale Grocery Territories, 434
Augusta, Georgia, 437, 442
Australia, 416
Avery, William Henry, 198

B-1 bomber, 398
Bafalis, L. A. "Skip," 242
Baltimore, Maryland: and 1920 value-added in manufacturing, 56n; and Merchant Marine Act, 160; and manufacturing belt, 207; and Maybank amendment, 283; and trade area criteria, 426; and Federal Reserve System, 431
Bankhead, William, 238
Barden, Graham A., 221
Batten, Barton, Durstine, and Osborn, 433–34
Bay St. Louis, Mississippi, 268
Beard, Charles, 111
Beck, James B., 70
Benjamin, Adam, 279n
Benson, Ezra Taft: supports Soil Bank program, 193; on agricultural supports and controls, 194, 203, 211n; on political reciprocity between agricultural commodities, 214n; on farm organizations, 214–15n
Berke, Joel, 289n
Berry, Brian, 264n, 417

Billings, Montana, 437, 443n
Billington, Ray, 116
Birmingham, Alabama: and 1920 value-added in manufacturing, 56n; supports continentalism, 101; supports McNary-Haugen plan, 142; supports Merchant Marine Act, 160; as civil rights symbol, 279
Bismarck, North Dakota, 443n
Black, John D., 129n, 140–41n
Black belt: description of, 12–13; southern congressmen and, 14; and cotton cultivation, 137; and McNary-Haugen plan, 141; and welfare dependency, 305
Blanton, Thomas, 230n
Blouin, Michael, 273–74n, 284–88
Blue Ridge Parkway, 147–48
Boatner, Charles, 95n
Bogue, Daniel, 422n
Bolling, Richard, 351n, 367n
Boll Weevils, 298n
Boston, Massachusetts: and 1920 value-added in manufacturing, 55n; and military preparations for WW I, 106–7, 115; opposes McLemore Resolution, 124; supports naval appropriations, 127; opposes Muscle Shoals development, 136–37; supports Merchant Marine Act, 160; and parity payments for agriculture, 165; and the committee system, 172, 357, 367n; and agricultural supports, 203; and the manufacturing belt, 207; and busing, 249, 250n, 251; cultural influence of, 257n; and Maybank amendment, 283; and the core economy, 314; and Amtrak, 324; and the ADA, 393–94; sectional alignment of, 411; Federal Reserve city, 427n, 428; trade area territory, 442
Boutelle, Charles, 84
Bradley, Sallie Ann, 65–66
Braudel, Fernand, 22–23n
Breckinridge, William, 77–78
Bremerton, Washington, 125–27
Brock, Clifton, 392n
Brooklyn, New York, 422, 426
Brown, Charles H., 193n
Browne, Lynn E., 276n
Buffalo, New York: and 1920 value-added in manufacturing, 55n; and military preparations for WW I, 115; opposes McLemore Resolution, 124; and busing, 249; and Maybank amendment, 283; and congressional party system, 375
Burdick, Quentin, 218
Bureaucratic discretion: and clarity of policy

choices, 26, 53; and sectional alignment in roll call voting, 29; party leadership favors, 30; and decline in sectional stress, 53; makes possible New Deal coalition, 105, 150–52, 171, 370, 391, 403, 405; and support for preparations for WW I, 113n; and formation of farm bloc, 139; and New Deal political economy, 149; southern opposition to, 168; and Public Utility Holding Company Act, 169; and congressional committee system, 172; and WW II, 176, 178–79, 181, 183, 190

Bureau of Foreign and Domestic Commerce, 434, 437

Bureau of Labor Statistics, 273n

Burggraf, Shirley P., 264n

Burnham, Walter Dean: on the emergence of the industrial core, 62; on the American party system, 371, 372n, 391n

Business Week: on relocation of industry, 263–64; on the future of the industrial core, 312–13

Busing for school integration: sectional stress on roll calls concerning, 224–25, 249; amendment to the Constitution, 242, 251; legislative consideration of, 247–51; court-ordered, 249

Butte, Montana, 437

Caine, M. R., 422n, 426n

California: and agricultural supports, 203; citrus production, 208; lynchings in, 228n; and civil rights, 241; and Land and Water Conservation Fund, 272n; AFDC and ESEA formula, 290, 293n; and government fuel assistance formula, 298; and revenue sharing formula, 299; and the core economy, 314–15

Callaway, Oscar, 106–7

Canada, 3, 5n, 416

Candler, Allen, 75–76, 82n

Cannon, Clarence, 149–50, 165

Cannon, Joseph, 332, 356

Cannon Revolt of 1910: and growth of the committee system, 151, 173; and power of the Speaker, 329, 332; and the party system, 403

Carter, James: and defense spending, 279–80; and the 1980 election, 388; and the ADA, 392–93

Carter, Tim, 304

Cartwright, Wilburn, 168

Cary, William J., 117–18

Cellar, Emanuel, 353n

Census of Business, 185–86

Census of Manufactures, 185–86

Chamber of Congress, 187

Chan, Steve, 92n

Chappell, William, 280–81

Charleston, South Carolina: WW II population growth in, 182; and trade area criteria, 422; trade area status, 437, 441–42

Charleston, West Virginia, 249, 437

Charlotte, North Carolina: and busing, 249; and New York City aid, 276–77; and the committee system, 319, 357; trade area status, 442

Chicago, Illinois: sectional alignment of, 37, 411; and 1920 value-added in manufacturing, 56n; supports McLemore Resolution, 124; and naval appropriations, 127; and parity payments, 165; and the manufacturing belt, 207; and dairy production, 208; and busing, 249, 250n; welfare dependency in, 305; and the core economy, 312n, 314; and the ADA, 393–94; central reserve city, 426n; Federal Reserve city, 427n, 428

Christaller, Walter, 417–19

Christian Century: on Roosevelt and anti-lynching legislation, 230–31; on class conflict and the poll tax, 232–33n

Cincinnati, Ohio: and 1920 value-added in manufacturing, 56n; supports imperialism, 101; and Muscle Shoals development, 133; and McNary-Haugen plan, 142; and New Deal Committee system, 172; and busing, 249; and Federal Reserve System, 428, 430–31

Civilian Conservation Corps, 165, 167, 181

Civil rights: and the District of Columbia, 191n; and political reciprocity between agriculture and labor, 222; sectional stress on roll calls concerning, 222–25, 245–53; bill of 1966, 222; and New Deal Democratic coalition, 224, 232, 245, 370, 372–73, 397, 405; bill of 1956, 225; bill of 1957, 225; bill of 1964, 225; and congressional reform, 233n, 254; and House discharge petitions, 239–40n, 241; party support for, 242; nationalization of, 246–47; and nationalization of the South, 256; and ADA ratings, 398; and the decline of the industrial core, 403–4; and sectional stress, 404

Civil Rights Act of 1866, 74

Civil Rights Act of 1957, 224, 244n

Civil Rights Act of 1960, 224, 240–41

Civil Rights Act of 1964: and the poll tax, 225; and school desegregation, 247; consideration of, 254; and the New Deal coalition, 403

Civil Rights Commission: sectional stress on roll calls concerning, 55, 224–25, 246; legislative consideration of, 235, 243n, 246

Civil service: comparative duration of system, 24;

Civil service (*continued*)
  recruitment and sectional stress, 52; bureaucracy and segregation, 152; employment and
  CCC, 165–66; and unemployment relief, 167;
  and patronage, 167*n*; and the committee system, 172; and expansion of the federal government, 173; and WW II, 190
Civil War, 415
Clark, Champ, 112, 122*n*
Clark, Timothy, 279
Class conflict: in the industrial core, 23; and attitude of periphery toward the central state, 52;
  and the Democratic party, 72, 78; in the South
  and suffrage restrictions, 81; and populism,
  89*n*; and the New Deal party system, 148,
  176; and New Deal political economy, 153; in
  agriculture and farm policy, 214–15; between
  North and South, 253–54; in the North and
  southern Democrats, 368–73; in the South
  and the party system, 369–73; and the New
  Deal coalition, 372–73; in the North and ideology, 397–400; in the North and decline in
  sectional stress, 409
Clawson, Marion, 196*n*, 198*n*, 199*n*
Clean Air Act of 1970, 303–4, 410
Cleveland, Grover: attitude toward military pensions, 63–64; vetos private bills, 64–66; com-
  mits Democrats to free trade, 69; appoints
  blacks to federal posts, 78; reelection kills
  Force Bill, 78–79
Cleveland, Ohio: and 1920 value-added in man-
  ufacturing, 55*n*; supports imperialism, 101;
  and Muscle Shoals development, 133; and New
  Deal committee system, 172; and civil rights,
  242; and busing, 249, 251; and the ADA,
  393–94; Federal Reserve city, 427*n*, 428,
  430–31
Cline, Cyrus, 124
Coalition of Northeast Governors, 279
Cohen, Robert, 312
Coleman, Hamilton, 75, 77*n*, 78
Colorado, 241
Columbus, Ohio, 249, 433
Commercial Atlas and Marketing Guide, 437–42
Committee on Energy, 367*n*
Commons, John R., 4*n*
Community Services Administration, 297
Comprehensive Employment and Training Act:
  sectional stress and the allocation formula,
  268, 284–88; and Northeast-Midwest Coali-
  tion, 275*n*; and the committee system, 325*n*
Compton, Barnes, 83
Comptroller of the Currency, 422, 426

Confederacy, 415
Congress: and sectionalism, 9–10; seniority in
  and sectional stress, 13; and imperialism, 91,
  93*n*, 96*n*; and WW II, 176, 180–81; 49th,
  38, 63, 65, 404; 51st, 79, 84, 329; 54th, 35,
  56, 73, 79, 84, 404; 59th, 35, 38, 88, 404,
  433*n*; 64th, 35, 38, 105, 131, 404–5; 67th,
  374–75; 68th, 135; 69th, 50, 332, 333, 405;
  74th, 37–38, 56, 128, 147–48, 158, 238*n*,
  405, 434; 79th, 35, 38, 50, 56, 176, 182,
  184, 186, 190, 349, 397, 399, 405; 80th,
  352–53; 81st, 239*n*; 84th, 190–91, 203–5,
  221, 223*n*, 405; 87th, 334; 88th, 362, 364;
  89th, 56, 174, 222, 223*n*, 239*n*, 254, 300*n*,
  334, 375, 378, 405; 92nd, 341; 93rd,
  357–61; 94th, 35, 38, 268–69, 279*n*, 284,
  364, 398, 406; 95th, 242; 96th, 242,
  321–22
Congressional committee system: comparative duration of, 24; and institutional norms, 29; and
  New Deal coalition, 30, 149–51, 153, 155,
  175, 218, 318–19, 370, 391, 401, 403,
  405–6; and decline in sectional stress, 53,
  409–10; encourages depolarization of party
  system, 56; and political cooperation between
  agricultural regions, 105, 139; and New Deal
  legislation, 157, 164*n*, 171–72; development
  of, 173, 335–53; and bureaucratic discretion,
  173; and jurisdictional conflicts, 189; and agricultural supports, 206–7; and civil rights legislation, 224, 228*n*, 232–35, 238*n*, 244; and
  political parties, 241, 275; and destabilization
  of the plantation elite, 257; and the decline of
  the industrial core, 275; and grant-in-aid formulas, 293–94; and the party system,
  317–19, 383; and fundamental sectional
  alignment, 318–19, 353–54, 411; and the
  national political economy, 319–29, 339–40,
  362; and welfare dependency, 321–29; and labor contributions, 327–29; incentives supporting, 335–53, 357–66; and electoral resources,
  337–38; and committee jurisdictions,
  339–40; and committee assignments,
  340–46; impact of membership expansion,
  345–46; and roll call frequency, 362–64; sectional stress on committee reform measures,
  367*n*; decline of, 357–67
Congressional Quarterly Weekly Report, 16–17
Congressional Record, 348
Congressional Research Service, 299
Congress of Industrial Organizations: and
  WW II, 180, 189; and draft for industrial
  labor, 187–88; and agricultural supports, 221

Connecticut: farm population in, 200; and regional redistribution of income, 260*n*; an energy-disadvantaged, union shop state, 264*n*; and Land and Water Conservation Fund, 272*n*; AFDC and ESEA formula, 290, 293*n*; and unemployment insurance program, 324*n*

Conoco, 316

Conrail, 324

Conservatism. *See* Ideology

Conservative coalition, 17, 160, 171

Constitution, United States, 329, 331

Consumer Credit Protection Act, 269

Conte, Silvio: on public works job formula, 269, 272; and the Maybank amendment, 284*n*; on government fuel assistance formula, 297–98; on Gypsy Moths and Boll Weevils, 298*n*

Contested election cases: and federal control of southern elections, 61, 87; sectional stress on roll calls concerning, 73, 84; partisan nature of, 84, 87; frequency of, 87; strengthen majority control of House, 87

Continentalism. *See* Imperialism

Converse, Philip, 388

Cooley, Harold C., 219–20

Coolidge, Calvin, 136, 143

Cooper, John Milton, 124*n*

Core-periphery relations: within a world-system, 18–21; retention of core-state status, 20; within the United States, 21; incompatibility of core and periphery economies, 23, 35, 37, 51, 92*n*; and sectional alignment in roll call voting, 29, 37; and the decline of the core economy, 38, 273, 311–16, 403–4; and development of regional division of labor, 51; effect of transport costs on, 51; and the federal bureaucracy, 52, 56, 59; and protective tariff, 52, 62, 101; use of descriptive terms, 55–56; and 1920 value-added in manufacturing, 55–56*n*; and emergence of the industrial core, 60; and imperialism, 61, 90–92, 93*n*; and military pensions, 66–67; and Reconstruction measures, 73–74; and 1890 Force Bill, 76, 79*n*; and statehood for western territories, 88; and contested election cases, 101–2; and American intervention in WW I, 104, 109, 115, 127–28; in manufacturing and agriculture, 137; and the New Deal political economy, 148, 150, 152, 169, 172; and southern economy, 152, 160–61; and New Deal fiscal policy, 159; and regional wage differences, 163–64; and the committee system, 172–73; and WW II controls, 183, 186, 190; and regionalization in agriculture, 197, 208; and ag-

ricultural supports, 199–200; and suffrage restrictions, 223–24; and civil rights, 230, 246, 251; and segregation, 256; and unionization, 258; and the 1973 oil embargo, 259; and the relocation of industry, 261–62; and regional growth rates, 264; and economic development of the periphery, 267; and the party system, 274, 317–18, 368–73, 380–81, 391, 401–2, 405–6; and federal grant-in-aid formulas, 287–88, 293, 299; and regional impact of energy regulation, 294; and labor regulation, 303; and environmental policy, 303; and the welfare state, 311; and the committee system, 319–29, 353–54, 362; and the centralization of legislative power, 334–35; and ideology, 370, 396–400; and the world economy, 407–8; future of, 408–9

Corn belt: economic imperatives of, 137; and McNary-Haugen plan, 140, 142; and export debentures for agriculture, 146; and the Soil Bank program, 193*n*; and regional specialization in agriculture, 197–98, 207; and agricultural supports, 203; trade area delegations, 209*n*; and political reciprocity with other commodities, 211–14; and the South, 213*n*; and the Republican party, 217

Corrigan, Richard, 259*n*

Cotton belt: economic imperatives of, 137; and McNary-Haugen plan, 140, 142, 146; and Frazier-Lemke bill, 170; and regional specialization in agriculture, 208; and political reciprocity with other commodities, 211–14; and the Democratic party, 217

Cotton, Incorporated, 269

Countercyclical Assistance. *See* Intergovernmental Anti-recession Assistance Act

Crisp, Charles, 333

Crude Oil Windfall Profits Tax of 1980, 297

Cox, Edward, 221

Cuba: necessary to American sea power, 91; American intervention in, 95–96; and Platt amendment, 98–99

Cummings, Amos, 78*n*, 97*n*

Dallas, Texas: sectional alignment of, 37, 411; and 1920 value-added in manufacturing, 56*n*; supports continentalism, 101; and McLemore Resolution, 124*n*; and the committee system, 171–72, 357, 367*n*; and New York City aid, 276–77; Federal Reserve city, 427*n*, 428, 431, 433*n*; trade area territory, 443*n*

Davenport, John I., 83, 84*n*

Davis, James H., 119*n*, 121

Delaware, 248n, 264n

Dellums, Ronald, 278–79n

Democratic party: sectional conflict within, 14; New Deal coalition in, 24–25, 30, 403–5; and northern urban machines, 25; two-thirds rule in presidential conventions, 25; and progressivism, 29, 392; retention of power by and bureaucratic discretion, 30, 52; and Tammany machine, 49; and decline of sectional stress, 53; and military pensions, 64; supports free trade policy, 69–70; and sectional alignment on tariff, 72; and 1890 Force Bill, 76–79, 77n, 78; and federal oversight of New York elections, 83; and continentalism, 90; and Cuban independence, 95; and statehood for New Mexico, 95; opposes statehood for Hawaii, 97–98; and the committee system, 105, 150, 155, 171, 218–19, 241, 318–19, 334–35, 348, 360–61, 367; divided over military preparations for WW I, 112–13, 122, 127; and McLemore Resolution, 122–24; and class-conflict in the industrial core, 148; bipolar coalition in, 152–53, 165, 173, 369–70; and the civil service, 152–53, 167; leadership and Wage and Hour bill, 161–63; leadership and Frazier-Lemke bill, 170n; and bureaucratic discretion, 171; and the Republican party, 175, 194; and agricultural supports, 203, 207, 218, 405; and high-risk agricultural regions, 215; and marginal agricultural producers, 215; and the cotton belt, 217; and political reciprocity between agriculture and labor, 219, 221, 222; white primary in, 224; and civil rights, 224, 230, 238, 242–45, 253; and anti-lynching legislation, 226; and the seniority system, 241n; and fundamental sectional alignment, 274; and federal aid to New York City, 276–77, 279; and AFDC recipients, 309; and nationalization of welfare, 310; and core-periphery relations, 318–19, 353–54, 368–73, 391; and centralization of legislative power, 334–35; and the Rules Committee, 333–35; caucus and preconditions for membership, 334n; and committee assignments, 341–46; Steering Committee and the Speaker, 353–55; deposes committee chairmen, 359–60, 362; as separatist party, 372; and the South, 381–85, 406; and the Populist party, 392; and the ADA, 391–400; and ADA ratings, 395–400; and electoral instability, 400; and contested election cases, 404; and working class interests, 405; and American liberalism, 411. *See also* New Deal coalition

Democratic Study Group, 393, 393n

Demonstration Cities and Metropolitan Development Act, 223n

Denver, Colorado: and 1920 value-added in manufacturing, 56n; supports McLemore Resolution, 124; and McNary-Haugen plan, 142; and New Deal committee system, 171–72; and busing, 249; sectional alignment of, 411; and Federal Reserve System, 431; trade area status, 442–43

Des Moines, Iowa, 249, 441–42

Detroit, Michigan: and 1920 value-added in manufacturing, 55n; and WW II demobilization, 189; and agricultural supports, 203; and busing, 249, 251; and AFDC, 278; and Maybank amendment, 283; and community development block grants, 288n; welfare dependency in, 305; and the ADA, 393–94

Dies, Martin, 119n, 162n

Dinsmore, Hugh, 95

Dirksen, Everett, 188–89

District of Columbia: federal policy toward and segregation, 88; segregation and sectional stress on legislation concerning, 191n, 222–23

Distribution through Drug Channels in the 84 Wholesale Trading Areas, 434

Dixiecrats, 386, 393

Drinan, Father, 393

Dulles, Foster Rhea: on imperialism and the Constitution, 90–91; on the political appeal of imperialism, 93, 95; on American intervention in WW I, 111n

Duluth, Minnesota, 208

DuPont, 316

Dyer, Leonidas, 225

Dyer bill, 225, 228n, 229n

East: and military preparations for WW I, 106, 116–17, 405; agrarian resentment toward after WW I, 129, 143; opposes Muscle Shoals development, 137; opposes McNary-Haugen plan, 141; and environmental policy, 303; and the Republican party, 403–6; and imperialism, 404; and the decline of the industrial core, 406

Eastland, James, 243

East North Central, 266n

Edgar, Robert, 299

Edwards, Don, 393

Edwards, Mickey, 278

Eisenhower, Dwight: and agricultural supports, 193, 200, 203, 211, 215–16, 217n; vetos farm bill, 203, 211n; and corn-cotton alliance,

214; and 1956 civil rights bill, 234; and the party system, 391

Elazar, Daniel J., 257*n*, 312

Elementary and Secondary Education Act: sectional stress on allocation formula, 289–94; description of Title I, 289*n*; allocation formula and AFDC, 290–94, 311; and Orshansky definition of poverty, 291; and the committee system, 325*n*

El Paso, Texas: and 1920 value-added in manufacturing, 56*n*; and livestock production, 208*n*; and Federal Reserve System, 433*n*; trade area status, 437, 441, 442, 443*n*

Emergency Fleet Corporation. *See* Shipping Board

Emergency Price Control Act, 178, 180

Emergency Relief Appropriations, 168

Emory, Frederick, 96*n*

Energy: 1973 oil embargo and the world economy, 259, 260, 316; regional growth and importation of, 264–65; regional impact of regulation, 294–95; legislation and ADA ratings, 398

Environmental Protection Agency, 303, 410

Executive discretion. *See* Bureaucratic discretion

Executive Office of the President, 184

Export debentures. *See* Tariff

Faddis, Charles, 167–68

Fair Employment Practices Commission, 224*n*

Fair Labor Standards Board, 160

Fargo, North Dakota, 443*n*

Farm bloc: formation of, 130, 135*n*, 137, 139; support for McNary-Haugen plan and Muscle Shoals, 135–36, 142–43, 146; divisions within, 139; and political reciprocity between commodities, 206, 213, 215; and political reciprocity with labor, 207, 218; and marginal producers, 215; and the Republican party, 401

Farris, John W., 65

Federal Bureau of Roads, 155, 157

Federal Energy Administration, 269

Federal Power Commission, 259*n*

Federal Reserve Board, 426–31

Federal Reserve System, 59, 421, 426–31

Firestine, Robert E., 258–59*n*

Fish, Hamilton, 161–62*n*

Fite, Gilbert, 130

Fitzgerald, John F., 96, 97*n*

Flood, Daniel, 220–21, 280

Florida: sectional alignment of, 50; and naval appropriations, 127; and WPA wage rates, 164–65*n*; and agricultural supports, 203; citrus production in, 208; lynchings in, 228*n*; dual school systems in, 248*n*; and Land and Water Conservation Fund, 272*n*; and government fuel assistance formula, 297–98; a right-to-work state, 300*n*; welfare program in, 309*n*

Foley, Thomas, 366*n*

Food for Peace, 193

Force Bill of 1890: opposed by Tammany, 49; introduction and provisions, 75; Republicans support, 76; and the tariff, 76, 79; compared to British colonial policy in Ireland and India, 77, 78*n*; sectional stress on roll calls concerning, 79; compared to 1965 Voting Rights Act, 102; and civil rights, 223, 225

Ford, Gerald, 398

Ford, Henry, 133–35

Ford, William D., 278

Fordney-McCumber tariff: sectional stress on, 71; effect on American trade, 129; and antilynching legislation, 226, 228

Fort Smith, Arkansas, 442

Fort Worth, Texas, 428*n*, 434, 437

Fox, Edward, 11–12*n*

Fox, William, 102–3

France: pays for American goods during WW I, 108; extension of credit to, 110; J. P. Morgan as agent for, 110; and American intervention in WW I, 115

Fraser, Donald, 393, 395*n*

Frazier-Lemke bill, 170, 173

Froman, Lewis A., 364*n*

Fuller, Claude, 167

Fuller, Hubert Bruce, 331*n*

Fulmer, Hampton, 143

Gallagher, Miriam, 351*n*

Galloway, George, 334, 351

Galtung, Johan, 92*n*

Georgia: restricts suffrage, 81, 223; and WPA wage rates, 164–65*n*; peanut production in, 221; lynchings in, 228*n*; poll tax in, 233*n*; and 1965 Voting Rights Act, 247; dual school systems in, 248*n*; a right-to-work state, 300*n*; welfare program in, 309*n*; and twenty-one day rule, 333

Globalism. *See* Imperialism

Goldwater, Barry, 334

Gonzalez, Henry, 281

Goodwin, George, 343*n*

Government Information Service, 184

Gramm, Phil, 298

Grand Army of the Republic, 63–64, 66

Grandfather clause, 224
Grand Rapids, Michigan, 441
Gray, Finly, 158–59
Great Britain: sectional stress in, 3; colonial policy compared to 1890 Force Bill, 77–78; as model for American imperialism, 96–97; supports American imperialism, 102–3; and American intervention in WW I, 104, 107, 111*n*, 115–16; payment for American goods during WW I, 108; extension of credit to, 110; J. P. Morgan agent for, 110; imports southern cotton, 120–21, 129; compared to American North, 276*n*; US aid to and liberalism ratings, 397
Great Falls, Montana, 437, 443*n*
Great Lakes region: sectional alignment of, 50; supports military preparations for WW I, 115, 117; and reapportionment of 1930, 129*n*; as part of manufacturing belt, 137; federal spending in, 267, 279; and unemployment, 273; and core-periphery relations, 311–12
Great Plains: sectional alignment of, 50; and populism, 89*n*; and globalism, 90; and military preparations for WW I, 115; and WW II controls, 183; and agricultural supports, 215; and trade area territories, 437
Griffin, Anthony, 229
Griswold, Glenn, 159*n*
Gulf Coast, 208
Gypsy Moths, 298*n*

Hagstrom, Jerry, 275*n*
Hamilton, Edward, 99
Hannaford, Mark, 288–89
Hansen, Julia, 367*n*
Harding, Warren G., 133, 374–75
Hardy, Rufus, 112
Harrington, Michael, 294
Harrison, Benjamin, 66, 75–76
Hartford, Connecticut, 437, 441
Harvey, Ralph, 213*n*
Haugen, Nils P., 74–75
Hawaii: necessary to American sea power, 91; annexation of, 96–97; AFDC and ESEA formula, 293*n*; in Honolulu trade area, 442
Hawley, Amos H., 420*n*
Hawley, Ellis, 148–49
Hayes, Rutherford B., 74
Heacock, Walter J., 161*n*
Hearst, Randolph, 148
Heflin, J. Thomas, 131
Helena, Montana, 56*n*, 433–34
Hepburn, William, 83

Hinckley, Barbara, 348*n*
Hinds, Asher, 149–50
Hoffman, Clare, 213*n*
Honolulu, Hawaii, 249, 442
Hoover, Herbert, 136, 146
House of Representatives, United States: as source of data on sectional stress, 7; and roll calls in the Committee of the Whole, 9*n*; roll call voting in, 25–31; institutional norms in, 29–30, 53, 149–51, 164*n*, 172–73, 244–45; committee system and New Deal coalition, 30; considers private pension bills, 64; and tariff votes, 70; records votes on 1890 Force Bill, 79; records votes on repeal of Reconstruction measures, 84; power over election of members, 87; authorizes American intervention in Cuba, 95; considers legislation for the Philippines, 99; reapportionment of, 129*n*; discharge petition in, 129*n*, 161–63, 170, 222–23, 233*n*, 235, 238–45, 332–33; committee jurisdictions in, 189; and suspension of the rules, 204, 238; and teller votes, 214; and twenty-one day rule, 239–41, 244–45, 333–34; and the power of the Speaker, 329, 331–32; quorum requirement in proceedings, 329, 331–32; major precedents of, 329, 331–35; sectional stress on precedents, 330–335; Reed's Rules, 332; career orientation of members, 336–40; and recorded votes, 364*n*; party system in, 371–91; sectional stress in, 404–6. *See also* Congressional committee system
Houston, Texas: and 1920 value-added in manufacturing, 56*n*; supports McLemore Resolution, 124*n*; and busing, 249; and core economy, 313; and trade area criteria, 426
Howard, William Schley, 112*n*
Huddleston, George, 119, 134
Hughes, Charles Evan, 368
Humphrey, Hubert, 244*n*, 393, 400*n*
Hunter, Andrew, 84

Idaho, 247, 309*n*
Ideology: comparative duration of, 25; and coalition structure of political parties, 25; function of, 25; and roll call voting, 28–30; political economy of liberalism, 28; and CETA formula, 288; and the party system, 370, 391–400, 406; and fundamental sectional alignment, 411
Illinois: sectional alignment of, 50; criticized by Tillman, 87; and road subsidy formula, 155; and WPA wage rates, 164–65*n*; and manufacturing belt, 197; and corn belt, 197; lynchings in, 228*n*; and civil rights, 241; and regional

redistribution of income, 260*n*; and federal spending, 267–68; and Northeast-Midwest Coalition, 267*n*; and Land and Water Conservation Fund, 272*n*; AFDC and ESEA formula, 290, 293*n*; and unemployment insurance program, 324*n*

Immigration and Naturalization Service, 190*n*

Imperialism: and sectional alignment, 23, 38, 404; periphery bears cost of, 51; supported by industrial core, 61; high stress roll calls on, 88, 101; definition of, 89; and 1890 depression, 89, 92; and continentalism, 90, 93*n*; and globalism, 90, 93*n*; and tariff, 92; and WW I, 102, 104, 117; and the party system, 372; and the world economy, 407

Income tax, 72

Indiana: sectional alignment of, 50; and WPA wage rates, 164; and the manufacturing belt, 197; and the corn belt, 197; farm population in, 200; and civil rights, 241; federal spending, 267–68; and Northeast-Midwest Coalition, 267*n*; and Land and Water Conservation Fund, 272*n*; welfare program in, 309*n*

Indianapolis, Indiana, 142, 434

Indian Territory, 88

Industrial core, decline of: causes, 258; and the 1973 oil embargo, 260, 263, 403–4; economic maturity, 262; sectional stress in roll calls concerning, 268–69, 276, 279*n*, 281, 283, 297, 298; and federal grant-in-aid formulas, 273, 284*n*, 287–88, 293–94, 298*n*, 299; and federal regulatory authority, 273; and the party system, 274; and the committee system, 275, 293–94; and defense spending, 279–80; and welfare dependency, 304, 311; consequences of, 313–14; and New Deal coalition, 370; and the Democratic party, 388; and ADA ratings, 397–99; and sectional stress, 406; and the world economy, 409–10

Insular Cases, 90–91

Interest-group liberalism, 173

Intergovernmental Anti-recession Assistance Act, 273–74*n*, 278–79*n*

International Magazine Company, 433

Interstate Commerce Act of 1887, 63*n*

Interstate Commerce Commission, 269

Iowa, 197, 267*n*, 300*n*

Isaacs, John, 395*n*

Jacksonville, Florida, 56*n*, 225

Jersey City, New Jersey, 422

Johnson, Albert, 369*n*

Johnson, Hugh, 141

Johnson, Lyndon: and agricultural supports, 194; and civil rights, 244*n*; and 1961 Rules Committee expansion, 334; and the congressional party system, 375, 378

Jones, Charles O., 208

Journal of the House of Representatives, 331, 348

Judiciary Committee, House: and civil rights, 235, 238*n*, 243*n*, 244; and anti-lynching legislation, 238*n*

Judiciary Committee, Senate, 243–44

Jusenius, Carol L., 266*n*

J. Walter Thompson Company, 433

Kahn, Julius, 125

Kansas: as part of wheat belt, 137; and wheat supports, 211; and high-risk agricultural production, 215; lynchings in, 228*n*; dual school system in, 248*n*; an energy-advantaged, right-to-work state, 264*n*, 300*n*

Kansas City, Kansas, 428*n*

Kansas City, Missouri: and 1920 value-added in manufacturing, 56*n*; supports imperialism, 101; and McNary-Haugen plan, 142; and New Deal committee system, 171–72; and trade area criteria, 426; Federal Reserve city, 427*n*, 428

Kennedy, Edward, 392–93

Kennedy, John F., 194, 334

Kentucky: and road subsidy formula, 157; lynchings in, 228*n*; dual school system in, 248*n*; and revenue sharing formula, 299; welfare program in, 309*n*

Key, V. O.: on sectionalism and national unity, 3*n*; on the extreme form of sectionalism, 4–5*n*; and the study of sectionalism, 11–13; on geographical determinism, 11; on sectionalism and the party system, 12; on seniority and sectional conflict in Congress, 13; on future of sectional conflict, 13; on the South in American politics, 251, 253

Keynesian economics, 173

Kirst, Michael, 289*n*

Kitchens, Wade Hampton, 161

Kitchin, Claude: critic of Wilson's war policies, 112, 122, 127; attacked by *New York Times*, 122*n*; and McLemore Resolution, 122*n*

Knox, John Jay, 426*n*

Knoxville, Tennessee, 50, 433

Kolko, Gabriel, 89*n*

Kondratieff cycles, 259–60*n*

Krock, Arthur, 231

Labor: supports tariff, 63; and imperialism, 93*n*; opposes McNary-Haugen plan, 141; and the

Labor (*continued*)
New Deal political economy, 149; and the Wage and Hour bill, 162, 172; and WW II controls, 175, 179–83, 186–90, 405; and agricultural supports, 207, 215–16; and political reciprocity with agriculture, 216–22; and civil rights, 230, 253; and New Deal coalition, 232; and the committee system, 241–43, 327–29; and destabilization of plantation elite, 257; and the post-civil rights South, 258; unionization and industrialization, 262; unionization and regional growth, 264; nationalization of regulation and unionization, 300–301; sectional stress on legislation concerning, 300*n*; and the decline of the industrial core, 315–16; contributions and welfare dependency, 327–29; in the Democratic party and the South, 368–69; and the party system, 371–72*n*; and the ADA, 392–93

Ladd, Everett Carll, 372*n*

LaFollette, Robert, 107, 332–33

LaGuardia, Fiorello, 134*n*

Land and Water Conservation Fund, 272

Ledebur, Larry C., 266*n*

Legislative Reorganization Act of 1946: and committee assignments, 341, 346, 349; and the committee system, 173, 351–53, 366, 403

Liberalism. *See* Ideology

Lincoln, Nebraska, 426

Lindbergh, Charles A., 118–19

Link, Arthur S., 109, 121*n*, 128*n*

Literary Digest: reports poll on American neutrality, 115, 117; and regional distribution of lynchings, 228*n*; and anti-lynching legislation, 230*n*

Littlefield, Charles, 99

Little Rock, Arkansas, 249, 442

Lodge, Henry Cabot, 75

Lodge Bill. *See* Force Bill of 1890

Longworth, Nicholas, 131, 133*n*

Los Angeles, California: sectional alignment of, 50; and 1920 value-added in manufacturing, 56*n*; and McNary-Haugen plan, 142; and busing, 249–50; welfare dependency in, 305

Los Angeles County, California, 288*n*, 308–9*n*

Losch, August, 417

Louisiana: and 1890 Force Bill, 78; restricts suffrage, 81, 223–24; and 1965 Voting Rights Act, 247; dual school system in, 248*n*; electricity generation costs in, 259*n*; and regional redistribution of income, 260*n*, 315; an energy-advantaged, right-to-work state, 264*n*, 300*n*;

and revenue sharing formula, 299; welfare program in, 309*n*

Louisville, Kentucky: and 1920 value-added in manufacturing, 56*n*; supports free trade, 70; supports continentalism, 101; and busing legislation, 225; and Federal Reserve System, 431

Lowenstein, Allard, 393

Lundine, Stanley, 288

Lynching: sectional stress on roll calls concerning, 224–25, 246; and the Dyer bill, 225; frequency of, 228; legislation concerning, 235, 238, 247

McCarthy, Eugene, 392, 393

McClellan, John L., 168

McConnell, Grant, 142

McCormack, John, 217*n*, 221

McGovern, George, 393

McKinley, William, 95, 96*n*, 98

McLemore, Jeff, 122, 123*n*

McLemore Resolution, 112, 122–24

McManus, Michael J., 258*n*, 259*n*

McNary-Haugen plan: and equality for agriculture, 105, 129, 139; and the tariff, 130, 142; and Muscle Shoals development, 135, 141; description of, 140; legislative introductions of, 140*n*; origins of, 141; provisions of 1927 bill, 142–43; sectional alignment on votes concerning, 142–46; and post-WW II agricultural supports, 192, 198, 209, 213; and anti-lynching legislation, 228; and sectional stress, 405; and the world economy, 407

Maguire, Andrew, 272, 299

Mahan, Alfred Thayer, 91

Maine, 67, 264*n*, 309*n*

Manufacturing belt: and agricultural production, 137; opposes McNary-Haugen plan, 141; and export debentures for agriculture, 146; and regional specialization in agriculture, 196–97, 200, 207–8; and the world economy, 199; and agricultural supports, 203, 211, 213*n*, 215–17, 405; trade area delegations, 209*n*; and legislative heritage of industrialization, 262–63; and federal grant-in-aid formulas, 273, 293–94; and federal aid to New York City, 275–77; and Maybank amendment, 283–84; and CETA formula, 287; AFDC recipients in, 290; and the decline of the industrial core, 312; future of, 312–13; and the interregional division of labor, 314–15; and cohesion of congressional delegations, 315; and the committee system, 319–21, 362*n*; and centralization of legislative power, 335; and the 1973 oil embargo, 403–4; and the party system, 406; and protectionism, 408–10

Marathon Oil, 316

Market Data Handbook of the United States, 433–34

Martin, John Frederick, 231*n*, 244*n*

Maryland, 248*n*, 290, 321

Massachusetts: reference to in debate, 73; and road subsidy formula, 155; and WPA wage rates, 164–65*n*; farm population in, 200; an energy-disadvantaged, union-shop state, 264*n*; and Land and Water Conservation Fund, 272*n*; and defense spending, 279; AFDC and ESEA formula, 293*n*

May, Andrew J., 187

Maybank amendment: and Defense Manpower Policy No. 4-B, 280; sectional stress on, 281, 283; effect of, 281*n*; language, 283*n*; and the Appropriations Committee, 283; compared to ESEA formula, 293

Mayhew, David R., 212*n*, 219, 222*n*

Mays, James H., 117*n*

Meany, George, 221–22

Medicaid, 325*n*

Medicare, 325*n*

Memphis, Tennessee: sectional alignment of, 37, 411; and 1920 value-added in manufacturing, 56*n*; supports free trade, 70; and New Deal committee system, 171–72; and 1965 Voting Rights Act, 225

Memphis Press, 228–29*n*

Merchant Marine Act of 1935: voting on, 148, 159–60, 171; description of, 159

Mertz, Paul, 160–61, 164*n*

Methodology: sampling procedure and development of themes, 31–37, 56; sectional stress index and identification of poles, 33; use of descriptive terms, 55–56

Meyer, Adolph, 97*n*

Miami, Florida: and busing legislation, 249*n*; and Maybank amendment, 283; and the core economy, 313; trade area status, 442

Michel, Robert, 195*n*, 206, 300

Michener, Earl C., 168

Michigan: and civil rights, 241; and regional redistribution of income, 260*n*; an energy-disadvantaged, union-shop state, 264*n*; and federal spending, 267–68; and Northeast-Midwest Coalition, 267*n*; and Land and Water Conservation Fund, 272*n*; AFDC and ESEA formula, 290, 293*n*; and value-added tax on

automobiles, 299; unionization, 300; and unemployment insurance program, 324*n*; and the ADA, 400*n*

Middle East, 313

Midwest: and military preparations for WW I, 107, 112, 117, 125; pacifist perspective of, 117, 119; and the Wage and Hour bill, 163; and the Frazier-Lemke bill, 170; and WW II controls, 183; and the manufacturing belt, 197; and relocation of industry, 260–61; and the Northeast-Midwest Coalition, 267; economic decline of, 272, 315–16; and defense spending, 279–80; and a competitive market, 284; and community development block grants, 288; and regional energy expenditures, 294; and the regulation of natural gas, 294–95; and the cohesion of congressional delegations, 315; and the party system, 375; and the revenue sharing formula, 395*n*; and the Republican party, 403–6; and imperialism, 404; and protectionism, 408; trade area territories, 441, 442, 443

Military pensions: and the tariff, 24, 70, 407–8; and the bipolar sectional alignment, 38; and New York City, 49; and the emergence of the industrial core, 49, 60, 62–63; nationalized by the Spanish-American War and WW I, 50, 72; general legislation concerning, 63; high stress roll calls on, 63; and the Pension Bureau, 63–64; private bills concerning, 64–66; proportion of federal budget, 66; geographical distribution of, 66–67; and Republican insurgency, 335; and sectional stress, 404

Miller, Clarence, 131

Milwaukee, Wisconsin, 208, 249, 442

Mink, Patsy, 393

Minneapolis, Minnesota: and 1920 value-added in manufacturing, 56*n*; supports McLemore Resolution, 124; and McNary-Haugen plan, 142; and civil service employment, 168; and busing, 249; and congressional party system, 375; Federal Reserve city, 427*n*, 428

Minnesota: military pension recipients in, 67; and McNary-Haugen plan, 146; and dairy production, 197; and the corn belt, 197; lynchings in, 228*n*; and Northeast-Midwest Coalition, 267*n*; and the ADA, 400*n*

Mississippi: restricts suffrage, 81, 223; farm population in, 200; lynchings in, 228–29*n*; poll tax in, 233*n*; and 1965 Voting Rights Act, 247; dual school system in, 248*n*; an energy-advantaged, right-to-work state, 264*n*, 300*n*;

Mississippi (*continued*)
ESEA formula, 290; AFDC formula, 308*n*; welfare program in, 309*n*; and twenty-one day rule, 333
Mississippi Plan, 81, 97, 223–24
Mississippi River Valley, 251
Missouri: and the Soil Bank program, 193*n*; and the corn belt, 197; lynchings in, 228*n*; and civil rights, 241; dual school system in, 248*n*; and Land and Water Conservation Fund, 272*n*
Mobile, Alabama, 181, 442
Moffett, Toby: on the regional redistribution of income, 260*n*; and gasoline rationing set aside, 295, 297; on federal grant-in-aid formulas, 298*n*
Monroney, A. S. Mike, 353*n*
Montana, 155, 164–65*n*, 299
Morgan, J. P., 110, 119*n*, 121
Morse, Elijah, 73
Mottl, Ronald M., 242
Moulton, Elma, 434, 437
Murphy, Raymond, 417–18*n*
Muscle Shoals, Alabama: and TVA, 105; development of in WW I, 125; debate over public ownership, 128; and fertilizer production, 131–37; sectional alignment on votes concerning, 131–37; and McNary-Haugen plan, 135, 141–42, 146; and New Deal coalition, 136–37

Nashville, Tennessee, 56*n*
Nation, 232*n*
National Association for the Advancement of Colored People, 231*n*
National Association of Manufacturers, 187
National Banking Act, 426*n*
National Defense Act of 1916, 124–25, 130–31
National Farmers Union, 215
National Industrial Recovery Act, 155, 157, 171
National Journal, 267–68
National Labor Relations Board, 188–89
National Oceanographic Office, 268
National Progressive Convention, 368–69
National Recovery Administration, 141*n*
National Weather Bureau, 297
National Wholesale Druggists Association, 434
National Youth Administration, 181, 184*n*
Naval appropriations bill, WW I, 125–27
Neal, Will E., 213–14*n*
Nebraska, 197, 215, 300*n*
Nevada, 155, 300*n*, 309*n*
Newark, New Jersey, 288*n*, 422
New Deal: and class conflict in the industrial

core, 23; Democratic coalition in, 24–25; and bipolar sectional alignment, 38; and attitude of the periphery toward the central state, 52; and formation of farm bloc, 137, 139; sectional stress on legislation during, 147–48, 157–71; and bipolar alliance in the Democratic party, 148, 150, 153, 155, 173; transforms national political economy, 148–49, 152; and core-periphery relations, 160; and the party system, 175, 378–79, 391; and WW II mobilization, 180; and the career orientation of House members, 336; and roll call frequency, 362; as democratic class struggle, 372. *See also* New Deal coalition
New Deal coalition: bureaucratic discretion makes possible, 26, 30, 171, 190; and decline in sectional stress, 53; and agriculture legislation, 105; and Muscle Shoals development, 136–37; and institutional norms in the House, 150–51; and segregation, 151, 372–73, 388; and federal civil service, 153, 167; and agricultural supports, 194, 203, 207, 215–22; and the Eisenhower administration, 216; and civil rights, 224, 230, 232, 238, 244–45, 253; and the committee system, 257, 318–19, 405–6; and centralized legislative power, 334–35; and the seniority system, 348–51; and the American political system, 370; and southern Democrats, 383, 385; and liberalism ratings, 397–400; prerequisites for, 401; emergence of, 403; and the 1964 Civil Rights Act, 403; and sectional stress, 405, 409–11. *See also* New Deal and Democratic party
New England: military pension recipients in, 67; reference to in debate, 73, 143; employment growth in, 266*n*; response to business cycles, 266*n*; and Northeast-Midwest Coalition, 267; and unemployment, 273; and Maybank amendment, 280; and gasoline rationing, 297; and the core economy, 314–15; and the Republican party, 369
New England Congressional Caucus, 266*n*, 272, 284*n*
New England Research Office, 259*n*, 266*n*, 267
New Hampshire, 67, 309*n*
New Haven, Connecticut, 422
New Jersey: farm population in, 200; and regional redistribution of income, 260*n*; an energy-disadvantaged, union-shop state, 264*n*; and Northeast-Midwest Coalition, 267*n*; and Land and Water Conservation Fund, 272*n*; AFDC and ESEA formula, 293*n*; and unemployment insurance program, 324*n*

New Mexico: statehood and sectional stress, 88, 95, 100–101; and dominance of Anglo-Saxons, 95*n*; and Wage and Hour bill, 162; dual school system in, 248*n*; and revenue sharing formula, 299; welfare program in, 309*n*; and Federal Reserve System, 433*n*

New Orleans, Louisiana: sectional alignment of, 37; and 1920 value-added in manufacturing, 56*n*; supports free trade, 70; supports Merchant Marine Act, 160; and New Deal committee system, 171–72; and 1965 Voting Rights Act, 225

New Republic, 232, 234*n*, 395–400

New York City, New York: federal aid to, 26–30, 268, 275–79, 406; sectional alignment of, 49, 411; and the emergence of the industrial core, 49; and 1920 value-added in manufacturing, 55*n*; supports free trade, 70; effect of 1890 Force Bill, 78, 84*n*; ethnic composition criticized, 100*n*; supports imperialism, 101; and military preparations for WW I, 106–7, 115, 118*n*, 125–27; opposes McLemore Resolution, 124; supports naval appropriations, 127; supports Merchant Marine Act, 160; and parity payments, 165; and New Deal committee system, 172; and agricultural supports, 203; and busing, 249, 251; cultural influence of, 257*n*; and mass transit, 263; and AFDC, 278; and Maybank amendment, 283; welfare dependency in, 305; and the core economy, 312*n*, 314–15; and floor reciprocity, 357; and the congressional party system, 375; and the ADA, 393–94; federal aid to and the ADA ratings, 398; trade area compared to New York State, 420*n*; and trade area criteria, 422, 426; banks and banking reserves, 426*n*; Federal Reserve city, 427*n*, 428; trade area boundaries, 441, 442

New York, state of: and federal election oversight, 83, 84*n*; and road subsidy formula, 155; and McNary-Haugen bill, 162*n*; and Wage and Hour bill, 162*n*; and agricultural production, 197, 203; and civil rights, 241; electricity generation costs in, 259*n*; and regional redistribution of income, 260*n*; an energy-disadvantaged, union-shop state, 264*n*; and the Northeast-Midwest Coalition, 267*n*; and Land and Water Conservation Fund, 272*n*; and federal aid to New York City, 276; and Maybank amendment, 281; AFDC and ESEA formula, 293*n*; and unemployment insurance program, 324*n*; and the ADA, 393; and the New York City trade area, 420*n*, 442

New York Sun, 79

New York Times: warns against German threat, 107; criticizes Democratic opposition to Wilson, 113*n*, 122*n*; on Roosevelt and anti-lynching legislation, 231; on fuel assistance formula, 298–99

Nixon, Richard, 279–80

Norfolk, Virginia, 125–27, 182

Norris, George, 135–36, 332

North: urban machines in, 25; military pension recipients in, 66–67; and 1890 Force Bill, 76–78; Democratic party in, 78; class conflict in, 149, 372; and exploitation of the South, 152–53; and civil service, 168; and lynchings, 228; and busing, 247–50; as model for southern political future, 253; and civil rights, 253; residential segregation in, 257*n*; negative business climate in, 258*n*; federal spending and economic development, 267; compared to Great Britain, 276*n*; and the Taft-Hartley Act, 300; welfare dependency in, 304–5; and the party system, 368–73, 375, 380–81; liberalism ratings and Democratic success in, 396–400; and segregation in the South, 403; and the New Deal coalition, 405; and southern plantation economy, 408; and traditional notions of sectionalism, 415

North Carolina: restricts suffrage, 81, 223; and naval appropriations, 127; and WPA wage rates, 164–65*n*; and tobacco allotments, 216*n*; lynchings in, 228*n*; and 1965 Voting Rights Act, 247; dual school system in, 248*n*; and Maybank amendment, 280; AFDC and ESEA formula, 290; unionization, 300; welfare program in, 309*n*

North Dakota: farm population in, 200; and wheat supports, 211; and high-risk agricultural production, 215; an energy-advantaged, right-to-work state, 264*n*, 300*n*; and revenue sharing formula, 299; welfare program in, 309*n*

Northeast: sectional alignment of, 37, 50; and imperialism, 93; supports military preparations for WW I, 112, 115, 122*n*, 125; opposes McLemore Resolution, 124; and reapportionment of 1930, 129*n*; and the manufacturing belt, 137, 196–97; opposes McNary-Haugen plan, 143; dominates Committee on Labor, 161; and the Wage and Hour bill, 163; and the relocation of industry, 181, 260–61, 264; and WW II controls, 183; and busing, 251; and revaluation of energy resources, 259, 294; and regional growth, 266*n*; economic decline in, 272, 315; and unemployment, 273; and

Northeast (*continued*)
   New York City, 276; and defense spending,
      279; and Maybank amendment, 281; and a
      competitive market, 284; and community de-
      velopment block grants, 288; and regulation of
      natural gas, 294–95; and gasoline rationing,
      297; and core-periphery relations, 311–12; fu-
      ture of, 312–15; and cohesion of congressional
      delegations, 315; and the conservative coali-
      tion, 348; and the Republican party, 371, 375;
      and the party system, 372; and the ADA,
      393–94; and revenue sharing formula, 395n;
      and protectionism, 408; trade area territories
      in, 441, 443
Northeast-Midwest Economic Advancement
   Coalition: and the industrial core, 266–67;
      membership in, 267n; and public works job
      formula, 272; policy priorities of, 275, 294,
      305; and Maybank amendment, 280, 281n,
      284n; and community development block
      grants, 288; on fuel assistance formula, 299;
      on future of the industrial core, 315

Obey Commission, 367
Occupational Safety and Health Administration,
   300–301
O'Connor, John J., 162n, 240n
Odum, Howard, 152
Office of Price Administration, 178–79
Office of War Information, 184–85
Ohio: sectional alignment of, 50; and the manufacturing belt, 197; and the corn belt, 197;
   lynchings in, 228n; and civil rights, 241; industrial capacity, 262; federal spending,
   267–68; and Northeast-Midwest Coalition,
   267n; and Land and Water Conservation Fund,
   272n; AFDC and ESEA formula, 290
Oklahoma City, Oklahoma, 56n, 441, 442
Oklahoma, state of: statehood and sectional
   stress, 88, 100; and cotton belt, 137; lynchings in, 228n; dual school systems in, 248n;
   electricity generation costs in, 259n; and regional redistribution of income, 260n, 315;
   and federal aid to New York City, 278; and
   revenue sharing formula, 299; welfare program, 309n; and Federal Reserve System, 433n
Omaha, Nebraska: and 1920 value-added in manufacturing, 56n; supports McLemore Resolution, 124; and busing, 249; and trade area
   criteria, 426; and the Federal Reserve System,
   431; trade area status, 437, 441–42
O'Neill, Thomas "Tip", 279, 315, 361–62

Orange County, California, 288n
Oregon, 264n, 293n

Paarlberg, Don, 192n, 212n, 216n
Pacific Coast region: and reapportionment of
   1930, 129n; and the Wage and Hour bill,
   163; and regional specialization in agriculture,
   208; AFDC recipients in, 290
Pacific Northwest, 137, 215, 251
Panama Canal, 88
Paterson, New Jersey, 422
Patman, Wright, 158, 170n
Patterson, James: describes voting on Wage and
   Hour bill, 160, 162n; on the South and the
   WPA, 164n; on discretionary distribution of
   relief funds, 168
Peabody, Robert L., 340n
Peek, George N., 141
Pennsylvania: and road subsidy formula, 155; and
   agricultural supports, 203; and civil rights,
   241; and Northeast-Midwest Coalition, 267n;
   and Land and Water Conservation Fund, 272n;
   AFDC and ESEA formula, 293n; and unem-
   ployment insurance program, 324n; impact of
   sectional alignment on party system, 371
Pension Bureau, 63–64, 65, 66
Pepper, Claude, 231, 297–98
Periphery. See Core-periphery relations
Perry, David G., 263n
Philadelphia, Pennsylvania: sectional alignment
   of, 35–37, 411; and 1920 value-added in
   manufacturing, 55n; supports tariff, 70; and
   military preparations for WW I, 106–7, 115;
   opposes McLemore Resolution, 124; supports
   naval appropriations, 127; opposes Muscle
   Shoals development, 136–37; supports Merchant Marine Act, 160; and New Deal committee system, 172; and busing, 249–50,
   251; cultural influence of, 257n; and Maybank
   amendment, 283; welfare dependency in, 305;
   and floor reciprocity, 357; and the ADA,
   393–94; Federal Reserve city, 427n, 428
Philippines: necessary to American sea power, 91;
   insurrection suppressed by United States, 99;
   and American imperialism, 99n; United States
   captures, 99n; debate over self-government for,
   100
Phoenix, Arizona, 50, 441–42
Pierce, Neal R., 275n
Pittsburgh, Pennsylvania: sectional alignment of,
   37; and 1920 value-added in manufacturing,
   55n; and military preparations for WW I, 115;

supports WW I naval appropriations, 127; and
Muscle Shoals development, 133; supports
Merchant Marine Act, 160; and agricultural
supports, 203; and busing, 249–50, 251; and
Maybank amendment, 283; and floor reciprocity, 359; and Federal Reserve System, 428,
430–31
PL 480. *See* Food for Peace
Platt amendment, 98–99
Poage, William R., 222
Polenberg, Richard, 188
Political parties: in Canada, 5*n*; Frederick Jackson Turner on, 5*n*, 9–10; V. O. Key on, 12;
comparative duration of system, 24–25; and
ideology, 25; and leadership influence on roll
call voting, 27–28; brokering in and ideological coalitions, 29; and sectional alignment
in roll call voting, 29; leadership favors bureaucratic discretion, 30; and vote trading, 30;
institutionalization of the House and depolarization of, 56, 318–19, 336; tariff and sectional alignment of, 71–72; and core-
periphery relations, 148, 317–18, 368–73;
and the committee system, 173, 258,
317–19, 403; and sectional stress, 176,
409–11; and regional specialization in agriculture, 214–15; and anti-lynching legislation,
225–26; and civil rights legislation, 241–42;
sectional alignment of and congressional reform, 242–43; and fundamental sectional
alignment, 274, 406; and CETA formula, 288;
and welfare dependency, 311; leadership and
centralized power in the House, 334–35; and
the sectional stress index, 373–74; nationalization of, 378; regional polarization and electoral
instability, 379–81; sectional stress and critical
elections, 379–81; natural sectional cleavage,
381, 400–401; decomposition of, 385; repolarization of the system, 399–400
Poll tax: sectional stress on roll calls concerning,
224–25, 246; and the South, 232; and the
committee system, 232*n*; legislation, 233,
235, 238, 243*n*, 247
Polsby, Nelson, 351*n*
Pomper, Gerald, 379
Populism: and the party system, 25, 406; and
sectional alignment in roll call voting, 29; and
imperialism, 89; as a sectional movement,
89*n*; and American intervention in WW I,
117, 120; and veterans' bonus bill, 158
Portland, Maine, 437, 442
Portland, Oregon: and 1920 value-added in man-

ufacturing, 56*n*; and busing, 249, 250*n*; and
trade area criteria, 426
Powell, Adam Clayton, 224*n*
Presidential elections, 385–91
Preston, Price H., 221
Pritchett, C. Herman, 133*n*
Professional Air Traffic Controllers Organiza-
tion, 328
Progressivism: and party system, 25, 406; and
sectional alignment in roll call voting, 29; and
imperialism, 89; and agrarian radicalism, 89*n*;
and career orientation of congressmen, 336;
and the Republican party, 368–69, 401; and
the Democratic party, 392
Providence, Rhode Island, 437, 442
Public Utility Holding Company Act, 169, 171
Puerto Rico, 91

Ramseyer, William, 118*n*
Rand McNally, 421, 437–42
Ray, George, 84*n*
Rayburn, Sam, 169, 334
Reagan, Ronald, 298*n*, 316, 391
Reciprocal Trade Agreement Act, 397
Reconstruction: and core-periphery relations, 74;
and repeal of federal election laws, 84, 225*n*,
403–4
Reconstruction Finance Corporation, 169–70
Reed, Thomas: supports 1890 Force Bill, 76; and
quorum ruling, 329, 331–32
Reed's Rules, 332
Republican party: sectional conflict within,
14–15, 403; and military pensions, 24, 64,
66, 70; and tariff, 24, 67, 69; and progressivism, 29, 89*n*; and Pension Bureau, 63–64;
supports Reconstruction measures, 73–74, 81;
and the 1890 Force Bill, 75–79; supports federal election oversight, 84; and contested election cases, 87, 404; and globalism 90, 96–98;
opposes New Mexico statehood, 95; supports
military preparations for WW I, 112, 113*n*;
vote on McLemore Resolution, 124*n*; leadership and Muscle Shoals, 133–34; and federal
civil service, 152, 167; and New Deal coalition, 155, 175, 216, 253; and the committee
system, 171, 241, 335–36, 348; and agricultural supports, 194; and prosperous agricultural producers, 215; and the corn and
wheat belts, 217; and anti-lynching legislation, 225–26; and civil rights, 230; and the
seniority system, 241*n*; and fundamental sectional alignment, 274; and federal aid to New

Republican party (*continued*)
	York City, 276–77; and the Taft-Hartley Act,
	300; and nationalization of welfare, 310; and
	core-periphery relations, 318, 368–73, 391;
	leadership and 1924 LaFollette supporters,
	332–33; and floor reciprocity, 360–61; as na-
	tionalist party, 372; and sectional stress in the
	party system, 379–81, 401; and the South,
	382; and ADA ratings, 395–400; insurgents
	and the party system, 401; sectional base of,
	405–6
Reserve Bank Organization Committee, 426–31
Reuss, Henry, 366*n*
Reuther, Walter, 221
Rhea, John S., 97
Rhode Island, 200, 264*n*, 272*n*
Richmond, Virginia: and 1920 value-added in
	manufacturing, 56*n*; and the Merchant Marine
	Act, 160; and voting rights, 246; sectional
	alignment of, 411; Federal Reserve city, 427*n*,
	428, 431
Ricketts, Edwin D., 117*n*
Roach, Hanna Grace, 22
Robertson, A. Willis, 162*n*
Robins, Raymond, 369*n*
Robinson, Kenneth, 283*n*
Robinson, William A., 331*n*
Robsion, John, 143, 161
Rocky Mountains, 50
Rodey, Bernard, 100*n*
Roll calls: economic interests and voting on,
	25–31; and the study of sectional stress,
	25–31; bureaucratic discretion and voting on,
	26, 29; party organization and voting on,
	27–28; ideology and voting on, 28; institu-
	tional norms and voting on, 29; sectional
	alignment and voting on, 29; sampling of, 33
Roniger, George, 268*n*
Roosevelt, Eleanor, 151*n*
Roosevelt, Franklin: abrogates Platt amendment,
	99; supports free trade, 102; New Deal pro-
	gram and the South, 150; indifference to civil
	rights measures, 151; vetos bonus bill, 158;
	and federal civil service, 167; and control of
	relief funds, 168; opposes Frazier-Lemke bill,
	170; and sectional stress on New Deal legisla-
	tion, 171; and WW II, 179, 181, 187; and
	anti-lynching legislation, 230–31; and 1932
	election, 400; and the New Deal coalition, 403
Roosevelt, Theodore, 99*n*; 368–69
Root, Elihu, 87–88
Rostow, Walt W., 259*n*; 268*n*; 276*n*
Rothbard, Murray, 116

Roybal, Edward, 297–98
Rules Committee: and civil rights legislation,
	234–35, 238, 254; 1961 expansion of, 241,
	334; and the Speaker, 242, 332–35, 355; and
	the twenty-one day rule, 333–34; Republican
	support for autonomy, 335; floor success,
	364–65; and the ADA, 393
Rundquist, Barry, 351*n*
Rural Electrification Administration, 153
Russia, 397
Rystad, Goran, 90*n*

Sabath, Adolph, 333
St. Joseph, Missouri, 426
St. Louis, Missouri: and 1920 value-added in
	manufacturing, 56*n*; supports continentalism,
	101; and McNary-Haugen plan, 142; and New
	Deal committee system, 171–72; and civil
	rights, 246; and busing, 249*n*; and New York
	City aid, 276; central reserve city, 426*n*; Fed-
	eral Reserve city, 427*n*, 428
St. Paul, Minnesota, 428*n*
St. Petersburg, Florida, 225
Salt Lake City, Utah, 56*n*, 208*n*, 249
Samoa, 91
Sanders, M. Elizabeth, 294, 410*n*
San Francisco, California: sectional alignment of,
	37, 411; and 1920 value-added in manufactur-
	ing, 56*n*; and imperialism/statehood, 101;
	supports McLemore Resolution, 124; and
	McNary-Haugen plan, 142; supports Merchant
	Marine Act, 160; and civil service employ-
	ment, 168; and truck farming, 208; and anti-
	lynching legislation, 225; and busing, 249;
	and the core economy, 313, 315; and floor reci-
	procity, 357; and the ADA, 393–94; Federal
	Reserve Bank city, 427*n*, 428; trade area sta-
	tus, 442–43
San Francisco Bay, 314
San Jose, California, 313
Satterfield, David, 304
Savannah, Georgia, 437, 441
Saylor, John, 280
Schattsneider, E. E., 388, 401–2
Schneier, Edward. *See* Turner, Julius
Schriftgiesser, Karl, 128*n*
Schultz, William J., 422*n*, 426*n*
Schumpeter, Joseph, 263
Seattle, Washington: and 1920 value-added in
	manufacturing, 55–56*n*; and busing, 249,
	250*n*; trade area territory, 442, 443*n*
Sebelius, Keith, 301
Second War Powers Act, 178

Sectionalism. *See* Sectional stress

Sectional stress: and ethnic identity / religious rivalry, 3; formal definition of, 4; as a complex fact, 5–6, 17; and geographical determinism, 11–12*n*, 20; future of, 8, 13, 14*n*; contemporary analysis of, 15–17; bipolar alignment of, 22, 35, 37–38, 55; fundamental nature of, 22–25, 29, 31–38, 52; and the party system, 25, 274, 368–91, 401–2; and bureaucratic discretion, 26, 29, 52, 56, 59, 176; and time horizon of vote trading, 30; identification of sectional poles, 33*n*; and major trade area alignment, 35; and cross-cutting cleavages, 38; and lower transport costs, 51; decline of over last century, 52–53, 174, 409; and the committee system, 275, 293, 318–19, 348; in presidential elections, 385–91; and ratings of liberalism, 398–400; most important events in evolution of, 403–4; and the world economy, 407–10; fundamental sectional alignment, 410–11; trade areas and the study of, 415–16; deficiencies of traditional notions of, 415–16

Sectional stress index: and identification of sectional poles, 33; and use of descriptive terms, 55; highest score on, 55; and the party system, 373–74; advantages of, 443, 449; formula for, 443, 449

Securities and Exchange Commission, 169

Segregation: influence on central state expansion, 59; in South after Reconstruction, 73–74; and the District of Columbia, 88, 191*n*; and New Deal coalition, 150–51, 176, 245, 372–73, 401; and federal civil service, 153, 167*n*; and suffrage restrictions, 223; and lynchings, 228; and plantation economy, 233; dual school systems, 248*n*; and nationalization of South, 256; and southern congressmen, 258

Select Committee on Committees, 367*n*

Selective Service System, 187

Senate: considers 1890 Force Bill, 79; considers Platt amendment, 98; filibuster and segregation, 151, 234–35, 243–44

Seniority system: and New Deal coalition, 149, 151, 173, 370, 403; and congressional parties, 241*n*; violations of, 254; and nationalized party competition, 318–19; and 1924 LaFollette candidacy, 332–33; and a strong committee system, 333, 336, 346–51; and career orientation of members, 338; and committee jurisdictions, 339–40; and the 1946 Legislative Reorganization Act, 351–53; and the ADA 393

Shallenberger, Ashton, 141

Shields, Mark, 276

Shipping Board, 128

Shreveport, Louisiana, 442

Shull, Leon, 395*n*

Sierra Club v. Ruckelshaus, 303–4

Sioux City, Iowa, 442

Smith, Al, 387*n*, 400

Smith, Howard, 254

Smith, Wint, 199*n*

Smith-Connally Act. *See* War Labor Disputes Act

Soil Bank, 193, 213*n*

Soth, Lauren, 204*n*

Soule, George, 140

South: suffrage in, 24–25, 61, 81, 83, 89*n*, 223–24, 256–57, 403; sectional alignment of, 37; and northern industrialization, 49; and central state bureaucracy, 56, 59; and contested election cases, 61, 85, 87, 404; effect of Reconstruction experience on, 61, 93*n*, 104, 120; shoulders costs of industrialization, 63; and military pensions, 66; and Reconstruction measures, 74–75, 81; reaction to 1890 Force Bill, 75–76, 79*n*; role of Democratic party in, 78; and imperialism, 93; opposes American intervention in WW I, 119–20, 127, 404–5; and cotton exports to Britain, 120–21, 129–30; opposes McLemore Resolution, 124; and McNary-Haugen plan, 130, 141–43; supports Muscle Shoals development, 134–36; and formation of farm bloc, 135*n*; and New Deal political economy, 150; colonial nature of, 152; and federal civil service, 153, 167; and Wage and Hour bill, 160–61; and WPA, 164; and the relocation of industry, 182, 261, 264, 312*n*; and WW II controls, 183; and agricultural supports, 213*n*, 215, 222*n*; and the 1965 Voting Rights Act, 225, 246; lynchings in, 228; and segregation, 233; and the seniority system, 241*n*; and busing, 247–48, 251; and preoccupation with race, 251; and Taft-Hartley Act, 254, 300; nationalization of and civil rights, 256; residential segregation and annexation, 257*n*; federal spending and economic development, 267; and the Democratic party, 274, 381–85, 406–7; and unemployment rates, 276*n*; and New York City aid, 279; and defense spending, 279, 283; and community development block grant formula, 288; and AFDC, 290; and fuel assistance formula, 298; welfare dependency and party competition, 311; and interregional division of labor, 314–16; and O'Neill's retirement, 315;

South (*continued*)
and the party system, 368–73; and core-periphery relations, 368–73, 380–81; disfranchisement and class conflict in, 369–71; suffrage expansion and the New Deal coalition, 370; and redistribution of national wealth, 391; and revenue sharing formula, 395*n*; and civil rights, 405; and core status in the world economy, 408; and end of Reconstruction, 411; and traditional notions of section, 415; and the economic structure of trade areas, 420; and Federal Reserve System, 431; and the urban system, 442–43

South Carolina: and military pensions, 67; and martial law during Reconstruction, 74; restricts suffrage, 81, 223; election practices noted by Tillman, 87; and WPA wage rates, 164, 165*n*; lynchings in, 228*n*; poll tax in, 233*n*; and 1965 Voting Rights Act, 247; dual school systems in, 248*n*; and the Maybank amendment, 280; ESEA formula, 290; and unionization, 300; AFDC formula, 308*n*; welfare program, 309*n*

South Dakota, 264*n*, 300*n*, 309*n*

Southeast, 131, 266*n*

Southern Politics in State and Nation, 253

South Dakota, 200, 215

Southwest: and revaluation of energy resources, 259; and relocation of industry, 264; and regional growth, 266*n*; and federal spending, 267; and unemployment rates, 276*n*; and fuel assistance formula, 298–99; and the core economy, 315

Spanish-American War: and nationalization of military pensions, 50, 72; beginning of, 95; and annexation of Hawaii, 96; support for, 96*n*

Speaker: and civil rights legislation, 234–35, 238; and the Rules Committee, 242, 332–35; increase in power, 329, 331–32, 353–57; referral of legislation to committee, 340, 353–57; and the seniority system, 348; and the Democratic Steering Committee, 355*n*

Spokane, Washington: and 1920 value-added in manufacturing, 56*n*; and busing, 249; trade area status, 437, 441–42, 443*n*

Standard Financial Digest, 115

State Department, 190

Stephens, John H., 124*n*

Stockman, David, 304

Stone, William, 107

Strong, James G., 134–35

Suitland, Maryland, 268

Sumners, Hatton, 228*n*, 235

Supplemental Security Income, 308

Supreme Court: rules on Reconstruction measures, 74; and imperialism, 90–91; sectional stress on legislation concerning, 223*n*; and civil rights decisions, 224; and anti-lynching legislation, 229–30; and school desegregation, 248; and Clean Air Act, 303–4

Syracuse, New York, 437, 442

Syron, Richard F., 266*n*, 276*n*

Taft, William Howard, 98–100, 143

Taft-Hartley Act, Section 14(b) of: and class-conflict in North, 149; sectional stress on roll call concerning, 223*n*; discussion of, 254, 300, 372; and right-to-work states, 300*n*

Tammany Hall: and sectional alignment of New York City, 49; effect of 1890 Force Bill upon, 78; allied with *New York Sun*, 79; Republican harassment of, 83; and federal election oversight, 84*n*

Tampa, Florida, 225, 442

Tansill, Charles Callan, 111*n*

Tariff: and sectional alignment, 23, 38, 52, 70–72; and military pensions, 24, 72–73; and sectional alignment of New York City, 49; and emergence of the northern core, 49, 60, 62, 404; and the Great Plains, 50; as tax upon the periphery, 62; political coalition supporting, 62–63, 70, 127; produces federal revenue, 67; and the party system, 72, 372; and 1890 Force Bill, 76, 79; and imperialism, 92–93*n*; and McNary-Haugen plan, 104–5, 140, 142; operation of before WW I, 107; after WW I, 109, 129; and export debentures for agriculture, 184; and agricultural supports, 199–200; and the decline of the industrial core, 314–15, 408–10; and Republican insurgency, 335; and the New Deal coalition, 388; and the world economy, 407–8

Tarrow, Sidney, 4*n*

Tarver, Malcolm C., 165

Tavenner, Clyde H., 118

Tennessee: and WPA wage rates, 164–65*n*; poll tax in, 233*n*; dual school system in, 248*n*; AFDC and ESEA formula, 290; a right-to-work state, 300*n*; welfare program in, 309*n*

Tennessee-Tombigbee waterway, 184*n*

Tennessee Valley Authority, 105, 136–137

Texas: restricts suffrage, 81; delegation opposed to military preparations for WW I, 121; supports McLemore Resolution, 124; and naval appropriations, 127; and expanding cotton belt, 137; and road subsidy formula, 155; and the Wage and Hour bill, 162; lynchings in, 228*n*; poll tax in, 233*n*; dual school systems in, 248*n*; electricity generation costs in, 259*n*; and regional redistribution of income, 260*n*, 315; and energy-advantaged, right-to-work state, 264*n*, 300*n*; and Land and Water Conservation Fund, 272*n*; and revenue sharing formula, 299; AFDC formula, 308*n*; welfare program in, 309*n*; and 1961 Rules Committee expansion, 334

Thompson, Joseph B., 125*n*

Tillman, Benjamin "Pitchfork," 87

Time, 233, 234*n*

Tincher, James, 146

Tindall, George, 137*n*, 152, 369*n*

Toledo, Ohio, 441

Trade areas: use of in the study of sectional stress, 17, 415–20; and interdependency between congressional districts, 26; and the bipolar sectional alignment, 35–36*n*, 38, 49–50; and 1920 value-added in manufacturing, 55–56*n*; agricultural commodity delegations, 209*n*; categorized by busing orders, 248; major federal policy interests of, 319–20; and deficiencies of traditional notions of section, 415–16; theory, 417–20; and the urban system, 419–20; criteria delineating, 421–43

Troy, New York, 437, 442

Truman, Harry, 280, 392

Tugwell, Rexford, 180

Tulsa, Oklahoma, 249, 441–442

Turner, Frederick Jackson: on sectionalism and political parties, 5*n*, 9–10; on the study of sectionalism, 7–11; on the future of sectional conflict, 8*n*; on sectional conflict in Congress, 9–10

Turner, Julius, 14–16

Udall, Morris, 351*n*, 366*n*

Underwood tariff, 71

United Auto Workers, 393

United Kingdom. *See* Great Britain

United Mine Workers, 189

United Nations, 397

United States Steel, 316

Utah, 264*n*, 266*n*, 300*n*

Vance, James, 418–20, 442

Van Riper, Paul P., 167*n*

Van Voorhis, John, 95

Vatter, Harold G., 191*n*

Vermont, 67, 200, 264*n*

Veterans' bonus, 158, 171

Virginia: restricts suffrage, 81, 223; and contested election case, 85–87; and WW I naval appropriations, 127; and tobacco allotments, 216*n*; lynchings in, 228*n*; poll tax in, 233*n*; and 1965 Voting Rights Act, 247; dual school system in, 248*n*; a right-to-work state, 300*n*; welfare program in 309*n*; and the District of Columbia Committee, 321; and the twenty-one day rule, 333

Voting rights, 224–25, 235*n*, 246–47

Voting Rights Act of 1965: compared to 1890 Force Bill, 102; sectional stress on, 225; Rules Committee support for, 239; and support for civil rights legislation, 242, 245; provisions of, 247; and Taft-Hartley Act, 254; nationalization of, 256

Wadsworth, James, 353*n*

Wage and Hour bill, 160–62, 171–72

Wallace, George, 388

Wallace, Henry, 186

Wallerstein, Immanuel: and the study of sectionalism, 17–21; and the modern world-economy, 19–21, 407–8; and geographical determinism, 20; and core-periphery competition within one nation, 20; and retention of core-state status, 20; approach of, 20–21; on the tariff and the emergence of the northern core, 49, 62; on semi-periphery status within the world economy, 314

War Industries Board, 141*n*

War Labor Board, 181, 188

War Labor Disputes Act, 179, 184*n*, 188

War Manpower Commission, 187*n*

War Mobilization and Reconversion, 187–88

War Production Board, 177–78, 187

Washington, D.C.: and truck farming, 208; and busing, 249*n*; suburbs and Howard Smith, 254*n*; AFDC and ESEA formula, 293*n*; and Amtrak, 324; and the ADA, 393; and trade area criteria, 422, 426

Watkins, Alfred J., 263*n*

Wayne County, Michigan, 278

Weaver, James B., 64

Weinstein, Bernard L., 258–59*n*

Weiss, Theodore, 278

Welch, Richard E., 99*n*

West: public lands and sectional alignment of, 50; military pension recipients in, 67; and military preparations for WW I, 115, 405; supports McLemore Resolution, 124; and Muscle Shoals development, 133; and McNary-Haugen plan, 141, 143; coalition with New

West (*continued*)
England criticized, 143; and relocation of industry, 182, 261, 312*n*; and regional specialization in agriculture, 208; lynchings in, 228; and revaluation of energy resources, 259; federal spending and economic development, 267; and withdrawal of public lands, 269; and unemployment, 273; and Maybank amendment, 283; and community development block grant formula, 288; and environmental policy, 303; welfare dependency in and party competition, 311; and O'Neill's retirement, 315; and interregional division of labor, 316; and redistribution of national wealth, 391; and the ADA, 393–94; trade area territories in, 437, 442–43

West South Central, 266*n*

West Virginia, 228*n*, 248*n*, 299

Wheat belt: economic imperatives of, 137; effect of McNary-Haugen plan, 140; and Frazier-Lemke bill, 170; and regional specialization in agriculture, 198, 208; and political reciprocity with other commodities, 211, 214; and high-risk agricultural production, 215; and the Republican party, 217; and the committee system, 325*n*

White, Walter, 231*n*

White, William Allen, 130*n*

White primary, 224

Whitten, Jamie, 199

Wholesale Dry Goods Institute, 434

Wichita, Kansas, 375

Williams, John Sharp, 97, 121

Wilmington, North Carolina, 442

Wilson, Woodrow: and periphery attitude toward central state, 52; and imperialism, 102; and American neutrality, 109–10; delivers war message, 110; and extension of military credits to Allies, 110; supports military preparedness measures, 111–12, 127; leadership of Democratic party, 113; war powers, 113*n*; accused of conspiracy, 119*n*; and McLemore Resolution, 122–24; and Muscle Shoals, 130–31; and WW I demobilization, 133*n*; and segregation in the federal government, 225*n*; and progressivism, 368–69, 400; and the South 369*n*

Winston-Salem, North Carolina, 437, 442

Wisconsin: sectional alignment of, 50; and McNary-Haugen plan, 146; and WPA wage rates, 164–65*n*; and dairy production, 197; and federal spending, 267–68; and Northeast-Midwest Coalition, 267*n*; and Land and Water Conservation Fund, 272*n*; AFDC and ESEA formula, 293*n*

Works Progress Administration: and regional redistribution of wealth, 153; and regional wage differences, 163–64; in the South, 164*n*; political conflict over wage rates for, 164*n*, 165, 171; and WW II, 181

World War I: sectional alignment on intervention in, 38, 105; demobilization from and sectional alignment, 50, 128; nationalizes military pensions, 50, 72; American intervention in, 89, 109–10; and imperialism, 102; and Anglo-American cooperation, 104; effect of on American foreign trade, 107, 110–11, 120–21; transforms US into creditor nation, 108; effect on American economy, 110–11, 115, 121, 129, 133*n*; and free enterprise, 180; and industrial development coalition, 404–05

World War II: sectional alignment on demobilization from, 50; and mobilization of the American economy, 175–82, 190–92, 405; political coalitions during, 183; sectional stress on roll calls concerning, 184–87, 189–90

Wyoming: dual school system in, 248*n*; an energy-advantaged, right-to-work state, 264*n*, 266*n*, 300*n*; and revenue sharing formula, 299; welfare program in, 309*n*

Yost, Jacob, 85–87